TETIAROA

MOOREA

TAHITI

MEETIA

TWO TAHITIAN VILLAGES
A Study in Comparisons

Douglas Oliver

Two Tahitian Villages: A Study in Comparisons

Published by The Institute for Polynesian Studies
Sponsored by the
Polynesian Cultural Center
and
Brigham Young University—Hawaii Campus

This work was set in 10/12 Baskerville on a Harris Fototronic Phototypesetter

Printed by Brigham Young University Press, Provo, Utah

ISBN 0-939154-22-6 (hard cover)
ISBN 0-939154-25-0 (paperback)

TWO TAHITIAN VILLAGES
A Study in Comparisons

Douglas Oliver

In loving memory of
Sheila and Andrew Oliver

CONTENTS

ACKNOWLEDGMENTS

It is a pleasurable duty to acknowledge the assistance received from several institutions and individuals in enabling this study. Most of the financial means for carrying out the field research were provided by the National Science Foundation, the Howard Foundation (Brown University), and the Tri-Institutional Pacific Program. I am also indebted to Harvard University for logistic support, and to the University of Hawaii's Social Science Research Institute (William Lebra, director) for providing facilities for analyzing research results. Professor Jean Guiart helped greatly to expedite the official permit to conduct research in the Society Islands, and in those islands my work was facilitated—indeed, made possible and congenial—by the top officials of the Administration, by Dr. Émile Massal, the late Dr. Henri Jacquier, Mlle J. Laguesse, Mlle Aurora Natua, M. Jullien, and Mr. and Mrs. M. R. Kellam. In addition, I wish especially to thank Dr. and Mrs. Bengt Danielsson for their warm hospitality, and Mr. R. G. White for his patient efforts to arm me with a working knowledge of the Tahitian language.

My colleagues in this enterprise were Ben Finney, Roger Green, Antony Hooper, Paul Kay, Robert Levy, and Richard Moench. To all of them I am indebted for their friendship and for their perspectives derived from their own researchers in the Society Islands.

And finally—needless to say—I am most grateful to the long-suffering residents of "my" two Tahitian villages, who treated me with unfailing hospitality and friendliness, despite their puzzlement as to why I was there.

PREFACE

This monograph is intended, mainly, to be an exercise in "controlled comparison"—a *genre* of anthropological research that has been practiced for a very long time and that has generated many interesting studies.[1] It has been claimed by some of its proponents that, because of anthropology's inability to conduct sufficiently controlled *experiments,* controlled *comparison* is the sole means at its disposal to arrive at "scientific," universally valid generalizations about cultural process. I am not convinced that that is so—or, for that matter, that *any* research method heretofore proposed or practiced is capable of producing such generalizations—but controlled comparison appears to be a method worth devoting more effort to.

The weakness of the method in most of its applications so far has been, it seems to me, that the societies that have been compared have shared too few characteristics to permit sufficient "control."

As an exception to this kind of widespread circumstance, Polynesia has long been cited as an ideal region for controlled comparison, and indeed some stimulating hypotheses about cultural process have been generated by comparisons made among some of its pre-European societies[2]—to the extent,

---

[1] A comprehensive review of the method and its applications is contained in F. Eggan's "Social Anthropology and the Method of Controlled Comparison," *American Anthropologist,* 56 (1954). That influential article covered the literature up to 1953 when field work for the present monograph was first planned.

[2] As, for example, Irving Goldman's *Ancient Polynesian Society* (Chicago: University of Chicago Press, 1970), and Marshall Sahlin's *Social Stratification in Polynesia* (Seattle: University of Washington Press, 1953). And for nearby Micronesia, Leonard Mason's "Suprafamilial Authority and Economic Process in Micronesian Atolls," *Humanités, Cahiers de l'Institut de Science Economique Appliquée,* Ser. V, No. 1 (1959). Or for Melanesia, see my "Horomorum Concepts of Southern Bougainville," in Peabody Museum Papers 20 (Cambridge, Mass.: Peabody Museum, 1943); Jill Nash's "Sex, Money, and the Status of Women in Aboriginal South Bougainville" (in press); and the torrent of studies, with comparative focuses, that has flowed from research in the New Guinea Highlands.

that is, that reliable records made such comparisons credible. In the case of present-day Polynesian societies, however, i.e., of those that have come to differ from one another not only in geographic setting and population size but in colonial history, etc., the requisite "controls" have become too exiguous to permit the generation of credible propositions or testable hypotheses.

So, what is the science-minded Polynesianist to do? Leave those Happy Isles to the archaeologists, or to the functionalist (or structuralist, or symbolist, etc.) ethnographers, and look for more tractable comparisons elsewhere? or concentrate upon a single "species" of present-day Polynesian society and try applying his comparative approach to its several subspecific varieties?

After about thirty seconds of deep deliberation, I decided upon the latter alternative and to focus my study on that species of Polynesian society located, appropriately enough, in the Society Islands—a decision that would probably have been made by most anthropologists who, like myself, had already experienced Tahiti and who did not consider the hair shirt to be a necessary uniform for field work.

Thus persuaded, I returned to the Society Islands in 1954, and for a year pursued my primary objective, first on the island of Huahine and then on Mo'orea. In doing so, however, I came to recognize that there were almost as many subspecific varieties of Tahitian societal cultures as there were communities, so that I determined upon having as many of them studied as possible. In the end, this turned out to be eight in number—two of which were studied by myself in 1954–55 and again in 1959–60, and six of which were studied, two each, by Harvard student-colleagues Ben Finney, Antony Hooper, and Paul Kay. In addition to these, another student-colleague, Richard Moench, was assigned the formidable and fascinating task of learning how the Chinese residents of these islands provided the connections by which the Tahitians were, mainly, integrated into the colony's European-dominated society. And we subsequently succeeded in persuading a Tahitiphile psychiatrist, Robert Levy, to devote several years of his life to study two of our eight communities from his complementary perspective. (The publications that have thus far come out of this research program are listed in the Bibliography, under the above participants' names.)

As usual, the student colleagues completed and published their parts of this enterprise sooner than their professor—*they* needed jobs and did not have to attend committee meetings!—but I am finally fulfilling one of my purposes of the enterprise with the publication of this comparison of the two communities I studied. If hardening arteries and softening resolve permit, I will someday combine the observations recorded about all eight communities within a single comprehensive frame—but for the next few years, there are other, more engrossing projects to pursue.

In this monograph, I have attempted to do three quite separate things. First, in line with my conviction that *description* of a vanishing way of life is an anthropologist's most urgent and most important professional duty, I have attempted to provide fairly comprehensive and fairly detailed pictures of the "public" behavior of the residents of the two rural Tahitian villages I observed. That they were vanishing—have indeed now vanished—is attested by recent reports from Tahiti. Secondly, I have attempted to exemplify and test the usefulness of the method of "controlled comparison"—which, as noted above, has been characterized by some to be anthropology's main way of achieving respectability as a social *science*. And thirdly, I have focussed on the "economic" aspects of the communities studied in an attempt to indicate that the "hard" *discipline* of economics could profit by some leavening by the "soft" *art* of ethnography.

In the long run, I expect that the descriptive portions of my monographs—*sans* comparison and *sans* "economics"—will prove to be the most useful part of it; what passes for science in today's world will inevitably change, and the boundaries of present-day academic disciplines will inevitably shift. But a description of a unique and vanished way of life, however small in scale and however inconsequential to the rest of the present-day world, will always have some value in the future's Museum of the Human Experience.

With regard to my third objective, to the "economics" aspects of this monograph, what I have *not* attempted to do is emphasize how the Tahitians I observed *deviated* from "classic" models about how economics, "primitive" or "modern," etc., operate. I have, of course, attempted to describe, and in some detail, how the Tahitians did the things popularly included under the dictionary rubric of "economic" but, as will be seen, my conception of what may be so included is rather wider than many such conceptions.

Thus, I have not made a point of distinguishing my subjects' "economic" behavior as being different from any "standard" form of such behavior. Why? Simply because I do not believe that the economy of any *whole* society, anywhere, conforms very closely to such a standard. In other words, while historians and theoreticians have formulated models about "the ways economies work," they are hypothetical models, useful for certain purposes (when applicable to certain limited segments of actual ethnographically localized behavior) but otherwise misleading and a source of fruitless and tiresome debate.

Of course, much of the Tahitians' "economic" behavior I observed differed from what I have seen occurring in the segments of American behavior I am most familiar with. (For example, the case cited on page 98 about Tahitians' apparent disinterest in sparing themselves *future* work by investing *present* effort in labor-saving devices.) But to characterize such propensities as "noneconomic," as being a deviation from some *universal* standard of economic behavior, would be like saying that a giraffe is a deviant kind of animal because it has a long neck.

In other words, in connection with my third objective, it is my limited purpose in this monograph to compare the economies of two small village societies *one* with *the other,* and not with *all other* societal economies, or *any other* known societal economy. In doing so, I have not hesitated to use words like "savings," "rent," "profit," "investment," etc., as convenient glosses to inform readers of what I am, broadly speaking, referring to. (If any reader objects to my usages, he is invited to substitute labels of his own.) In my view, the arguments over such terms—and such other ones as "primitive," "rational," "surplus," "maximization," and the like, have long since passed their point of usefulness. Like many of the words argued over in medieval scholasticism, they served in the beginning to sharpen awareness of certain intellectual issues but should now be relegated to our art's version of the *Oxford English Dictionary*—i.e., the dictionary containing not necessarily *correct* but rather historically dated usages of words.

CHAPTER I

INTRODUCTION

The Society Islands

The archipelago now known as the Society Islands was first visited and reported on by Europeans in 1767, when Captain Samuel Wallis, commander of the H.M.S. *Dolphin*, touched briefly at small and isolated Me'etia, the easternmost island of the chain, and then went on to anchor and tarry at Tahiti, the largest island of the chain. At that point in its history, Tahiti had an indigenous population of about 35,000, and all the other inhabited islands of the archipelago another 12–15,000 more (Oliver 1974). Though divided into numerous separate and often warring tribal units, all of the inhabitants spoke a common Polynesian language and shared a common culture. Recent archaeological finds indicate that the Society Islands had begun to be populated in about A.D. 800 and that the early inhabitants were culturally very similar to their contemporaries in other central and eastern Polynesian archipelagos; but by the time of Wallis's visit, the populations of these various archipelagos had long since become relatively or absolutely isolated from one another, and had all evolved some distinctive beliefs and practices, including widely dissimilar dialects or mutually unintelligible languages.

After Wallis, and except for a gap between 1777 and 1788, Tahiti and one or more of its neighboring islands provided anchorage and various kinds of hospitality to a succession of European ships—English, French, and Spanish, but mostly English—all accompanied by the characteristic types of interchanges: material, sexual, pathogenic, etc.—and cumulatively resulting in the historically familiar conditions of political turbulence, population decline, and changes in material life.

In 1797, a band of representatives of the London Missionary Society landed on Tahiti and began the process of religious transformation, which added to the political turbulence for a while but culminated, in 1815, in the establishment of a unified monarchy over all Tahiti and Mo'orea by one of the leading chiefly converts, Pomare II.

During the following twenty-eight years, contacts with Europeans multiplied, but the islands' several tribal regimes—the Pomare monarchy of Tahiti-Mo'orea, and the three Leeward Island "kingdoms" of Huahine-Mai'ao, Ra'iatea-Taha'a, and Borabora-Maupiti—remained more or less separate and independent although influenced weightily by their resident British missionaries and by the assurances of international "protection" received from various other British subjects, who visited the islands with increasing frequency.

This situation changed in the Windward Islands (i.e., Tahiti, Mo'orea, Me'etia, Tetiaroa) in 1842, when France established a political foothold, which became formalized in 1847 as a Protectorate and consolidated in 1880 as a fully annexed Colony. Meanwhile, in the petty kingdoms of the Leeward Islands, the influence of British residents, though complicated by German commercial activities, remained paramount until France succeeded, in 1897, in annexing them as well (although under the euphemistic label of a *régime de l'indigenat*). Thereafter, the Leeward Islands were joined to the Windwards, the Tuamotus, Marquesas, Gambiers, and Australs into a single unit, the EFO (*Etablissements Français de l'Océanie*, subsequently changed to *Polynésie Française*), which was administered by governors and other top-level officials sent out from Paris.

In 1940, some resident and mainly French de Gaullists succeeded in overriding the local (and also largely French) Pétainistes and brought the EFO into the Free French camp. (The presence of a United States base on Borabora undoubtedly contributed to keeping it that way.) Finally, in 1946 under the postwar Fourth French Republic, the whole Colony became an overseas Territory and all its Polynesian indigenes French citizens. Although increasing amounts of local self-government were subsequently meted out to the latter, at the time of my field studies in 1954–55 and 1959–60, on which this book is based, the Territory's status was still that of a colony, in fact if not in name.

The principal islands of the Society archipelago are spread out for about 480 km along a northwest-to-southeast axis. The widest gap in this chain is the one of 120 km separating Tahiti from Me'etia, but from their mountain heights even these two islands are within sight of each other. The next widest gap is the one of about 80 km separating Mai'ao (which with Tahiti, Mo'orea, Me'etia, and Tetiaroa are now called the Windward Islands), from Huahine (which with Ra'iatea, Taha'a, Borabora, Maupiti and Tupai are called the Leeward Islands). This ocean gap between Windwards and Leewards is now administratively formalized; it also contributed to the evolution of some cultural differences between the two groups of islands during pre-European times (except that Mai'ao, now in the Windward administrative *circonscription,* was formerly a part of the Huahine chiefdom).

Tetiaroa and Tupai are coral atolls; all the others just listed are volcanic, or high islands, although Mai'ao's highest point rises only 185 meters above its broad atoll-like lagoons. Tahiti is the largest of the islands by far, measuring 52 km along its axis.

All these islands are the remnants of cones raised by successive extrusions of lava from the ocean floor, and many of the physical differences among them derive from their differences in geological age. The atolls are oldest of all, then Mai'ao; all the others are relics of a more recent succession of eruptions, which progressed from northwest to southeast, thereby making Maupiti oldest (hence most degraded and with more reefs) and Me'etia youngest (hence least degraded and with no barrier reef at all).

Atoll topography is well enough known so as to require no further description here. Mai'ao is little more than an atoll with a hill dividing its two large lagoons. As for the other high islands, they all consist of one or more central mountain peaks or ranges, valleys ranging from broad and open to narrow and confined, and of littorals varying from vertical cliffs to mile-wide coastal plains. Corresponding differences occur in types of soils, from rich alluvial to relatively sterile coraline sand.

The year-round high temperatures that would otherwise attend these islands' latitude (i.e., center 17° south) are tempered by their location in the sweep of the southeast trades, which blow almost continuously from May to October and intermittently the rest of the year, when they alternate with calms or with winds from the west. These variations and their accompanying changes in humidity and rainfall make up two seasons—a warmer and wetter one from November to April, with a mean maximum temperature of 31.6 C, and a cooler and drier one from May to October. The differences between these two seasons are not wide; the mean maximum temperature of the hottest month is only 2.2 C higher than that of the coolest, and the rainfall of the wettest month is only about twice as much as that of the driest. However, these figures are but averages for the whole inhabited part of the archipelago; more pertinent for this study is the fact that local variations in climate are considerably greater than the averaged seasonal differences just mentioned.

Different combinations of types of topography, soil, and climate served to permit the indigenous growth of various types and combinations of plants; and this natural inventory and arrangement of vegetation has been altered, in some places totally, by human agents, both recently and prehistorically. From the viewpoint of scientific taxonomy, the islands' indigenous plant associations have been divided into four major zones—atoll, coastal, mesotropical, and wet tropical—and the last three of these in turn subdivided as follows:

Coastal. This zone, which extends from the foot of the mountain flanks to the lagoon or ocean and includes the lower floors of the valleys, is divided into three subzones: (1) submangrove—muddy flats containing ferns, grasses, and the following economically noteworthy trees: hibiscus, Thespia, Barringtonia, Calophyllum and Hernandia; (2) littoral—a narrow, saline-dominated strip of shoreline containing some of the submangrove and atoll vegetation, along with Inocarpus (Tahitian chestnut), Casuarina (iron-wood), Ximinia, and several other shrubs, legumes, and grasses; (3) adlittor-al plain—the most extensive part of the coastal zone, extending from the littoral to the mountain slopes and up into the bottom of the valleys. Most trees found in the littoral zone also grow here, along with the pandanuses, banyans, and numerous species of vines, shrubs, etc.

Mesotropical. This zone extends from the adlittoral to altitudes up to about 300 meters and is in places characterized by intense sunshine and moderate rainfall. The dominant indigenous plants of this zone are acacias, shrubs, and a ground cover of grasses, legumes, ferns, woody herbs, and mosses.

Wet-tropical. This zone is divided into four subzones: (1) lower reaches of valleys—Spondias (Tahitian mango), Taetsia (the ritually important *ti*), Amomum (native ginger), etc.; (2) plateaus and middle slopes of mountains—this subzone consists of three types of vegetation landscapes: myrtle forests; moors and pseudosavannahs, covered mainly with Gleichenia fern; and steep high slopes, sporadically populated by myrtles; (3) rain forests; (4) mountain summits of Tahiti and Ra'iatea, dominated by myrtle, saxifrage, ferns, epiphytes, and lycopodes.

The indigenous plant geography just listed has undergone some major transformations since humans arrived in these islands twelve or more centuries ago. These changes may be most conveniently summarized by treating them as having taken place in two stages, pre- and post-European.

During the ten or more centuries prior to European contact, the islands' Polynesian inhabitants wrought, directly or indirectly, the following changes in the prehuman landscape.

First, many areas of adlittoral and lower valley subzones were cleared of their original vegetation and replaced with houses, temples, groves, and gardens of introduced plants—mainly breadfruit, taro, *taruā* (*Xanthosoma*), sweet potato, yam, arrowroot (*Tacca pinnatifida*), sugar cane, paper mulberry, and giant taro (*Alocasia*). Some of these subsequently "escaped" from gardens and groves and became established in other settings.

Second, several kinds of useful prehuman plants were encouraged to proliferate by deliberate planting and protection, mainly in the coastal and lower valley areas, e.g., coconut palms, mountain plantains, bananas, kava (*ava, Piper methysticum*), ti (*Cordyline terminalis*), and turmeric.

Third, considerable inroads were made into natural growth of certain plants for food, construction, and other purposes. For example, natural stands of mountain plantain had been drawn upon heavily, and men had to go farther and farther inland in search of suitable trees for canoe hulls and house timbers.

Fourth, the pigs introduced by the Polynesians have succeeded in destroying some of the original plants in some areas, but much more destructive in this respect were the brush fires set by humans, accidentally or in connection with pig hunting, garden clearing, and warfare.

In summary, by the time Europeans had arrived on the scene, the Tahitians had, deliberately or otherwise, brought about extensive changes in some parts of the islands—mainly in the adlittoral parts of the coastal zone, the lower slopes of the dry tropical zone, and the lower parts of the wet tropical zone—areas which European visitors were to describe as parklike, reminiscent of "the Elysian fields."

The vegetation changes resulting from European contact have been much greater, in numbers of new plants and in spatial extent, although the zones mainly affected are the same as those modified by the Polynesians, namely Tetiaroa atoll and the atoll-like flats of Mai'ao, and the coastal and mesotropical zones of the high islands.

In the coastal and mesotropical zones such Polynesian-introduced plants as breadfruit and coconuts have been augmented with Indian mangoes, citruses, sweet bananas, sugar cane, coffee, papaya, and guavas, along with several new shrubs and grasses. Throughout much of the mesotropical zone, frequent brush fires and the wasteful methods employed by the (largely Chinese) market gardeners have resulted in considerable soil erosion, the near disappearance of casuarinas, a further spread of the Gleichenia fern, and invasion of a number of introduced plant pests such as lantana and guava.

It is in the coastal zone, however, where the greatest transformation has been effected. The Polynesian-era stands of coconuts have been added to by mile after mile of commercially-planted groves. And the Polynesian inventory of fruit plants and ornamentals has been expanded and widely extended. Along with these changes, numerous weeds and other troublesome plants have moved in, including particularly the ubiquitous guava. In addition, large areas have been planted in vanilla, pineapples, melons, cassava, sugar cane, and other cash crops; and the Tahitians' gardens now contain a number of new food plants of European and American origin.

Before humans arrived in these islands, there evidently were no mammals there at all, and reptiles consisted only of blue skinks and geckos. The most noteworthy freshwater fish present were perches, gobies, pipefish, and eels. There were numerous species of land and freshwater prawns. Upon their arrival, Europeans found there scorpions, centipedes, house flies, fleas, and two kinds of mosquitoes, the *Cultex fatigans* and the filaria-bearing *Ardes polynesiensis*. It is not known whether any of these were present before the Polynesians, or were brought there, accidentally, by them. On the other hand, it is almost certain that it was the Polynesian immigrants who (purposely) introduced pigs, dogs, and chickens, and (probably unwittingly) a small, brown species of rat.

The most noteworthy birds that inhabited these islands prior to human occupation were frigate birds, boobies, tropic birds, ducks, terns, sandpipers, curlews, pigeons, parakeets, cuckoos, kingfishers, shrikes, and Old World warblers. It is unlikely that the Polynesians added to this list.

Since 1767, the faunal inventory of these islands has been changed in several ways. In the first place, several entirely new mammals have been introduced—e.g., horses, cows, cats, goats, and sheep—along with new varieties of pigs, dogs, chickens, and rats. The effects of these introductions have been varied and far-reaching. The immigrant rat, for example, has replaced the pre-European variety; crossbreeding with the newcomers has completely transformed the local pigs, dogs, and chickens; and goats, especially, have denuded many places through their close-cropping grazing. Some new species of freshwater fish have been deliberately introduced, but with what effects I do not know, nor do I know of any change having taken place with respect to molluscs, crabs, and prawns. As for insects, the durable Polynesian varieties are still thriving and have been joined by such stowaways as cockroaches and doubtless several new varieties of house flies and fleas. (As on most other Polynesian islands, however, malarial mosquitos have not yet established a base.)

The bird population has also been expanded during European times—most conspicuously and noisily by the irascible mynah (*Acridotneris tristis*). It is plausible to suppose that some of the fauna introduced during the European times—e.g., cats and egg-eating rats—have served to reduce the variety and quantity of the indigenous birds, but I do not know whether that is in fact the case.

The marine world encompassing these islands plays almost as important a part in the lives of many present-day Tahitians as it did with their ancestors two centuries ago, and the geography of that world appears not to have changed much since that time. In terms of the uses made of it by present-day Tahitians, it consists of several distinctive zones.

At one extreme are those places such as the southeastern tip of Tahiti where mountains plunge vertically into the sea with no beachline and with no offshore barrier reef protecting the coast from the ocean's swells and waves. Except in very calm seas, such waters are hazardous for both swimmers and small boats; hence, fishing of most kinds.

Somewhat similar but less hazardous conditions prevail along windward coasts that are sheltered only discontinuously by reef but are fringed with strips of beach, usually consisting of black basalt sand. Fishing did and continues to take place here, both angling and netting, but the waves often run prohibitively high; and the water is usually too turbid for underwater spear fishing.

The more continuous barrier reefs, which occur most typically along the islands' leeward coasts, provide several different kinds of environments for fishing. The shallow waters along the shore, with or without fringing reefs, supply gastropods, molluscs, crustaceans, octopus, eels, and small fish (used mainly for bait). In addition to these, the deeper waters of the lagoons contain a large variety of free-swimming fish; and fishing is facilitated here by the relatively calm waters and the white-sand bottom, which improve visibility. The barrier reefs themselves also harbor molluscs, etc., and provide footing for casting or spear-diving into the deeper waters outside.

Finally, the open seas around and between the islands are regular feeding grounds for such pelagic fish as bonito, dolphin, albacore, cavally, swordfish, and shark. The waters around openings in the reefs are especially populous because of the small fry and other food discharged from the freshwater streams (which also inhibit the growth of coral and hence gave rise to the openings in the reef).

Two other distinctive marine environments in these waters worth noting are the extensive shallow and muddy sea flats found in the southern angle formed by the join of Tahiti's two major parts and the nearly landlocked lagoon at the northern end of Huahine. The former is particularly well supplied with crustaceans and other shallow-water animals, and the latter forms a natural trap for fish entering the long narrow channel from the sea.

What emerges from the above summary is that, along with some environmental features found throughout these islands, e.g., fairly similar year-round temperatures, fairly similar kinds of vegetation, close access to fairly similar kinds of pelagic fish, etc., there also occur some marked local differences in the relative quantities of various environmental features.

With respect to topography, for instance, some settlements were (and are) spread thinly over wide coastal flats while others are concentrated along narrow, steep-backed beaches. Some settlements front quiet lagoons while others face turbulent open seas. Climate, too, presents some wide local variations—not so much in temperature as in insolation, rain, and wind. For instance, Tahiti's southern isthmus receives more than one and a half times as much rain as its northwest coast; and for anyone fishing or having to travel by sea, there is a crucial difference between the wind velocities off windward and leeward coasts.

Comparably wide local differences occur with respect to soils, to vegetation, and to accessible marine resources; and these and other differences just mentioned exerted much influence upon present-day gardening, commercial agriculture, and fishing during the period of this study. For example, breadfruit grew almost everywhere throughout the inhabited zones, but the kind and quantity of root crops produced depended greatly upon soil type and ground moisture. And while coconuts will grow at lower altitudes nearly everywhere, vanilla requires very special combinations of soil, insolation, and ground moisture. Also, the location of a place with respect to other populated places was an aspect of differentiation that should not be overlooked. For instance, Huahine's long distance from Tahiti limited commercial fishing to the scale of what could be locally consumed, whereas Mo'orean fishermen produced copiously for the nearby Pape'ete market.

However, it would be erroneous to attribute to the physical environment too decisive an influence on what mid-twentieth-century Tahitians produced for their own consumption or for sale. For example, for all its distance from the Pape'ete market, remote Maupiti Island produced masses of watermelons and sent them there for sale. And for all its unavoidably difficult and hazardous boat-loading procedures, Mai'ao Island regularly exported large quantities of copra and fresh fish.

The census of 1951 (Tessier 1953) listed the residents of the Society Islands under the following labels:

Métropolitains	1,389
Créoles et Métis	11,677
Autochthones	26,581
Chinois	6,475
Européens et autres étrangers	533
Total	46,655

Unfortunately, it is not entirely clear what some of the census's ethnic labels signify. *Métropolitains* evidently refers to French citizens born outside the EFO; presumably most of these would have been Caucasian in physical type, but that is not certain (nor is it particularly relevant to the present study). Also the *Européens et autres étrangers* include the many Americans and the handful of other non-French, non-Chinese aliens residing there. And by *Chinois* is presumably meant all those who classify themselves as such, whether born locally or not, and including perhaps some who may not be of wholly Chinese descent. But the major problems arise in connection with the labels *Autochthones* and *Créoles et Métis*.

Autochthones translates, not surprisingly, as "autochthons" (*The Concise Oxford French Dictionary*, London: O.E.P., 1958, p. 73); and the latter has the conventional meaning in English of "native to a particular place," "indigene," "aborigine," etc. Unfortunately, the census does not specify which place is referred to—the Society Islands? the EFO overall? Polynesia? or Oceania in general? And although the implication seems to be that the individuals in question contain large proportions of Pacific-islander genes, it does not specify how large; and it would be rash judgment indeed to claim that *any* Pacific islanders now residing in the Society Islands possess no non-Pacific islander genes.

Some clarification of the question of provenience is provided by comparison with another tabular breakdown, *Démembrement par nationalité*. With respect to the Leeward Islands, all the *autochthones* are included under the label *Océaniens citoyens français*, which signifies at least that they are native to a French Pacific dependency; no comparable clarification is, however, provided for the Windward Islands.

Turning now to the label *Créoles et Métis*, the former evidently refers to locally-born (?) French citizens of mostly (or at least self-identified) Caucasian descent. As for *Métis*, this identification was deduced (according to the explanation) if the "mixed-blood" in question was now a French citizen and possessed a surname of "foreign origin, either European or Asian." (Teissier 1953, p. 6.) The numbers of combinations of elements included under this label—biological, geographic, national—are potentially and in fact so numerous that I shall not even attempt to identify them.

To estimate the corresponding numbers in these census categories for 1954-55, the period of my first field study, it would be logical, though not demonstrably accurate, to add to the listed numbers about 75 percent of the increase deduced from the next census of 1956. Again, unfortunately, the 1956 census[1] classifies the population under labels that differ in some cases from those of 1951:

---

[1] *République Française: Territoire de la Polynésie Française: Recensement Général de la Population* (December 1956). *Résultats définitifs*. Paris 1960.

Français de Naissance

D'origine métropolitaine 1,618
De Polynésie 22,841
Autres Français non-métropolitaine 1,087

Naturalisés

De souche Asiatique 237
Autres nationalités 175

Etrangers

Nationaux d'Europe 103
Chinois 3,793
Autres nationaux d'Asie 19
Autres nationalités 208

In fact, any attempt to sort out and enumerate these islands' population in terms of conventional labels is doomed to partial failure. Not only are some of the criteria employed locally to classify persons mainly behavioral, but even these criteria are subject to change, according to context.

A simpler, but more socially significant, everyday classification of persons in these islands is provided by Tahitian-language usage: *popaʻa* (Caucasian), *tinito* (Chinese), *Maʻohi* or *Taʻata Tahiti* (Polynesian), and mixed-blood (French, *Demi*; Tahitian, *ʻafa*). *Demi* and *ʻafa* are used mostly to refer to an alleged mixture of Polynesian and Caucasian; when the non-Tahitian component is Chinese, the person in question is usually called *demi-Chinois* or *ʻafa Tinito*.

However, biological race constitutes only one aspect of the distinction. As noted above, there are probably very few living Tahitians who do not contain some Caucasian genes, or Chinese genes, or both. Moreover, in many instances the proportions are large enough to be recognized even by the most anthropologically uninformed. Even so, some individuals who are dominantly Caucasian in physical features, e.g., white-skinned, blond-haired, blue-eyed, and who are positively known to have had a European parent or grandparent, are nevertheless called "true Tahitians" by their neighbors. And the converse is also sometimes the case. For, as Finney puts it, the prime criteria for the labeling are cultural and behavioral: "To use the term common in French colonial practice, *Demis* are *evolués* Tahitians: persons who have "evolved" to the point where they speak French in preference to Tahitian, follow French table manners and avoid the Tahitian practice of eating with the hands, and, in general, act more European than Tahitian." (Finney 1973, p. 22.)

As a first approximation, Finney's characterization of *Demis* is a useful enough one, but situationally the matter becomes far more complicated. For instance, some persons may act and identify themselves as *Demis* in some situations and as *Tahitians* in others. Also, a person's location, behaviorally, on what might be called the Tahitian-European continuum, will tend to influence how he labels another person, however others may label the latter, or however the latter labels himself (Kay 1963, Appendix 1).

More will be said about the demography of the more Tahitian portion of the Society Islands population in Section B, but it may be useful at this point to say a few words about the other ethnic categories in terms of their histories, their occupations (if any), their population trends, and their geographic distribution.

Europeans began visiting these islands in 1767 with the arrival of the British ship *Dolphin*. During the following three decades after that came many others in ships commanded by Cook, Bougainville, Boenechea, Bligh, Vancouver, etc. Some crew men remained for months or even years after their vessels departed, notably several of the *Bounty* mutineers. But aside from a few beachcombers, the first Europeans to settle in these islands with the firm intention of making them their homes were members of the London Missionary Society who arrived in 1797. Since then, these islands have never been without some Europeans; and with the imposition of French rule, beginning in 1843, the numbers have continually (but not steadily) increased. Several of the earlier immigrants married Tahitian women, acquired land, established plantations and other enterprises, and founded European-style family lines that have survived to this day. Others also settled down into liaisons with Tahitian women but produced progeny that have become submerged into the *Autochthone* population. And still others have succeeded—if such is one's notion of success—in founding family lines that are European both genealogically and in style of life. Among the Caucasians, individuals of metropolitan French extraction preponderate, but there have also been many British, American and other European immigrants who made these islands homes for themselves and their progeny.

In addition, large numbers of Europeans have remained in the islands for shorter periods, or without having established recognizable, or even unrecognizable, lines of descendents there. Adventurers, escape-minded romanticists, etc., have figured prominently among these latter; but probably the largest segment of nonpermanent European residents have been functionaries posted there from France.[2]

---

[2]It should be kept in mind that the period referred to by this and other statements in this chapter is 1954-60 and before. With the undertaking of atom bomb experiments in Moruroa in the 1960s, Tahiti became its principal supply and operational headquarters, which brought in large numbers of additional Europeans (Danielsson and Danielsson 1977).

The second large non-Pacific-islander component of the population is the Chinese, who numbered 6,475 in the 1951 census and who were at that time evidently still on the increase. The first sizeable influx of Chinese arrived in the 1860s; these were laborers recruited in Canton and Hong Kong for a cotton plantation established on Tahiti (to exploit the market shortages occasioned by the American Civil War) (Coppenrath, Moench). With the failure of this enterprise—another example of the familiar South Sea Bubble—most of the Chinese were repatriated, although those who remained were eventually joined by others seeking work. Until about 1907, the numbers remained fairly constant, i.e., 300–400 and nearly all males, and included a large proportion of transients. The 1911 Revolution in China induced another large influx; and although many of those returned eventually to China, their numbers had increased to about 4,000 by 1926, including hundreds of women. Since then, the rise in numbers has come about mainly through local births. In 1954–55, probably less than 10 percent of the local Chinese population were naturalized French citizens; the rest were considered citizens of Taiwan-based Nationalist China, which maintained a consulate in Pape‘ete. However, the source of most of the immigrants was mainland South China, largely from the Hakka-speaking regions. Most of the islands' Chinese resided in Pape‘ete and Uturoa, where they dominated retail and wholesale commerce and where their younger members were prominent in the skilled trades and in white-collar jobs in private firms. Being aliens, they were barred from most Administration jobs.

The Chinese who figure directly in this study were those living in the rural areas where they were the principal (indeed, in most places the only) storekeepers, the buyers (and sometimes the dryers) of copra, and the buyers and dryers of vanilla. Their roles in rural villages will be described later on.

In addition to all the above, there has been a continuous influx of other Pacific islanders into these islands during the last two centuries, including numbers from other Polynesian archipelagos. Those who remained have become Tahitianized in varying degrees, and most of them now are labeled as such.

Prior to 1767, the Tahitians satisfied most of their material needs for food, clothing, and shelter within the social bounds of their household groups; and they appear to have done so amply and without excessive toil. Food and other valued objects circulated outside the households in the form of hospitality, taxation, gift exchange, and religious offerings; but commercial trade was confined largely to contractual exchanges between some more specialized gardeners and nearly full-time fishermen. Some items that were characterized by craft specialty (such as finely-made stone adzes) or by localized raw materials (such as bowls made of a kind of basalt found only on Maupiti) also moved about and may have done so in part by barter, but most objects that circulated outside household groups did so in non-commercial ways.

Similar conventions typified the circulation of services and the exchange of services for objects. Some specialists (e.g., canoe makers, architects, entertainers, priests, physicians, magicians, warriors) exchanged their services for food, barkcloth, etc., on a barter-like basis; but most of the skilled labor performed for persons outside the specialist's own household was in the non-commercial ways listed above.

Another characteristic of Tahitians' pre-European economy was the paucity of wealth in terms of large, long-term accumulations of valued objects. Valuables were assembled periodically and turned over to chiefs, but such of these that were not quickly consumed within the latters' households were just as quickly exchanged again for "social credit."

Neither the indigenous forms of transactions nor the unconcern with tangible wealth underwent much change among the Tahitians during the first half-century or so of European contact. Tahitians traded pigs and other native produce for European tools, textiles, mirrors, muskets, and so on; but even many of these transactions were carried out in the idiom of gift exchange (to the delight, at first, of the Europeans; then to their bafflement; then irritation). And some Tahitians also traded occasional services, including especially sexual services, for Europeans' goods; but they were either unwilling or culturally unprepared to engage in steady wage labor for the latter except for service on European ships, which seems to have been regarded more as adventure than as routine toil, and except for domestic services in European households, which involved little modification in work habits or social ambiance.

After 1815, when Tahiti and Mo'orea became united under the Christianized regime of Pomare II and when a kind of *pax* (and *dux*) *missionaris* began to prevail throughout the Leeward islands as well, the islands underwent more radical economic change. The export of native products—especially coconut oil and pork—increased considerably, as did the local sale of food and labor to the numerous European vessels; and the list of exports had expanded to include pearl shell, arrowroot, molasses, lime juice, wood, *bêche-de-mer*, whale oil, and cattle. Some rum was also exported, and a lot more consumed locally, by visitors and Tahitians alike. Tahitians engaged in most of this commerce, but only as small-scale producers or occasional laborers. The larger-scale planters and processors were nearly all Europeans, as were the traders and merchants. Many of these latter cohabited, legitimately or otherwise, with Tahitian women and sired mixed-blood lines of progeny; some of these mixed-bloods continued to maintain their inherited estates and businesses for generations and indeed up to the present in some cases; but others (perhaps most) of them merged into rural Tahitian communities, economically as well as socially.

In the 1860s, the French authorities began a more deliberate campaign to Westernize the Windward Islands' economy through such measures as encouragement of colonization (mainly from France), through assistance to the development of larger-scale export crops and through individualization of land holdings. More Europeans did, in fact, immigrate, including several married couples; but those first efforts to transform Tahitians into individualist land-holding peasants or steady wage-laborers fared poorly. And the principal plantation venture, a scheme to produce cotton in Tahiti's district of Atimaono, ended in political scandal and economic disaster. That is to say, the enterprise itself ended; but one of its effects persisted and served to shape the islands' economy, ethnic composition and social structure for all conceivable time to come. I refer here, as already mentioned, to the introduction into the islands of large numbers of Chinese, which began with this enterprise. Having long since come to believe that Tahitians themselves were disinclined, to say the least, to engage in the kind of work required by the plantations of those times, the European promoters imported Chinese coolies for the job. And although many of the original batches later returned to China, those who remained, along with subsequent arrivals from China, eventually pioneered or gained control of the islands' rural commerce and of much of its urban retail and import-export business as well.

The need for labor also resulted in the import of scores of other Pacific islanders, particularly from the Cook and Gilbert Islands; but unlike the Chinese, those islanders who remained eventually merged into rural Tahitian communities, a process facilitated by their similarities to Tahitians in both appearance and way of life.

From the 1860s to World War II, the economy of the islands underwent some change in emphasis but little in its basic components. Copra became and remained the principal cash crop overall, but it was complemented or even superseded in many places by vanilla. Copra continued to be produced both on small, mainly Tahitian, holdings and on larger plantations owned by Europeans or by families of mixed European-Tahitian descent. Many Tahitians also turned to vanilla growing but the largest vanilla plantations were worked by Chinese, mainly on land leased from Tahitians or Europeans. Throughout this period, Tahitian producers usually dried their own coconuts but the more protracted and extracted process of vanilla-bean drying was carried out by Chinese traders, for whom this and bread baking became the principal sources of income in their nearly ubiquitous rural stores.

Meanwhile, Pape'ete remained the commercial center of the Territory. Through its port, nearly all overseas goods and people moved; and virtually all of this trade remained in European or Chinese hands. Pape'ete's population was enlarged by a sprinkling of tourists and by metropolitan French functionaries. In addition, increasing numbers of Marquesans, Tuamotuans, Austral Islanders, etc., went to the capital for long or indefinite stays, as did many rural Tahitians as well; however, most of the latter retained their homes and their economic bases in their home communities.

World War II brought straitened economic conditions for all the islands' ethnic elements, but the postwar era (up to the time of my first study in 1954–55) witnessed a resumption of copra and vanilla "prosperity," and a considerable increase in tourism (the latter augmented through seaplane connection with Fiji). However, neither during this nor in the preceding periods were locally generated revenues sufficient to pay for the costs of administering these islands or for providing for the inhabitants' health, communications, or educational needs. The islands remained strongly attached to France commercially as well as administratively, but at the cost of an increasingly large financial subsidy from Paris. Moreover, although a certain amount of local economic diversification developed in response to local demand, much of the islands' food (e.g., beef, canned fish, butter, rice, flour) and nearly all of its manufactured goods continued to come from overseas.

The Society Islands, along with the Marquesas, Tuamotus, Gambiers, and Australs, make up the French Overseas Territory of *Polynésie Française,* which in 1954–55 was called *Etablissements Français de l'Océanie* (EFO) and which has for its governmental headquarters the town of Pape'ete on the island of Tahiti. In 1954–55, the EFO had an administrative structure along with what can be called a legislative one—the former headed by *fonctionnaires* appointed and sustained by the government of the French Union, the latter by representatives elected by voters of the EFO.

Administratively, the EFO was composed of *circonscriptions,* divisions thereof, and districts—in that order of subdivision, plus the urban communes of Pape'ete and Uturoa. The Society Islands, which are our concern, were divided into two such *circonscriptions*: (1) the Windward Islands (*Iles du Vent*) comprising Tahiti (twenty districts, or *mata'eina'a,* and the commune of Pape'ete), Mo'orea (five districts), Makatea, Mai'ao, Tetiaroa, and Me'etia; (2) the Leeward Islands (*Iles Sous-le-Vent*) comprising Ra'iatea (five districts and the commune of Uturoa), Taha'a (six districts), Borabora (three districts), Maupiti, Huahine (five districts), and Bellinghausen.

Each *circonscription* was presided over by an *administrateur* (*tāvana hau*) who was a career civil servant of metropolitan extraction and who reported to the territory's governor (*tāvana rahi*) who was also a civil servant from France. At the head of each *circonscription* division was a member of the

Gendarmerie, called by Tahitians the *muto'i farani,* and also usually of metropolitan extraction. In contrast, the district-level official (*muto'i*) in this hierarchy was typically a local (district) resident of at least part-Polynesian extraction. The official duties of the *muto'i,* although a salaried civil servant, required only part-time attention; when he was not delivering mail, investigating breaches of government regulations, etc., he was farming and fishing, or doing nothing, like his neighbors.

All the above officials had certain judicial and police powers; but in addition, the Territory contained a staff of judicial officers tied into the judicial hierarchy of the French Union. Judges sat regularly at Pape'ete and Uturoa, and also made circuits periodically around the districts. And in addition to all these functionaries, there were numerous other governmental organizations whose agents occasionally had dealings with the Territory's residents—agricultural experts, surveyors, public works engineers, doctors, nurses, etc.

Each district had its own government council consisting of five regular and two alternate members. These were elected by those residents of the district who were French citizens of at least twenty-one years of age and who had not been disenfranchised by court order. District elections took place periodically, and there was no limit to number of terms of office. From among their number, each district council elected one individual to be *chef* (*tāvana,* from English "governor"), one to be secretary, and one to be treasurer—all elections having been subject to approval by the colony's governor on advice of the *chef de circonscription.* The district *tāvana* received a small salary from the Colonial Administration plus a modest fund that was used mainly in the entertainment of visiting officials; the other council members served without pay.

Tāvana were officially described as "auxiliary agents" of the Administration. They and their council associates were supposed to meet at least once a month; they were charged with carrying out specific instructions of the *chef de circonscription* and, in general, to maintain their district's civil order as an official body of first resort. In addition, the *tāvana* himself was authorized to perform civil marriage ceremonies.

By terms of official decree, the *tāvana* possessed certain police powers locally, but the statutory delimitation between the roles of *tāvana* and *muto'i* was vague enough to permit some conflict of authority between the two officials if they disagreed. In fact, the circumstance that the latter was appointed by the Administration, rather than elected by themselves, led many Tahitians to consider him somewhat alien and thus suspect—if not in character then at least in his job.

As in colonies elsewhere, these islands have been for decades the scene of efforts on the part of some of their local residents to obtain a larger voice over their own affairs. Prior to World War II, the metropolitan government instituted a series of local colonial "councils," etc., to meet—or appear to meet—some of these desires, but maintained its control over the more important public aspects of life—political, economic, fiscal, judicial, educational, constabular, etc. Moreover, these jobs were performed in the main by functionaries sent out from France for relatively brief tours of duty and with salaries and perquisites generally superior to the ones of local residents of comparable background.

Predictably, the requests of local residents for more autonomy and fewer metropolitan functionaries became more vociferous after World War II and has increased steadily ever since. The metropolitan government's first response in the Territory was to institute a representative assembly consisting of ten elective members from the Windward Islands (mainly Tahiti) and ten from the rest of the territory. The powers given by the government to the first representative assembly were limited mainly to economic affairs, including voting the local budget (which, however, was drafted by the Administration and contained several expenditures over which the assembly had no say). Also, the assembly was privileged to be "consulted" by the Administration but was forbidden to debate "political matters" (Thompson and Adolff, p. 29). The first assembly was composed largely of men prominent in Pape'ete's commercial, political, and social life, most of them urban European in life-style and evidently conservative enough in attitude to tolerate a slow evolution in local political development. Stimulus for more rapid political change came from other segments of the population.

The first viable political party to become established in the colony was the RDPT (*Rassemblement Démocratique du Peuple Tahitien*), which grew up around the most remarkable culture-hero to develop in the islands since Maui, the demigod of legendary fame. The man in question was Pouvana'a a Opa'a, who was born on Huahine in 1895 and who was a veteran of World War I. Although thoroughly Tahitian in upbringing and manner, the very epitome of Tahitianness to his host of Tahitian and largely rural admirers, Pouvana'a was more Nordic than Polynesian in appearance, having inherited blue eyes and a fair complexion from a Danish forebear. His Leeward Island origin, which inculcated fundamentalist Protestantism, nostalgia for the nineteenth-century "British" era, resentment against Chinese commercial dominance, and a generally anti-French attitude, brought him into conflict with the firm-handed Free French authorities during World War II. On Tahiti Island, where he worked as a carpenter, he circulated petitions and founded organizations aimed at achieving more local autonomy and more equitable treatment of Tahitians (*vis-à-vis* European and Chinese privileges). As a consequence, he was exiled to his home island but later escaped in a canoe and made what was to become legendized as an epic journey to Borabora (which, in fact, is only about fifty miles distant), where an American force was based. On Borabora, he requested the American commander to forward his letter of protest to de Gaulle; instead of which, the officer delivered Pouvana'a to the French authorities, who this time deported him to isolated Bellinghausen Island.

After the war, Pouvana'a's widespread appeal among rural Tahitians provided several locally born, more urbanized but at least partially Tahitian, critics of the Administration with a titular leader for the movement which eventuated in the RSDP. At first, the platform of the movement included the familiar demand for more local self-government and civil rights and fewer imported metropolitan functionaries, but did not advocate any weakening of ties with France. In time, however, its attitude became more radical and anti-French, demanding, for instance, that Tahitians replace all nonlocal officials, that they take over the official bank and all Chinese-run commerce, that Tahitian rather than French be used as the official language, and that the French flag be replaced by one which had originally been given by the British to Queen Pomare a century earlier.

These developments alarmed not only the Administration but the pro-French, urbanized, affluent, and largely *Demi* population residing in Pape'ete, who consequently formed another political party, the UPO (*Union Populaire Océanienne*) to oppose the RSDP.

In the elections of 1953, RSDP candidates won eighteen of the twenty-five seats in the recently enlarged Territorial Assembly, and these then elected two of their leaders to represent the territory in the French Union Assembly and the Council of the French Republic, respectively, thereby constituting, with Pouvana'a, the Deputy, the entire elective representation of the Territory in Paris. By 1954–55, the period of my first field study there, the only representative elective institutions of government in the Territory were thus firmly under the control of the rural-based, Protestant-oriented, antimetropolitan RSDP. The municipal commune of Pape'ete remained in the camp of the UPO, and signs of factional strife were beginning to appear among the RSDP leaders, but in the villages I studied, Pouvana'a and his movement retained much of their original lustre.

The first systematic attempt to introduce Christianity into these islands was begun in 1797 by members of the London Missionary Society. Eighteen years later, after numerous vicissitudes, when its principal chiefly convert Pomare II finally and decisively defeated his pagan rivals and unified Tahiti and Mo'orea into a single kingdom, the new Protestant religion became the official one of the kingdom. Thereafter, until France established its rule, the connection between the kingdom and the mission was so close that the polity resembled a theocracy. The influence of the English missionaries was pervasive and powerful in administrative organization, in lawmaking, in conventions of dress, and so on. Protestant ritual displaced pagan ritual and Protestant myths eclipsed the pagan ones. Also, sustained official efforts were applied to inculcate Protestant ethical and moral principles in individual consciences as well as in social practices, with results evidently varying from profound success to total failure.

France's political control over the Tahiti-Mo'orea kingdom also paved the way for a Roman Catholic Mission which eventually led to some conversions to that creed, but Protestantism has continued to command the allegiance of most of Tahiti's and Mo'orea's indigenes ever since. In 1863, a French Protestant Mission (*Société des Missions Evangélique de Paris*) replaced the London Missionary Society and continued to exercise control over parish affairs until 1963, when *l'Eglise Protestante à Tahiti* became autonomous. The Catholic mission has throughout its history been conducted by members of the *Société de Picpus,* and their local adherents have, since the beginning, been mainly Europeans of French extraction and a scattering of French-Tahitian *Demis* practicing a more westernized way of life (O'Reilly, 1969).

In the Leeward Islands where French administrative control was not consolidated until 1897, the Protestantism first established by the English missionaries has continued to maintain a strong hold over the indigenous and largely rural population.

Meanwhile, the Mormons have made some inroads into the Protestant strongholds. Mormon missionaries first arrived in French Polynesia in 1844. For the next few years they had some success, mostly in Tubuai and in the Tuamotus, where London Missionary Society agents had not been active; but local difficulties and home-church neglect proved to be so discouraging that the Mormon missionaries returned home to America in 1852, leaving some converts in Tahiti and elsewhere who continued on their own and split up into numerous and bizarre sects. In 1873, two more American Mormon missionaries arrived, representatives of the breakaway Missouri (i.e., Reorganized) branch of the Mormon church—i.e., those who followed the leadership of Joseph Smith III and who were opposed to the Utah or Brigham Young branch. The Polynesian converts, and reconverts of these "Reorganites," became known as *Kanitos* (Saints). In 1892, some representatives of the Utah branch were transferred from Samoa to Tahiti and began their mission, including attempts to win over the *Kanitos* (Ellsworth, 1959). By 1954–55, the local congregations of the two branches in the Society Islands were still apart, and their total membership in these islands (1,200 in all) about equally divided in numbers.

The Tahitians

As noted earlier (refer to pages 1–15), the 1951 census of the Society Islands listed 26,581 *autochthones*. This figure includes many Polynesians born elsewhere (e.g., in other archipelagoes of the EFO, in the Cook Islands, etc.), but how many is not specified. And while it is true that many of the latter would, as in the past, eventually become wholly assimilated and thus became as Tahitian as the local born, others listed as *autochthones* in the 1951 census would probably return eventually to the places of their birth.

Another uncertainty in the figures is introduced by the census's category, *Créoles et Métis* (more popularly *Demi* in French, *'afa* in Tahitian), signifies racial mixture, but the label is more cultural than biological; if genetic criteria alone were involved, most if not all of those now labelled *autochthones* would have to be called *Métis*.

These and other ambiguities in the published census data also make it impossible to list age and sex characteristic of the whole *autochthone*, or true Tahitian, population of 1951. As an indication, however, such figures for the population of the Leeward Islands will not be too misleading, since 11,500 of the total population of 12,920 are labelled *Océaniens citoyens français*. (Although this category would appear to include *Créoles* and *Métis* along with *autochthones*, it is my impression that the latter constitute a far smaller proportion of the total population than was the case in Tahiti itself.)

For what it may be worth, there were listed 6,759 males and 6,161 females, i.e., a sex ratio of about 1:1.1, and an adult-child ratio of 1.2:1, adults being those twenty-one years of age and older. To apply these figures to the total "true" Tahitian population of the Society Islands (whatever that is) involves considerable risk of inaccuracy, but it is all there is to go by.

By comparison with the estimate offered for 1767–75, i.e., 35,000 for Tahiti and 12–15,000 for the rest (Oliver, 1974), the Tahitian population for 1951 had not yet recovered from the decline in numbers that took place soon after Europeans appeared on the scene. That decline was most precipitous during the first century of European contact, when, for instance, the population of Tahiti Island itself dropped to about 8,500, mainly as a result of introduced diseases combined with the reproduction consequences of infanticide. According to the evidence of subsequent censuses (e.g., McArthur, 1967), the locally born Polynesian population of these islands remained at less than one-half of its 1767–75 figure until after World War I, when it began to increase by natural process at an accelerating rate.

Most of the Tahitians of 1954–55 (henceforth, I shall use this label, unadjectivized, for what they themselves call *Ta'ata ma'ohi* or *Ta'ata Tahiti*) were residing in the archipelago's rural areas; but that, of course, is a tautology, inasmuch as the label is as much cultural as genetic and refers to a way of life basically rural in style. In any case, since it is mainly in the rural areas that a distinctive Tahitian way of life can be discerned, and since the communities described in this book are rural, the rest of this stage-setting section will apply to this part of the islands' "pluralistic" society.

Before the arrival of the Europeans, the Tahitians obtained their food by collecting breadfruit, coconuts, wild plantains, Tahitian chestnuts, native mango, cordyline roots, etc.; by gardening taro, *taruā,* 'giant taro,' plantains, yams, sweet potatoes, arrowroot, sugar cane, etc.; by raising pigs, chickens, and dogs; by fishing; and on rare occasions by hunting birds and feral pigs. Most of the early European reports agree that food was plentiful for all people most or all of the time, although there were seasonal scarcities of specific items. When in season, two or three times a year, breadfruit was the staple and required little or no cultivation; coconuts were harvested year round and appear to have been abundant. Little has been reported about horticultural methods except that their gardens were judged to be "untidy" by European standards. (The absence of written descriptions could mean either that the European observers did not consider the subject worthy of reporting, or that Tahitians did not devote much time to gardening—or both.) Some care was devoted to raising pigs and perhaps to raising dogs as well; both these animals were eaten, mainly on festive occasions. In contrast to reports about gardening, the sources abound in descriptions of the varieties of techniques and the fine skills utilized in fishing, which, again, may have been partly a reflection of the visibility of this activity and of the Europeans' interest in it, but only partly so; fishing was and remains a popular, highly skilled, and fruitful occupation among these islanders.

With a few exceptions, most pre-European Tahitian households—a unit composed of people who usually slept together and shared at least part of their daily food—produced virtually all the food they consumed. There was, of course, a division of labor in food production and processing among household members, and probably some small-scale interhousehold food exchanging, but usually of the same kinds of food. Moreover, this statement holds true for most households of all kinds, from the small nuclear-family units found mainly among commoners to the large establishments of *ari'i* chiefs. A few of the latter, it is true, obtained some of their daily food on a periodic basis from distant gardens and groves worked by residentially separated servants, but these servants acted as household adjuncts and not as tribute-paying tribal subjects.

The most noteworthy exceptions to domestic self-sufficiency in food were cases involving regular exchange between pairs of households, one specializing in fishing and the other in gardening. Other than this, there appear to have been no commercial transactions in food. Food did, however, figure in other kinds of transactions, e.g., as periodic and mainly symbolic tributes to chiefs, as ceremonial tokens or substantial grants of hospitality, as offerings to spirits, as accompaniments of social rites, etc., so that domestic consumption surpluses were occasionally required and, in fact, produced as a regular and universal aspect of social life. On the other hand, with three exceptions, the perishable nature of these islanders' food did not permit their physical accumulation in the form of social capital. (A donation of food to another person, mortal or spiritual, did often serve to build up social credit for the donor, but that is another thing.) The chief exception was pigs, which constituted a highly valued form of asset. Another exception was ripe coconuts, which remained edible for months on the trees. And the third was fermented breadfruit, which remained edible even longer. However, despite their durability, none of these three kinds of capital figured in commercial exchange in pre-European times.

Turning now to sleeping houses and other domestic shelters, most of these were evidently constructed from readily available materials by the household members themselves or with the help of neighbors and kinfolk, who received at most a meal or two for their services. In the case of larger buildings, e.g., the residences and guest houses of chiefs and other persons of social importance, the materials and labor were usually required as tribute from the owners' subjects, who may have been, but not necessarily, tokenly rewarded with food. Sometimes the owners utilized expert architects to plan and supervise the work, and these latter were either compensated for their services with extra food or valued objects, or, in some instances, these experts were regular members of the chiefly owners' household staffs.

The *marae,* the religious structures of pre-European times whose components consisted mostly of stones and slabs of coral, were constructed by their own congregations. Except for the experts who planned and supervised the building of the larger ones, and who, in some cases, received compensation in the form of food, barkcloth, mats, etc., for their services, the laborers were evidently not paid.

The same kind of arrangement obtained in the building of the larger canoes intended for official purposes, e.g., war canoes and travelling canoes for tribal chiefs. In the case of canoes intended for other purposes, however, the owner either built it himself or employed an expert to build it, or part of it, and paid him for his services in food and textiles.

Nearly everyone past early childhood had some competence in making barkcloth and plaiting the mats that served for garments, bedding, floor covering, etc. There was some division of labor practiced in these crafts and, of course, certain individuals excelled in them; but every household probably produced enough of these articles for its members' personal needs, and there does not seem to have been much commercial barter involving them.

On the other hand, barkcloth, particularly, was used in tribute levies, in diplomatic gift-exchanges, and sometimes for compensating experts for their services. Indeed, in view of its durability and its widespread use in exchanges for both services and other objects, it approximated somewhat to some writers' definition of "money."

In addition to all the above, there was a certain amount of other kinds of "economic" activity over and above the kinds of transactions that took place among members of any one household. Some individuals were more proficient than others in fabricating objects such as stone adzes or fine woodcarving and in performing such services as tattooing, dancing, and curing. And while some of these carried out their specialties as members of chiefly households and received compensation in the form of keep, some of those objects and services undoubtedly circulated commercially, the specialists having been paid in food, barkcloth, and the like.

And that about exhausts the list of activities conventionally included under the rubric of "economics." The pre-European Tahitians did not have places, i.e., *market* places, where people met regularly to barter or to buy and sell. Nor does there seem to have been much, if any, deliberate effort made to fabricate objects or acquire skills with a view to exchanging them commercially in response to *potential*, as distinct from specifically expressed demand.[3] (Later in this book, in the analysis of the social relations of the 1954–55 villagers that are the focus of my study, "economics" will be defined in a more comprehensive way, but this is not the place to describe pre-European Tahitian society in such terms.)

Tahitians played some modest but basic roles in the mid-twentieth-century economy of the Society Islands. Many, perhaps the majority of them, continued to supply much of their own requirements for food and shelter directly by their own gardening, collecting, fishing, and fabricating, although all of them were dependent in some measure upon goods that required money to obtain.[4] To obtain this money, the modern[5] Tahitians

---

[3]The Maupiti stone bowls may have been an exception here. And the occasional trading expeditions to Me'etia, a midpoint to the Tuamotus, may have included objects fabricated with this potential outcome in mind.

[4]The generalizations recorded in this subchapter, which are meant to refer to Tahitians throughout the Society Islands, are impressionistic, to say the least. Although they are founded on the observations of myself and my fellow researchers in eight communities, selected to represent a wide range of differences in economy, etc., they are not demonstrably representative of the full range of such differences throughout the archipelago. And although I travelled extensively around the islands and gained many impressions, I did not undertake a comprehensive and systematic collection of economic data. Nor had anyone else done so prior to or during my visit; in fact, the difficulty, if not impossibility, of sorting out Tahitians from other elements of the population would have ruled out precision in any such survey.

[5]Here and henceforth, I use the adjective "modern" to describe people, conditions, practices, etc., of the period focused on by this study, namely, 1950–60.

engaged in a number of occupations, full- or part-time, but the types of such occupations were somewhat limited and the incomes from most of them were small relative to the earnings of other elements of the islands' population. In a word, although by 1954–55 all Tahitians were participating in some degree in the westernized, monetized economy of the islands, for many the participation was fairly marginal. And now for some details.

Nearly two centuries of contact with Europeans had brought about few changes in Tahitian gardening. A few new staple food plants were being cultivated, e.g., South American manioc (cassava) replaced the native arrowroot, but taro (*taruā*), yams, and sweet potatoes continued to be grown. And although steel axes had replaced stone and shell ones and some gardeners used iron digging sticks in place of the traditional wooden ones, garden layouts and site preparation methods had not perceptibly changed.

Many modern Tahitians also grew introduced garden crops such as corn, eggplant, tomatoes, melons, and lettuce, but they were nearly everywhere viewed as supplemental to the traditional starchy staples. It was the same with tree crops. Breadfruit, native plantains, coconuts, Tahitian chestnuts, and native mangoes continued to be gathered and eaten as before (although the fermenting of breadfruit was no longer practiced). Some introduced fruits were widely produced and relished, e.g., the Indian mango, numerous varieties of sweet-eating bananas, and several kinds of citruses, but these were eaten as supplemental foods and involved no new techniques of cultivation or processing.

A more noteworthy addition to food production was the introduction, cultivation, and widespread consumption of coffee. Some modern Tahitians bought their daily, or even twice-daily, portions of coffee (whole beans, ground, or brewed), but many others grew, dried, roasted, ground, and brewed their own.

However, the major change that had taken place in the Tahitians' food habits was the universal reliance upon certain foods obtainable mainly or only by purchase, mainly bread, rice, and sugar. Tea was also favored by many persons, and there were probably few households that did not at times use butter in place of coconut oil.

In 1950–60, many households continued as before to raise pigs and chickens for home consumption, and a few did the same with cattle. But, in addition, probably all households, at times, consumed large quantities of canned meat purchased at stores. Modern Tahitians also ate large quantities of canned fish; but the larger part of the fish they consumed was, as before, caught by the householders themselves or acquired through gift or purchase from other Tahitians.

A look at modern Tahitian fishing would reveal much that was new (e.g., a partial, but not total, replacement of native hooks by purchased metal ones, the use of spear guns, swimming flippers and goggles for underwater fishing, nets made of nylon rather than local plant fibers, motor instead of wind-driven boats for deep-sea fishing), but it would also turn up many traits from the pre-European past (e.g., techniques for driving fish into nets, use of torches for night fishing, trolling from hand-paddled canoes).

As for the animal production techniques employed by modern Tahitians, poultry raising had undergone little change, that is, no more deliberate effort was expended than before. Pig raising, on the other hand, had undergone some change, mainly in response to the introduced breeds, which, because of their larger size, required and encouraged special and regular feeding. Cattle required even more special and constant tending, which accounts in part for their rarity as home-grown animals.

Unlike Tongans and Samoans, the Tahitians gave up their *kava* drinking many decades ago. In its place, they produced home brews in the form of fermented starch and fruit juices for special occasions; but during 1954–55, they drank mainly purchased wine, beer, and liquor. Tobacco was also a post-European introduction, and most modern smokers used store-bought tobacco.

Modern Tahitian houses ranged in architecture and materials from totally self-supplied native style to European-style buildings constructed entirely with nonnative lumber, cement, roofing, etc. Most of them, however, were blends of the two—floors made of purchased lumber and roofs thatched with coconut leaves, or floors of concrete and roofs of metal but walls of locally split bamboo. Most households retained the pre-European pattern of separate buildings for sleeping, eating, and cooking, while a few maintained the same pattern in the form of separate rooms under the same roof.

Inside most modern Tahitian houses one would find European beds, although many individuals continued to sleep, by preference, upon mats on the floor. Many houses also contained a sewing machine, a phonograph, and, more rarely, a radio. Other new features in most modern Tahitian houses were chairs, tables, and lamps. The mats found in most modern houses were made elsewhere, mainly in the Austral Islands, where most of the native coconut-fiber cordage (sennit) used by Tahitians was also manufactured. Outside of the towns, nearly every Tahitian house possessed an earth oven for daily or occasional cooking of the principal meal; but most modern Tahitian households contained some type of European, and usually kerosene-fueled, stove as well. Also, most of the cooking and eating utensils used by modern Tahitians were purchased, European-style ones.

For clothing, the modern Tahitians had gone over almost wholly to European materials, and largely to European-style garments as well. Barkcloth and mats had long since been replaced by imported textiles, although many Tahitian women continued to tailor clothes for themselves and their families. Both males and females often wore a *pareu* (a wrap-around kiltlike garment), but in modern times these consisted of imported fabrics. Even the females' hats made locally and out of local plant fibers were old fashioned, but unmistakably European in shape. On the other hand, imported perfumes, pomades, and skin lotions had not yet fully replaced locally made, flower-scented coconut oils.

Pre-European medicines were also depended upon by many modern Tahitians, i.e., "pre-European" in terms of the local source of their ingredients and of the logic of their efficacy. Increasingly, however, modern Tahitians had turned to European remedies and medical practitioners to relieve their real or imaginary ailments.

Modern Tahitians still depended upon their own legs to get about their own districts; but for longer overland travel, they usually depended upon public buses, when available, or on bicycles and motor bikes, very few of them having owned motor cars. For local water transport, they continued to use native-style, hand-paddled canoes; but many owned and used motor-driven boats even for local use, including fishing. And for interisland travel, these descendants of yesteryear's intrepid maritime adventurers were almost entirely dependent upon the large motor-powered boats owned mainly by Europeans and Chinese. In fact, constraints were exercised, with good reason it appears, by the Administration to discourage interisland travel in smaller boats.

Finally, although some modern Tahitians continued to amuse themselves some of the time in time-honored ways, most of them had come to rely on new forms of recreation that cost money—including cinema, musical instruments, and, last but certainly not least, European alcoholic beverages.

Thus, the need for money had become universal for all modern Tahitians, although there were some differences between communities and between households and individuals within communities in this respect. Some communities, like Papeʻete's Polynesian enclaves and its suburbs were preponderately monetized; others, like isolated Maiʻao, were much less so. But, as just stated, every modern Tahitian made use of some objects and services that cost money to obtain. The question is: how did they acquire that money?

Although it would be tedious, to say the least, to document it, my impression is that most of the money acquired by modern Tahitians came from the sale of objects produced by themselves, mainly copra, "wet" (i.e., green) vanilla beans, fish, pigs, cattle, fruits, native vegetables, cassava, and roof-thatch-plates. In this respect, Tahitians differed markedly from the local Europeans and Chinese, most of whom acquired their money incomes from sale of their services and as rent from their capital assets.

It is also my impression that most of the objects that modern Tahitians exchanged for money were produced by individual or small-group enterprises, few of which involved large land holdings or costly equipment or wholly non-Tahitian patterns of work organization.

Moreover, although most of the modern Tahitians' money income, as a whole, came from objects commercially sold, that money came largely from the production labor itself; the transport and marketing of the products (with the attendant profits) having been carried out mainly by Chinese or European middlemen.

Modern Tahitian communities also differed widely with respect to what their residents produced for sale and how their products were marketed; but contrasting them as a whole with Europeans or with the Chinese, the characterizations just offered seem, to me at least, to be apt.

Some modern Tahitians worked full time for wages or salaries, and many others did so on a part-time or occasional basis; but as stated above, money obtained in this manner earned for Tahitians as a whole less than such averages earned by the local Europeans or Chinese and less than the money earned by the Tahitians from sale of objects produced by themselves.

The salaried occupations which were occupied nearly exclusively by Tahitians were rural Protestant pastorates and district chieftainships and police. Many of the teaching positions in primary schools were also held by Tahitians, as were many of the paramedical positions in the Administration health service. In addition, a few Tahitians held clerkships and minor administrative posts in the Administration, but all of the higher-paid Administration positions were held by Europeans or by *Demis*.

Most modern Tahitians who worked for money did so as wage earners. For those working full time for wages, the principal jobs were domestic service, boat-crewing, stevedoring, truck driving, and a variety of other unskilled or semi-skilled occupations. Although there was no official distinction between Tahitians and others in terms of scales of pay, the fact that Tahitians worked mainly in the low-paying jobs and that such jobs were held almost wholly by Tahitians resulted in their receiving, on the average, a far smaller income than did the average European, Chinese, or *Demi*.

Notwithstanding these differences, of which most of the adult Tahitians I knew were aware, the desire among them for wage-earning jobs was powerful and widespread. A few of my Tahitian acquaintances disdained wage labor, preferring either to earn the money they needed by farming or fishing or to reduce their need for money to amounts that could be provided by kinfolk or friends. Many others I knew, however, were so eager for money that they left their home communities, which offered few wage-earning opportunities, for the discomforts and uncertainties of living and working elsewhere. Other motives were also involved in some of the moves, but the desire for money was weighty in most cases I knew about.

The widespread desire of modern Tahitians for wage work, or rather, their willingness to engage in such work however hard, menial, tedious, and relatively low-paying it may be, represented a marked change in attitude from the one ascribed to them a century ago, when, it will be recalled from an earlier paragraph, hundreds of Chinese, along with other Pacific islanders, had to be imported to man the European enterprises of that era.

Some modern Tahitians—how many I do not know—obtained money income—how much I cannot even venture to guess—from rent, mainly of land. Judging by the instances I knew, the average amount of such income was much smaller than that earned by sale of objects and services, although in some particular cases the rents from land holdings were quite large. In this connection, in the communities I knew best, a double- or even a triple-standard rent rate prevailed; Europeans and Chinese paid up to four to five times as much as other Tahitians, and close kinfolk sometimes paid nothing at all.

In comparison with local Europeans and Chinese, the modern Tahitians' involvement in commerce was small in scale and limited in range. The retail stores owned and operated by Tahitians were few in number and characteristically short-lived, due perhaps mainly to the importunities of kinfolk and neighbors for credit and the social difficulty attending collection of debts. As they themselves said, most Tahitians are too *maru* (soft-hearted, easygoing) to succeed in this trade. On the other hand, as occasional vendors, some of them I knew did quite well; such were the ones who sold soft drinks, home-baked cakes, melon slices, etc., to their neighbors on cinema nights. (Perhaps it was due to the "cash only" rule for such transactions that such trade succeeded.)

In some rural districts, Tahitians retailed beer and wine through lease of Administration licenses, for which they paid large fees. These franchises tended to bring in small but steady incomes for the fortunate owners I knew, but there may have been cases elsewhere that failed.

Some modern Tahitians owned and operated trucks and boats to transport people and goods, but most of this kind of service was in the hands of non-Tahitians.

A few, but only a few, Tahitians acquired some income in the form of interest from bank savings. I have no figures for the Society Islands as a whole, but in the communities I knew best, such savings accounts were few in number and small in size.

Finally, a few modern Tahitians acquired some money income in the form of veterans' pensions, welfare payments, or child-support allocations. In the rural communities I studied, such payments were few in number and small in amounts—much smaller, in fact, than in the more urbanized neighborhoods in and near Papeʻete, where, for example, in the Papeʻete enclave of Manuhoe, child-support allocations ranked fifth in terms of total community income (Kay 1963, p. 34ff).

In the 1950–60 period, virtually every Tahitian was professedly a Christian. So important indeed was Christianity to most of them—its cosmogony, its "historical" authenticity, etc.—that their most usual way of epitomizing Tahiti's past was into three eras: *tau 'etene* (era [of] heathenism), said to be a time of savagery and stupidity;[6] *tau māramarama* (era [of] enlightenment), i.e., the time when everyone believed and lived according to Biblical teaching; and *i te'ie nei*, the present time, i.e. of religious backsliding.

In fact, very few Tahitians I encountered anywhere (and none in the rural communities I studied) knew anything about the religious beliefs and practices of their heathen-era ancestors. Or rather, although many of them held beliefs and engaged in practices that were in fact continuities from pre-Christian times (e.g., beliefs in ghosts, spirit-possession, and divinition practices), they did not usually recognize them as such. For most modern Tahitians, the Bible, which was translated into Tahitian over a century ago and which was the only book most of my neighbors possessed and consistently read, was the most authoritative source of truth and the most publicly venerated (though not necessarily the most consistently followed) guide for living.

As noted above, in 1951 about 80 percent of the total population of the Society Islands was Tahitian (as distinct from European, Chinese, Creoles, *Demis*, etc.). From available sources it is not possible to determine precisely how many of them could be labelled "Protestants," but an estimate of 75–80 percent of all Tahitians would probably not be far off the mark. Among these (according to the 1951 Census) 1.1 percent (of the total Society Islands population) were orthodox (i.e., Brigham Young) Mormons, 1.3 percent *Kanitos* (adherents of the break-away Mormon sect), and 0.9 percent Seventh Day Adventists. The remaining non-Catholics were associated, in one way or another, with the *Société des Missiones Evangéliques*, successor to the London Missionary Society. In fact, rural Tahitians, with whom this study is concerned, were so preponderately Protestant (Tahitian: *Porotetaṇe*, the term I shall apply henceforth to this sect), that some information about its archipelago-wide organization and practices is called for.

---

[6] *Tau tahito*, time-ancient, was also used by some modern Tahitians to refer to pre-European and pre-Christian times, but in most conversations about "history" that I heard or was engaged in, the *heathen*-ness of that era was the aspect that was most stressed. In the communities I knew best, some Tahitians expressed the view that the paganism of their heathen-era ancestors was indeed due to the latters' "stupidity," that they had been informed about Christ and the Christian God long before the arrival of the Europeans, but had rejected that information in favor of their "stupid" and "wicked" pagan beliefs. Just how that information had reached them was not explained.

Throughout modern rural Tahiti, the boundaries of Administration districts (*mata'eina'a*) and Protestant parishes (*paroita*) were conterminous, and had been more or less so since the 1820s, when matters of church and state were more closely interlinked. Heading each parish was a Tahitian pastor ('*orometua a'o*) assisted by several deacons (*teatono*); together they constituted a deacon's council ('*āpo'ora'a teatono*), which was under supervision of a Territory-wide Great Council ('*apo'ora'a rahi*), consisting of the Mission's president (a European) and two other officials, along with representatives—pastors and deacons—from each island. The Great Council ('*āpo'ora'a rahi*) had final jurisdiction over all Mission property; over the selection, training, ordination, and assignment of pastors; over the disposal of money collections; and, indeed, over most aspects of Mission organization, administration, theology, and ritual. For example, while the decision to repaint a parish church building rested in the hands of its own deacons' council, permission to acquire land for building a new church had to come from the Great Council.[7] And while a parish was empowered to raise money locally in order to assist a nearby parish to, say, build a new church, the money collected at the regular Sunday Service went into the coffers of the Great Council.

The reasons why some young men decided to undergo training to become pastors I found to be varied. According to the general consensus, in order for an individual, usually a young male, to qualify for pastoral training he had to be devout, industrious, sober in conduct, firmly and faithfully married, and to display signs of being *māramarama* (intelligent, knowledgeable about matters profound). In some instances, evidently, one young man in any community possessed these qualities to such an obvious and widely acknowledged degree that he was impelled in this direction by a culmination of popular opinion and self-modeling. In other instances I inquired about, encouragement came from a visiting (European) missionary, whose attention had been caught by some youth's display of religious devoutness or mental agility. In still other instances, the fact of being a pastor's son proved decisive. And in at least one instance I heard about, the choice was evidently made because of the opportunities it seemed to offer for wealth and social power.

Perhaps few established pastors ever acquired outstanding wealth, but most, if not all of them, managed during some periods of their incumbencies to achieve considerable amounts of social influence over local affairs, secular as well as religious, as later chapters will reveal. Formerly, it

---

[7]Between the local parish deacons' council and the Great Council were several divisional councils consisting of representatives of several neighboring parishes (e.g., in the case of Mo'orea, all of its parishes); some parish petitions to the Great Council had to pass through this body, but whether the divisional council could take any initiatives of its own I did not inquire about.

was customary for pastors to serve in the parishes in which they grew up; but in recent years, it appears to have been mission policy that they serve elsewhere in order to minimize nepotism, etc., and the stresses of local factionalism that so often fractured along kinship lines.

Whatever wealth a pastor may have acquired certainly did not come in the form of his salary, which was only 1,750 Pacific francs a month, i.e., the average amount earned by a man for fourteen days of unskilled plantation labor. Pastors were provided with rent-free housing, and they were often the recipients of food from sympathetic parishioners; but the wealth that some of them came to acquire resulted from the uses they made of their better-than-average intelligence and education, or from the favors they received from parishioners in terms of services, tools, and land use—or all of these combined.

The duties of a pastor were not very onerous. They, of course, presided over the principal Sunday mid-morning service and delivered the sermon, but the service as a whole followed an invariant ritual and the latter a prescribed monthly program of topics. As described to me by one pastor, this program consisted of the following sequence:

—First Sunday, a vehement (*ha'apūai*) harangue (*tā'iri*), followed by Communion and baptism.

—Second Sunday, instruction in the ways of righteousness.

—Third Sunday, a recounting of Biblical events.

—Fourth Sunday, *te 'ōro'a e fare* (house ceremony).[8]

Moreover, the sermons themselves adhered to a time-honored pattern that took shape over a century ago. This pattern was described in 1933 by a former mission president, Charles Vernier, whose characterization of these services, which I shall freely paraphrase, is more widely representative than any I could present; also, it provides some insight into the relationships that obtained in 1933 and was still evident in 1954–55 between the European shepherds and their Tahitian flocks:

> The Tahitian sermon is very distinctive and its structure somewhat archaic. It had been instituted by the London Missionary Society missionaries at the time when it was necessary to teach the native Christians the principal ideas and events of Protestantism in simple and unambiguous terms. And present-day native Christians—pastors, deacons, and brethren—have been loath

---

[8] Another pastor described to me the order somewhat differently, i.e., first Sunday: Communion and house ceremony; second Sunday: strong harangue; third Sunday: instruction; fourth Sunday: Biblical history. In fact, during the countless Sunday services I sat through, reduced almost to coma but ever hopeful of obtaining some ethnographic tidbit, I witnessed much variation in the "standard" order.

to change the pattern of the sermons, which in fact provides them with a simple and easily remembered formula, based on the metaphor of a tree. Thus, a sermon is divided into one or more tree "trunks" and the trunks' "branches" into "leaves" and "fruit." The "trunks" are the main parts of the sermon, consisting of basic themes expressed often in the form of questions. The "branches," etc., are given in the form of answers to those questions. Finally, the sermon is concluded with the *shutting of the door*. (An effective metaphor, however mixed!) Granted that the mechanics of the standard Tahitian sermon is a bit old fashioned, nevertheless it does have the advantage (and especially for the natives) of serving to expound two or three themes in easily understandable terms. . . . To our native parishioners nothing is more interesting than to follow the development of a sermon given at the Sunday service. To them it is an intriguing pleasure to try to anticipate what the "branches," etc., will be, once the "trunk" has been described. And pastors are judged by their Biblical erudition and by the science or art they display in expressing it in tree-metaphor logic." (Vernier, 1933.)

In addition, Vernier points out, the Tahitian pastors of his day (like those of the mid-twentieth century I knew) showed a marked predilection in their sermons for the Old Testament, with its emphasis on stern and uncompromising leaders and on large, fateful events.

The principal prayer of the main Sunday Service was also delivered by the pastor, and while it was sometimes as long as the sermon itself, and was prescriptively "extempore," the countless numbers of them that I sat through (on perhaps the most uncomfortable church benches in Christendom) followed an invariable and, to me, mind-paralyzing pattern that included long lists of the Deity's attributes (remarkably similar in style and hyperbole to the litanies contained in the pagan Tahitian prayers that have been recorded), countless allusions to Biblical episodes, and perfunctory salutations to all and sundry categories of people, local and elsewhere, old and young, sick and well, etc.

In summary, this part of a pastor's job, though obviously requiring a solid familiarity with Biblical personae and episodes (extended and reinforced by their seminary training) along with some talent for oratory and permutational invention, did not necessarily involve lengthy weekly preparation. Of the two pastors I knew best, one informed me that he chose his sermon topic while walking to church (a distance of about 200 meters), and the other said that the topic usually "came to him" while he was digesting his Sunday morning coffee and talking with parishioners while waiting to enter the church.

Other duties of a Protestant pastor included officiating at christenings, weddings, and funerals; teaching Sunday School (optional); instructing and testing would-be communicants; and, of course, leading an exemplary Protestant life (which permitted some wine with meals but no excessive recreational imbibing).

Although it was widely and popularly held that a parish's pastor had the heaviest responsibility for conducting parish affairs, for serving as a parish's leader as well as its spiritual minister, the governing functions were statutorily vested in the council consisting of pastor and deacons. By rule, parishes numbering two hundred or less Protestant residents (minimum age unspecified) had four deacons; those numbering more had one deacon for every additional fifty residents. Deacons were elected by majority votes by local Protestants twenty-one years of age and older, male and female.[9] Eligibility for deaconship included at least three years of church membership (as a communicant) and, if married, a wife who was also a communicant. (A man living with a woman but not legally married to her was thus ineligible.) The rules also specified that no ascendant, descendant, or brother[10] of a deacon could hold that office in the same parish.

A parish council was required to meet at least once a month and was under the presidency of the pastor. Its responsibilities, as set forth in the rules prevailing in 1954–55, were as follows:

1) to maintain proper ecclesiastical discipline among local parishioners;

2) to construct and maintain in good repair the church and other parish buildings;

3) to safeguard and administer the use of all other parish property;

4) to accept legacies and other gifts made to the parish; and

5) to regulate the disposition of regular church collections.

In connection with the first of these rules, the council was empowered to suspend an erring member's right to partake of Communion for a period of up to three months. In addition, the deacons were required to assist the pastor in the performance of regular church services and rituals, including Communion and prayer meetings, and they were also delegated the responsibility of supervising the two or more sodalities into which each parish was divided.

---

[9]Although, in the two parishes I knew best, it was the pastor and the incumbent deacons who, in fact, did the "electing" by presenting nominations which were then usually agreed upon by all other parishioners.

[10]I do not know what the official policy of the mission's leadership was at the time on the question of female officials, but there were no female deacons in the two parishes I studied, and the residents I queried about the matter were emphatic that, in *their* parishes, there never would be!

A sodality (*pupu paroita*) was composed of parishioners who met together, usually on Sunday evenings but at some other times as well, to engage in exhibitions of Biblical learning and verbal skill, and generally to socialize. Each sodality had its own meeting house (*fare putuputura'a*), usually a long rectangular building, typically of wooden construction and thatched roof, with seats only for the unit's leader and distinguished guests. In contrast to the kind of deportment prescribed but seldom followed in church, behavior in these meeting houses was easy and informal; occupants sat on the floor, chattered, laughed, smoked, ate snacks, snoozed, and moved about at will.

The singing that took place at sodality meetings was of two kinds: learning and practicing the European-style hymns for performing at the main Sunday Church Service, and harmonizing old favorites for what was obviously the sheer joy of vocalizing. Concerning the former, except for the very old, most members of each sodality tended to sit together during the Sunday Service, mainly to exhibit their vocal powers and repertoire. Concerning the old favorites, the *himene ru'au* (old-time hymn), I turn again to Vernier, for a description of this moving, consummately *Tahitian* art form:

> These indigenous melodies, which are sung in three or four voices, produce in the listeners a powerful effect because of their strict rhythms, minor-key tonality, and interminable, organ-like coda.... Indeed, when heard from a distance the effect of this singing is that of an organ, and of an organ made to sound like waves receding and then thunderously breaking on the reef.... The basses are powerful and steady, the tenors somewhat nasal, the sopranos and altos pure. Occasionally, in the midst of a *himene*, someone, male or female, will launch upon a *perepere*, a phrase pitched much higher than the rest of the song, which has the effect of refreshing and renewing the whole song. (freely translated from Charles Vernier, 1933: 197–8.)

The focus of most sodality meetings[11] was, however, the *tuāro'i*, a competitive exercise involving Biblical learning, idea development, and riddle-solving skills. The following description is based on my own observations, supplemented by Charles Vernier's rich and full account (Vernier 1933:214ff).

The performance of a *tuāro'i* centered on a Bible verse, selected by the pastor or other church official who would preside over the session, and the overall purpose of the session was to arrive at the "true" meaning of the verse through the concerted efforts of those attending. For the larger and

---

[11]In some parishes, the *tuāro'i* was on occasion a whole-parish affair.

more formal sessions (e.g., one attended by a visiting Church dignitary) the younger and less experienced parishioners prepared for their roles by memorizing verses neighboring the thematic verse and by learning more about the events, etc., contextual to the theme itself. (The older parishioners usually depended upon their respective stores of Biblical knowledge and oratorical experience to see them through.)

A *tuāroʻi* session opened with the usual singing, prayers, and salutation, followed by reading of the thematic verse. Then, like sermons, the program proceeded according to a metaphor-based plan. One such plan, described by Vernier and witnessed frequently by myself, had to do with house construction. In it, the participating children in the audience, first boys, then girls, provided the *foundation stones* for the house with their short and mechanically delivered recitations. Then followed the "young" people (*taureʻareʻa*), again, males first, whose recitations provided the house's *cement*. Then the communicants, whose addresses provided the *walls*, and the nonpresiding deacons and other more elderly communicants, the *roof, doors,* and *locks*. Finally, the key to the completed "house," with a lengthy (usually a *very* lengthy) summation of the night's proceedings and a final, and authoritative, clarification of the thematic verse's "true" meaning. (Far from being perfunctory, at the sessions I sat through, this final clarification was accorded fully as much attentive curiosity as that shown by a European audience during the *dénouement* of a mystery play.) Meanwhile, the progress of constructing the "house" was frequently interrupted by singing and was accompanied by the crying of babies, the fidgeting of children, and the snores of those unable to keep awake throughout the three- to five-hour sessions after the Sunday's heavy meal and several previous hours in church.

The *tuāroʻi* deserves much fuller treatment than I am able to give it here,[12] and I must at least draw attention to the lively interest which the Tahitians I knew continued to show toward its century-old content. Even after decades of experience with cinema and other European-type entertainments, and with the products and, for some people, the principles of Western science, they continued to derive their principal intellectual pleasure from the practice of this ancient Bible game.

In many parishes, its sodalities also undertook other kinds of activities, including conducting life crisis celebrations for their members, money raising, etc., but hymn singing and *tuāroʻi* were, to my knowledge, the only activities engaged in everywhere, so an account of those subsidiary doings will be given later on when describing life in the two villages I studied.

---

[12]For example, much might be learned about Tahitians' cognitive processes from their metaphors, etc., used in their recitals, and much about their symbolization of social relationships.

All of a parish's professing Protestants over fifteen years of age (and not just its full-fledged communicants) were eligible for membership in one of its sodalities, and most of those eligible seem to have belonged, although in a range of participation from constant commitment to total inactivity. In parishes composed of spatially separated neighborhoods, the residents tended to belong to the nearest sodality; in the less dispersed parishes, where sodality houses were nearer together, factors such as kinship and friendship seemed to influence an individual's choice of association.

Generally speaking, every sodality counted at least one deacon among its membership, and it was usual for one of these to serve as sodality leader. In fact, in some parishes the deacons attained that office by sodality election, subject finally to endorsement by the parish's pastor and by the Great Council.

These islands' parish sodalities were among their oldest and most indigenously conservative post-European institutions. In some parishes, they were very dynamic parts of community life; in others, they had survived only as fossils. The difference between the two villages that form the substance of this study were, in this respect, quite striking, as will be described later on.

At the time of first European contact, the natives of these islands were divided into numerous more or less autonomous tribes; eleven or twelve on Tahiti, twelve on Mo'orea, one on Huahine-Mai'ao, one on Rai'atea-Taha'a, and one on Borabora-Maupiti. The tribes differed widely in size of population from 14,000–15,000 (comprising Tahiti's peninsula) to less than one hundred. They also differed considerably in their intertribal relations, including long-standing and stable confederations, short-lived and opportunistic coalitions, and endemic states of war. The hostilities that served to define tribal boundaries were mitigated somewhat by transtribal kinship ties and occasionally by supratribal religious cults as well. But at times such cults also conduced to the hardening of tribal boundaries, with some of the bitterest of enmities between chiefly kinfolk.

Tribal chiefs were recruited on the dual basis of primogenitural succession, mainly male but occasionally through females, and administrative ability. (The ability was essential for acquiring and maintaining leadership, succession for legitimating it.)

Contact with Europeans set events in motion[13] that culminated, in 1815, in the assimilation of all Tahiti and Mo'orea into one "Kingdom," which

---

[13]The question of whether or not these islands' tribes would eventually have "evolved" into a single unit without the stimuli of European contact and the assistance of European guns cannot, of course, be answered. For a discussion of this question, see Oliver 1974.

remained united until French rule was established in 1843 and which was allowed to persist, in ceremonial guise, until it was officially abolished in 1880. Elsewhere, in the Leeward Islands, the several petty tribal kingdoms persisted a little longer, under a light-handed and "unofficial" British "protectorate," until French annexation in 1897.

This book is not the place for tracing the history of these islands' governmental structures from the form that prevailed in 1767 to the one of 1954, which was summarized in Section A of this chapter. Suffice it to say that the structures had undergone many changes. The focus of power had shifted to metropolitan France, and although Tahitians were represented there as well as in the territorial assembly in Pape'ete, their role in decision making was ineffectual, to say the least. Even in the administrative hierarchy concerned with governing them locally, they held positions only at the lowest (i.e., district) level, where they were concerned with such trivial matters as reporting lawbreakers to higher authorities and urging villagers to keep their pigs off village streets (a far cry from some pre-European chiefs, who were able almost at will to confiscate their subjects' goods and snuff out their lives).

The total transformation of the Tahitians' governmental system under European control was accompanied by metamorphosis of the class structure with which that system was closely geared. When Europeans first arrived, Tahitian society was stratified into three major classes—castes, actually, since the principal mechanism that divided them, or at least that separated the upper (*ari'i*) class from the middle (*ra'atira*) class, was the proscription against marriage across class lines. (Marriages between a *ra'atira* and a *manahune* (commoner) were probably less strictly prohibited, but positive information on this point is lacking.)

By 1954–55, the labels *ari'i* and *manahune* were no longer being applied. (*Manahune* would have been considered insulting, and *ari'i* anachronistic, except in Honolulu's night clubs where nearly every Tahitian entertainer was billed as such!) Meanwhile, the meaning of *ra'atira* had expanded to mean both captain (for example, of a ship, a team) and citizen-resident (of a district). This does not mean that the modern population of these islands was socially unstratified. Even in the rural, almost wholly Tahitian communities that I knew, some stratification could be inferred from marriage preferences, to say nothing of the social levels that could be deduced from housing, income, consumption, etc.

In any description of the kinds of social relationships that prevailed among these pre-European Tahitians, those referred to by the English word "kinship"[14] would have to feature prominently not only in everyday life situations but in descriptions of government, class, and even religion. In other words, statuses in those other social subsystems were to a large degree derivative of relations among kinfolk, and especially consanguines.

The sources of information about kinship in pre-European Tahiti concentrate on the interpersonal relations of certain socially prominent persons; generalizations about wider aspects of the topic must rest on inferences, some direct and some indirect. The English missionary lexicographers listed several words referring to kinship, but with glosses too "English" to indicate the kinds of relationship or social units implied either by the lexicographers (if they really knew) or by the Tahitians themselves. Examples of such words, recorded in the London Missionary Society Dictionary, are: "*fēti'i*, a family; the relations of a person; to tie or bind; a binding or knot," "*hiva*, a clan, or the company of a canoe." (Oliver 1974, p. 616ff.) Inferences from other kinds of evidence do, however, persuade me that the Tahitians of that era distinguished, conceptually, between *consanguines, adoptive kin,* and *affines*; and further, that they conceptually distinguished several types of categories of kin (in addition to the categorization implied by classificatory uses of such kin terms as *metua,* "parent," and *tupuna,* "grandparent"; for example: *firia, fēti'i,* descent line; *huia,* or *'āti,* cognatic stock; and *aveavefēti'i,* branches of a cognatic stock.

There is also evidence that the pre-European Tahitians conceptualized (and associated together) in residential, co-worshipping groups, consisting of a core of consanguines and their spouses, along with other individuals adopted into these groups. The focus of each such group was a *marae,* or temple, at which the members (usually only the adult males) communicated with and presented offerings to their tutelar spirits (who usually included one or more ancestral spirits). With each of these groups was also associated one or more tracts of land (and in some cases, adjacent portions of the lagoon or sea). Lacking unambiguous information on what the ancient Tahitians themselves called such units, I use the label *kin-congregation* to refer to them (to emphasize the religious character of the group).

There is also evidence that most kin-congregations segmented over the course of time, and that, when feasible, such segments maintained links with each other, mainly by worshipping together at common "parental" temples. Moreover, as I interpret the sources, this genealogical pattern exemplified in co-worship had its parallel in land tenure. That is to say, the "parental"

---

[14]The inverted commas around *kinship* are added to express the usual *caveat* about this troublesome label, i.e., the familiar warning that what English speakers or anthropologists mean by the label is not necessarily what they (in this case, the Tahitians) may mean. And now, having performed this verbal ritual, I leave the question to its long overdue rest.

unit (the word "parental" is mine) held residual rights in the territories of offshoot units, and so on down the genealogical line. These rights were symbolically expressed in first-fruits offerings, and in other token ways.

Internally, each kin-congregation had a leader, who was normally (but not invariably) a male, and who usually attained the office by primogenitural succession. Such offices included both secular and religious functions, but in the case of the larger units the latter were usually delegated to priestly functionaries.

It is tempting to regard the cores of these "genealogically" linked sets of kin-congregations as segmented cognatic stocks, but if they were so, the segmentation appears not to have followed a wholly consistent pattern, and the reality (in contrast to the Tahitians', and to my, conceptualizations of it) might have been much more complex than I have proposed.

In any event, from the logic of the arrangement and on the basis of actual reports, some individual Tahitians held membership rights in two or more separate kin-congregation units, as a result of their having been able to trace descent from individuals in such units. In these and other instances however, most individuals utilized their rights only in the one in which they resided most of the time.

For the "commoners" of pre-European times, "marriage" consisted of living together, sharing household tasks, and reproducing offspring; it is not altogether clear that such unions had to be legitimated by any nuptial rites or transactions. It is, however, fairly certain that among "commoners" at least, marriage was interdicted between "close" consanguines—how "close" was not reported.

At the top level of society, marriage had a quite different focus. Among the *ari'i*, its principal objective appears to have been the reproduction of offspring hereditarily suitable to bear their respective parent's physical, spiritual and social endowments. It was consequently entered into with elaborate ceremony and sumptuous and bilateral exchanges. And, reversing the rules pertaining to "commoners' " choice of spouses, the higher ranking *ari'i* were permitted and encouraged to marry close consanguines, in order to produce offspring of similar quality.

Kinship also figured weightily among modern Tahitians, but to a somewhat more limited extent. In government, for instance, offices were no longer inherited, although kin ties undoubtedly played parts in district elections. Attendance at a parish's church was open to individuals regardless of kin ties, although individuals not officially married to their sexual mates were ineligible for full membership as communicants; also, kin ties did, to some extent, influence people's sodality affiliation. In addition, (bilateral) ties of kinship continued to be activated at marriage ceremonies and funerals, and marriage continued to be proscribed between "close" consanguines. And, most importantly, French laws regarding inheritance served even to reinforce some aspects of traditional land tenure, although unofficial Administration policies and economic circumstances tended to promote the subdivision of jointly-owned tracts and the individualizing of land titles.

From all the foregoing, the reader will have inferred, correctly, that the modern Tahitians were all very much alike in some respects; that is, alike in comparison with the European, the Chinese, and even with the more European-like *Demi* segments of the islands' population. On the other hand, the Tahitians of this "modern" era also displayed behavioral dissimilarities among themselves, i.e., dissimilarities over and above those attributable to differences in age, sex, native intelligence, individual pathologies, etc. I surmise that with appropriate inquiries one would find nearly a full range of individual behavioral types in nearly all Tahitian communities, but that a clustering of such types would be found to differ from place to place.

However, in this monograph I am not concerned with individuals per se, nor with types of individuals per se, nor, for that matter, am I professionally qualified to conduct the type of inquiries that would discover such types.[15] Rather, my study is concerned with differences between two communities of Tahitians as exemplified in their institutions—economic, religious, recreational, etc., but mainly economic—and with the more plausible reasons for those differences. It may well be that the dissimilarities in institutions were responsible for some of the differences in clustering of individual types, but that is an hypothesis that I will not test.

As noted earlier, this study was carried out as part of a larger research program that sought to compare eight modern Tahitian communities. And as noted, the choice of those eight was guided by their locations in relation to Pape'ete. At one extreme was Manuho'e, a neighborhood of wage earners in Pape'ete itself; at the other extreme was Maupiti, the island most distant from Pape'ete and the one having had the least volume of contact. In the original formulation of the research design it was surmised that those locational differences, and what was expected to be their correlative differences in the volume and frequency of contact with Pape'ete, would result in social-relational and other cultural differences among the eight places. This, indeed, may yet turn out to have been an accurate surmise, but the present monograph is concerned with only two of the places (which I shall call *Atea* and *Fatata*), which I studied, first and mainly in 1954–55, and then with follow-up visits in 1959–60.

---

[15]For this aspect of modern Tahitian life, the reader is referred to Robert Levy's outstanding study, *Tahitians* (Levy 1973).

Both Atea, on Huahine Island, and Fatata, on Mo'orea, were near the midpoint in our distance-from-Pape'ete axis, and were alike in many of their residents' institutions and activities (and hence more comparatively "controlled"). On the other hand, the two communities were dissimilar in many other respects, including their travel-time distance from Pape'ete, and it is the principal objective of this monograph to summarize those differences (mainly those having to do with their economies) and to try to account for them. In order to summarize the differences, however, it will be necessary first to describe their *similarities*, which I will do under the label of *Te Piti* (literally, The Two or Both).

Before embarking on a description of Te Piti's (and Atea's and Fatata's) activities and institutions, it will be useful to summarize their historical, geographic, and demographic peculiarities, some of which may be found to have been influential in differentiating other aspects of the two communities' ways of life.

Atea and Fatata

Throughout this monograph, I will refer to the separate villages I studied as Atea (and the Ateans) and Fatata (and the Fatatans), respectively.[16] In the case of the former, the people studied, the Ateans, comprised all but a few of the residents of a whole administrative district, which will be referred to as the District of Atea; the only other persons residing in the district were a European planter, his Tahitian spouse, and their offspring, who lived on his small, family-size plantation across the bay from the village itself and who had very little to do with the villagers themselves. In contrast, the place (and people) I label Fatata formed only part of the area and population of one of Mo'orea's five administrative districts; for the sake of anonymity, I will give this district the fictitious name of Toerau. This difference between the two study areas makes for some degree of noncomparability between them, which is, of course, a flaw in a comparison designed to be controlled, but, regrettably and inevitably, ethnographers cannot stage their inquiries with the kinds of controls available to laboratory scientists.

Fatata was much closer than Atea to Pape'ete, in terms of crow-fly distance and actual travel time. Fatata's most direct and quickest route to the metropolis was about 30 km long, which with the boats that routinely made the round-trip every day of the week in 1954–55 averaged a travel time of about three to three and a half hours each way. To travel from Atea to Pape'ete one had to go by boat to Huahine's one interisland port, Fare, about 12 km away, and then by schooner the rest of the approximately 150

---

[16]In fact, the Tahitian words so represented are *ātea* and *fātata*, but will be written hereafter without the long vowel marks, in the interest of simplification.

km. During 1954–55, the boat trip to Fare took about one to two hours[17] and the weekly schooner trip to Pape'ete another twelve hours or so. A seaplane also plied somewhat irregularly between Fare and Pape'ete, but the high cost of its fare discouraged its use by Ateans and, of course, absolutely ruled out the transport of their goods.

The land area occupied by the Ateans for residing and for most of their working and other usual activities, and the one in which most of their land-ownership rights were located, comprised about 680 hectares and, as noted above, was approximately conterminous with the administrative district of Atea.

Atea District encircled two deep bays, and most of its land area consisted of the steep and thickly vegetated bay-side slopes of old volcano rims. The Ateans' principal dwellings were "crowded together" (as the Ateans themselves characterized them) on a long and very narrow flat along the larger bay's northwest shoreline. The houses were located on both sides of the village's one street, many of those on the bay side having been built on piles over the water. As for the street itself, both ends trailed off into narrow paths leading only to gardens and groves.

Near the western (seaward) end of the village was the wharf, and directly inland from it a plazalike open space faced by the schoolhouse, church, parsonage, parish assembly house, one of the village's three sodality houses, and one of the village's two stores, the other store having been located halfway down the eastern (inland) stretch of the street. At the "seaward" end of the village were also located most of the village's larger and better-built dwellings—which, with some attendant economic and social factors, led Ateans to label it the *teitei* (high, lofty) end, in contrast to the inland, *ha'eha'a* (low, humble) end.

Ateans' gardens and groves were located elsewhere around the two bays. Some families had second, smaller houses near their gardens and for occasional use but spent most of their time in their village houses.

A tortuous footpath connected Atea with an even smaller settlement to the northwest, but all travel and transport to other Huahine settlements had to be carried out by boat. The nearest settlement of any size was Fare, about 12 km away, which served as a transshipment place for the Ateans' exports and imports and where Ateans could purchase a somewhat larger range of retail store goods than was available in their own local stores. But

---

[17]By 1959–60, a few Ateans had acquired high-powered outboard motors for their small boats, and occasionally used them for faster "emergency" trips to Fare—such as replenishing the liquor for a drinking party—but continued to transport their agricultural products and store imports by the slower launches. A road link between Atea and Fare was not completed until after 1960.

neither Fare nor any other Huahine locality offered Ateans opportunities for wage employment, or for direct contact with the urban side of Tahitian (or European) life.

Historically, Atea village had had a short and uneventful past. In pre-European times there was a thin scattering of habitations around its two bays, but the only evidence of human activity on the modern village site itself was a collection of stones alleged to be the remains of a small and probably domestic temple; Huahine's main centers of residence, religious activity, and chiefly power were at the northern and southern ends of the island, at Maeva and Tiva, respectively. In due course, the representatives of the London Missionary Society established their principal Huahine station at Fare, which on account of its position at the only passes through the island's leeward barrier reef, became and remained the center of the island's political, administrative, and commercial activities. As for Atea, during the early decades of this century a few houses were built at the present site of the village, but their occupants continued to travel to Fare to buy supplies and to attend church services. Then, about 1920, a church was built at Atea itself and a resident (part-Tahitian) pastor appointed; and with that, the District's other residents began to move into the village from their former houses around the bays, a movement that had been more or less completed only a few years before my visit there.

Contrast Atea's history and location with those of Fatata. Fatata had been one of Mo'orea's largest religious centers in pre-European times, and the residence of some of its highest ranking and politically most powerful chiefs. Later, it became the island's principal Christian mission center, and was, until recently, the island's administrative headquarters as well.

The present village is located opposite a large, readily navigable opening in the reef, and, as described above, was served by a boat going daily to and from Pape'ete. In addition, Fatata's main street was part of the all-weather vehicular road that encircled Mo'orea and that gave quick and easy access to a well-stocked Chinese-owned emporium about 12 km away. Even closer at hand were three European-owned plantations, which provided wage employment for some Fatatans, full- and part-time.

Fatata, that part of the district of "Toerau" focused on in this study, comprised 695 hectares, i.e., almost the same size as the 680 that comprised the area identified with Atea. Fatata's location with respect to the rest of Mo'orea's physical features and in comparison with Atea's to Huahine's, were similar in some respects and markedly different in others. While most of Fatata's dwellings were, like *all* of Atea's, situated on the flat coastal strip fronting bay and lagoon, Fatata's strip was much wider than Atea's, for the most part, and some of its dwellings were situated well up into the large valley behind the main part of the settlement. In fact, the existence of Fatata's valley immediately behind the main settlement was another marked difference between it and Atea, whose most comparable valley was much farther away and reachable only by boat or roundabout trail.

Like Atea, Fatata had, in social geographic terms, "lofty" and "humble" sides, a wide freshwater stream having served, more or less, as a divide. However, the social implications of the division derived more from past than from current affluence, as will be described.

In both Atea and Fatata, the lands behind the coastal strips and valleys rose steeply and culminated in mountainous peaks and ridges, the difference being that Fatata's highest peaks, of 500–760 meters, surpassed Atea's highest by 250–300, thereby making for steeper slopes on the average in Fatata. This difference was, however, compensated (in terms of human use) by Fatata's somewhat larger area of relatively level coastal and valley bottom land.

To people as agricultural as the Ateans and Fatatans, factors such as soil types and drainage figured importantly in their lives, and extensive surveys of such matters have been carried out in some other places in the Society Islands. I am, however, unaware of any such data on Atea and Fatata, and did not even attempt to undertake any such survey myself. I did, however, elicit the ways the Te Pitians (i.e., the Ateans *and* Fatatans) themselves classified and labelled the lands which they considered to be arable, namely:

—*fenua* (land) *mato*: broken and with rocky outcrops (suitable for melons);

—*fenua vari, fenua paruparu*: soft and muddy (suitable for taro);

—*fenua mea maro*: dry (suitable for *tarua,* cassava, yams, vanilla, pineapple, etc.); and

—*fenua varivari*: sandy, muddy, damp (suitable for coconuts, breadfruit, mangoes, etc.).

In addition, there were places within their environs so steeply sloping—or so rocky, or swampy, or thinly soiled, or clayey, or so overgrown with jungle or huge trees, etc.—to be considered by the Te Pitians as useless for agriculture, or as requiring more labor to clear or drain or terrace than their farming would repay.[18] In terms of scientific agronomy, of course, this classification may have little merit, but it provided the Te Pitians with their one and only technical standard for choosing where and what to plant, and hence, in this *ethnographic* study, it is more relevant than one based on laboratory-type scientific inquiry.

---

[18]While in the field, I lacked the time and the knowledge to attempt to correlate the Te Pitians' categories with those set forth in Papy's detailed monograph (Papy 1954)—a regrettable gap, but one, I believe, that does not reduce too greatly the accuracy of the general conclusions drawn from my study.

Using this "folk" classification, I attempted to map the land areas associated with Atea and with Fatata. As the reader will doubtless postulate, there was some disagreement among my guide-informants about how to classify certain places, especially some of those having "mixed" features. Nevertheless, the agreements were close enough to permit a rough comparison of the two places in terms of the amounts of their respective land areas constituting this or that "folk-classification" type, a comparison rendered more cognate by the similarity in size of the areas compared, namely 680 hectares for Atea and 695 for Fatata. (I must reveal however, that many of the identifications of my informants were not made directly on the basis of their personal knowledge of an area's soil or drainage, etc., but indirectly, on the basis of what was in fact growing there, a deduction, by the way, which was not invariably accurate and diminishes somewhat the consistency of the classification itself. Nevertheless, it is the only one available to me, and hence the only one I am able to use.)[19]

To begin with, the lands described by most informants as "useless" for agriculture amounted to about 110 hectares in Atea and about 380 in Fatata.[20] The remaining areas deemed to have agricultural potential were distributed as follows:

Table 1A. Distribution of land types (hectares)

	ATEA		FATATA	
	number	percentage	number	percentage
mato (rocky)	22	3.2	41	5.9
vari, paruparu (soft and muddy)	57	8.3	26	3.7
marō (dry)	105	15.4	60	8.6
varivari (sandy and muddy)	386	56.8	188	27.1
"useless"	110	16.2	380	54.7

The amounts of such lands actually devoted to agricultural use will be specified in Chapters II and III. As for the areas not used agriculturally or

---

[19]Surprisingly, there was no perceptible difference between Ateans and Fatatans as a whole regarding their classifications. I say "surprisingly" because I had expected that the former, with their heavier dependence upon agriculture, would have been somewhat less particular in their criteria of arability.

[20]In this connection, I knew of several Chinese farmers who were successfully growing vanilla outside Fatata but on terrain like that considered "useless" by the Fatatans. And when I apprised the latter of this, the stock answer was to the effect that "the Chinese do indeed work harder than Tahitians, but that is because they are so mercenary." Needless to add, the typical Chinese countercharge was that "Tahitians like money, but they are too lazy to work hard for it."

for house sites, roads, etc., the vegetation was a mixture of indigenous and introduced forms, and varied in phytogeographic patterns like those described in Papy's monumental work summarized above. As such, they did not differ markedly between Atea and Fatata, overall, or in terms of the resources they provided, e.g., wood for canoe hulls, bamboo for house walls, leaves and bark for medical remedies, etc. From my cursory inquiries about the matter, there seem to have been more extensive stands of acacia in Fatata than in Atea (i.e., a valuable resource for cattle feeding), and more wild plantains in Fatata's hinterland than in Atea's, but these advantages appear to have had only slight influence in differentiating the two villages' ways of life.

Nor did I discover any noteworthy differences between the array and quantity of wild fauna that inhabited the areas being compared; the mosquitoes and house flies were just as numerous in both places, the bird and rodent populations alike. In fact, the only difference I perceived with respect to human-related wild fauna was in the larger reported number of Fatata's wild pigs, a difference probably connected with Fatata's more extensive undisturbed hinterland.

In addition, Fatata was better situated than Atea with respect to fresh water. A sizeable stream flowed through the middle of the village and, had it been needed, would have provided ample clear water for all local domestic needs. As it was, piped water from the local reservoir rendered the stream's water superfluous, but a few women continued to use the stream for washing clothes.

Ateans' only readily available natural fresh water consisted of two small and somewhat muddy springs, which were used (actually overused) for some laundering and bathing; the only fresh water streams were located elsewhere around the main bay. Usually Ateans made do with rain catchment for their domestic needs—either from their own roofs or from the larger cistern at the schoolhouse—but during dry spells had to go to the distant streams for their laundering, or collect water from them and take it back to the village by canoe.[21]

The only other technological uses made by the Te Pitians of their freshwater streams was for occasional shrimping and for soaking timber and other plant products designed for use in construction. In this respect, Fatata's centrally located stream was more convenient than Atea's distant (and smaller) ones, but the latter seemed to harbor more shrimps; and the Fatatans had to go elsewhere, to outsider-owned streams, for the little shrimping they did.

---

[21]That was the situation at the time of my 1954–55 visit. Subsequently, pipes were laid from a distant reservoir so that during my second visit in 1960, Ateans had the use of piped, running water which, however, they were required to use frugally because of limited supply.

Turning now to their marine settings and resources, Atea and Fatata were alike in some respects, different in others.

Both villages were adjacent to deep bays. Fatata's one was longer and somewhat deeper than either of Atea's two, but none of these bodies of water was much resorted to for fishing because, I was informed, the encircling lagoons contained more fish. With regard to the latter, Atea's lagoon was somewhat wider than Fatata's, about 1.2 km against an average of 0.9 km at Fatata. There was, however, no reason that I was aware of that would have rendered them markedly different in varieties and quantities of marine life.[22] The generally shallower depths of most of Fatata's lagoon made it better suited to fixed seine-net fishing, but angling and spearfishing were equally feasible in both places. The most obvious difference between Atea's and Fatata's lagoons lay in the shapes of their enclosing reefs. Fatata's reef was broken by two passes, one of them navigable only by canoes but the other by very large boats. The nearest reef passes to Atea village were a narrow and shallow opening some 5 km to the south and the navigable ones opposite Fare, 10 and 12 km to the north. In 1954–55 as well as in pre-European times, the locations of those reef passes influenced Atea's and Fatata's contacts with the world outside and hence their respective sizes and characters.

The climates of Atea and Fatata also differed, but in only small and minutely influential ways. According to my regular but short-term observations, the temperatures and rainfalls of the two places were about the same, although I formed the impression that Atea was subjected to more overcast weather. It is true that there were more marked differences in the two villages' winds. Fatata's shoreline was subjected to fairly brisk and seasonally continuous trades; Atea faced directly the more infrequent winds coming from the south and west, but was also buffeted, occasionally, by brief but powerful overland gusts from the northeast. In any case, most of the Fatata houses were situated far enough inland from the shore to escape the full force of the trades, and Atea's were exposed enough to benefit from its lighter sea breezes. And outside the residential areas I did not perceive that the differences in the two places' wind patterns had any marked effect upon their agriculture. (The relative importance exerted by the winds on fishing will be described in Chapters II and III).

Finally, a comparison must be made between Atea's and Fatata's human populations, whose activities and institutions are the subject of this work.

---

[22]This is not to say that there were no differences. The different average depths of the two lagoons may have fostered differences in quantity and variety of their marine life. And the passes that opened Fatata's lagoon to the sea may have encouraged more influx of pelagic fish. About such matters, however, I cannot speak with any authority.

For strict comparability, censuses should, of course, be conducted on the same night or day. This I obviously could not physically accomplish. Moreover, while I conducted my "definitive" census of Atea in mid-March 1955, towards the end of my stay there and after having learned enough about the community to be able to ask relevant questions about who lived where, I did not begin work in Fatata until mid-April of that year, and it was not until late May that I knew enough about its populace to carry out a similar survey.

Like most anthropologists who have attempted to make censuses in their study of communities, I found myself first confused, then frustrated, and finally humbled by the task. To begin with, in the process of making the tally on a household basis, some people were reported to "belong" to the household in question but to be "absent," others (I later discovered) were overlooked, and still others kept turning up in neighboring households as well. As for those whose names were volunteered but declared to be absent, some had been so for years and seemed to me unlikely to return, to reverse which there were others who had left the village quite recently and would probably return after a while but who were considered by their former household mates to be gone indefinitely, and hence perhaps, in their views, forever.

Moreover, in communities like those studied where the comings and goings were so intrinsic a feature of life, where, for example, visits ranged in duration from a day to a year or more, and where people went elsewhere for schooling or for "temporary" jobs that lasted from weeks to years, the term *resident* can only be defined in arbitrary ways, as I perforce did.

I gave the label of *resident* (and hence included in the census) all those who were residing in the household in question on the census day, including those who were said to have come from elsewhere whose stays were not to be ended by completion of a specifically named objective (such as attending a wedding, or harvesting a coconut grove) and who were participating fully in the household's "pool-sharing" economy. (For definition, see Chapter X.) I also counted as residents those reported as usually living there but currently absent on specific missions for limited periods of time. (In this sense, a child attending school in Pape'ete was classified as a resident, whereas a young man or woman who had "gone to work in Pape'ete" was not.) Predictably, there were some borderline cases which I "neutralized" by classifying one out of two as a resident.

In contrast to the uncertainties regarding who was a *resident*, the information on individuals' birth dates was, in most cases, gratifyingly definite and reliable. The birth dates of nearly everyone under about age fifty were known to the subjects themselves or to their near kin; and for all those born locally, I was able to confirm such dates or correct the few uncertainties by referring to the local Civil Register (*Etat Civil*). Even for those over about fifty, nearly all of them were able to name the year, if not the month, of birth—information, by the way, which was in some cases recorded in the individual's family Bible.

For those interested in minutae per se, figures for a one-year interval breakdown of the censuses will be supplied on request. For other readers the results are shown below in Tables 1-B and 1-C in five-year interval pyramids.

If the pyramids I have constructed represented complete and more or less isolated populations, they would deserve some attention, as a whole, as biological phenomena. As it is, however, the only aspects of them that appear to have large and direct biological relevance are the categories comprising individuals under age fifteen and those sixty and over; this seems to be on account of the circumstances that individuals in those age cohorts very rarely changed their village of residence, once born there or otherwise established there so late in life. There were of course cultural reasons for that immobility; but with respect to the under-fifteen category, those cultural factors served mainly to maintain underlying biological events.

As for most other characteristics of these population pyramids, cultural facts must be included in any attempt to account for those in which the two communities differed, an exercise that will be undertaken in Chapter XII.

Table 1-B
ATEA'S POPULATION 1955

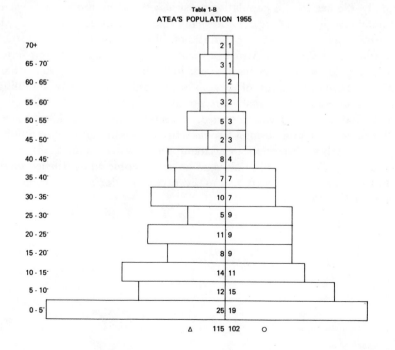

Age	♂	♀
70+	2	1
65 - 70	3	1
60 - 65		2
55 - 60	3	2
50 - 55	5	3
45 - 50	2	3
40 - 45	8	4
35 - 40	7	7
30 - 35	10	7
25 - 30	5	9
20 - 25	11	9
15 - 20	8	9
10 - 15	14	11
5 - 10	12	15
0 - 5	25	19

Δ   115   102   O

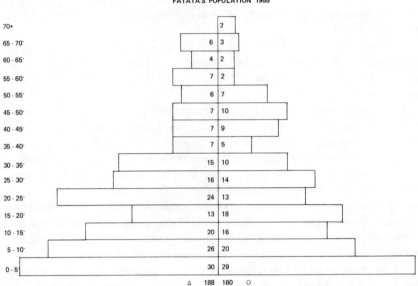

Table 1-C

FATATA'S POPULATION 1955

Age	△	○
70+		2
65 - 70	6	3
60 - 65	4	2
55 - 60	7	2
50 - 55	6	7
45 - 50	7	10
40 - 45	7	9
35 - 40	7	5
30 - 35	15	10
25 - 30	16	14
20 - 25	24	13
15 - 20	13	18
10 - 15	20	16
5 - 10	26	20
0 - 5	30	29
	△ 188	160 ○

Finally, the health of a population must also be taken into account when considering its members' capacity for work, play, etc. In light of this, I will record my impressions—based, of course, on obvious and external evidence alone—that the residents of Atea and Fatata were much alike in their states of health, which were, in general, good. In both communities, people had their (pan-human?) shares of discomforting and temporarily disabling illnesses—respiratory, intestinal, etc. To these must be added occasional bouts of filariasis and, I was informed, of venereal disorders, old and new. On the other hand, aside from a few cases in both communities of crippling caused mainly by elephantiasis or accident, the Te Pitians were a physically sound and capable lot—until, that is, some catastrophic ailment felled them or until about the age of sixty-five to seventy, when, for most of them, decrepitude began to set in.

Quayside Papeete: Loading the launch to Fatata

Arrival at Fatata

Atea's usual links with outside world

Rare event in Atea: Interisland boat makes a call

Atea looking inland (with Assembly House at left)

Atea looking seaward

Fatata shoreline

Fatata fish seining crew

Atea Main Street

Atea backyards at high tide (latrines at right)

Fatata Main Street

Fatata: Old "Vanilla" house

CHAPTER II

SUBSISTENCE

Food

The ordinary weekday eating routine of most Te Pitians consisted of a light breakfast shortly after sunrise and a large meal in the afternoon—early, middle or late, according to the schedules of the households' more actively productive members. Then, unless the day's main meal was very late, there was usually another light meal partaken in the early evening, typically of bread and coffee or tea.

Or such at least was the common preference. However, if circumstances interfered with this routine, e.g., a journey, an unusually long fishing expedition, a meeting or ceremony, Te Pitians appeared to tolerate much longer periods of abstinence, or to eat much larger than average meals early in the morning or late at night. (That is to say, their food appetites seemed not to be closely synchronized with any actual or imagined clock.)

Breakfast for most usually consisted of coffee and bread, the former mixed with coconut milk or canned condensed milk and heavily sweetened with sugar, and the bread spread with coconut oil or butter. Some individuals drank tea in preference to coffee, and sometimes leftovers from the previous day's meal supplemented the usual bread and beverage breakfast.

Many Te Pitians recalled an era before coffee or tea or bread were readily available: then (they recalled) breakfast and supper consisted only of fruit and perhaps leftovers from the previous day's main meal. By 1954, however, coffee or tea and bread or some other baked goods were regarded by virtually everyone as the essential, if not indispensable, fare for beginning and ending a day.

For most Te Pitians, the day's main meal consisted of *mā'a*, *'ina'i*, and *miti*. *Mā'a* was the term used for any kind of starchy vegetable, e.g., breadfruit, taro, yam, sweet potato, plantain, rice, or cassava. *'Ina'i* referred to fish and animal flesh (pork, beef, chicken, etc.). And *miti*, the term also used for sea and seawater, referred in this context to salty or savory liquid seasonings— sea water, *miti ha'ari* (a mixture of sea water and coconut cream), *miti hue* (soft coconut meat fermented in shrimp 'water') *fāfaru* (fish fermented in sea water).

Bread was also eaten in some households at main meal time, but usually as a supplement to, or unavoidable substitute for, *mā'a*.

To most Te Pitians, a main meal consisting of *mā'a* alone was regarded as inadequate and unpalatable. On those rare occasions when no *'ina'i* was available, one could make do with *mā'a* flavored with *miti*, but every main meal worthy of the name required at least a few morsels of *'ina'i*.

Breadfruit, taro, and plantains (i.e., cooking bananas) were the most highly favored kinds of *mā'a* for most, but *taruā*, sweet potatoes, yams, etc., served as occasionally or circumstantially acceptable substitutes. Many individuals also ate rice now and then, either by choice or necessity, but I came across no one who preferred it as a steady diet.

The most commonly eaten *'ina'i* was fresh fish either cooked or marinated raw. Fresh chicken, pork, and (rarely) beef were customarily eaten only on special occasions. Canned meat and fish were also eaten sometimes but usually only when fresh fish or meat was unavailable or when work or some other activity made cooking inconvenient or too time consuming.

On special occasions, e.g., Sundays, celebrations, when entertaining important guests, meals sometimes included such delicacies as *pota* (taro leaves cooked with chicken or pork and coconut cream), *po'e* (a gelatinous cake made of cassava starch, sugar, and various kinds of flavor components, e.g., bananas, pineapple, lemon juice), Tahitian chestnuts, crayfish, prawns, homemade or store-bought cake, gelatinous Chinese noodles, and perhaps one or two Chinese or European canned goods.

The fruits and melons found growing in Te Piti, e.g., mangoes (native and introduced), papayas, watermelons, oranges, grapefruit, were eaten mainly as between-meal snacks and did not qualify as *mā'a*.

The beverage usually drunk with the day's main meal was water, sometimes slightly salty and sometimes in the form of homemade lemonade. A few, but only a very few, households accompanied their main meal with wine, typically a harsh Algerian red wine to which some drinkers added sugar. Other alcoholic beverages, including beer and homemade brews, were usually reserved for separate occasions, and the relatively few bottled soft drinks (*siro*) that Te Pitians consumed were drunk mainly during celebrations or at cinema time.

The foregoing account refers to all Te Pitians past infancy (*aiura'a*, eat-milk-hood). Once a child had graduated from an all-milk diet, a very early threshold in most cases, it was permitted, even encouraged, to eat and drink anything except, in most households, alcoholic beverages. Thus, all Te Pitians past infancy ate some food purchased from stores or other vendors, but most of them also ate some foods grown, gathered, or caught, etc., by themselves or their household mates.

Most of Te Piti's residences were divided into three kinds of space: one for sleeping, one for everyday eating, and one for cooking. In some instances, these constituted three separate structures; in others, separate rooms under the same roof. On formal occasions in some residences, adult guests were fed in the sleeping room where they were also able to view and admire the colorful bedspreads and pillows displayed on the surrounding beds. At such times most females and younger male members of the households ate separately and later, after having sat behind the diners listening to the table talk and watching for signs of approval for any delicacies provided.

Every household owned store-bought utensils—cups, bowls, and plates or china or enamel, and metal knives, forks, and spoons—and these were used in common European[1] style, except that coffee and tea were ordinarily drunk from bowls, tougher meat was typically cut with one's personal knife, and hands served more often than forks to convey food to the mouth.

The usual method of eating *mā'a* (breadfruit, taro, plantain, etc.) was to mold it by hand into a large mouth-filling ball and then dip it into one's individual bowl of seasoning (usually the blander types of *miti*) before stuffing it, *all* of it, into the mouth. Bread and other baked goods were also customarily dipped, but in coffee or tea, before eating.

Fish was eaten in smaller morsels, sometimes separately and sometimes along with a mouthful of *mā'a*; raw fish, especially, was dipped into a seasoning, typically the more pungent *fāfaro*, before eating. Other kinds of *'ina'i* were eaten separately in very small pieces, meat as well as fish. In the case of the latter, each small morsel was likely to contain a bit of bone, gristle and flesh, cut seemingly without reference to the animal's anatomy. Until I grasped the rationale of this procedure, I judged my hosts to be either ignorant of animal anatomy or wholly indifferent to the gustatory rewards of skilled carving; but, in time, I came to appreciate the advantage of their way of carving: no matter how small the supply of meat, every diner received at least a taste, and one that lasted longer for having to be cracked, chewed, and sucked. (I was never able to elicit from the Te Pitians

---

[1]Here and henceforth, "European" refers to persons and customs of originally European (as distinguished from, say, Asian) background, including English, French, American, Australian, etc.

themselves this rationale for their method of carving, but its effects were as described.) Moreover, the importance of meat, however little people were able to get of it, is indicated by the answer I often received to my query of why people spent money acquiring false teeth: namely, "to be able to chew meat." (For young and especially unmarried women, cosmetic reasons also applied; but for most other persons, teeth were valued mainly for their aid in chewing.)

By some European standards, Te Pitian eating was a single-minded and noisy affair. While engaged in this favorite activity, people devoted *all* their attention to it, evidently not considering it socially essential to vary chewing and sipping with small talk. Usually, the sounds that accompanied it were in the form of loud slurping, smacking, and sucking, punctuated with hearty belching. Also, conventions did not impose limits on quantities consumed; on the contrary, any guests happening to be present were urged vociferously to "eat, eat," and "finish it up"—which leads to the question of what ideas the Te Pitians held concerning the amounts and kinds of food one should, or liked to eat.

To calorie-conscious Europeans, most Te Pitians would appear to consume unreasonably large quantities of food, principally starchy *māʻa,* at their main daily meal. (I did not undertake any systematic measuring of individual consumption, but gained an impression from numerous occasions that most men regularly put away about four to five times an amount my stomach could comfortably accommodate.) Three considerations seem to be relevant here. In the first place, their traditional food prepared in the conventional manner was judged to be one of the best, if not *the* best, things in life; and the more there was—up to the point of satiety—the better. Secondly, as far as I could discover, Te Pitians were not constrained in their eating by any nutritional doctrine, scientific or otherwise, concerning desirable consumption limits. And thirdly, corpulence was not narrowly discountenanced; on the contrary, a certain degree of plumpness was considered to be comely and healthy, especially in females. (For example, male informants characterized plump women as better for sexual intercourse, and thin women were generally considered to be ill.) What Europeans would label gross obesity was decried also by Te Pitians—the high cosmetic value accorded such excess fatness by ancient Tahitians no longer obtained (Oliver 1974, pp. 434ff)—but to Te Pitians, the line between permissible plumpness and unsightly obesity was considerably higher on the scale. (Perhaps one reason behind this difference between Te Pitian and European views is the fact that corpulent Tahitians in general, and Te Pitians in particular, carried their pounds better than corpulent Europeans; I rarely saw among Tahitians such disfigurements as large sagging paunches associated with spindly arms and legs.)

Given, then, that the Te Pitians took great pleasure in eating and that they at least once a day liked to eat large quantities of food, it was only the rare individual who ate in a way that can be described as gluttonous. When circumstances provided, most individuals ate to the point of satiety—which, as described, was a very high level by European standards—but thereupon stopped eating. Although hospitality required that guests be urged to "finish it up," left to themselves most Te Pitians appeared not to continue eating just because some food was still there. It is true that there were one or two gluttons in both communities—mainly middle-aged men of no affluence—but these were held in some contempt because of it.

Turning now to the kinds of food Te Pitians considered most beneficial or palatable, it should be noted at the onset that most of them either did not make such a distinction verbally or expressed no opinions about the nutritional value, beneficial or noxious, of particular foods. Some young women voiced disapproval of coffee as being "poisonous" (*ta'ero*), and I occasionally heard pious statements about "fresh food being better than canned," but that was all, despite some lessons on nutrition given in school. Once when I stepped out of role and suggested a possible connection between their generally wretched teeth and their heavy consumption of sugar—an average of half a kilo a day for a family of four—I was accorded the polite incredibility due to a respected but hopelessly naïve guest. In fact, Te Pitian food preferences were based not on cryptic characteristics like calories or proteins but on such palpable properties as consistency and flavor. For example, sweetness was almost universally preferred over bitterness—as witnessed by the very high consumption of sugar (even, by some, in wine)—and many individuals I queried preferred soft oily foods to sinewy dry ones, e.g., the fatty squill (*varo*) over the juiceless *langouste* (*oūra miti*), and mushy pâte (*pōpoi*) to bake-dried *po'e*. On the other hand, tastes differed considerably with respect to seasonings, i.e., some people (mostly adults) were fond of *fāfaru* while others found it nauseatingly rank. And although most individuals rated breadfruit, taro, and plantain above *taruā*, sweet potato, and the other starchy foods, there was considerable difference of opinion concerning which of the most favored staples was "best."

As in the case of seasonings, some differences in food preference seem to have been due to one's age, but I discovered no correlation between such preferences and the person's sex or formal education or experience in more Europeanized settings. Nor did I discover any consistent differences between the food preferences of Ateans and Fatatans. More highly educated and more generally European-experienced individuals were to be found in Fatata than in Atea; and some of the Fatatan females were capable of preparing many French-style recipes (which were far tastier to my European palate); but they did so mainly for European guests. When left to themselves, even these sophisticates appear to have preferred, or at least to have eaten, Tahitian-style foods and recipes.

In contrast to food preferences, however, there were some noteworthy differences in food consumption patterns between Atea and Fatata. Breadfruit was a favored staple in both places but Ateans as a whole ate much more aroids and plantains than Fatatans did—not, as I have noted, because of differences in preference, but because smaller amounts of these foods, on the average, were grown in Fatata than in Atea. A few Atean households produced no aroids of their own (exactly how many I did not investigate), but all of these regularly obtained supplies of them from neighbors by purchase or "gift." In Fatata, the situation was quite different. Only a few households produced aroids, and what they did produce was mainly consumed by themselves. Most Fatatan households—again, I did not collect exact figures—produced no aroids at all; and those they ate, which in some cases happened very infrequently, had to be purchased, some from neighbors, some from the local trade store, and some from the Pape'ete market. (In the latter instances, by order placed with the daily boat.)

Instead of a daily staple of breadfruit or aroid, most Fatatans ate breadfruit or rice. Ateans also ate rice on occasion but usually as an addition to breadfruit or aroid, or when there was not time or inclination to bake, which was the normal method for cooking breadfruit and aroids.

Fatatans, on the average, also ate such canned foods as peas and baked beans much more frequently than Ateans, and bottled ketchup was a more familiar sight on the tables of the former. Moreover, in addition to their larger consumption of locally caught fish, Fatatans ate, on the average, about as much canned fish as Ateans, as well as considerably more purchased meat (either canned meat from the local stores or fresh meat brought from Pape'ete).[2] Fatatans also ate (and produced) more chickens and eggs than the Ateans did. In the case of dog flesh, Ateans were more open about their liking for it than Fatatans—a consequence, perhaps, of the latters' greater sensitivity to Europeans' abhorrence of the practice; but whether Ateans actually ate more of it, I cannot say.

No such uncertainty prevails about the consumption of alcoholic beverages. With one exception, the few households that regularly accompanied their main meals with wine were all in Fatata, where beer was also drunk by a few men as a regular, almost daily practice. All this was done quietly

---

[2] These generalizations are based on records kept for me by several household heads in both communities. However, I hasten to add, they did not even attempt to record quantities of items eaten, but only lists of the kinds and sources of foods served; adequate and accurate measure of a household's food consumption would have required much more time and attention than my study warranted.

and discreetly, facilitated by the presence in Fatata of a licensed beer and wine seller and by the daily boat to and from Pape'ete. In sharp contrast, Ateans had to go to Fare for their supplies of wine and beer, which they either brought back in their own skins, in everyone's view, or in containers just as obvious to their neighbors. Moreover, when Ateans acquired wine or beer they usually drank it—*all* of it—forthwith and within close hearing (literally) of their neighbors. Fatatans also indulged in noisy drinking sprees occasionally; but much more of their drinking was done regularly, more moderately, and much more quietly. The greater circumspection attending Fatatan drinking was of course facilitated by the greater distance between most of their houses; but in addition, Fatatans were prone, less so than Ateans, to regard drinking as a sociable event.

According to my admittedly uncertain estimates, Ateans consumed about 40,400 francs worth of imported alcoholic beverages in 1954 as compared with the Fatatans' 105,000.

Another difference between Atean and Fatatan drinking habits obtained with respect to homemade brews. I knew of only two Fatatans who made a regular practice of brewing those potent beverages—usually out of cassava starch flavored with pineapple or bananas, whereas a score or more Ateans engaged in this mildly illegal practice. In Atea, most brewing was done during December in preparation for New Year, but much of the liquor was consumed beforehand in numerous preliminary "tastings" by the maker alone or in company with friends. In fact, for a fortnight before New Year itself, one of the villagers' main conversational topics centered on the progress and relative merits of their numerous brews—a topic that required of the ethnographer a feat of diplomacy as difficult as the one involved in the actual sampling of those corrosive drinks.

Finally, while tobacco smoking was widespread among Te Pitians, I have the impression that they were as a whole less addicted to the practice than most communities of Europeans I know. I knew no one who chain-smoked and few who smoked the equivalent of a twenty-cigarette pack a day. In fact, most men I knew well smoked only two or three cigarettes or pipes a day, mainly after meals; and some women I knew well smoked not at all (although some of the heaviest smokers were elderly women).

Causes for the Te Pitians' comparatively mild attachment to smoking were various. A few individuals, mainly young women, abstained (they said) for reasons of health. (However, I heard few parents or other adults actually prohibit or discourage smoking among children.) Other Te Pitians traced their infrequent smoking to the high cost of tobacco, which during my visits all came from the stores. In addition, I can suggest (but by no means demonstrate) that the infrequent smoking of some Te Pitians may have been due to smoking's incompatibility with many of the activities they pursued, i.e., active, physical movements requiring constant use of both hands.

Te Pitians obtained their food by producing it themselves (by gardening, collecting, fishing), by purchase, and in the form of "gift" from others. There are some salient differences between the two villages with respect to the relative amounts obtained by production as opposed to purchase. The present section will be devoted to describing the methods of food production utilized in common by both villages and such differences that existed between them in this regard.

Coconuts (*Cocos nucifera L.*; *niu, ha'ari*). Te Pitians used the liquid of unripe coconuts as a beverage, the meat—both ripe and unripe—for food and seasoning, and the creamy oil for frying, breadspread, and confection. Unlike some Pacific islanders, they did not derive a toddy from the plant and they seldom ate the spongy pulp of the germinating nut. Nor, although they appreciated its flavor, did they have many opportunities to eat the heart of palm since this is obtained only by destroying the palm itself.

Coconut palms grew throughout both of the villages' residential areas, interspersed among the houses; and they also grew in large and small groves outside the residential areas. Nuts from the former were the ones usually used as food while those in the groves were used mainly for making copra for sale. The only new plantings I witnessed were in the groves, and the only "cultivation" I saw practiced consisted of nailing strips of zinc around the trunks in order to foil nut-eating rats. Mature nuts were collected either by picking them off the ground, by climbing the trunk and cutting or twisting them free (in Atea)—a task usually performed by boys—or by cutting them loose with a knife attached to a very long pole—a feat requiring considerable strength and practice, and one almost invariably performed by males. Nut husking was also done mainly by males, but females could and did perform this job if no male was available.

Tahitian coconut palms reach nut-bearing age about five years after planting and continue to bear for about sixty years. It may be that nuts mature somewhat faster during the summer months, but I heard nothing to indicate that Te Pitians actually thought this to be so; and for eating purposes they were harvested year round.

As far as I could tell, both villages were endowed with natural resources for producing enough coconuts for ordinary food and drink requirements, i.e., enough land of suitable slope, insolation, etc. What differences there were between them with respect to coconut growing affected their "surpluses," i.e., the quantities of nuts available for copra-making about which something will be said in Chapter III. Within each village, however, there were some wide differences between households with respect to numbers of nut-bearing palms owned.[3] Some households owned hundreds of palms, some only a few. But even the latter were allowed to take nuts, *gratis,* from acquaintances' or relatives' palms for ordinary eating purposes—typically, from one to four nuts a day, depending upon menu and size of household. In other words, during my stays in Te Piti, coconuts for eating were not exchanged among local Tahitians for money or other goods; and unlike some other locally grown staples, they were not even sold to the Chinese stores for local resale. I assume that people who "gave" eating coconuts to others on a fairly regular basis expected some eventual reciprocation in objects or services, but this was disavowed by those to whom the question was put.

Viewed comparatively, I could not discover any noteworthy differences between Atea and Fatata with respect to the acquisition—or processing or consumption methods and levels—of coconuts used in household cuisine.

Breadfruit (*Artocarpus altilis* [incisa?]; *'uru, mai'ore*). Breadfruit and taro were the Te Pitians' favorite kinds of *mā'a*. Some individuals rated one of them higher than the other; but in nearly everyone's expressed opinion, these two stood at the top of the list of preferred staple foods. If breadfruit had ripened year round—which was not the case—it is likely that many Te Pitians would have been content to eat it every day. Others preferred to vary their diets somewhat even at the expense of growing or purchasing other staples. In any case, breadfruit was available during only seven to eight months of the year so that taro or other staples had to be obtained by gardening or some kind of exchange.

The breadfruit grown in Te Piti were seedless and were propagated by shoots and root cuttings; young plants were usually protected by individual fencing until large enough to withstand wandering pigs. Trees began bearing five to seven years after planting and thereafter produced fruit for some fifty years more (Wilder 1928). The only care I saw being given a breadfruit tree was an occasional pruning, which a few, relatively well-educated men undertook in the belief that it increased the quantity and quality of the fruit—a notion regarded with skepticism by some of their neighbors.

During my visits, those breadfruit trees growing in or near the residences produced edible fruit three times a year: a brief "preliminary" fruiting in March; a full one from late May to early August; and another full fruiting during November, December, and early January. I was informed that no

---

[3]The subject of Te Pitian property ownership is a very complex one and will be described in Chapter XI. In the present context, I use "own" to mean that one or more members of a household held proprietary or use (including consumption) rights, exclusive or joint, officially or widely acknowledged, to the item in question.

two years were the same in terms of beginning and ending dates or quantity of fruit, but I could not establish that any such irregularities did actually occur or, if in fact they did, what might have accounted for them.

Te Pitians distinguished three stages of breadfruit ripeness: *'uru pī,* when the outer skin is green; *'uru maoa,* when the skin is yellower and the fibrous pulp riper, softer, and "sweeter"; and *'uru pē,* just prior to falling, when it is even softer. (Fallen and hence overripe fruit splatters on reaching the ground and is eaten, if at all, only by pigs feeding nearby.) The riper fruit tended to be used more in culinary mixtures; but Te Pitians ate the fruit at all three of its edible stages, some favoring one stage over another.

Although individuals often picked the fruit with no help, the easier and preferred method was for one of a pair to climb the tree and twist loose the fruit, which the other person caught by hand or with a bag; any fruit at an edible stage would otherwise burst open.

Unlike their Tahitian ancestors, who used to eat some of their breadfruit raw and after lengthy fermentation, the Te Pitians I observed ate theirs cooked and within a day or so of picking. Cooking was done either in an earth oven or over hot coals or in a pot or frying pan. Most informants agreed that earth-oven baking was best in terms of flavor and consistency, and that the other methods were resorted to only for lack of time or industriousness, or in the absence of a proper oven and heating stones.

Botanists point to the existence in the Society Islands of several varieties or kinds of breadfruit (Wilder 1928). Te Pitians also made distinctions among them on the basis of shape of fruit and leaf; but on the few occasions when I sought (not very systematically, I must confess) to elicit a common taxonomy from my informants, I did not get very far—there having been both a large measure of ignorance and a considerable lack of consensus.

As previously stated, most Te Pitians regarded breadfruit (along with taro) as one of the best of foods in terms of flavor and consistency. A few even claimed, without elucidation, that these two foods were also essential for maintaining one's "strength." In fact, chemical analysis of breadfruit has determined that it consists of about 83 percent water by weight, and the rest mainly starch.

There were no discernible differences between Atea and Fatata with respect to techniques of breadfruit production or processing, and adequate supplies were available to both communities to satisfy local needs. However, Fatata's trees were on the average more accessible than those of Atea. In Atea, there were only a few bearing trees in the residence area itself; most of them could be reached only by long walks or canoe trips across the bay. In Fatata, on the other hand, large numbers of trees grew within the residential area itself, which, it will be recalled, was spread out more thinly over a wider coastal and lower-valley plain. And, although I did not make a precise enough record of its consumption in either place, I gained the impression that on the average more of the fruit was eaten in Fatata than in Atea.

Aroids. Te Pitians grew three species of Araceae: taro (*Colocasia esculenta L. Schott*), 'ape (*Alocasia macrorrhiza L. Schott*), and *taruā* (*Xanthosoma sagittifolium*), the latter a post-European introduction.

Taro, by all odds the most highly favored food of the three, was grown in wet, friable soil (but not under water). The parts eaten were the root and tender young leaves. The plant was propagated by burying the stalk and top of the root in a hole about 20 cm deep, with plants about 80 cm apart. It was planted and harvested year round, but the recognized local experts said that it was best planted in October, at the beginning of the hotter and rainier time of the year. Opinions differed widely concerning taro's ripening time; some persons claimed that it ripened in four months, others said six months, still others said eight or nine. Differences were also voiced concerning the length of time the ripe root could be left in the ground before rooting, i.e., from a few months to a year. Some of these differences may have been due to local and seasonal variations in growing conditions, but I suspect—although did not test—that much of the disagreement derived from most Te Pitians' unconcern with measurement of time.

In pre-European times, Tahitians distinguished and labelled some twenty-nine varieties of taro (Henry, p. 35); but even the expert gardeners I questioned could name only nine, of which the root of the variety known as 'ura (red) was considered best.

Taro roots were cooked by baking, toasting over embers, frying, or sometimes boiling. The favored way of preparing the tender, edible leaves was oven-baking with pork.

Most Te Pitians considered *taruā* inferior to taro as a food, but it had some qualities that led them to plant more of it, i.e., it grew well in drier soil (*fenua mea marō*), which was more abundant than taro-growing soil in both villages; it was less vulnerable to insect pests; and it could be "stored" without rooting by leaving it in the ground for a longer time after ripening. (In fact, *taruā* becomes self-propagating if left long enough in the ground.) It was said to have grown best when planted in August–September and to have been ready for harvest after nine months.

Taruā also has the advantage of being more productive and of growing satisfactorily in mixed-garden sites. For example, in one such garden that I measured, some 4,800 square meters in area, about 1,250 *taruā* plants grew interspersed with numerous banana, breadfruit, and papaya plants and a few coconut palms. At an average of four kilos a tuber, this provided a total yield of about 5,000 kilos. The few other *taruā* gardens I measured led to fairly similar estimates which, when compared with estimates derived from measurements of taro plots, showed *taruā* to provide a slightly more productive yield, area for area, and at the cost of considerably less labor.

Taruā was recognized by Te Pitians as being a post-European introduction (and, "consequently," it was widely reasoned, inferior to taro in flavor and texture, but also "consequently" destined to supplant taro altogether). It was cooked and eaten exactly like taro.

The giant-size *'ape* was occasionally planted by Te Pitians but occurred mainly growing wild in swampy out-of-the-way places. It was described as a famine-time food for humans and I knew of none having been eaten during my visits. It had the advantage of remaining storable in the ground for five years or more after ripening, but its bitter-tasting oxalate crystals must be removed by long soaking before the root is palatable. Also, it is tougher and more sinewy than *taruā* and taro. I saw pigs occasionally being fed chunks of the root but even they seemed to prefer the parings of taro and *taruā*.[4]

Both taro and *taruā* gardens require weeding soon after planting and for some time thereafter until the large leaves produce enough shade to inhibit weeds, but the weeding period would appear to vary from site to site. Although aware of the potential significance of local differences in this matter, i.e., the extent to which local differences in geography may have required differences in weeding labor, I made no systematic observations regarding it and was unable to elicit reliable opinions about it. In any case, this deficiency turns out to be fairly irrelevant in the face of another, overriding difference between the two villages, namely, in the amount per capita of land devoted to root-crop gardening, i.e., the figure for Atea was not only significantly larger, but it was only in Atea that taro was grown at all. Fatatans did occasionally eat taro, but only by buying it at the Pape'ete market.

In both places, both males and females engaged in gardening; and in both places, it was the verbalized convention that males should do the heavier work of clearing and planting and females the weeding. However, Fatata females tended to leave more of the latter as well to their mates.

Sweet Potato (*Ipomoea batatas*; *'umara*). The native, pre-European varieties of this tuber are reported (Barrau, p. 74) to have been superseded by better and more productive varieties of recent introduction; but even so, Te Pitians in general planted few of them and ate them only when other vegetable staples were not available. The principal advantage of sweet potatoes derives from their rapid growth and their adaptability to marginal soils, but evidently neither of these advantages had to be taken into account in Te

---

[4]I was informed that there were two kinds of *'ape*: *mā'aro*, the less bitter variety eaten by humans, and *mā'ero*, the variety fed to pigs.

Piti during the times of my visits. Te Pitians claimed that they grew best when planted in July, and that they were harvestable after four months.

While I did not systematically measure the garden areas devoted to each root crop in either community, I did form the impression that those Fatatans who actually produced root crops (and these, it will be recalled, were relatively fewer than in Atea) grew more sweet potatoes on the average than the Atean gardeners, for the expressed reason that sweet potatoes required less work.

Yam (*Dioscorea alata L.*; *'ufi*). Te Pitians considered yams inferior even to sweet potatoes in flavor and much more difficult to grow, i.e., the soil required special preparation and poles had to be planted to support the climbing leaves. Consequently, few yams were grown for food. On the other hand, the spectacular sizes that carefully nurtured yams can attain (some of them nearly two meters long), led some men to grow them mainly for show. To produce very large yams, it was necessary to excavate a hole a meter or more in depth, refill it with lighter top soil, weed the surrounding area scrupulously, and train the leaves to climb around a high pole. When left to grow to full maturity, such a yam was considered far too dry, tasteless, and sinewy for human consumption and even poor food for a pig, but its size gave evidence of the producer's gardening skill and, as such, was a source of pride and prestige.

Yam growing was pursued much more actively in Atea than in Fatata, stimulated mainly by the holding in Atea of an annual agricultural contest, which will be described below.

Cassava (*Manihot dulcis*; *maniota*). The multiple, starch-rich roots of this plant (which was introduced around 1850) were extensively gardened in Te Piti for local consumption and as a cash crop. Occasionally, the roots were cooked and eaten like other root crops, but more often their starch was extracted and sold or used in the producer's household for making puddings (*po'e*). Extracting the starch was a laborious process. After they were washed and peeled, the roots were shredded and placed in large wooden troughs. Fresh water was then poured over the shreds to wash out the starch, the water and starch-free fiber were dipped out, and the remaining white starch was spread out and left to dry. The peelings and fibers were sometimes saved for pigs, although it was recognized that they were of slight value as food.

As elsewhere in the Society Islands, the alien cassava had completely supplanted the indigenous arrowroot (*Tacca leontopetaloides*) in native cuisine, probably because of its higher productivity and copious starch yield (about 35 percent by weight). The root was usually planted in May and reached maturity after four months to a year, depending upon variety and growing conditions. It remained edible in the ground for a year or more thereafter. Relatively fewer households in Fatata grew cassava than in Atea for either domestic consumption or sale.

Banana (*Musaceae*). Te Pitians ate several varieties of *Musaceae,* including *M. paradisica, M. sapientum,* and *M. troglydatarum.* Some of them were deliberately cultivated; others grew wild; some required cooking; others were eaten raw. I attempted on several occasions to match up the two native terms, *mei'a* and *fē'i,* with distinctive botanical species, or cooked versus raw-eaten types, but without general consensus among my informants, except for the tendency of restricting *fē'i* to the wild-growing, cooking varieties.

In any case, Te Pitians seemed to prefer their bananas cooked, either in the form of puddings, or baked or boiled whole. The recently introduced "Samoa" (*mei'a hamoa*)—the sweet, noncooked varieties favored by Europeans—were also planted and eaten by Te Pitians but served more for snacks than for solid, meal-time fare. Bananas were propagated from shoots and were observed growing in a wide variety of locations and conditions, from seaside to high mountain slopes, in houseyards or gardens or forests. Informants stated that cultivated bananas were best planted in July–September, and required about nine to twelve months to ripen, and did not remain edible very long thereafter.

Occasionally, a Te Pitian male would spend a whole day in the mountains searching for a bunch or two of the now scarce wild-growing fruit—the cookable type usually labelled *fē'i.* To bring some home was considered a laudable feat, not only because of its highly-prized flavor but because of the strength and endurance involved in this adventurous and very "Tahitian" (*mea mā'ohi*) endeavor.

Ateans, on the average, grew and ate more bananas than Fatatans, but the latter collected and ate more of the wild-growing *fē'i,* probably because of the accessibility to Fatata of large areas of higher altitudes where the few remaining sources of this vanishing fruit were still to be found.

Coffee. A few Te Pitians preferred tea; but for others past childhood (and for many children as well), coffee was considered to be an absolute necessity. Along with bread (usually "buttered" with coconut oil), coffee formed the principal, indeed almost the only, part of their morning and evening meals. It was brewed black and strong and drunk with coconut cream and very large quantities of sugar. I was unable to collect enough reliable figures to report per capita consumption for all Te Piti, but one household I knew well, consisting of three adults and three children, used about six kilos of coffee a month, and another with eight members used nine—an average of one kilo a person each month, which I believe was about the same in most households.

Except for occasional purchases in Fare or Pape'ete, all the coffee consumed by Te Pitians (which was the *arabica* variety) was grown locally. Not every household grew its own beans, but others grew enough to provide for themselves with enough left over to satisfy local demand, by gift or sale; and a few households produced enough for export to Pape'ete as well.

From what was said and seen, coffee bushes grew best on sites a hundred or more feet above sea level and in places having deep soil, good drainage, and protection from high winds. In some cases, the bushes grew in groves of a score or more each; and in other cases, they were scattered among other kinds of vegetation. As with other cash crops, the Administration expended much effort in trying to instruct farmers, including Te Pitians, in proper coffee-growing practices; but most of the Te Pitians I observed either misunderstood or pointedly ignored such advice. For most Te Pitians, the only service desired of the Administration in this activity was maintenance of a high price for coffee beans.

According to my observations, the beans ripened from March to June. They were said to be best when picked directly from the bush; those falling on the ground began immediately to rot. Bean picking was a slow and reportedly tedious process, so much so that some individuals not engaged in producing for sale bought their coffee-making beans hulled and dried and left those growing in their own bushes to fall and rot or permitted more energetic neighbors to collect them, more or less *gratis.*

In both Atea and Fatata, the owners of raw coffee berries removed the outside skin and pulp in hand-cranked machines supplied *gratis* by the Administration. They then dried the bean-like kernels in the sun in an average time of five days and hulled them by hand, the Ateans with mortar and pestle and the Fatatans by beating the bagged kernels with a bamboo stick. If any were to be sold, it was done so at that stage. For home use, however, the dried beans were roasted in a frying pan and then pulverized either by mortar and pestle or in a hand grinder. (To add a personal note: despite—or perhaps because of—the haphazardness of all this processing, the resulting brews made by pouring boiling water over the grains were the best flavored coffee I have ever drunk.)

Gardening. To anyone familiar with the preoccupation of many Melanesians with gardening—technically, magically, aesthetically, and socially—the gardening in Te Piti would at first appear to be offhand, pragmatic, utilitarian, and socially irrelevant. Closer observation revealed it to be quite efficient in terms of labor expenditure; but the Te Pitian gardeners I watched seemed to devote no effort, for example, to the shape of their gardens or the

uniformity of their yam-vine poles. And except for their avoidance of planting on the sites of ancient pagan temples, they employed no magical actions
or devices in gardening as far as I could discover. (Some of them did, however, state that they prayed to God for the prospering of their crops; and
cases were reported of crop failures having resulted from sorcery or from the
gardener's social misdeeds.)

As for the relevance of gardening to social, in contrast to purely "economic" concerns, longer observation revealed to me that Te Pitians did indeed
reward skillful performance in this activity. In both villages there was widespread consensus concerning the identities of the best local producers of
each major food crop; and the manner in which the ranking was discussed
indicated that some prestige was attached to this form of skill. In Atea,
moreover, the winners received more than verbal rewards.

Atea's vegetable-growing contests (*parie ma'a*, from French *pari*) mentioned
earlier were said to have been instituted by the Administration in about
1950 in order to encourage more and better homegrown food crops. They
were annual events held usually in mid- to late May. The one I witnessed
involved twenty-eight entrants, all of them male. In addition, most of the
rest of Atea's population attended in order to view the judging and prize-
giving and to partake of the accompanying feast. In fact, so solid was the
attendance that the more conspicuous absentees, i.e., certain male heads of
households, were noted and their reasons for staying away discussed, e.g.,
"too old to walk," "still angry about last year's judging," "considers the custom unprofitable in money terms," "ashamed at having grown nothing
worth exhibiting."

Four kinds of crops figured in the contests: watermelons, sweet potatoes,
taro, and yams. The prizes went to the largest specimens produced, by
weight, provided they contained no visible rot. In the case of yams, the
larger specimens were usually too old and stringy for human consumption;
but that did not disqualify them. At the contest I witnessed, only yams and
taro were actually exhibited and judged; the entrant melons and sweet potatoes had been weighed previously, then eaten at the time of their ripening
because of their brief spans of edibility.

Each year's contest was initiated a year in advance, when prospective entrants would indicate which crops they would enter and how much money
each of them would wager. (If, for example, ten individuals decided to enter
the contest and to compete for prizes totaling 5,000 francs, each of them
was committed to contribute 500 francs.) Prizes were usually awarded to the
five highest winners in each crop category, and the first prize in the taro
and yam categories—the most popular and widely contested—were reported
to have reached as high as 15,000 francs in some years, i.e., an amount
equaling the total money income of most local adult males. In the contest I

witnessed, the purse for all categories totaled 24,000 francs; and the largest first prize (for the largest single yam) was 10,000 francs.

In addition to this "official" wagering, many of the entrants in each year's contest, along with some nonentrants, waged side bets which, in some instances, produced for the winners amounts as high as 5,000 to 10,000 francs. Thus, the interest engendered by this simple contest of gardening skills was greatly intensified by the very large money gains (and the not inconsiderable money losses) that accompanied it.

The only practice in Fatata comparable to Atea's vegetable-growing contest was the annual public announcement, by the Administration, of Mo'orea's top performing gardeners, i.e., those who had taken the trouble to register their noteworthy products with Administrative officials. Some Fatatans occasionally took part in this competition;[5] and now and then, even won and had the satisfaction of having their neighbors know about their successes—should the latter happen to learn about them.

Finally, regularities in times of planting and harvesting some of Te Piti's food crops served to structure the annual cycle—not as decisively as societies elsewhere that are subjected to sharper climatic variations or that are more preponderantly self-subsistent, but perceptibly and acknowledgedly so. Informants differed somewhat in their dates but agreed upon a three-season cycle: (1) *āva'e pa'urā* (months [of] dryness), June-July-September, the season of sparse rainfall when food plants die; (2) *āva'e ahuni* (months [of] hotness), October-December, the season of heat and heavy rainfall, hence of planting; (3) *āva'e o'otira* (months [of] cutting, i.e., harvesting time), January-May.

Fishing. Some very wide differences existed between Atea and Fatata with regard to fishing, and these had far-reaching effects upon other activities in the two communities. Some of these differences may have derived from local environmental conditions, but others resulted directly from Fatata's proximity to Pape'ete, which provided a large and generally profitable market for locally caught fish. These matters will be described later on; for the present, I shall focus on the techniques of fish-catching insofar as they were common to both communities.

From my own—doubtless ethnocentric—perspective, I envisage Te Piti's fishing techniques under five general headings: collecting, angling, spearing, netting, and a residual "miscellaneous."[6]

---

[5]These annual awards, which included small money prizes, were part of a comprehensive competition involving also fishing catches, plantation improvements, etc.

[6]Te Pitians themselves used the word *hi* for angling, and applied the word *'upe'a* to all kinds of fish nets, large and small; otherwise, it is doubtful that they mentally classified all their fishing techniques as I have done. A systematic "cognatic" approach to this topic would doubtless be interesting but is dispensable in terms of the objectives of this study.

Collecting land crabs qualifies as "fishing" only because it was done to provide fishing bait. It was engaged in mainly by children, who derived lively entertainment from trying to entice these cautious animals out of their holes by means of a leaf attached to a string.

The freshwater streams around Te Piti sheltered quantities of prawns (*Malacostraces decapodes*; *'oura pape*), which Te Pitians regarded as luxury food, mainly for feasts, and which they caught at night with the help of lamps or flashlights. Certain saltwater crustaceans were also regarded by some as luxury food and caught for special occasions. These were, mainly, *langoustes* (*Panulirus penicillatus*; *'oura miti*) and squills (*Pseudosquilla ciliate*; *varo*). The only mollusk regularly caught and eaten, and this only for festive cuisine, was the tridacna clam (*Tridacna elongata*; *pāhua*). Unlike some other Tahitians (especially those living on Tahiti itself), those of Atea and Fatata did not make a regular practice of collecting oysters (*tio*), mussels (*'u'u*), or cockles (*'ahi*); nor did they consider it worth the effort to collect sea urchins (*vana*) for the tiny morsels of food thus obtained. While I heard no opinions expressed regarding the division of labor most appropriate to this activity, all collecting of crustaceans and mollusks I knew of was done by males.

Angling was practiced in several ways. Some patient souls were content to sit on a wharf or point of land and manually trail a line—for what appeared to be a usually unrewarding catch. Others went out into the lagoon in canoes, alone or in pairs, and fished either while anchored or while paddling slowly along; this was engaged in mainly by women and some elderly men. More robust and active male anglers found it more rewarding to take their canoes beyond the reef or to cast into the ocean while standing on the reef. (The type of pelagic trolling from a powered boat engaged in by Pape'ete's professional fishermen was practiced by only one Te Pitian and with such uneconomic returns that he finally gave it up.)

Some individuals set out shore-attached lines with devices for signalling when a fish was hooked, but the rewards from such arrangements were not large or frequent enough to encourage their widespread use.

When poles were used in angling, they were usually of local bamboo. As for the hooks and lines, these were nearly all manufactured imports obtained from the local Chinese stores. However, I did see an occasional fisherman—typically, a youth with no money or store credit—use hooks fashioned by himself out of nails.

Fish spearing was more physically demanding than most kinds of angling and was consequently practiced mainly by young men. It was also usually more rewarding in terms of catch and at the same time was regarded by many of its practitioners as an especially pleasurable, even exciting, sport. Some spear fishermen continued to use a homemade, manually propelled spear (*'auri pātia*), a wooden shaft tipped with one or more metal prongs.

Others used a speargun (*pupuhi*), either a metal commercial manufacture or one made locally out of wood, tire-tube rubber, and iron bolt. The goggles used by spear fishermen were nearly all homemade. These consisted of small oblongs of glass set into hand-carved wooden frames and held in place by rubber bands. Usually, every fisherman made his own, cutting the frame to fit his own face; such goggles, according to most, provided a closer, more watertight fit than any commercial type known to them. A few spear fishermen also owned and used a flipper, only one having been worn at a time; and they were all of commercial manufacture.

Sometimes a spear fisherman went out alone, swimming all the way hour upon hour and trailing a float-attached line or a floating basket-shaped container for carrying his catch. At other times, fishermen went out in canoes and usually in pairs; then, while one of them dived for fish, his companion kept the canoe nearby and reloaded the speargun after each shot. Upon surfacing after each long dive—and some of them seemed to me to be dangerously protracted—while refilling his lungs, the fisherman would emit a curious kind of whistle, which served as a self-consciously proud symbol of this kind of expertise.

More often than not, the canoes of spear fishermen would congregate and move about in a solid fleet. In the beginning, this struck me as an uneconomic maneuver, i.e., fanning out might have provided each canoe with larger harvest. Indeed, when I questioned some fishermen on this point, they readily agreed; however, they added, it was more pleasurable to fish within talking distance of friends—which highlights the enjoyment most Te Pitians seemed to derive from fishing, a matter that will be returned to later on.

Fish spearing was occasionally engaged in at night with the help of a waterproof flashlight attached to the diver's head. On the average, nighttime spearing was more productive than in daylight; but some fishermen refrained from doing it because of its discomforts: the water itself was warm enough but the night air was considered too chilling. This fact, along with the danger from sharks, served to restrict nighttime spear diving beyond the outer reef to a handful of adventurous young men. The reason usually put forward for engaging in this arduous and hazardous activity was economic—"for every dive a large fish"—but it was also clear that the men who did so derived much pleasurable excitement from it and were in addition rewarded with special esteem from other fishermen.

When individuals teamed up in the canoe of one of them for angling or fish spearing, they usually shared the catch equally. When, however, an individual or a team used the canoe of someone in another household, it was customary to "give" (*hōro'a*; not *tārahu*, "pay interest/rent") some of the catch to the owner if the catch was not too small—"too small" having

usually meant an amount less than that required by the fisherman's household for that day's main meal. A fisherman using a borrowed speargun
would also tend to "give" a portion of his catch to the gun's owner, especially if it was a store-purchased gun, but this usually depended upon the
size of the catch. (For example, if only two or three small-to-medium-size
fish were caught, the owner would not usually expect or receive a share.)

Nets (*'upe'a*) were employed in fishing in several ways. Shallow scoop nets
were used mainly for catching bait fish and for collecting larger fish already
entrapped within a seine. Throw nets were used in the shallows for catching
small-fry both for bait and eating, but such nets were few in number and
infrequently (and, it appeared, not very expertly) put to use. Far more important was the use made of seine nets, both in terms of subsistence and
money income. During my visits, seining was practiced only in Fatata;
Ateans had owned a large seine net shortly before but had disposed of it for
lack of use.

All the seine nets operated in Fatata were of commercial manufacture.
They were purchased (usually in Pape'ete) in separate strips fifteen to
twenty spans long and then joined together into longer lengths to suit the
owners' needs—the latter classified by finger width. For example: an *'upe'a
ōeha* was of average (three spans) depth, large (i.e., three to four fingers)
mesh size, and thin (i.e., no. 6 to 9 size) cord; an *'upe'a oniti* was of average
depth, small mesh (one to two fingers), and no. 9 to 12 cord; an *'upe'a
(tautai) pāpa'i* was of average depth, small mesh, and no. 18 cord; and an
'upe'a 'ōrare was of small mesh, medium cord thickness, but four to five spans
deep. Various techniques of seine fishing were practiced, and each of these
called for a different type of net.

Pārava consisted of extending a net of *ōeha* type in a more or less straight
line across a lagoon channel by fastening the ends to reef coral. The net
tenders, usually only two men in a small canoe, then beat the water with
their paddles to drive fish into the net; or they simply waited nearby to collect the fish as the latter netted themselves.

Hapua was a larger-scale enterprise. It required at least two canoes and
three to four men. With it, a large *ōeha* net was arranged in a ⟨ shape by
fastening its lower border to coral outcrops on the lagoon bottom—a job requiring much underwater work and, hence, goggles. The placement of the
net varied with tidal direction, and, thus, with time of day—the fish having
been driven against the tide. After the net was secured, men in canoes or
swimming converged toward the trap formed in the center of the net, meanwhile beating their paddles or hands on the water. The swimmers then entered the trap, enmeshed the fish into one part of it, and tossed them into a
larger canoe standing nearby. (A variant of this technique consisted of clos-
ing the trap and then scooping up the entrapped fish.) The fish thus

caught were placed in a large floating basket-cage towed by the larger canoe. Typically, a drive of this kind lasted one or two hours, including net placement, and was repeated once or twice in different locations in the course of the expedition, much additional time having been used up in going from one location to another. Both *pārava* and *hapua* techniques were practiced daytime and nighttime, the former having been particularly effective at night.

When after "stronger" fish, e.g., during a run of bonito (*'auhopu*), a *tautai pāpa'i* net was used, i.e., one made of thicker cord. On some such occasions when there was no time for fastening the net uniformly to the lagoon floor, the ends had to be held by wing canoes; and larger numbers of canoes and men were engaged in corralling and catching the entrapped fish.

Some Atean fishermen also used to employ seines—usually the type called *'ōrare,* i.e., one, four to five spans deep—but were no longer doing so during my visits. The reasons given for discontinuance were various: paucity of fish, danger from high seas or sharks, and the familiar explain-all, "fedupness" (*fiu*).

Obviously, seine fishing required more equipment, more manpower and more organization than angling or spearing. A seine net was an expensive item, and the cost of maintaining it was high in terms of the owners' own time or of paying for its repair. In addition, to engage in *hapua* seining on a regular basis required at least one larger-than-average canoe and a dependable, experienced crew. During my 1955 visit to Fatata, there were seven large seine nets in more or less active use and a dozen others in various stages of decay. All of the former were individually owned (two of them by the same man), and all of them were used regularly to catch fish mainly for sale. Each of these latter was assisted by a fairly permanent crew of relatives or friends.

The economics of seine fishing differed according to the end-use of the catch. When two or more individuals from the same household seined together and the catch was sufficient only for home consumption, it was served up for all to eat. Also, if members of separate households teamed up to seine and managed to catch only enough fish to provide the respective households with a meal or two, it was not customary for the net's owner to receive a larger share. (It might have been right had he been treated so, I was told, but such a man would have experienced difficulty in finding regular helpers if he always insisted on a larger share.) The situation altered, however, when any of the catch was exchanged for money. In such instances, the net owner invariably received a larger share of the proceeds—the exact formula for sharing tended to vary somewhat according to the ages of members of the crew. This formula will be described in detail in a later section; put briefly, the owner of net and large canoe usually received one-half of the (net) cash proceeds, the other half having been divided equally among all the adult or near-adult members of the crew—near-adult meaning those youths past the stage of childhood dependency.

Mention was made above of the "cost" of maintaining a seine net. This did indeed constitute a large expense to the nets' owners in terms of their own time and, in some cases, of money spent. During my visits to Fatata, a few nylon nets were in use, and even these required a great deal of work in repairing the breaks made by coral and large fish. As for the local natural fiber nets, keeping them mended and dry was a never-ending chore. Some nets were kept in repair in the owner's own households, by themselves or other members, male or female. In other cases, owners employed neighbors to do the job, there having been several men who made of this a part-time specialty. (One of these, a man crippled with elephantiasis, was engaged in making whole seine nets; and while his neighbors praised his skill and occasionally bought strips of net from him as charitable gestures, they purchased most of their netting, at less expense, from stores.)

I made no systematic effort to record the varieties of fish caught by Te Pitians with their different techniques. Such a study would have been a major undertaking and would have required a zoological knowledge I did not possess, along with a degree of attention my objectives did not warrant. I did record that Te Pitians deliberately caught and ate almost any free-swimming fish exceeding 100 or so grams in weight, except for such oddities as the long pencil-thin 'a'avere (*Tylosorus stongylurus*) and for fish believed to have "poisonous" flesh, either seasonally or year round. Even the grotesque scorpion fish (*Synanceia verrucosa*; *nohu pu'a*) was eaten with appreciation after removal of its poisonous spine and sac. On the other hand, sharks were not eaten and were killed only because of their threat to life, nets, and other fish. And mammalian dolphins were left to frolic unharmed, with justifications ranging from sentiments of *aroha* (sympathy, fellow-feeling) to attributions of supernaturalism.

Moon phases, weather, and longer-range seasonal changes had strong effects on Te Pitians' times, locations, and techniques of fishing; and local weather, in relation to weather conditions simultaneously prevailing on nearby Tahiti, played a large role in Fatatans' fishing for money.

Bright moonlight was considered unfavorable for nighttime fishing in general and for spear-diving in particular. Household needs or market conditions led many individuals to angle or seine for fish even on full-moon nights, and not without some success, but diving at such times was said to be fruitless. In addition, most Te Pitian fishermen possessed many bits of knowledge or opinion about where to find what varieties of fish during successive phases of the lunar cycle, but this did not add up to any explicit, comprehensive calendrical guide for fishing such as the ancient Tahitians possessed (Oliver 1974, p. 303ff). Many Te Pitians were aware of the former existence of such guides; and one individual owned a copy of one of them in a volume from a Mission series.[7] However, no one attempted to obtain or follow such guides, saying—what was perhaps true—that they did not apply to conditions at Atea or Fatata. And no local fishermen troubled to systematize local knowledge into a guide for themselves or others.

Air temperature, degree of cloudiness, and force of wind exercised strong influence on Te Pitians' fishing activities. Chilly temperatures discouraged fishing of all kinds, especially diving (in which the wider difference between water and air temperatures was considered especially uncomfortable). High winds, in addition to affecting temperatures, also rendered most kinds of fishing, especially angling and seining, more difficult or even impossible. And cloudy skies tended to improve all fishing in nonturbulent waters—or so many fishermen said.

To the extent that the factors just mentioned were seasonal, so did seasons influence Te Pitians' fishing. Thus, July and August were considered by many to be "too cold" for much fishing, whereas the many calm and cloudy days occurring during the southern summer led some Te Pitians to describe this season as ideal. In addition, the more expert fishermen were aware of and guided by the seasonality of the schooling of certain fish.

Another cyclical factor that influenced fishing was the weekly round. Fridays and Saturdays nearly always saw people out spearing or angling for Sunday's big meal, while on Mondays little or no fishing was to be seen. Then, fishing for home consumption was usually renewed on Tuesdays; and if no leftovers remained, again on Wednesdays or Thursdays. This pattern obtained particularly in Atea; in Fatata, it was complicated and superseded for many fishermen by the proximity of the Pape'ete market, which provided a daily outlet for some fish and high peak demands on Fridays and Sundays. Also, Fatata's fishing for this market was influenced by weather conditions along Tahiti's western coast; when conditions there were very unfavorable for fishing, they were usually less so near Fatata, thereby reducing the market's usual supply and raising the price paid for Fatata's fish. (The converse, of course, also obtained.) Fatata's more commercially minded fishermen made it their business to be informed about Tahiti's condition, sometimes through the daily radio news but more typically through word of mouth, facilitated by the daily boat service to and from Pape'ete.

---

[7]Volume 5 of the *Ramepa Api* (New Light), published in 1904 by the Protestant Mission at Uturoa and under the editorship of G. Brunel. The fishermen's guide contained in this publication's list of "Nights of the Moon" closely resembles the one published in Teuira Henry's *Ancient Tahiti*.

Returning to the technology of fishing, much—and perhaps most—of the catch was cooked and eaten within hours of catching, but there were ways of preserving some of it for later eating or marketing. Some fish left over from one day's meal was simply recooked and eaten the following day. In the case of one very large fish I came to know all too well, it was recooked and eaten at for three days after catching before consignment to the household's dogs and cats. In a few other cases, the fishermen kept some of their extra fish in kerosene-powered refrigerators, either their own or those belonging to the local Chinese storekeeper. A third way was provided by the bamboo basket-cages already alluded to. These cages were practical only for fish not badly wounded, i.e., for those caught by netting. Judging by actual practice, fish kept alive in this manner remained fit for consumption for no longer than about three days after catching.[8] Finally, many fishermen made a practice of preserving fish in excess of their immediate household requirements, or ability to sell, by presenting it to other households. This transaction was invariably phrased as a "gift" (*hōro'a*), although some such donors revealed that they did so in expectation of eventual return. (One Pape'ete-wise sophisticate described it as being "like putting your fish in a savings bank"!)

There remain to be listed certain less "practical" beliefs and actions associated with Te Pitian fishing. First of all, before embarking on a fishing expedition involving the coordinated efforts of several individuals, it was the usual practice for one of them to utter a (Christian) prayer for their success and safety. (I failed to observe or inquire whether a prayer was also said after a successful catch.) Also, some fishermen told me that they, individually, uttered silent prayers even before going out alone, especially before engaging in nighttime, spear-gun fishing beyond the barrier reef. It was also the practice of some of the more devout seine-net owners to have a new net "blessed" by the pastor or deacon prior to its initial use.

After a good deal of probing, I elicited statements from some individuals to the effect that a fisherman would be unsuccessful if he went out soon after quarrelling with a close relative or if his wife were sexually unfaithful while he fished. However, I never heard of any specific fishing failure directly attributed to such causes and suspect that the elicited statements may have been speculative; and in any case, such beliefs, if in fact they were such, evidently were not very compelling.

To all this must be added the value attached to fishing as a diversion and a basis for prestige. I have already mentioned the evident pleasure many spear fishermen derived from their labors. Something of the same attitude

---

[8]Basis for this judgment was my observation that the owners usually tried to dispose of such fish within that time by eating, selling, or even giving it away.

was evident in other forms of fishing as well, especially when it involved numerous participants and fast movement, as in a bonito drive, or when it held out promise of large rewards, as during some seining operations. Even lone anglers fishing from the shore or going out in their canoes appeared to be enjoying themselves; this included males and females, old and young. Indeed, some individuals readily stated that to be their prime reason for fishing on some occasions.

The prestige attached to fishing was exemplified by the admiration many Te Pitians displayed towards the fisherman after a successful catch. This was especially true of the individual angler or spear fisherman; and the admiration was directed more towards size of individual fish than towards total quantity and weight of catch—another example of the "diseconomy" that prevailed in fishing, should the reader insist on defining "economizing" in the narrow sense. News of the landing of a very large fish was sure to become widespread—helped along, in some instances, by the fisherman taking his prize to the store to be weighed.

In contrast to this positive attitude towards fishing as a pleasurable pastime was the negative one voiced by other individuals, who disparaged it as "time-wasting play" except in the case of the few net-owners who earned regular and substantial incomes from it. But even in reference to the latter, some of the older and more affluent copra and vanilla producers compared fishing unfavorably with farming, calling it a source of "quick profits" (*moni'oi'oi*) in contrast to the slower but longer-range and allegedly more dependable rewards of cash-crop farming. It was of course recognized, and usually with sympathy, that some men, lacking land for cash cropping, must rely on fishing or other quick-profit sources of cash income, but something approaching contempt was occasionally expressed by the more solid farmers for men who neglected their coconut groves for fishing.

Differences between Atea and Fatata in terms of fishing had to do mainly with the far greater importance in the latter of fishing for an external market, but a few differences between the two commmunities obtained also in the domain of fishing for self-consumption and for local exchange.

Compared with Fatata, Atea was more consistently a sellers' market. I learned of no instance in Atea where a successful fisherman was unable to sell his surplus fish, if he wished to do so, but recorded several episodes in Fatata in which a fisherman was obliged, for lack of local buyers, to give or throw away fish. (This usually occurred when a catch was deemed too small to send to Pape'ete, or when Pape'ete prices were believed to be too low.) In Atea, when someone not going fishing wanted fish for the day's main meal, he nearly always put in his order in advance with someone known to be going fishing. This kind of procedure was also followed by some Fatatans, but most prospectivĕ buyers there did not have to rely on that kind of foresight.

Again, fish constituted a "gift" exchange between households more characteristically in Atea than it did in Fatata despite, or perhaps because of, its larger and more widely obtained supply in Fatata. Also, the better supplied Fatatans were less given than Ateans to comment about exceptional catches; there was nothing in Fatata comparable to the triumphant march of an Atean carrying an especially large fish along the village street. Nor was there anything in Atea even remotely similar to the kind of unspoken, but perceptible, social distinction that obtained in Fatata with respect to fishing and farming as differently focused styles of life.

Finally, it was my observation that despite Fatatans' greater preoccupation with fishing, females engaged in fishing more widely and more frequently in Atea than they did in Fatata as, it will be recalled, was also the case with subsistence gardening and, as will be shown, with vanilla production.

Pigs. Te Pitians raised scores of pigs. Of these, some were destined to be eaten in the owners' own households on special occasions and the others were intended for sale, locally or elsewhere. I was told repeatedly that pig-raising was a profitable enterprise because the animals "cost nothing" to raise, being fed on food leavings that would otherwise have been thrown away. I will question the accuracy of this proposition below, but it appeared to me at the time that Te Pitians did, in fact, view pig-raising mainly in those terms.

This view of theirs was sharpened by the conventional manner in which they obtained pigs for raising, again, "without cost." When someone (more often a young man) wished to embark on pig-raising, he usually obtained the loan of a sow from a kinsman or friend and fed the sow until she littered. (Only a sow not clearly pregnant would be lent out in this way.) Then, after the litter was judged old enough to survive without nursing, the borrower returned half of it and the sow to its owner.[9] Instances were also reported to me of individuals purchasing a young shoat in order to raise it, but the method just described, labelled *faʻaʻamu teʻāfa* (i.e., *feeding* [in return for] *half*) was far more common.

Pig-raising was an onerous undertaking and was regarded by most Te Pitians as such. The animals had to be fed daily, and with considerable amounts of food. Some of the food did, indeed, consist of a household's inevitable leftovers, but even one mature animal usually required a

---

[9]If the sow failed after a long time to reproduce, I was told that it was sold and the receipts split evenly between owner and borrower. However, I was unable to confirm this with respect to any specified case and suspect that in actual life the original owner would demand a larger share.

supplement of, say, *taruā* or breadfruit or manioc, which meant that an owner had to produce or acquire more food than usually appeared on his own table if he wished to feed any pigs.

Most pigs were kept within fenced areas outside the residential parts of the villages. Those few kept in the settlement itself were by law required to be corralled or tied up and hence had to be fed all the food they ate, whereas the ones kept outside the settlement were able to supplement their daily feed by foraging in what were larger enclosures or runs.

But keeping one's pigs outside the village settlement involved difficulties of other kinds. First, there was the daily chore of carrying heavy loads of food to them; in Atea, this meant for most people a long trip by canoe, in Fatata, a shorter, but nonetheless burdensome one, overland. Pigs kept outside the village were troublesome in still another way: if they were not fed with sufficient quantities and regularity, they could be counted on to escape their enclosures or leashes and either become feral, which represented a total loss, or break into someone's garden, which invariably led to troubles and fines.[10] Pigs kept in the village also occasionally moved about at will, either by breaking their leashes or through their owners' carelessness, and also became the source of troubles, but they at least did not escape into the wilds.

Burdensome and troublesome as they were, nearly every household owned at least one or two pigs, and some of these animals were evidently treated as pets. (A poignant sight, in Atea, occurred daily when an elderly man visited the pig he had had to sell to a neighbor because of a critical need for cash. Sometimes he actually wept when he patted and talked to his former pet, and the latter clearly recognized its old friend.) I recorded two instances, and heard of others, of owners exchanging one of their pigs for another to avoid killing and eating their own animal on an occasion that required festive food. Also, some pig owners out of sympathy for their pigs used cordage made out of hibiscus bark for leashing them, in place of the stronger but harder and more abrasive sennit.

On the other hand, Te Pitians displayed a large measure of callousness to pigs in general (other than a treasured pet) as exemplified by the way they transported them or left them immovably bound up for hours in the blazing sun awaiting transport.

The usual method of killing a pig was by piercing the throat with a sharp short knife, which seemed to be quickly effective and which tended to reduce external bleeding. The outer skin and bristles were then scraped away

---

[10]In Fatata, such fines were levied by a circuiting judge and (I was told by a Fatatan, but cannot otherwise confirm) amounted to 100–200 francs plus a prorated percentage of the judge's travel costs. Several such fines were levied in Fatata during my visits there, but no parallel cases occurred during my visits to Atea.

by means of knife and hot water; the head cut off and entrails removed; and the body washed, quartered, and cut into long strips, each one containing some of the animal's prized fat.

All of the killing and butchering of pigs that I witnessed was done by men, as was the cooking of pork destined for a feast. In fact, pigs were, in general, usually identified with men; women and children often shared in feeding them if the men were otherwise employed, but "pig work was man's work" (*te 'ohipa pua'a ta te 'ohipa tāne*), as Te Pitians liked to assert.

Cattle. Altogether, there were 108 head of cattle in Te Piti when I carried out a property census there in 1955. In neither place were the beasts milked or killed by their owners for their own household consumption. Only two or three Atean cattle owners sold any of their animals; the other cattle in this community were used to keep the vegetation cropped in their owners' coconut groves. In Fatata, on the other hand, cattle were regularly sold, almost all of them to buyers in Pape'ete. In both places those cattle dying of sickness or old age were either left where they fell to rot or, if near the lagoon, were dragged into it and allowed to float away. (In Fatata, the tides and currents conspired to deposit these carcasses immediately in front of my house; in Atea, they providentially drifted out to sea.)

Starting a herd of cattle was like starting pig-raising, i.e., a man borrowed a cow from a kinsman or friend, fed her until she had calved twice, then returned her and one of the calves to the original owner.

Keeping cattle required access to and usually ownership of enough land for grazing and enough cash for barbed wire to fence in that land. Several Te Pitians kept herds of two or three animals without having to spend much time in their feeding or care. But those keeping larger herds (which occurred only in Fatata) had to spend much time in moving them about from lot to lot to keep them well fed. Leaves from acacias were regarded as good cattle food, and careful owners spent much time in making this food available to their cattle (including cutting down branches and transporting them.)

Of the 108 cattle kept in the two communities during my 1954–55 visits, the thirty in Atea were distributed among ten of its forty-one households, and Fatata's seventy-eight among nine of its sixty-two households.

Other Domestic Animals. Many Te Pitians kept dogs, partly as pets and partly for rat catching. And although they did not deliberately raise them for eating, many often were all too pleased to eat dog flesh when an animal happened to die. The treatment of dogs varied from pampering with food and attention, to total neglect—or what might appear to a tender-hearted European to be callous cruelty. Generally speaking, Fatatans were more

"European" in their attitudes to dogs, but even in Fatata, the average canine was more skin and bones than flesh.

Cats were also to be found in both communities and were subjected to the same range of neglect. Most cat owners questioned said they kept them for rat catching; it did not appear that they were valued as pets, and, to the best of my knowledge, cats were never eaten.

In the case of both dogs and cats, when litters arrived they were usually all allowed to live until their lives would, in most cases, eventually be ended by starvation and neglect.

One Fatata household kept a herd of goats, the legacy of a European once resident there. I was told that occasionally one of these animals was killed and eaten and that the flesh was considered good; but during my visits the only thing these animals did was graze peacefully, and destructively, on the hill behind their owners' house.

Horses were also present in both Atea and Fatata, where they were used for transport and sport. In Fatata, especially, their owners used them for transport, mainly for carrying coconuts, copra, and breadfruit. In Atea, where road distances were shorter and distant gardens and groves more accessible by canoe, horses were left to graze out their lives unfettered or were occasionally raced by daredevil youths along the muddy shoreline.

As for differences between Atea and Fatata in this respect, a somewhat larger proportion of Fatata's households kept horses, but the average numbers per horse-owning household were about the same, i.e., 1.2 in Fatata and 1.1 in Atea.

Finally, a few words may be said about Te Piti's chickens, a very athletic breed. Although they seemed to spend most of their days chasing large insects or pecking over the ground, some of them were occasionally fed, most typically with grated coconut. Some Fatata owners went even further and kept a score or more each, feeding them carefully with table leavings and collecting their eggs for home consumption or local sale. In such cases, the chickens were also occasionally sold locally, thereby providing a small but useful income for their feeders, who were invariably female. For, as pigs were "the work of men," chickens were considered to be "the work of women."

Comparatively, about an equal proportion of each village's households "kept" chickens, i.e., about two-thirds of them. Otherwise the numbers of fowls per household were considerably larger in Fatata, having averaged about twenty per household to Atea's six.

Hunting. Wild pigs roamed over the mountainous terrain surrounding both Atea and Fatata, and Te Pitians evidently found high excitement and pleasure in hunting them. In fact, some males went pig hunting mainly for the sport, the flesh of the wild animals having been considered less succulent than domestic pork and hardly worth hunting just for food. In most cases, however, a hunt took place in order to kill some wild pig that had damaged the hunter's crops.

The conventional hunting weapon was a spear, although a few individuals hunted with guns. Dogs were nearly always taken along to hunt out the animals and help run them down.

It was generally asserted that the successful hunter was expected to give some of the flesh to the owner of the land on which the pig was killed, but it was also generally conceded that hunters avoided doing this except when the place of the kill was publicly known. In any case, the issue did not often arise, for during my entire visits to Te Piti only four wild pigs were actually killed.

The only difference I could discern between the two villages with respect to hunting wild pigs was that the "experts" in hunting were singled out more in Fatata than in Atea, quite possibly because it was regarded more as a sport in the former. Some Te Pitians spoke of having shot wild ducks in the past, but no one did so during my visits.

Summary of Differences

In these summaries, which will be added to each section or subsection of the descriptive chapters of this book, only those differences between Atea and Fatata will be recapitulated that appeared to be prominent and relate to the economic focus of the study.

1. While there were no discernible differences between Atea and Fatata in terms of stated food preferences, there were some major differences between them with respect to the kinds and sources of foods actually eaten. In general, Fatatans ate more store-bought foods than Ateans, e.g., rice, canned vegetables, and meats, and more self-caught fresh fish. In comparison, Ateans ate more starchy root vegetables (which they themselves grew) and more money-bought fish.

2. In line with those differences, Ateans devoted much more land and labor, including females' labor, to the growing of root crops, and much more interest in gardening expertise, as manifested in the annual vegetable-growing contest. Conversely, Fatatans devoted much more labor to fishing, and, although most of that was aimed at export money earning, it had the spillover effect of yielding more fish for domestic consumption.

3. Per capita consumption of fresh pork and beef (nearly all of it produced by the consumers' own households) was almost the same in both places, the difference between them having been that the Fatatans produced, in addition, more for sale. (Fatatans also produced and consumed more

eggs, but the economic significance of the differences, both in terms of consumption patterns and earned money incomes, was small.)

4. It could perhaps be asserted that dogs had more positive economic value in Atea (where they were more frequently eaten) than in Fatata (where they were more often kept as pets). Conversely, Fatatan horses might be said to have been more economically valuable than those of Atea, inasmuch as they were more often used for transport. However, neither of these differences merits any emphasis in comparison with the major ones listed in paragraphs one and two.

5. Although of minor economic significance in itself, the contrasting attitudes held by Ateans and Fatatans towards hunting may have derived in part from more economic bases. That is to say, the Ateans' more serious-minded, less recreational engagement in pig-hunting may have been related to their larger acreages of root crops against which unfettered pigs were a costly menace.

6. Finally, the Fatatans' somewhat larger consumption of alcoholic beverages, in general, and of money-bought ones, in particular, was undoubtedly of economic importance; but the extent of that importance will have to be measured, in a later chapter, in relation to money incomes.

Clothing and Body Care

Cleanliness. Most Te Pitians bathed all over at least once a day and sometimes as many as three or four times. They did not attempt to avoid activities that resulted in becoming dirty, but, as soon thereafter as possible, they bathed. Most adults appear to have considered it desirable after immersion in salt water, however dirt-free they were. In fact, cleanliness was regarded not only as requisite for physical comfort but as a mark of social worth as well; that is, while cleanliness itself in a person evoked no particular comment, individuals who were chronically dirty, mainly certain middle-aged and elderly males, were typically described as being "disgusting" (*faufau*).

Cleanliness itself was probably not the only satisfaction gained from bathing. For many Te Pitians, the daily bath appeared to provide the kind of pleasure that is derived from a ritual regularly expected and regularly performed. And in addition, watching some of them at their daily bath, soaping, rinsing, soaping, rinsing, etc., convinced me that they were experiencing a large measure of sensual enjoyment in this simple routine.

Soap was nearly always used when available (except perhaps to remove saltiness from an otherwise clean body) and thus was a regular item of purchase from the local stores. In both Atea and Fatata, some individuals used laundry soap for bathing, while others used more expensive toilet soap, the latter having been used more commonly in Fatata.

Readers familiar with eighteenth-century descriptions of Tahitians will be struck with the persistence of their descendants' concern for body cleanliness, as for example in the following excerpt:

> They are certainly as cleanly a people as any under the sun except in their lousyness, every one of them wash their whole bodies in the running water as soon as they rise in the morn, at noon, and before they sleep at night; and if they have not such water near their houses as often happens, they will go a good way to it; as for their lice had they the means only they would certainly be as free from them as any inhabitants of so warm a climate could be. Those to whom combs were given proved this, for those who I was best acquainted with kept themselves very clear while we staid by the use of them; as for their eating lice it is a custom which none but children and those of the inferior people can be charged with. Their cloths also as well as their persons are kept almost without spot or stain; the superior people spend much of their time in repairing, dying, & the cloth, which seems to be a genteel amusement of the ladies here as it is in Europe. (*The Endeavour Journal of Joseph Banks*: 1768–1771. Edited by J. Beaglehole. Vol. I, p. 337.)

I discovered no differences between Atea and Fatata in people's bodily cleanliness, but the former had to expend more energy than the latter to keep themselves clean.

In 1954–55, nearly every Fatatan residence had its own water tap with a seemingly endless supply of clean, fresh water from the local reservoir. In fact, some taps ran continually, either from faulty plumbing, oversight, or deliberate intent. Some enterprising householders even went so far as to rig up showers from their taps. In sharp contrast, in 1954–55 Ateans had no supply of running water. A reservoir had been partly completed and pipes awaiting installation were piled up in the central plaza, a favorite place for sitting and dozing; but the Ateans were waiting for the Administration to complete the reservoir and lay the pipes or pay them to do so, complaining that they should not have to work "for the government" without wages.[11] Two Atea residences maintained small but fairly continuous supplies of rain water by runoff from their tin roofs, but all the others had to obtain fresh water from the village's only rain catchment tank at the schoolhouse, a chore usually left to children, or from Atea's few small springs and streams.

---

[11]In a sense, they were, of course, justified in this view since the government had paid elsewhere for such work.

Some of the latter, thereby, served as centers of social congregation where women went regularly to do their households' laundry, and where many males and a few females bathed.[12]

The Te Pitians' preoccupation with body cleanliness extended to their hair and clothes. Most males kept their hair washed, fairly short, and well trimmed. Several made a practice of barbering their kinsmen and friends, and without pay except for the social esteem they received in the form of comments about their "true Tahitian-ness." Young unmarried men would, on occasion, oil their locks, either with store-bought preparations or with homemade flower-scented coconut oil (*mono'i*).

For most of Te Piti's females, hair grooming was a daily concern, and for young women a major preoccupation. Some of them spent an hour or two every day several days a week engaged in combing, brushing, and oiling their own tresses or those of a relative or friend. Something approaching dismay was expressed by some of them towards the few females who chose to keep their hair cut short; who, by the way, were to be found in Fatata but not, during my visit, in Atea.

Proper grooming also included manual de-lousing. Presumably most Te Pitians had this service performed for them by family members or friends at some time or other, but the only times I saw it performed in public were by mothers for their young children, or by older siblings for younger ones.

Grooming standards did not require men to be clean shaven at all times. In fact, a once-a-fortnight scrape (usually with a very dull razor) was sufficient to keep these mostly thin-bearded Polynesians fairly clean shaven. Those possessing higher proportions of European genes grew thick stubble in a day or two, but local conventions did not require them to shave more than once a week or fortnight, even for church.

Teeth presented a much larger cosmetic problem, at least to the young females. I have already indicated how susceptible many Te Pitians were to dental decay. Such decay had one of two outcomes: it either progressed to the point of a mouthful of ruined, unsightly stubs, or, if accompanied by pain, by the removal of the offending tooth. There were no dentists readily available for tooth repair;[13] tooth-pulling, on the other hand, was performed

---

[12]An ethnographer focusing on "social integration" could appropriately characterize these water places as having had a positive influence in Atean society, and one that had no exact counterpart in Fatata. But, in this sense, their influence was occasionally the reverse when, for example, heated words passed between women who were trying to wash clothes and males who were bathing and splashing or muddying the water. In fact, I witnessed several such episodes, including some that resulted in lengthy interhousehold feuds.

[13]Ateans could have gone to Ra'iatea for dental repair work, and Fatatans to Pape'ete, but the costs of these errands were considered too great a price to pay simply for repairing or saving a tooth.

not only by nearby government medical orderlies but by several wholly untrained Te Pitians as well. For most males and for older women, the crucial disadvantage of tooth damage or loss had to do with eating (see above pp. 56–57), but for most young women it meant impairment of beauty. I know of no instance wherein a young woman with toothache suffered it to continue in order to save a tooth, but for most of those missing several teeth, a new set of artificial ones was one of the most longed-for objects in life.[14]

I did not count instances of tooth loss in either village but retain the impression that they were not noticeably different in this regard.

Te Pitians' reactions to corpulence would be somewhat surprising to any observer familiar with accounts of ancient Tahiti, where obesity was considered a mark of beauty and privilege. The Te Pitians I knew deplored skinniness in individuals of all ages, having considered it evidence of sickness or gross undernourishment or terminal senility, but full rotundity was felt to be appropriate only in infants and in those well past youth.

There were some fat infants but no fat children in Te Piti during my visits; the dimpled flesh so admired by some in infants simply did not survive the regimen of childhood. Later on, during the period of youth, a few young women had reached stages of obesity that even their contemporaries considered to be unsightly and a subject of some derision. Several men, young and old, confided that they enjoyed having sexual relations with fat women, but most young men I queried displayed distaste at the thought of having a very fat woman for a wife. Of course, the level at which a Te Pitian woman's amplitude reached the point of being "too fat" was considerably higher than the European fashions decree, but a level was nevertheless recognized. When I told them about the ancient custom of *ha'apori* (to make fat), a custom no informant had previously heard of, the universal reaction was one of amused incredulity (Oliver 1975, p. 434ff).

Obesity in a young man simply did not occur. As described earlier, several older men in Te Piti might have been called obese by European standards, but two or three of these were considered to be too fat by local criteria as well.

One might suppose that Fatatans, who in general engaged in less physical exertion than Ateans and who probably ate just as much, would on the average weigh more than the latter; but while I did not actually weigh individuals in either place, my visual impression is that the two populations did not differ in this regard.

---

[14]And also one of the most costly. According to Fatatans, a private Pape'ete dentist's charge for installing an ordinary white tooth was about 1,500 francs, a gold one twice as much. One informant who made enquiries in Pape'ete, reported that the cost of supplying his toothless wife with upper and lower plates would have been 15,000 francs—"just to improve her looks!"

Clothing. Turning now to clothing, Te Pitian conventions were closely geared to the wearer's age. First, with regard to infants, except when on exhibit (e.g., at Sunday church services, when they were clothed in elaborate European-inspired baby finery) they were generally unclothed. When somewhat older, some female children were kept in minute pants or skirts as soon as they began to toddle, while others remained unclothed until about four, when the taunts of their playmates, rather than the concern of their parents, finally drove them to cover their genitals. Upon boys, these pressures were exerted a year or two later and were considerably weaker. In fact, males of all ages could undress to change or bathe in full public view, only perfunctorily covering their genitals while doing so, without causing comment.

Female modesty standards were more complicated. As just noted, it was generally considered desirable that girls begin to cover their genitals earlier than boys, and, thereafter, that this part of their anatomy never be exposed in public. Breast modesty, on the other hand, was much less strict. As far as I could tell, it was the girl herself, rather than her elders, who insisted that she cease exposing her breasts when they began to fill out, influenced, evidently, by the teasing of other girls and boys. For the next ten or so years of her life, a female's "shame" (*ha'amā*), it was said, moved her to keep her breasts more or less covered from public view, rather than any publicly voiced precept. This period of modesty began to end when babies arrived and had to be nursed, often in public; after that, breast-modesty "shame" apparently diminished with age, so that many women past forty or so worked in and around their houses, in full view of neighbors, with their breasts fully exposed.

I obtained the impression that Atean women were more casual about breast-baring than those of Fatata—*vis-à-vis* Europeans and strangers, that is; I had no way of knowing how far the latter exposed their breasts among fellow householders and neighbors.

Dress style, as distinct from considerations of modesty, involved some highly patterned popular conventions in terms of sex and age. First of all, there was a general precept that all garments worn in church ought to be spotlessly clean; this applied to both sexes and all ages. The nearly universal attitude was that elegance and unshabbiness are fine for those who can so afford, which is not everyone, but that cleanliness in clothing is within everyone's reach.

Alongside this "utopian" precept, there were, however, some differences in expectation based on sex and age. In general, females were expected to be more scrupulous in clothing than males, and the clothes of older people, especially males, were not expected to be as unsoiled as those of youth and early middle age.

With regard to style, the period of "youth" (*taure'are'a*) was recognized as being the time of life when both males and females quite naturally liked to adorn themselves in new and fashionable garments, although no older person acknowledged this to be the "right" thing to do. Like many other habits of youth, lavish grooming was in the opinion of many older persons one of the immutable facts of life, neither desirable nor wholly undesirable, but just another bit of evidence to confirm the opinion that young people are by nature rather ignorant and silly.

For people between "youth" and old age, public opinion was not very specific about what *should not* be worn. Men exposed themselves to some friendly joshing if they continued to dress in the flashy style of youth, but some women continued to wear the gay figured-print frocks of youth without meeting any disapproval, provided they left off such accessories as bright lipstick. There came, however, a time in the middle period of life when dress style began to take on a more positive significance.

Judging from pictures and other evidence, the standard "dress" uniform of most adults in rural Tahiti until the 1920s was mainly black; for women, a long, loose, black Mother Hubbard gown and a black, homeplaited broad-brimmed hat; for men nondescript trousers but a high-collared tight-buttoned black jacket. It may well be that this costume was once a badge also of church going piety, but in the 1950s it was simply "old fashioned" and, derivatively, a mark of respectable old age, being the invariable Sunday dress of many of the Te Piti's most pious old people. Several younger men also occasionally affected this costume (or at least the jacket), as did a few young women; but there was a difference to be observed in such cases. When a man of thirty or thirty-five dressed in this manner it occasioned little or no discernible public reaction; it was as merely another sign, not, however a necessary one, that so-and-so was well past youth and admirably preoccupied with the serious concerns of life. In contrast, the few younger women who affected this old-fashioned dress were criticized by some of their contemporaries for being or trying to appear *too* solemn and pious.

Finally, in this listing of age-graded clothing, there is the important matter of shoes. Mothers took delight in covering their infants and toddlers in finery for all public occasions, including knit booties or new sandals, but thereafter footwear did not become a social issue until boys and girls began the transitions to "youth," wherein proper dress for public occasions called for pretty sandals or high heels for young women and heavy-soled leather shoes for young men, an obviously painful sacrifice on the altar of Pape'ete fashion. After this period of immolation, to wear or not to wear became again a matter of individual taste and need.

In matters of clothes style, the younger women of Fatata were more up-to-date with Pape'ete fashions than those of Atea. My inexpert judgment on this point was confirmed by the young household helper brought along by my wife from Atea. While she criticized her Fatatan peers for their pre-occupation with clothes, she was sensitive enough to the difference to express "shame" in having to appear in their company with her more rustic Atean Sunday best. Fatata's modernity in this regard, which was paralleled in the clothing of a few young men, was clearly due to the fact that its residents, as a whole, spent more money on their clothing than those of Atea, and to the circumstances that the former visited Pape'ete more often.

In connection with this difference in fashionableness, Fatata's women tended to buy more clothes ready-made than those of Atea, but even in Fatata, women tended to make most of their dresses themselves. The local stores in both places stocked dressmaking materials and patterns, rather than ready-made dresses, and nearly every female from childhood to senility engaged in some sewing. A few of the more expert helped others less experienced or made whole garments for relatives or friends, but, I was assured, not for pay.

Nearly one in every four households in both villages contained a hand- or treadle-operated sewing machine, usually of ancient vintage, which had been passed on down the generations.[15] Only one new machine was purchased in each village during my 1954–55 visits; in both cases, they were bought by female owners out of their own earnings.

Women customarily made most of the garments for their own younger children, but when past childhood, most girls made their own. Most of the garments of males past childhood were bought ready-made.

Such figures that I was able to collect concerning expenditures for clothing cannot be regarded as altogether representative or reliable. Some households kept records of purchases of ready-made garments and large amounts of cloth, but the common practice of buying one needle at a time, or one spool of thread, etc., was seldom recorded. Moreover, records of purchases for the previous year were, in most cases, unrepresentative inasmuch as several years might elapse between purchases of some size. I can, however, reiterate the impression already repeated that Fatata's women spent more on clothes than those of Atea. As for males, I have the impression that the youths of Fatata did the same, but that the older men of both places simply "had" their clothes and were moved to buy new ones only when the old ones became unmanageably threadbare.

Health. In addition to their common norms and practices regarding cleanliness, the Te Pitians shared certain ideas and habits regarding other

---

[15]Fatata contained one antique machine that served as the gravestone of its owner. The story was that her children and other relatives treated her so shabbily during her old age that she had directed that this, her most precious possession, be placed on her own grave.

aspects of their bodies. Mention has been made of their views, etc., on body weight and teeth; some observations can also be reported on their attitudes, etc., regarding body deformations, bodily malfunctions, and pain.

Except for baldness, which was an object for ribaldry, and except for extremes of obesity and skinniness, as locally defined, Te Pitians seemed rather indifferent about their own and others' acquired blemishes, such as scars, missing joints, and fracture-twisted limbs, but reacted with what appeared to my Western tender-mindedness to be heartless levity to other persons' infirmities, such as crabfoot, elephantiasis, and humpback. On the other hand, even this ridicule did not succeed in moving the victims of such infirmities to seek to correct them.

A similar degree of fatalism seems to have been prevalent in both Atea and Fatata regarding bodily malfunctions, recognized as such; I refer here, for example, to feebleness induced by illness, to subnormal hearing and vision, to morbid symptoms like nausea and chill, and to premature impotence, whatever its cause. (The feebleness, etc., accompanying advanced age were regarded as normal and irreversible, and hence wholly unremediable.[16]) When any of these conditions was accompanied by persistent pain,[17] measures were sometimes taken to alleviate the pain and to cure the cause of it by use of herbal remedies, by consulting native therapists (*tahu'a*), or, as a last resort, visiting an Administration medical specialist. All of these measures cost some time and effort, but little or no money or other goods except for the expenses incurred by the relatives of hospitalized patients who accompanied the latter to Uturoa or Pape'ete.

In both Atea and Fatata, there were individuals reported to be expert in diagnosing or curing, or both, one or another type of physical or psychic disorder.[18] And for disorders not serviceable locally, there were experts in nearby villages whose services were known about by Te Pitians and occasionally used. The noteworthy thing about most of the above services was that they were rendered freely in the spirit of "the Tahitian way." Grateful patients sometimes repaid such specialists with small presents of food or tobacco, i.e., consumable things, but payment in the form of money was

---

[16]Similarly, I found no evidence of Te Pitians taking active measures to minimize or delay senile enfeeblement, e.g., no diet to reduce what Westerners would call overweight, no exercising for the sake of health, etc. As noted earlier, some individuals repeated Western-learned cliches about the unhealthfulness, e.g., of alcohol, of coffee, or of "too much canned food," etc., but no elderly Te Pitians that I knew of acted on such advice.

[17]The reader is referred to Levy (1973) for a detailed and profound discussion of Tahitians' perception of and reaction to pain, a subject that has a fundamental bearing on what Levy calls the "private" world of Tahitians but one having only marginal relevance to the "public" and mainly economic aspects of Tahitian behavior that are my concern.

[18]For a full account of rural Tahitian folk medicine, see Hooper 1978.

usually neither demanded nor proffered. In fact, several informants made this point by telling how one elderly midwife had indignantly refused to accept a Christmas gift of cloth from a man whose wife she had tended through a long and difficult confinement, saying: "That's not a matter for pay (*tārahu*); I'm not Chinese." The exceptional practitioners (all, of course, resident in other villages!) who did charge fees or accept them, were criticized for their "Chinese-like" attitudes.

In connection with the above, I found Te Pitians' reactions to what I would regard as physical discomfort to be extraordinarily indifferent: either their "discomfort thresholds" were very high or their measure of stoicism heroic. Whatever the explanation, I never ceased to wonder at their ability to sit and lie, even sleep, for hours on surfaces and in positions that by most Western standards of comfort would be adjudged unbearable for people of comparable age.

Finally, acknowledgment should be made of the fact that Te Pitians experienced and defined (or vice versa!) certain conditions that might be called "psychic disorders," and that they spent some of their resources, energy, and money, but more of the former than of the latter, in efforts to cure them. (For a professionally qualified discussion of this subject the reader is again referred to Levy 1973.) Looked at from the public and economic viewpoint, it is enough to record that these disorders served to disable some of them for some of the time, and one or two of them for most of the time, from performing economically useful actions. Also, it should be noted that some goods were expended (somewhat more in Fatata than in Atea) to alleviate disorders, although, compared with the money, etc., expended in Western societies to alleviate comparable disorders, the Te Pitian figures were infinitesimal.

Summary of Differences

Some Fatatans, mainly women and to a lesser extent young males, devoted more time and money to clothing than their Atean counterparts. This was also the case with expenditures on health, but with respect to all other aspects of body care, e.g., cleanliness and hair grooming, the residents of the two villages behaved about the same.

Houses and Furnishings

Te Piti's dwellings comprised a bewildering assortment of styles, sizes, and materials; and they ranged in quality from shoddy to substantial, from dilapidated to shipshape. They all, however, consisted of at least three functional divisions: a room or set of rooms mainly for sleeping, another one for eating, and a third for cooking. In addition, some dwellings had a place set aside for bathing and a latrine, usually outside, and many of them had a verandah, which typically faced the street. As for house yards, some (mainly in Atea) were virtually nonexistent. The accompanying photos provide a better impression of dwelling-house differences than any words can do, but it will be useful to point out certain of their features that appear to have some significance, historical, social, or economic.

First of all, it was possible to distinguish several architectural styles. At one extreme were the "vanilla houses," so named because of their having been built in an era, mostly in the 1910–20s, when their owners were receiving sizeable incomes from their cash crops, especially vanilla. Vanilla houses were entirely of European colonial inspiration; they were built on posts, some of them very high, with plank floors and metal roofs. The walls of some of the older ones were of coral-limestone plaster, the others were of wooden planks. Their boxlike rooms had proper windows and doors, and most of them had verandahs in front, in front and back, or all around. By 1954, some of Te Piti's "vanilla houses" were still in fair shape, but most of them had reached stages of partial or total disrepair, giving to them a melancholy appearance of economic and social decline, however affluent their current residents happened to be.

The mid-fifties economic equivalent of the "vanilla house" was what might be termed "Pape'ete suburban," because of its popularity in that part of Tahiti Island. It was built on a solid concrete slab and was much less European in style. The more substantial but less "Polynesian" ones had thick cement walls and metal roofs; others, more deliberately and picturesquely "Polynesian," had thatch roofs and walls of tastefully plaited bamboo.

At the other extreme, in terms of building costs and durability, were those houses made almost entirely of local materials and in indigenous shapes. Whereas ownership of a "Pape'ete suburban" house betokened current affluence and residence in a "vanilla house" recalled an affluent past, the type of "grass-shack" dwelling, as I shall label it, served as a mark of its owner's poverty and, if he appeared content to live there indefinitely, his lack of social ambition.

Between these extremes were structures exemplifying numerous permutations of different shapes, sizes, and materials, e.g., of metal roofs with bamboo walls, of thatch roofs with plywood walls, etc. Despite their numerous differences all these composite dwellings had one important feature in common: they appear to have been designed more in keeping with the owner's spatial needs and current resources than in conformance with any conventional architectural style. That is, while the principal nuclear part of these houses was of the usual rectangular shape, the partitioning, if any,

Atea: "Grass-shack" houses in foreground

Atea: Family seated outside "grass-shack" houses

Fatata: Large "Vanilla" house

Atea: Small "Vanilla" house

Atea: "Composite" house

Atea: "Composite" house

Atea: Modern cement house

Fatata: "Tahiti Suburban" house

varied from house to house as did the number, size, and arrangement of attached units, dining room, kitchen, additional bedrooms, etc.

Even more varied were the nature and combinations of the materials used in these composite houses. One house, for example, would have bamboo walls, masonite partitions, and a metal roof; another, masonite walls and partitions and a thatch roof, etc. In this connection, I believe it is safe to say that most of Te Piti's adults preferred metal, plywood, etc., to their native building materials.

Except for the few aesthetically-minded ones who deliberately chose to live in a more Polynesian house, most house owners, actual or incipient, sought to replace native materials with manufactured imports, metal roofing, plywood, etc. A metal roof was undoubtedly hotter to live under, but it lasted much longer and did not harbor as many insects. A wall of planks or plywood may have restricted ventilation somewhat, but it was easier to put up and take down.

In connection with the last point, it was not unusual for whole houses to be taken apart and reconstructed elsewhere, or for their various components, plate of thatch, metal sheets, floor boards, etc., to be divided among the co-owners and used by them in building separate houses.

I wrote above of the lack of "social ambition" popularly attributed to those who seemed content to live indefinitely in "grass-shack" dwellings. This criticism did not extend to individuals obviously unable to improve their housing, e.g., to those with incapacitating infirmities, or to the aged waiting out their end, but it served to point up the fact that many, perhaps most, Te Pitians considered a good house to be one of life's most desirable goals. What was considered "good" in housing varied considerably with individuals, but it always included some elements of European inspiration or manufacture, e.g., metal roofing, cement foundation, or plank flooring.

The descriptions of house types just given apply to both Atea and Fatata, but there were some noteworthy differences between the two villages with respect to the percentage of types found in them. These differences are recorded below in Table 2A. The categorization given is mainly, but not entirely, my own. Te Pitians also distinguished the type that I (and they) labelled "vanilla houses," but they would not, perhaps, have distinguished as sharply as I have done between large and small vanilla houses. Te Pitians also distinguished the type I label "grassshack" with the label *fare ni'au* (house [of] palm leaf); but for all other houses, they used labels like *fare tima* (house cement) and *fare punu* (house metal) for whole houses even though the adjective may have referred only to walls and roofs. It could be argued that their taxonomy, such as it was, is more relevant to ethnography than the one I have devised. On the other hand, for purposes of comparison, it is not as exhaustive as the one I use; nor does it give enough weight to what I believe to be an important economic factor, namely, the degree of recent or current affluence represented by possession of a "Pape'ete suburban" type house or of a "composite" house, consisting largely of imported materials. Also, my distinction between large and small "Pape'ete suburban" houses represents a fairly significant one in terms of degrees of recent affluence, as does the similar distinction applied to "vanilla houses" about affluence a generation or more in the past.

Table 2A. House Types*

	ATEA		FATATA	
	number	percentage	number	percentage
"Vanilla":				
small	8	20	12	19
large	0	0	15	24
"Pape'ete suburban"				
small	0	0	5	8
large	2	5	7	11
"Grass shack"	7	17	5	8
Composite				
A—more native materials	11	27	8	13
B—more imported materials	13	32	11	17

*Note: Only those houses inhabited during 1954–55 are listed.

Several noteworthy differences between Atea and Fatata are revealed in this comparison:

(1) With regard to "vanilla houses," while Atea and Fatata contained nearly identical percentages of small ones, a fourth of all inhabited Fatata houses can be classified as "large vanilla," thereby attesting a quite prosperous past, as compared with no such houses in Atea.

(2) With regard to "Pape'ete suburban," Fatata is revealed as having had four times as many (relative to total number of houses) as Atea. This may be viewed as a measure of Fatata's greater affluence in the current or recent past, although the difference between the two places is seen to be smaller when the comparison is made in terms of large Pape'ete suburban houses alone.

(3) The relatively larger number of "grass shack" houses in Atea can, I believe, be traced almost wholly and directly to that community's relatively smaller supply of money, currently and in the recent past.

(4) The percentages for "composite" houses are more equivocal. While such houses are twice as prevalent in Atea as in Fatata (59 percent versus 30 percent), the proportion of A and B subtypes are quite similar in both villages. The large differences may perhaps be accounted for by the availability in Fatata of so many more older but still usable "vanilla" houses, but reasons for the similarity just noted are more obscure.

Utilities. The widespread desire for houses constructed of European materials did not extend so effectively to modern European patterns of cooking, illumination, and plumbing. In almost every household, even of the more spacious "vanilla houses," most cooking was done in a separate building. Also, even some of the most affluent persons were content with ordinary nonpressure lamps, and with only one or two of these. And with regard to plumbing, inside toilets and inside bathing facilities were to be found in only a few houses, and those of the "Pape'ete suburban" type. In fact, of those houses individually supplied with piped water (and in 1954–55 this included only those in Fatata, and not all of these), one, usually outside, water tap served all the household's needs.

The Te Pitians' view regarding their water supply was part of an attitude towards savings in general, at least with respect to labor-saving devices. In 1959–60, both villages were served by water piped in from government-constructed reservoirs. Prior to that, Atea was dependent upon rainwater for drinking and cooking, and streams or springs for all other purposes, its rainwater having been stored in cisterns containing the runoff from metal roofs. Even after installation of piped-in water, Atea's supply remained somewhat limited, so that a rule of one tap per household was imposed. In Fatata, there was no such shortage or rule; nevertheless, no one troubled to increase his household's water outlets by extending the pipes to additional taps, although many households possessed the economic capacity to do so. I used to view with wonder (from my American viewpoint!) the sight of my neighbors moving back and forth between their single taps and the distant places where the water was actually required. In fact, there were several tapless households whose members made dozens of trips each day to their neighbors' taps, one almost fifty meters away, evidently without having felt any need to acquire taps of their own which, in most cases in question, would have been well within their resources to do.

Furniture. A notable feature of Te Piti's dwellings was the nature and arrangement of their furnishings. In a word, the principal rooms in most dwellings were filled, literally, with beds, or alternatively, with beds and large wooden wardrobes. Even those rooms used occasionally for social entertaining, where one might find a few chairs and a table, were typically dominated by a large bed or two. The beds in question, mostly double-sized, were provided with homemade kapok-filled mattresses and fat rock-hard kapok pillows. Over most beds were coverings bearing characteristic flowerlike designs (*tīfaifai*); these bedspreads were among a household's most prized possessions, and women skilled in their sewing were widely praised.

I did not discover how regularly the Te Pitians actually slept in their large double beds. I know that many men and boys preferred to sleep on simple cots, or on mats on the floor, which were said to be cooler. Some females undoubtedly slept on the beds in question, mainly with a smaller child or two, but others preferred, like men, to sleep on a simple cot or mat.

Another characteristic feature of many of Te Piti's bed-sitting rooms was its collection of photographs, mostly of relatives, along with colorful pictures cut out of magazines. Some dwellings contained a few decorative sea shells and a vase or two of flowers, artificial blossoms having been especially favored. A few houses also contained a hand-cranked phonograph: two in Atea and eight in Fatata. About the only book present in Te Piti's houses was a Tahitian Bible, and several houses did not contain even that. In 1955, only one Atean house contained a radio, as compared with the three Tahitian-owned ones in Fatata.

The dining division of a house usually contained one long table, with benches, and a wire-screened cabinet for perishable foods. A few houses also possessed kerosene-fueled refrigerators, which served mainly for storing fish; there was one of these in Atea, as against five in Fatata. In several dwellings, the dining room also contained a sleeping cot or two.

Nearly every household did most of its cooking in a separate little house, which was usually built directly on the ground and usually of native materials. The principal feature of the cook-house was its earth oven, a hole dug in the middle of the earth floor and supplied with a number of stream-rolled stones and large round cover mats made of leaves.

As just noted, Fatata's Tahitian dwellings contained relatively more phonographs, radios, and refrigerators than Atea's; on the other hand, I recorded the impression (I did not systematically count) that the residences of the two villages were much alike with regard to other household furnishings: beds, tables, chairs, lamps, kerosene-fueled stoves, cooking utensils, etc.

The income and expenditure survey previously mentioned included a question on amounts spent by the households on house furnishings during 1954. For Atea the extrapolated total was 75,300 francs, for Fatata 130,500, which works out, respectively, to 339 and 385 francs per capita.

House yards. Atea's narrow and densely-built residential area did not permit much in the way of house yards. In contrast, many of the houses in Fatata were built in the middle of spacious house lots, most of which were grassed over and surrounded with coconut palms, breadfruit trees and decorative shrubs and flowers. Characteristically, in most of the houses with spacious yards the residents kept the yards tidier than the inside of their houses, although I did not once hear anyone comment on the appearance of a yard, save for a few cases where the sordidness and disarray were impossible to ignore and were generally described as "disgusting." In this connection, several of the ancient "vanilla houses" of Fatata were in such states of decay that the government had ordered them to be either repaired or torn down, a ruling with which, needless to say, few Fatatans agreed.

House building and repair. During the periods of my visits, the building and repair of Te Piti's houses was accomplished in three different ways. In some cases, an individual built or repaired his own house largely by himself with only occasional assistance from relatives or friends. In other instances, he employed some specialist to manage all or part of the job. And in still others, he utilized the services of a local house-building (or house-thatching) work group.

Building one's house oneself tended to be a very long, drawn-out job. Usually the man in question sandwiched it in with farming and fishing and spent only an hour or so a day at it two or three days a week. (One such project I followed had been begun a year before my arrival and was still incomplete when I left.) The advantage of this method of house building was, I was told, that it "cost nothing" (except, of course, for the materials used). In this connection, most men were handy with simple carpentry tools and some were quite expert, a skill learned through imitation, or informal instruction, or apprenticeship elsewhere.

When the build-his-own man called upon friends or relatives to assist him, he usually remunerated them with a meal or a few drinks of wine, or both.

Few Te Pitians were affluent enough, or willing, to build their houses from the ground up. It occurred only once during all of my visits; and, according to my enquiries, of the dozen or so houses that had been constructed during the decade of the 1950s, only three had been built in this way. The one such incident that I witnessed involved the construction of a large, cement-floored and cement-walled house with a metal roof. It was located in Atea, where no one, at the time, possessed the requisite architectural or constructional skills. For this reason, along with the owner's desire to have "only the best," a highly-priced builder was brought in from Ra'iatea to plan and supervise the whole job, using local labor.

Most houses built with the help of paid construction labor also involved the use of the owners' labor and of one or more of their kinsmen or friends, who were usually compensated with food and/or wine and, tacitly, with the expectation of reciprocal assistance at some future time.

The third arrangement used in house building (or major repair) operated only in Atea; it involved the services of an organized house-thatching group (*pupu fare ni'au*). During my visits, such groups engaged only in rethatching projects, but they were qualified, conventionally, to build whole houses or to carry out other projects of major repair.

The nucleus of each Atean house-thatching group consisted of a number of houseowners who joined together on occasion to help each other rebuild or repair each other's house. Several members of each of these groups were interrelated through ties of kinship, but only incidentally so. The immediate rewards for one's service were the meals provided on the day of the work, usually including some food delicacies, but the long-range return was, of course, the right to have the services eventually reciprocated. In addition, when the job involved rethatching, each member was called upon to supply an equal number of thatch-plates.

Some Ateans asserted that "bookkeeping" was not practiced in connection with the activities of house-thatching groups, that it was all a matter of friendly fellow-feeling and assistance. Friendly it may have been (the rethatchings I witnessed were indeed jolly, festive affairs), but bookkeeping was most definitely practiced. Every nuclear member of such a group could verbally specify his credits and debits in terms of labor, and some of them kept written accounts of everyone's thatchplate contributions going back for years. Also, during the times of my visits, some group members were publicly vocal about the inequities they were experiencing from the arrangement.

In addition to the nuclear members taking part in a house-thatching project, it was usual for a number of other youths and men to participate, explicitly in return for the food and drink provided, but implicitly also for the pleasure derived from this festive activity.

As a variant on their regular reciprocal arrangements, rethatching groups were occasionally employed by nonmembers and were repaid with a meal and a lump sum of money, which was sometimes distributed and sometimes kept in the group's "treasury" to be used to buy wine for future feasts. The money paid for such work invariably amounted to less than the sum the house owner would have had to pay for labor hired on an individual basis. However, the thatching group members evidently looked upon the arrangement as equitable, if the food, and especially the wine, was ample. Also, the camaraderie typical of all such occasions probably added an incentive (which motive, however, Ateans did not explicitly articulate).

Still another variant of Atea's house-thatching arrangements were the general work groups, i.e., associations of males who pooled their labor not only for thatching houses but for other activities as well: ground-clearing, firewood cutting, copra making, etc. Some of these groups were entirely "secular" in composition; others were composed of the male members of each of the church parish's sodalities. As was the case with the house-thatching groups just mentioned, kinship ties among such groups' members were only incidental. When the secular ones worked for a nonmember, they usually shared their earnings in the form of money or wine. In the case of the sodality work groups, however, their money earnings usually went into their treasury.

In both Atea and Fatata, women usually contributed their own money in constructing or repairing their own houses, but the only part they played in house building itself was in the making of thatch-plates. Males also manufactured thatch-plates on occasion, but it was mainly an activity of females.

A standard unit or plate of thatch was made by splitting the midrib of a coconut frond and plaiting the adhering leaflets into a diagonal checkerwork pattern (see W. C. Handy, p. 65). Green coconut leaves were used on some occasions, e.g., for thatching a temporary shed, but Te Pitians claimed that greenleaf thatch remained rainproof for only two years or less; for longer-lasting thatch, they utilized older, dried-out leaves, which remained rainproof for three to four years. A leaf was regarded as properly dry when its frond had fallen naturally from the palm. Thus, many Te Pitians made a regular practice of collecting and saving all fallen fronds they found. At home these fronds were stored in places off the ground, to prevent their rotting; then, before being made into plates, their leaves were soaked in fresh water for a day or two in order to make them more pliable.

To the best of my knowledge, all of Te Piti's women and girls, and many males as well, made thatch-plates on occasion, but several women did so regularly, as a source of money income. Indeed, some women were highly skilled in this craft, capable of plaiting from sixty to ninety plates a day of uninterrupted work. When sold commercially, thatching brought from fifty to sixty *tara* (250–300 francs) per 100 plates, as against their 25-*tara*-per-100 evaluation when contributed to other members of the maker's own thatch-making group or to her husband's house-thatching group.

The thatch-making groups just referred to were composed solely of women who assembled on occasion to plait plates and, of course, to enjoy each other's company. Those active during my visits were composed according to sodality membership.

Thatch-making groups usually worked only to supply specific demands, i.e., to provide thatch for a house about to be built; they did not convene to build up stocks against potential future demand. The leaves so used were supplied by the group members themselves, and their earnings went into a common treasury, not to be shared out among them but to be used for a common purpose, such as the refurbishment of their sodality meeting house.

As far as I could discover, no precise bookkeeping was kept, written or otherwise, of any individual's share in terms of number of leaves supplied or plates made on any one occasion. Women differed widely in thatch-making speed; and while this was a matter of pride for the experts, it did not lead to complaints against the slow. On the other hand, if some member of the thatch-making group spent consistently less time than the average in the co-operative work, this inevitably led to recriminations, provided there were no extenuating circumstances, such as illness of herself or her child.

One of the most telling differences between Atea and Fatata was in the socioeconomic ways in which residences were built and repaired. In Atea, since the "vanilla house" era, only one residence had been constructed mainly by employment of an imported specialist architect-builder who, however, used local men for ordinary labor. All other houses in existence or in process of being built or repaired during my 1954–55 visit were done so by the occupants themselves, either alone or with occasional help of a relative or friend, or by means of work groups, of which there were two large ones devoted solely to house building or repairing, and several smaller ones devoted to group work in general. In Fatata, in sharp contrast, no such work groups were in existence during my 1955 visit. When questioned on the subject, most Fatatans knew about this type of organization and recalled instances of attempts by individuals to institute them, principally by immigrants from the Leeward Islands, but all voiced the opinion either that they "wouldn't work equitably" in Fatata, or that it was far less troublesome and more economic to do it on one's own or to employ a carpenter for money, which, in all cases I could learn about, had been or was in process of being done. Consistent with this expressed view, Fatatans rarely called on relatives or friends outside the household in question to assist in repairing or rethatching.

In view of the large amounts of unrecorded labor that went into this activity, either unpaid or uncosted, I am unable to produce an accurate quantitative comparison of Atea and Fatata for this aspect of house building and repair, although, as just noted, the proportion of labor thus engaged was much higher in Atea than in Fatata.

With regard to recorded costs of both labor and materials, Fatatans' expenditures for house building and repair during 1954 were twice as large, per capita, as those of Ateans, i.e., 800 francs to Atea's 550 (see below, Chapter III, p. 175). Some of Fatata's higher figure in this statistic is doubtless due to the fact, just noted, that much more of the labor involved in house building and repairing was paid for in money and actually recorded. Also, a much larger proportion of the materials that went into building and repairing Atea's houses was acquired by means other than purchase.

Summary of Differences.

(1) There were some striking differences between Atea and Fatata with respect to residential houses—in size, style, and quality of construction. Some of these differences, e.g., those relating to "vanilla" houses, were residues of a quarter-century or more past, but Fatata's superiority in numbers and kinds of recently built houses was a tangible sign of current economic differences between the two villages as well.

(2) In terms of such house equipment as beds, chairs, tables, lamps, and stoves, the two villages were not noticeably different, but with respect to such costly and recently purchased items as phonographs, radios, and refrigerators, Fatata's houses contained relatively more.

(3) In 1954–55, Fatata was far better equipped with running water. Indeed, Atea had none at all; but this difference was due to Administration intervention and not to any larger expenditures on the part of the Fatatans themselves.

(4) Fatata's house yards were also far larger than those of Atea. But, again, this was due to topography and to historic circumstances long since past and not to any current economic differences between the two villages.

(5) A major difference between the two villages which did, however, involve economic aspects was the organization and financing of house building and repair. Ateans' preference for, and Fatatans' widespread opposition to, organized labor exchanging may have been due in part to deeply-rooted "custom," but was also a consequence of Ateans' relatively greater dearth, now and probably in the past, of ready cash.

CHAPTER III

EARNING AND SPENDING MONEY

Every Te Pitian was in some measure dependent upon objects and services obtainable only with money, and nearly every Te Pitian male over fourteen or fifteen was engaged some of the time in money-earning activities, the same having been the case with many females. Such activities included production (copra, vanilla, kapok, cassava, coffee, fruit and vegetables, cattle, pigs, fish, firewood, boats, and thatch-plates), services (transport, processing, teaching, laboring), vending, and renting. Individual engagement in these activities ranged from forty or more hours every week to an occasional hour or so. I begin with a description of the production of copra, i.e., dried coconut meat, the oldest of Te Piti's money-earning industries.

Growing Cash Crops

Copra. In both Atea and Fatata, copra (*pūfā*) was made by harvesting ripe coconuts, by manual removal of the meat from its shell, and by drying it in the sun. Methods of meat removal and drying were the same in both villages, but there were some differences between the two in methods of harvesting and in protection provided for the growing nuts.

The major natural factors limiting copra production were uncurbed ground cover and uncontrolled rats. There were some locations, mostly near the shore, where the soil discouraged undergrowth, but elsewhere, unless some efforts were made to restrict or remove the grasses and shrubs growing under the coconut palms, it became difficult, if not impossible, to find and collect fallen nuts. A few owners pastured their cattle in their groves, which seemed to keep the undergrowth sufficiently low; others had to keep it cut low by hand. In both villages, however, there were some proprietors who, for some cause or another, allowed their groves to become unharvestable from excessive undergrowth.

Rats destroyed coconuts in two ways: by eating into immature nuts and causing them to fall prematurely, and by eating into mature nuts on the ground. Some owners employed dogs in an effort to discourage rats from attacking the fallen nuts and some nailed collars of zinc sheeting around their palms to stop rats from climbing to the growing nuts. The zinc was supplied free by the government, which also paid cooperating proprietors a subsidy of three francs for every collar installed.

Coconut palms are propagated by planting of a nut that has progressed past maturity to the stage of sending forth rootlets and stem. In the Society Islands, it takes about five years for a palm to reach nut-bearing stage, and thereafter it continues to bear year round for about sixty more years. To the best of my knowledge, only about 800 palms were purposefully planted in Te Piti during my visits, and those mainly in groves intended for copra production. Nuts were harvested in Te Piti in either one of two ways, by collecting fallen nuts from the ground or by detaching them from the palms either by climbing the palm and cutting (or twisting) their stems or by cutting them from the ground with a knife blade attached to a long bamboo pole. Both collecting of fallen nuts and detaching involved some disadvantages. Collection was, of course, much easier than cutting, provided the undergrowth was sparse, but the fallen nuts were exposed to damage from rats if not promptly collected. Detaching a nut reduced the possibility of rat damage (even when the palm was not protected by a zinc collar) and hastened somewhat the harvesting time; on the other hand, it led to some harvesting of premature nuts (thereby reducing the weight of the copra) and it was a difficult and tiring job either to climb the high palm or to handle successfully the long-poled cutting knife.

Because the coconuts ripened continuously without discernible seasonal variations in growth rate, harvesting could have proceeded year round at an unchanging rate. However, other influences intervened to make harvesting discontinuous. For example, in the case of a specialist fisherman or of a large-scale vanilla grower, the seasonally fluctuating demands of these occupations usually led them to neglect their copra-making jobs at such times. Some grove owners put off harvesting until June through September, the season of steady trade winds marked by sunny days and little or no rain, when the meat of the coconut dried at a faster rate. The celebrations occurring at year end for Christmas and New Year also resulted in some variation in nut harvesting; many individuals were active in copra-making in late November and early December in order to obtain money for these events, and few undertook this or any other kind of cash-earning work during the three to four weeks devoted to the celebrations.

Atea: Clearing a garden site

Atea: Husking and shredding coconuts for a feast

Atea: A prize-winning yam

Atea: Judging taros and yams for prizes

Atea: Drying copra on an old-type dryer

Atea: Processing manioc

Atea: Weighing green vanilla beans for sale

Atea: Awaiting her turn to weigh-in vanilla beans

Another factor influencing the timing of copra-making was the kind of harvesting arrangements shared by a grove's co-owners. Many of Te Piti's "commercial" coconut groves (as distinct from the smaller stands of palms found near the houses whose nuts were used for food and drink) were held in joint ownership—say, by a set of siblings or by two or more such sets. This situation came about through the operation of colonial property-inheritance laws, which resulted in devolution of property to all the legitimate offspring of an owner in equal shares. In the case of a parcel of land, the inheritors were thereby presented with the alternative of dividing it physically into legally separate estates, or of dividing use of it on a time-allotment basis. Te Pitians tended to follow the second alternative until friction among the co-inheritors, or some other specific event or situation, induced them to divide the estate.

It came about, then, that many coconut groves (as well as other kinds of property) were owned jointly by two or more individuals. The simplest type of arrangement adopted in such instances was that involving two or more siblings; in such a case, each one held harvesting rights for an equal and specified portion of a calendar year—six months each in the case of two siblings, four months in the case of three, and three months in the case of four. Three months was considered to be the minimum unit for the purpose and six months optimum. When more than four equal-share owners were involved, the cycle was usually extended to two or more years. More complicated arrangements resulted when an estate was owned by two or more sets of equal share owners, as represented in the following diagram:

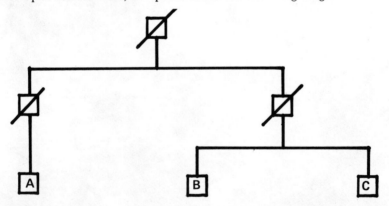

In this case, A would have had the right to harvest coconuts from the estate for six months of every year, while B and C only three months each.

Even more complex share-owning arrangements were in operation during my visits to Te Piti, but enough has been said to indicate how harvest sharing operated—ideally, at least.

The practice of time-use allotment resulted in some discontinuities in nut harvesting. Each co-owner, during his use period, usually attempted to harvest as many nuts as possible. This led most of them to clean out their grove of all mature nuts at the end of their respective use periods, with the consequence that the next user had to wait for several weeks before enough nuts had matured to warrant the effort of harvesting. In view of the continuous growth of coconuts, such a practice did not result in any apparent inequities, provided, of course, that all the users employed the same harvesting techniques. However, if one of two co-owners harvested only fallen nuts while the other cut them down from the palms (which was typically done just before the end of the use period), the former invariably had to wait longer to harvest and in the end harvested fewer nuts. Te Pitians were keenly aware of the inequities resulting from such a practice, and there was general agreement that it was "unethical," i.e., "Chinese-like," "un-Tahitian." On the other hand, the few individuals who engaged in the practice were grudgingly admired for their enterprise and energy—nut-cutting, it will be recalled, having been a difficult exercise.

Not infrequently the full owner of a coconut grove would sell his harvesting rights to it for specific periods of time, either at a fixed rate (payable in advance and calculated on a percentage of the previous year's profits) or for a share of the profits. Similarly, some co-owners sold their harvest rights in jointly held estates, either to fellow co-owners or to other individuals. Summarizing the economics of these arrangements on the basis of several that took place during or just prior to my visits, the rights owners received rents of about 40 to 60 percent of the profits of the groves' average net profits for corresponding periods of time (i.e., by European standards, a very high rent indeed).

In those cases in which the sellers of harvest rights were domiciled and present in the community throughout the period in question, the reasons given for sale varied. In some cases, the estate in question obviously was too large for even the most industrious owner to harvest alone or with the assistance of his fellow householders. Some other rights sellers were men who were either too old or too sickly to carry out the heavy work of harvesting and cutting nuts. Others were men in need of immediate cash or those employed full time in lucrative jobs. And still others, it was widely said, were men simply too lazy to exert the required effort.

In several other cases, the sellers of harvest rights did so because, for one reason or another, they chose to be away from home for lengthy periods of time. A common variant on this arrangement occurred when one of a set of co-owners (say, one of a pair of brothers) was absent from home for an indefinite period of time. In such instances, it was not unusual for an explicit contractual agreement to be made; the stay-at-home merely undertook, implicitly, to "look after" (*ha'a pa'o*) the whole of the jointly owned grove. If, then, the absentee did not stay away too long, and if his relationship with the stay-at-home remained good, the latter would usually set aside for the absentee one-half of the profits derived from working the absentee's part of the estate. However, an absentee who stayed away too long and did not enjoy good relations with his stay-at-home co-owners risked losing most or all of his share of profits from the joint estate.

The last situation was a common one in Te Piti; it resembled, somewhat, the biblical Prodigal Son theme, except that the outcomes were not always so happy for the returnee. One variant thereof occurred when a youth left home, spent years on Tahiti mainly 'pleasure-ing' (*āre'are'ara'a*), and returned to replenish his cash. The returned prodigal was usually housed and generously fed, but his demands for share of profits from a jointly-owned estate were invariably contested with loud recriminations from his stay-at-home co-owners. The outcomes of such situations varied for reasons that are not relevant in the present discussion, but it rarely happened that the returned co-owner received all of his claimed and otherwise acknowledged share.

This resolution exemplifies two propositions that were basic to several kinds of transactions among Te Pitians. First, that when money was involved in an exchange, the bookkeeping tended to be more precise than with exchange involving other kinds of goods. And second, that social relations entailing long-term exchange needed to be periodically revalidated to continue in effect.

The second proposition was typified by another situation commonly met with in Te Piti, namely, the arrangements that obtained for sharing copra profits with permanently nonresident co-owners of a local estate. Through the normal operation of inheritance rules, it often transpired that an estate would include among its co-owners some individuals who resided permanently in other districts, including those of other islands. In such cases, it was the common practice for one of the resident co-owners (usually the "senior," i.e., *matahiapo*, first-born among siblings) to manage the estate's copra production and parcel out its profits (after having subtracted his additional one-half share as payment for his services). In the case of estates earning large profits and having few co-owners, the manager usually sent to each nonresident his (or her) share by mail. But when the amounts to be distributed were quite small (say, less than about 200 to 300 francs), the money was commonly kept by the manager unless and until the nonresident co-owner specifically asked for it, and even then the latter's claim tended to lose its weight if it was not presented within two or three years.

Many Te Pitians owned portions of distant copra-producing estates; but unless these were monetarily valuable (say, 200 to 300 francs or more a year), they shrugged them off as inconsequential and made little or no serious effort to collect, i.e., effort that involved letter writing. However, some individuals did utilize the existence of such credit ties as one justification for visiting distant places where the hospitality they received would, tacitly, serve to balance any outstanding credits.

Now to return to the technical processes involved in turning coconuts into marketable copra. After the coconuts had been collected, they were assembled in piles inside the grove and their meat extracted on the spot. The most common method was to split the whole coconut in half, usually with an axe, and remove the hard white meat by means of a small and sharp knife. This was said to be a difficult job, requiring deftness and considerable strength. Conventionally, it was a job for youths and adult males, but I occasionally saw women engaged in it, helping their men.

The extracted meat was put into burlap sacks for the dryer. Two sizes of sack (*pūtēi*) were used, the smaller held about 65 kilos of "green" (undried) meat, the larger about 80. A fast worker could cut enough to fill about ten of the smaller bags in a single working day (about seven to eight hours), but for most men an average day's cutting was five to eight of the smaller bags.

Freshly cut coconut meat contains 40 percent water by weight. Unless most of this is removed by drying, the meat quickly becomes rancid; hence, drying must be carried out as soon after cutting as possible. In Te Piti, all the meat was dried locally before transport to Papeʻete, where it was stored for overseas shipment. Elsewhere in the Society Islands, some copra was also dried by smoke and some by artificially produced smoke-free hot air. Formerly, I was told, there were a few hot-air dryers in Fatata, but during my visits, both there and at Atea, all copra drying was by sun and virtually all of this was carried out on specially constructed drying platforms (*paepae pūfā*), each one big enough in area to permit large quantities of coconut meat to be thinly spread out. In addition, each platform was provided with baffles against rats and had attached to it a roof that could be rolled or slid over it, when needed, to protect the drying meat from rain. Most of the dryers in use during my visits had metal platforms and metal-top roofs that moved along on wheels. There were, however, still in existence two exemplars of an older type model with leaf-thatch roofs and wooden runners (which had the advantage, according to their builders, of having "cost nothing" to construct). I also came across one example of an even older method of sun-drying, consisting of a string of a dozen or so husked half-coconut shells still containing their meat and hung up on a tree to dry. My companion at that time guessed, probably accurately, that the owner's object was to obtain only enough dried meat for making coconut oil for culinary, cosmetic, or medicinal use.

To sun-dry copra adequately—according to government standards—required a minimum of three to four days of sunny, cloudless weather, but because of adverse conditions (occasional cloudiness, rain showers, extrahigh humidity) most drying in Te Piti required five to eight days and some a fortnight or more. The task of overseeing the drying was considered by most Te Pitians to be extremely boring since it necessitated a continuous weather-eye against unheralded showers and allowed the overseer no other occupations during daylight hours—not even a long siesta.

During 1954–55, there were ten small copra dryers in operation in Atea (including one each owned by the two Chinese stores) and four larger ones in Fatata. Some of the latter constituted large investments of labor and of costly materials. For example, one of them had cost its co-owners 12,500 francs in new materials plus the unestimated value of all the metal which had been taken from a dismantled house. Another, also in Fatata, which had a drying platform eight by ten meters square, had cost 20,000 francs to build in materials and paid labor.

For those producers without dryers of their own, there were four options open to them for drying their coconut meat. A few were allowed rent-free use of a kinsman's dryer provided, of course, it was not otherwise in use. The second arrangement was for the copra producer to rent the use of the dryer from its owner, and then proceed to manage the drying himself. In 1954, most Atean dryer-owners permitted friends and relations to use their dryers gratis; in Fatata, even siblings of the owners had to pay rent, which averaged ten francs per large sack of dried copra. The third arrangement was for the dryer-owner himself to manage the drying of the producer's green copra for a price of ten francs in Atea or twenty in Fatata for a small sack of dried copra—or fifteen to twenty-five francs for the larger-size sack.[1] A fourth kind of arrangement, which was followed by most producers in Atea, was to sell their green copra to one of the two local Chinese stores, whose proprietors then dried it on their own dryers.

To insure that all copra be adequately dried, the government maintained an inspection system at the source. This consisted of a committee (*tōmite*) of three local residents appointed by each island's resident gendarme. When the owner or paid dryer of a harvest of copra considered it adequately dried, he informed one of his village's inspectors, who then examined it and approved it in writing or ordered it to be further dried. Annually, the

---

[1]As noted earlier, unless otherwise specified, all money figures in the text are given in francs for purposes of consistency with official statistics, etc., but it should be recalled that the Te Pitians themselves reckoned mainly in *tārā* (i.e., five francs) units to the extent, even, of translating franc-given figures not divisible by five as, e.g., twelve or thirteen as "*e piti tārā e te afa*" ("two *tārā* and a half).

committee reported to the gendarme the total amount they had inspected and approved, and were paid by the Administration for their services at the rate of two centimes (*peni*) per kilo. This payment they then divided equally among themselves. The sanction behind the program appeared to be effective, i.e., if, subsequent to approval, any copra was found to be spoiled due to inadequate drying, the inspection committee itself was fined.

Now to list the differences between Atea and Fatata with respect to copra making. First, although Atea contained larger areas on which coconut palms could grow (see Chapter I), the areas actually planted in palms were less extensive than those of Fatata—a consequence, I suggest, of Fatata's longer history as a center of population and cash-cropping enterprise. On the other hand, it was my solid impression, although I did not make systematic measurements, that Fatata contained larger areas of unharvested mature coconut groves than Atea, both absolute and relative to population size. Most of these, in both places, included groves with undergrowth up to a meter or so high. In addition, there were some groves, mainly in Fatata, that contained secondary-growth trees so large that it would have required a great deal of labor to clear, almost as much as that involved in clearance of growth for a new site. Most of those unharvestable groves, it is true, were located on relatively large estates whose owners had other, more accessible, plots elsewhere. Nevertheless, even their landless neighbors were evidently not motivated strongly enough to lease and clear these idle groves themselves, an opportunity that Ateans would have been much more likely to seize.

In the absence of good aerial photographs, I was unable to measure the amounts of land planted in coconuts in either village. However, based on local production figures and on estimates for other Society Islands locations (which established an average of 750 kilos of dried copra per hectare[2]), Fatata's producing groves would have covered at least seventy hectares and Atea's at least fifty-seven (to which must be added both village's areas of unharvested grove areas).

In contrast to Ateans' more intensive, less prodigal use of land containing mature coconut palms, was their more conservative, less scientific attitude towards production. That is to say, whereas most Fatatans took pains to protect their growing nuts from rats by installing the Administration-issued zinc collars, most Atean growers refused these handouts, reasoning that the zinc would kill the palm.

---

[2]*Situation Economique et Perspectives d'Avenir, 1959–60.* (Polynésie Française: Service des Affaires Economiques et du Plan). This study characterizes per hectare copra production throughout French Polynesian as "meager" (*faible*), p. 7.

Another difference between the two villages' production techniques had to do with nut-harvesting, i.e., Fatatans, on the whole, engaged in much more nut-cutting than Ateans did. As described earlier, harvesting a still-attached nut (by cutting, or by climbing and twisting) involves much greater effort than picking up a naturally fallen nut off the ground; how then account for this difference between Atea and Fatata, a difference that was reinforced, it will be recalled, by Ateans' public condemnation of the practice? It cannot be explained by differences in work ethic—on the whole, Ateans were, if anything, harder working than Fatatans and even more eager for money. And it seems not to have been motivated by any Fatatan's desire to protect against ground-based rat damage or any Atean's concern that cut nuts were not wholly ripe, and hence contained less meat—at least, no such reasoning was expressed to me. The explanation lies in the differences in social relations and in the tenure arrangements under which coconut groves were harvested, a subject that was introduced above and will be discussed further below.

As recorded in my diary of work schedules, Ateans tended to harvest their coconuts more continuously than was the case in Fatata—partly, perhaps, as a consequence of the latter's greater preoccupation with fishing during certain times of the year, but also because of the tenure arrangements for harvesting mentioned in the previous paragraph.

I was unable to discover any differences between Atea and Fatata with respect to the methods used in removing coconut meat from its shell, but some technical (and perhaps environmental) differences were discoverable at the drying stage.

On the one hand, Atea contained more dryers (ten to Fatata's four), despite the latter's larger population and despite the circumstance that most Ateans sold their copra green. On the other hand, three of Fatata's four dryers were very much larger and more modern in construction than any found in Atea. One possible explanation for this disparity was the availability of more cash in Fatata for the kind of sizeable money investment required to build a large, technically advanced dryer. Yet even Fatata's somewhat impulsive economists would probably not have made such investments unless they had thought that the quantity of any one copra-drying commission would be large enough to fill the dryer. In other words, although Fatata's regular copra producers were fewer in number than Atea's, their episodic harvests were, on the average, larger in size.

The more pervasive monetization of Fatatan copra-making was manifest in several ways. For example, it was the practice of some of its grove owners to hire casual labor to assist them in harvesting and cutting; in Atea, on the other hand, in cases where groves were of a size beyond the capacity of their respective owners to harvest by themselves (including, of course, their household members), they were more likely to lease profit-sharing harvest rights to others, having on the average possessed less cash in hand than their Fatatan counterparts to pay for casual labor. Again, Atean dryer-owners were more liberal than their Fatatan counterparts in lending their dryers rent-free to other residents. While the latter were, in most cases, close kinsmen of the dryer-owners, in Fatata not even siblings allowed one another rent-free dryer use if they resided in separate households.

A comparison of meteorological data might reveal some differences between Atea and Fatata with respect to sunlight, i.e., to copra-drying conditions. Regrettably, I did not record such data during my visits and official records are not geographically specific enough for purposes of this comparison. I have the impression (but it is only that) that Fatata was, on the whole, sunnier than Atea, but this is not enough basis for predicting copra-drying times. I also recorded numerous statements from individuals in both places about both average and actual drying times, but here again the statements were too varied to be reliable. Thus, although such information might reveal some significant conclusions regarding environmental influences on the copra economy, etc. (e.g., discontinuous drying would probably result in more spoilage, hence more work for less money, etc.), I myself am unable to prove it.

Marketing procedures differed considerably between Atea and Fatata. Most Ateans sold[3] most or all of their green copra to the local Chinese storekeepers, who then dried it on their own dryers and shipped it to Pape'ete buyers. The rest of Atea's green copra was dried on their owner's or on neighbor's dryers through arrangements already described, and then freighted to nearby Fare where it was sold either to some Fare storekeeper or to the agent of a Pape'ete-bound boat. The transport to Fare was done by launch, either by one of the two owned and operated by Ateans or by one owned and operated out of a neighboring village. In contrast, very little of Fatata's copra passed through local storekeepers' hands. Most producers shipped it, dried, by interisland launch to Pape'ete, at a cost averaging 500 francs per ton, and sold it directly to any of the numerous buyers in business there; the seller either accompanied his shipment and negotiated the sale himself, or sent it to a regular consignee, or deputized the captain of the launch to do so in return for a commission.

A few Fatata producers incurred additional costs by paying to have their copra trucked from grove to dryer and from dryer to wharf—transfers which other growers in Fatata and Atea made by hand cart, canoe, or horse, or on their own backs.

---

[3]Actually, "sold" is not an accurate term, since the green copra transferred to the storekeepers was in most cases payment against store debts.

Turning now to the economics, strictly speaking, of copra production, I can begin by attempting to estimate the numbers of local copra-producing palms actually owned by Ateans or Fatatans.[4] I write "attempting" advisedly: I did not myself carry out an actual tree count—a task for which the required effort would have far exceeded the reward—but relied mainly on interviews, which I confirmed or revised in only a few instances by actual counting. Moreover, the attribution of ownership was, in many instances, difficult to decide.

Unlike the situation in some other Pacific island societies, the coconut palms growing in Te Piti were not, in 1954–55, distinguishable from the lands themselves in terms of ownership. (The same did not always hold for shorter-lived crops like vanilla.) And, as will be described, most of Te Piti's land parcels, including those with coconut palms, were held in joint ownership, which meant, of course, that the palms themselves were jointly held. This complication was kept in mind when residents were queried about "their" palms in order to avoid duplicate counting and in order to calculate each owner's actual assets, i.e., a one-half ownership in two palms was recorded as full ownership of one. However, I would deceive myself and the reader by holding that the resulting tallies are highly accurate.[5] And my tallies do not take into account the differences in productive value *between* palms—between, say, one with a productive life of forty years and one near the end of its nut-bearing life. It would be comforting to believe that the differences between properties averaged out in this respect, but from my impressionistic observations, that was probably not the case. For, not only were the palms of Fatata somewhat older, on the average, than those of Atea, but in both places there were discernible differences between the ages of many groves.

Nevertheless, with these qualifications in mind, I estimate that the thirty-three Atean palm-grove owners possessed the equivalent of full ownership rights in about 12,500 mature coconut palms, while the thirty-seven Fatatan owners possessed such rights in about 28,900. Thus, the Atean palm-owners owned an average of 379 local palms each and their Fatatan counterparts 781, i.e., just over twice as many.

---

[4] I exclude from this count the groves nearby but outside Fatata owned by Europeans or non-resident Europeanized part-Tahitians; although some of these plantations employed Fatatans as full- or part-time laborers, the resident owners or managers were not active members of the communities under study, and their influence upon local affairs was limited mainly to the wages they paid to local residents. I also excluded the palms located near the Te Pitians' dwellings whose nuts were used wholly or mainly for food and drink.

[5] Even less confidence is warranted by published official statistics, which seem to have been based on enquiries even more equivocal than mine.

In this setting, the mere ownership of a capital resource as important as mature coconut palms would appear to confer economic advantages upon their owners. In this sense, the palm-owning residents of Fatata were on the average twice as advantaged as those of Atea—as indeed was Fatata as a whole, since (ignoring the fact that not all residents, nor even all adults, owned such palms), its total of 348 residents "owned" in 1954–55 an average of eighty-three palms each, to Atea's per capita average of fifty-eight.

Thus, the Fatatans as a whole would appear to have been potentially wealthier than the Ateans in this respect, but this is only part of the picture and does not take into account the palms owned by Ateans and Fatatans elsewhere. Regrettably I cannot even guess with any measure of reliability what those numbers were. I recorded instances of residents going to harvest some of their "foreign" groves as well as instances of money received by some of them from the co-owners who harvested such groves, and I recorded several statements from Te Pitians about distant properties that they co-owned but received no income from. More particulars about these "foreign" holdings will be given below, in Chapter XI; for the present, however, it is sufficient to state that, in terms of ownership alone, I cannot estimate which village was the more advantaged in this respect.

In any case, despite—or perhaps because of—their relative disadvantage in local palm ownership, Ateans tended more than did the Fatatans to convert their growing coconuts into actual money income. Not only did Atea contain smaller areas of unharvested palms than Fatata, as was earlier mentioned, but Ateans also obtained, by one means or another, more money from their foreign groves, as a later section will describe.

Averages aside, the most noteworthy thing revealed in the figures on local individual holdings (Table 3A) is the far larger number of Fatatans in the over-500 palm class, a statistic that could be the reflection of an important socioeconomic difference between the two villages if the palm owners in question had regularly converted their growing nuts into copra, which, as has been noted, they were less inclined than their Atean counterparts to do.

Table 3A. Palm Ownership

Number of Palms Owned	Number of Owners	
	Atea	Fatata
less than 100	6	5
100 to 500	22	21
over 500	5	11

In 1954, Ateans produced from local groves and sold the equivalent of 42,700 kilos of dried copra. Of this, 67,389 kilos of green copra were sold to the local storekeepers (who dried it to become about 40,500 kilos) and 2,200 kilos, which they dried themselves and sold at Fare.[6] During the same period, the Fatatans produced from local groves and sold (mainly in Pape'ete) about 52,000 kilos of copra dried by themselves. Thus, per capita, the Ateans actually harvested more coconuts in 1954 than the Fatatans, which, when dried, came to 192 kilos, as against the Fatatans' 153.[7]

However, the Ateans' larger (per capita) coconut harvest, despite the relatively fewer palms growing in Atea, did not bring them correspondingly more profits.

In the first place, the average prices paid for the Atean copra, green and dried, were significantly lower than those paid for Fatata's, i.e., the green copra they sold brought an average price of 3.5 francs per kilo and the dried a price of 7.5, resulting in a total revenue of about 252,362 francs. In comparison, the 52,000 kilos of dried copra sold by the Fatatans brought an average price of 10 francs per kilo, or a total revenue of 520,000 francs.[8]

From these revenues, the sellers had to pay out some direct costs, such as drying and transport, which amounted to 40,000 francs for the Fatata copra and about 1,500 francs for that of Atea, the large difference being due to the circumstance that most of the Atean copra was sold locally and undried. Thus, the average gross-profit price received (sale price less drying and transport money costs) for a kilo of dried copra or its equivalent amount of green was about 9.23 francs in Fatata and about 5.87 francs in Atea. While it is true that some of the Fatatans' larger profit resulted from the extra labor that they expended in drying and transporting their copra; and while it is true that the Ateans, by selling their copra locally and green, were thereby saved a corresponding amount of labor for possible use in other money-earning work, the fact of the matter was that for most of the Ateans there

---

[6]The figures given here pertain only to copra produced locally by Tahitian residents of Atea and Fatata and will be found to differ from the official statistics, which also included copra produced by other persons residing in the districts in question.

[7]The population figures used in this calculation were 222 for Atea and 339 for Fatata, which differ from those established for 1955 (namely 217 and 348, respectively). The 1954 figures, which will be used throughout this study for comparisons of income and expenditures, were arrived at by questionings based on the residential populations of 1955, i.e., by determining which of those present in 1955 were there during most of 1954, plus others who were there in 1954 but no longer present in 1955. Admittedly, this is not a very precise procedure for determining past censuses of populations as mobile as those of Atea and Fatata, but was the only one I could pursue.

[8]I did not collect production or price statistics preceding 1954 but was informed, in both communities, that they had been "about the same" as in 1954.

was no other local form of money earning to which they could have applied that saved labor.

In addition to the direct costs of drying and transport, some of the copra producers of Atea and Fatata had to pay rent, which was of three kinds: (a) flat-fee rent money for long-term occupancy; (b) share-crop money receipts; or (c) payments to grove owners for short-term harvest rights. The approximate amount of such rents paid in 1954 on coconut-bearing land were as shown in Table 3B.

Table 3B. Rents Paid in Coconut-Bearing Lands

Village	TYPE A		TYPE B		TYPE C	
	To Outsiders	To Residents	To Outsiders	To Residents	To Outsiders	To Residents
Atea	5,000	0	85,000	9,000	5,300	1,400
Fatata	1,000	0	62,000	13,000	4,700	7,400

In sum, out of their sales revenues from copra, the Atean seller-producers paid rents to other local Tahitians and to outsiders, amounting to about 105,700 francs, and those of Fatata paid about 88,100, which, when added to drying and transport costs, resulted in net profits of, respectively, 145,162 and 391,900 francs, thereby reducing the net profits per kilo of dried copra (or equivalent) to, respectively, 3.39 and 7.54 francs.

Thus, despite their concern to harvest all the coconuts accessible to them, the Ateans were handicapped *vis-à-vis* the Fatatans by their farther distance from Pape'ete and by their chronic indebtedness to their local storekeepers, which either inclined or impelled them to sell their copra to their creditors in an unprocessed state. This constraint was particularly unfortunate for the Ateans, inasmuch as their labor, which might have been applied to drying copra, was virtually the only thing many of them had to sell. Fatatans also piled up debts with their local storekeepers by obtaining goods on credit and by receiving money loans, but they, more than the Ateans, had other and less constraining ways for paying off those debts.

Turning now to the question of how such profits were distributed among the residents of Atea and Fatata, a simple calculation will show that, on a straight per capita basis, those of Atea received 654 francs and those of Fatata 1,156—but the profits were, of course, not actually distributed in this per capita way.

Although the storekeepers in Atea and the freight agent in Fatata recorded the names of the individuals selling or shipping copra, the persons named were not necessarily the ones who had produced the copra in question, or the ones to whom the payments belonged. In some instances, the seller in question sold only what he himself had produced, whether on his own behalf or on behalf also of co-owners of the harvested grove, both those living locally and those living elsewhere. In other instances, the seller sold under his name not only his own production but that of other producers, including, usually but not invariably, members of his own household. And in still other instances, the listed sellers were not the actual producers, but had received their allotments from the producers in proportion to their ownership rights of the harvested groves.

Thus, regrettably, but perhaps inevitably, I cannot provide figures on how money proceeds from the Te Pitians' copra making were actually distributed.[9] However, the lists of *recorded* sellers will provide a rough approximation to those figures, as shown in Table 3C.

Table 3C. Copra Sellers, 1954

Number of Kilos	Atea*		Fatata	
under 100	6		5	
100–499	20		31	
500–999	13		16	
1,000–1,499	8		10	
1,500–3,999	5		8	
over 4,000	1	(7,017)	1	(6,176)
Totals	53		72	

*Note: the Atea figures were made comparable to those of Fatata by reducing the weight figures on green copra by 40 percent.

---

[9] If, as I suspect, the reader is becoming increasingly irritated by my inability to provide precise, unambiguous quantification for many of the activities described in this study, I can only say that I have often felt much the same. In partial extenuation, I can add that some of the imprecision is inherent in the behavior itself (most Te Pitians did not keep records or retain memories of the precise amounts of their earnings), and some in the circumstances attending this kind of research, i.e., a lone observer simply cannot physically pursue in detail all the inquiries that a comprehensive ethnography entails. A more legitimate excuse for the imprecisions in economic statistics, however, is the intent that this study be concerned with quantities only insofar as they relate, directly and importantly, to social relations.

To a resident of an industrialized society, perhaps the most striking thing about these figures relating to this most basic Te Pitian money-earning activity is the trivial amount of income it produced, considering the Te Pitians' preoccupation with it as a focus of labor, as a topic of interest and conversation, and (in the expressed views of many of them) as the most important economic basis of their "Tahitian way of life."

In Atea, every 65 to 70 kilo bag of green copra turned over to the buyer, at a price of about 236 francs, represented collecting and cutting and carrying labor of from three to five hours. Compared with the 100 francs a day that could occasionally be earned from unskilled labor, this was a profitable return if the coconuts were from land owned by the producer. If not, a circumstance that prevailed in many instances, the return from three to five hours of copra-making labor was, on the average, only 200 francs, which was still better than ordinary wage employment, but a very limited source of income in terms of opportunity. For even the largest producer-seller in Atea earned a net profit of only about 25,000 francs (the equivalent of U.S. $278 at that time), and the average of all sellers only about 2,740 francs.

Fatatans fared better than the Ateans in their copra-making, even after discounting the extra labor they expended in drying and marketing it. But even so, the average net profits received in 1954 by its seventy-two sellers came to only 5,443 francs—which was, for example, about five times the average amount spent by Fatatan men on wine and beer!

Another way of looking at the economics of Te Piti's copra industry, and of all other money-earning activities, is in terms of the sources of its Tahitian money-earners' revenues, whether from other local Tahitians or from outsiders, i.e., from persons and organizations located outside Atea or Fatata, and from non-Tahitians residing locally (which in this context means the local Chinese storekeepers). The two villages under study, for all their small size, were like whole nation-states: if their Tahitian residents obtained goods from outside sources, they had to deliver other goods in exchange, and in the long run at a money-equivalent rate. As we shall see in Chapter VI, the Te Pitians regularly received certain objects and services from "outside" (including government) sources, for which they delivered little or no money-equivalent objects or services in exchange (although many Te Pitians did not view it in this way); but for most other goods received by them from "outsiders," they had to pay with money that had originated "outside," and in this sense, one of the points on which this study's comparison will be made will be the amount of each village's balance-of-payment credit or debit.

With respect to its copra industry, Atea's copra, as a whole, earned a total of 156,762 francs from the "outside," i.e., a total sales revenue of 252,362 francs minus amounts paid in rent to outsiders (95,300 francs) and in transport payments to outsiders (about 300 francs). The other costs borne by the Atean producers, i.e., 10,400 francs in rent and 1,200 in transport charges, were paid to fellow Ateans and hence did not enter into their "foreign" exchange.

In comparison, Fatata's copra earned from the "outside" a total of 443,300 francs, i.e., total sales revenue of 520,000 francs minus rents of 67,700 and transport charges of 9,000 francs paid to outsiders. In addition, the Fatatan producers paid to fellow Fatatans 20,400 francs in rent and 31,000 francs in dryer and transport charges.

A final point on copra production concerns Te Piti's copra dryers. Earlier in this chapter, I characterized the dryer facilities of the two villages—ten small ones in Atea, four large ones in Fatata—as well-suited to distinctive local needs. Some correction should be appended to that judgment lest the reader receive a false impression about the "rationality" of Te Pitian economic practice.

In terms of costs, the best documented copra-dryer in Te Piti was one constructed in Fatata in 1954 which cost about 20,000 francs to build and had a drying capacity of about 1,200 kilos of green copra per load. If this dryer had been in continuous use year-round and received a new load of copra every eight days (the average drying time year-round), it would have processed about 54,000 kilos a year and would have earned about 6,770 francs in rent; in other words, the investment would have paid for itself in about three years' time, and so said the proud owner when he was describing to me the advantages of the enterprise. In fact, so evident was his pleasure in his prospective affluence that I did not have the heart to point out to him the unlikelihood of keeping the dryer continuously employed, inasmuch as Fatata's total production of green copra in 1954 amounted to only about 65,000 kilos!

Vanilla. *Vānira* was introduced into the Society Islands in 1848 and flourished there as a cash crop until 1967, when production dropped to a very low level. It was grown both in Atea and Fatata during my visits there in 1954–55 and 1959–60 and provided some residents with substantial cash incomes.

According to agricultural experts, vanilla grows best in humus-rich, well-drained soils and on partially-shaded sites. I found it growing in a number of different situations—on hillsides, in valleys, even in house yards along the shore. I could not discover any obvious connection between location and plant quality, and the only such judgment I could elicit from growers was that the plant yielded better on "new" garden sites.

Land intended for vanilla growing was first thoroughly cleared of low-growing vegetation. Vanilla was propagated from cuttings and the stalk trained up a pole about two meters high. After that, it continued to produce marketable pods for several years, but at a decreasing rate, evidently due to soil exhaustion. August and September appeared to be the best months for planting in Te Piti. Annually, pods tended to ripen between October and May, the largest harvests having been in March and April.

The larger vanilla plantations I examined in Te Piti contained about 8,000 stalks per hectare—the closest spacing possible, according to Te Piti's most experienced growers, who also calculated that a stalk properly planted and tended could be counted on to yield about one-fifth of a kilo of pods per annum during the plant's first two or three years of life.

Vanilla plantations had to be continuously weeded, both for better growth and for ease of access when fecundating and harvesting.

The vanilla grown in these islands required manual pollination. This was done by pressing the pollen-bearing anther down onto the pistil, an operation requiring good eyesight, dexterity, and patience. Every stalk bore several blossoms (ten to twenty according to informants), hence a hectare-size plantation could contain tens of thousands, each one requiring a separate manual operation.

To most Te Pitians, vanilla pollinating (*fa'atito i te vānira*, literally, "marrying the vanilla") was considered a tiring and boring job. The average "marryings" accomplished by most males were said to be about 1,000 per working day; women were described as being able to work more persistently and two to three times faster, as were some Chinese men. (I was told that some of the latter were capable of performing five thousand and more "marryings" a day, but I cannot vouch for that, or any of the figures given.) Compared to pollinating, picking ripe vanilla beans was a relatively easy and, of course, much more satisfying task.

After picking, the green-colored pods had to be dried before commercial use. This was done in Te Piti by sun drying, which required about three months and which reduced the pod to about one-fourth of its weight at harvest. During my 1954–55 visits, all vanilla grown in Te Piti was dried by the Chinese storekeepers of Te Piti or neighboring villages, who purchased the pods from the growers in the green-colored state and carried out the drying in their own establishments, an operation requiring continuous attention, turning and re-turning the pods and protecting them from rain and pests. (Indeed, vanilla drying constituted the principal occupation of most of the local storekeepers, and was probably the source of most of their revenues.)

By government regulation, vanilla growers sold their pods to the dryers on one or two fixed days every month throughout the harvest season. In Te

Piti, the sale always took place in public and was supervised by members of the local (Tahitian-manned) Vanilla Committee, whose job it was to inspect and weigh each grower's produce on scales periodically checked by a government inspector, to discard substandard pods, and to record and attest in writing the amount each seller sold to each buyer. For this, the committee was paid a fixed amount per kilo by each buyer for all the approved pods purchased by him. Subsequently, if any of the lot thus purchased was found by the buyer to be substandard, the committee itself, and not the seller, was required to indemnify the buyer.

In Atea and in Fatata, the committees consisted of four members each, who were elected from their number by all the local vanilla growers and who held office for one year. In former years of high production, the annual commission of a committee inspector reached as high as three to four thousand francs in Atea (somewhat less in Fatata), which made the position attractive enough to be contested for. But during the years of my visits, the harvests, and hence commissions, were so small that few men were willing to accept the responsibility entailed.

Te Pitians wishing to grow vanilla had several ways of acquiring use of the necessary land. Some growers had land of their own through inheritance. Others purchased it for that specific purpose; this, of course, required a large amount of ready money, which few possessed, and a more than average amount of profit-seeking determination. For those holding joint ownership in land which their co-owners were unwilling or unable to divide, it was necessary to obtain the approval of all co-owners before planting vanilla, and thereafter, in some instances, to pay the latter a percentage of the sales revenue. (In contrast, a person growing food crops was not usually required to pay his co-owners any rent in the form of money nor to obtain the permission of nonresident co-owners, the explanation having been that vanilla tied up the land indefinitely and that money was earned from growing it.)

Another alternative for the prospective vanilla grower was to rent some land; this invariably required a notarized contract (*tontara parau fa'a'au*), and was usually for a period of nine years. The rent paid, retroactively, was based on a fixed percentage of the sales revenue, typically about 20 percent, i.e., in Te Pitian terms, one *toata* (or franc) from every *tārā* (or 5 francs). Still another alternative was to rent an established plantation; that is, a land owner cleared and planted a patch of land, either his own or one rented by him, and then commissioned someone else to keep it cleared, to pollinate the blossoms, and to harvest and sell the pods, for a percentage of 50 percent to 70 percent of the sale price. The fact that individuals could be found to sharecrop land at such high rents indicates not only the economic advantage that accrued to the land owner and the disadvantage of owning none, but also the lengths to which some individuals were willing to go to earn money when no other means were available—a point that will be documented in a comparison between Atea and Fatata, to which I now turn.

I discovered no noteworthy difference between Atea and Fatata with respect to the technical side of vanilla growing. One Fatata grower used a chemical herbicide in helping to keep his garden free of weeds, but his lead was not followed by his neighbors who characterized the practice as being "too expensive" (although, in fact, none of these critics was able to quantify that judgment).

More noteworthy were the differences between the two villages with respect to the land tenure arrangements followed by vanilla growers. Most of the vanilla growers in both places, who numbered seventy in Atea and seventeen in Fatata, had their gardens on land in which they or their spouses or parents owned rights acquired by inheritance. In some of these instances, the gardens were on portions of larger tracts still held in joint and legally undivided ownership with others, but such portions had been informally allocated to the current users by consensus among all the co-owners, with no rent charged inasmuch as the portions in question were considered to be about equal, in size and quality, to the users' fair share of the tract (i.e., the share that would be allocated to the user were the tract to be legally divided). In the remainder of these instances, the users had planted their vanilla on portions of jointly-held tracts considerably larger than their own due, and it was in these cases that differences were apparent between Atea and Fatata.

In Atea I recorded only one case out of twelve in which the larger-than-own share-user was required to pay rent to his tract co-owners, a rent that consisted of about 5 percent of the sales revenues. In Fatata, on the other hand, all six of such users were required by their co-owners to pay rent (which averaged about 10 percent of sales revenues). In connection with these rent-paying cases, it will be recalled that in both Atea and Fatata land use was willingly and gratuitously tendered to land-poor neighbors, including, of course, kinfolk, for the purpose of planting subsistence crops (which tied up the land for only a year or two); hence, it might be supposed that the reason for exacting rent for growing vanilla was based on the fact that a planting in vanilla usually tied it up for five or more years. The reason I heard expressed was not, however, the longer period of preemption, but the fact that *money* was earned from the land's use in the case of vanilla growing. ("When people need land for food, we give it to them out of *aroha*; when they earn *money* from it that is another thing.")

During my 1954–55 visit, the only resident of Te Piti who had actually purchased land mainly for vanilla growing was the pastor of Fatata. In Atea there was a part-time resident who owned several vanilla-growing tracts inherited from his European father who had, himself, purchased the land a generation previously; but in 1954–55, no year-round resident of Atea possessed cash enough or commanded credit enough to purchase land.

Differences between Atea and Fatata were also exemplified in the sphere of sharecropping arrangements. One such arrangement, it will be recalled, was to lease land from its owner for a nine-year, contract-sanctioned period, at a rent of about 20 percent of revenues from vanilla grown and marketed. Eight of Fatata's seventeen vanilla growers were involved in this kind of arrangement in Atea only two out of seventy. One basis for this discrepancy was the larger quantity of land in and near Fatata available for leasing, but another, more intrinsic reason was the Ateans' lesser readiness to engage in such undertakings, there having been fewer possessing enough ready cash or credit to invest in the development of such properties and fewer having enough self-assurance to take on such long-term and uncertain risks. In fact, the other five Ateans who grew vanilla on a sharecrop basis submitted to the more usurous practice of weeding, pollinating, and harvesting already-planted plots for one-half share of the sale price of the green beans. No Atean I queried had calculated the cost of his labor involved in this arrangement, but according to my rough estimates the money they earned from this kind of labor amounted to about 50 francs a day, i.e., one-half of the amount conventionally paid for wage labor of other kinds. The landlords involved in these five sharecropping arrangements were all nonresidents; no true Atean, I was informed, would charge a fellow resident such a high rent. In other words, although the sharecroppers did not actually calculate the cost of their rental payments in terms of their labor, they felt them to be very "high." Moreover, two of the five landlords in question were nonresident Chinese who themselves had leased the lands in question from absentee owners and who had paid their current Atean subtenants to clear the tracts and plant the vines, another striking and poignant example of the costs in labor which Ateans sustained in a monetized world in consequence of their poverty in money.

Two Fatatans also sharecropped vanilla plantations under the kind of arrangement just described, but in these cases they received 70 percent of the proceeds of the vanilla they had pollinated and harvested (but not planted), and one of these sharecroppers stated that he had undertaken the job mainly to help out the owner, who was a kinsman employed full-time in Pape'ete.[10]

---

[10]The fact that the numbers of land-use type examples listed in this section exceed the numbers of actual vanilla producers—seventy-seven in Atea, twenty-two in Fatata—is due to the circumstances that some producers had two or more separate plantations that were tenanted in different land-use arrangements.

Finally, lest the reader infer from the foregoing that the difference between Fatata and Atea was that between "capitalist" and "labor," it should be noted (as will be later on described) that some Fatatans worked as full- or regular part-time laborers on vanilla and copra plantations in which they owned *no* share of the products at all, a situation not found in Atea. Ateans did work as paid laborers on others' vanilla and coconut plantations, but only infrequently and casually, and more typically as members of organized work groups whose charters tacitly included noneconomic purposes as well.

Several important differences between Atea and Fatata were exemplified on their respective vanilla-selling days. In Atea, where production was considerably larger, even a light, off-season selling attracted several onlookers, all eager to compare the growers' productions and to witness the drama of the sale. For drama there was; on no other occasion I observed was there evident such overt tension between Tahitians and Chinese—the former the sellers, the latter the buyers. First of all, the price offered by the buyers was usually a source of argument, some of it bitter and accompanied by threats and insults on the part of some sellers. Also, any buyer who appeared to interfere in the operation, to check on the weights or question the committee's judgment, was angrily shouted down.

There was also a quota of comedy on most Atean vanilla-selling days as, for example, when some individual pretended to stagger under the weight of his two or three kilos of pods, or when a committee member made a mistake in reading off a weight. And there was usually a loud murmur of speculation when someone delivered pods suspected of having been stolen, especially when the seller was known to have planted no vanilla of his own.

The Ateans' treatment of the Chinese buyers was conditioned in part by their attitude toward the latters' profits; that is, while the sellers were paid, say, only 225 francs per kilo for their undried pods ("which we worked so hard to produce"), the latter would receive about 1,250 francs per kilo for the cured pods ("which required nothing but time to dry"). Most of the growers acknowledged, grudgingly, that drying reduced the vanilla's weight to one-fourth, but complained, nevertheless, that the dryers' true profit, i.e., about 350 francs per kilo of dried pods, was unjustly large. But then, when I asked, "Why don't you dry it yourself?" the answer that usually came was to the effect that "Tahitians, as everyone knows, haven't the patience required for drying vanilla," i.e., at least three months of constant care, with all the restriction on movement that this would involve.

The Tahitian vanilla growers of Fatata also grumbled about the prices they received for their undried pods, but their complaints were directed against "the government" (*Te Hau*), which was accused of keeping the export price low in order to benefit the ultimate buyers in metropolitan France.

In Atea, vanilla-selling day was also a time for the settlement of debts and promises. Regarding the former, most of every grower's production would have been already obligated through charge-account purchases at the buyer's store. And, in cases where the sellers' revenues exceeded the debts owed to their buyers, some of the balance was sure to have been owed to kin or friends, which served to increase the interest of some of the onlookers in the sale.

Vanilla-selling day in Atea was also the time for discharging less commercial pledges, for example, for making contributions to the church or to one's parish sodality. Typically, all the vanilla-growing members would promise in advance to donate a specific amount of vanilla (not money) from the harvest of a certain month, and the buyer would either pay this directly to the donor-seller or to the donee institution in question. Occasionally, sellers waited until the sales day itself to announce the amount of their contributions, a gesture that was certain to elicit loud approval from the crowd and that was doubtless calculated to produce just such an effect.

Vanilla-selling day in Fatata was an altogether different kind of event. In the first place, only twelve of Fatata's Tahitian residents had pods for sale during the months of my visit in 1955. Several others were engaged in establishing or pollinating new plantings at that time but had not yet attained the harvesting state. The first sales I witnessed there took place at the store of the community's principal Chinese buyer and were attended only by the actual sellers and the buyer himself. Later, on instructions from the island's gendarme, the sale was held elsewhere at a more "neutral" spot. While there was some argument over price and some remarks about "Chinese tight-fistedness," it was accompanied by much less heat and anger. And while there was some interest shown in each seller's production, the mood of sportlike rivalry was muted and the air of festivity entirely absent. Moreover, the sales I observed in Fatata were not accompanied by donations and, according to informants, never were.

The sellers present at the Fatata sales I attended were all adult males, whereas Atea sales included several women and children. Some of these latter were selling the produce of their own vanilla patches, and the money they received was described as being their very own. In the case of a few of Atea's children, it was explained that while they had no vanilla patches of their own, they had, in fact, assisted in the planting, etc., of their parents' and were consequently receiving the rewards of such work.

The more neutral, commercial nature of the Fatata sales also came out in connection with the handling of the plaited coconut-leaf baskets in which the sellers delivered their vanilla pods and in which they were weighed. In Atea, the weights of these baskets were only roughly estimated; in Fatata, they were separately and carefully weighed. Finally, while the Atea sales were announced and recorded in *tārā* and in Tahitian, in Fatata they were done so in francs and in French.

Another way in which Fatata differed from Atea with respect to vanilla was in the activities of their respective Vanilla Committees. In Atea, the committee's only job was to supervise, etc., the sales that took place locally, which in 1954–55 comprised all of the locally produced crop; for this, the committee received five centimes for each kilo of green beans inspected. In Fatata, on the other hand, the committee received one franc for each kilo inspected and undertook to sell elsewhere all locally produced vanilla that was not sold locally. It happened only occasionally that the committee had to carry out this responsibility, but when it did, it required a trip to either a neighboring district or to Pape'ete. In return for performing this additional service to the seller, a committee member was paid a commission by the latter amounting to 10 percent of the sale price.

Turning to other facets of vanilla-growing, I could not discover precisely when this form of cash cropping began in either Atea or Fatata, but evidently it had had long and fluctuating histories in both.

It Atea, the memories of some individuals reached back to a time, said to be in the twenties, when "vanilla made everyone rich," a statement as imprecise as it was, undoubtedly, inaccurate. In any case, many Ateans recalled a time, said to have been in the forties, when local production exceeded thirty tonnes a year. In this connection, the statistic mostly remembered was not the *annual* production of thirty *tonnes,* but the size of the largest single *monthly* cutting and sale of fourteen *tonnes,* a telling example of Te Pitians' concern with concrete events rather than time-unit averages when discussing economic matters. From that high point on, however, it had been all downhill, and the production for 1954 totalled only 5,080 kilos (not including the amounts grown locally by nonresidents).

Various explanations were given for the decline, e.g., droughts, insect pests, plant disease, soil impoverishment, low prices, and, according to some moralists, laziness or irresponsibility on the part of some individuals to provide for the long-term security of their dependants. All these explanations contain some measure of truth. For several years prior to my visit, Society Islands vanilla had been afflicted with a root-rotting fungus and a stem-eating insect. Also, with continuous use and the lack of artificial fertilization, some of the local soils had, indeed, become impoverished, and the erratic fluctuations of vanilla prices would have confused and discouraged growers anywhere. As for "laziness," there undoubtedly were some Ateans who were "lazy" by standards anywhere, but there is no basis for believing that there were more of such individuals in 1954 than there were in the bumper years of the forties. "Irresponsibility" is a more complicated charge; it derived from Ateans' opinions about economic welfare and the nature and function of investment.

As mentioned earlier, some Ateans, mainly of middle age but a few younger ones as well, drew a sharp distinction between agricultural and other sources of money income, such as fishing and wage labor. Income from the former was *moni tāere* (slow money), from the latter, *moni 'oi'oi* (fast money). And when verbalizing that distinction, they would almost invariably add: " *'oi'oi roa'a*; *'oi'oi ha'apau*" (Quickly earned; quickly spent). Expanding on that theme, the critics of *moni 'oi'oi* usually referred to the plight of the offspring of men unwilling or unable to invest their energies in establishing or maintaining a source of long-term income, such as that provided by an agricultural cash crop. (The principal reference was usually to vanilla and coconuts, but cassava, coffee, cows, and pigs were included as well.) A few of the critics also spoke of the desirability of a man to provide, as well, for his own and his spouse's old age, but this appears to have been less of a preoccupation or, at least, it was a less conventional explanation than was the concern for offspring.

Even the most sententious of these moralists acknowledged sympathetically that some of their neighbors were unable to undertake cash-cropping either on account of infirmity or of lack of suitable land and absence of helpful kinfolk. But against all those other noncash-croppers with dependants, the charge of laziness or irresponsibility was levelled. And underlying this critical attitude was something more than endorsement of the general concept of investment; it represented a more specific, almost mystical, admiration for agriculture itself.

In any case, during the 1954 vanilla-harvesting season seventy-seven Ateans (35 percent of the 1954 population) sold a total of 4,772.6 kilos of green vanilla beans to the Chinese buyers at prices averaging 225 francs the kilo, a total of about 1,073,925 francs. The average sale per individual was 62 kilos, the smallest having been 0.9 kilo and the largest 380.7. A breakdown of sales figures is shown below:

Under 10 kilos	14 sellers
10 to 20 kilos	16 sellers
21 to 40 kilos	10 sellers
41 to 60 kilos	7 sellers
61 to 90 kilos	11 sellers
over 90 kilos	19 sellers

Some of those selling less than 10 kilos were the wives or children of larger producers; and the beans they sold were, in most instances, the shares they had received as a result of the labor they had contributed in pollination and harvesting.[11]

---

[11]This arrangement accounts for the discrepancy between numbers of growers (who totalled seventy, as reported above) and sellers.

In addition to the above, during 1954, Atean growers turned over a total of 309.5 kilos of green beans to the account of the parish as part of their annual church contributions.

Turning to Moʻorea, vanilla growing became very widespread at the turn of the century, and it is likely that Fatata shared in the industry at that time, as well as in the peak prosperity it experienced around 1914, when some of Fatata's large colonial-style "vanilla houses" appear to have been built. Subsequently, however, Fatatans turned more to copra production and fishing as sources of money, so that in 1954 only twenty-two of the residents sold any vanilla at all. In addition, several other Tahitians living elsewhere in the Toerau District produced and sold vanilla, as did several Chinese renters or sharecroppers living within the district.

The twenty-two sellers of 1954[12] sold a total of 552.8 kilos of green beans, or an average of 25 kilos per seller, and at an average price of 250 francs per kilo. These sales ranged in size from 1.7 to 149.7 kilos for the whole year and were distributed as follows:

Under 10 kilos	9 sellers
10 to 20 kilos	6 sellers
21 to 40 kilos	2 sellers
41 to 60 kilos	4 sellers
61 to 90 kilos	0 sellers
over 90 kilos	1 seller

In Fatata, no children offered any vanilla for sale, and only three females did so, all of them widows (as compared with twenty-one female Atean sellers, seventeen of whom were living in marital unions).

The reasons given for Fatata's decline in vanilla production were the same as those advanced in Atea, namely, plant disease, insect pests, soil impoverishment, "laziness," and peoples' preference for "quick-money" jobs as reputable sources of income.

Summarizing the above, the total amount of green vanilla sold for cash or against debts by Ateans in 1954 brought a price of about 1,074,000 francs as against 138,000 francs by Fatatans. This was in addition to 3,095 kilos, worth about 70,000 francs, the Ateans turned over to their parish during this period, bringing the total revenue to 1,144,000 francs. Also, as the previous figures on sellers reveal, 35 percent of Atea's 222 residents of 1954 took significant parts in the selling and hence production of vanilla, as compared with only 6 percent of Fatata's. The figures on sellers also reveal large differences between Atea and Fatata in overall amounts grown and in the relative amounts sold by each seller, e.g., only one of Fatata's twenty-two

---

[12]See footnote 11.

sellers sold more than 60 kilos, while thirty, i.e., 39 percent, of Atea's seventy-seven sellers did so.

On the other hand, the figures on sales, just given, do not signify that the sellers themselves disposed of all the money received, or even that the proceeds of the sales remained in Atea or Fatata. As noted above, some growers were obliged to pay about 10 percent of their sales revenues to their land co-owners for the use of larger-than-average portions of co-owned land; this was the case with six growers in Fatata, but only one in Atea. In addition, eight of Fatata's seventeen growers, compared with only one of Atea's seventy, grew vanilla on leased land per se, for which they were obliged to pay rents of about 20 percent of their net profits. The Atean in question rented his land from an outside owner, as did four of the eight Fatatans, hence part of the revenues of these growers went elsewhere. On the other hand, five Atea sharecroppers, as against none in Fatata, worked under the lease arrangement that obliged them to pay one-half of their profits to their landlords, all of whom were outsiders. I did not obtain exact figures on all these cases; but averaging from those for which I did, I estimate that 150,000 francs of Ateans' revenues from vanilla growing was paid to outside landlords as against about 17,000 francs of Fatatans'.

Putting these 1954 figures together, the Ateans produced vanilla amounting to 1,144,000 francs (including 70,000 francs worth contributed directly to their parish) from which they paid rents totalling about 150,000 francs. This works out to a per capita "profit" (sales revenue minus rent) of 4,477 francs, which may be compared with the corresponding Fatata figure.

Kapok. Several varieties of "silk cotton" (*Gossypium; vavai*) grow throughout the Society Islands. The pods ripen and burst open annually during September and October, and their silky fibers may be carded and used as fillers for mattresses and pillows.

Kapok trees grew in abundance in Te Piti, enough to provide for all local requirements plus some for export. In fact, most of the fallen pods were allowed to rot on the ground since carding was considered by many Te Pitians to be a tedious and financially unrewarding job. During 1954–55, however, some residents of both villages processed kapok for export, which was marketed by selling it to the local Chinese storekeepers, who then shipped it to Pape'ete. The current price was 12.5 to 15 francs a kilo, a decline from the previous year's 20 francs.

Fatata contained a very large number of kapok trees, many more than Atea, but produced a far smaller amount of carded fibers for sale. In fact, during my visits to Fatata, several residents purchased imported ready-made pillows (something which no Atean did), despite there having been kapok pods going to waste in their own yards.

In Atea, thirty-seven persons sold a total of 4,950 kilos of carded kapok in 1954 for a total revenue of 68,685 francs. Individual sales ranged from 14 kilos to 708 and were distributed as follows:

Under 50 kilos	14 sellers
50 to 99 kilos	15 sellers
100 to 199 kilos	11 sellers
200 and over kilos	7 sellers

In Fatata, only a handful of individuals reported income from this source and none of these could or would recall how much he or she had earned, saying that the amount was "too small to recall." This was confirmed by the local Chinese buyers, who provided their usual explanation, that "Fatatans are too lazy to process kapok."

In Atea, kapok collection and carding for sale was carried out mainly by elderly individuals, male and female, who had few other sources of money income. There were also several individuals of this type in Fatata, but there the work of carding was evidently considered too tedious and unrewarding, even by these.

I did not make systematic observations or inquiries about kapok carding, but in the one instance I witnessed, an elderly neighbor of mine worked at it for eighteen hours to produce about 8 kilos, which sold for 104 francs, yielding a labor rate of about 5.8 francs an hour as compared with the standard Atea rate for unskilled labor of about 12.5.

An interesting sidelight on the Atea sales was provided by the situation wherein one of the storekeepers paid a lower price than the other; nevertheless, about half of the Atean kapok sellers sold all of their product to him, and three of them sold to both. This, of course, exemplifies the circumstances that many Ateans used their production of kapok, as they did copra and vanilla, towards paying off store debts. It would have been possible for such persons to sell their kapok to the 15-francs buyer and then use the proceeds toward settling their debts with the other buyer, but it evidently occurred to no one to do that.

Coffee. There were enough coffee plants growing in both Atea and Fatata to satisfy all of the residents' own, rather heavy, demands (an average of about one kilo of dried beans per person per month) and for export as well. As mentioned earlier, many households produced their own beans; the others obtained their supply by "gift" or by purchase from fellow villagers.[13]

---

[13]A few households occasionally purchased roasted coffee in Pape'ete or Fare, but more for novelty and labor-saving than for better flavor, the local products having been satisfactory to most tastes (including my own).

(Coffee was not included in the popular rule against selling vegetable foods to other Tahitians, and the prices asked from neighbors tended to be the same as those then obtaining for beans sold for export.) I did not record the quantities of coffee that circulated locally among Te Pitians or the revenues earned from this commerce; with a few exceptions, my efforts to do so produced either patently invented figures or amusement that anyone could be interested in such trivia.

Earnings from exports were another matter. Not only did the sellers recall how much they had sold, but many of them were accurately, and indignantly, acquainted with the wide and frequent price changes that seemed to characterize the coffee bean market. Moreover, some sellers, typically the larger Fatatan producers, deliberately delayed selling for a few weeks at a time, awaiting higher prices.

Fatata contained many more productive coffee trees than Atea; I did not make a systematic count but gained the impression that the ratio was about four to one. During 1954, Fatata also surpassed Atea by far in volume of coffee exports; and from the scattered evidence I collected, this had been the case for many years. In Atea that year, only seven persons sold beans for export, the total amount having been 360 kilos (at an average sales price of 75 francs per kilo); the largest individual quantity sold was 68 kilos. In contrast, during that same year, some twenty-two Fatatans sold beans for revenues totalling about 96,700 francs; at the prevailing prices, this represented a volume of about 7,440 kilos.

Fatata's largest producer was the pastor, who employed helpers, all females, to pick the beans at 120 to 150 francs a day, according to quantities picked. Males expressed amazement at this pay, the highest rate paid locally for female labor, but disdained the employment as being too boring for them.

Coffee bean pulping in both villages was done by males and in hand-cranked machines supplied gratis by the Administration which, however, received no acknowledgment for this service to subsistence and money earning, except complaints when the machines broke down.

Vegetables.

> No Tahitian would sell *mā'a* [vegetable staple] to another Tahitian; that would be a shameful thing to do. If someone is hungry and without *mā'a*, anyone with *mā'a* would give him some [free]. That's the way Tahitians behave.

Such was the standard answer to my queries on this matter. And, when I pressed with the further question: "But perhaps the donor would expect to be repaid at some future time, if not with money then with some other object or service?" The usual answer was, "No; no Tahitian wants anything in return for *mā'a*. He would be ashamed (*ha'amā*)."

And so it usually was, at least with respect to breadfruit. On the other hand, some Tahitians regularly sold cassava flour to other local Tahitians, and some even sold *Xanthosoma* (*taruā*), sweet potatoes, and yams. The common procedure, and the only one in Atea, was for the producer to sell to the Chinese storekeeper, who would then sell to Tahitian buyers (at a markup price of about 20 percent)[14]—thereby (and deliberately) preserving the convention that "No Tahitian sells *mā'a* to another Tahitian." Some farmers in Fatata also followed this procedure, but others there sold directly to other Fatatans, who, it will be recalled, included many individuals who grew no root crops at all. Notwithstanding this, Fatatans were no less definite, verbally, than Ateans about the impropriety of such sales. The statistics I managed to collect on this activity are spotty and unreliable.

For Atea, seventeen persons reported to me that they had sold vegetables during 1954; and in all cases, they said, to the storekeepers (for what ultimate disposal, they said, they did not know!). Those reporting (and there were probably others who did not wish me to know about their traffic in this slightly "un-Tahitian" business) reported 1954 incomes of from 150 to 4,000 francs from this source. On the other hand, the storekeeper-buyers stated that they themselves bought, altogether, no more than about 5,000 francs' worth during the entire year; thus, either the sellers and/or buyers were incorrect in their figures, or some of the sellers had sold directly to other Tahitians.

For Fatata, only seven Tahitians reported selling any vegetables (other than cassava) during 1954, and some of these reported receiving from 5,000 to 10,000 francs from this source—figures too suspiciously rounded for credibility. The storekeepers themselves claimed that they kept no records of their purchases, but since their store bins nearly always contained such wares, mainly *taruā*, and since many Fatatan households grew no vegetables of their own, the commerce in these staples must have been more active and voluminous than reported (certainly much more so than in Atea). How much more so I can only guess, namely, that they sold about 40,000 francs' worth to the Chinese storekeepers (who kept some for themselves and sold the rest to the local Tahitians), and another 20,000 francs' worth directly to other Fatatan Tahitians.

---

[14]Evidently, the fact that their neighbors had to pay extra for such vegetables (an extra amount that went to the storekeeper!) was, ethically, less objectionable than selling directly to other Tahitians—or so my informants rather sheepishly admitted when I pointed out the realities of such transactions.

Fruit. Bananas (*hamoa* [Samoa]), lemons (*tāporo*), oranges (*'ānani*), grapefruit (Fr. *pamplemousse*; *'ānani popa'ā*), etc., circulated among Ateans and Fatatans, and usually without pay; but, in addition, one or two Ateans and several Fatatans sold some fruit to Uturoa or Pape'ete. The eating bananas and grapefruit thus marketed, and some of the lemons, came from the sellers' own trees; the other lemons came from a plantation near Fatata whose owner permitted them to be collected, for a token payment, out of sympathy for the collectors' poverty. And the oranges were collected in the trackless mountains, a feat of strength and climbing ability locally much admired. In addition, one elderly woman of Fatata used to collect nuts of the *'ati* tree (also called *tāmanu*; *Calophyllum inophyllum* L.) in her "spare" time for sale in Pape'ete at 25 francs per kilo, equal to about 400 nuts and the work of about six to eight hours, an occupation that no other Fatatan, however, poor, considered profitable enough to engage in.

As for how much income was derived from all these marginal and occasional money-earning activities, I can only venture a guess—a guess based on the mental memories, most of them obviously vague, of some of the collectors (who also regarded this form of money earning as minor and incidental). The guess is that the profits derived from all of these activities for 1954, i.e., sale price minus transport and cost (if any), would have been no more than 2,000 francs for Atea and at least 20,000 francs for Fatata.

During my 1955 visit to Fatata, a few individuals were beginning to grow pineapples (mainly for the Pape'ete market), but only one of the growers reported any 1954 income from this source, and that was about 5,000 francs.

Cassava. As noted earlier in Chapter II, several individuals in Te Piti grew this starch-rich vegetable for sale as well as for their own household consumption, and most of the purchasers were their local Tahitian neighbors—who either grew none themselves or required, on festive occasions, more than they themselves produced. Unlike most other food crops, cassava was not classified as one that "no Tahitian would sell to another Tahitian." In Atea, I was given the names of nine persons who "occasionally" sold cassava to fellow Ateans; most of these whom I questioned recalled having received amounts that averaged about 350 francs during 1954 from this source. In Fatata, only eight persons had made a practice of selling cassava locally, but their revenues from this source averaged about 600 francs a year.

In addition, one individual in each village regularly produced much larger amounts of cassava for sale in Pape'ete. In both cases, the producers were the local Protestant pastors, and, to the amusement of their more cynical neighbors, the purchaser, in both cases, was the brewer of Pape'ete's famous Hinano beer. During a typical year, Atea's pastor exported to

Pape'ete about 4,000 francs' worth of cassava, and Fatata's pastor about twice as much. In both cases, the labor used in processing the starch was "free," having been supplied by fellow householders in Fatata and by fellow householders and "volunteer" parishioners in Atea.

Cutting Firewood

The firewood used by the Chinese storekeepers of Te Piti for baking bread was supplied by local Tahitians on a contract basis for 100 francs a cord, i.e., a pile two meters long, one meter wide and one meter high. The wood—acacia, hibiscus, guava, etc.—was cut in two-meter lengths and delivered to the buyer in bundles. A hard worker was capable of cutting up to one and a half cords a day, thereby earning up to 150 francs.

The only figures I was able to obtain on this form of money earning came from some of the woodcutters themselves; the Administration collected no records on this activity nor did the buyers. When wood was supplied to the latter, they simply checked off its value against the suppliers' store debts or, less commonly, paid them in cash.

In Fatata, there were six men who regularly supplied the storekeepers with firewood. When questioned, none of these was able (or willing?) to estimate his total earnings from this source, but all of them asserted that it was "not much," and that it was very hard work, which they undertook because they were otherwise "very poor," as they owned little or no coconut- or vanilla-growing land and were not successful fishermen. Some of them cut their wood from other people's land, but only one of these reported paying the landowner for it; in his case, 5 francs a bundle, or 5 percent of the price received from the Chinese buyer.

Firewood cutting in Atea was engaged in by many more individuals. Nearly every youth and adult male queried reported doing so at some time. And although it was regarded there too as being hard work, it was also said to have the merit of "costing nothing," as the growing trees required no money investment. A few men had verbal contracts to supply the stores with firewood on what was said to have been a regular basis, but since these particular suppliers were evidently less productive than the demand, the storekeeper buyers were nearly always eager for additional supplies, which they obtained from casual suppliers. Some of these latter worked individually, in response to their own immediate cash needs, while some of this additional wood was supplied by work groups working for common or shared purposes.

The only record I was able to obtain on Atean firewood income came from the eight individuals who had kept written tallies of this source of their incomes. Of these, the smallest earnings for 1954 was 250 francs, the largest about 5,000, and the average about 1,650.

As far as I could discover, no Te Pitian female engaged in firewood cutting, which was described as being both "too difficult" for them to manage, and, in any case, inappropriate for females. ("Inappropriate" it surely was, but many females I knew there were physically capable of both cutting the wood and carrying the bundles.)

Raising Livestock

Nearly all the pigs raised by the residents of Atea were consumed locally. Most of them were eaten either by the families that raised them or by those that purchased them from the farmer in order to celebrate some special occasion or to fete a guest. A few other locally raised pigs were eaten by the Chinese storekeepers, who bought them regularly to accompany their everyday meals. In those transactions I knew about, the going price was six *tārā* (30 francs) when sold to a fellow Tahitian, six and a half (32.5 francs) when sold to a local Chinese storekeeper. Occasionally, an owner took one of his animals along when traveling to Pape'ete, but usually for the purpose of giving it to some kinsmen there, either as a "gift" or in return for bed and board. Altogether in 1954, Ateans sold pigs worth about 24,000 francs to "outsiders" and about double that amount to other Ateans.

The only Atean who regularly sold cattle locally did so once a year, when he slaughtered an animal and sold shares in its meat to other Ateans for their New Year feast meal. In 1954, the price was 30 francs a pound, the same as the price for pork. A few other Ateans occasionally sold an animal to the Fare Chinese from the herds that grazed their coconut groves.

Fatatan pig owners also sold some of their animals locally, but most of their sales were to Pape'ete buyers, mainly Chinese. As far as I could discover, all cattle sold by Fatatans were bought by Pape'ete Chinese. In the case of both pigs and cattle, the buyers were in the habit of visiting Fatata when needing meat. When there, they sought out the known livestock raisers and arranged the purchases; the animals were subsequently freighted to Pape'ete at an agreed-upon time.

During my 1955 visit to Fatata, cattle buying had slowed considerably and the price offered, 40 francs a kilo, was 10 to 20 less than the previous rate, a result, people complained, of Pape'ete's having become surfeited with cheaper New Zealand beef, a situation that "the government ought not to permit." In fact, buying by brokers from Pape'ete had fallen off so sharply that some Fatatans were "considering" taking both their pigs and cattle into Pape'ete for sale. But since this would have cost an additional one franc per kilo in freight, plus the owner's own fares, and a market tax of 10 to 40 francs per animal, depending on its size, no one actually did so while I was there.

Fatata's leading cattleman maintained a herd of around forty animals; he attempted to dispose of all in excess of that number, holding that his land could not support more. Cattle raising was his principal source of income, and he was diligent about learning and using scientific practices in his work. Among his fairly healthy-looking herd were many Holsteins, but none of his cows was milked. According to his explanation, Tahitians "don't know how to milk," and in any case, "few of them like to drink milk, which is infants' food." His 1954 income from this source was reported to have been about 45,000 francs.

Comparing Atea with Fatata, relatively more residents of the former owned cattle, but those of the latter who did so possessed larger herds and sold more of their animals. In fact, in addition to the Fatatan who made cattle raising his principal occupation, the five other Fatatans who reported having sold cattle during 1954 received a total of 120,000 francs for them. In contrast, the Ateans' total income from cattle sales during 1954 amounted to only about 20,000 francs, one-fourth of which came from local sales.

In the case of pigs, relatively more Ateans owned them than did the Fatatans, and individual household herds were, on the average, somewhat larger (about four animals to three). On the other hand, more Fatatans than Ateans made a regular business of raising pigs for sale as against consuming them at home and, during 1954, received a total of about 300,000 francs from this source, 210,000 from "outsiders" and the remainder from other Fatatans.

As noted earlier, about two-thirds of the households of each village kept chickens, but the individual flocks of Fatata averaged about three times the size of Atea's (twenty chickens to six). Moreover, while Ateans disposed of few of their chickens or eggs by sale, and that to the local Chinese, for a total of about 2,500 francs, the thirteen Fatatan households that reported income from this source received a total of 11,600 francs for their chickens and eggs, which were sold partly locally, to the Chinese and to fellow Fatatans, and partly in Pape'ete. Most of this money went to the households' women, who were the ones mainly engaged in feeding the chickens and collecting the eggs.

Thus, in all three phases of livestock production, Fatatans went in for more individual specialization and commercialization than Ateans and obtained more money, both totally and per capita, for their produce.

Fishing for Money

Four Atean men fished "commercially," but only one of these did so with any regularity. He did so alone and by trolling in an outboard-motor-driven boat. Sometimes he made large hauls, sometimes he caught nothing.

Atea: Roughing out a canoe hull

Making coconut leaf thatching

Atea: Rethatching a roof

Atea: After rethatching comes the reward

Over the months during which I recorded his fishing, he earned only enough profits by sales (to Ateans) to permit him an occasional alcoholic fling, his subsistence needs having been met by money earned from canoe making and the sale of a little copra.

Atea's demand for fresh fish was substantially greater than its own residents were able to supply through their small-scale, largely individual, fishing activities. The difference was made up by purchase from sellers residing in other Huahine villages. When conditions in the eastern and southern Huahine waters were favorable, fishermen from these neighboring places went out in their motor-powered boats with nets or lines and caught quantities of fish, which they then peddled from village to village. The arrival of one of their boats at Atea's pier was announced with conch trumpet, and the sellers nearly always found local buyers for fifty or more kilos of fish. Thus, although it could not match Pape'ete in scale, Huahine Island did provide a market for some commercial fishing; however, few Ateans made any effort to supply that market, and those only irregularly.

In sharp contrast to Atea, the fishermen of Fatata not only supplied all local requirements for fresh fish but were a major source of supply for the Pape'ete market as well.

Over half the households in Fatata were supplied with all their fresh fish by their own members, fishing individually or as members of crews. All other households obtained their fresh fish from other local fishermen either in the form of "gifts," or regular barter arrangements, or purchase.

In Fatata, the traffic in fish "gifts" took place most frequently between close relatives, e.g., from a man to his parents or parents-in-law, but also occurred between friends and neighbors. The aged or infirm, whether kin or not, were regularly supplied with fish by neighbors, out of *aroha*.

A few fishermen maintained regular barter arrangements with non-fishermen, whereby they supplied the latter with fish once or twice a week in return for root crops and other vegetables or occasional labor as part of a fishing crew. These transactions typically occurred between neighbors who were also friends, but, in some cases, they involved close kinsmen, including siblings. I was assured most emphatically that bookkeeping was not involved in these understandings but recorded some instances in which such arrangements had lapsed because of insufficient returns from the nonfishing partner.

Local sale of fish in Fatata took place in two ways. Sometimes a householder desiring fresh fish for that day's main meal would approach a neighbor known to be going fishing and bespeak a certain part of the catch, for cash or credit. Or, occasionally, a fisherman whose catch was more than he could dispose of by household consumption or by other fixed arrangements but less than would warrant a shipment to Pape'ete peddled his surplus up and down the community's main street, or, rather, deputized a child or two to do so. When even this method did not succeed in disposing of all of it, what was left was thrown away; indeed, by that time, the remaining fish was usually past its prime.

Some of the above kinds of intravillage arrangements prevailed also in Atea, although in fewer numbers of cases and on a much smaller scale. In Atea, however, I heard of no recent instance in which a local fisherman (other than the "commercial" fisherman mentioned above) was reduced to peddling his surplus catch.

By far, most of the fish caught by the Fatatans that was surplus to their own households' consumption was sent to the Pape'ete market, and virtually all fixed-net fishing was carried out with that end in view. Having already discussed the technical and organizational aspects of such fishing, it now remains to describe the procedures followed in marketing such fish and the economics of the activity as a whole.

The Pape'ete marketplace, a huge open-sided, iron-roofed shed furnished with tables for display of all kinds of fresh produce, was crowded with people every morning from its opening, about five o'clock, until midmorning. Tahiti's remarkable buses—remarkable for their limitless capacity in terms of human bodies and freight—converged on the market place from all parts of the island, jammed with people and piled high with produce, and then returned to their distant terminals bearing the same people, and, what often seemed to be, the same kinds of produce, plus fish, which Tahiti's fishermen rarely seemed to be able to catch enough of to satisfy demand. Pape'ete's fleet of open-sea, troll-line boats appeared able to satisfy local demand for tuna and bonito most of the time (Anderson 1963, Ottino 1965), but other kinds of fish in local demand were supplied by fishermen operating along the coasts of Tahiti, Mo'orea and (occasionally) Mai'ao. Fish was sold at the market every day of the week, but the greatest demand occurred on Fridays and Sundays, the latter especially since that was the day when the market drew the largest crowds.

Accordingly, Thursdays and Saturdays were the most active fishing days of the week for Fatata's fishermen, unless the waters of all accessible fishing sites were too rough. In this connection, while there were winds that made fishing conditions unfavorable along Mo'orea's northern and western coasts, there were others that affected one coast but not the other. Thus, when Tahiti's customary fishing waters were too rough but most of Mo'orea's west coast still feasible, many of Fatata's fishermen proceeded to the calmer areas by boat or truck.

Fish was transported from Fatata to Pape'ete by launch. Prior to my visit, four locally-owned boats were engaged in this traffic, but they were subsequently withdrawn and the job was taken over by a larger, more seaworthy, more comfortable nonlocally owned launch that plied daily between Fatata and Pape'ete, a trip that required about three hours each way. When a load of fish was to be transported, the launch made an extra trip, leaving Fatata about midnight so as to arrive in Pape'ete in time for the market's opening. The standard charge for transporting fish on this launch was ten francs per *tui,* a *tui* being a string of fish averaging 5 to 10 kilos in weight.[15]

Some men accompanied their own fish to market and sold them there, either directly or through a broker; others commissioned a fellow Fatatan, or the launch's captain, to dispose of the catch by payment of a commission that averaged 100 francs plus breakfast in Pape'ete. The two Fatatans who were considered experts in this trade made a practice of accompanying any fish shipment, and undertook three to four commissions each trip. Perhaps using the facilities provided by the Pape'ete market to sell their wares paid a small fee to the municipal administration; in the case of fish, this amounted to 2 francs 50 centimes the *tui.*

The prices fetched in the Pape'ete market varied somewhat with the species of fish. In addition, prices fluctuated widely over time, mainly as a result of changes in volume of supply. For example, when supplies were short, the most highly favored species of fish brought 100 francs the string, a price which Fatata's fishermen considered very good. At other times, when Tahiti's fishermen brought in large catches, the Fatatans had to dispose of their catches for prices as low as 25 to 30 francs the string, and occasionally they were unable to sell all their fish at any price and had to throw some away. At such times the frustrated sellers were usually able to persuade the boat owner or agent to reduce the price of transport. It was this kind of situation, coupled with chronic motor troubles, that resulted in the withdrawal of the four locally owned boats from the fish-transport trade. After a series of low-price episodes, the boat owners who had not reduced their charges lost their customers out of disgruntlement, and those who had reduced their charges received too little revenue to induce them to maintain their boats and motors sufficiently to continue in the business.

---

[15]Unlike such cash crops as copra, vanilla, coffee, and cassava (which were carefully weighed when sold), the smaller lagoon and reef fish that made up most of Fatata's catches were sold by the string (*tui i'a*), which varied considerably in weight, from season to season and year to year. During 1954–55, the *tui* that I measured averaged 5 to 10 kilos in weight, a figure also confirmed by an anthropologist who made a study of Tahitian pelagic fishing and of marketing fish in general (Eugene Anderson, personal communication). For detailed descriptions of this and other aspects of modern Tahitian commercial fishing, see Eugene Anderson, "Tahitian Bonito Fishing," *Kroeber Anthropological Society Publication* No. 28, Spring 1963, and Paul Ottino, *"La Pêche au Grand Filet ('Upe'a Rahi) à Tahiti."* (Ottino 1965).

As mentioned earlier, some of Fatata's commercial fishermen endeavored to anticipate Pape'ete market conditions by keeping themselves informed about each day's prices and about weather conditions at Tahiti's principal fishing grounds. Weather conditions were not always stable enough, or predictable enough, to permit price forecast two or more days in advance, the lead time required for a large-scale fishing expedition. Hence, the returns obtained by Fatata's fishermen from single operations ranged from high profits to net loss.

In this connection, the results of a marketing mission were clearly visible in the behavior of the returning fishsellers as they disembarked from the boat bringing them home from Pape'ete. If some of them staggered from too much wine or beer or were loaded down with purchases from Pape'ete's stores, it could be assumed that the mission had been a financial success. If, on the other hand, they wandered homewards empty-handed and relatively sober, their neighbors knew that the trip had been a loss. A Sunday morning return was especially dramatic in this sense. The road from the pier led directly by the church, from which the pastor himself joined the congregation in peering out the windows in order to gauge the homecomers' mood and hence the outcome of their trip.

An example of what the Fatatans themselves regarded as a highly successful fishing operation is provided by the following case.

On one Thursday morning in late July, a man I shall call Teahau sampled the wind, took a look at the lagoon, and decided to go fishing to take advantage of the situation of the large number of people still crowding Pape'ete for the final days of Bastille Day celebrations. After passing on the word to his four regular fishing helpers, he spent all of Thursday and Friday working on his nets and tinkering with his outboard motor. On Saturday morning, he and his four helpers, none of them close kinsmen, began their fishing, using his net and large canoe (and motor) and the smaller canoes of two of his helpers. By midafternoon and after four net operations, they had caught what all of them described as a very good haul. After a quick meal, bought by Teahau at the store, they spent the next few hours stringing the fish, totalling 202 *tui* in all. At midnight they loaded their catch onto the interisland launch (which also carried the catches of several other fishermen, working individually or in crews) and set out for Pape'ete. Teahau and all four of his crew went along in anticipation of a good sale, although the mission could have been carried out by any one of them alone or by someone else.

True to his forecast, all of Teahau's fish were sold and at an average price of 100 francs a string, a total of 20,200 francs. From this, he paid out the following:

Transport .... 2,010 francs
(because of the large size of the shipment, the launch captain
charged nothing for transporting Teahau, himself, and his crew)
Market Tax 505
Food 725
(Breakfast in Pape'ete and the previous afternoon's meal in
Fatata)
Total .... 3,250 francs

Deducting this from the proceeds left 16,950 francs. Of this, Teahau kept
half for himself and divided the other half equally among his four compan-
ions, 2,120 francs each.

Everyone involved considered this a successful, even memorable, operation, as indeed they should have, in view of the fact that the standard
wage for one day's labor on government projects or on plantations was 100
to 125 francs plus food.

Needless to say, profits of this magnitude were the exception. More commonly, an expedition's manager (and principal equipment owner) realized
a net profit of no more than 1,000 to 1,500 francs and his helpers not more
than 250 to 300 francs each; and, as mentioned earlier, some expeditions
had to sell their fish for less than the costs of transport and food. Nevertheless, the memory of an occasional windfall not only provided many men
with incentive enough to keep on fishing but imbued some of them with ir-
repressible enthusiasm for the financial possibilities of commercial fishing.
For, as in other types of money-earning activities, most Fatatans did not as-
sess economic returns by explicitly averaging their profits and losses over a
lengthy period of time. A series of unmitigated losses tended to cause them
to abandon fishing altogether in favor of some other more predictable
source of money. One or two windfalls, however, served to remove the memory of past failures for a while. In fact, only two of Fatata's five large-scale,
net-owning, and fairly persistent commercial fishermen kept year-round accounts of their operations. One was the Protestant pastor, who kept a written record of all of his income and expenses, including his varied and extensive agricultural ventures. Other Fatatans looked upon his profitable and
cost-controlled activities with mixed feelings. On the one hand, they mar-
velled at his entrepreneural shrewdness and financial success; on the other
hand, they considered his business preoccupations unbecoming in a pastor.
And they explained his economic attitudes and behavior as the result of his
having been born and raised in the Leeward Islands (in Ra'iatea, to be specific), where "most people are like that."

The second account-keeping commercial fisherman was a fine old man,
reportedly in his eighties but still active and vigorous. Unlike the pastor,

this man, whom I shall call Old Puai, pursued no economic activities other than fishing; even his vegetables he bought from neighbors or stores. He owned no land on Mo'orea and was not interested in acquiring any. Old Puai's fishing crew consisted largely of his "sons," all adopted, or the sons of these "sons." Throughout the favorable fishing months of the year, he fished two to three times a week and spent the remainder of his waking hours keeping his nets and boats in repair. He and his large household lived securely and comfortably off his profits, but, so far as I could learn, he had not managed to save any money more than that required for occasional purchase of a new net. In contrast to the pastor, he was universally and un-qualifiedly respected and praised for his success, which was explained as due not only to his Leeward Islands origin but to his part-American Negro an-cestry ("like Joe Lewis"), his father having been of that race.

I obtained figures from Old Puai and the pastor concerning the long-term economics of their commercial fishing, and from several other fish-ermen concerning the detailed economics of particular fishing operations (especially of large windfalls, and of memorable, or at least plausible re-cords of their fish sales) but for the remaining money-earning males of Fa-tata, I had to be content (as I hope the reader will be!) with the following indications of the part that fishing played in individual Fatatans' lives.

Thus, out of Fatata's 102 active money-earning males during the time of my 1955 visit, one of them earned all his money from commercial fishing; thirteen of them earned less than all but more than half of their money in this way; eighteen of them earned between a quarter and a half of their money in this way; forty of them earned up to one-quarter in this way; and thirty of them earned no money in this way. These figures do not, of course, provide exact parallel estimates of the amounts of time these individuals de-voted to commercial fishing, e.g., some of those earning about half of their income in fishing spent more or less than one-half of their money-earning time so engaged.

Fortunately, I can be somewhat more specific about the amounts of fish marketed in Pape'ete by Fatatans during 1954, because of the efficient re-cord keeping by the launch captains that carried most of the fish to market. The amount thus transported totalled about 17,000 strings (*tui*) of fish, plus small consignments of langoustes and crabs. As described earlier, the prices fetched in the Tahiti market varied between 25 to 100 francs a string (leav-ing out of account the occasional strings that were not sold). By reckoning the average profit of all fish transported to market to have been 50 francs, a conservatively low estimate, the total profits to the fishermen would have been about 850,000 francs, which, with the addition of profits derived from the sale of langoustes and crabs, would have come to at least 860,000 francs.

Turning to some other aspects of Fatata's commercial fishing, I mentioned earlier the attitude held by some residents about the relative merits of fishing and farming as sources of money income, i.e., the merits of fishing's "quick money" (*moni 'oi 'oi*) versus those of farming's slower but longer-lasting and allegedly more dependable returns. It would be convenient to conclude and report that "quick money" was generally held to be somehow "less respectable"; the distinction is, however, not quite so clearcut. As with most attempts to rank-order social values, and especially in societies undergoing rapid change (which is the case with Tahitian society), the researcher's question must include "*whose* values," it being highly unlikely that all residents' norms will be found to be alike. Differences in age and sex, at the very least, will be found nearly everywhere to differentiate people's norms; and in mid-century Tahiti, such variables as land ownership, education, religion, and politics—perhaps all interdependent to some degree—may have served to influence an individual's social values, including his relative evaluations of commercial farming and commercial fishing.

Regrettably, I did not investigate this matter systematically, but I did gain the impression that the more affluent, church-going, and politically conservative Fatatans considered commercial farming to have longer range rewards than commercial fishing, although some of them engaged in both. As for land ownership, the connection between that and occupation was all too clear; men without land suitable for vanilla or without groves of bearing coconut were almost obliged to engage in sharecropping or to seek "quick money," either by wage labor or commercial fishing. A few of the more enterprising of these had managed to save enough money to purchase full title, or long-term use rights, to land which they then proceeded to farm; but, for most landless men, the difficulty involved in taking that giant step kept them bound to the sharecropping or "quick-money" way.

The social differences between farming and fishing were embodied in some measure in Fatata's residential layout, the stream that divided the community physically having been something of a social boundary as well. East of it the "colonial vanilla" and "Pape'ete suburban" types of houses predominated, and most of these were set far apart and surrounded by spacious and generally well-tended lawns. In contrast, the houses west of the stream were predominantly of "grass shack" or "composite" styles in architecture and materials and were located much closer together. There were, it is true, a few "vanilla" houses in the western section, and a few unsubstantial shacks in the east, but the proportionate differences were as stated.

Similarly, several "easterners" engaged in commercial fishing and several "westerners" in commercial farming; however, the proportion of fishermen to farmers was higher in the west and all the half- to full-time fishermen resided there.

Thus, the visible facts revealed an association between occupation and neighborhood, and between neighborhood and, at least, architectural suggestions of differences in life-style. On the other hand, I encountered a great reluctance on the part of Fatatans to acknowledge these differences verbally or to generalize about their community in terms of social class. They talked at length about "class" differences on Tahiti Island and used terms like *ha'eha'a* (low, humble) and *teitei* (high, lofty) to describe specific behaviors of other Fatatans but seemed intent on maintaining the fiction (which I believe it was) that "we Fatatans are all true Tahitians, hence fraternally equal."

But, returning to fishing itself, what are the explanations for the very marked difference between Atea and Fatata with respect to the place of commercial fishing in their residents' lives?

To my untrained eye, the waters off Atea appeared as likely a haunt of fish as did those off Fatata; the Huahine lagoon was wider and generally deeper, but otherwise quite similar.[16] Some Ateans stated flatly that it contained few fish, others asserted the reverse; in any event, the more determined fishermen of nearby villages did manage fairly regularly to obtain large catches.

Nor could Ateans' disinterest in large-scale fishing be attributed mainly to lack of equipment or skills. When I arrived in Atea in 1954, there were two very large canoe hulls pulled up onto the shore and left to rot, all interest in preserving them evidently gone. They turned out to be souvenirs of a large-scale enterprise that had operated in Atea until about two years previously. It had been, I learned, a community-wide net-fishing project. The net had been 100 spans long and had been purchased with contributions from all of the community's adult residents. All the canoes used in the project, including the two large ones just mentioned, had been owned by individuals. The net required about thirty men to operate and as many more to man the canoes. "A grand sight," everyone agreed, "and a great deal of excitement and pleasure." Every household received some of the catch whatever its contribution had been in terms of equipment or labor. "It was a good custom; truly Tahitian."

Nevertheless, that "good custom" was eventually abandoned and the nets, still in good condition, sold to some residents of Taha'a Island. "Several poor catches" was the standard explanation for discontinuance of the project, but, based on my observation of other Atean events, I suspect that other factors were contributory. For one, despite many Ateans' pleasure in

---

[16]However, Fatata's shallower lagoon was better suited to fixed-net seining; and, as postulated earlier, the nearby break in Fatata's outer reef may have resulted in its lagoon having had more fish.

fishing, a meal or two of fish (which could be obtained with much less effort) was not reward enough to sustain interest in the day-long project after the novelty had worn thin. Also, while the initial euphoria produced by good company and excitement may have encouraged open-handed generosity for a while, I doubt that those who had contributed heavily in equipment and labor were content to share out the catches equally and indefinitely to persons who persisted in contributing little labor or equipment to the enterprise.

In the end, I suspect that the Ateans' smaller concern with commercial fishing, relative to that of the Fatatans, was due mainly to their lack of an accessible and generally receptive market. As mentioned earlier, there was, in fact, a steady market for fish in Atea itself and in other Huahine villages, a market that was supplied mainly by fishermen from nearby villages, but, compared with Pape'ete (and hence the whole island of Tahiti), the Huahine market was enough smaller and less dependable to discourage (or rather fail to encourage) Ateans from undertaking the costly move in equipment and effort that commercial fishing would have involved. The circumstance that more Ateans than Fatatans possessed substantive use-rights in cash-crop-producing land was probably also a factor in this differentiation, although some Fatatans without inherited or affinally acquired land-use rights did turn to measures other than fishing to supply themselves with cash incomes.

Craftwork

Another way some Te Pitians earned money was by fabricating objects, mainly thatch-plates and boats. A few women also made hats, dresses, bedspreads, and pillowcases for others, but usually as "gifts," or in return for services.

I described earlier the "commercial" thatch making of some Te Pitian women in organized thatch-making groups, or individually. In both cases, the products were disposed of locally.

In the case of those groups, the income received always went into their "treasury," to be used for some common purpose, such as the construction of a sodality meeting house or as a donation for some parish cause. In addition, some women regularly made thatching individually and sold it for cash. It was strongly emphasized to me that the money thus earned belonged solely to the sellers to use as they wished. In fact, although a few of these women spent all such incomes for clothes, dental plates, etc., for themselves, most of them used some of it for clothes and other items for their children, or for food and other household expenses.

Atea: A typical one-man canoe

Fatata: Anchoring the net for fishing

Fatata: Impounding netted fish into basket

Fatata: Drying nets

Some women working individually made thatching in advance of orders, but more typically, the regular thatch makers accumulated the fronds and then made the thatching in response to specific orders—"otherwise," they explained, "the thatching might rot before it was sold" (whereas, the implication was that if any of the fronds themselves were to rot the work of plaiting would not have been lost).

It will be recalled from Chapter II that an experienced thatch maker could plait from sixty to ninety units a day. During 1954–55, the standard prices for "commercial" thatching, i.e., that sold outside the context of co-operative group work, were 250 to 300 francs per hundred. This means that the expert completed thatching worth from 150 to 270 francs a day, which would be a relatively high return but for the fact that the figure does not include the labor spent in collecting and preparing the fronds for plaiting—an amount that would be undoubtedly large but impossibly difficult to calculate.

I was unable to collect comprehensive figures on the earnings of Te Piti's women engaged in making thatch-plates for sale. The male household heads I queried about this invariably expressed lack of knowledge: "That's her concern; not mine." A few women told me, with evident pride, of their earnings from the last sale or two, or their present accumulated savings from this source, but were unable to estimate their average yearly earning from this source.

Nevertheless, I am convinced that Atea's women, on the whole, were much more actively engaged in this work than were those of Fatata, both in terms of the numbers so occupied and in average output and income derived from it. And as a guess, I would venture that the latter made and sold at least 6,000 francs' worth per annum and the former about twice as much.

Almost every household in Te Piti had the use of one or more canoes for fishing or transport, or both. Also, many of Te Piti's men were capable of making and repairing canoes and did so for themselves, but only twelve in all were considered by themselves and their fellows to be experts, that is, skillful enough to be able to sell their services or their products to other Te Pitians (a criterion supplied by the Te Pitians themselves). Actually, the canoe-making experts sold only their *services,* on commission or wage basis; I know of no instance of an expert making a canoe and then putting it up for sale. (I did, however, record an instance of a man commissioning the making of canoes for sale in Pape'ete, of which more will be said later.)

When someone wanted a new canoe, he commissioned an expert to do it for him, specifying the desired length in terms of 'eta'eta (an adult's arm span) and the kind of wood desired for the hull. The price paid to the canoe maker was usually set at the start; informants stated that some canoe makers worked on a daily-wage basis at an average of 175 francs, but they could not provide an instance of this in recent years.

The commission charged by canoe makers varied according to the hardness and durability of the hull wood, the softer and thus more easily worked woods, e.g., kapok, costing about two-thirds the amount charged for working the harder woods such as breadfruit, *mara*, hibiscus, and mango.

In this connection, I tried in vain to learn why some experts charged more than others, no one having been willing to compare their skills. ("That's just their custom; one charges more, the others less.") And when I inquired why specific individuals had not dealt with X, who was more experienced, than with Y, who was less so, the invariable reply was *"feti'i"* (i.e., a kinsman).

Another aspect of pricing which I never succeeded in translating into "rational" economic terms was the attitude towards canoe length, or, more specifically, that towards the measurement unit called *'eta'eta*, armspan. The question first arose when I commissioned one of the experts to make a canoe for me. At the time, the price seemed relatively high to me, but in my concern not to antagonize a prospective informant (a predicament familiar to ethnographers everywhere), I agreed. However, shortly thereafter, when I complained mildly to another neighbor about that price, I was told: "Not really expensive; you'll get your money's worth because he [the canoe maker] has a very long span." Subsequently, I heard much talk about "long spans" and "short spans" and concluded that there must exist some consensus about how long non-long or non-short spans should be; however, I was never able to elicit a more precise definition. Now, this would not be surprising in some societies, but most Te Pitians were familiar with metric measurement, and many of them used meter measures for carpentry, etc. Nevertheless, when I asked why meter measures were not used for canoe measurements, the rather proud answer was, "Because *Tahitian* canoes are always measured in spans."

Te Piti's canoe makers, expert or not, all used the same kinds of tools—axe, adze, machete, and plane. They also used such store-purchased materials as metal nails and synthetic calking fibers; there was general agreement that the more traditional wooden nails and coconut-husk calking were more durable but required too much labor to manufacture. Sennit continued, as in pre-European times, to be used for attaching the outrigger, but that in most common use during my visits was made in the Austral Islands and sold in the Chinese stores. Sails were no longer in use but had been so in Atea as recently as about 1950.

The making of a canoe was a fairly leisurely occupation and usually attracted an onlooker or two, who sat around exchanging talk with the canoe maker and spelled him now and then with adzing. During the few occasions I watched a hull being shaped, no means of measurement were utilized other than the craftsman's eye.

In Atea, there were slightly more canoes per household than in Fatata (1.3 as against 1.1), but the average sizes of the latter were larger—in line with Fatata's focus on commercial fishing.

Canoe making was also a somewhat more exclusive and specialized money-earning occupation in Fatata than in Atea. In the latter place, there were eight individuals who were occasionally commissioned by others to build canoes, in Fatata only four. (Although I suspect that some other Fatatans were as competent in this craft as some of Atea's so-called specialists, there was wider acceptance in Fatata of the principle of specialization and hence perhaps higher standards applied to recognized expertise.)

During 1954, only seven canoes—all of soft woods—were manufactured on commission and the five canoe makers so employed—two in Atea and three in Fatata—received an average of 2,250 francs a canoe. Thus, it is clear that money income from this source was not sufficient to relieve the canoe makers of either village of the necessity of engaging in other kinds of money-earning occupations.

During my stay in Atea, the village's most expert carpenter (and not one of its regular canoe makers) was commissioned by another resident to build for him a small rectangular flat-bottom scow, to be used for hauling bulky items within the bay. For this the owner supplied the materials and paid the carpenter for his services at 150 francs a day. No one else assisted in this nontraditional work, and the boat's launching was not accompanied by prayer.

Working for Wages and Salaries

Te Pitians were accustomed to performing some kinds of service for one another without specific pay, such as hair trimming, babysitting, midwifing, and doctoring (both physical and "psychic"). That is to say, specific fees for such services were neither proffered nor expected at the time. Indeed, in one case I recorded, the offer of a fee was angrily declined. On the other hand, I suspect that, despite their disclaimers, the parties to some of these kinds of transactions may have regarded each of them as one of a series that should more or less balance over time. For example, when the elderly T. "developed" powers of divining supernatural causes of illness and of bringing about cures (a skill claimed by several elderly persons when, it would appear, they became too decrepit for more active occupations) he did not put a price on his services, but most of his patients kept him provided with food before and after the treatment—not, it was said, to "pay" for the treatment, but because of *aroha* for his decrepitude.

In contrast to the above, many of the services performed by Te Pitians for one another called explicitly for payment, in money or in kind. First to be described are those services performed for money; services paid for in kind are described elsewhere.

To begin with, it should be noted that the Te Pitians usually distinguished sharply between working for other Tahitian Te Pitians and working for the local Chinese. They expected payment for almost all services performed for the latter, whatever the service happened to be, including some kinds of jobs, e.g., child tending, carrying things to and from the pier, which they did without pay for other Tahitians. Some Te Pitians were in the full- or part-time employ of the local Chinese—drying and sorting vanilla, bread baking, or nursemaiding; for this, they received wages that averaged about 75 francs a day for girls and women. Rates for casual, short-term labor were higher for males, i.e., about 100 francs a day, but for females about the same as for long-term employment.

In addition to boat making described above, the kinds of money-paid work done by Te Pitians for other Tahitian Te Pitians consisted mainly of carpentering, transport, copra drying, and manual labor of several kinds.

Concerning specialized carpentry, each village contained one resident who was better skilled than the rest in this trade and who was occasionally called upon to do jobs on a day-by-day basis for other residents.[17] The pay received by Atea's resident carpenter was 150 francs a day; the Fatata one received 150 to 175. Evidently, neither of them was considered skillful enough for major construction jobs, because when such projects were undertaken, e.g., construction of a general meeting house and of a large cement-walled dwelling, professional builders from elsewhere were brought in to supervise the job. I was unable to learn precisely how much either of the local carpenters earned per annum as neither kept records, but, calculating from the projects they recalled having been employed at, it was probably about 15,000 francs for the Fatatan, 10,000 for the Atean.

During my 1954–55 visits, two Ateans owned boats that they used to transport people and goods between Atea and Fare. Prior to my visit to Fatata, four of its residents were similarly engaged in transport, carrying fishermen and their catch to Pape'ete, but outside competition and decrepit boat engines persuaded them to cease. The Atean boat owners had also to compete with outsiders in this traffic, as well as with one another, but managed to secure small but steady profits from it—or so they said. In fact, their manner of calculating profits provides insight into one form of Te Pitian economic bookkeeping—in this case, a form practiced by two of its most "business-minded" residents. Both of them claimed to have kept tallies of "net" profits from their transport business, i.e., the fares and freight fees

---

[17]In addition, both villages counted among its long-time residents two expert carpenters who plied their trade on Tahiti and returned home only occasionally.

received, less costs of fuel, until these incomes had totalled the original costs of their boats. After that, they ceased tallying such "profits" and considered that they were still doing well so long as the income from fares exceeded the costs of operating fuels by a hundred or so francs a week. Meanwhile, no account was taken, past or currently, of their boats' depreciation (which had been and continued to be very rapid) nor of the labor each man had expended, or continued to expend, in operating and maintaining the boats.

As described earlier in this chapter, some Atean copra-drying owners undertook the job of drying the green copra of their fellow villagers, i.e., of actually tending the drying and not merely leasing out the use of the dryer. I was unable to learn the exact amounts of money earned in this way but know them to have been small, infrequent, and limited almost entirely to Fatata. When obliged to use another's dryer for drying one's own copra, even Fatatans chose to rent use of the dryer and to oversee the drying themselves, rather than pay the dryer owners for that service.

Turning to other forms of money-earning labor, a few Te Pitians worked regularly and frequently for other Te Pitians, one instance having been the fishing crew employed by Old Puai, the seasoned Fatatan fisherman. While all the members of his own crew were Puai's foster children and grandchildren and members of his household, he invariably distributed part of his profits among the older ones of them. And even when he realized no profits from a catch, he paid his crew members for their labor: to spare them, he said, the necessity of seeking other sources of money (and to provide himself, it can be added, with a dependable and experienced crew.)[18]

The other kind of employment wherein Te Pitians worked regularly for their fellows was domestic service. In each village, there was one household that employed a local woman—in both cases a kinswoman—to assist in housework.

Several Te Pitians worked occasionally for Tahitian neighbors and in a variety of jobs, including fishnet repairing, gardening, coffee bean collecting, copra cutting, vanilla pollinating, and cassava processing. The standard wage for such work was 100 to 125 francs a day for males and 60 to 75 francs a day for females. The major exception to these standard wage rates applied to work done for Atea's pastor, who paid nothing or considerably less, on the tacit understanding that the laborers' smaller wages were compensated by the pastor's religious services to the village. When questioned

---

[18]Another instance of this kind was the job held by a Fatatan youth who worked full-time for his uncle in the latter's copra-making enterprises. In this case—the only one of its kind involving a Te Pitian "officially" working for another Te Pitian—the uncle-employer paid a registered wage, and its associated employer tax, in order to qualify the nephew to receive the Administration's Family Welfare Allowance (*Afata Aufaura'a a Tua Tamari'i*).

on the matter, some of the people so employed complained of the inequity; but, so long as relations with the pastor remained good, they continued to provide him with such labor. In sharp contrast, the pastor of Fatata scrupulously paid going rates for all extra household labor he employed, explaining that he considered it improper to take advantage of his pastoral position for personal economic gain. In fact, it is unlikely that any adult Fatatans not related to him by kin ties would have worked for him at less than the going rate, not necessarily because of personal dislike, but in tune with Fatata's more commercially minded social ambience.

None of the Te Pitians who engaged in this individual, casual labor for each other kept regular long-term records of their earnings, nor did their employees keep records of wages paid out. On the basis of my short-term and fairly representative sampling, however, I estimate that the average annual income of Ateans so engaged was about 2,500 francs, as against 4,500 of their counterparts in Fatata. Also, compared with the twelve or so Ateans who engaged fairly regularly in this kind of work, around twenty-five did so in Fatata.

One other feature of wage work that distinguished Atea from Fatata, and very sharply so, was the existence in the former of the "secular" house-thatching and general work groups already alluded to. There were five of the latter operating very actively in Atea during the first months of 1955, with memberships ranging from four men to eight. Their rules for cooperation were quite strict: if a member failed to turn up for a group job, he was required either to supply a suitable substitute or to pay a fine of 100 francs.

The custom of fining non-shows made sense in connection with work performed for each other on a reciprocal basis; its application to money-earning jobs done for others was perhaps less "rational" from a purely economic point of view but evidently helped hold such groups together and thereby postponed, for a time, the day when such groups would fall apart, which they inevitably did.[19]

There appears to have been some seasonality in the activities of the Atea "secular" work groups. They were particularly active from mid-January to mid-March during my 1954–55 visit, and I was informed that this was the climax of such activities during most years. This timing may have been influenced by some ecological factors (which, however, I was unable to fathom) but was in part determined, I am convinced, by the mood to replenish the money spent during the celebrations that attended New Year, when many Ateans became avowedly *"fiu"* (bored, fed up) with the long period of idleness and carousing.

---

[19]This purpose may have been in the minds of the groups' members but was never so expressed to me. For the men involved, it was simply a "Tahitian custom"—"The way we do things."

As to why so many Atean men chose to earn the needed money by working in such groups—a choice, it should be recalled, not made by men in Fatata—they were quite explicit: "It is more pleasurable to pool labor, and the jobs get done faster that way."

But not all of Atea's men chose to work in such groups. In fact, some of the older men were as cynical about such arrangements as were their Fatatan counterparts, and they usually traced their negative attitude to specific examples of inequities they had personally experienced in the past.

In addition to the above, several Te Pitians—all of Fatata—were regularly employed as semi-skilled, full- or part-time laborers at nearby European plantations, such opportunities not having been available to the Ateans. Also, one Fatatan woman was employed as laundress at a European plantation nearby, her wage having been reportedly 1,300 francs a month. Undoubtedly, others in Fatata, and many in Atea, would have undertaken such work had it been available, since everyone past childhood needed and wanted some money, and since opportunities for earning were limited in both villages. In fact, several Te Pitians did leave their home villages for months or years at a time for employment elsewhere, e.g., in Tahiti, Makatea, and New Caledonia; and while the reasons for these absences were not always or solely economic, the quest for money income was an influential factor in most of them.

Some resident Te Pitians also received regular salaries from outside sources, namely the schoolteachers, pastors, chiefs, and policemen of both villages, and Fatata's water reservoir inspector. Each pastor received 1,750 francs a month from the denomination's Pape'ete headquarters, along with free use of the parish parsonage, while the chiefs, policemen, and reservoir inspector received, respectively, about 2,250, 4,000, and 500 francs each month.[20] The work required of these officials will be described in Chapter VII; suffice it to say here that none of them worked full time at these official jobs, nor relied upon their salaries as sole sources of money income.

In 1954–55, Atea's sole schoolteacher was a native of and, in his own words, an "exile" from, Tahiti Island. As far as I could discover, he received from the Administration about 14,000 francs a month in salary and dependency allowances. Two of Fatata's three schoolteachers were long-time residents of the village, and widows with several dependents; the third was a European. In addition to their basic salaries, each of the two Tahitians

---

[20]These figures are approximations only. I was told by several persons, including the incumbents themselves, what they thought the basic salaries were, but the figures were not consistent, and the ones I list represent averages. Unlike some other kinds of money income, Te Pitians seemed reluctant to give out their fixed salaries in such jobs, possibly because of their fear of public criticism for what could be perceived as their lack of appropriate performance.

received substantial dependency allowances, bringing their total combined incomes to about 36,000 francs a month, making them the highest salaried residents in Te Piti.[21]

Also, it will be recalled, the government paid each village's copra committee two centimes for every kilo of copra approved by them. The vanilla committee was, on the other hand, paid its fees by the Chinese buyers.

During my 1954–55 visit, the government also provided Fatatans with incomes in the form of wages for installing a water pipe from the local reservoir to a neighboring village. Most of the local men still capable of sustained physical labor were employed in this project, which consisted mainly of ditch digging. The proximity of the job and the relative high wages paid for it, i.e., 110 francs a day for digging a length of ditch three meters long, which most men were able to do in less than five hours, made it very attractive to Fatatans and led several of them to clamor for more of such projects.

During 1954, thirty-three men worked on this project and earned a total of 457,045 francs (range: 10,430 to 41,460; average 13,850).[22] Most of the men employed in this project gave up or postponed other money-earning occupations while doing so. Thus, while the project was a one-time opportunity, and in this sense a windfall, its nonoccurrence would probably not have reduced Fatatans' money earnings very much. The attraction of the project was not that it provided the only, or the most revenue-producing opportunity at the time, but that it was, day to day, the least arduous way in sight for earning money—or so said several of its employees.

Work on the pipe-laying project continued into 1955 but in a desultory way, most of the Administration's allocation for it having been spent. This, of course, meant that only a few men were able to work it, which inevitably led those not chosen to accuse the *tāvana* (who supervised the project) with favoritism based on kin ties and politics.

The money-hungry men of Atea were also vocal about the lack of Administration-financed work projects in their district. One such was in the offing, namely, the completion of a reservoir for the village and installation of a water pipe; but little progress was made on it during my 1954–55 visit.

---

[21]I cannot vouch for the accuracy of these figures, but they represent a consensus of informants' views, not including those of the teachers themselves, who indicated that the matter was none of my business (which in a sense was quite true!).

[22]From the list given me by the District Council's clerk and paymaster, several workers appear to have been underpaid due to the latter's mistakes in multiplication, which, interestingly, none of the payees seems to have recognized. I pondered whether to point this out to the paymaster but decided in the end against doing so inasmuch as the 1954 budget had already been used up. Had any of the underpaid workers learned of the mistake, a minor revolution would undoubtedly have ensued.

For one thing, the Ateans declared themselves adamantly opposed to working on the project without pay, even though the Administration supplied the materials. The fact that the project was intended to provide them, and them alone, with running water was considered to be irrelevant.[23]

Now I shall attempt to summarize the amounts Te Pitians earned through their working, specifically, for money, and to compare Atea and Fatata in this respect.

As I have indicated, the information of this kind I was able to collect is spotty and meager, to say the least; there is, however, enough of it to point up some sharp differences between the two villages, not only in the amounts earned from various sources but in the ways in which they were earned. With regard to amounts, I can provide reliable figures for only one source of income, namely, the wages paid to the Fatatans for their work on the pipe-line project; all the other figures must be given in rough calculations or in impressionistic judgments about differences between the two villages with respect to certain sources of income.

Moreover, in order to keep these data consistent with those on money income from other sources, especially vanilla and copra, I have limited them to the calendar year 1954, only part of which I spent in Atea and none of which I spent in Fatata. This, of course, is based on the assumption that in most respects the money-earning activities were about the same, in type and scale, in both years. Shaky as it may appear, the assumption is in fact founded on some historical probings that lend credence to it. In any case, because of the marked seasonal variations in money-earning activities that obtained, use of the whole of 1954 as a time unit will provide a more accurate picture of Te Piti's economy than could be obtained by extrapolating from my shorter-term observations.—After which mountainous prologue I shall proceed with constructing a molehill out of the sparse information I was able to collect.

In Atea, only about four individuals worked regularly for the local Chinese, and those only part time. I estimate that these four earned a total of no more than 30,000 francs or an average of 7,500 each. In Fatata, three persons worked full time for the local Chinese storekeepers, earning an estimated annual income of 20,000 francs each, and six more worked part time, earning about 6,000 francs each. Neither of these figures includes the money earned by Te Pitians supplying the Chinese with firewood, which was discussed above.

Again, six resident Fatatans worked full time on nearby European-owned plantations, earning an average of 32,500 francs per annum. Another

---

[23]Needless to say, the Ateans' attitude was reinforced by the news they received about the Fatatan and similar Administration-financed public works projects.

thirteen Fatatans worked on those plantations as part-time regulars; I could not obtain specific figures on amounts earned by all these part-timers, but a sampling of them showed an average figure of 8,000 francs each per annum. In sharp contrast, no resident Atean was engaged in such regular outside work, either full- or part-time.

At the time I left Atea in March 1955, general-labor work groups were still going strong, so again I must revert to the calendar year 1954 to obtain some impression of the full amounts earned through such activities. By questioning a fair sample of the thirty-two individuals so engaged, I turned up only four who had kept written accounts of their earnings, but through them, and through several others who had kept mental tallies, I estimate that the full thirty-two work-group participants had earned a total of about 60,000 francs in this way, or an average of about 1,875 each. (This was in addition to the food and wine with which they had been compensated.) Except for those parts of these earnings that were received from the local Chinese storekeepers, all of this money came from other Ateans and did not, therefore, count as external in source.

These and other figures on money earned for services are summarized on Table 3D given below.

Table 3D. 1954 Money Incomes from Wages and Salaries (Francs)

"Outside" Sources	Atea	Fatata
Government:		
Salaries and Allowances	[243,000]*	[513,000]
Copra Inspection	854	1,037
Public Works	0	457,045
Protestant Church:		
Pastor's salaries	21,000	21,000
Local Chinese Storekeepers:		
Wages	[30,000]	[100,000]
Vanilla inspection	2,540	553
European Plantation (Wages)	0	[300,000]
Total	297,394	1,392,635
Per Capita	(1,340)	(4,180)

"Internal" Sources	Atea	Fatata
Domestic Wages	7,500	15,000
Transport	[10,000]	0
Carpentry	[10,000]	[15,000]
General Labor (Individual)	[30,000]	[112,500]
General Labor (Group)	[60,000]	0
Copra Drying	0	[2,000]
Total	117,500	144,500
Per Capita	(529)	(426)

*[] = Rough Approximation.

Leasing Property

Some Te Pitians obtained money by leasing property owned by themselves—boats, copra dryers, houses, land, and money itself. (Fatata's pastor owned an ancient truck which he used in agricultural enterprises and which he, very occasionally, rented out, although not during the period of my visits.)

The two boats in question were outboard, motor-propelled skiffs at Atea; their owners occasionally rented them to local residents for troll fishing or for transport. Only in Fatata was any money reportedly received from rental of copra dryers, the amount in 1954 having totalled about 3,000 francs. And the houses in question were rented to nonresident cinema film distributors, whose agents showed up once or twice a week to present their films. In Fatata, the "theaters" were designed and built especially for that purpose and were used only as such. In Atea, the one theater consisted of an ordinary dwelling, whose occupants periodically piled their possessions into a corner to make room for the filmgoers. The rent paid for such uses totalled about 6,000 francs in Atea and about 18,000 in Fatata.

There were a few houses in both villages owned by resident or nonresident Tahitians and occupied by local kinfolk or "friends" without rent. ("Why no rent?" "Because they were *feti'i*," or because the occupants were "taking care of" the house.) The house in Fatata occupied by the "outsider" (European) schoolteacher was owned by a local resident and brought a modest rent. In contrast, the house the ethnographer was privileged to occupy in 1955 added considerably to its owner's income, who, however, lived in Pape'ete. The house occupied by Atea's sole teacher, an "outsider" Tahitian from Tahiti, was owned by the Administration, having been donated for that purpose by its previous owner, Atea's current *tāvana*.

Land rental in Te Piti was of two kinds[24]—sharecropping and nine-year lease, both of which were described above.

During my visits, there were a few cases of local residents, in both villages, renting agricultural land (mainly for vanilla growing) on nine-year leases. Most of these cases involved outside owners, but a few Te Pitians also leased land to fellow villagers in this way.

Much more usual was the practice of sharecropping, whereby the land owner was paid a percentage of the sales revenue of the crop. During 1954, Atean landlords received about 58,400 francs in rent from other Ateans for use of their lands located in Atea—10,400 from land planted in coconuts and 48,000 for land planted in vanilla. In addition, during the same year Ateans received a total of about 2,500 francs from outsiders on crop lands located within Atea.

In comparison, during the same year Fatata's landlords received about 25,400 from their local resident tenants (20,400 on coconut land, 5,000 on vanilla land) and about 12,000 francs from outsiders on lands located within Fatata.

The sale of coconut harvest rights—a kind of "grove rental"—was engaged in in both villages, but more frequently in Fatata, where about 7,000 francs were reportedly received by local landlords in this kind of rent money during 1954. As far as I could discover, no such transactions took place in Atea during 1954, but people recalled instances of it in previous years.

The information collected about rent revenues received by Te Pitians from lands they owned elsewhere, i.e., revenues derived from share in crop profits, I suspect was not altogether reliable and was certainly incomplete, but it indicates that Ateans received about 8,000 francs from that source in 1954 and Fatatans about 19,000.

Only two Te Pitians, both of them in Fatata, reported having received interest during 1954 on money lent, i.e., to fellow villagers, one having received about 1,000 francs, the other 1,500. I suspect that there were more who had done so but who were ashamed to acknowledge profiting from the money difficulties of their Tahitian relatives and neighbors.

Finally, four Te Pitians, all in Fatata, received interest from savings accounts during 1954; I did not learn the exact figures but was informed, probably accurately, that the amounts were "very small."

---

[24]In addition, the owner of the Fatata land on which the local Football Club practiced and played was paid 300 francs per annum in rent, which, however, was supposed to be used for keeping the grass cut. And the owner of the Fatata land on which the Football Club had built one of the village's two theaters, which was leased to a film distributor, received 1,200 francs a year, being 10 percent of the rent paid to the club.

Table 3E. 1954 Income from Rent (in Francs)

	From "Outsiders"			
	Houses	Theater	Land	Money
Atea	0	6,000	10,500	0
Fatata	?[6,000]*	18,000	31,000	?[1,000]

	From Fellow Villagers				
	Boats	Copra Dryers	Land	Harvest Rights	Money
Atea	?[500]	0	58,400	0	?[0]
Fatata	0	?[3,000]	25,400	7,000	?[2,500]

*?[] = "Informed Guess."

Vending

Some Te Pitians made a practice of selling special foods and beverages to others on occasions; for example, two or three enterprising individuals in each village sold Tahitian chestnuts, thin slices of watermelon, soft drinks, etc., to cinemagoers, and one resident of Atea occasionally baked batches of cakelike bread and sold them to his neighbors for Sunday treats.

Atea's two "regular" cinema vendors asserted that their revenues were "too small to recall"; from the few observations I made, they could not have brought in more than about 3,500 francs (net) each per annum. Two of Fatata's three regular vendors asserted that they had sold goods worth about 15,000 francs in net profits each per annum. Fatata's third regular vendor was its *tāvana,* who conducted a very lively business selling soft drinks and cakes in front of one of the "theaters." He feigned ignorance, i.e., lack of records—indeed, he was nearly illiterate—of his revenues from this source, but, according to my observations and extrapolations therefrom, they would have been not less than about 40,000 francs during 1954, or about 30,000 in profits.

A few enterprising Fatatans also sold refreshments—soft drinks, home-made cakes, etc.—at the only interdistrict football match that was held there during my visit. Of the three out of the four who did so and who were willing to describe their transactions to me, one acknowledged a net loss (in terms of revenues, less money cost of materials—some of which had spoiled), while the other two, quite proudly, reported "profits" of 3,000 and 4,500 francs, respectively, but did not, of course, include in their costs their own self-grown fruit or the labor of themselves and their helpers.

Also, during Fatata's New Year celebrations of 1960, seven individuals operated booths for selling refreshments and for conducting games of skill and chance—pale imitations of Pape'ete's Bastille Day midway. During the three to four days of their operations, two of these operators were reported as breaking even, i.e., revenues minus out-of-pocket money costs, and one as having suffered a loss. Of the four who were reported as making profits, one—the district *tāvana*—was said to have gained "more than 4,000 francs," and the others considerably less. A similar midway was conducted in Fatata over New Year 1954–55. It occurred, however, before my arrival there, and I learned nothing more about it than that the only one who made "much" money from it—how much I did not discover—was the selfsame *tāvana*.

During my 1954–55 visit, only in Fatata were any alcoholic beverages sold locally. Residents of Atea were able to tank up on their periodic visits to Fare, and some of them bought beer or wine there and carried it home, where it was promptly consumed. In Fatata, however, two local Tahitians sold wine and unchilled beer, either for drinking on the premises or for taking home. One of these enterprises was largely inactive, the licensee, an elderly widow, having become "*fiu*" (fed up) with the carousing that attended it; the other remained active and, evidently, profitable enough to warrant its continuation.

The latter establishment was located in an open shed attached to the house of its manager who, however, was not the licensee. The license itself was owned by another Fatatan, a veteran of the company of Tahitian volunteers that had fought in North Africa in World War II—the basis, evidently, for his having been granted the license. Not choosing to sell from his own house, the licensee "rented" his license to the actual seller, because (he said) of friendship and sympathy for the latter, who was too badly crippled to do other work.

According to one possibly reliable account (I was unable to get details from the owner or retailer), the license fee was 5,000 francs per annum. The owner purchased his wine (a red Algerian, which constituted the bulk of his sales) from Pape'ete by the barrel at about 22 francs a liter and sold it for 35. According to this same source (a man who was a frequent enough customer to be in a position to know!), the annual profits were about 5,000 *tārā* (25,000 francs), which were divided equally between licensee and retailer.

Remittances

My inquiries turned up only three cases of Te Pitians living and working "outside" and sending regular remittances home. All three of these were from Fatata. One was a middle-aged carpenter employed in Pape'ete; he regularly sent or brought to his sickly Fatatan wife about 3,000 francs each month. Another was a man in his early thirties employed in the phosphate works on Makatea; his wife lived there with him and he made regular remittances to his elderly Fatatan parents of about 1,200 francs a month, which represented nearly all of the latters' money income. And the third was a young woman who worked as a clerk in Papeʻete and sent about 1,300 francs a month to her widowed Fatatan mother—a deed that won for her widespread praise (but not emulation) and that was used by several elderly Fatatan parents to contrast with the "neglect" and "ingratitude" shown by *their* offspring living and working elsewhere.

Otherwise, several Fatatans, and Ateans, living and working elsewhere, used to send occasional gifts of money or objects to their kinfolk (usually parents) at home, but not enough in value or in frequency to mute the oft-heard complaint of "neglect."

Conversely, a few Te Pitians occasionally sent gifts of money or objects (usually food) to relatives elsewhere, but nowhere near as much, in the aggregate, as the incoming flow, small even as that was.

Several Fatatans received regular special allowances from the Administration. Of these, three elderly widows received old-age payments of 195 francs a month, and a fifth received 295 a month, reportedly because of a son's death in the armed forces. Two veterans, one of each world war, received small pensions, the amounts of which I could not discover. And one elderly woman, who had "retired" from long service with a nearby European plantation, was paid by her former employer a pension of 200 francs a month.

As noted previously, another Fatatan family received regular payments from the colony-wide *Allocation Familiale* program, whereby the dependents of the workers of certain registered employers received, directly, a percentage of the workers' wages made up of a withheld percentage of their wages and contributions from the employers and the program. The total "outside" money received by these Fatatans from this source in 1954 probably amounted to no more than about 200 francs a month.

No resident Atean worked regularly for an outside employer, hence none of this type of income was received there. Several Ateans were, however, eligible for old age or welfare-type remittances, but, as far as I could discover, no one there received any—whether because of official neglect or local ignorance of rights, I failed to learn.

Summary of Differences in Money Earning

Copra. Within Fatata's boundaries, there was less land suitable for growing coconuts than in Atea, but there were more mature plants. On the other hand, Fatata also contained a larger number of unharvested palms than Atea.

I did not measure per-hectare production in either place, but, judging by results obtained elsewhere, Fatata's more widespread practice of banding palms against rats should have given an advantage to it in this respect. Conversely, the Fatatans' greater inclination to harvest still-attached, and hence possibly less mature, nuts, an adaptation perhaps to their larger measure of time-based grove-sharing, may have reduced somewhat their palms' copra output, but I know of no evidence that would support this surmise.

Many of the palms in both villages were owned by outsiders. Of those owned by Te Pitians, there were in Fatata about eighty-three productive palms per capita, against only fifty-eight in Atea. In terms of individuals, relatively more Ateans than Fatatans had actual ownership rights in productive local palms, although their average holdings were less than half as large.

Fatata produced more copra than Atea in 1954—52,000 kilos to Atea's equivalent of 42,700—but this works out in per capita terms to 153 against Atea's 192.

Relatively more Ateans (24.4 percent) than Fatatans (29.6 percent) actually sold copra during 1954, but, for reasons already stated, these figures do not necessarily indicate how many individuals were actually engaged in copra making.

In any case, while Ateans produced more copra per capita during 1954 than the Fatatans, the copra produced by the latter produced higher net profits per kilo, i.e., 7.54 francs against Atea's 3.39.

In the case of both villages, some of the costs that served to reduce the producers' profits went to their local fellow Tahitians in the form of rent, wages, dryer rental, and transport charges, and some to outsiders, mainly in the form of rent. Thus viewed, while Fatata's copra brought into the village as a whole (i.e., to producers, landlords, dryer owners, wage earners, and boat owners) about 443,300 francs or 1,308 per capita, Atea's copra brought into that village only 156,762 francs or 706 per capita.

It should be recalled that the above figures relate to ownership and income from palms located within the defined boundaries of Atea and Fatata. Te Pitians also owned and sometimes worked and/or received incomes from palms located elsewhere; differences between the two villages in this regard will be summarized later on.

Finally, comparison between copra making in Atea and Fatata reveals some differences of a kind that is less susceptible to statistics but, nevertheless, is important in terms of social relations. One such had to do with harvesting methods, namely the practice, involving Fatatans more than Ateans, but which was adjudged to be "selfish" in both villages, of cutting down nuts during an allotted harvesting period. Again, Fatatan producers used more paid labor in their copra making than did the Ateans, who relied for help almost entirely on members of their own households. And third, Atean dryer owners were more liberal than their Fatatan counterparts in allowing others some use of their equipment.

Vanilla. Vanilla growing engaged 35 percent of Atea's residents during 1954 as against only 5 percent of Fatata's. During the same year, the Ateans produced 5,082 kilos of green beans, worth about 1,144,000 francs, as against 553 kilos, worth about 138,000. (In Atea another seven individuals, and another five in Fatata, assisted the above growers to the extent that they received shares in the crops, which they sold as separate lots.) Thus, vanilla growing is revealed as having been much more important in Atea than in Fatata. In fact, as comparison with other sources of income will reveal, vanilla growing was by far Atea's most important, i.e., most revenue-producing, industry; whereas, as we shall see, in Fatata, it ranked as a revenue producer behind wage work, fishing, copra, and even livestock. Within this broad context, there were some noteworthy differences between the two villages regarding vanilla growing.

In the first place, Fatatan sellers received higher prices for their green beans than those of Atea, by an average of about 25 francs per kilo. Secondly, Atea's larger vanilla growers, i.e., those producing over 60 kilos in 1954, outnumbered Fatata's thirty to one. Thirdly, although the rents paid by vanilla growers amounted to about the same percentage of sales revenue in both villages (150,000 francs in Atea, of which 102,000 went to "outside" landlords; 17,000 in Fatata, of which 12,000 went to "outside" landlords), the rental arrangements undertaken, in the case of both local and outside landlords, differed somewhat. In Atea, only one grower was required to pay "rent"—and that only 5 percent of sales revenue—to his land co-owners for use of jointly-held land, whereas in Fatata there were six, who paid rents amounting to 10 percent of sales revenue (revealing, thereby, a more "commercial" attitude to money earning, even towards kinfolk). Again, only two Atean growers leased land outright (for 20 percent of sales revenues) for vanilla growing, as compared with eight Fatatans, an indication of the latters' greater readiness to undertake long-term, i.e., nine-year, commitments of this kind. And also, whereas five Ateans engaged in working outsider landlords' vanilla plantings for 50 percent share of sales revenue (a rent regarded by Ateans as usurious but occasionally unavoidable), only two Fatatans chose to undertake this kind of arrangement, and that for a rent of only 30 percent of sales revenue.

Finally, the social ambience of vanilla production differed in the two villages to a very marked degree. Whereas in Fatata the selling of green beans took place as a solemn and strictly commercial transaction between sellers and buyers, in Atea it was an occasion for a community-wide gathering, due not only to the larger number of sellers but also to the widespread economic and social interest in this harvest-festival-like affair.

Kapok. Kapok grew profusely in both Atea and Fatata and was harvested and processed in both places for local use, but Ateans processed more of it for use locally and much more of it for sale "outside." In contrast to a handful of Fatatans, who sold amounts described by them as being "too small to recall," there were thirty-seven Ateans engaged in this tedious and relatively low-paid work in 1954, to earn a total of 68,685 francs (which amounted to an average of 1,856 francs per producer and a per capita sum of 309).

Coffee. Some of the coffee grown in Te Piti circulated commercially, both locally and "outside." I was unable to discover the volume or values of the former, but the reported export figure seems fairly reliable and complete. During 1954, the seven Atean export-producers received a total of about 27,000 francs for their beans, while the twenty-two Fatatans who engaged in this commerce received a total revenue of about 96,700 francs.

Vegetables and Fruit. Some Te Pitians earned money selling vegetables. According to my queries and rough estimates, the Ateans sold about 5,000 francs' worth to "outsiders" (mainly to their local storekeepers, who resold some of them locally) and the Fatatans about 60,000 francs' worth (40,000 to their local storekeepers, for themselves and for local resale, and 20,000 directly to other Fatatans). In addition, a few Te Pitians took along other local products, mainly fruit, for sale on their trips to the "outside." Fatatans were much more active than Ateans in this kind of commerce, another advantage accruing to them as a result of their easier access to Pape'ete. My guess is that the Fatatans earned about 25,000 francs from this source in 1954 and the Ateans no more than 2,000.

Cassava. Several individuals in both villages grew and processed enough cassava for sale, in addition to the amounts grown for their own households. Most of that sold was done so locally; in Atea at least 3,150 francs' worth circulated in this way during 1954, and in Fatata at least 4,800. In addition, one man in each village produced and exported cassava in larger quantities, the Atean about 4,000 francs' worth and the Fatatan about 8,000.

Firewood. Because of Fatata's larger consumption of bread, totally and per capita, more firewood was used by its Chinese storekeeper-bakers than in Atea. And since the only source of this firewood was from local Tahitian woodcutters, those of Fatata earned more, aggregately, than their counterparts in Atea. Fewer men engaged in this arduous labor in Fatata than in

Atea, and those who did so earned correspondingly more. I was unable to discover specifically how much more that was, but based on some Atea figures (wherein the eight most "regular" cutters earned yearly average incomes of 1,650 from this work), the six Fatata "regulars" probably earned an average of 6,000 or more.

Livestock. In all three kinds of animal production—cattle, pigs, and chickens (and eggs)—Fatatans sold more during 1954 than did the Ateans. More of Atea's households kept cattle, but mainly for the purpose of controlling the ground covers of their coconut groves. In contrast, the Fatatan cattle owners kept their animals mainly for sale. The latter (including one man whose principal occupation was cattle raising) sold beef animals, all to Pape'ete, worth a total of about 165,000 francs, as compared with Ateans' revenues of 20,000 (including 5,000 francs' worth sold to other Ateans).

Ateans raised relatively more pigs than did the Fatatans but, again, disposed of fewer by sale either to local Tahitians or to non-Tahitians, local or elsewhere. During 1954, the Ateans sold pigs to the aforesaid non-Tahitians worth about 24,000 francs, compared with the Fatatans' sales to outsiders of pigs worth about 210,000 francs. And with respect to chickens and eggs, Fatatans sold all of them locally, and mainly to the Chinese, in amounts worth about 11,600 francs, whereas Ateans sold virtually none except to the visiting ethnographer, who paid prices as high as the odor of most of the eggs.

Fishing. The difference between Atea and Fatata with respect to commercial fishing was as wide as it is easy to state: in Atea virtually no one earned any money from this kind of activity, whereas in Fatata it was a gainful occupation for about two-thirds of all money-earning men and the principal occupation of some of them. According to my admittedly labyrinthine calculations, Fatata's fishermen earned profits during 1954 approximating a total of 860,000 francs from sales in the Pape'ete market and another 40,000 francs' worth in sales to other Fatatans.

Craftwork. Some Te Pitian women earned money for themselves by making coconut-leaf roof thatch-plates for sale. My guess as to the amounts earned in this way was about 6,000 francs in Fatata and about twice as much in Atea. In Atea, there were eight men who occasionally worked as canoe makers and in Fatata, four. Such work was, however, very sporadic and the money earned was aggregately small, i.e., about 4,500 in Atea and about 11,250 in Fatata.

Wages and Salaries. The differences between Atea and Fatata in this domain of money earning were summarized in Table 3D. During 1954, the

Fatatans earned about three times as much, per capita, as the Ateans in wages and salaries from "outsiders"—their advantage having come about through the existence of a large public works program (which, however, was a one-time opportunity) and through the location nearby of European plantations (which, at the time, provided continuous sources of money for several Fatatans and occasional wages for several more who worked part time).

As for the money earned by Te Pitians working for other Te Pitians, the positions of the two villages were reversed in 1954. Ateans earned a total of about 117,500 francs in this way (i.e., 529 per capita) and Fatatans 144,500 (426 per capita). Moreover, the kinds of services involved in that internal exchange differed in the two villages in two important respects: namely, most of the boat transport used by Ateans was supplied by other Ateans, and the general money-earning labor employed in Fatata was supplied on an individual basis, while that employed in Atea was carried out by Atean men working collectively in groups.

Leasing. Differences between Ateans and Fatatans with respect to monies received in rent in 1954 were summarized in Table 3E. (The more noteworthy differences between the two villages revealed in this table have to do with the houses, theaters, copra dryers, land, harvest rights, and money "lent" to fellow villagers and to savings accounts.) Efforts to explain these and the other noteworthy differences revealed in this chapter must be postponed to Chapter XII.

Vending. The two regular cinema-time refreshment vendors of Atea earned profits of about 3,500 francs each in 1954, whereas the three regulars of Fatata earned amounts totaling about 45,000 francs. An even wider difference occurred with respect to two other kinds of vending operations. In one of these, which had no counterpart in Atea, a few Fatatans earned money selling refreshments, etc., at a local interisland football match and at the village's New Year midway. Of the profits from these activities, which totalled about 20,000 francs, around three-fourths came from sales to other Fatatans. In the other vending operation, which also had no counterpart in Atea, Fatata's two men engaged actively in the selling of wine and beer realized between them profits totaling about 25,000 francs during 1954.

Remittances. The total amounts of money received by Te Pitians in 1954 in the form of remittances from kinfolk living elsewhere and from pensions, welfare payments, etc., came to about 85,000 francs in the case of Fatata and no more than about 2,000 in the case of Atea.

Table 3F. Money from "Outside" Sources, 1954

	Atea		Fatata	
	Total	Per Capita (N = 222)	Total	Per Capita (N = 339)
Copra	156,762	706	443,300	1,308
Vanilla	1,042,000	4,694	126,000	372
Kapok	68,685	309	[0]	[0]
Coffee	[27,000]	[122]	[96,700]	[285]
Vegetables	?[5,000]	?[23]	?[40,000]	?[118]
Fruit	?[2,000]	?[9]	?[25,000]	?[74]
Cassava	[4,000]	[18]	[8,000]	[24]
Firewood	[18,200]	[82]	[53,000]	[156]
Livestock	[41,500]	[187]	[376,600]	[111]
Fish	0	0	860,000	2,537
Wages and Salaries	297,394	1,340	1,392,635	4,108
Rent	16,500	74	49,000	145
Vending	0	0	[5,000]	[15]
Remittances	?[2,000]	?[9]	[85,000]	[251]
Totals	1,681,041	7,572/3	3,560,235	10,502/4

Note: [] = Rough Approximation; ?[] = Informed Guess.

Money Spending

Most of Te Piti's money earners quickly spent, or overspent, their money earnings. As previously noted, some were in debt to the local storekeepers for months at a time and few of them put aside money into savings accounts. Nor did I hear of any instances of the private hoarding of substantial sums and I believe that information about such situations, had they existed, would have circulated widely among these acute and zealous auditors of their neighbors' affairs.

The information I was able to obtain about what they spent their money for came mainly from three sources. One of these was in the form of answers to a questionnaire. Another source was the actual written records kept by a few individuals in both villages. And the third consisted of records of receipts kept by persons who took in some of the money spent.

The questionnaires were composed after I had lived for several months in each village and was thus better able to formulate pertinent questions and

Table 3G. Money from "Internal" Sources, 1954

| | Atea | | Fatata | |
	Total	Per Capita (N = 222)	Total	Per Capita (N = 339)
Vegetables	?[5,000]	?[23]	?[20,000]	?[59]
Cassava	?[3,150]	?[14]	?[4,800]	?[14]
Coffee	Some		Some	
Meat	[53,000]	[239]	[100,000]	[295]
Fish	?[5,000]	?[23]	[40,000]	[118]
Canoe-making	4,500	20	11,250	33
Thatch-making	?[12,000]	?[54]	?[6,000]	?[18]
Wages, including transportation	117,500	529	144,500	426
Rent	[61,000]	[275]	35,000	104
Vending	14,000	63	80,000	236
Totals	275,150	1,239/40	441,550	1,303

Note: [] = Rough Approximation; ?[] = Informed Guess.

to interpret and evaluate answers. In both places, they included expenditures for the whole year of 1954 and were addressed to individuals who were the "money managers" of their respective households or to individual money earners who managed the expenditures of household subunits or of themselves alone. In Atea, I obtained answers on twenty-six of these questionnaires, comprising the expenditures of, or on behalf of, about 55 percent of the village's average population (of 222) during 1954. In Fatata, the forty-two questionnaires administered represented the expenditures of about 48 percent of that community's average 1954 population of 339. In both places, I did most of the questioning myself and thus have some feeling for the degree of reliability of the results, which I believe to be somewhat better in the case of Atea, based not only on its larger (relative) sample size but also on the generally greater ingenuousness of the respondents there.

In neither case, however, do I attach equal credence to the responses of all respondents, or on their responses for all parts of the questionnaires. Some of them quite obviously gave trumped-up figures, e.g., for the amounts spent on wine and beer; and many others gave figures, e.g., for cinemagoing and clothing, which were so neatly rounded as to be highly suspect. But in many other instances, their reports on expenditures for such items as, e.g., building materials, were detailed enough to appear genuine, or their contributions to church causes were such as could be confirmed elsewhere.

As for the information obtained from individuals' written records, I copied nine of them that appeared to be complete for the whole year 1954 (six in Atea and three in Fatata), another seven that covered all expenditures of one or more months but less than the whole year, and another twelve that covered current purchases (on credit) in 1954 from the local stores, i.e., records that had been kept "to insure that the storekeepers would not cheat them."

The principal weakness of the comprehensive year-long records is of course their small number, and for Fatata, their unrepresentativeness, i.e., two of Fatata's record keepers having been among the village's largest money earners.

With regard to information on receipts of the money spent, some of this was manifestly accurate and served either to confirm or to correct figures obtained from the written records or the verbal questionnaires. The most dependable of these were those having to do with church contributions, overall cinema receipts, local store credit purchases in Atea,[25] and local alcohol purchases in Fatata.

The table below (Table 3H) consists of figures derived from all three sources of information as "corrected" (when necessary and possible) by each other and as "audited" (when they were patently improbable) by myself on the basis of other kinds of information I possessed (including some comparable records on 1955 expenditures). Clearly, these figures contain too many guesses, however well informed, to warrant use as statistics in reports on economics per se, but they do provide some insight into how Ateans and Fatatans, separately and comparatively, ranked their needs and wants for the things that money could buy.

Details about some of the above expenditures have already been given; those about other categories will be given in the chapters that follow. And, after all such details have been provided, some comments, and explanations where possible, will be offered concerning the many noteworthy differences between Atea and Fatata in the ways their residents spent their money.

Finally, I cannot resist the urge—such moments occur so rarely in an ethnographer's work—to point to the circumstance that the reconstructions of expenditures herein presented do not differ greatly from those of the earnings reported above. Whether this is a case of interdependent convergences or accidental coincidences, I, of course, cannot positively say, but the resulting similarities do provide some basis for the comforting thought that all those tedious and at times painfully ticklish inquiries were not entirely in vain!

---

[25]To my surprise and delight, the storekeepers of Atea gave me full access to their credit ledgers (because of the "importance of your work"[!]); their counterparts in Fatata were more wary, evidently suspecting a link with officialdom.

Table 3H. Money Spent in 1954

	Atea		Fatata	
	Total	Per Capita (N = 222)	Total	Per Capita (N = 339)
Food	721,400	3,250	1,621,700	4,784
Clothing	132,400	596	337,000	994
Medical	14,100	64	57,500	170
House Building and Repair	122,000	550	271,300	800
House Furnishing and Utensils	75,300	339	130,500	385
Tools, etc.	155,400	700	333,000	982
Vehicles	0	0	12,000	35
Cinema	200,000	901	210,000	619
Cinema Refreshments	8,000	36	55,000	162
Wine and Beer	40,400	182	105,000	310
Musical Instruments	4,300	19	12,500	37
Travel	102,800	463	107,900	318
Church	98,200	442	102,600	303
Political	[2,350]	[11]	[3,400]	[10]
Feti'i	90,200	406	123,600	365
Taxes, Fines	0	0	[1,115]	3
Totals	1,766,850	7,959	3,484,115	10,278

Note: [] = Rough Approximation

I turn now to a description of Te Piti's Chinese-owned retail stores, through which some of the Te Pitian's money incomes were acquired—more, however, in Atea than in Fatata—and where much of their money earnings were spent.

CHAPTER IV

THE STORE (*Fare Toa*)

On a visit to isolated Mai'ao Island, I was for a time affected by what seemed to be a pervasive atmosphere of torpor, one I had never before experienced in any other rural Tahitian community. After a while, I realized its cause: the island had no Chinese store. In lively contrast, Atea had two and Fatata three; and their presence, however foreign their origin, rendered these communities more typically "Tahitian" than all-Tahitian Mai'ao.

The stores of Atea and Fatata were all centrally located—indeed, they largely defined both communities' centers—and they were all of the same wholly functional architectural style, namely, a principal wood-walled, tin-roofed shack housing the store itself, to which had been added, as need dictated, several other rooms of various uses, sizes, shapes, and materials. In addition to their stocks of retail goods, all of the Te Piti stores contained porches for drying and rooms for sorting vanilla; four of them contained bakeries; and two of them contained copra-drying racks. And, along with these more or less public facilities, they all contained two or three private rooms where the storekeepers and their dependents carried on their secluded and somewhat mysterious domestic lives.

Turning first to the stores' retail trade, all of them stocked and sold the following items: flour, rice, sugar, canned meat and fish, canned milk (condensed and powdered), tea, canned butter and cheese, tomato sauce, salt, laundry soap, combs, kerosene, flashlight batteries, sewing materials, tobacco and matches, and fishhooks and lines. In addition, four of them stocked coffee, some clothing and dress-making goods, lanterns, table and kitchen ware, axes and knives, and soft drinks—chilled or unchilled. Occasionally, other items would be added to the shelves, e.g., candies, canned vegetables, sandals, cosmetics, mirrors, etc., but the overall impression made

Selling produce to owner of Atea's larger store

Watching the world go by at Atea Store

Fatata Store. Catching up on the news

Atea Store. Chinese owner drying vanilla beans

upon an observer from a supermarket civilization was one of meagerness and lack of variety. Not so, evidently, to their Tahitian customers, some of whom seemed to spend hours gazing at the shelves in mute wonder.

The quantities of items sold by Te Piti's stores were indicated above; here I wish to describe Te Pitians' buying habits, at their local stores and elsewhere.

Accustomed as I was to American homes and their shelves filled with week- or month-long supplies of consumables, I was struck with the paucity of such—indeed, with the absence of shelves in most Te Piti houses. It would not be too farfetched to say that most Te Pitians were accustomed to buying what they needed just prior to using it and in quantities only large enough to satisfy their immediate needs. It was not unusual to see someone go to a store and purchase only enough tea or sugar, or rice, or flour, etc., for the midday meal and then return in a few hours to purchase some of the same items, in like quantities, for that day's supper. Even more, on one occasion I was present in a store when a child obtained about an ounce of laundry soap for his mother, who was then washing clothes, and then returned about an hour later to obtain another ounce so that she could finish that wash. And the storekeeper assured me that this was not an unusual kind of episode.

Five explanations may be put forward and tested for this characteristic mode of purchasing, which, I suggest, is not a trivial or isolated feature of Te Pitians' behavior.

1. Te Pitians were in general not given to longer-range planning and were accustomed to provide only for satisfaction of immediate needs. (This explanation would appear to be valid, if it referred only to this particular kind of behavior. But there are other activities in which the Te Pitians did display foresight and long-range planning, so that their way of store shopping cannot be explained by deriving it from a general mental set.)

2. Their everyday lives were so monotonous that a trip to the store was regarded as a welcome break, to be repeated as often as possible. (*'Ua fiu*—I am bored—was indeed often expressed by Te Pitians with respect to many of their activities, including staying at home. And a trip to the store did indeed provide opportunities for pleasurable talk, etc., hence this explanation may be valid in part—but only in part, in view of the fact that the individual needing the store item often sent someone else to get it.)

3. They did not place much value on time, hence that spent on numerous shopping expeditions was not regarded as "wasted." (This too has some validity, but more in the sense of not exercising a constraint than of being a cause.)

4. Their cash in hand and the credit limits imposed on them by the pragmatic storekeepers were usually so small that they were unable to buy larger

quantities at a time. (It was undoubtedly true that most households did not keep enough cash on hand to permit regular large-scale purchasing. And it was also quite true that Te Piti's storekeepers would not have extended credit for quantities which they knew, from experience, that particular customers would find difficult to pay for. But the quantities I am talking about were smaller in many instances than either of these constraints would account for.)

5. It was safer and more economical to store things not immediately needed in the easily accessible store than at home, where they were subject to spoilage at the purchaser's cost and to unauthorized consumption. (I never succeeded in eliciting this explanation from a Te Pitian, but it does make sense. In any case, even if it were not a conscious reason influencing them in their shopping behavior, I suggest that it may derive from a more general disposition among Tahitians, and one due largely to ancient ecological necessities, namely, a tendency to use up immediately all consumables on hand.)

Te Pitians on occasion also purchased things elsewhere, including items which their local stores did not stock (e.g., construction materials, tools, outboard motors, fishnets, clothing, medicines) and some that they did. One reason for purchase of the latter was that such items cost generally less in larger centers than in the local stores, and Te Pitians would undoubtedly have availed themselves more often of those lower prices but for their lack of ready cash. But here again, their distance from the lower-price stores—in Fare for Ateans, in Paopao and Pape'ete for Fatatans—was a potent constraint, regardless of the frequency with which boats plied between Atea and Fare, and Fatata and Pape'ete.

This last observation points to a more general tendency of Te Pitians' economic behavior, that is, to their inclination to engage in exchange transactions only on a face-to-face basis. For example, despite savings in money, they rarely ordered items by mail even when money was available and even though money-transmitting procedures were simple and mails fairly frequent. Illiteracy, undoubtedly, accounted for some of this, but I knew of several literate and well-travelled persons who spent days negotiating for on-the-spot but second-hand articles that could have been obtained newer and cheaper by mail order. If a trusted relative or friend would act as a direct face-to-face agent in "foreign" purchases that was usually acceptable—although the criteria for "trusted" tended to be very narrow when money was involved—but most Te Pitians seem to have been either unable or unwilling to conduct such transactions by post.

As indicated above, many—indeed, most—Te Pitians made their purchases from the local stores on credit. Some of these did so on a monthly basis, others on a semiannual basis, and still others settled their bills only when their cash crops were harvested and disposed of. Concerning the latter, a very common arrangement was for a local storekeeper to extend credit to a customer in return for a commitment to sell enough of his vanilla or copra or kapok to the former to settle the account. Several customers produced only enough vanilla (and, in Atea, green copra) to pay off their store debts, so that, lacking other sources of money income, they were never able to accumulate any cash for current or future expenses and, thus, always lived on credit and expectations of future crops. In fact, some of them charged that the Tinitos (Chinese) deliberately encouraged cash-cropping customers to pile up debts in their stores in order to acquire most of the latters' crops for processing and/or marketing. True or not, the willingness of the storeowners to extend credit—in effect, an interest-free loan—provided those customers with goods that they might not otherwise have been able to purchase.

A few Te Pitians kept written records of their store purchases on credit, not, purportedly, to keep their expenditures within practical limits but "to keep the Tinitos from cheating." Those record keepers I queried were unable to cite any instance of having been cheated but explained that the mere information that they "kept records" served to keep the storekeeper honest. Among those who did not keep tally of their store debts, some did charge the storekeepers with fraud but, of course, were not able to support their charges—and in any case kept on buying. (This situation moved one Atean to tell me he felt sympathy for the storekeepers, whom he considered were being untruthfully and unfairly accused—one of the very few instances I observed of a Chinese being defended by a Tahitian.)

From their side, the Chinese storekeepers appeared to deal with their Tahitian neighbors on an individual basis, based not only on their own experiences with them but also on a profound knowledge of each individual's current resources, activities, character, and crop prospects. To some they granted extensive and indefinite credit, from others they demanded cash or provided credit to them only by a written agreement (*parau tarahu,* 'talk [concerning] loan')—with various arrangements in between. In the event of a persistent default, they could resort to taking the matter to the island's gendarme and eventually to court. The fact that these measures seldom had to be resorted to indicates either shrewdness on the part of the storekeepers or fear of government authority on the part of the customers, or both.

When on several occasions, after being regaled with complaints about the local storekeepers' stinginess, hard-dealing, trickery, extortion, profiteering,[1]

---

[1]Regarding profiteering, it was a common view that Te Piti's storekeepers earned enormous profits by "doing nothing," i.e., that their mark-ups involved no work on their part: "They merely order goods and put them on their shelves."

etc., I asked why no Tahitian operated a store in the village, the answers were not that "Tahitians have too little money to start such a business," but rather, that "Tahitians are not clever enough," or "Tahitians would not be hard (*pa'ari*) enough to refuse giving or lending all their goods to relatives and friends." (Evidently such attempts had been made in both villages in the recent past, with invariably disastrous results.) My reminder to informants that the refreshment vendors at the cinema were suffering no such fate was met with the answer that such enterprises were "different" from the store. And different they indeed were, but not in the sense meant. For my informants, the difference lay in the kinds of goods sold—the refreshments being luxuries, the store goods essentials. The fact that the stores' goods represented a considerable investment in slow-moving or no-moving items was not mentioned. Nor was the circumstance that the cinema refreshments were usually sold for cash.

Four of Te Piti's Chinese stores baked bread six or seven days a week, and nearly every household bought at least one loaf a day. I did not inquire into the economics of these enterprises, but I constantly wondered how a profit could have been realized with the sale of those large, delicious, French-style loaves whose price was set by the government at 5 francs each.

Baking was supervised by the Chinese themselves, but much of the labor was supplied by Te Pitian employees, one or two of whom—usually youths— were employed on a long-term basis in each bakery. A second way in which the bakeries provided some Te Pitians with money was, as described earlier, through purchase of firewood or, in some cases, through employment of labor to cut the wood.

Occasionally, some Te Pitians borrowed money from other Te Pitians or from their local storekeepers. The general expression was that it was better to borrow from a Tahitian than from a Chinese because the former never charged interest (*taime*, 'time') and the latter always did. In fact, few Te Pitians possessed, or acknowledged possessing, unobligated money in quantities large enough for lending beyond a few hundred francs. And although loans to close relatives or friends were in fact usually without monetary interest, some kind of quid pro quo was invariably expected. Moreover, although a Chinese storekeeper occasionally charged interest for loans of any size—and up to 20 percent per annum in interest—most of their monetary loans were advances on vanilla purchases and involved no interest at all.

While retailing and breadbaking may have been the most public aspects of their activities, the business of processing and marketing locally grown crops—vanilla in both communities, copra and kapok in Atea only—was probably the economic mainstay of Te Piti's stores. Vanilla, especially, made the difference between operating at a bare survival level, or even at a loss, and operating at a level of profit sufficient to enable most storeowners to partake regularly of Chinese cuisine and to indulge in certain luxuries not available to most of their Tahitian neighbors, including (in particular instances) drinking costly whiskey, gambling for large stakes, pampering extravagant Tahitian mistresses, and providing offspring with expensive educations—which leads me to add a few words about the social, less specifically economic, position of Te Piti's Chinese in their respective communities. While I did not focus any attention on their domestic lives, I became very much aware of the nature and amount of their social interactions with their Tahitian neighbors, customers, and employees.[2]

The attitudes of the Te Pitians towards their Chinese neighbors were influenced by certain stereotypes that prevailed among Tahitians throughout these islands. For example, one of these pictured the Chinese to be harder working and generally cleverer than Tahitians, and while this was considered admirable it was felt to be overbalanced by the Chinese preoccupation with money making. Another view held them to be Shylockian, deceptive, even fraudulent in their business dealings with Tahitians. A third formula widely current among Tahitians was that all Chinese were clannish, inscrutable, and given to ridiculous practices—culinary, sexual, ritual, etc. Corollary to these and similar Tahitian-held attitudes was the widespread assumptions that Tahitians' most effective defense against the alien Chinese was through their own physical superiority, their greater sexual prowess, and their larger numbers. Thus, disputes between Chinese and Tahitians typically led to physical threats by the latter; and few subjects delighted Tahitian audiences more than descriptions of beatings handed out to Chinese. Consequently, it was widely held that the principal, indeed the only comprehensive reason for a Tahitian woman to live with a Chinese man was for the material advantages thereby provided, especially food delicacies, a large wardrobe, and little domestic work.

Te Pitians knew, by everyday observation, that their own local Chinese deviated from the stereotypes in some or many respects, and this knowledge encouraged some mutually sympathetic and generous acquaintanceships. Nevertheless, if even minor differences occurred, the Tahitians involved tended to evoke the old and comfortable *Tinito* stereotype. It is against this background that the reader should view the social position of Te Piti's Chinese in their respective villages.

In the first place, all of Te Piti's stores were social centers for their Tahitian customers—in fact, the villagers' most continual gathering places, from daybreak, when people went there for the morning's bread, until after supper, when they sat around there exchanging the day's news.

---

[2] For more comprehensive accounts of the Chinese in the Society Islands, see Moench 1963 and Coppenrath 1967.

Secondly, as already related, the stores provided long- or short-time wage employment for several Te Pitians as vanilla sorters, bakery assistants, firewood suppliers, and domestics. The wages paid were usually the standard ones, and relations between employers and employees were generally friendly. When differences occurred, they usually resulted in termination of employment, either by firing or quitting, and by threats from the Tahitians involved. However, some other local Tahitian could always be found to fill the vacancy, so eager were people for local wage-earning jobs.

Something has already been said about two other aspects of Te Piti's Chinese and Tahitian relations, namely those of retailer-customer and of buyer-seller of produce. Both were subject to ups and downs, to moods of mutuality and of tension; within the institutional framework of the current economy, Te Piti's Chinese and Tahitians were indispensably linked, and both parties appeared to recognize this (with identical sentiments of regret!).

Turning to the sexual aspect of Te Piti's Tahitian-Chinese relations, both co-owners of one store were "married" to Tahitian women, i.e., they had maintained unofficial but long-lasting unions with them. One of these unions was troubled by frequent quarrelling and by the long absence of the woman (visiting her home village on another island), but both unions had produced children (who were obviously the apples of their father's eyes). All other male store owners in Te Piti had Chinese wives; the only female store owner was widowed and lived with her fully Chinese children. To the best of my knowledge (and in a Tahitian community such knowledge tends to be widely held), none of Te Piti's storekeeping Chinese, male or female, was involved in casual sexual liaisons with any Tahitians during my 1954–55 visits, although one of the Chinese wives was said to have made herself available to local Tahitian males in years past. (Some male informants asserted that she had sought out partners and had "paid" them for their services, but others scoffed at this and claimed it had been the other way around.) In any case, judging by genealogies and physical appearances, sexual relationships involving Tahitians and Chinese were fewer and more stable during my visit than had been the case in the past.

A substantial number of older Te Piti women had had sexual liaisons, of varying duration, with Chinese men in the past; this information was common knowledge, and with a few exceptions was discussed by the women in question with no discernible sign of embarrassment or regret. Also, several Te Pitians, of all ages, were acknowledged by themselves and others to have had a Chinese father or grandfather. With most of these mixed-breeds (all of whom were culturally Tahitianized), the fact of their Chinese descent was entirely disregarded by themselves and others in their everyday social lives. In a few somewhat aberrant cases, however, the individual's personality peculiarities were explained away by reference to this Chinese ancestry. This was especially so in the case of those preoccupied with money and given to "hardness" in their exchanges, whether they were successful or not.

Thus, like their stores, which provided the Te Piti Tahitians with objects and services essential for their economic needs, the Chinese themselves provided their Tahitian neighbors with a useful set of symbols with which to contrast and thereby help to preserve their self-imagined Tahitian-ness.

Summary of Differences

In all the foregoing, the Chinese of Atea and Fatata were much alike in the circumstances and conduct of their lives, but there were some noteworthy differences between them with respect to the quantity and quality of their interactions with their Tahitian neighbors.

In the first place, Ateans sold relatively more of their products to and bought relatively more of their "imported" goods from their local Chinese store than did those of Fatata. As noted earlier, Ateans sold virtually all of their cash crops—vanilla, copra, and kapok—locally. The Fatatans on the other hand sold only part of their vanilla crop locally, the rest having gone to Chinese buyers from a nearby district; and they sold all of their copra, pigs, and cattle, and most of their fish, to buyers in Pape'ete. As for wage labor, the only nearby markets for Ateans were the local Chinese stores, whereas several Fatatans resided at home and worked in European plantations within easy walking or boating range.

Ateans bought most of their "imported" foods, tools, utensils, fuels, sewing materials, etc., from their local stores. A few of them went occasionally to Fare where they bought special tools, building materials, ready-made clothing, etc., but not many Ateans possessed enough ready cash, or credit accounts in Fare, to do so regularly. For many Fatatans, the local stores were utilized only for such daily staples as bread, rice, soap and canned meat, which, incidentally, were priced on the average of 2 to 3 percent lower than in Atea. Most other of their purchases were made in Pape'ete (and at even lower prices), either by themselves on visits there or by the captain of the interisland boat acting as agent and usually without commission.

The differences between the two villages in commercial exchange between local Tahitians and Chinese were paralleled in other forms of interaction. The families that owned and operated Fatata's three stores were entirely Chinese, and they all lived their domestic lives quite separate from their Tahitian neighbors and employees. In contrast, each of the two owners of one of Atea's stores resided with his Tahitian "wife" (and usually with several "visiting" members of her family), while the owner of the other store and his Chinese wife resided in an almost symbiotic relationship with their next-door Tahitian neighbors. In addition, while Atea's Chinese were invited not infrequently to attend their customers' ceremonies, such as wedding feasts and funerals, those of Fatata were only rarely included.

CHAPTER V

DIVERSIONS

Contemporary Tahitians use three words of overlapping meanings to refer to the activities to be described in this chapter. Dictionaries tend to translate these words as follows:

> *ha'uti*—to play, to frolic, to play a game, e.g., soccer, cards; to play-act a role (in a film, stage play).
>
> *perē*—to play a game involving other persons (from English "play"?).
>
> *'ārearea*—amusement, diversions; *fa'a'ārearea*—to amuse, etc.

According to my (unsystematic) lexical inquiries, Te Pitian usage conformed fairly closely to the above, with the added specificity of applying *ha'uti* to the play of children and *perē* to the more goal-focused play of older persons. Also, *'ārearea* tended, in my hearing, to refer more to the action and feelings of people past childhood.

In this same search for meaning categories—for chapter headings—I also attempted (again, very unsystematically, in comparison with the precise strategies of current cognitive research), to discover what words the Te Pitians used to contrast with the above. Because my reams of recorded verbatim conversations were little help here, I tried to elicit responses to two other dictionary listings that seemed potentially contrastive to the above, namely, *'ohipa*, which is usually glossed as "work"; and *fiu*, usually glossed as "tedious, dull, wearisome, satiated." Predictably, it turned out that in the opinion of many informants, some "work," e.g., fishing, house thatching with friends, could be amusing and playlike, i.e., *mea 'ārearea*, and some games could become exceedingly tedious, i.e., *mea fiu*—all of which persuades me to abandon this attempt at cognitive mapping and proceed along more familiar, comfortable lines.

Into this chapter, then, will first go descriptions of activities that were engaged in by Te Pitians explicitly for purposes that I, with *my* cultural background, label diversion, play, or amusement. Under this heading, the diversions engaged in both by Ateans and Fatatans included children's games, "youth" activities, moviegoing, drinking parties, social visiting, and festivities associated with New York and Bastille Day. In addition, the youths of Fatata engaged in competitive soccer playing during my 1955 visit; Ateans formerly did the same and were to resume it before my second visit but were not doing so in 1954–55.

Ha'uti covers a wide range of activities: organized games, self-entertainment with a toy, horseplay, joking, etc.; people of all ages engaged in *ha'uti* sometimes, according to situation and temperament, but with "children," it was said to be so unceasing as to be almost distinctively characteristic. Also, the element of conflict deemed appropriate—or tolerated—in play differed in degree: mature and old people may have bantered words and young people have engaged in sharp raillery or mild scuffling, but most adults considered it inevitable that children at play would jeer and wrestle one another until tears began to flow.

Te Piti's children played sometimes in gangs, sometimes in pairs or threes, and sometimes alone. Their games were widely diverse: tag (in the water or on land), ball games, mock fights, etc. The cinema provided many themes, particularly war and cowboy films. Also, toy fads appeared, lasted for a week or so, were abandoned, and then reappeared; among such were homemade carts, boats, stilts, bows and arrows, etc. (Imported manufactured toys were not to be seen.) Play groups of younger children nearly always included both boys and girls. Older boys—not yet "youths"—tended to play without girls; or if some older girls were also involved in their games, the encounters were often complicated by undertones of sexuality, such as grabbing at each other's clothes or genitals.

While *ha'uti* was regarded as the natural activity for "childhood" amusement, *'arearea* was so of "youth"—which, indeed, was the label given to that period of life, i.e., *taure'are'a*, "period of pleasure."[1] Females as well as males went through this stage of life, but male "youthing" was a much more distinctive pattern of behavior.

In comparison with many other peoples, Tahitians in general, and Te Pitians in particular, were an unfrowning lot, but their life was not the carefree idyll tourists to Pape'ete may imagine it to be. In the villages, one did

---

[1] I am not certain about the historical basis of this etymology, but some Te Pitian informants made the connection.

not often see an adult face hardened into a scowl over the hardships or life or the perversities of mankind; the prevailing facial expression was one of matter-of-fact solemnity or even blank affectlessness. In the course of everyday activities, laughter came rather easily for most of Te Piti's adults, but it was frequently ironic; social interaction did not demand set smiles or simpering displays of good will.

All of which heightened by contrast those occasions calling for *'ārearea*, i.e., for more or less obligatory expression in the form of continuous, unrestrained merriment. At almost any formal, secular meal celebrating a wedding, a national holiday, an arrival or departure, after the food had been consumed and the speeches exchanged, the hosts would refill glasses and press all present to "*'ārearea*, everybody, *'ārearea*." And thus it would begin. Such a party would usually continue as long as the alcohol lasted—for several hours or even several days. Some guests would sleep *in situ*, others would go home and return, sometimes with more drink. Singing, stamping, dancing, not infrequently some fighting, accompanied the festivities, which would usually include only males, but in some cases a sprinkling of women as well. If the pastor attended such a banquet, he and a few like-minded adults would usually leave before the *'ārearea* began, but for most other adults in Te Piti, such affairs were either watched with pleasure or joined in with zest. The greatest *'ārearea* of all occurred at New Year, when all productive work stopped and parties went on for days—including, in Atea, a truly bacchanalian parade involving the whole population either as active participants or more or less approving onlookers (less, in the case of the pastor and one or two of the more teetotalling deacons).

Thus, most adult Te Pitians occasionally set aside the serious business of making a living or being a Christian to engage in periods of just as earnest pleasure-making. In contrast, with "youths," it was said, the proportions of time were "naturally" reversed (if, that is, one includes the pleasure "youths" were said to derive from work itself.

The only organized sport pursued during my 1954–55 visits was soccer (*tu'era'a pōpō*, "kicking ball") and this at Fatata. Soccer had also been played at Atea; it was abandoned two years before my 1954–55 visit, because of *fiu*, but was to resume two years later. (Conversely, soccer playing ended at Fatata a year after my visit, and my inquiries turned up the fact that there and in other rural districts the sport characteristically had a cyclical life of about three years of activity followed by about an equal time of nonplaying.) In both Atea and Fatata, the players, who included almost all the young men, constituted a club (*tiete pōpō*, "society [of] football") and maintained a club treasury that was used to finance away-from-home games. The Fatata club played in a league made up of Mo'orea and Tahiti clubs; the Atea club had played mainly against other Huahine teams. Money for the club treasuries was collected from admissions charged to spectators at interclub games, from (in the case of Fatata) rental of the club's Cinema Theater, and occasionally (when it could be collected) from fines levied against members for missing practice.

The practice sessions I witnessed at Fatata were disorganized, instructionless affairs characterized by more shouting than running and including very little teamwork. The interclub games themselves were somewhat faster and less dispirited but still lacking in teamwork. (Nor could the wine and beer, with which many players quenched their thirst, have added to their powers of concentration.) There was little evidence of camaraderie during practice sessions or games, and I often heard complaints from members concerning the stewardship of the treasury, the high cost of shoes, the fatigue resulting from practice, the failure of absentees to pay their fines, etc. Also, many club members had to listen to criticism from their elders concerning the time and energy-wasting inutility of the sport (*'aita faufa'a*, "it is without [monetary] value"). In fact, the whole activity provoked such a spate of negative responses, both among players and community members at large, that I sometimes wondered why it was kept alive at all.

One partial explanation for its recurrent existence emerged from the talk I often heard among young men away from the playing field, and especially over wine or beer. In this setting, their experiences in soccer playing were recalled as moments of high adventure, of heroics on the field, of great victories and narrow (accidental!) defeats, and of journeys to other places and their sexual conquests there.

The only other organized sport engaged in by Te Pitians within recent memory was canoe racing at Bastille Day celebrations (at Fare for Atea, at Pape'ete for Fatata). Fatatans had evidently given up the pastime many years previously, Ateans more recently (the long hull of Atea's racing canoe was still to be seen, rotting away). In answer to my queries as to why the sport had been abandoned, the stock answer in both communities was: "*'Aita faufa'a*," "it was without value," i.e., an activity without [monetary] rewards.

In pre-European times, the Tahitians had no alcoholic beverages. The closest equivalent was the mildly narcotic kava (*'ava*), an infusion made from the root of the pepper plant, *Piper methysticum*. Evidently, kava was a scarce item among the ancient Tahitians and was imbibed mainly by affluent, high-status people. In contrast to the elaborate ceremonial practices associated with its use in Samoa and Tonga, those few ancient Tahitians who regularly imbibed it did so informally and in no special ceremonial context. After the arrival of Europeans, many Tahitians became habituated to alcoholic beverages, especially rum and a drink made of the fermented root of the *tī* plant. According to reports by nineteenth-century observers, excessive alcoholic drinking was very widespread and contributed weightily to the physical decline and social malaise said to characterize the Tahitians of those times. If that were truly the situation during that era, it was certainly no longer so in Te Piti in 1954–55. During my first visits there, some of the residents made a fairly regular practice of drinking a little wine or beer with their meals, plus larger amounts on festive occasions like New Year, weddings, and work-completion celebrations, but only a very few individuals could be accurately described as "heavy" drinkers, and none at all as alcoholics.

The "heavy" drinkers of Te Piti met together to do their imbibing, and they usually kept at it until the beverage had been consumed (which might have been a few hours, a whole day, or two or more days at a time). A good deal of singing accompanied such sessions, along with a great deal of boasting and airing of grievances. Fighting sometimes broke out, but during my visits it never became overly destructive to property or seriously damaging to person. Occasionally, such groups would be joined by a woman or two—the wives of the male drinkers—but the usual membership consisted only of males, i.e., males past thirty or so.

Individual reasons for drinking (other than light drinking with meals) varied. Some drinkers said that it was good for one's health, others that it made one feel stronger, several others implied that it reduced the awkwardness they usually felt in unfamiliar social situations, and still others stated that it relieved the boredom (*fiu, ha'uamani*) of everyday life. Whatever the motivations,[2] even the heavier drinkers usually stopped short of total inebriation or spaced their bouts widely enough apart so that they were able to keep up with their domestic chores—although, admittedly, the "usual chores" of two or three of these were minimal by their communities' average standards of work. In fact, to the extent that heavy drinking constituted a social problem in Te Piti, it was not due to any excessive work absenteeism it may have caused (some of the heaviest drinkers were also the most industrious and productive of workers) and not to any habitual drunken rough handling of spouse and children, but rather to the reduction in household living standards resulting from the relatively large sums spent on wine and beer.

Atea and Fatata differed somewhat with respect to drinking habits. As described in Chapter III, Fatata had an active licensed seller of wine and beer (and a second one that was licensed but inactive during my stay), whereas Atea had none. (Nor were any Ateans permitted to obtain one by

---

[2]For a detailed description of the psychological—"private"—aspects of Tahitian drinking, see Levy 1973.

the Administration's island representative headquartered at Fare—a prohibition, by the way, that was supported by most of Atea's adult residents, including even some of its heavy drinkers.) This difference in access served to
reinforce—or possibly determine?—the differences in drinking habits just referred to.

When a Fatatan wanted a drink, he had only to walk to the vendor's
house and imbibe there, quietly, in the company of the sociable but somewhat abstemious seller, or to carry it home and drink it privately, usually
with his meals. Drinking also took place at celebrations—weddings, etc.—but
drinking parties as such were rare. In addition, many Fatatans travelling to
Pape'ete returned with the staggers but not, typically, as prologue to a
party.

When an Atean wanted a drink, he—specifically *he* (the drinkers of both
villages having been preponderantly male)—usually had to travel to Fare
for it, a trip by boat that took an hour or two. (The home brews made by
some Ateans [see above] were mostly concocted for and drunk during New
Year.) Most such drinkers tanked up in Fare and returned home with all
the alcohol inside. Or, if they returned with any still left in the bottle, that
fact became quickly and widely broadcast and the balance was drunk by
the owner and his friends in a noisily publicized party that lasted until it
was consumed. A few Ateans managed to keep small stocks of alcohol on
hand for longer periods—usually wine, beer, and sirupy liquors—to be imbibed more gradually at mealtimes or when entertaining special visitors,
but for more of the village's drinkers, the possession of alcohol invited finishing it off, and usually in the company of friends.

The quantitative records I was able to obtain on the consumption of alcohol are spotty, to say the least. As part of the survey I carried out on household incomes and expenditures, a question was included on amounts spent
on alcoholic beverages, but I am under no illusions about the accuracy of
the responses. The survey did confirm what I already knew, namely, that
many households—about one-third of those in Atea and about one-fifth of
those in Fatata—purchased (and probably consumed) none at all. But the
figures collected on expenditures for the others were so suspiciously
rounded, and in some instances I knew better about, so preposterously inflated or deflated, that I have had to reject them, as a whole, out of hand.
In fact, the only fairly objective data I was able to collect about this matter
was on the sale of wine by Fatata's one active licensee (above, p. 165). According to one well-informed customer, this outlet sold about 2,300 liters of
wine per annum at a total cost to the (local) customers of about 80,000
francs. To this must be added the money spent by Fatatans for alcohol in
Pape'ete and consumed mainly there—an amount I, of course, cannot document but would guess to be in the neighborhood of 25,000 francs.

As for Ateans' expenditures of this kind, my naively hopeful survey inquiry turned up a figure of 40,400 francs for the year 1954. From other things I knew about the respondents in this small and crowded-together community where privacy scarcely existed, some of them had greatly understated their alcohol expenditures and some boastfully overstated them, but I would guess that the total figure was not very far off the 40,400 mark.

In any case, by adding these figures—more or less "hard" data, inferences, and informed guesses—I can state, with some small degree of credibility, that Fatatans spent at the rate of about 105,000 francs per annum on alcoholic beverages during the time of my visit and Ateans about 40,400—which works out, per capita, at about 310 francs in Fatata to Atea's 182.

Throughout the Society Islands, Bastille Day (14 July) was marked by week-long celebrations—patriotic rites, exhibitions, contests, parties, etc. Some forms of celebration continued to be held at the administrative center of each island, but more and more of the activities had come to be centered in Pape'ete itself. During my 1954–55 visits, many Ateans attended the celebration at Fare, but from Fatata only a handful were interested enough to make the three-hour trip to Pape'ete.

Formerly, both villages participated actively in the proceedings by entering boats in the canoe-racing events, but in 1954–55 the Te Pitians who attended the celebrations went mainly to watch, to visit with relatives, to shop, and to engage in drinking sessions with friends.

New Year was a more important event by far. In both villages, it consisted of a week or more of holidaying, marked by family reunions and by festive eating and drinking. It commenced with special services in church and ended, for most, only after the last of the visitors had left for home a week or so later. The two villages differed considerably in their attitudes towards and behavior during the long holiday, but in both places the event possessed certain common features of social-relational importance:

—it provided Te Pitians with a temporal climax, a once-a-year high point of social interaction, accompanied by good food and (for some) much drink, a respite from ordinary work, a relief from everyday routine, i.e., a time par excellence for *'arearea.*

—it served for many as a strong incentive to increase their "economic" activities—to acquire money for buying extra food, drink, clothing, etc.; to produce more food for domestic consumption; to repair and refurbish their houses; etc.

—it brought together kinfolk from all parts of the archipelago, although most of the visitors came from Tahiti and were former residents of Te Piti who were returning home.

In comparison with New Year, Easter and Christmas were minor events, celebrated almost exclusively by church services.

In Atea, the celebration of New Year was an event of climactic social and economic importance. People began planning for it weeks, even months, in advance and some of them drew out the actual festivities for two or more weeks into January. By the beginning of December, work had already begun—refurbishing houses, assembling food stocks, fermenting home brews, acquiring or repairing clothing, etc. And even before then, some other jobs had to be done, such as communicating with intended homecoming guests and ordering joint barrel-lots of wine from Uturoa or Pape'ete. And, of course, many of the individuals involved in what were extraordinary money expenditures had to make their arrangements, with storekeepers or neighbors, for loans or additional credit.

By Christmas Day (which was celebrated by special church services but was itself only a prelude to New Year), Atean life was wholly dominated by preparations for and talk about the forthcoming events. A few men continued to work in their gardens or grove, but everyone else remained around home making last-minute preparations and discussing their approaching festivities. It was not unusual to see children actually shiver with excitement when sharing their expectations. And even otherwise impassive men revealed animated signs of pleasurable anticipation when they met together to test the stage of maturity of one another's home brews.

The visitors—most of them offspring or other near kin temporarily working and living elsewhere—began to arrive before Christmas, so that in some households the festivities—the homecoming feasts, leisurely visiting, drinking parties, etc.—commenced before New Year itself, but the public, community-wide celebrations opened with a solemn and colorful late-night church service on New Year's Eve. During this long ceremony—which was attended by every ambulatory Tahitian resident and guest, all dressed in their very best—the usual singing, praying, and sermonizing were supplemented by the christening of all local infants born during the preceding two to three months. Then, at midnight (which was attested by the ethnographer's watch, the church's three clocks having long since run down) the church bell was rung and everyone filed out of the building, shaking hands with the pastor and deacons, and then filed in again for more singing and prayer.

After that opening, Atea's religious services continued for a week. Three or four prayer meetings were held every day, each under the supervision of one or another of the congregation's members, who took turns at this *chore*— for so it was viewed; indeed, some of the meetings were attended only by the convenor himself or herself.

Meanwhile, the secular side of the celebration got underway with a mid-morning gathering (of youths and adult males, with most of the village's older children and some of its wives looking on) in the schoolyard at the seaward end of the village street. There in the blazing sun, tables had been set up and laden with large flagons of red *vin ordinaire,* donated for the occasion by the village's more affluent household heads. After a few words of greeting by the *tāvana*—"Enjoy yourselves, but don't become too drunk"—the drinking, singing, and dancing began, punctuated by occasional speeches that hyperbolized the *tāvana's* (mostly actual) virtues and the village's (partly mythical) fraternal solidarity. Then, after an hour or so of that, those still able to walk formed into a kind of line, headed by a man carrying a banner, and began to parade down the village street. Along the way, they stopped off at the several houses where more wine had been set out for the occasion, so that the marchers dropped out or thinned out as they progressed, leaving paralyzed or sleeping bodies along the way. Finally, upon reaching the last house, the handful of hardy survivors stopped off to sleep or to drink some more.

Needless to say, Atea's pastor viewed these events (from afar!) with some distress, but even he excused them as "a Tahitian custom." (He had also served to legitimize them by granting some *temperance* pledgers a temporary release from their promises.)

After New Year's Day itself, the village settled down into less public forms of diversions. The heavier drinkers continued their revels in smaller parties at home, the visitors were passed around among the various households where they had kinfolk, the young men and women met along the street for bouts of music and dance, and the faithful continued to attend, in diminishing numbers, the daily prayer meetings in church. Then, after about a week or ten days, the visitors began to leave, the alcohol ran out (along with the money to buy more), and the mood of festiveness became more and more forced—in a word (in fact, in their *own* words), people became *"fiu"* with celebration and idleness and gradually resumed work and everyday life, including extra work in efforts to repay money borrowed for the celebrations and idleness just experienced.

I cannot begin to estimate how much money income the Ateans had to forego through their idleness during the New Year celebration, and I was not able to collect credible figures for all the money all of them spent. I did, however, manage to collect a few expenditures from households that ranged from "affluent, hospitable, and heavy-drinking" to "poor, nonhospitable, and abstemious." Two of the former spent between 10,000 and 12,000 francs on their celebrations, the three latter I recorded spent less than 500 each, and the two households about the middle of this range reported expenditures of about 3,000 francs each. On the basis of this (admittedly small) sample, and informed by the knowledge I had of the styles of other Atean households, I estimate that the village as a whole spent between 100,000 and 120,000 francs on New Year—an average of about 2,500 to 3,000 per household.

Fatata's New Year celebrations were in marked contrast to those of Atea.[3] The religious side of the activities followed the same general format except for the christenings (which in Fatata took place at regular church services), and except that a larger proportion of parishioners did not attend.

The public, nonreligious part of Fatata's New Year festivities consisted of a dozen or so booths set up by as many residents, for chance-taking and for the vending of homemade food delicacies, homegrown fruits, nonalcoholic beverages, and a few manufactured novelties purchased in Pape'ete—all in pale imitation of the commercial side of Pape'ete's (fortnight-long) Bastille Day celebrations. On New Year's Day and for a few days thereafter, numbers of Fatatans would hang around their little midway talking, playing, drinking, and eating, but most of the celebrating consisted of entertaining friends and visiting kinfolk at home.

For some households with guests, the break from everyday activities lasted as long as a week, but for most other Fatatans, "New Year" was a matter of only two or three days. Except for money spent at the midway and for the larger-than-average consumption of wine and beer, the only extraordinary money outlays accompanying Fatatans' New Year celebrations were those of the nine households housing visitors—a cost I am unable to specify but one that probably would not have averaged more than 2,000 francs.

Finally, as was the case with Ateans, while I am unable to specify the income losses to Fatatans resulting from their New Year holidays, I am confident that they were much smaller on the average than those of the Ateans. Moreover, some of the Fatatans who operated booths at the village midway actually made some money profits from New Years (see page 165).

The cinema (*teata,* from "theater") was a regular part of Te Pitian life; in Atea, films were shown once or twice a week, and in Fatata, two to four times a week. In Atea, the showing took place in a small "colonial vanilla" house whose owner cleared most of it of furniture before each performance and rented it for a percentage of admissions receipts, plus free attendance for himself and his household-mates. In Fatata, the two film distributors who serviced the village rented separate "theaters"—large thatch-built sheds

---

[3]Having been in Atea at the time, I could not, of course, observe Fatata's 1954–55 New Year celebrations; but I did see those of 1959–60, and collected verbal accounts of the 1954–55 events, and so am reasonably certain that my description, so far as it goes, of the earlier one is correct.

made specially for film showing and otherwise unused. (Until shortly before my 1955 visit, the rival distributors used to show their films on the same nights but were persuaded by the theater owners to change to separate nights in order to increase the latters' revenues, which were based partly on attendance.)

The films that circulated around the rural districts of the Society Islands, including Atea and Fatata, were an extraordinarily assorted lot—cowboy, musicals, historical dramas, drawing-room comedies, slapstick, etc. Their only common characteristic was their great age; I saw some dating back to the late 1920s and none that was later than the late 1930s. (One *News Report* I witnessed pictured Marshal Foch—who died in 1929!—placing a wreath on the Tomb of the Unknown Soldier.) Most of the sound tracks were in English, the rest in French; no matter—the projection man who accompanied the films on their rounds usually made up for this shortcoming by "explaining" the action and the dialogue in terse Tahitian phrases and in a booming voice that had to compete with the deafeningly loud sound track and the audiences' continual top-of-voice commentaries. (To add a personal note, nothing I encountered in fieldwork could match the discomfort and ennui of cinema attendance: sitting for hours on floors or narrow wooden benches in stifling enclosures in an ear-splitting bedlam of sound and watching, for example, an ancient Mickey Mouse, or a publicity short advertising heavy snow-moving equipment. While realizing that my Te Pitian neighbors had different standards of comfort, noise tolerance, etc., from mine and different reactions to what they were viewing, I was nevertheless struck with their good-natured tolerance of film breakdowns, reel-sequence reversals, and the triteness and, yes, *fraudulence* of most of the subject matter itself—a fraudulence so blatant in some cases as to be commented on humorously by themselves.)

In Fatata, the distributors brought their films and equipment in a truck, unnoticed until their loudspeakers blared forth to announce the imminent performance. One of the theaters was owned by a partnership of five local men, who rented it to the film distributors for a percentage of the admissions receipts. The second theater was owned by the local Football Society, whose members had built it and whose treasury was paid 1,000 francs a month in rent by the distributor. During cinema evenings, refreshments were sold outside each theater by some enterprising residents.

Cinema evenings in Atea were much more community-wide affairs. The film crew arrived by boat to the accompaniment of loud blasts from a conch shell. Thus alerted, several young men would meet the boat at the wharf and carry the equipment, paradelike, to the theater and thereby earn free passes to the evening's performance. Unlike Fatata, where the occasions were generally sparsely attended and prosaic, cinema evenings in

Atea were very lively; nearly everyone went along, either to view the film or join in the crowd outside. Here, as in Fatata, admission cost 10 francs for children, 25 for everyone else except infants and the pastor, who entered free. In addition, some people spent from 10 to 100 and more francs for refreshments, including items like melons and fruit of which they usually had ample supplies at home, a few paces away. Unlike Fatata, the Atea theater was usually filled to overflowing, but (another source of wonder to me) I know of no instance in which a ticket-holder unable to find a seat inside the theater received or demanded a refund. (Nor, in Atea, were refunds ever received or demanded in the event of a curtailment caused by film breakage or equipment breakdown, once the showing had proceeded for a half-hour or so.)

The money spent by Te Pitians on films, and on film-time refreshments, was cumulatively very large in both villages but larger per capita in Atea than in Fatata. Few individuals kept records of their own expenditures, but approximated total figures are available for Atea, based on the rent received by the theater-house owner from the film distributor—the rent having been calculated as a percentage of the total admission money received. On this basis, Ateans spent about 200,000 francs on filmgoing during 1954, or about 901 francs per capita. In Fatata, even with its two theaters and three to four film showings a week, the populace spent much less per capita, i.e., about 619 francs.

When the costs of film-time refreshments are added to these figures—an estimate based on a few recorded individual outlays and on general observations at that time—the total per capita expenditures on this form of diversion would have come to about 937 francs for Atea and 781 francs for Fatata.[4]

This study, with its focus on economics, is not the place for an account of what the Te Pitians received in return for their large outlays on the cinema. Without question, many of them were amused or otherwise diverted, else they would probably not have continued to go. (However, there were individuals in both villages who deliberately stayed away from the cinema, asserting that the events shown in films were "not true!") Some of the things the filmgoers saw may, for example, have served to change or reinforce their desires for imported goods, with consequences for their work habits and expenditures—all matters of economic import. However, I did not follow up this line of inquiry and so cannot do more than raise the possibility here.

---

[4]The fact that Ateans spent on the average more money than Fatatans on cinema admissions but less on refreshments was due to the circumstances that many Fatatan males congregated around the refreshment booths on cinema evenings—to socialize and consume soft drinks—but did not attend the films.

Fatatans engaged in two kinds of diversions not met with in Atea, namely, billiards and *"pique-niques."* The billiard playing was housed in a shed
next to the house of the table's owner. It was not in operation during my
1955 visit, the owner having been away in Tahiti on some "business" venture no one was clear about. When in operation, I was told, it catered
mainly to the village's young men, who used to congregate there evenings
and play for 5 francs a game. *Pique-niques* (evidently of European derivation!) were engaged in mainly by young unmarried people, principally
those who were nearer the demi-European point in the ethnic behavior
scale. Those that I knew about included about a dozen participants, male
and female, and took place at the district's best swimming beaches. The
food was characteristically European: sandwiches, quiches, salads, cakes,
fruit, soft drinks, and sometimes wine. Besides swimming, the picnickers
played music and sometimes danced. According to gossip, these outings also
provided opportunities for more open flirtations than everyday village life
afforded or condoned; but they seem not to have been the erotic revels that
some older Fatatans suspected them to be.

A comparison can also be made between the amounts of money spent by
Ateans and Fatatans for the phonographs and music-making instruments
that some of them cherished. In Atea, this amounted to about 4,300 francs
in 1954, in Fatata 12,500.

In summary, when one compares the "diversions" just described with
comparable activities that were engaged in by the pre-European Tahitians,
the list seems very small. The ancient Tahitians possessed a large and varied
repertory of such, including dances, dramas, concerts, games, and sports;
and these reportedly used up much of their time and resources and involved
the services of many specialists (Oliver 1975:315–49). Of course, the "diversions" just described were not the only activities from which the 1954–55 Te
Pitians derived recreation or amusement or the like, but compared with
their ancestors of two centuries before they did seem to lead humdrum
lives—the consequences, largely, of decades of the austere puritanism introduced and enforced by Protestant missionaries.

Just as suggested, Te Pitians did quite evidently derive amusement, etc.,
from some other activities that were not engaged in wholly or primarily for
diversion. One such was participation in sodality activities, especially in
competitive singing and *tuāroʻi*. Another was fishing, still another chatting
with friends and neighbors, especially at the end of the work day. For
Ateans (but not Fatatans), there were four other kinds of activity that they
found highly diverting, namely, vanilla selling, work-group projects, the annual contest of gardening skills, already described, and women's sewing
bees.

Sewing bees in Atea were either "organized" or "unorganized." The latter, and more common, consisted of a few women getting together occasionally at the home of one of them for two or three hours of conversation and individual sewing projects. The former were parish or sodality affairs held at the parsonage or in one of the sodality meeting houses for the purpose of making, jointly, a large bed cover (*tīfaifai*) as a contribution to some worthy cause. (For example, the bed cover was sold and the proceeds donated to the sodality treasury, or it was given to a neighboring parish where it was sold and the proceeds added to the latter's building fund.) The sewing materials used for the "organized" sewing bees were contributed by the women themselves, as were the coffee and cakes sometimes partaken.

Compared with the men's house-building or reroofing gatherings, or even with the women's thatch-making ones, sewing bees were sedate, muted affairs. Nevertheless, they provided one of the few opportunities open to Atean women to display, in some respects competitively, their expertise in this almost solitary relic of Tahitian, albeit Europeanized-Tahitian, decorative art.

Finally, a few more words should be said about the practice of the ancient and durable Tahitian custom of social visiting. Te Pitians seemed to me to spend a large part of their lives visiting relatives in other places or being visited by them. At the beginning, I attempted to keep a record of these events but gave up after a while, defeated by their ubiquity. People went visiting singly or by family, and the purposes for going were varied. Some visits were for attending weddings or funerals, some for collecting shares of the profits from jointly held estates. At times, a parent went in search of a spouse for a son or daughter, or sometimes the latter would undertake the mission for himself or herself. Occasionally, a man, either alone or with his whole family, would accompany his produce to a distant market—Uturoa (in the case of Atea) or Pape'ete (in the case of Fatata). And it was common practice for an invalid's family to accompany him or her to a hospital in Uturoa or Pape'ete.

Visiting thus fulfilled a number of functions—social, economic, educational, etc. In addition, it also constituted one of the Te Pitians' cherished, and certainly one of their most talked-about diversions from what they themselves sometimes characterized as the monotony of their everyday lives. And, inexpensive as it was by some travelling standards, it cost some Te Pitians large percentages of their money incomes.

I did not record the total amounts actually spent on travelling for either Atea or Fatata. An item on "travel costs" was included in the survey I conducted among the heads of households, but, in most instances, the figures "recalled" and the methods of "recalling" were, like those for expenditures on alcoholic beverages and other "luxuries," not such as to inspire credibility, to say the least!

I did, however, collect enough detailed and credible accounts from a few returned travellers soon after their return home to provide some basis for estimation. Thus, in the case of the Ateans who travelled outside Huahine during my stay there (mostly to Uturoa and Pape'ete), the person-trips undertaken (not including non-fare-paying infants and children) cost an average of about 3,000 francs each—for transportation and food; lodging was usually with kinfolk—bringing Atea's total annual expenditure on this item to about 102,800 francs, or 463 francs per capita.

Based on a similar kind of sampling and averaging, supplemented by fare records kept by the Fatata-Pape'ete launch captain, the total annual figure for Fatata for the same period was about 107,900, and the per capita one about 318. (This does not include the trips made by fishermen to market their catches.) The cost per trip for Fatatan travellers (mainly to and from nearby Tahiti) was far less than that for most Atean travellers, but more of the former took such trips and did so more frequently.

CHAPTER VI

BEING A PROTESTANT

In Chapter II were described some features of the "native" Protestantism that prevailed throughout the Society Islands, including Atea and Fatata. I now turn to some additional features of church-related belief and practice that I observed in Atea and/or Fatata, but first a word about the two parishes' pasts. To begin with, the two communities had had markedly different experiences, historically, with Christianity.

Fatata was a major religious center in pagan times, having been the site of numerous temples, including a large and awesomely sacrosanct one, Taputapuatea, which was dedicated to the god 'Oro. ('Oro, a god of war—among other attributes—was the Society Islands' principal deity from sometime before 1767 to 1815, the one to whom human sacrifices were offered and whose sanction was required for the validation of the islands' highest-ranking kin titles.) In contrast, the site where Atea now stands was inhabited in pagan times by only a thin scattering of households, and the only surviving evidence of religious activity there was a small set of stones alleged to be the remains of a temple (probably a domestic shrine). The principal centers of Huahine's pagan religious structures and activities were several miles away, at Maeva in the north and Tiva in the south.

Fatata had also been a principal center of early Christian missionary activity. In 1809 when the first missionaries and their sole Tahitian patron, Pomare II, were obliged to flee from the latter's pagan enemies on Tahiti, they took refuge in Fatata. Thereafter, when most of the missionaries continued their exodus by going to Australia, one of them remained at Fatata; and it was to Fatata that most of the missionaries repaired to in 1811, after their return from Australia. When Pomare embraced Christianity in 1812, Fatata became the major site of missionary activity, and it was there that the high priest of Taputapuatea temple announced his own conversion by consigning to the flames the dread 'Oro image of the temple.

In 1819, there were enough converts in Fatata to form a church, the first in the islands, and shortly thereafter its members began to construct a stone chapel (the predecessor of the present one of the same shape). Thereafter, Fatata remained a premier center of mission activity; according to an early history of the mission it was the "nursery from which originated every church not only in Eimeo [Mo'orea] and Tahiti, but also in each of the Leeward Islands" (Newbury, 1961, p. 305).

Atea, on the other hand, had no church of its own until 1927. Before that, some of the people residing scattered around its two bays went to Fare to attend church services and the others went to Tefare, on Huahine's east coast. At one point, there developed such a schism (over dogma) between the Fare and Tefare pastors that many of Atea's residents moved to Tefare or Fare in order to support their respective pastors. The first resident pastor of Atea was a local man, a mixed-blood descendant of one of the first English missionaries on Huahine, who was selected and trained for the position by the mission authorities. This man (two of whose daughters were residing in Atea in 1954–55) was also the first to conduct school in Atea. When he died, he was succeeded in the pastorate by the man who held the position in 1954–55.

However, the differences between Atea and Fatata with respect to their religious histories were not reflected in the content of the religious *beliefs* of their 1954–55 residents, which it will now be useful to summarize.

In Te Pitians' belief,[1] a human consisted of a physical palpable body (*tino*) and a separate spirit (*vārua*), or soul. The latter sometimes left the body during sleep—hence dreams—or during states of accident, sickness, or induced unconsciousness, and finally at death. Upon occurrence of the latter, the soul did one or both of two things: (1) in line with Protestant doctrine, it went to the right hand of God to await judgment; (2) following persistent pre-Christian ideas it became a ghost (*tūpāpa'o*) and remained nearby. (This seeming contradiction was either ignored by believers in some contexts or "solved" by the positing of two souls.) I will return to the Protestant side of Te Pitians' belief after a few words about the pagan side but meanwhile

---

[1] I did not make a systematic attempt to discover the full range of Te Pitians' beliefs about the various matters that ethnographers conventionally include under "religion." I did sound out several informants about their views on those aspects of religion in general, and Protestantism in particular, which seemed to have a direct bearing on the "economic" focus of my field study but even for this narrower purpose, my data are so sparse and shallow that I depend upon Robert Levy's remarkable work to broaden and deepen my own understanding and to provide the reader with a helpful summary. What follows in this section then is based partly on my own data and partly on Levy's.

Atea: The dying art of hat-making

Atea: Old ladies' fashions never change

Atea: A matron's pride—

Atea: Public laundry

must stress that all Te Pitians I knew anything about believed in both sides.[2]

Some ghost-spirits were mildly benevolent, more were characteristically mischievous or even malevolent, and most were usually quite neutral though capable of harm if angered or if pressed into service by a sorcerer. Harming was done in a number of ways, including accident-causing, sexual seduction, and possession; and consequences ranged from mild discomfort or illness to death. Humans courted those fates by breaking social-relational rules—wittingly or not; by violating old pagan tabus, e.g., moving stone land boundaries, defacing pagan temple remains—again, whether wittingly or not; and by angering another human sufficiently to induce him to utter a (spirit-invoking) curse or to utilize a sorcerer to employ his spirit-familiar to attack.[3]

Some spirit-caused disorders were amenable to remedy through one of the poultices or brews of native plants (which may therefore be inferred to have some spirit-associated efficacies). Others were cured through the services of a *tahu'a* (spirit doctor), who used his own spirit-familiar to drive away or otherwise neutralize the attacking spirit. As Levy notes, sorcerers may in fact exist only in Tahitians' fantasies; curative *tahu'a*, on the other hand, were real, there having been one in Atea and one in Fatata during my 1954–55 visits.[4]

Neither of the above practices—the use of native medicines nor the utilization of a spirit-doctor—had any large economic significance. As described earlier, Te Piti's several herbalists neither expected nor received any tangible kind of fee from their clients, and only one of the local spirit-doctors was recompensed in any tangible way; he was a very old man and was given some food from time to time by grateful patients. Economic implications can, however, be read into the beliefs about some of the causes of spirit-attack, namely, those aimed at persons thought guilty of such specific misdeeds as theft or such societal improprieties as overweening ambition, excessive wealth, and over-conspicuous consumption. Such persons were believed to be vulnerable either to direct attack by an offended spirit or by

[2]As Levy noted, the Protestant pantheon introduced to Tahitians by the LMS missionaries also included a variety of lesser spirits, benevolent and malevolent, in addition to the Holy Trinity.

[3]In Levy's opinion, the Tahitians he studied believed themselves vulnerable to most kinds of spirit attack only if they felt and allowed themselves to express anxiety of the spirits' presence. I myself happened only upon fragmentary symptoms of this attitude, not enough for generalization.

[4]*Tahu'a pifao* was the Tahitian term for sorcerer in contemporary Te Piti as it was throughout these islands in pre-Christian times. *Pifao*, a kind of fishhook, refers to the agony experienced by the sorcery victim, like that of a hooked fish.

some human whom they had harmed or who was envious or scandalized by the other's wealth or ambition or display.

Turning now to the more distinctly *Protestant* side of religion, Te Pitians derived their beliefs about it from reading the Bible and from hearing it read and explained by their pastors. Few Te Pitian adults considered the Bible to be true in all historical details, but for nearly all of them it was the most authentic source of information about God's relations to man and the most authoritative guide for human conduct. (Many Te Pitians also read the Bible for pleasure, it having been the *only* reading matter for most of them, and—besides the cinema and local gossip—their only source of narrative.)

Of the various supernaturals named in the Bible, Te Pitians concerned themselves mainly with God (*te Atua; Iehova*). Jesus (*Ietu*) was referred to occasionally, the Holy Ghost (*Vārua Maita'i*) figured in prayers, and angels were acknowledged to exist—especially Satan (*Tātani*), who served as a kind of avatar for the pagan deities that Te Pitians had heard about; but God, and a distinctly anthropomorphic God, was overwhelmingly predominant in their pantheon, the focus of their prayers and worship. (Mary was also acknowledged and sometimes honored, but Mary-worship was said to be a distinctively Catholic and hence somewhat alien practice.)

Following Robert Levy's analysis (Levy 1973: 180ff), one may consider Te Pitians' relations with God as having three bases: (1) His role as Creator of the cosmos and sustainer of cosmological order; (2) his day-to-day concern with mankind's affairs; and (3) his role (with Jesus) as Final Judge over the fate of human's souls.

I found no trace of disbelief in the role played by God as Creator of the cosmos (including mankind) and as sustainer of the larger aspects of cosmological order. On the other hand, outside of perfunctory sermon references, I recorded no sentiment to the effect that mankind in general, or Te Pitians in particular, owed God any tangible return for His services. (In this respect, the attitude towards God resembled that of many Te Pitians towards the Administration, i.e., officials endowed with *so much* wealth and power neither needed nor were entitled to repayment for their services to mankind, and particularly not from people as poor as themselves.)

Levy states that his Tahitian informants believed God to be concerned with their everyday behavior in three ways. First, for those actively associated with the Protestant Church (and this included nearly all adults in Atea but a significantly smaller proportion of those in Fatata), that association carried a publicly enunciated and personally accepted commitment to obey church rules, e.g., regarding church attendance, Sabbath sanctity, familial morality, etc., 'and expectation of divine punishment in the event of rule breaking. (This represents another example of Levy's interesting point about the consciously *contractual* nature of some types of Tahitian relationships.) Secondly, my own findings serve to confirm Levy's opinion that "... God also takes a limited role in the active protection of individuals in this world ... in response to prayer" (p. 181) and regardless of the moral worth of the suppliant. In this respect, as Levy notes, God is similar to ancestral spirits and ghosts, who also occasionally protected individuals in response to prayer entreaty. And thirdly, God was viewed as intervening in Te Pitians' daily affairs by way of punishing individuals who exceeded certain limits of natural or social order. In Levy's words, "It is God who punishes violations of the natural limits, which for the villagers and many urban Tahitians means in particular acts involving ambition, striving, or pride. The man who wants too much, who strives too much, who is too ambitious about accumulating wealth or developing his lands. The man who is not humble enough, who is too aggressively self-confident, will be punished by God in this world. He will become ill and lose the fruits of his striving." Thus, Levy goes on to say, his informants viewed the biblical tribulations of Job as "... the natural response of God to a man who has too much" (Levy 1973:181-2). Needless to say, this belief contains some important implications for the economic behavior of those who hold it, which many Te Pitians did.

Levy uncovered two rather widely different sets of opinion concerning God's role as (in his terms) "Gatekeeper of heaven and hell." One, shared by his more traditionally oriented informants, held that proper action was the key to heaven; as Levy says:

> People must obey what they call the "don'ts," the *'eiaha*, which are the Ten Commandments. Many villagers have violated the commandments concerning stealing, adultery, and honoring one's parents. But for those who accept action as a guarantee of salvation, the goal is to have put oneself in some sort of conformity with the Ten Commandments before dying. This is a matter of reading the Bible frequently, legitimizing one's relationship with one's spouse, establishing some household stability, and, if one is within the church, becoming a Communicant. This takes care of the "true" soul while the perhaps more important part of one's personality prepares to be transformed into an earthbound ghost. [183]

The other opinion held, according to Levy, by a few more ambitious, more "modern" individuals, viewed salvation to be dependent not only upon right actions but, in addition, upon conscious thoughts and urges whether or not these are expressed in actions. According to Levy's probings, some individuals of this opinion considered themselves destined for hell because of their sinful thoughts and wishes despite their success in curbing them, inasmuch as God read their thoughts and judged them accordingly.

On the basis of my fragmentary and less profound probings, I can attest to having found exemplars of both of these opinions in Te Piti but received the impression that one's afterlife destiny was of little concern to most people living there, including those who seemed most assured of their fate in heaven or in hell. It appeared to me that, for most Te Pitians who gave the matter much thought (these having been relatively more numerous in Atea than in Fatata), the immediate opinions and reactions of fellow villagers, and the prospects of immediate divine retribution, were more influential censors of behavior than were any hopes or fears about afterlife.

As stated at the outset, I found no noteworthy differences between Atea and Fatata with respect to the *content* of religious beliefs held by their residents. This is not to say that all residents of either village subscribed to all of the beliefs just listed. In fact, towards some of the beliefs, e.g., in fiery hell and in the "reality" of (the metaphor of) communion, there were sceptics, even outright disbelievers, in both villages. Regrettably, I did not attempt to probe the degree of such scepticism in either place. There is some plausibility in supposing that the Fatatans, with their generally higher level of (secular) schooling and their more frequent exposures to Pape'ete's secularizing influences, were on the average less "religious" in their beliefs than the Ateans, but I cannot prove that to have been so.

On the other hand, there were some appreciably wide differences between the two villages in the ways their residents engaged in *actions* associated with their Protestant beliefs—to which subject I now turn.

In both Atea and Fatata most residents were identified in one way or another with the Protestant faith. Atea contained only one individual associated with another denomination—in this case, Mormon; Fatata contained several individuals affiliated with the Roman Catholic Church and one Seventh Day Adventist (a man from Tahiti married to a local woman). There were, however, some notable differences between the two villages with respect to the proportion of each populace taking active parts in church-associated affairs, i.e., the average amount of time active Protestants devoted to church activities, and so on. There were also some differences in the content and organization of the activities themselves.

Regular church services were held every Sunday and consisted in both parishes of an early-morning session, a Sunday School session, and a main service that began about an hour or two before noon. The early session was usually attended by only a handful of the older stalwarts and consisted mainly of prayer. Sunday School was, of course, for children, and the turnout was generally as large as it was boisterous. The main service was usually well attended, including people of all ages, from newly born to decrepitly senile. Occasionally, also, the full-fledged church Communicants returned or remained to attend an afternoon prayer session as well.

Sunday night meetings in both parishes were usually devoted to singing combined with *tuāroʻi*, the gamelike Bible-knowledge bees described earlier. In Fatata, these sessions were separate sodality affairs; in Atea, they usually took place in a common Assembly Hall (*Fare Putuputuraʻa*), which was built especially to accommodate the whole congregation's more secular meetings.

Events like Christmas, New Year, and Easter were celebrated with special services, which were alike in both parishes in some respects and different in others. The similarities do not warrant description; they conformed to Protestant ritual patterns that are probably worldwide in form and content. The differences do, however, merit some mention.

In the first place, while all three services—Christmas, New Year, and Easter—drew larger attendance than ordinary Sunday services in both villages, the additions to the Atea congregation on these occasions were barely noticeable (nearly all Ateans having been regular attenders throughout the year). In contrast, large numbers of Fatatans attended these services who rarely or never appeared at the regular Sunday services.

Secondly, while Christmas was the more elaborate service in Fatata, the New Year's Eve one was such in Atea, which corresponded, on the religious side, with the differences of emphasis on the secular side. As previously noted, for Ateans, the New Year celebrations lasted for a week or more and climaxed weeks of preparations, whereas for Fatatans they represented a relatively brief and low-key festival. Conversely, in Fatata, Christmas was marked by some gift-giving (especially to children) and a few other simulations of European custom, while in Atea such practices were conspicuously absent. Some Ateans I queried knew about some European Christmas customs but asserted that they themselves were "too poor" to practice them, particularly the giving of gifts to children or anyone else.

The May Offering (*ʻaufauraʻa mē*) took place once a year and usually in the month of May.[5] To it all members of the congregation were morally obliged to contribute as large an amount of money as possible, for support of the mission as a whole. The day of the collection varied from place to place and from one year to the next, depending upon the itinerary of the mission

---

[5] Similar meetings take place in Protestant communities in other parts of the Pacific islands, but the only ones I have observed firsthand were those in the Society Islands, where they constituted one of the many practices introduced by missionaries of the London Mission Society that have persisted ever since. For a classic description of such a meeting, this one in Tonga, see Basil Thomson, *The Diversions of a Prime Minister* (Edinburgh and London: William Blackwood and Sons, 1894).

official (usually the president) who presided over the affair. It took place in the church, to the accompaniment of prayer, singing, and sermons.

One that I witnessed in Fatata lasted four hours until, it appears, the visiting mission leaders were convinced that no more donations could be extracted from the congregation. The meeting began with a sermon about people's obligations to God and the mission (including the need to send missionaries to places not yet fortunate enough, as was Tahiti, to be "enlightened"). Then numerous prayers to the same effect, followed by some general and some sodality singing, and the collection began.

The assembled children led off the procession to the table, which had been set up in front of the pulpit and behind which sat the pastor and visitors. The children marched up to the table in line and placed their offerings on it—coins or tight little wads of bills. When they were done, two of the visitors counted the money and reported the sum to the mission leader, who announced the count to the congregation with the remark that it was "very, small; not nearly enough; not even as much as last year's." At this, a few of the children marched forward again and tossed down additional coins, which were counted and adjudged "better; but still not enough." After two more rounds by a dwindling line of children it was reckoned, evidently, that no more would be forthcoming, and the next category of donors, the communicants, was invited to come forward. This was done by a representative of the latter, the parish *Orator*, who went forward and handed over a roll of bills containing the money which the Communicants had been assessed, by prior agreement among themselves, i.e., 100 francs each. When this sum, called the *foundation money* (*moni tumu*) had been received (and counted and announced), the communicants were exhorted to come forward with additional donations—*support money* (*moni tauturu*). This they did, one by one, some of them returning several times.

All this was accompanied by singing, a continuous harangue from the leaders, and by much noisy moving about among the congregation. Some of the donors placed their money on the table, almost furtively; others flung their coins and bills down with what looked like disgust and contempt. (Later I was informed that many in the congregation had indeed become angered by the ceaseless exhortations but felt obliged to keep on giving.)

Meanwhile, some members of the congregation left the church for a while to obtain money for more donations. And during all this, one of the Chinese storekeepers operated a refreshment stand on the roadside nearby, thereby diverting many a franc that might otherwise have gone to God.

In this way were presented a number of other donations, *foundation* (assessed) and individually given *support* money, by each of the sodalities, by the Football Club, and by sets of the relatives and friends of persons who had died in recent years.

Finally, when all these "institutional" groups and causes had been canvassed and the resulting tally found to be less than the previous year's, individuals *qua* individuals were exhorted to contribute, which many of them did, one by one, until the leader's apparent objective had been reached—a sum of 41,410 francs, which was about 2,000 more than the previous year's. With this, the donations ended and shortly thereafter the meeting itself.

As the congregation dispersed homeward, I was struck with the exhausted and somber color of most adults' moods—not exhilaration at the sum given (which they knew to be relatively large) and not self-satisfaction in their magnanimity, but what appeared to be anger at the way the support-money had been wrenched out of them and self-reproach that they had succumbed to the harangues.

Most intriguing of all about this exhibition of large-scale "giving" was the anonymity of much of it. Unlike comparable manifestations I had witnessed in Melanesia, where the value of each individual's "gift" was explicitly and loudly proclaimed, the larger part of the total money donated at the Fatata May Collection—that comprising the various individually donated *support* monies—was unattributed; no donor made a point of revealing how much he gave and no announcement of the amount was made by the recipients. Later on after direct questioning, I managed to learn from some individuals how much they themselves had donated, but to the best of my knowledge, few donors made any point of revealing such information to others. In a word, there appeared to be no effort made on the part of the donors to obtain any returns in the form of social approval for their largesse. And, judging by the attitude of most of the donors I questioned, there was little, if any, expectation on their part that their gifts would be reciprocated in any form by God. Of course, the fact that a contributor made repeated trips to the table could have been—probably was—noted by others, but at the time, few in the congregation would have known how much money was being given. (And I never heard a cynical word, from these oftimes cynical Fatatans, suggesting that anyone had attempted to deceive by dividing their total contribution into smaller payments in order to make more trips and hence a better show.)

I did not witness a May Collection in Atea during my visit but was informed in considerable detail about previous ones there. From such accounts, it appears that they had differed from the Fatatan one in several respects.

In the first place, most of the money donated in Atea had been in the form of foundation money—from the Sunday Schoolers, the Communicants, and the three sodalities—all of which had been assessed and collected prior to the meeting and which was presented by a representative from each group. Also, the relatively small donations of support money given by

individuals were handed over by each of them in toto (and not in installments), to the attentive interest of the whole congregation. (Evidently, the
amounts of these individual donations were not announced at the time but
were widely known anyway.)

Secondly, the entire proceedings were relatively brief and were carried
out quietly and solemnly, with none of the harangue that marked the Fatatan session I saw. It should be recalled that my evidence is hearsay, and my
informants may have been concerned to suppress the discreditable side of
the occasion—for such they considered it when I later on described to them
the Fatatan proceedings. On the other hand, if their accounts were true—
and I take them to be so—the reason for this difference between the meetings was due not to any contrast between the temperaments or religious attitudes of Ateans and Fatatans but to the knowledge on the part of the visiting mission leaders that no amount of exhortation could have extracted
from the former more money, because more money they did not have.

Comparing the two parishes with respect to contributions to the May
Collection, 41,410 francs were donated by Fatatans in 1955, as against
32,000 by Ateans that same year.[6] This would result in an overall per capita
contribution of 95 and 152 francs, respectively, if the population figures
used in this calculation included all *Tahitian* Protestants residing in each
parish at the time.[7]

The figures on relative numbers of actual donors and the amounts per
donation provide another comparison. In these terms, in 1955, 168 of Atea's
216 Protestants—78 percent of them—donated 31,000[8] francs for an average
of 184.5 francs per donor. Most adults gave 100 to 150 francs each, while
one gave 200, another 250, and the pastor and his household 900. At Fatata's May Collection for 1955, the method of giving the *support*-money
rules out a wholly accurate count, but I estimate that the 237 resident Tahitian donors—54 percent of all resident Protestant parishioners—gave an average of 160 francs each. Since several of the donors gave amounts of over
500 francs each, this reduces the average of the others to about 140 francs
each.

In other words, in this domain of money spending, while a few of the
more generous Fatata parishioners donated larger sums than any of the
Ateans, a relatively larger number of Tahitian Protestants residing in Atea

---

[6]The reported figures for 1954 were approximately 39,000 for Fatata's parish and 32,100 for
Atea's parish.

[7]In the case of Fatata, there were at this time 437 Tahitian "Protestants" (including infants)
living in the whole parish, including 107 who resided outside the community studied.

[8]Some of the contributions to each village's collection came from absentee (Tahitian) residents and from non-Tahitians, e.g., from the local Chinese storekeepers.

village gave to their church, and gave more than was the case with their counterparts residing in Fatata village.[9]

While the May Offerings were higher in drama, the basic ritual of Te Piti's Protestantism was the ordinary Sunday midday service. Indeed, no other event epitomized so many patterns of Te Pitian social behavior as did that long-drawn-out test of an ethnographer's measure of dedication to his job.

First of all, the seating plan itself exemplified some of the basic ways the Te Pitians classified themselves, as will be described.

Secondly, the Sunday midday service was Te Piti's only regular occasion for which people—some people—specially dressed. Infants were outfitted in beribboned pink, blue, and white garments identical with Western baby fashions, including knitted bonnets and bootees (in church-house temperatures that regularly climbed to 100 degrees Fahrenheit!). Children were neatly clothed in dresses or in shorts and shirts. Young men and women, whether married or not, usually wore the latest Pape'ete fashions, including sandals or shoes. Middle-aged men and women were less fashionably dressed, but even some of them made the painful sacrifice of wearing shoes, which, however, were usually eased out of once inside the church. (Another badge worn by some men in church—and *only* in church—was dark glasses; why, I could never fathom. Not, it would seem, to be able to conceal their closed eyes; many of them slept unashamedly without such a disguise.) Finally, even the elderly dressed up for church; that is to say, elderly women usually put on their straw hats and old-fashioned and usually black "Mother Hubbards," and elderly men donned their black high-collar jackets. However, few elderly churchgoers bothered to wear shoes; and elderly men often did not even bother to shave. (It was never clear to me whether the elders' mode of dress was due to an unconscious disinterest in self-adornment or was deliberately meant to express a conventional age-based attitude towards the fashion foibles of youth.)

Elders possibly aside, for most Te Pitians past childhood correct Sunday-service attire was a major cultural objective. A large proportion of most families' money income went into buying ready-made clothing or the materials for making some. (For some females, this provided the principal incentive to work at a money-earning task.) Many girls and women devoted every Saturday to laundering and ironing, and Sunday mornings before church were men's usual, and sometimes only, time for shaving and trimming hair.

---

[9]This calculation is based on the assumption—a fairly safe one, I believe—that the Tahitians residing in the Fatata community under study gave the same amounts, on the average, as those residing elsewhere in the parish.

The Te Pitians' customary bearing in church also requires description—although I am not sure what it signifies other than exemplification of general behavioral modes. Let me say to begin with that postures suggesting *reverence* were, to say the least, uncommon. Babies were allowed to cry for long periods before being taken outside. Children—especially little boys—poked one another continuously. Older people chatted in stentorian whispers—or quite out loud. For a while, I thought that old men, and they alone, displayed signs of quiet solemnity but later discovered that they were often sound asleep. Sometimes the din reached such volume that it drowned out the sermon and moved even the normally patient pastors to ask for quiet. Now and then the children became so unruly that an adult, usually a deacon, intervened, but never with lasting effect. (On one occasion I witnessed, when the pastor admonished a particularly unruly boy by name, the latter's parents became so affronted by this usurpation of *their* authority that they widely criticized the pastor and remained away from church for weeks.)[10]

The general monthly program of sermon topics was listed earlier (Chapter I). It was my observation that this program was adhered to quite faithfully, although the particular subjects treated within that framework varied widely from one month to the next. There was one kind of topic, however, that was notable by its absence: I refer here to sermons dealing with local affairs. Rarely did the pastor in either congregation use the pulpit as a rostrum for inveighing against parishioners' behavior, religious or otherwise; and on the few occasions when he did he was usually criticized (though not to his face) for having done so ("that's not his job"). Only twice did I hear such pulpit-delivered criticism elicit support: once, when it concerned the heedless prank of some youths in removing the district's tricolor from its flagpole; the second time, when it laid into certain unnamed people who had allegedly ridiculed an indigent neighbor for attending church service in tattered clothes.

During my visit in 1954–55, the Atea church was filled almost to capacity nearly every Sunday. In fact, the only Tahitians in Atea who consistently stayed away from the Sunday midday service were a handful of infirm old men and a middle-aged woman who professed contempt for the religious hypocrisy of her neighbors' churchgoing. In Fatata, on the other hand, the Sunday midday service usually drew less than half of the parish's nominal Protestants; in fact, many of the absentees openly voiced their disinterest in local church matters, and a few went so far as to express an active dislike for all aspects of Christianity except the truth of the Bible itself.

---

[10]This lack of reverence on the part of those merely attending religious ceremonies, in contrast to the bearing of the main officients, was noted by Bligh at pagan rites (Oliver 1974:85–86; Levy 1973:148).

Differences were also discernible in other ways in which the two communities observed the Sabbath. In Atea, it was a day for church attendance, good eating, and rest. Except for a little early-morning (prechurch) fishing, and except for preparation of the large Sunday noon meal, little or no productive work was carried out. People strolled or sat about quietly; occasionally there was a public meeting to discuss government or parish affairs, but no organized sports, no partying, and especially no publicly noticeable drinking.

In Fatata, quite the reverse. Although few people engaged in productive work on Sunday, the day there was the usual one for partying, including an occasional noisy drinking party (even within hearing of the people gathered for services in church). It was also the usual day for football matches (and in later years for cockfighting) which were sometimes attended by the pastor, who expressed no opposition to them—"provided they did not take place at church-service time."

In the view of the Atean girl who accompanied my wife and me to Fatata, the two sharpest, most distressing differences between the two places were the unelaboratedness of some Fatatan weddings (in Atea *every* wedding ceremony, civil and/or religious, was accompanied by a celebration), and Fatatans' lack of reverence towards the Sabbath.

Differences between the two villages with respect to the celebration of Christmas, New Year, and Easter and with respect to the conduct of the May Collections have already been touched on.

Besides attending Sunday services with some regularity—weekly, monthly, or only yearly—many of the Protestants of Te Piti assisted in one way or another in maintaining the physical facilities of their respective church buildings. In each place, these buildings consisted of the church itself, the pastor's residence, and the land on which they stood; titles to these properties were held by the mission, headquartered in Pape'ete. In Fatata, the mission also held title to a large tract of land located in the center of the village. This was provisionally allocated to the local pastor for his personal use; while I was there, he did so by collecting from its breadfruit and other fruit trees and keeping his pigs there. In Atea, there was an additional building, a new and costly meeting house (*Fare Putuputura'a*), in which the congregation as a whole met to engage in activities considered too secular to carry out in the church itself—including *tuāro'i* sessions and business meetings for the congregation as a whole. Some incidents in the history of the building throw light on the congregation's organization, and in the place occupied by the church in Atea, as distinct from Fatata, where no such building existed. (In Fatata all *tuāro'i* sessions there took place in the separate sodality meeting houses, and all other secular parish-wide business was conducted by the pastor in conference with the deacons or with the Communicants as such.)

The Atea parish meeting house was a handsome, cement-floored and -walled building that had been built a few years previously under the supervision of an expert builder brought in for the purpose. It was the pride of the parish—and a major source of its conflicts.

When an architectural plan for the building had been agreed upon—a process that in itself had provoked much strife—and the estimated cost put at 350,000 francs, the parish leaders decided to raise the necessary money by assessing each parishioner age fifteen and over the sum of 2,500 francs, to be paid in five annual installments. And to insure payment, a rule (*ture*) was adopted (by vote of a large majority of the parishioners) that defaulters would be denied access to the building and, more weightily, would be denied the services of the local pastor for marriage rites, funerals, etc., although not for church services themselves) until their debt had been paid. This rule, which was deemed too draconian by some parishioners but adopted anyway, was considered by the majority (and on sound evidence!) to be necessary in order to insure completion of the building. (Ateans had seen around the islands several uncompleted public buildings left so by financial default, and they were on whole cynical about their fellow Tahitians' determination regarding unsecured financial obligations.) Residents reaching age fifteen, or outsiders moving to Atea, after completion of the building would not be required to pay, but residents living temporarily elsewhere were assessed.

In due course, the building was completed, and duly dedicated—but what a dedication! The mission official invited to dedicate it described it as being "so beautiful" that he declared it, in his prayer, to be too "sacred" for some of the activities for which it had been built (including consuming food) and for tobacco smoking. This meant that *another* and even more secular parish house was required; and another such house was begun nearby—but only begun, since it had been located, without permission, on Administration-owned lagoon land and since no sanctions regarding the financial assessments had been instituted to insure its completion.

Meanwhile, during my 1954–55 visit, the parish meeting house was regularly used for the parish-wide Sunday night *tuāro'i* sessions—by most parishioners, that is. Some parishioners continued to be denied access because of their failure, in a few instances purposeful, to pay their assessments. One such was Fati, whose "case" surfaced during my first visit.

Fati was one of Atea's largest landowners and by all reports received a large money income from cash crops and rent. He was, however, residing in Pape'ete while the meeting house was under construction and, upon his return, he announced his disinterest in utilizing the building and therefore his unwillingness to pay his share of its cost. But that was before he decided to get his two nubile daughters married safely, i.e., before their maidenly reputations in the village had been compromised. The double wedding envisaged for this important event (one of the grooms was the son of another of Atea's wealthier men) called for a bang-up church wedding and some use of the meeting house, so Fati ate his earlier words and asked the pastor to conduct the services, promising to pay part of his meeting house assessment immediately and the rest later on, after regaining the solvency he would sacrifice in paying for the large expenses such a wedding would entail. The pastor agreed but convened a meeting of the whole parish—a necessary action in view of the important principle involved.

The meeting was long and stormy. Except for the local groom's father (who argued that since he himself had paid up his son should not be penalized by enforcement of the rule), everyone suggested that the rule should be applied. The break in ranks came over the suggestion that Fati be allowed to pay part of his assessment later on; a few sided with the pastor on this point, but most agreed that full payment should precede pastoral service and meeting house use. (Some of them pointed out that a few other residents—poorer ones—were being denied such rites because they had been unable up to that point to pay all of their assessments.)

In the end, the rule was upheld according to its strictest interpretation, and Fati managed to pay the full amount before the wedding, but the incident led some of the more philosophic parishioners to conclude out loud that the meeting house, for all its splendor and usefulness, was creating more strife than it was worth.

As reported at the beginning of this anecdotal *détour,* Fatata contained nothing equivalent to Atea's meeting house. I would, in fact, predict that without a major change taking place in their social relationships, most Fatatans would not wish for or support a parish-wide project of this kind. (The church itself and its building had "always" been there and required no extraordinary parish-wide effort to maintain its program.)

Maintenance of Te Piti's church buildings and parsonages devolved upon the congregations. In both places, relays of women and girls met together periodically to sweep the churches and surrounding yards, and during my 1954–55 visit to Atea the church building and parsonage were repaired and repainted by a crew made up of most of the parish's able-bodied youths and men; the few able-bodied males who did not join in contributed money, which went towards buying the paint. The Fatata church building was also, acknowledgedly, in critical need of repair and paint. The last major repair job had been carried out "many years" previously by skilled workmen who had been paid money for the job—money levied from the congregation—but during my visit, the pastor appeared unwilling to stir up a controversy, which another such levy would have surely set off. In contrast to this attitude, the Atea church painting was carried out willingly and in good spirits, although there was some grumbling when they were instructed by the pastor to put a second coat of paint on the parsonage.

When I described to some Fatatans how the Ateans had accomplished their church and sodality house repairs—by work bees rather than money assessments—they reacted with amusement at the "rural backwardness" of the latter.

The two congregations were also required from time to time to provide hospitality for visiting Communicants from other parishes and to contribute funds or services to other parishes engaged in constructing new churches.

Finally, another kind of activity engaged in by Te Piti's church congregations—or by pastors representing those congregations—was the performance of certain rites for individual members, namely, christenings, nuptials, and funerals. Virtually all children born of Protestant parents were christened in church. Also, all religious wedding rites uniting Protestant couples were performed by the pastor in the church. (Civil rites were performed by the *tāvana* in the schoolhouse.) And except in the case of some prechristened infants, the pastors usually presided at the graveside rites of their parishioners. In fact, the exceptions were not really such, because even after their christening children did not count as full-fledged parishioners until they had entered Sunday School.

The foregoing activities were engaged in by each community's parish congregation as a whole. In addition, each one of the congregations was divided into sodalities (*pupu*) which had activities of their own.

As noted in Chapter I, all Tahitian parishes were subdivided into two or more such sodalities, each with its own assembly house (*fare putuputura'a*), where members met together to sing and engage in *tuāro'i* and other semi-religious activities. The general features of the parish sodalities set forth in Chapter I apply equally to those of Atea and Fatata and hence need not be reviewed here. I am unable to judge whether Atea and Fatata shared features of sodality organization, etc., not shared with those of other parishes, but it will be useful at this point to describe in greater detail some of the features that they had in common.

By local precedent in both parishes, girls and boys were eligible for membership in a church sodality upon reaching the age of fifteen, which was also the conventional age for leaving Sunday School. And in both parishes there was a slight numerical tendency for people to choose a sodality mate for a spouse, but this was rarely verbalized as a norm. According to my enquiries, an individual marrying into a parish from outside almost invariably joined the sodality of his (or her) spouse, and this was said to be "right." Also, in the case of a marital union between locals belonging to different sodalities, most opinions expressed on this score said that a woman ought to transfer to the one of her spouse—which was merely a specific application of the general postulate concerning male superiority. In actuality, my queries established that almost as many men had transferred as had women, and in some cases spouses had remained in separate sodalities.

Even more emphatic was the opinion that children should join the sodalities of their parents, or at least of their father; the former they almost invariably did, but in cases where parents belonged to separate sodalities their offspring tended to follow suit on sexual lines.

But all this has only background relevance; the point of present interest is that the members of a sodality were not, normatively, classified by age criteria—at least not explicitly so. Every sodality was headed by one or two "leaders" (*ra'atira*), and these were in most cases parish deacons and usually men past forty or so, but there were no formally enunciated regulations regarding behavior based specifically on age. At sodality gatherings there was the tendency for members to segregate by age and for leadership to be exercised by people in their middle years; but these actions were expressions of more general age-linked norms. Officially, once a person became a member of a sodality, his membership rights and duties were full-fledged.

I was struck repeatedly by the amount of rivalry that prevailed in both congregations between their respective sodalities. This rivalry was exemplified most actively in singing, but it surfaced in other contexts as well—in mutually disparaging remarks about the other's meeting house, meeting attendance, size of treasury, etc. The singing rivalry took place in church at the Sunday midday service, where members from each group sat together and at a point in the proceedings performed some song specially practiced for the event. The singing was not staged as a contest—in fact, it was not usual for all sodalities to perform on the same Sunday—but a particularly good or bad performance was noted by the congregation and mentally chalked up to the relative credit or discredit of the group over time. The singing was judged partly on performance—in terms of harmony and loudness—and partly on the novelty of the hymn. Concerning the latter, the objective was to produce one that had never been sung locally before. This ruled out the old favorites and moved the more active choristers to search out new hymns, which they could then dramatically unveil (better: *unleash!*) in church, to the discomfiture of their rivals.[11] To produce the desired effect, the new hymn had to be practiced in secret—a relative term of course,

---

[11]In the eyes of some Te Pitians, nothing served better to secure our acceptance in their midst than the efforts of my wife and myself to teach them new hymns, especially Negro spirituals, which I translated into Tahitian lyrics and which my wife then taught them to sing. Needless to say, we were most careful to bestow our services evenhandedly among all the sodalities, although it was suggested to us occasionally that we ought perhaps to favor one of them over its rivals.

absolute secrecy about *anything* having been unattainable in either Atea or Fatata. All of this led to charges and countercharges between sodalities—of spying, of prior disclosure, and of song stealing. And while some of the older members of the congregations expressed amusement or even disdain at the heat of these rivalries, for some of the principals themselves they were matters of major and continual concern.

Each of the sodalities maintained a treasury with which to finance building repairs and feasts, but the ways in which the treasuries were replenished differed markedly between Atea and Fatata.

The Ateans' way of maintaining their religious buildings carried over into their way of replenishing their sodality treasuries. When money was needed for some sodality activity, e.g., providing hospitality for visitors or raising money for the sodality's May Collection assessment, it was usually done by the members' joint labor. For example, young men earned their assessments by clearing someone's garden site for pay, and women joined together to make roofing thatch for sale. In Fatata, on the other hand, such money came from individually levied contributions.

The same contrast obtained with respect to some other sodality activites. In Atea, virtually the entire active church congregation took part regularly in sodality affairs, whereas in Fatata the Sunday night sodality meetings usually drew only a handful of people, and those mainly the young members interested in the competitive aspect of sodality singing.

Another noteworthy difference between Atea's and Fatata's sodalities had to do with the treatment accorded the weddings of their older members. In both villages, when a person died, his sodality mates played prominent parts at the graveside rites and at the wakes preceding them. Also, in both Atea and Fatata the large gala weddings held for "virgins" (veiled-bride weddings) were arranged and financed by the families of the principals, but the villages differed in their treatment of older couples, and especially those already cohabiting. In Fatata when such couples were persuaded, for some reason or other, to legitimatize their union, they did so privately; if there was any celebration at all, it usually consisted of a modest feast held in a private dwelling. In Atea, the weddings of such couples were usually public and festive and were often financed and celebrated by each couple's sodality. Typically, such ceremonies were also mass affairs, with up to eight or more couples—some of them in their fifties—becoming legally and ecclesiastically married at the same time.

As elsewhere in the Society Islands, the congregations of Te Piti's parishes (*paroita*) should by prescript comprise all Protestants within the respective parish boundaries—which, it will be recalled, were conterminous with the boundaries of the Administration districts (*mata'ein'a*) of those names. In fact, both parishes counted among their regular church attendants a few individuals who lived in neighboring districts; and conversely, a few residents of Atea and of Fatata's districts maintained their parish ties elsewhere. But these exceptions, which were mainly the result of interparish marriages, were so few in number and consequences that they may be ignored.

From what I could learn, most individuals became Protestants, officially, by being christened as such in infancy. I heard of a few instances outside Te Piti of individuals changing from Catholic to Protestant but neglected to inquire how this change had become officially validated. There may also have been a few individuals whose Protestant parents had neglected to have them christened and who, nevertheless, were recognized as Protestants—indeed, I would be surprised if there were not—but no such case ever came to my attention.

After christening, the next step that most Protestants went through was catechism training, mainly in Sunday School. (Again, I neglected to inquire whether this was an official requirement for remaining a Protestant, but, in fact, I knew of no instances in Te Piti of Protestant children not undergoing catechism training, at least for some period of time.) In both Atea and Fatata, Sunday School was conducted regularly by either the pastor or his wife, and sometimes with assistance from a deacon or some other biblically versed member of the congregation. Children began their Sunday School careers at around six years of age and were enjoined to continue until about fifteen or sixteen and until the successful passing of a catechism test. (Until "graduation," all such persons were labelled, in Church parlance, *tamariʻi*—which was the term applied generally to persons of this life-stage.) In fact, boys tended to drop out earlier, and many girls also left before completing the course. (Also, while still in the Sunday School stage, girls were enjoined to remain virginal—a rule that was more often honored in the breach, thereby occasioning much mirth among the local cynics when such girls continued to attend Sunday School.)

In both Atea and Fatata, the Sunday Schoolers were seated in three age groups (of both sexes), each presided over by a teacher and usually under the watchful supervision of the pastor. Hymns were sung and catechism memorized. Even beginners were taught to perform in the unaccompanied (and unrestrained) multivoice harmony characteristic of Society Islands church singing. Religious instruction was almost entirely in terms of catechism drill, i.e., by shouted chorus answers to printed question-answer texts (e.g., "What was the Sea the Israelites crossed?" "The *RED* Sea.").

The culminating step in being a Protestant was to become a Communicant (Tahitian, *ʻētāretia*, from *ekklēsia*). To achieve this status, one had to have reached the age of fifteen, undergo further instruction in biblical lore and in church rules, and agree to abide by a code of conduct that prohibited excessive alcohol drinking, extramarital sex, and "dishonesty." It was permitted for an unmarried person believed to be abiding by these rules to become a communicant, but there were very few such. And, of course, an unmarried *couple* was ruled out no matter how firm their unions or upright their conduct. (In Te Piti, some of the most devout parishioners were in this limbo because of their inability or neglect to secure legal divorces from long-departed spouses.)

According to the pastors of both Atea and Fatata, it was their decision, and only theirs, as to when a candidate was qualified to become a Communicant. Also, according to them, it was within their authority, and theirs alone, to expel a parishioner from the position of Communicant, e.g., for flagrant adultery, chronic drunkenness, notorious dishonesty, etc., but only after warnings.

In 1954–55, Atea parish contained sixty-seven resident Communicants out of a total number of 216 Protestant parishioners of all ages. During the same period, that part of Fatata's parish included in this study contained only forty-five (out of a total parishioner population of 348).

As noted earlier, some of the Communicants became deacons (six active ones in Atea and five in Fatata). Conventionally, these were elected by majority vote of all local Protestants twenty-one years of age and older. In fact, in both Atea and Fatata, most of the incumbents during my visits had been elected by their respective sodalities, which they then, ex officio, supervised. Also present in both parishes were one or two "retired" deacons, near-senile men who took little part in secular parish affairs but who were venerated to some extent because of past status and present calm decrepitude (which, evidently, passed for piety and wisdom). One of these latter in each parish bore the title of *'auaha paroita* (parish orator) and served, as far as I could discover, as a kind of senior steward over the parish's morals.

Finally, all other adult Protestants, i.e., all those past *tamari'i* (i.e., Sunday-School age) who were not Communicants, were labelled *taure'are'a,* which in general nonchurch contexts was also the term applied to both males and females who were, in age and behavior, between "children" (*tamari'i*) and "adults" (*ta'ata pa'ari*).

Cutting across these membership "age" categories in each parish were the church sodalities (*pupu*)—three in Atea, two in Fatata. Each sodality included Communicants, *taure'are'a,* and one or more deacons. (The *orators* tended to dissociate themselves from sodality affairs, and the pastors were unaffiliated.)

As identical units in the mission-wide organizations, Te Piti's congregations were supposed to follow the same rules regarding the relations among the several categories of members. In fact, there were some striking differences between the two parishes in social organization, and this will be described in due course. First, however, I will describe the organizational norms which the two congregations shared and in some respects actually complied with.

As noted in Chapter I, it was the official responsibility of the parish council as a whole to "maintain proper ecclesiastical discipline among local parishioners" and to exercise stewardship over parish property, including money. While Te Pitians in general were aware of this official mission-wide principle, they subscribed to the local convention that it was the pastor (who was also the president of the parish council) who had overriding authority. During my 1954–55 visits, this authority was not widely questioned in either village; there was, however, a significant difference between the two villages in this respect. In Fatata, there was some individual grumbling against some of the pastor's "arbitrary" or "inappropriate" actions, but no situation developed in which his authority was actually tested—as did occur in Atea.

The Atean episode took place on a Friday night, when one of the sodalities met to practice a new song for the coming Sunday church service. The practice was attended largely by women. Meanwhile, several men, including the husbands of some of the women attending the choir practice, were drinking wine and beer in a dwelling nearby, and their din reached such a volume that it became difficult for the choir practice to proceed. Finally, one of the women went to the dwelling (where her own husband was in full song) and requested the carousers to lower their voices. With this, her husband staggered over to the sodality house and laid into the choir practicers, vehemently and abusively, for presuming to ask *adult males* (!) to be quiet. The sodality's (male) leader sat quietly, and probably fearfully, through the long tirade, but the pastor, who had been awakened by the drunk's shouts, appeared on the scene and demanded that the latter withdraw. The drunk then challenged the pastor and raised an arm as if to strike him. At this point other men watching the proceedings, including the *tāvana* and *mūtoʻi*, seized the drunk and warned him of arrest, for daring, of all things, to disobey and actually *threaten* the pastor. By this time the drunk had sobered enough to realize the enormity of his actions, and he broke into sobs, explaining that he was really scolding the sodality members and not the pastor.

All this had a subduing effect even upon the partying men, who broke up and went home, where the wives of some of them (I was later informed) also laid into them for having helped to precipitate such a serious crisis. Subsequently, I was told, the guilty drunk went to the pastor and abjectly asked his forgiveness. And for several days thereafter, various Ateans took occasion to reassure me how shocked they had been by the dreadful affair, and how in their opinion their pastor's word was law and his person sacrosanct.

The only comparable episode during my visit to Fatata took place during a funeral wake. While the deceased's relatives and friends (including his sodality members) were singing and praying in his house, a regular film-showing proceeded on schedule in the "theater" nearby. Evidently, the mourners did not object to the film showing but the blast of noise from the film's sound track disturbed them so much that they asked the *tāvana*—not the pastor, who was at the wake—to intervene, which he did forthwith. (The *tāvana* was also owner of the theatre, which he leased to the film projection-ist, and that may have been why the mourners acted through him and not directly to the projectionist himself.) When I asked some of the mourners why the pastor had not acted, the answer was, "That is not his job."

Another kind of evidence of the differences in authority possessed by the two pastors had to do with the custom of *sinie* (from the French, *signer,* to sign—in this case, the *Croix Bleu,* or temperance pledge; even people with no other knowledge of French used this term). To *sinie* consisted of going to the pastor and pledging in writing to abstain from some undesirable behavior, usually gambling or the drinking of alcoholic beverages. The sanction against pledge breaking was the pastor's personal and official reprimand. An unspecified supernatural penalty was also involved, but the more pal-pable censure by the pastor was clearly the decisive factor and appeared to have been very effective—in Atea, at least, where pledgers usually returned to the pastor and "un-*sinied*" before resuming their drinking, etc. Or, if they wished to take up drinking for a limited period (e.g., during the New Year celebrations) they obtained verbal permission from the pastor before doing so. (In Fatata I was informed that "unpledging" did not take place; in fact my informants there, including the pastor, expressed surprise and somewhat amused contempt when told of the Atean practice.)

Pledging also applied to sexual behavior, in the case of the unmarried. (In the case of married persons, the vows pronounced, and particularly the religious ones, were said to make pledging, in this sense, redundant.) Some-times a younger and unmarried cohabiting couple who did not wish to mar-ry pledged themselves to abstain from sexual relations with other persons, as an earnest of their short-range intentions to remain faithful to one another. More often, the pledge was taken by a man only, in response to pleas or warnings from his unmarried mate.

The point of the above in the present context is that pledging was prac-ticed very commonly in Atea and very infrequently in Fatata. And the rea-son for this disparity that was given by Fatatan informants, when informed of the Ateans' practices, was that "perhaps the Atean pastor has more *mana*" (i.e., more powerful sanctions behind his authority).

The only sphere in which a deacon exercised any individual authority in parish matters was over the sodality in which he was leader. It was my observation that this was a very circumscribed authority, which consisted more of encouraging and guiding a consensus than of issuing fiats. A sodality's leader also customarily chaired proceedings at its regular *tuāro'i* sessions, and supervised the collection of assessments, but the funds in a sodality's treasury were usually safeguarded by the pastor himself.

In addition to these palpable and more or less explicitly prescribed lines of authority, some parishioners asserted that the "parish orator" (*'auaha paroita*) was "over" everyone else, including the pastor, and that he could "dismiss" (*fa'arue*) the pastor if the latter was at fault. An *orator* of forceful personality might indeed have been able to mobilize incipient parish opposition to an unpopular pastor and thereby move the mission authorities to remove him, but Te Pitians were unable to recall that this had ever been done in their parishes. And in the case of the two men who occupied the office during my visits, it was unlikely that they commanded influence enough, or were forceful enough, to play such a role.

Other than the above hierarchies, there were no other official ones among parish members: Communicants were not superior to *taure'are'a,* nor either of them to Sunday Schoolers—in parish matters, at least.

Relations among parish members were, however, manifested in *spatial* terms, but in this the arrangements corresponded more closely to everyday (chronological) age categories than to the type of membership categories just described.

In both Atean and Fatatan churches, people sat in (chronological) age groups: children (i.e., Sunday Schoolers, aged from about six to sixteen); late teenagers and young adults; married and unmarried; middle-aged people; and elderly people. Within each of these aggregates, males and females tended to sit in separate rows, with males usually behind. In other words, although the category that comprised "children" included the same individuals in both church and "secular" contexts (and in seating place in church), throughout the rest of the church a communicant (or a non-communicant adult—*taure'are'a*) tended to sit with age-mates rather than with others of his membership category.

In the rectangular Atea church, the aggregates were arranged according to their relative ages, with the youngest in front and the oldest in the rear. In the octagon-shaped Fatata church, the pattern was somewhat more complicated but was in general plan much the same.

An additional complexity in both churches was provided by the tendency of sodality members to sit together, especially when each sang separately as a group. However, this involved only minor role ambiguities, since most of the active singers were (chronologically) young adults. Also, in some instances, younger and older singers joined their sodality mates for singing and then returned to their proper age-based pews.[12]

It remains now to consider the transactions that, normatively, character-ize interpersonal relations among Te Piti's parishioners.

First of all, there was the overarching theological proposition propounded by the pastors that God's gifts are too bountiful for mankind ever to be able to repay but that mankind should at least reciprocate as much as possible in terms both of *worship* (*ha'amori*) and of money contributions towards mission support.[13] It may be that some parishioners other than the pastors actually subscribed to this theological doctrine; if so I was unable to discover it. In fact, the more prevalent view appeared to exclude God from the exchange circuits and to conceptualize transactions as taking place entirely among human members of the denomination.

With respect of each parish's external transactions, the official view was that the regular Sunday collections and the special one of May, both of which went into the central mission coffer in Pape'ete, were reciprocated in the form of salary for the pastor and other unspecified services provided by the the mission's high officials. I was unable to discover whether the ex-change was in act approximately equivalent in monetary terms, but I can report that some parishioners complained from time to time that the ser-vices they received counted less than the money they contributed.

The May Collection differed from the regular Sunday ones not only in the sums contributed but in the rationale of the giving. Officially, it was, like the Sunday collections, represented as a contribution to the mission for value received, but the officials that I saw conducting the meeting also en-couraged more giving by representing it as a means of outdoing other parishes—implying thereby, I suggest, that the extra contributions would be repaid in terms of prestige-building approbation for the parish in question.

Again, I do not believe that many Te Pitians subscribed to this latter "of-ficial" view. From what I saw, their own rationale for making extra contri-butions (i.e., *support money*) was more immediate and local. Insofar as the size of those extra *support money* donations was proclaimed—which was not al-ways the case—the rationale was to gain praise—or escape censure—from neighbors, rather than to enhance their reputations throughout the mission

---

[12]The symbolic aspect of Tahitian church seating is discussed more fully in Antony Hooper's " 'Blood' and 'Belly'—Tahitian Concepts of Kinship and Descent" in *Èchanges et Communications (Mèlanges offerts à Claude Lévi-Strauss)*, Paris: Mouton. Hooper's discussion is based on the seat-ing plan of the church in Maupiti, which is closer to that of Fatata than to that of Atea but, like both of the latter, exemplifies the Tahitian way of classification by age and sex.

[13]This generalized and highly abstract conception of exchange between the Christian God and mankind was markedly different from the forms and rationale of the exchanges that took place between humans and divinities in pre-Christian Tahiti (Oliver 1975).

area as a whole. To gain reputations for generosity outside their own parish, Te Pitians undertook more direct measures—i.e., by providing hospitality for visiting Communicants and by making contributions to specific parishes in need of material aid. The hospitality usually consisted of a special meal or two provided and attended by the local Communicants. And the contributions consisted either of money (needed, say, to build or repair a church), or of some object (say a large *tīfaifai*) made by the parish women. The money thus given was raised either from individual contributions or from the earnings of work projects. While all such donations—hospitality and contributions—were represented as having been pure "gifts," most such "giving" was transparently motivated by and based on calculations of past transactions with the recipients and on expectations of eventual repayments.

Focussing now on transactions among parishioners of Atea and Fatata, those between pastor and congregation were the most comprehensive.

As noted earlier, each pastor received a regular salary from the mission and part at least of the money from the salary came originally (I suppose) from his congregation's contribution. In other words, the arrangement can be viewed in the abstract as an exchange of money for services, and statements by some Te Pitians indicate that they did so view it. Their views differed however regarding the equivalence of values exchanged: as just noted, some stated verbally that the services rendered were worth less than the money paid, while others indicated by their actions (but not in so many words) that their pastor deserved compensation in addition to the salary and perquisites paid him. It would not be surprising if the pastors themselves took this latter view of exchange, and one of them did in fact so verbalize it. The surprise is occasioned by the Fatatan pastor's perception of his role in the exchange equation, and since this differed markedly from that of his Atean colleague, it warrants description.

During my 1954–55 visit to Atea, the local pastor appeared to take full material advantage of his special status in the community. He accepted presents as if by right. On cinema nights, he attended the film showings without paying and barely acknowledged the tidbits that the food sellers pressed on him. Fish and other food was given to his household, evidently without expectation of reciprocation and with no intention on his part to do so. Again, when he employed a work group to do some job for him it was tacitly understood, and generally accepted, that he would pay its members less than the going rate. And when he and his family members extracted starch from his cassava harvest, several youths in the congregation "volunteered" their services without any prospects of receiving shares of the profits he realized from sale of the starch (which was used by the buyers, by the way, to brew beer!).

A few Ateans occasionally grumbled at this one-way flow, but usually quite good-naturedly, and kept on giving as before.

Contrast this with the corresponding situation in Fatata. There, the pastor was offered few if any objects or service gratis, nor—evidently—did he request any. When I queried him on the matter he explained his attitude in the following terms:

> It is wrong for a pastor to beg (*tāparu*), as they do in many places. A pastor, rather, should be a servant (*tāvini*) to his parishioners. He should give to them instead of they to him. He should support himself entirely; that is the reason I spend so much time on my various enterprises. A pastor should pay for everything he buys, at the going rate.

This pastor did indeed support himself, and support himself well—so well, in fact, that some of his parishioners accused him of spending too much of his time seeking money (*i te ʻimiraʻa moni*). And although he was a demanding and somewhat tight-fisted employer, he made a practice—a virtue, even—of paying for all services received from persons outside his immediate household. In two matters only did I hear him criticized for taking advantage of his special status in the community. One, already noted, was the use he made of the mission's tract of land in the center of the village (where the early English missionaries had had their dwellings and groves). During my visit to Fatata, he evidently reserved the land for his own private uses, whereas previous pastors (I was told) permitted other villagers to gather breadfruit and keep their pigs there. The other matter concerned his commercial fishing activities. Formerly, it was said, when fish used to be carried to Papeʻete in locally owned boats, the pastor had attempted to monopolize the transport by sending the one he owned before midnight on Saturdays and by criticizing the other owners, whose fishing arrangements made it difficult for their boats' departure before about 3:00 A.M. Sunday, for engaging in money earning on the Sabbath (his own boat, he claimed, having been out of his jurisdiction before the Sabbath began!).

The only worldly compensation that Te Piti's deacons received for the services they may have rendered was in the form of status enhancement, represented by the votes that served to elect and maintain them in office. A couple of them complained to me that this was not an adequate return, but their dissatisfactions were evidently not deep enough to move them to resign.

It is possible that expectation of heavenly rewards also served to motivate the Te Piti deacons, as well as the pastors, to perform their services, but about that I did not inquire, nor record any evidence that could be thus interpreted.

The transactions that took place among members of each sodality are best viewed, analytically, as instances of pool-sharing, and the members themselves viewed them as such. The activities engaged in differed in the two parishes but the exchange patterns involved in these activities were, normatively, alike.

Summary of Differences

1. Atea and Fatata had had markedly different histories in terms of their contacts with Protestantism, and these contributed to differences in the ways the two parishes practiced Protestantism, and perhaps also in the numbers of persons—relatively more in Fatata—who were skeptical of some Protestant-derived beliefs. But among the Protestant believers of both parishes, the contents of those beliefs were alike. (Nor were there any discernible differences between the two villages with respect to the contents of pagan beliefs still held by many, if not most, of their residents.)

2. Regarding the standards of Protestant ritual practice, the calendars and programs of church services were the same in both parishes (as they were, probably, throughout the Society Islands), except for minor features such as Atea's New Year's Eve christenings and Fatata's more elaborate Christmas services. The major difference between the church services of the two parishes was in service attendance, the Ateans having been much more faithful than the Fatatans. Moreover, this difference was reflected in the ways the two congregations observed the Sabbath as a whole, Ateans having been much more pious in this respect.

3. The procedures followed in the May Collection service also differed somewhat, but this was due to differences in the forms in which the donations were made, i.e., Ateans made most of their donations in the form of precollected, more voluntary, *foundation* money (*moni tumu*), whereas Fatatans donated much of theirs in the form of *support* money (*moni tauturu*), which was given more reluctantly and only in direct response to publicly voiced harangues.

4. Comparison of the May Collection services of 1955 also reveals differences between the two parishes. Although a few members of Fatata's parish gave amounts larger than any given by individual Ateans, a larger percentage of Ateans made donations than did their Fatatan counterparts—78 percent to 54 percent—and those doing so made, on the average, larger contributions, i.e., 184.5 francs against Fatatans' 160. Moreover, per capita differences are seen to be even wider when the total local donations are divided by the total number of professed Protestants, donors and nondonors, residing in each parish at the time, namely, 152 francs for Atea's parish and 95 francs for Fatata's.

5. Differences between Atea and Fatata parishioners were also revealed by the goods which they contributed to help maintain their church buildings, the Fatatans having given money, the Ateans both money and labor. Moreover, in recent years at least, Ateans were more supportive than Fatatans in this regard, not only in connection with the existent parish buildings but also as shown by their large money donations to the building of a costly new assembly hall.

6. While Atea's and Fatata's parish sodalities were alike in their organization and choral activities, they differed in some other respects. Of first importance was the fact that their members attended sodality meetings much more faithfully in Atea. Another sign of the Ateans' deeper commitment to this Protestant institution was the sponsoring role it played in the weddings of its older members, whose Fatatan counterparts were left to celebrate their weddings in private.

Ateans also differed from Fatatans in the ways the members supported their sodalities materially, i.e., Ateans with their own labor, Fatatans with money.

7. Finally, in terms of congregational social relations, the principal, in fact the only wide, difference between Atea and Fatata had to do with relations between the pastors and their respective parishioners. In Atea the pastor exercised a strong effective authority not only over church affairs but over other community and individual affairs as well. The Fatatan pastor also provided effective enough leadership over all church matters per se, but neither sought, nor was delegated, authority or even much influence, over other community or individual affairs. And correspondingly, while the Atean pastor welcomed and even encouraged his parishioners to contribute goods and services to his personal endeavors, his Fatatan counterpart was scrupulous to keep his parish and personal economic activities strictly separate.

CHAPTER VII

BEING A RESIDENT-CITIZEN

Chapter I outlined the official governmental structure of the Society Islands and the history of its major political parties, insofar as these touched on the lives of the Te Pitians and other residents of rural districts. The present chapter will describe how those and related institutions worked in Atea and Fatata—what things the Ateans and Fatatans did as *citoyen* and/or as *ra'atira* of their respective districts (*mata'eina'a*), and as members of one or another of the Territory's political parties.

Citoyen and *ra'atira* had somewhat different but overlapping meanings for Te Pitians. In French law all Tahitians were *citoyens,* and all *citoyens* had certain rights and obligations, graded according to age, e.g., all of them twenty-one years of age and older and not otherwise judicially constrained had the right to vote for district officers provided they had been domiciled in the district during the previous six months (*Code Civile,* Article 102ff), and all of them between ages six and fourteen inclusive were obligated to attend school.

In Te Pitian usage the label *ra'atira*—sometimes glossed as "*citoyen*" or at times as *chef* (of a team), *capitaine* (of a boat), or *directeur* (of a business), etc.— was less clear-cut even in the context now under discussion. In this latter sense however the word was most usually applied to any French *citoyen,* male or female, residing locally (for however long a time), who was about fourteen to sixteen years old or older, i.e., anyone fourteen or older who had either dropped out of or completed elementary schooling. It was possible for a person to count as *ra'atira* in two districts simultaneously, provided he (or she) spent lengthy periods of time in each; on the other hand, young people even over sixteen who attended higher schools outside their home district were apt not to be counted as *ra'atira* at home. And finally, although no distinction was made between males and females in listings of a district's *ra'atira*, most corvées involving all able-bodied *ra'atira* included only males under about sixty, and in meetings at which community decisions were made, e.g., to petition the Administration, few females ever attended and fewer still voiced opinions or cast votes. (In the words of some of Atea's and Fatata's *least* diffident women, "Such matters are the province of men.")

The government organization, it will be recalled, consisted of district and municipal (geographic) units, a Territorial (legislative) Assembly, and a Territorial Administrative hierarchy. Like other rural Tahitians, Te Pitian *citoyens* elected the officers of their own district and had a voice in the election of the officials who represented their respective islands in the Assembly—but no voice at all in the selection of the administrative officials (from the island gendarme to the Territory's *gouverneur*) who had most to do with governing them. They were sometimes consulted in the appointment of their local *mūto'i* (constable), but that was all.

District Government

As related earlier, each rural district had its own council, to which members were elected every five years. The council consisted of the five candidates who received the largest number of votes; the two receiving the next largest number were named alternates. Candidates for the council were required to submit their names to the island's chief administrative officer (the gendarme), who was empowered to confirm or deny their eligibility in terms of their civil records. There were no limits on the number of terms a council member could serve, but with one or two exceptions the turnover rate in office holders had been fairly high in Te Piti in recent decades.

Any French citizen over age twenty-one with at least six months' residency in the district could vote in the "secret" ballot, provided he (or she) had not been disqualified by court order—for some illegal act. From what I could learn, the turnouts at Te Piti's district elections were usually nearly complete.

Upon election, the five successful candidates voted among themselves for *tāvana* (*chef*), deputy *tāvana*, treasurer, and secretary. Of these only the *tāvana* received any pay, i.e., 2,250 francs a month, plus an allowance for entertaining visiting officials.

In addition to its elected officials, both districts included in this study contained a more or less official "public orator," whose implicitly recognized duty—and privilege—it was to deliver the opening address on formal public occasions, e.g., when welcoming visiting dignitaries or (in Atea) when starting off the New Year festival. The principal—indeed, the only—

qualification needed for this role was an ability to orate: sonorously, floridly, and lengthily. The incumbents in Te Piti had not been formally elected to their positions; they had evidently simply moved into them, through personal initiative and public acknowledgment.

Te Pitians also had the right to join with other villages of their respective islands in selecting an island representative to the territorial Assembly. In both Atea and Fatata, the representatives during my 1954–55 visits were residents of other villages—of Fare for Huahine and of Afareaitu for Mo'orea, and, according to their local supporters-turned-critics, once elected those representatives showed no further concern for Atea or Fatata.

As for Te Pitians' views concerning the selection of the host of civil servants comprising the Administration that governed them—from governor (*tāvana rahi*) down through the judges, *gendarmes*, office bureaucrats, agricultural extension officers, etc.—they believed, quite accurately, that they themselves had no vote in the process at all. They did, in fact, have minor and indirect voices in the selection of the Territory's delegates to the French Union Assembly and to the Council of the French Republic, but these officials appear to have had no influence in the decisions made by those large bodies.

In Te Piti, the councils met when summoned by the *tāvana* and usually in response to some district problem or some interpersonal conflict among the residents requiring resolution; in Fatata[1] this turned out to be every two to three months, in Atea less frequently so and with considerably less formality than in Fatata. Reasons for this difference were various. In the first place, in Atea most local problems and most interpersonal conflicts that were at all solvable were settled either among the principals themselves or by recourse to the *tāvana* alone, who was held in affectionate regard and respect by nearly every Atean—in contrast to Fatata's *tāvana*, who was an unsociable and unsmiling figure admired for his industry and self-earned affluence but liked by few. And secondly, the council members of Atea, in contrast with those of Fatata, saw one another frequently enough in the course of their other activities to reduce the need for formal meetings.

In both Atea and Fatata, the district councils were empowered to enact ordinances concerned with local (and characteristically trivial) matters, e.g., the prohibition of music and other loud noises at parties after 11:00 P.M. and the keeping of pigs off village streets. In addition, the *tāvana* themselves

---

[1]The population of the village of Atea constituted almost the whole of its district's population, while the district in which Fatata was located, which I have labelled Toerau, contained one large hamlet and a string of separate households outside the village itself. Throughout this chapter, however, for the reader's convenience, I will use Fatata to refer to the larger, Toerau District except when the sense requires otherwise.

Fatata: Church Sodality Meetinghouse

Atea: Sunday afternoon in front of Parish Assembly House

Fatata: Waiting for church to begin

Atea: Generational differences in church-going dress

were authorized and required to conduct civil marriage ceremonies, to pub-
licize laws and regulations coming from the Administration, to safeguard
and supervise the keeping of the Civil Register, and to entertain visiting Administration officials. Also, they were empowered to adjudicate—subject to
the right to higher appeal—disputes of purely local interest, such as those
having to do with land boundaries or marauding pigs.

In addition to the council meetings, which were usually closed to nonmembers, the *tāvana* of both districts occasionally convened meetings of all
local *ra'atira,* i.e., all their fellow citizen-residents, male or female, past
school-leaving age. The agenda of these meetings, which were held every
two or three months or so, usually included explanations of new Administration regulations, e.g., concerning stricter copra standards, and announce-
ments of council decisions, e.g., concerning preparations for an official vis-
itation. Sometimes non-council members raised questions and objections,
e.g., about the depredation of unknown pigs or the theft of vanilla beans,
but the more characteristic direction of information, instruction, etc., was
from council to citizenry, with reactions from the latter being expressed *after*
the meetings and in smaller gatherings.

The tone of such meetings were alike in Atea and Fatata—low-key, non-
histrionic, listless, and extremely slow moving—but those of Atea differed
from Fatata's meetings in two noteworthy respects. For one thing, such
meetings in Atea were very well attended, including most of the male citizenry and a few females as well. In Fatata, they were usually very sparsely
attended and rarely by any females at all. And secondly, while such meetings in Fatata were usually concerned with district government matters
only, those of Atea (which nearly always took place on Sunday afternoons)
concerned government and parish matters and sometimes political-party
matters as well.

In terms of *economics,* the above governmental structures and activities had
effects in Te Piti both direct and indirect.

Directly, the salaries paid to the *mūto'i* and *tāvana* constituted that much
added spending power to their communities' resources—for, as far as I could
discover, nearly all of the money was spent locally. It could be proposed, I
suppose, that the time the above officials devoted to their jobs decreased by
that much the time they would have devoted to other jobs, like cash-
cropping, which also would have added to the communities' money resources. Regrettably (for this theory) the proposal cannot be maintained,
for, not only did the officials in question devote little time to their duties—
Fatata's even less than Atea's—but for themselves and for other Te Pitians,
time itself, as a factor in economics, was not sufficiently scarce to figure importantly in this way.

Drawing on parallels in Western democracies, and even in Melanesian Big-man societies, it could be proposed that the Te Pitian elections had economic implications, in terms of "campaign spending." It was indeed true that some of the successful candidates received some of their votes in return, implicitly, for services rendered and goods bestowed in the past, but as far as I could discover, no Te Pitian in recent years had purposely campaigned for office in that way.

More indirectly, economic implications were also contained in some of the decisions made and enforced by the councils, or by the *tāvana* acting singly—such, for example, as those concerning unconfined pigs (in both places), the prohibition of alcohol selling (in Atea), and the distribution of public works and welfare monies (in Fatata). It is even possible that representation by a council or a *tāvana* may in the past have been responsible for obtaining extra Administration assistance of a material kind. However, the only such item that was received during my 1954–55 visits was Atea's coffee-bean pulping machine, which the *tāvana* had requested but which in all likelihood would have been issued eventually anyway.

Aside from voting for the officials that governed them locally, four other kinds of duties—all more or less obligatory—were performed by Te Pitians in their roles as citizens. One was to have the socially critical turning-points of their lives recorded in their district's Civil Registry, i.e., birth and parentage, civil marriages and divorces, and death. Another obligation was to keep their children in school from age six to fourteen inclusive. A third was to pay certain "taxes" in the form of money or services. And a fourth obligation of citizens was to maintain their residences in conformity with official standards of sanitation and repair. In addition, Te Pitians were of course required, subject to penalties, *not* to do all the many things proscribed in French laws and regulations, e.g., committing homicide, deliberately marketing subgrade copra, etc.

While the Civil Register maintained in each district was the official responsibility of its *tāvana*, the actual job of posting entries in it was in most places, including Atea and Fatata, entrusted to one of the local school teachers (mainly because of the latter's literacy in French), some *tāvana* having been without French and some even wholly illiterate.

In 1954–55, all adult Te Pitians seemed to be impressed with the need to keep the Registry up to date and accurate respecting entries for themselves and their close kin, chiefly for purposes of proving inheritances and contracting new civil marriages. Indeed, some of each village's stock hard-luck stories concerned local people who had become irreparably disadvantaged through mistakes or omissions in Registries, e.g., surnames reversed, divorces unrecorded, paternities not officially acknowledged, etc. For example, one devout long-married couple who aspired to church respectability was unable to marry, and thus become church Communicants, as a result of the woman's inability to obtain the record of her (Pape'ete) divorce. Nor could their many children use their own father's patronymic, nor automatically inherit interest in any of his land. (A written testament by the father would have resolved the inheritance question, but the man in question was evidently unable to undertake such a mysterious and conceivably difficult step.)[2]

The official obligation of Te Pitians to keep their children in school for the prescribed time was regarded by some parents as arbitrary, labor-wasteful, and fruitless; by others as onerous but perhaps ultimately fruitful; and by a rare few as the best possible place for children to be in, both for present advantages and future benefits. The official goal of public schooling was to prepare the students for a Territory-wide test, by passing which the student received a certificate permitting him (or her) to continue in a higher school, or, in the case of students manifestly unable to obtain a certificate (*certificat d'études primaires*), to provide them with some basics of literacy, arithmetic, history (mainly French), geography, etc. Certificate testing did not usually occur before age sixteen; students in the noncertificate track were also encouraged to remain in school until age sixteen but all students were officially allowed to withdraw upon reaching fifteen.

Another official educational goal was for all instruction to be in French, and although anyone passing by the schoolhouse during class time would sometimes hear lessons being chanted in monotone French, once out of class the scholars (and those of their teachers who were Tahitians) would revert to Tahitian.

Atea's school was not firmly established until 1939; before that, there were some short-lived attempts to keep one going, but the only continuous organized schooling took place in Sunday School, where successive pastors succeeded in teaching nearly all the local children of those generations the rudiments of reading and writing in Tahitian. Up to 1955, only seven of the children who attended Atea's school had earned certificates, and three of those had done so only after receiving some additional schooling elsewhere. At the time of my 1954–55 visit, the school's one teacher was a Tahitian from Tahiti Island, evidently from a comparatively well-educated and affluent "suburban" family. This teacher was outspoken in his view that his task in Atea was hopeless and his assignment there an "exile" (or as he put it, "St. Helena") among "primitives." According to this conscientious and

---

[2]Needless to say, these Registries proved to be a rich mine of demographic and sociological information for me and, occasionally, some amusement as well, as, e.g., when I came across evidence of cinema influence in the appearance of names like "Bridgette-Bardot à Vahinemoea" and "Kowpoi à Pahi."

aggrieved man, Atea's dismal educational record (in terms of certificate earning) was due largely to parental disinterest, ranging from lack of positive support to outright opposition. As evidence, he listed the following:
  —Children possessed insufficient energy for concentrating in school. According to him, they breakfasted on coffee only and lunched entirely on fruit. In addition, he claimed, the older boys were often kept awake all night fishing.
  —At home, children spent nearly all of their time doing chores, and even at night, when chores were done, they were not permitted to use lanterns to study by, because of parental objections to "wasting fuel," or because their parents had other uses for the lanterns.
  —Most parents regarded schooling (which they said *they* did not have) as a waste of time, and they kept their children in school only so long as required by law—and that because of fear of the Administration.
  —Even those parents with some formal education, including the few having a smattering of French, did nothing to encourage their children to do homework—holding to the view that all "education" should be carried out in school.
My own observations (which were only incidentally concerned with schooling itself) lend support to most of the Atean teacher's complaints, but, of course, the reasons given by him were only part of the explanations that can be given for Atea's educational shortcomings. Other factors I could add would include:
  —the inappropriateness of the curriculum itself, i.e., its irrelevance to rural Tahitian life; and
  —the uninspired method of teaching.
Nor were the impediments to schooling confined to parents and instruction alone.

The desire of most fourteen- to fifteen-year-old boys to move out of the stage of "childhood"—to which all school attenders were popularly assigned—and into the unfettered and adventurous status of "youth" was impelling enough in many instances to overcome even parental desire that they remain in school (when such existed, as it rarely did). Peer pressure added a powerful fillip to this incentive, e.g., many such dropouts occurred in pairs and threes. Similar pressure led many girls to drop out of school early; and while the urge to begin "youthing" may not have been as impelling as with boys, some girls had already begun to be involved in coresidential sexual unions by that age.

In Fatata, the schooling provided by the Administration had been underway for several decades, and in 1955, the school there employed three teachers, a (metropolitan) Frenchman and two local middle-aged Tahitian women. I was unable to learn how many of the school's former students had won certificates in the past (based on local schooling alone) but know that their number far exceeded Atea's, relative both to total numbers of students and years of school operation. (In addition, six children domiciled in Fatata in 1955 were at that time attending schools in Pape'ete, and such had been the situation for a number of years previously.)

On the other hand, I was informed by the European teacher in Fatata that for most of his students the parental support, or lack of it, resembled that of Atea. Added to that, he as a European found it next to impossible to maintain discipline among the older boys of his classes. Fear, he said, instilled by physical chastisement, was the only sure way to keep such boys in line, and since he did not wish to use physical force (and as a European would have been subject to parental revenge had he done so) was unable to exercise control.[3]

On the positive side, there were several parents in Fatata (as compared with two couples only in Atea, according to Atea's teacher) who evidently valued schooling highly and provided some support for their children's education both in and out of school (even going so far—Fatata's European teacher said—as to permit their children full-time use of a pressure lamp for homework!). Also, as noted earlier, during my visits to Fatata there were six local children enrolled in advanced schooling in Pape'ete, as compared with only one from Atea.

Now to summarize some *economic* implications contained in this phase of Administration-sponsored activity in Te Piti. First and most tangible, the salaries received by the school teachers added considerably to local income, inasmuch as most of it was spent locally. The Atean teacher's pay was about 10,000 francs a month, plus a substantial dependants' allowance for his wife and child. According to him, most of that income was spent locally for food, he having produced none of his own beyond collecting coconuts and breadfruit from nearby trees. The two Tahitian teachers of Fatata received annual salaries and dependants' allowances of about 19,000 and 16,000 francs, respectively; most of this was spent in local stores, but since both of these women were of local origin and owned land locally they were able to obtain much of their food without money and put some of their earnings into savings accounts.

Secondly, and less tangible, the negative or apathetic attitude of most Te Pitians towards schooling may be viewed as an example of widespread local

---

[3]With his Tahitian colleagues, he declared, the problem was reversed. They were able to maintain discipline through frequent and severe beatings which, they being Tahitians in positions of some authority, provoked no effective parental objections; but (in this informant's judgment) their teaching was so unskillful that their cowed students learned from them nothing except keeping quiet in class.

attitude towards *investment* in general: that is, a disinterest in or unwillingness to postpone present consumption—in this case their own or their children's time and energy—on behalf of future and larger benefits. Of course, this diagnosis is apt only insofar as Te Pitians believed in the reality of those future benefits, and some of them clearly did so, e.g., by reference to the high earnings of some well-educated individuals they knew, and by attribution of their own money-earning disabilities to their lack of schooling. But several other Te Pitians seemed to perceive little or no connection between formal schooling and economic success or failure in the Te Pitian setting—in which, by the way, they might have been correct![4] As for other, noneconomic benefits which formal schooling beyond mere literacy might have conferred, not one of my informants ever mentioned such a possibility—indeed, it is unlikely that the thought ever crystallized.[5]

A third kind of economically relevant implication that can be seen in Te Piti's school institution has to do with its dropouts, namely, to the extent that the school programs, etc., encouraged—or did not discourage—dropping out, they thereby added some extra labor hours to local subsistence and money-earning activities.

And finally, the attitude of most Te Pitians concerning their schools may be viewed as another example of the economic aspect of their overall view towards the Administration. That is to say, even for those who looked upon the school as a valuable and desirable institution, it was held to be a service *owed* to them by the Administration, and one for which they should not be required to contribute any specific return. When I raised this point with some of them, by referring to the "school rates" that property owners are required to pay in some U.S. tax jurisdictions, a few retorted that although they did not pay school rates as such these were covered "by all the other taxes they paid." For most respondents, however, the question of tangible payment for schooling was irrelevant; for these, the relationship between themselves and the Administration, between ruled and rulers, poor Tahitians and rich (European) Frenchmen, *obligated* the latter to provide schooling and, as we shall see, many other goods and services besides.[6]

---

[4]The only justification I heard mention concerning the utility of formal schooling for local economic activity was that a knowledge of arithmetic would help in bookkeeping and in the cost-planning of a cash-crop project.

[5]Literacy was, however, universally acknowledged to be a desirable skill for noneconomic as well as economic purposes, e.g., for Bible reading, account keeping, defense against a storekeeper's cheating, letter writing and letter reading. (As one man explained: "If you can't read, how can you learn whether a letter received by your wife isn't from a lover?")

[6]Two respondents supported this generic rationale with the opinion that, in fact, the Administration ought to *pay* Tahitians for attending school—or more specifically, for learning French.

What in fact were the goods received by Te Pitians from the Territorial Administration—for being *citizens,* as it were?

First can be listed the numerous kinds of services, in addition to schooling, provided gratis by Administration departments: medical, judicial, police protection, agricultural advice, radio transmission of news and entertainment, the building and maintenance of principal roads, etc. To these can be added their heavily subsidized postal services, help when needed with hospitalization, and assistance with public works projects of purely local utility (such as wharves and farm-access roads).

In the form of tangible objects, the Administration supplied some persons in Fatata with old-age pensions or other welfare allowances and assisted would-be cash-crop producers with low-interest loans (see above, Chapter III). Fatata also received a free supply of water and free maintenance of the circumisland road that ran through the village. In 1954–55, Atea's planned water system still awaited completion, but some water was obtained from the Administration-built storage tank attached to the school.

The Te Pitians I talked with about these matters freely acknowledged the volume and comprehensiveness of the flow of services and objects in their direction, but as previously noted, nearly all of them either held them to be balanced by their "tax payments" or expressed the view that such goods should be theirs by right. Indeed, a complaint I often heard expressed was, "Why doesn't the Administration do *more?*" e.g., provide *free* copra dryers, subsidize *higher* prices for copra and vanilla, keep out New Zealand beef (which served to lower the prices paid for local cattle), force storekeepers to lower their prices, build sodality houses, etc.

Let us consider now the direct taxes actually paid by Te Pitians to the Administration (apart, that is, from indirect taxes, such as the duties levied on the imports they purchased and on the exports they helped to produce—both of which many Te Pitians viewed as taxes in themselves—and apart from their submissiveness to French rule, which some Te Pitians considered to be a service more than sufficient to balance the exchange).

Taxes were levied throughout the islands—but evidently quite sporadically—on certain types of houses: e.g., on "vanilla" houses in good repair and on new cement-based ("Pape'ete suburban") houses, beginning five years after construction—but not on houses of mostly native materials. During 1954–55, *no* Atean houses were thus taxed, and only two in Fatata village (averaging 45 francs a year each).

A modest tax was levied on motor vehicles, but the only Te Pitian who owned one was Fatata's pastor. A purchase tax of 300 francs was levied on new motorbikes; one of Fatata's two motorbike owners had paid such a tax (before 1954) but the other, inexplicably, had not done so.

In Fatata, three residents paid 136 francs each year for licenses to sell refreshments at the cinemas; as far as I could discover, their Atean counterparts had so far escaped paying this impost. Also, the two Fatatans possessing licenses to sell alcoholic beverages paid fees of 10,000 francs a year; no such license was held in Atea.

Formerly, I was told, Fatatans paid small fees for (piped) water use, road tax, and dog licenses—all subsequently abolished. Having neither a vehicular road nor a piped water supply, the Ateans had no such obligations, and as far as I could learn, they had always successfully evaded paying dog licenses. Older people in Atea could recall a time, decades ago, when all local male residents from eighteen to sixty years old were required to pay a head tax of 50 francs a year, along with labor two days a month on some public works project; I have found no official confirmation of these imposts and heard of nothing similar in Fatata.

Te Piti's Chinese were required to pay license fees for retailing and for refrigerator ownership (as well as for vanilla processing), but it had evidently occurred to none of their Tahitian customers that these fees were also taxes on themselves, inasmuch as they were passed on to themselves in the prices they paid for store purchases. (Compare in this regard the Te Pitians' attitude towards duties levied directly on imports, which they considered to be [indirect] taxes on themselves. Evidently, their satisfaction in seeing the Chinese "lose" money, directly, served to distract their attention from the parallels between the two kinds of imposts.)

Military conscription was the most comprehensive kind of tax paid by Te Pitians in the form of service, but few individuals were in fact required to serve. No Ateans had been conscripted since 1948, and prior to that only a handful had ever served. As far as I could learn, Fatatan youths were still subject to a term of fourteen months' military service, but none was thus engaged during my visit in 1955.

Prior to obtaining French citizenship, I was told, Ateans were "required" to participate in the Administration's Bastille Day celebrations at Fare—with canoe racing, singing, dancing, etc., but after gaining their "freedom," this service became voluntary and was in fact no longer performed. For their part, Fatatans had long since ceased to participate, corporately, in Bastille Day celebrations, and while it was reported that the Administration encouraged such participation, no Fatatan averred that it was obligatory—and I suspect that that had been the pre-"freedom" situation in Atea as well.

Another "service'" required by the Administration—or, so Te Pitians viewed it—was the responsibility for keeping their yards "tidy" and their latrines "sanitary" (whatever that signified). Despite several notorious and perennial violations in both villages, neither of the respective *mūto'i* (the responsible officials) took any steps that I could discover to enforce the rules—one of them having been both lazy and cynical, the other having been afraid to ruffle his neighbors' feelings.

Some Te Pitians viewed the Administration rule about burial sites to be not only an unreasonable violation of their traditional customs but as a costly expenditure of labor. I refer here to the regulation that graves be located at some distance from residences and, ideally, in one common cemetery. Most Ateans ignored this rule altogether and continued to bury the bodies of their household-mates next to their houses; the others obeyed half of the rule and buried their kin outside the residential area but in separate sites located on family-owned lands.

Fatatans in general accepted the burial rule with more equanimity and violated it only infrequently. When the rule was introduced, several landowners donated bits of their adjacent holdings to the Administration for the site of a cemetery, and the district council was made responsible for its upkeep, which was accomplished by corvée—every able-bodied male between school-leaving and age sixty having been required to work there about two or three hours a month or pay a fine of ten francs. (The money went into a special treasury, the *Afata Menema,* and was used to buy fence wire and a horse-drawn hearse.) Individuals who refused to contribute labor or pay the fine were forbidden burial in the cemetery—thereby creating a dilemma, because of the Administration regulation against burial elsewhere. (I could not discover what might happen in the cases of family members of such evaders; the only evader in residence during my 1955 visit was an unkempt, misanthropic unmarried man without dependants who announced that people could "throw my body to the sharks," for all he cared.)

Another taxlike service (or so it was viewed) that Fatatans performed more frequently than Ateans was in the form of receiving and entertaining visiting Administration officials. (The refreshments supplied on these occasions were provided either by the visitors themselves or by the entertainment allowances regularly advanced to the *tāvana.*) With its proximity to Tahiti and its more "historic" past, Fatata was a favored point of call on the visitor circuit. The standard program for receiving important official visitors included speeches of welcome and songs by school children (and by any other voice-proud residents that could be assembled by the *tāvana* for this occasion). Except for the local officials (including the pastor), few other adults attended these gatherings, unless occasionally out of curiosity; some, in fact, made a point of staying away.

Ateans would, undoubtedly, have turned out in force for such occasions (and complained about their onerousness later on!), but alas, no important officials ever visited remote Atea; and few Ateans voluntarily troubled to travel to Fare to greet them there. (Some of the stay-at-homes did so out of indifference; a few others explained their nonparticipation as a deliberate protest against this form of "tax.")

Summarizing, while neither Fatatans nor Ateans can be described as having been heavily tax burdened—and not even in terms of their rather broad conception of "taxation"—the former paid more taxes than the latter and did so less unwillingly, it would appear. The contrast between the two villages in this respect is exemplified in two taxationlike episodes I will now describe.

In 1954, the Fatata (i.e., Toerau District) council decided to widen and improve the path leading from the main circumisland road up into the main valley, in which there were several residences and many gardens and cash-crop lands. The Administration provided assistance in the form of a bulldozer and truck, with driver, and pipe for water drainage. All other labor was contributed, gratis, by Toerau's able-bodied males. Although many of the latter gained no personal advantage from the road, they all nevertheless worked on it—or paid fines of 110 francs for each day when not working—for several days and with little grumbling on their part. A few, I was informed, asserted that the Administration should have paid wages for their labor, but most of them agreed that it was a legitimate kind of "tax."

Turning to Atea, I have already described how its local citizenry had delayed completion of its water-piping project by refusal to work on the project without wages—a project of direct value to all of them. Another episode of this nature had to do with the deepening and cementing of a spring-fed pool used by many Ateans for bathing and washing clothes. (The natural pool was shallow, with muddy bottom and banks—a quagmire after rains.) The women who regularly did their laundry there had for years been urging their husbands to improve the facility. Finally, the *tāvana* requested the Administration for assistance, and the latter responded by providing a few bags of cement, which a few of the husbands reluctantly proceeded to put to use—a matter of a few hours of work for half a dozen men. When, midway along, it was discovered that more cement would be needed and that the Administration would not supply it, three husbands of the users—the pastor, the *tāvana*, and the latter's son-in-law—made the well-publicized gesture of contributing one bag of cement each, which served to complete the job—all amidst complaints about the Administration's meanness.

The contrast between Atea and Fatata in this context is further sharpened by comparison with the respective views of the two citizenries concerning cooperation viewed as having purely local relevance. That is to say, those very same Ateans who objected strongly to including the Administration in their exchange transactions were willing and generous exchangers, even pool-sharers, of their own labor in activities viewed by them as being traditional and purely local functions. Fatatans, on the other hand, who out of individualism and cynicism were unwilling to labor together in exchange for pool-sharing activities of a more traditional kind seemed willing to contribute labor, in partnership with the Administration, for advantages which some of them could not share.

So much for the activities engaged in by Te Pitians as *citoyen* and/or *ra'atira*. I will focus now on the social relations that exemplified their behavior in such roles.

Relations among the *ra'atira* qua *ra'atira* of Atea (or of Fatata) consisted largely of those between the *tāvana* and all others, individual or en masse. In both villages, once its council had reached a decision on some matter—occasionally after considerable discussion and argument—it was usually the *tāvana* himself who publicized it and undertook to enforce it. Occasionally, in Fatata, the *tāvana* deputized the council secretary—at the time a young man who seemed to enjoy such assignments—to circulate the council's decisions as well as new Administration rules. In Atea, however, the *tāvana* himself usually passed such messages along—in fact, some Ateans I queried could not even list the names of all their councilmen, having "forgotten" them. Also, in both villages pressing complaints were usually made directly to the *tāvana* himself—although in Fatata (more typically than in Atea) people occasionally addressed questions about government matters to other council members or asked the latter to intervene with the *tāvana* about matters of less consequence to themselves.

In neither Atea nor Fatata did the Administration's local constables, the *mūto'i*, interfere with the direct nature of the linkage between the *tāvana* and his fellow villagers, as the ambiguities between the statutory roles of *tāvana* and *mūto'i* rendered possible and as actually eventuated, I was told, in some other districts. In Atea the *mūto'i* was a faithful aide to his *tāvana*, on the rare occasions when an aide was required. And in Fatata, the local *mūto'i* (who had obtained his sinecure as an army veteran) bestirred himself only to collect and deliver mail and was happily content to leave all other matters of governance to the *tāvana* and his council.

Given, then, the direct, personal relationships between *tāvana* and *ra'atira*, which comprised virtually the entire district administrative social structure in both Atea and Fatata, what was the nature of that kind of relationship?

Generalizing about contemporary "*tāvana*-ship" for the Society Islands as a whole, some non-Tahitian observers I talked with professed to see continuities between it and the chieftainship of pre-European times, while others regarded it as totally different, the very antithesis of ancient Tahiti's tribal governance: which raises the question of what chieftainship in ancient Tahiti actually was.

A very lengthy chapter would be required to answer that question exhaustively inasmuch as ancient Tahitian society was pervasively hierarchical in structure, and inasmuch as the distinct hierarchies characteristic of governmental units—of tribes—were the society's most complex and preponderant ones by far (Oliver 1974). I will list here only enough of the features of those tribal hierarchies to indicate that while some of the mid-twentieth-century district hierarchies may have shared some of the features of the ancient tribal ones, the two kinds of hierarchies in most respects were widely different.

To begin with, the tribes in existence when Europeans first arrived on the scene varied greatly in size (from a few hundred to over fourteen thousand), as well as in degrees of durable autonomous separateness from one another. (For example, some remained fiercely independent and "permanently" unallied, while others oscillated between independence and partnership or subjugation, or drifted from one alliance to another.)

Secondly, in most of ancient Tahiti's tribes, chiefly authority was based on a combination, in varying proportions, of ascribed rank and achieved power, and achievement was measured in several ways, or combinations of ways, e.g., fighting deadliness, military leadership, diplomatic finesse, priestly impressiveness, shamanistic luck, oratorical persuasiveness, etc.

And thirdly, the governing styles of tribal chiefs ranged from benevolent paternalism to arbitrary despotism—with the majority of chiefs nearer the latter extreme. In even earlier eras, when Tahiti's tribes were probably more conterminous with kin units, their chiefs were self-motivated, or constrained, by the more beneficent values of kinship. By mid-eighteenth century, however, all the tribes then extant consisted of several more or less distinct kin units, and tribal chiefs were separated from most of their subjects by wide gulfs in kin ties (and also in caste). This is not to say that no eighteenth-century chiefs were generally benevolent—for there were such in several tribes. And this is not to deny the presence of some checks on chiefly power even in the larger and more kin-disparate tribes. But when the chief in question possessed ascribed social rank *and* martial skill *and* personal ruthlessness, there was little to constrain him other than rival chiefs having similar attributes.

Thus, comparisons between ancient chieftainship and mid-twentieth-century *tāvana*-ship are not very useful, in terms of either unit size, leader recruitment, or leadership style. And of course there is the overriding consideration that the modern districts (of 1954–55) were but small parts (and functionally very insignificant parts) of the vast "tribal" unit that is the French Union.

Published observations about modern *tāvana*ship are scarce. Hooper, generalizing about "political" relationships in the islands' rural communities, characterizes them as "highly egalitarian and nonhierarchical" and adds that ". . . with the Administration of the Territory controlled by the French . . . there are indeed very few occasions when an overriding community organization is called for" (1975:373).

Finney contrasts *tāvana*-ship in Pa'ea, a district on Tahiti Island that is suburban to Pape'ete, with that of isolated Mai'ao Island, in the following words (1973:44–45):

> District organization is now little more than a relic of 19th century colonial rule. The modern tendency has been for the Administration to treat local officials as instruments for direct rule rather than as representatives of the will of the district constituents (West 1961:98). This is especially apparent in Pa'ea, mainly because it is so close to Administration headquarters in Pape'ete. There the saying (in French) is that the *Tāvana* is nothing but the "orderly of the administrator," and that the *Mūtoi* is the "orderly of the gendarme." The district council rarely meets, and the *Tāvana* rarely acts in an official capacity, except perhaps to initial the request of some church group in Pa'ea to hold a benefit dance, or to officiate at a civil wedding ceremony. Few of the 2,000-odd residents of Pa'ea, and none of the Europeans among them, go the *Tāvana* about matters needing adjudication. Instead most people go directly to the administrator, to the courts, to some government bureau in Pape'ete or to the newly established *Gendarmerie,* less than one kilometer from 'A'ou'a.
>
> In contrast, on Mai'ao district organization is still viable, mainly because of the island's isolation. Since administrators and gendarmes seldom visit the island, regulation of many local matters is left to the Mai'ao. The *Tāvana,* for example, periodically convenes the district council to discuss local problems, he leads the men in fortnightly work days devoted to clearing the village path or to other civic projects and is able to adjudicate successfully some local disputes. Nonetheless, his powers are limited and he refers serious cases, such as those involving aggravated personal assault or tangled land claims, to Pape'ete officials.

Levy's observations on *tāvana*-ship apply specifically to "Piri," his pseudonym for the rural community he studied on Huahine, but there is an implication in some of his statements to the effect that they apply generally to rural districts throughout the Society Islands. I can attest to the appositeness of his observations to Atea but am dubious about extending them to *all* rural districts in the Society Islands, including Fatata, until a wider sample has been studied. However, with reference to Atea, his statements are so remarkably perceptive and lucid that I quote them here in extenso:

> In situations requiring decisions people tend to involve the smallest number of people whose consensus is deemed necessary (family, kin segment, village), but they resist the overt and autonomous decision-making authority of an elder, an "expert," or the *tāvana*.
>
> People are resentful of overt power. Many group activities in the village (e.g., work groups) often have different leaders for different activities. But in those situations in which there are fixed leaders (e.g., the *tāvana* or the island gendarme) leadership should have certain qualities. Ideally, a leader should not tell people what they should do; he should help them find out. He should help them come to a consensus and get things done by "helping them find their own way."
>
> Such a leader may fail in two directions, according to the frequent discussions in Piri about various *tāvana* and gendarmes. A leader may be too willful, intrusive, or controlling. [The present] *tāvana*'s predecessor, appointed under the "old" law (people say that he never would have been chosen by the people themselves), was a leader of this intrusive sort. But, it is said, it is also possible to be too easy. A *tāvana* or a gendarme may be too easygoing, too much involved in just enjoying himself instead of seeing that "people get on with each other." The [present] *tāvana* of Piri is considered by most people to be an excellent leader. He is there when important things are going on. He listens. He encourages people to formulate their own thoughts and say what they think. He helps people discover what the other people in the village are thinking. But he is not proud and he does not put on airs. He does not push his own ideas. He loves the people. This kind of leadership is a very delicate job. It might be noted here that the qualities which make for good village leadership—unintrusiveness, sensitivity to group consensus, humility and the lack of any obvious ambition, a desire for harmony—are by no means the virtues for political leadership or for a political representative at the *territorial* level, let alone at the metropolitan level in France. At both these levels partisanship, aggressiveness, and the ability to represent one's people against the interests of other legislators or executives seem to be necessary virtues. But these are the very characteristics the people of Piri find suspect, unpleasant,

un-Tahitian, and dangerous in a leader. This has been one of the factors hindering the development of supervillage leadership in the Society Islands.

The ideals people have for the *tāvana* are those by which they evaluate the islands' administrative gendarme. Gendarmes and other colonial administrators are rated as good men or bad men, depending on the villagers' perception of their intrusiveness and their proper nonauthoritarian stance.

The Tahitian language has many words indicating "stuck-up," "putting on airs," proud, making oneself high. The administrator, the *tāvana*, and the villager should avoid such behavior. The lack of such tendencies is considered to be one of the characteristics of a *mā'oui* [true Tahitian] and one of the frequent descriptions of an *'afa* [*demi-*] is that he is becoming "proud and inflated." [Levy 1973:204–6]

There is little I can add to Levy's description about this aspect of *tāvana*-ship, insofar as it refers to Atea, but the comparable aspect of *tāvana*-ship in Fatata during my 1955 visit was different in some noteworthy respects.

To begin with, the Fatata *tāvana* at that time had been elected to office on the basis of strikingly different qualities. He differed also, I was told, from his two immediate predecessors. One of those, now deceased, was a hard-drinking, profligate man, a native-born Cook Islander who had come to Mo'orea on a pleasure-seeking visit and had married an affluent Fatatan woman, on whose resources he lived without doing much productive work. He was, however, a jolly fellow with lots of social charm and a very generous one (mainly with his wife's goods). He was, Fatatans recalled, not only "soft" but ineffectual as well, liked by all but respected or obeyed by few. He died in office. His successor was a much "harder" man, who kept the district "straight" (*tano*). He had many relatives locally and these—and others—elected him to the council deliberately to "straighten" the district after his predecessor's slipshod administration. He too was a congenial man, generally liked, but before he could "straighten" the district, he was brought to trial and relieved of office because of his participation during a party in mass copulation with a drunken woman; after that he left the island in "shame" and had not returned while I was there.

In contrast with these two previous *tāvana*, the 1955 incumbent was a taciturn, unsociable man who worked all day and nearly every day of the week tending, improving, and enlarging his many money-making enterprises— copra production, pig raising, land renting, cinema managing, refreshment retailing, etc. He had come to the district as a penniless plantation worker—

the offspring of a German father and a part-Tahitian mother (he was quite Scandinavian in appearance)—and through single-minded industriousness, austere living, money saving, and land buying, had acquired what was considered to be a fortune by local standards. He spoke only Tahitian, could neither read nor write, had no close friends (as far as I could see) and few friendly acquaintances. His charming and well-educated (Tahitian) wife made up for some of his social shortcomings, but most of his neighbors considered him "difficult," "hard," and "un-Tahitian." And finally, although nominally a Protestant, he attended church services only on ceremonial occasions, took no other part in church or sodality affairs, and maintained correct but tenuous relations with the pastor.

Why then had he been elected to the council by the local voters, and then to the *tāvana*-ship by his fellow councillors? "Because," I was informed by nearly everyone I asked, "he was expert in earning money," and because the territorial leader of the RDPT Party, the hero-worshipped Pouvana'a, had instructed his local followers to do so. The *tāvana*, it was said, had made generous financial contributions to the RDPT and was regarded by Pouvana'a as a shrewd and potentially influential ally. (Also, it might be added, the two men resembled one another physically in many respects.)

In contrast to all these Fatatan *tāvana*, the Atea incumbent had been elected because he was well liked *and* respected by nearly every Atean voter. He worked hard—but not *too* hard—and improved his material conditions—but not *too* much, and not at the expense of generosity. His leadership style was "soft" and (in Levy's words) "unintrusive," but he managed by tact and diplomacy to get people to decide and do the "right" thing on nearly all occasions. He was a deacon in the parish and worked closely with the pastor, but he was not "too" puritanical—having been in the habit of indulging in one-day drunken sprees every month or two. And unlike two of the Fatatan counterparts just described, his kin ties with other village-mates were numerous and close.

Once in office, neither of the current Te Piti *tāvana* exercised leadership obtrusively, but I suspect the influence of Atea's was much more pervasive. And the sanctions that served to enforce the respective standards and decisions of the two officials differed quite markedly.

With respect to judicial decisions, for example, appeals against the Fatata *tāvana*'s judgement required money in the form of the cost of a road trip to Afare (where the Mo'orea gendarme was headquartered) or of a boat trip to Pape'ete—costs large enough to discourage all but the most determined litigants. For Ateans the boat trip to Fare, where the Huahine gendarme heard appeals, was quicker and cheaper and consequently was not in itself an effective constraint to appeals. Instead, in Atea, people were more effectively discouraged from opposing their *tāvana*'s decisions by the solid support he enjoyed among their neighbors and kinfolk.

In the case of both *tāvana*, their authority was implicitly supported by their official right to deny applicants permission to receive free hospitalization and old-age welfare payments (which in the event were extended only to individuals whom their *tāvana* attested to being indigent). In Fatata, it was a fairly common occurrence for people to apply for free hospitalization, and although the local *tāvana* usually went along with certification there were known instances of denial—instances so blatantly fraudulent that even close kinfolk agreed with the *tāvana*'s decision. In Atea, however, I could turn up no instance of a refusal by the current *tāvana*, who evidently did not question the motives or circumstances of anyone seeking such help. And when I queried him on this point he replied that "it was not up to him to question people's wishes" (especially when it involved getting money from the Administration!).

I turn now to the economics of *tāvana*-ship in Te Piti, to inquire how Atea and Fatata were alike and how they differed concerning the goods that passed between each *tāvana* and his "subjects."

In ancient Tahiti, the flow of goods between a tribal chieftain and his subjects was immensely disproportionate. Chiefs periodically received tributary food and other objects from their subjects and, while some of these were "redistributed" in token amounts, many of these objects were used for the direct benefit of the chief himself. Chiefs also received services from their subjects in numerous forms: labor for construction and repair of buildings and temples; verbal praise and other expressions of deference; attendance at ceremonies honoring the chief and his close kin; military service—including the possible loss of life itself; sacrificial victims for increasing the chief's own benefits from the gods; etc. In return—although it is unlikely that the transactions were at the time conceptualized as *exchange—the chief* transferred few objects to his subjects other than the token "redistribution" just mentioned. And his services to them were limited mainly to priestly intervention with the gods (for tribal as distinct from personal welfare); some occasional support of some subjects against members of other tribes; and some occasional—but not consistent or comprehensive—intervention in his subjects' affairs for the purpose of maintaining public order and (in rare instances) social justice.

Compared with those pre-European transactions, the flow of goods between Te Piti's two *tāvana* and their respective subjects differed immensely from them in both volume and kind. And in addition, some differences in such transactions can be detected *between* Atea and Fatata.

In Atea, the services performed by the *tāvana* for his people were many and varied. He—like *tāvana* in other districts—passed on messages from higher Administration. He also served as a messenger-advocate for his people to higher officials and acted continually and effectively to settle local conflicts locally, i.e., to "protect" his people from the possible hardships resulting from the intervention of higher authorities. One or two older men complained that he was too "soft," that he did not intervene enough in local affairs, e.g., to keep the village street cleaner or to curb noisy drinking parties—but for most other Ateans his "softness" was exemplary.[7]

The Atea *tāvana* also contributed objects to the community beyond the amounts required by the official definition of his duties. Whether he did this consciously, as *tāvana*, or as a generous public-spirited citizen and parish deacon, I cannot say, but more often than any other Atean he made his house and furniture available for local celebrations, he contributed money or other objects to community projects (e.g., a bag of cement for a laundry basin which his own wife did not make use of), and he gave more generously than most other Ateans to parish causes.

What did he receive in return? (Or rather—since I cannot say that such transactions were conceptualized by Ateans as exchange—what did he receive from Ateans because he was their *tāvana*?)

First, in the form of *services*, he received praise in the shape of the votes that had put him into office and of the frequent verbal reassurances that he would continue in office as long as he wished. (I cannot of course measure the value of such praise in terms of other goods. I do not even know how much satisfaction the *tāvana* derived from it—he was a modest, reticent man, not given to readable expressions of self-satisfaction—but I suspect that some gratification was there.) As for more tangible services, I could see none that was performed for him in his role of *tāvana*. When work had to be done on public projects, e.g., on carrying cement for the reservoir, he worked as hard and as long as any man (despite his fifty-two years of age), rarely if ever shirking physical labor to play the part of a nonworking supervisor. Nor did he ask for or receive—as far as I could discover—any free or low-paid labor services from villagers (other than his own close kinfolk) in connection with his own personal affairs, e.g., clearing garden sites or making copra.

As for *objects*, on only a few occasions that I knew of did Atea's *tāvana* receive things from his people, as *tāvana*. Like the local pastor, he was proffered free soft drinks and pastries on the rare occasions when he attended the cinema, but it was only on the most festive occasions, e.g., a large wedding or a large family reunion, that he was invited and treated as an honored guest. His household regularly participated in food exchanges with

---

[7] His principal, indeed his only severe critic, was the local schoolteacher, who was an unwilling "exile" from his home island of Tahiti and who complained repeatedly about the *tāvana's* disinterest in the school, public hygiene, gossipmongering, etc.

some other local households, but his network of such exchanges was no wider than any other local networks of this kind, and the portions of food received by his household were no larger, relatively, than those received by other households in his network.

Indeed, the most tangible compensation received by the Atea *tāvana* for his services to the community came from the outside. One was in the form of his official salary; the other was his low-rental lease of a parcel of *domaine* land. Whether these were in fact adequate compensation for the services and objects he contributed to his community, or whether he *considered* them to be such, I am unable to say. In any case, by Atean or other standards, these compensations could logically be viewed as payment for services rendered to the Administration, and not to Ateans exclusively—or even primarily.

Turning to Fatata, the transactions there between the *tāvana* and the populace differed markedly from those of Atea.

I was unable to discover whether the Fatata *tāvana* derived any satisfaction from the votes he had received to put him in office but he showed no wish to be reelected, and even if he had done so, the opinions I heard—which would also have been known to him—could not have reassured him on that score. As for more tangible services, like his Atean counterpart the Fatata *tāvana* neither received nor evidently expected free or low-cost assistance from any nonkin neighbors on his own work projects; but unlike the Atean *tāvana*, he himself always played the part of nonlaboring supervisor on public works projects.

In terms of *objects*, the Fatatan *tāvana* received from the populace even fewer than those received by his Atean counterpart. And the wage he received from the Administration was significantly less, relative to his total money income, than was that of the Atean *tāvana*.

Reversing the direction of the flow: the services and objects contributed by the Fatatan *tāvana* to his "subjects" were also significantly less than were those contributed by his Atean counterpart. Unlike the latter, he referred nearly all matters of local misbehavior or conflict to the islands' gendarme for adjudication. (The fact that this officer visited Fatata once a week, compared to the much less frequent visits of the Huahine gendarme to Atea, may account for some of this difference, but—I believe—not much.) Moreover, even when the Fatatan *tāvana* passed on local petitions to higher authorities, he did so—or so people complained—as mere messenger and not as an advocate of local interests.

On the other hand, the Fatatan *tāvana* resembled his Atean counterpart in his disinclination to enforce Administration regulations regarding public hygiene, etc., and for this he received local approval, although his nonintervention was explained as deriving from his disinterest in the community rather than (as was the case with the Atean *tāvana*) his *aroha* (affection, compassion) for his community-mates.

Political Parties

Chapter I described the origin (postwar) of political parties in the Territory. Most Te Pitians held beliefs about the nature of those parties, favoring the program of one or the other of them; and some Te Pitians, mainly adult males, engaged in activities connected with the party of their choice.

Three political parties were represented or known about in Te Piti in 1954–55: the Pouvana'a-led RDPT, the Poroi-led UPO, and the de Gaullist. (The first two had supporters in both Atea and Fatata; the third in Fatata only.) I will not attempt to describe the official ideologies and programs of these parties, but only the beliefs held by Te Pitians about the more salient aspects of them—which, in any case, is all that is directly relevant to this study.

Every Te Pitian I talked with about the subject knew the high points of the Pouvana'a legend described earlier: his Huahine origin and thorough (rural) Tahitian-ness; his trade as a carpenter; his outspoken championing of Tahitians' rights, i.e., *vis-à-vis* Europeans and Chinese, during the austerities of World War II; his "exile" to Huahine and epic escape-journey to Porapora; his capture and confinement; his postwar political crusade and eventual victory; etc. Several of his supporters retold the story with almost religious fervor[8] and accepted it as sufficient basis for supporting the RDPT. Even those supporting a different party accepted the story as authentic, and most of these expressed admiration for Pouvana'a himself—or, at least, for his activities during the pre-RDPT days.[9]

In addition to the legend of Pouvana'a's wartime adversities and early postwar political rise, there were several other beliefs and judgments expressed about him and his party by various informants in Te Piti, namely: the RDPT wished the Territory to cut all ties with France and go it alone, or link up with the United States. The RDPT (including Pouvana'a) wished the Territory to remain French, but in the form of a separate *département,* so that territorian residents (mainly Tahitians) and not metropolitans, would staff all Administration positions; the RDPT (including Pouvana'a)

---

[8] Indeed, several of his more ardent admirers drew attention to the parallels between Pouvana'a and Jesus, e.g., in their carpentry trades, in their concern for the poor, in their arrest by authorities, etc.

[9] Although one cynic, in Fatata, voiced a popular view that during Pouvana'a's epic escape from Huahine to Porapora his seamanship had been so poor that he had travelled "hundreds of miles" to cover a direct navigable distance of only fifty.

wished to make laws to improve the economic conditions of Tahitians especially *vis-à-vis Demis,* (European) Frenchmen, and, of course, Chinese; the RDPT was at least socialistic and possibly even communistic with regard to property ownership—including property held by affluent Tahitians.

A variant on some of these themes was that Pouvana'a himself was not "really" anti-French, or communist, etc., but had been pushed into such positions by his more radical and shrewder, i.e., evil, self-seeking aides.

Nearly all of the "political" opinions I heard expressed by Te Pitians were in terms of agreement or disagreement with the speakers' own beliefs about Pouvana'a and the RDPT. In other words, those self-described as supporting the UPO or de Gaullist parties did so in terms of opposition to one or another of the alleged RDPT policies and not in terms of direct, personal commitment to de Gaulle, or to Poroi and other leaders of the UPO.

Some of those supporting Pouvana'a (and by implication the RDPT) seemed to do so mainly on the grounds of his being a "real Tahitian" and a one-time martyr to the "Tahitian cause," but most of his admirers explained their support on economic grounds, e.g., Pouvana'a wished to bypass France and sell copra and vanilla directly to America (and hence obtain higher prices for those products by cutting out the French middlemen); and by replacing metropolitan French officials with Tahitians, the salaries would go to the latter and thus official "stealing" from Tahitians would cease.

Alternately, while some of the opposition to Pouvana'a and his party was rendered in religiouslike judgments, e.g., "Communism is wicked, anti-Christian"—most of it was expressed in economic terms, e.g., "the RDPT wished to take away my land, etc., and give it to worthless drones"; "they continually promise to arrange higher prices for our products but prices continue to fall"; "Pouvana'a's aides want to collect all our 'taxes' and use them for themselves"; "the cooperatives they have started have failed, so they cannot be counted on to manage the Territory's financial affairs"; etc.[10]

Comparison of Atea and Fatata on the basis of these beliefs and assessments reveals some sharp differences between the two villages.

Ateans, almost to a man (women there rarely talked publicly about politics; most of them appear to have accepted the view, at least publicly, that, being female, they "knew nothing about politics"), esteemed Pouvana'a very highly—with gratitude (for his championing of Tahitians), with pride (for

---

[10]The last theme refers to Pouvana'a's efforts to establish a cooperative restaurant in Pape'ete—presumably to serve also as a party meeting place. Many Fatatans paid the 300 francs' membership fee, which was lost when the venture eventually failed—or so my informants reported.

his Huahine origin), and with approval for what they believed his economic program would be (i.e., to increase the receipts from copra and vanilla, force the Chinese to lower prices, hire Tahitians instead of metropolitan Frenchmen in administrative jobs, etc.). Unlike most of Pouvana'a's admirers in Fatata, they seldom if ever distinguished between their paragon and his aides. Moreover, I heard no Atean accuse the RDPT of "communism," and only two of them referred—in these instances, disapprovingly—to the party's alleged plan to equalize people's economic resources. There were three Ateans—the *tāvana*, the *mūto'i*, and the pastor—plus the wives of two of them, who did not vocally express support for the RDPT (i.e., for Pouvana'a), but their silence—I was told—derived from the offices they held. ("They actually prefer Pouvana'a but were warned by their superiors to avoid party affiliation.") As far as I could discover, only one other Atean actually supported the UPO—"because of his wealth," I was told.[11]

In contrast to Atea, there was a wide range of belief and preference in Fatata regarding party policies and activities. While most Fatatan voters supported the RDPT at the polls and considered Pouvana'a to be an admirable or at least well-intentioned champion of (rural) Tahitians, and an honest one, some of these held him to be either personally ineffective or a cat's-paw to his brighter and largely unscrupulous aides.[12] In addition, there was a substantial number of people who spoke out against—and presumably voted against—what they believed to be RDPT economic and political policies. The numerical lineup and other features of party social structure in Fatata will be discussed farther on; I turn now to the activities engaged in by Te Pitians as supporters of one or the other of the political ideologies, or personalities, just listed.

First of all, many Te Pitians engaged in much political talk while lounging at the stores, waiting for church services to begin, etc., but such talk that I overheard included little or no argument. In Atea, this talk usually consisted of solemn agreement with Pouvana'a's latest economic proposal (e.g., to sell copra directly to America) or political gesture (e.g., his refusal to speak French with some French official). Among Pouvana'a supporters in Fatata, such talk tended to be less adulatory, with criticism of RDPT policies and officials, even including Pouvana'a himself, occasionally expressed; but again, such talk consisted mostly of assertion and assent and not debate. In Fatata, I also overheard a few "political" conversations between

[11]One Atean woman had also voted for the UPO, "because she is stupid and didn't know what she was doing."

[12]On the occasion of Pouvana'a's visit to Fatata in 1955, the gathering listened respectfully to his speech but then questioned him critically and sometimes sharply about some of his points—a reaction, I believe, that would not have occurred in Atea.

Pouvana'aists and Poroists (or de Gaullists), but usually in the form of "Pouvana'a (or Poroi, etc.) says," and rarely in the form of debate. On the rare occasions when arguments took place about the relative merits of this or that opposing policy, the debaters were usually jokingly good-natured— deliberately so, it seemed to me. During my 1955 visit, I was told about a few cases of intrafamily estrangement caused by political arguments, but such arguments were evidently fought out at home.

Meetings held by party members differed markedly in Atea and Fatata. In Fatata, the UPO and the de Gaullists held none during my visit, and the members I questioned said that none had ever taken place except for some of them discussing their shared views when they happened to be together on other occasions. Nor did the Fatata RDPT supporters meet during my 1955 visit there, but I was informed that they had done so twice during 1954— mainly to elect officers for the local party chapter and to collect membership dues (50 francs per annum). Those meetings, I was told, were held at the *tāvana's* residence, he having been one of Pouvana'a's strongest supporters, and despite the "law" (it was called) against officials engaging in party politics.

In Atea, party meetings took place fairly frequently, but not as separate events. At about monthly intervals, meetings were called by the *tāvana* and the pastor to discuss district, parish, *and* RDPT affairs. The meetings were held in the central plaza and were usually attended by all but a few of the village's male *ra'atira,* together with a sprinkling of females (who however sat apart and took no part in the proceedings). At the sessions I witnessed, party items were intermixed with other business, e.g., an announcement by the *tāvana* of an impending visit of the circuit judge, then a listing by the local RDPT chapter president of members in arrears for dues, followed by the pastor setting the date for repainting the church. At one such meeting, it was decided to send a representative—the local RDPT branch president—to Pape'ete to petition Pouvana'a to intercede with the Administration in order to speed up the laying of water pipes from reservoir to village (with villagers being paid for their labor); and to pay for the trip, every male *ra'atira* paid (or promised to pay), including the village's own avowed Poroist. Also, the business of electing RDPT officers was carried out at one of these general community meeting, and when I remarked at the commixture, I was reminded that Pouvana'a was the champion of *all* Tahitians.

As noted earlier, the only active party branches in Te Piti were those of the RDPT, the Atea branch having contained forty-seven dues-paying (i.e., 50 francs per annum) members and the Fatata branch thirty. Each branch elected its own officers, whose duties—as far as I could learn—were as exiguous as their rewards.

The only other public activities engaged in by Te Pitians (and these by Fatatans only) to which the label of *party* can be applied consisted of sub-scribing to party journals (and presumably reading them) and (in years past) of buying shares in the defunct RDPT cooperative restaurant men-tioned earlier. Evidently, every one of Fatata's dues-paying RDPT members had joined the cooperative. As for subscribers to political journals, in con-trast with Atea, where only the school teacher and two others did so, several Fatatans spent money in this way: seven for the RDPT journal, nine for the UPO's, and two for the de Gaullist.

I turn now to the social-relational contexts of party beliefs and activities—first, to the question of party membership: What connection, if any, can be discovered between such membership and other socially significant attributes?

As noted previously, there were forty-seven dues-paying members of the RDPT, or Pouvana'a Party, in Atea, i.e., *all* males of voting age except for the village's three top-officials, socially inactive seniles, and its one avowed Poroist.[13] The latter told me he admired Pouvana'a but did not approve of his aides, who wished to "take away people's hard-earned property." This one political dissenter was genetically a half-caste (and more European in appearance than Tahitian), a deacon,[14] and one of the village's best edu-cated and most industrious and affluent men. No other Atean criticized him within my hearing for his political stand; it was described as being "... something of concern only to himself, the result of his own reflections."

Fatata's thirty dues-paying RDPT members constituted about 31 percent of the village's qualified male voters; but rather than attempt to account for their membership on the basis of their other community roles, etc., it will be simpler to consider those Fatatans who expressed preferences for other par-ties—or at least, those who denied their votes to the RDPT.

The most vocal Poroists were the members of the two extended families—one of them centered around the community's ineffectual but highly re-spected parish "orator" (*'auaha paroita*); the other around the schoolteacher widow of a former *tāvana* husband, who allegedly had had many friends among the affluent Pape'ete *Demis* who constituted Poroi's inner circle.

Fatata's avowed de Gaullists were put at eight males ("... and their wives?" I had asked. To which was replied, "Perhaps."—as if it didn't really

---

[13]As far as I know, females were not excluded from membership in the RDPT, but in 1954–55 the branches in Atea and Fatata contained only males.

[14]It was this man who in 1957–58 mobilized and led a faction that broke away from the es-tablished parish-church organization. This breakaway, which will be described in the Epi-logue, was partly political in cause and, ironically, was more Pouvana'aist than Poroist in po-litical color.

matter.) Of these eight, one had served in Africa and Europe during World War II and was a warm admirer of de Gaulle. Another two were brothers and large landholders. Another was the pastor. Another pair were close affines and comparatively affluent. And the remaining two worked part time in Pape'ete, having had close connections with several *Demis* there. In summary, all eight de Gaullists were somewhat better educated, or at least more cosmopolitan, than most of their fellow villagers, and most of them above average in material affluence as well.

As noted earlier, neither Fatata's Poroists nor de Gaullists associated together in active local party chapters. Several individuals among them subscribed to their respective party journals, but whether they paid other dues to their territorial party coffers I neglected to ask. In contrast, Fatata's thirty dues-paying Pouvana'aists (or dues-promising—twenty-one of them were in arrears during my 1955 visit) did occasionally hold meetings where, among other things, they elected their own officers. In 1955, their three-member executive committee included the *tāvana* and two other members of the district council. Of these, the *tāvana* was a wealthy man by local standards, although illiterate. The second member was also fairly wealthy—in land at least; but the third was quite poor. According to their fellow Pouvana'aists, they were elected because of their strong party sentiments.

In this connection, their leadership in party affairs probably accounted for their election to the district council—the latter event having followed the former in time. As for the role conflict that this clearly involved, i.e., its violation of the rule that district officials take no part in party affairs, not even the local Poroists or de Gaullists criticized them in those terms.

The elected leaders of Atea's much larger RDTP branch were notable mainly for their inconsequential positions in other village affairs. In fact, while all three had stood for office in the most recent district council election, none had won a place. Other Ateans' "explanation" for their leadership—such as it was—in the party and failure to win positions in the district hierarchy, was a rather smugly put, "The *hau* [Administration] says that council officials should not take part in party affairs." A perhaps better explanation is that since virtually *all* of Atea's adult males were more or less active Pouvana'aists, the district council itself constituted the de facto party leadership, leaving for the local party officials only subsidiary parts in party affairs. (This in fact appeared to be the common sentiment attending the new RDPT committee election that took place at the end of my visit there, i.e., some men had to be urged to stand for election—"to help the work for Pouvana'a.")

Finally, it will be recalled that, while Atea party matters were attended to at general community-wide meetings in conjunction with matters concerning both district and parish, those of the Fatata RDPT were convened in entirely separate sessions. And while these latter meetings were held at the residence of their "president," who was also the district *tāvana,* and were attended by three other members of the district council (including the two who, along with the *tāvana,* constituted the executive committee of the party), the identity between district and party leadership was not complete, inasmuch as one of the district's five councillors was a de Gaullist and an outspoken opponent of RDPT "communism."

Summary of Differences

The polities made up, respectively, of the citizen-residents of Atea District and of Fatata's Toerau District differed from one another in function, in cohesiveness, in style of leadership, in relations with other local social units, and in relations with the encompassing territorial Administration.

In function, Atea's district polity played a larger role than Fatata's in the handling of local problems, including cases of conflict, while Fatata's polity was more active than Atea's in the execution of programs of public works.

In cohesiveness, the periodic meetings of the district polities were much better attended in Atea than in Fatata. In style of leadership, the *tāvana* of Fatata tended to govern by fiat and delegation and to refer many matters requiring decision to his Administration superiors. In contrast, Atea's *tāvana* exercised a "softer" and more personal leadership and tended to solve interpersonal problems locally rather than refer them to higher authority.

In their relations with other social units, Atea's district polity was much more conterminous than Fatata's. In Atea, there was an overlap in membership and leadership between (male) district polity, (male) *ra'atira*-ship, and (RDPT) party that amounted almost to identity, and nearly as close a relationship between these and (adult male) parish membership and its lay leadership. In Fatata, there was a close coincidence between district and (RDPT) party in official leadership but some marked divisions in party membership and in *ra'atira* support for the district leadership, and little if any coincidence between parish leadership and that of the district or (RDPT) party. (The lack of identity in Atea between the district leadership and the *official* leadership of the RDPT party is explained by the circumstance that the former were in effect de facto leaders of the party.)

Thus, in terms of *local* considerations, Atea's district polity was a more active and firmly rooted unit than Fatata's. In terms of *external* relations, however, Fatata's district polity had much stronger ties with the rest of the territorial Administration of which it was a part.

For example, the Fatatans paid more in "taxes"—house tax, vehicle license, retailing permits, etc.—than their Atean counterparts, and received more in services and utilities—schooling, medical aid, adjudication services, roads, water supply, etc.

There was also some difference between the two communities with respect to their residents' *views* of their relations with the territorial Administration. In both places, the relations were viewed as unsatisfactory—as weighed in favor of the Administration—but the Fatatans were on the whole less dissatisfied than the Ateans with the relationship.

CHAPTER VIII

SEX AND MARRIAGE

Sexual Behavior

It will come as no surprise to most readers to be informed that Te Pitians looked upon heterosexual intercourse as a pleasurable and, within certain bounds, harmless activity. Christian rules have imposed some constraints upon its practice outside officially sanctioned marriage, but in Te Piti these rules were applied, by the populace at large and even by the respective pastors, with considerable latitude. Some other constraints were imposed on its practice in the form of local proprieties concerning age of commencement, the ages of partners relative to each other, and—in some small but influential measure—the social class of each partner. Contrarily, there existed in Te Piti what Levy[1] has felicitously labelled certain "cultural encouragements" to premarital intercourse, namely peer-group pressure upon boys to prove their manliness and a belief by girls that they will contract "filled-up sickness" (*ma'i fa'a'i*) if they do not engage in at least one act of intercourse within a few years after the onset of menstruation. ("Filled-up sickness," which was considered to be dangerous to the point of causing insanity or death, was believed to be caused by the trapping in the body of menstrual blood, which intercourse serves to liberate.)

Some males told me that they had begun to engage in heterosexual play during their earlier childhood, but they and other male informants gave twelve to fifteen as the age when males usually began to have intercourse. A few males were reported as having begun as late as their early twenties, but

---

[1]Levy 1973:124–25. While some of this section is based on my own field notes, much of it is derived from or confirmed by Levy's pages on "Sexual Intercourse," pp. 122–30.

these cases were held to be exceptional and due to special circumstances such as unusual shyness or personal characteristics considered to be repulsive (*faufau*) by females. As for females, I was informed that some of them avoided sex until their early twenties, but for most of them sex play evidently began much earlier.

Between experienced partners, the method of sexual intercourse seems to have been fairly uniform, with the male lying on top of the outstretched female. Occasionally, the couple would lie on their sides facing each other, but other positions, though heard about, were disavowed. A certain amount of male-performed foreplay—from five minutes to half an hour—was practiced, including breast fondling and kissing, clitoral manipulation, and cunnilingus; mutual orgasms were expected and, according to my informants, nearly always achieved.

Further details on contemporary sexual interaction can be found in Levy (1973), Danielsson (1956), and Marshall (1961), and comparisons with former practice can be made by reference to these authors and to my *Ancient Tahitian Society*; for purposes of this study, it will be sufficient to note that among Te Pitians most acts of heterosexual intercourse between experienced partners, "married" or unmarried, were popularly believed to have been mutually voluntary, mutually active, mutually enjoyable, and mutually satisfying—in other words, in the language of transactions, they could be labelled instances of balanced exchange.[2] I recorded some instances involving both casual encounters and stable marital relationships in which one of the partners, male or female, was much older than the other, and in which the older one was expected to balance the exchange with tangible contributions of some kind. Also, in some cases of casual encounter, the males gave, and the females demanded, payment in the form of gifts—money, cinema tickets, cigarettes, etc.—even when the partners were similar in age. In most stable relationships, however, the act of sexual intercourse was evidently considered to be mutual enough to require no balancing in the form of extra objects or services.

The most adventurous form of sexual encounter was *mōtoro,* the practice by a male of slipping into a female's house at night and either seducing her there, amid the nearby sleeping members of her family, or persuading her to go outside for a brief and secret embrace. Otherwise, trysts were initiated by

---

[2]I heard of only two cases of rape having taken place in Te Piti in recent times. One was perpetrated by several youths acting together to punish a local girl, a notorious teaser, who had led them on, individually, and then refused them sex. The other case took place at a wedding reception, where several youths and men took turns at a promiscuous, middle-aged, unmarried woman who was very drunk at the time. Informants generally agreed that the first of these "rape" victims got what she deserved but that it was improper for any man to take advantage of a drunken female.

meaningful signs (those having been exchanged in church were considered specifically audacious), by written messages, or by peer intermediaries. Although males probably took the first initiatives in most of these meetings, the roles were sometimes reversed—indeed, according to some males, this was mostly the case.

The closest equivalent in contemporary Te Piti to the former practice there of youths going in groups to other communities in search of sexual adventures was the Fatata football team's actions on tour. After one trip to Tahiti, for example, the team's sport losses were more than compensated (according to some members) by their successful sexual conquests—two of which had resulted in "engagements." During my 1954–55 visit to Atea, the local football team was inactive, but stories were still being told about their earlier sexual success abroad.

Types of Marital Union

Among present-day Te Pitians, *ha'aipoipo* has come to have the meaning of *marriage* duly instituted by French civil procedures, involving the posting of banns, performance of a legally correct civil ceremony, etc.; and in 1954–55, there were many Te Pitian couples who were married in this sense. But there were many other couples residing together without sanction of civil ceremony who were nevertheless considered by their neighbors to be well and truly "married" for all but certain legal and religious purposes. In fact, Te Pitians themselves recognized several kinds (or degrees?) of marital union. At one extreme was the union of a couple instituted by civil and church ceremonies, with all the trappings of bridesmaids, best man, etc., and celebrated by a series of sumptuous wedding feasts for relatives, officials, and friends. At the other extreme was the coresiding of a couple instituted by nothing more than their mutual consent to subsist and to sleep together, more or less exclusively, for an indefinite period of time. As a matter of observation, the threshold between the latter kind of relationship and casual sexual encounters (*'ohipa ha'uti noa*) was sometimes difficult to locate as Te Pitians themselves did not all agree on where to draw the line. The consensus, however, was that a female became a man's *vahine,* and he her *tane* (i.e., they become widely recognized as spouses) when, in addition to sleeping together more or less exclusively, they lived and ate together in the same house. And the very fact that this "definition" of a marital union was anything but sharp is itself a reflection of Te Pitian flexibility in this matter.

Te Pitians themselves often categorized marital unions according to their manner of institution. First of all, they distinguished unions that were *ha'aipoipo* (i.e., sanctioned by civil ceremony) from couples that *fa'aea noa* (i.e., those who "only live together"). And within these categories they made further distinctions:

Table 8A. Types of Marital Unions*

	ATEA		FATATA	
	Number	Percentage	Number	Percentage
HA'AIPOIPO				
I. Veiled-bride	5	8.9	16**	22.5
II. Parish	16	28.6	13	18.3
III. Pastor's	14	25.0	9	12.7
IV. Civil	0	0	0	0
FA'AEA NOA				
V. Firm (A)	1	1.8	4	5.6
VI. Firm (B)	12	21.4	17	23.9
VII. Temporary	8	14.3	12	16.9

*Not including the Chinese, or three "outsider" couples employed and stationed there by the Administration.
**Including two couples married by Roman Catholic rites.

Ha'aipoipo: I. *pūro'u* (veil): sanctioned by civil and church ceremonies and by large kin-sponsored wedding feasts; II. *paroita* (parish): sanctioned by civil and church ceremonies and by parish- or sodality-sponsored wedding feasts; III. *'ohipa to'o 'orometua* ("work of the pastor"): sanctioned by civil and church ceremonies and sometimes by a modest family wedding feast; IV. *tivira* (civil), sanctioned by civil ceremony only, with or without a modest family feast.

Fa'aea noa: V. *tāmau* ("firm"): unions disabled only by technical requirements from becoming legally (and hence ecclesiastically) sanctioned; VI. unions that were "firm" but whose principals expressed no wish for civil or ecclesiastical sanction; VII. more or less "temporary" unions (i.e., not yet *tāmau*).

Type I. A veiled-bride (*pūro'u*) wedding was a bang-up affair—an event organized, financed, and ofttimes even initiated by relatives, and a matter of considerable pride to them. (Such weddings, it was said, were staged to *fa'ateitei*, "elevate" the couple and their kinfolk.) Normatively, the bride was *'āpī* (unused), i.e., she was not known to have had sexual intercourse with a man—not even with the groom, according to the strictest view of the institution. But here Te Pitian flexibility again asserted itself, i.e., veiled-bride weddings were sometimes held for brides who were not eligible to wear veils. In fact, only those brides "really" *'āpi* were supposed to wear a full-length veil during the ceremony, that is, those young women who were not only generally considered to be *'āpi*, but those whose parental regimes were known to have been so strict that there could have been no opportunity for any sexual encounter. And unless a young woman was confident not only of her own innocence but of public acceptance of her innocence, she would have been reluctant to don a veil for her *pūro'u* wedding for fear of arousing skeptical comment. (Twenty years after the event, people were still discussing with barbed amusement the case of the veiled bride who on her wedding night was discovered by the groom to be six months pregnant.) In view of these requirements, *pūro'u* brides, even nonveiled ones, tended to be young, most of them still minors and legally subject to parental control (which had the additional meaning among Te Pitians of being subject to parental choice of mate).

The *pūro'u*-wedding groom also tended to be young, since it was generally thought fitting that such a wedding be reserved for males who had not previously been "married" even in the broadest meaning of that term. But here the range between the most fitting and the acceptable was much wider than in the case of the bride, and I recorded instances of *pūro'u* grooms with legally-recognized (*'ite*) offspring from previous marital unions. As the puzzled reactions of informants clearly indicated, the notion of an *'āpi* youth or man was not only ridiculous but virtually unthinkable.

So the chief ornament of a *pūro'u* wedding was a relatively chaste young woman, a subject of evident pride not only for her own relatives but for relatives of the male who wed her. The relatives of both bride and groom at a *pūro'u* wedding received several rewards in return for their contributions of money and objects and services, including the pleasure of feasting with kinsmen and friends; but it was one of the seeming paradoxes of Te Piti society, which in other respects placed little valuation upon chastity, that its members derived much evident satisfaction from publicizing it on this one occasion.

Type II. A "parish" (*paroita*) wedding differed from a *pūro'u* one in several respects. To begin with, it served to formalize, legally and ecclesiastically, a union already in existence, or to establish the formal union of a woman who had been previously "married." In many instances, a parish wedding was carried out in response to a pastor's urgings, or to more general pressures from fellow parishioners. Among Protestants, one of the most powerful incentives for formalizing in this way an already established marital union was the opportunity thereby provided for full church membership, for, unless there were extenuating circumstances, people living in marital union could not become Communicants ('*ētāretia*) until they had been duly married by civil and church officials.

Another difference between "parish" and "veiled-bride" unions lay in the ceremonies themselves. Usually such refinements as bridal gowns and attendants were dispensed with in the former, and the feast following the civil and church rituals of a "parish" union was provided and attended by fellow parishioners or fellow sodality members and was not a strictly kinship affair, i.e., an affair of the *fēti'i* (although there were always some relatives among those present).

Occasionally, a "parish" wedding ceremony involved only a single couple, but more often it involved more—one such with eight couples was celebrated in Atea just before my arrival there, and parish weddings with five or six couples were not rare in the past.

Because of the circumstances just mentioned, the brides and grooms of "parish" weddings tended to be older than "veiled-bride" couples.

Type III. Sometimes an established *fa'aea noa* union received the additional sanction of civil and religious rituals but without any accompanying parish or sodality feast and either with or without a small family celebration. One such wedding took place during my 1954 visit.

When the pastor of Fatata expanded his vanilla plantings, he hired the young man, Teva (this and all other personal names used in this work are fictional) of Afareaitu, as a live-in laborer. Soon after Teva began living at his employer's, he and the latter's daughter began sleeping together, regularly but on the sly. This went on for months before the pastor discovered it; when he did—after his daughter reached obvious pregnancy—he became very angry and insisted upon their marrying, which they did. The church ceremony was conducted by the pastor. There were no spectators at either civil or church ceremonies and no celebration afterwards. (When an Atean visitor remarked with surprise at the lack of any nuptial festivities, even for such an occasion as this, her Fatatan hostess explained that the event had no special significance in view of the circumstances—that there was "no point in spending money or energy for it.")

Such weddings were called "pastor's weddings," because of the latter's influence in arranging them. A variant occurred when a civilly married couple later went through a religious ceremony, mainly to become eligible for church membership. Such occurrences were infrequent and happened mainly with couples who had met and become civilly wed in Pape'ete. (I know of no instance having taken place in Te Piti of a civil wedding unaccompanied by a religious ceremony.)

Type IV. There were, however, three outsider few couples currently living in Te Piti who had been united in civil ceremonies elsewhere and who had not yet succumbed to local pressures to go through religious ceremonies as well.

Type V. One consequence of the application of the *Code Civil* to Tahiti was to promote (unwittingly!) what it refers to as "notorious concubinage." As we shall see, Te Piti marital unions were in general pretty fragile affairs, and this was particularly true of many persons' first unions. Moreover, legal divorces were either too expensive or too slow for many Te Pitians, who did not see the necessity of regulating their sexual and domestic lives according to an alien and, to them, largely unreasonable set of norms and technicalities. Since this view was very widespread and was shared by many of Te Piti's most faithful parishioners, I found in both Atea and Fatata a few previously married couples of unassailable respectability living together in the legal limbo of "notorious concubinage." Disabled by the technicalities of divorce procedure from contracting a new legally correct union, they consequently could not become church Communicants, and the ambiguity attending their new union created problems for their offspring as well (see below); but these circumstances tended, if anything, to gain sympathy for their positions from their neighbors.

Legal technicalities of another sort sometimes blocked the legal marriage of minors, for whom parental consent was required to perform a civil ceremony. The case of Timi and Ami illustrates this and other consequences of applying French law to Tahitian society. Ami was the daughter of Henere and Tetua, a couple who had been "only living together" (*fa'aea noa*) for some twenty years and who had borne several children. Henere and Tetua could not go through a legal ceremony because technically the latter was still wed to her first husband, who would not go to the trouble to give her a divorce. This, of course, meant that her former (and legal) spouse was legal father (*père*) of all her offspring, including those, like Ami, sired by Henere, and that person's consent was required by French law before the minor, Ami, could become legally married.

Similar in many respects was the position of the couple unable to go through with the civil ceremony because they could not produce authentic birth certificates as required by French civil law—or so the couple said. There may indeed have been cases of complete loss of such records, but I suspect that more commonly the inability to secure them from the district of birth was due to the reluctance of most Te Pitians to communicate by post. In one such case, I was informed that a Fatata couple had been "trying for ten years" to get the data on the woman from her home district of Atea. I know that the record in question existed because I had copied it, along with other demographic data recorded in Atea's civil register, and I discovered that their "trying" had consisted of sending one verbal request to a relative in Atea to "bring along the record when and if he came for a visit." (Prodded by my enquiry, they made the difficult move of sending off a letter and were soon in possession of the certificate, which permitted them to marry, in both civil and religious ceremonies, and to become church Communicants.)

How many such instances of nonlegal marriages "because of inability to produce birth certificates" were sincerely just that, and how many were a disguise for the desire to remain legally unwed, I cannot say.

Type VI. Numerous long-established couples did not go through a civil ceremony because one (or both) of the principals did not wish to. The most common reason given for such a stand was that, in the event of separation, a divorce would be too costly. In a few other cases, the reason given, usually by the man, was "Why bother?" And in addition, I turned up several special cases, as for example that of the man who had been willed land by his former wife under condition that he hot remarry, legally.

In terms of their wider social relations, such couples as these differed from those classed as Type V in being considered somewhat less respectable in parish terms. Even so, many such couples were observed to participate fully in all parish activities open to noncommunicants.

Some couples formerly of this type eventually went through the civil marriage ceremony without direct urging from church officials. A European planter told me about one such case involving a couple employed by him. The pair had been living together for about twenty years, with children of their own and with fairly respectable positions in their community. Then one day, they announced their intention of going through with a civil (and church) wedding ceremony; the reason given by them for this long-delayed action having been that they owned a large pig and wished to use it by having a feast.

Type VII. Finally, there were many couples living together openly and unashamedly in unions not yet considered *tāmau* ("firm"). Some of these were in the nature of deliberate "trial" marriages, e.g., of a young man and a young woman not yet certain whether they wished to remain together. Others were unions of older couples who knew themselves well enough to realize the unlikelihood of any permanent attachment. Still others involved an older woman and a younger man—the former wishing for permanence and trying to secure it through gifts, the latter remaining around only as long as nothing better turned up. And last, there were some instances of "trial" marriages not only sanctioned but actually arranged by parents of the principals, as in the case of Mana and Mina.

Mana, aged about seventeen, and Mina, aged fifteen, lived and slept together regularly and openly in Varua's household. Mina was a foster daughter of Varua's first wife (deceased), Mana the son of one of Varua's local friends. When Varua learned of Mina's affair with Mana, he encouraged it and invited the youth to move into his household to cohabit with Mina and to assist himself, Varua, in the latter's many enterprises. According to Varua, it was a good match, much better than Mina's previous one with another youth who turned out to be lazy. Varua, however, did not encourage Mana and Mina to marry, neither he nor Mana's father having wished to bear the expense of a wedding "until the couple became *tāmau*." After about a month of this arrangement (Mana meanwhile having proved himself a willing and able helper to Varua), a small feast was given in their household for the young couple but a marriage ceremony was indefinitely postponed.

The differences between Atea and Fatata with respect to types of marital unions are summarized in Table 8A. The most noteworthy differences revealed in this table were Fatata's preponderance of Type I ("veiled-bride" marriages) and Atea's preponderance of Types II and III (i.e., those in which church affiliation was the organizing principle).

Age at Marriage

By French law, individuals were qualified to marry upon reaching age twenty-one or after legal emancipation. Or, with parental or parent-surrogate consent, they could marry earlier—a male upon reaching eighteen, a female fifteen. Even earlier marriage could be authorized by special administrative dispensation (presumably, e.g., in the event of pregnancy).[3]

According to my records of civil ceremonies, most of the males in Te Piti who had gone through this legally binding ceremony did so between the ages of eighteen and twenty-six and females between seventeen and twenty-five. But these statistics reveal very little about the age factor in other types of Te Pitian marriages. They do not tell us whether the ceremony was a first one for the principals, and they provide no information at all about the noncivil unions which, as indicated, comprised some 43 percent of marital unions among contemporary Te Pitians. In fact, it is very difficult to locate the ages at which most Te Pitian first marital unions began. It is easy enough to discover that a certain percentage of them were legally wed between such-and-such ages, but it was not possible to discover if and when

---

[3]For French laws respecting age at marriage, see *Code Civil,* articles 144 ff.

these couples had commenced a "marital" relationship prior to the legal ceremony. And I am entirely pessimistic about the reliability of the results I obtained by asking: "How old were you when you started living together?" (When social scientists legislate—God forbid!—perhaps they will require all people to keep diaries!) What I can be more sure of, however, were my direct observations concerning who were and who were not married and the opinions of informants concerning such unions, and concerning persons who were in every sense unmarried.

It is my guess that few of the married females residing in Te Piti in 1954–55 had married before reaching the age of sixteen, and it was my observation that there were few who had *not* married before reaching twenty. With males, the corresponding ages were eighteen and twenty-four. The common reaction to marriages at ages earlier than these was: "They are too young." And the common reaction to unmarried women over twenty, and to unmarried men over twenty-four, was given in the form of an explanation of why they had not yet married. (I am referring here, of course, to people who had never married.)

Here are some of the more common explanations offered concerning why certain individuals of marriageable age had never married. Tini (Atea) gave as her reason for not marrying, and not wishing to marry, her desire to remain independent, to go where she pleased and do as she pleased. She had engaged in several short-lived affairs and probably could have had her pick of local youths. By age twenty-five, she had borne two offspring, whom she nurtured and exhibited with evident pride, but she continued to live with her parents and to disavow any desire for marriage.

Sona (Fatata) offered as her reason for not marrying her fear of being beaten by her spouse. Such beatings, she asserted, were an invariable accompaniment of marriage, especially to a young man; and since men were ordinarily stronger than women the latter were not always able to defend themselves. (Unlike Tini, Sona did eventually marry; and her fears were evidently not realized during the first year of marriage.)

Mona (Fatata) presented a different kind of case. She was a handsome, languid young woman, with little or no evident household chores to consume her energies or soil her large wardrobe. During her frequent visits to Pape'ete, she was alleged to lead a promiscuous life—but that was not the reason given by her detractors, who asserted that no right-thinking man would wish to marry her. The real reason, they said, was her incestuous relationship with her father, which was described as "disgusting." Some young men went so far as to disavow any desire to fornicate with her, but others said in private that such was not to be believed. In fact, some older male informants claimed that Mona's single state was not forced upon her but was of her own choosing: "Why should she risk marriage with one of the local louts while she had what she wanted, in sex and in clothing, without work or loss of independence?"

In the case of Ana (Fatata), her father explained that her single state was due to his own unwillingness for her to marry any of the local youths—because of their "low" family origins and their lack of promising economic prospects. Eventually, in return for assurances of Ana's financial security and for a sizeable "loan" to himself, he arranged for her to become the housekeeper and bedmate of an affluent and evidently honest-intentioned Pape'ete Frenchman thirty years her senior. The latter claimed that his wife, in France, would not grant him a divorce because of her Catholic faith—a point emphasized by Ana's father in attempts to justify his consent to a nonlegal union.

Turning now to confirmed bachelors—who, incidentally, were more numerous than their female counterparts—I came across only one past thirty who had remained so deliberately, and emphatically. As for males consigned to permanent bachelorhood through their inability to find a willing mate, these included notorious drunkards, some individuals of habitually filthy personal appearance or with disgusting physical defects, two of the villages' three *māhū*,[4] and one otherwise eligible man whose secluded, unsociable existence was explained as both cause and consequence of his bachelor state. He was characterized as a *"marae"* (pagan temple), into which no woman "would wish to enter."

Finally, I listed the names of several young bachelors, in their twenties, whose single status was put down to their lack of energy and enterprise, i.e., they were not in principle against entering into marriage, but being on kinship grounds unable to marry locally they were described as being too lazy or disinterested to seek a mate elsewhere.

A comparison of Atea and Fatata reveals no noteworthy difference between them with respect to the number of otherwise "eligible" but not yet married—or presumably unmarried—individuals.

Choice of Mate

In going over case histories of marital unions, I initially formed the impression that Te Pitians tended to marry the nearest prospect around. Proximity of residence did indeed turn out to be a factor in choosing a spouse, as I shall indicate, but there were other factors as well, including kinship, age, class, cult, and ethnic identity, along with some others that may be described

---

[4] In contemporary rural Tahiti, *māhū* had the general meaning of a "male who acts like a female." The activity, however, can be either wearing female clothes, or doing females' work, or playing a female role in sexual activity—or two of these, or all three.

as "personal." Some of these factors were verbalized quite explicitly in the form of rules; others had to be inferred from observed trends. Their relative importance in mating people depended upon who did the spouse-choosing.

By far the most explicit and frequently verbalized criterion for spouse-choosing was: "One must not marry a *fēti'i.*"

The official *Code Civil* served to add weight to this norm, although the range of applications specified in the *Code* was narrower, including only as-cendants and descendants of the same line,[5] offspring of same parent, and a person and his or her parent's sibling.[6] In respect to affines, however, the *Code* went further than Te Pitian norms, by proscribing marriage between a person and the former spouse of an ascendant, a descendant, or a sibling.[7]

Needless to say, most Te Pitians, even including those literate in French, were quite unaware of the above legal proscriptions; and in those instances where their own norms were in conflict with the legal ones—as for example in the case of the marriage of affines—it was doubtful that even the local civil clerks were either aware of the conflict or would have insisted on fol-lowing the letter of the law.

In answer to my direct question as to whether a person could marry any consanguine, most Te Pitians replied in the negative: "No person descended from the same ancestor or ancestress should have sexual intercourse." There were some, however, who asserted that the proscription applied only to "near" (*piri*) consanguines and not to "distant" (*ātea*) ones. There was some disagreement on where to draw the line, but the statement of one informant to the effect that it was all right for fifth-generation descendants of a com-mon ancestor to marry was rejected by most others as being "too near."

The response was somewhat different when my question was phrased more specifically, using names of neighbors of known relationship: i.e., "Could X marry Y?" Here there were also a few respondents who rejected the possibility if there was *any* known consanguineal tie, one going so far as to assert, for example, that two particular residents of Fatata should not marry in view of the fact that both had ancestors born on Mai'ao and were thus probably related because of the small population of that island. On the other hand, for most respondents the permissible range tended to become narrower when phrased in terms of specific individuals.

---

[5] "*En ligne directe, le mariage est prohibé entre tous les ascendants et descendants légitimes ou naturels.*" Art. 161.

[6] Art. 163. For the code's definition of parent, etc., see below.

[7] This proscription could be relaxed, by presidential decree, if the connecting relative were deceased. Similarly, if the reason were sufficiently pressing ["*pour des causes graves*"], a presiden-tial decree could permit marriage between a person and his or her parent's sibling (Art. 164).

The acceptance range became narrower still in terms of people's reactions to known cases of the marriage of consanguines. In one such case of the veiled-bride marriage of a couple known to share a common great-grandparent—the most closely consanguineal spouses I encountered—it was agreed among their neighbors that the relationship was in general "too near" but that it was all right in this instance since the parents, who arranged the union, had previously secured the consent of their *fēti'i*. It is not without significance that the families involved in this union were among the village's most highly respected and influential, and their neighbors were thus understandably guarded in their comments. In fact, reticence in accusing one's neighbors of incest—a serious charge avoided usually even in jest—may account for the narrower range of proscription expressed in this context.

In summary, I would say that most if not all Te Pitians asserted, and probably believed, the marriage of consanguines to be in principle a bad thing but that most of them also recognized the necessity of compromise under some circumstances. As many of them took pains to point out, the Bible itself "approves" such compromises as, for example, in the case of Abraham. In fact, some went on to recognize and even approve of the inevitability of "incest" in view of the small size of their society: *'ōpu ātea, 'ōhure fātata*: "womb distant, arses close together," i.e., "if the common ancestor/ress is remote in time, it's all right for the descendants to copulate." (Translation assisted by Ralph White)

Persons who marry "too near" were described as "cannibals" (*'amu ta'ata*, literally, "eat [a] human"). But besides experiencing the feeling of "shame" (*ha'amā*) and of having the anger of *fēti'i* and the gossip of neighbors directed against them, such persons were believed to suffer no other consequence. In some instances, informants added, deceased *fēti'i* (i.e., their ghosts) were probably also angered and applied sanctions in the form of sickness, but I suspect that this stereotype "explanation" was added for my benefit and did not really enter into Te Pitians' own calculations. I was well acquainted with several individuals described by some as having married "too near" but failed to discover any effects upon their positions in the community or upon their own behavior patterns, but this may be the result of the shallowness of my knowledge. Also, several of my informants agreed that it was not necessary to terminate a marriage of *fēti'i*, after the fact, if the principals had not known of their relationship prior to the marriage.

In the case of a legally adopted child, the legal proscription against marriage applied only between the child and its adopting parent (*Code Civil*, Art. 358). Te Pitian norms about relations involved in fostering (*fa'a'amu*) went further than this. According to Te Pitian precepts, a person should not marry any other child of its foster parents, real or foster—at least such was the rule that my informants stated in reply to the general question. But again, when I dealt with specific cases, the replies were less categorical and hinged on the "firmness" of the foster tie—which varied widely, as I shall describe later on.

Finally, I recorded no instances of persons being considered unable to marry because, and only because, of close friendship between their fathers, a proscription that applied in pre-European times to the offspring of *taio*, i.e., persons interrelated through ritually initiated "friendship" pacts (Oliver 1974: 842 ff.).

At several stages of fieldwork and data analysis, I set out to compare Atea and Fatata with respect to the "consanguineal distance" of current marriage pairs—classifying unions by use of "proximity" index, e.g., first cousins = 1, second cousins = 2, etc., but in the end I abandoned the exercise out of frustration, e.g., incomplete cases, contradictory or ambiguous information, etc., and decreasing trust in the significance of the indexing system itself. I can only report, on the basis of some small but credible samples, that the two villages were not markedly different in this regard. At first reaction, this might appear somewhat surprising, given Fatata's large size and hence, *ceteris paribus,* its residents' wider field of choice. On the other hand, Atea's smaller population may have served to remind its residents more forcibly of the (likelier) prospect of marrying "too near," thereby making them more conscious (i.e., than the Fatatans) of the requirement to avoid doing so.

So far I have been describing marriage *proscriptions* based on kinship; there were also two *preferences* worth noting. The best possible kind of marital union, said many informants, is that of siblings being married to siblings. The invariable reason given for such unions was that they helped to keep family property—and mainly land and houses—from being dispersed. I recorded no extant instances of such unions in Atea or Fatata—which might be taken to indicate that property itself was not an overriding factor in the actual choosing of a spouse.

Also, to marry an affine was considered not only permissible but actually desirable. As some informants explained, such persons had already established a relationship of affection (*here*), this having been especially true of siblings-in-law. ("By marrying your brother's widow, or your deceased wife's sister, you do not have to start over again. You already have love for each other and for each other's children. The children are not ill-treated by either parent and hence do not have to be fostered elsewhere.") I was unable to test this generalization, there having been no extant unions of this kind in either Atea or Fatata at the times of my visits. There were, however, a few instances in both communities of marriage between other kinds of affines, including two, both in Fatata, of a person marrying (the word was *haru,* seizing) a sibling's spouse while the sibling was still alive. In both cases the public reacted more with mirth than with moral disapprobation, and in one of them the deserted spouse and his daughter continued to live next door to his brother and former spouse, on apparently amiable terms. The outcome of the other instance was not so amiable; it resulted in unbroken coolness (*fe'i'i*) between the brothers. In addition, I recorded two other historical instances in Fatata in which spouse-seizing had resulted in the legal division of the brothers' jointly held patrimonial lands.

Relative age was a factor of considerable importance for Te Pitians in choosing a spouse.[8] Under ordinary circumstances, people chose spouses of about the same age, and this was considered to be "right" as evidenced in general statements or in comments about specific unions.

In contemporary Te Piti, most of the unions extant in 1954–55 involved spouses whose ages differed by no more than about five to six years. In most of these, the elder spouse was male, which informants characterized as "a good thing" (*mea tano*), although in such unions as these I suspect that the question of who was older was unimportant.

In instances of wider age discrepancy, informants' reactions varied. When forty-year-old males were married to thirty-year-old females, the age factor was rarely if ever discussed. But when Te Pitians commented on an older man marrying a much younger woman—say, a forty-year-old man and a twenty-year-old woman—some of them condemned it as morally bad (*mea 'ino*), others made witty and dire predictions about the man's sexual energies, and most asserted that the union would probably not last. (Some young women I knew were heard to counsel others that in choosing a European to live with one should deliberately pick an oldish man who would presumably be more affluent and generous [and more easily cuckolded?].)

On another kind of union there was also near-universal agreement: it was considered not entirely "right" for an older woman—say, one in her thirties—to marry a much younger man, but it was thought to be a most profitable kind of union for the young man. For in the few such unions I knew, and these varied from well-established civil and church-sanctioned marriages to some rather unstable "trial" unions, the women had brought to the union considerably more material resources than the man. In some cases, the men themselves acknowledged ("confessed" is not the word; I could discern no embarrassment on their part) that their spouse's superior

---

[8]As the reader has already noted, I use the words, *marriage, marital, married, spouse, husband,* and *wife* for any and all of the unions and relationships categorized earlier, but not for the casual affairs that Te Pitians called *'ohipa ha'uti noa.* This follows Te Pitian usage, which—as will be described—refers to all persons participating in such relationships as "her *tane*" (literally, "male") and "his *vahine*" (literally, "female").

wealth had been decisive in their choice. Once, after commenting on the physical unattractiveness and bad temper of one such woman, an informant added: "But she could have had any man she wanted—because of her property."

The only unions of this kind extant in Te Piti during my visits were five in number, all in Fatata. Two of these were nonlegalized unions, with short histories and predictably short futures; the women in question were relatively affluent and the men were obviously having a "good thing." The three other cases were long-established legalized unions from which all three husbands were believed to seek younger sexual partners occasionally but not enough, or flagrantly enough, to endanger what was generally regarded as advantageous by themselves and others.

In Atea, there was only one extant union that resembled this kind, the wife in question having been only about ten years older than her husband. However, the Ateans did feel obliged to "explain" this discrepancy, which, they said, was due to the wife's greater wealth. There was one other woman in Atea, a fifty-year-old widow, who had extensive land holdings there and elsewhere, but she seemed to be content with her role as mother and grandmother, having had no lovers as far as I could discover and no wish for another marriage. (Nor did unattached male Ateans, as far as I knew, even consider her in such terms.)

The question of denominational affiliation as a criterion in choosing a spouse did not arise for most Te Pitians inasmuch as most of them and their actual or potential associates were Protestants. The only interfaith union in Atea involved a Protestant woman and a Mormon man; the nuptial ceremony of this couple was of the veiled-bride type and was held in the Protestant Church (there having been no Mormon chapel in Atea at the time). The husband in this union, who had previously resided in a nearby village, was a devout Mormon but felt, he said, no reluctance about engaging in the Protestant rite (or in attending Protestant church services, which he regularly did), explaining that "the two denominations are practically the same."

Fatata contained two Catholic couples, who had been married by Roman Catholic rites. There were three other unions in Fatata in which the women were Protestant and the men (all from Tahiti) Catholic, or at least vaguely so. One of these unions was of the Type I Number VI; the other two had been nuptialized in the Protestant Church.

What part, if any, did considerations of ethnic identity play in Te Pitians' choice of spouse? To begin with, I believe it is safe to say that Te Pitians considered it a "good thing" to marry a European whereas most of them considered it a "bad thing" to marry a Chinese. (I should point out that any choice in the matter concerned that of a Tahitian woman for either a

European or Chinese man; instances in Te Piti of Tahitian males being married to non-Tahitians occurred only in the case of a temporarily resident public works supervisor in Fatata, who was married to a Wallis Island woman.)

I can go even further and say that many marriageable Tahitian women in Te Piti would have preferred a European spouse to a Tahitian (or Chinese) one. Skin color alone was not a factor (admired though it was in ancient times), since many Chinese and some Tahitians had lighter skin color than some Europeans. In fact, the reasons for this preference, stated and implied, were quite varied, e.g., more money, less household chores, better treatment (including, especially, less beating). Some of the same reasons were given, or implied, for defying norms and marrying a Chinese man: more varied foods, more clothes, less hard work, and in general a less demanding and more generous spouse. However, most Tahitian women I knew who were living with Chinese men, even including those with offspring by them, appeared to regard their situations as more or less temporary (and comfortable) expediencies, destined to end at a time of their own choosing. Moreover, I met with the same attitude, in retrospect, in several women currently wedded to Tahitians but with year-long liaisons with Chinese in their past. Other Tahitians' reactions to such unions varied somewhat, but such reactions were frequently flavored with disapprobation. At one extreme was the flat statement by a man of Fatata to the effect that no "respectable" Tahitian woman would ever live with a Chinese no matter what the material gains. While at the other extreme was the explanation given by the witty and highly "respectable" wife of the *tāvana* of Atea as to why she had lived so long with a Chinese (who, incidentally, had sired most of her children). What she said in effect was that it was every Tahitian's right to get as much as possible out of the Chinese by every means short of thievery; and even if it were not entirely right, had she not done well?

Thus, although the specific reasons (or excuses) given for living with a Chinese man were much the same as those listed in favor of a union with a European, the former situation was nevertheless regarded as "bad" and the latter as "good." In other words, ethnic identity per se did play a (verbally unarticulated) part. (In this connection, the American Negro heritage of Fatata's aged master fisherman seems to have entered into his neighbors' evaluation of him only in the sense that it helped to explain his industriousness and skill. Otherwise, his marital union to a Tahitian woman was not viewed as being "mixed.")

I come now to the question of social class as a criterion for spouse selection, a question that is difficult both to frame and to answer. Ancient Tahitian society was most definitely stratified into at least three social classes—castes, almost—across whose boundaries jurally valid marriages were normatively prohibited. And, as I stated earlier, some class-colored attitudes still survived throughout the Tahitian segment of mid-twentieth-century island society. Those attitudes prevailed more strongly among the more urbanized Tahitians of Tahiti Island, but they were also present in small measure in Te Piti during my visits. There it entered into the favorable view held about marriage with a European, but it also applied to marriage between persons considered to be thoroughly "Tahitian." Some of the Te Pitians, who were regarded by others as *teitei* (high, highly placed, proud, etc.; also haughty, arrogant) and who may have considered themselves to be so, were visibly part-European in appearance and claimed one or more European forebears (whom they could usually name). But there were others just as *teitei* in the eyes of others or of themselves or of both, who may have had but claimed no European mix. And there were still others, more European than Polynesian in appearance, who were regarded by themselves and by others as *ha'eha'a* (low, modest, humble).

More directly relevant than (some) European ancestry was descent from forebears who had been large landholders in the recent past. Respect, along with some envy, was generally expressed towards those currently having large incomes or extensive land holdings, but the attribute of *teitei* I am discussing was applied more typically to persons whose parents or grandparents had been wealthy, even if the living descendants were average or even relatively poor in money and/or land.

European-type education was also a factor in distinguishing between the *teitei* and the *ha'eha'a*, but it was not wholly definitive. There were some individuals of *ha'eha'a* family backgrounds who had become fairly literate and relatively unprovincial, through schooling and travel and through work experiences elsewhere, yet who were still regarded as *ha'eha'a*. And there were others of *teitei* status whose formal education had been largely forgotten through disuse.

In any case, whatever its rationale, the principal role played by social *teitei*-versus-*ha'eha'a* in Te Piti during the times of my visits was a criterion for choice of spouse. That is to say, some parents of *teitei* status exercised what influence they possessed to match their offspring, and especially their daughters, with individuals of similar status. And along with this was the somewhat sharper vigilance exercised by *teitei* parents over their unmarried daughters' social life, and the tendency, when financially possible, to celebrate the latters' nuptials with veiled-bride rites.

There were some differences between Atea and Fatata with respect to the pervasiveness of this kind of social-class attitude, and these will be summarized in a later chapter. In the present context, it will suffice to note that it appeared to be a somewhat weightier factor in Fatata than in Atea as a constraint on choice of spouse.

Within the limits imposed by kin avoidance, so-called "personal" factors outweighed all others when a spouse was being chosen. Even the factor of age was subsumed under this heading, the important thing having been how old a person looked and acted and not when he or she was born.

When parents chose a spouse for their son, they searched, among other things, for a girl who was industrious and nonpromiscuous. And on behalf of a daughter, they searched for a mate who was industrious, thrifty of his material resources, and not given to sustained heavy drinking. Young people doing their own choosing favored these traits too, but in combination with some others.

Provided she was not altogether lazy or notoriously promiscuous, a young man was probably swayed more by a girl's physical attractions than by any other factor. She should not be bony thin or superfluously fat, but within these limits the precise size and shape of her body was of no great consequence, at least not overtly so. Her color should be at least no darker than average, though beyond this point there was no direct correlation between "beauty" (*nehenehe*) and light pigmentation. Her skin, and particularly her facial complexion, should be reasonably clear of sores and scars, although it was unimportant that her feet and lower legs bore the expected marks of barefoot walking over rough and tangled terrain. She should have a more or less complete set of teeth and whether these were false did not really matter. And she should, of course, be free of any crippling or otherwise disfiguring physical defects.

To a young man, the ideal mate was also clean and well brushed except when work demanded otherwise; and her leisure-time clothes should be spotless and as near as resources permitted to the styles set by Pape'ete's fashion leaders. Formal schooling was not an important criterion, in the eyes of most youths, but the young woman who was socially awkward (*ma'au*)—either from sheer rural ignorance or from excessive shyness—was certainly less wanted than the one with some poise. Skill in dancing, Tahitian or European style, may have been an added attraction, but I saw little evidence that it was—not in terms of a prospective spouse, that is. Much more decisive was the factor of drinking: there were probably few young men in Te Piti who would have chosen to marry a heavy drinker unless this defect were outweighed by such factors as wealth. It was the general expectation that a heavy-drinking woman was either promiscuous or lazy or spendthrift or bad tempered, or all of these.

The factor of sexual behavior is more complex. The pleasure expressed by older relatives in staging a veiled-bride wedding undoubtedly reflected some pride in the chastity of one of themselves, and it would be strange indeed if some of this attitude had not been shared by younger men as well. (As noted before, "chastity" in Te Piti referred less to the condition of the hymen than to the supposed effectiveness of parental chaperonage.) In a sense, a veiled-bride wedding may be regarded as a ceremonial display of a kindred's wealth and generosity, having for its principal exhibit, and *raison d'être,* the chastity of one of its young female members. In this context, the young groom expected his bride to be chaste, at least with respect to other males; and I have the impression that this expectation had more to do with the technical requirements of the ceremony itself than with the young groom's criteria for choosing a mate. For in the contexts of all other kinds of marital union, there seems to have been little or no onus attached to a woman's previous sexual activities short of notorious promiscuity. In fact, in Te Piti the only young women whom most young men agreed to be too promiscuous for them were three who had spent time as pick-ups on the Pape'ete waterfront; and two of these eventually settled down into marriages having the appearance of some permanence. In this connection, some informants stated that it was actually better for a woman to have had several affairs prior to settling down in the marital union: "By doing such she will become sated and bored with copulating and will thus have less urge to sleep with men other than her husband." Indeed, some men asserted, overstrict parental chaperonage of a young woman led her to be sexually insatiable after marriage and thus more apt than others to be unfaithful.

From the vantage point of a young woman the ideal spouse was one who was both handsome and dependable. Dependability, perhaps the most decisive factor, meant that he would provide more than the bare bones of subsistence for herself and her children. It was more or less assumed that any man not seriously handicapped physically would be able to provide enough food for survival, enough shelter to keep the weather out, etc.; the mark of the dependable husband was that he would provide money income for goods beyond bare subsistence. And in this sense it was not only the amount of income that counted but its prospects of continuation or increase—a salaried job with tenure having been considered superior to daily wage labor, a large patch of vanilla superior to fishing for the fickle Pape'ete market, etc. (I have heard young women discuss these matters with the objectivity of investment bankers!)

The ideal husband was not necessarily a teetotaller, but he should not spend on beer and wine the money required for food and other household needs; and although some bouts of drunkenness were considered to be tolerable, these should not be frequent or lead to public brawls or beatings at home.

Handsomeness in a husband was the wish of every young woman I knew, although not at the expense of dependability. Comparing the young men said to be handsome with those said to be not, the term seems to have had a very wide range of meaning. In males, only the very darkest skin color was a stigma; beyond that, no particular value was attached to lightness. Tallness was not specially favored, except that the husband should be no shorter than his wife. Bony skinniness was in disfavor as were folds of superfluous fat, but such physiques were so rare among young Tahitian males as to be regarded almost as freaks. In fact, most young Tahitian males possessed such splendid physiques that this factor was taken for granted by young women choosing a spouse. Crippling or disfiguring physical defects were handicaps, but less so than with females, and this was particularly true with respect to teeth. A more serious handicap for a young man was baldness, but again this was so rare a phenomenon among young Tahitian males that it can almost be ignored as a criterion of handsomeness.

A periodically clean body, a combed and glistening head of hair, and a wardrobe containing some tight-legged trousers, two or three fashionable aloha shirts, and a pair of shining leather shoes—all these were possessions of nearly every young Te Pitian male, and young women seemed to attach no particular importance to a larger-than-ordinary wardrobe or a more-than-average scented pomade.

Of much more importance was the behavior that accompanied these traits of physique and plumage. To begin with, the young women I knew were as scornful of the *māhū* as her American counterpart used to be of the "sissy" five decades ago, the words having had some of the same kinds of meaning in this context; and her opinions on the subject were usually expressed with considerably more candor and bluntness. Strength and courage, endurance and physical skill were undoubtedly valued, as witnessed by the admiration young women expressed for the sports hero or the daring and successful speargun fisherman.

Aside from *māhū,* young women seemed to assume all young men were more or less experienced in sexual technique. Some were reputed to be kinder and more generous to their sexual partners than others, and they were consequently more highly esteemed; but the conventional sexual technique was so simple and direct that there was little room for refinement, and I could discover no evidence that lovers were publicly graded according to sexual skill.

Preliminary courtship behavior is, however, another story. To my age-jaundiced eye, there was nothing more comical than a young Te Piti male in courting posture: wandering along the road or sitting beside it with others like himself; his fine physique hidden in poor-fitting garments decorated with Hong Kong versions of Polynesian designs; his great spreading feet painfully inserted into unaccustomed and unlaced shoes; his head brilliantined with oily scent and crowned with flowers; and his heavy-browed and usually handsome face drawn up into a sick-cow expression as he sang to the accompaniment of somebody's guitar the latest Pape'ete inanity about love and moonlight and absence. But, fortunately for population survival, this performance appears to have had quite another effect upon susceptible young Te Piti females. Moreover, it had behind it the association and authority of Paris and Hollywood, since European parallels of this behavior pattern were to be seen all too frequently at the local cinema. In any event, the shy and awkward young man who did not possess these social graces, such as they were, was at some disadvantage in the quest for a mistress and presumably for a spouse as well.

In addition to all these generally applicable criteria, individual young women most certainly had individual requirements to guide them in their search for a husband, but on one other factor they nearly all seemed to agree: the short-tempered youth with a propensity for manhandling his mistress may have been all right as a temporary lover but was to be avoided as a spouse. As I have noted elsewhere, the fear of husbandly beatings figured high in the reasons given by some young women for remaining unmarried; and certainly one of the attractions of a European mate, or of the stereotype thereof, was his reputed restraint in this regard.

At this point, I must add a corrective to the above generalizations about choice of spouse. It is true that males no less than females had their opinions about the attributes of an ideal spouse; and males did indeed tend to take the initiative in starting love affairs. But, as one young man explained, "Males are lazy about marriage. It's the female who chooses which of several males she wants to stay with; and usually the male is pleased enough to agree."

In discussing these so-called personal factors, I have dealt in terms of what young men and women looked for in a spouse. Now, most Te Pitians did, in fact, marry during their youth, but a very large percentage of them also had occasion to choose spouses later on in their lives. (In Te Piti the record in this respect was held by a woman who, at the age of fifty-five and after nine unions that I know of, optimistically entered into another marriage with a man of about fifty-seven.) Needless to say, expectations altered with increasing age. To a forty-year-old man, a prospective spouse's teeth were perhaps less important than her ability and willingness to conduct an orderly household or aid him in pollinating his vanilla plants or in mending his nets. And for the older woman, except for some who were already assured of the material basis for a good life, probably the most desirable trait in a man was his dependability as a provider. But the hope for a handsome and gracious young lover died hard, as anyone knows who has attended a Tahitian cinema theater and observed the rapturous expressions on some older women's faces while watching a particularly romantic love scene.

And finally I return to the first factor mentioned in this section, the question of accessibility. I did not happen to hear a Te Pitian verbalize the formula in any such general terms, but my data on where spouses lived before their marriage makes it clear that the alleged principle of energy conservation operated quite frequently in this sphere of behavior. A surprisingly large number of Te Pitians seem to have settled down with whatever potential and unattached person happened to be nearest at hand (see below, page 300). Nor was unattachment always decisive; I knew of several instances of spouse-changing among near neighbors. The oral literature of ancient Tahiti contains many accounts of heroes voyaging through danger-ridden seas to distant islands in search of mates; in 1954–55, however, even with the ease of sea travel by motor launch or by motorbike over well-kept roads, the modern Te Pitian saved his travel energy for other enterprises and was usually content to settle down in marriage with someone, however short of ideal, who happened to live nearby.

Arranging Marriages

Young Te Pitians entered marital unions by one of three routes:
—They followed the dictates of their parents, who sought out a suitable mate and made all arrangements for betrothal and nuptials;
—they chose a mate and then left it to their parents to arrange the ceremonies; or
—they chose a mate themselves and began living together without further ado.
Veiled-bride weddings were always parentally arranged and occurred most frequently in connection with marriages in which the parents also selected the mates.[9] An example of this kind of arrangement was the union of Tamu.

Tamu lived with his father and stepmother at Atea. His economic prospects were excellent, since he would eventually receive large landholdings from both his father and his maternal relatives. There was no suitable match for him at Atea; girls there of about his age were ruled out either on the grounds of kinship or, implicitly, of "class." It was quite understandable that his ambitious and enterprising father should try to make the best possible connection for him, which meant the daughter of a wealthy man of *ari'i* stock who lived some five miles away. The wedding duly took place, one of the largest and costliest in recent Huahine history, but the bride soon thereafter left her husband, complaining of physical mistreatment, and divorce proceedings were begun—all to the disgust of parents and other relatives, because of the money "thrown away" for the wedding.

---

[9]Older informants recalled the times when parents used to betroth their offspring during the latters' childhood, or even before birth, but added that this practice had not been followed for a decade or more.

It also occasionally happened that parents stepped in and arranged a veiled-bride wedding for a young couple who had made their own choice. This occurred in the case of Timi and Purea who had met in Pape'ete while working there. The wedding celebrations took place at Fatata, at large expense to the relatives of both brides and groom and against a backdrop of cynical amusement occasioned by widespread skepticism of the bride's justification for wearing a virgin's veil. Most of the skeptics I talked with pointed their criticism at the bride's relatives, not at the bride, and blamed family arrogance for the pretence. ("They wish to appear *teitei*.")

A wedding held at Atea in 1955 combined elements of free choice and parental agreement. It began with an affair between a local girl, the previously well-chaperoned daughter of affluent parents, and a youth she met on a visit to relatives at the island of Taha'a. When word of the affair reached her Atea parents, they, fearing the worst, promptly arranged for the pair to wed, veiled-bride fashion, before that option could be closed by obvious signs of pregnancy.

In line with their economic resources and social pretensions, the girl's parents planned for a lavish, costly celebration which, their reasoning developed, would in fact "kill two birds with the same stone." (To the best of my knowledge there is no close Tahitian equivalent to this apt English metaphor, but I am reasonably certain that Te Pitians did reason in this way.) The other "bird" in this case had to do with the bride's younger sister, still unmarried and apparently still uncompromised. The decision was to make it a double wedding, which would have the additional double purpose of getting the younger sister safely married, in veiled-bride style, and at no additional cost. (With restraint perhaps unbecoming an ethnographer, I refrained from querying the girls' parents on this point, but most of the fellow-villagers I questioned expressed the view that of the two kinds of motive the economic one had been foremost in the parents' minds.)

The problem then was to find a groom for the younger sister—not a difficult problem, because there was an excellent prospect ready at hand. The youth in question was nineteen years old, still unattached, the son of another of Atea's most affluent and socially *teitei* couples. As I reconstruct the episode, the girl's father approached the boy's, who readily agreed, on both social and economic grounds, i.e., the proposed wedding would spread the cost into four equal shares, two of which would be borne by the two brides' parents and one each by the respective parents of the two grooms.

After the decision had been reached by the parents, the younger sister and her intended were informed—to their stunned surprise and mutual distress. (Apparently they knew and liked each other well enough, but that was all; neither wished to be married at that stage in their lives.) The distress

continued up to the time of the wedding, but evidently it occurred to neither of them, nor to anyone else, that they should or could disobey.

Parental arrangements did not always involve veiled-bride weddings, or
even civil-church rites. In some cases the parents who were short of money
or of social aspirations, or of both, had their children married in private civil and church rites and in small family-only celebration meals. And there
were other instances during and just prior to my visits in which young
couples were permitted or persuaded to cohabit in one of the parental
homes without even a civil rite.

Turning now to unions not arranged by relatives, many of the first
unions of young people began with no formal ceremony at all. Finding each
other compatible, after experimenting around, they simply ceased being
surreptitious in their lovemaking, began living together in a separate house
or in one of the parental homes, and commenced complementary subsistence roles. As indicated earlier, many of these unions may be regarded as
"trial" marriages; of those that endured, some eventually became sanctioned by civil-religious ceremonies, while others did not. In the beginning,
some of these unions received parental blessing but even if they did not, inasmuch as there was no civil ceremony involved, parental disapproval was
usually relevant only in cases where considerable property was at stake, as
no Te Pitians had any inkling of the nature of "parental authority" as defined in the *Code Civil.*

The case of Pepe is fairly typical of the beginnings of current unions of
Types III and VI. Pepe was the daughter of Mano from Ra'iatea, who had
arrived in Fatata twenty years previously to work on a European plantation. There Mano met and started living with Nora, who was born at Fatata and was the owner through inheritance of a small coconut grove and a
patch of land suitable for growing vegetables. After twelve years of living
together, Mano and Nora went through civil and church ceremonies,
mainly to become church Communicants. Meanwhile, Mano had legally
"recognized" their four children, including Pepe.

Pepe herself started having affairs with boys her own age when she was
eleven or twelve. By the time of my first visit, when she was fifteen, she had
three "regulars" but was beginning to favor Tapei more than the others. At
this point, when she became pregnant, she told her parents that Tapei was
"probably the father." They were angry (her father beat her every day for a
week, she said) but raised no objection when several months later she asked
their permission for Tapei to move into their house. Tapei said it was all
right with him too—his widowed mother sulked for a day or two but then
moved to another district to stay with a married daughter—so the union
took place without any further ceremony. ("There wouldn't have been time

for one," explained Tapei, "because the baby was born about a week later.") A year later, Pepe was expecting another child, and her mother had assumed the major job of looking out for the first baby, which she doted over. Meanwhile, Tapei helped his father-in-law with copra-making and vegetable growing and fished for the whole family, in addition to which he earned two or three hundred francs a week at casual labor and used part of this money for buying bread and canned beef for the household. The family was a peaceful one, i.e., none of the males drank to excess and Nora had been less shrewish since the arrival of her grandchild, and there seemed to have been no intention for Pepe and Tapei to become legally (and religiously) married or to move into a house of their own.

The union of Pepe and Tapei exemplified a fairly common sequence of events; another even more common sequence resembled it except for the detail that the girl moved in with the boy's family; eventually, however, most such couples moved into households of their own. It should again be noted that in such unions as these it was nearly always the woman who exercised the initiative in converting a casual affair into a more or less durable union.

Most *fa'aea noa* unions took place between residents of the same village, but now and then young people found their mates in distant places, either by chance or by conscious search. Pape'ete was one important source; young men and women went there for school or work and sometimes returned home with a mate.[10] When Fatata's football team was active, its members looked forward to matches on Tahiti Island where, in their roles as athletic heroes, they usually had no difficulty finding sweethearts and occasionally mates as well. Large veiled-bride weddings also provided opportunities for young people to survey matrimonial possibilities in other communities. And finally, one consequence and, in its turn, one of the maintaining causes of the geographically extensive scattering of relatives throughout the islands was the opportunity thereby provided for people to travel and, if necessary, search for spouses in distant places.

Young people also went occasionally on deliberate spouse-searching tours, sometimes (in the case of males) combining this pleasure with some business, namely, the collection of their share of the profits from a jointly owned plantation.

Older people tended to acquire their new spouses near home, but occasionally a widow or widower would visit distant relatives or take a job in a distant community with the express purpose of finding someone congenial to live with. Also, when abandoning one spouse for another, the new one would in most cases be from a nearby house, a solution which implies an

---

[10]Compare Kay 1963A:72, where the author aptly labels Pape'ete as a "territorial marriage market."

economy of effort and at the same time provides a clue to the cause of the change.

There is little to be reported about "courtship" in the context of marriage which has not already been reported in other contexts. It should only be added that a couple betrothed and destined for a veiled-bride wedding were supposed to be circumspect in their relations. Convention permitted them to be together, in company, during the daytime but required them to remain apart after dark—a rule that was more often honored than not, for a prospective veiled-bride maiden was to be seen usually surrounded by female relatives and friends, planning and giggling over the coming event.

Formal acts of betrothal usually took place only in connection with unions which parents or parental surrogates had some hand in arranging, although they were not limited to veiled-bride weddings or even to other legally sanctioned ones. In the case of Tapu, for example, when his foster mother found a suitable mate for him she formalized the arrangement by giving an engagement present (*hōroʻa momoʻa*, gift-engagement) to the girl through her parents, consisting of some bed linen and two new dresses.

The decision to hold a veiled-bride wedding was usually ceremonialized in a little feast attended mainly by the principals and their parents, and at about this time the parents of the boy presented an engagement gift (usually of clothes) to the girl through her parents. In some cases, there was also a religious ceremony performed at about this time. The young couple and their parents appeared before the pastor, and perhaps the deacons of their sodalities, to arrange a date for the wedding, and occasionally the boy presented an engagement present to his fiancee at this time. Some informants asserted that once a marital arrangement had been formalized in this manner it was difficult to withdraw from, and my evidence supports this assertion.

In addition to the familial and religious preliminaries for weddings, the law of the land required the posting of banns for at least ten days prior to the civil ceremony, and this in turn required a note from a medical officer certifying the couple to be medically fit for marriage (*Code Civil,* Articles 63, 64).

French law also provided detailed and comprehensive procedures for the disposition of the property of marrying couples, e.g., which properties of the spouses were to be pooled, which held separately, etc. Presumably such contracts are common enough in metropolitan France and sometimes accompanied the unions of Tahitians and Europeans and of some affluent *Demis,* but I did not hear of any having been drawn up in connection with the marriage of Te Pitians. In fact, most Te Pitians I queried about this matter had never heard of such procedures.

Veiled-Bride Weddings

Veiled-bride weddings were one of the three most ceremonious kinds of occasions engaged in by mid-twentieth-century Te Pitians (the other two having been New Year and the parish May Collection). I actually witnessed only four of them but collected fairly full accounts on twelve others, along with several general accounts describing how Te Pitians thought they *ought* to be conducted.

A full veiled-bride wedding celebration lasted at least three days. On the first day, there took place the civil and church ceremonies and a banquet for the wedding party and specially invited guests. The second day featured a feast for relatives who had come from other places. Then, if there was food and drink left over, all the relatives and friends who had contributed their services were fed at an informal meal, usually on the third day and after the banquet pavilion had been taken down.

Preparations for a veiled-bride wedding usually required several weeks' time—to collect money to cover the basic costs, to construct a banquet pavilion, and, very important, to acquire proper clothes. For the groom, the best man, and the bride's official "giver," this was not difficult; if they possessed no suitable coat or shoes of their own, they could easily buy or borrow some. But for the bride and her attendants the matter was much more complicated. After agreement had been reached on styles and colors—no easy matter in itself—the wedding gowns had to be obtained, either from a Pape'ete or Uturoa dressmaker or sewn locally by relatives and friends. Shoes also presented a problem, since they had to match the gowns; and the question of whether or not to wear a veil had to be honestly faced. Needless to say, all these activities provided numerous loopholes for crises, and crises invariably occurred, e.g., not enough dress materials, wrong shoe sizes, etc., and these provided the community's females with much conversational material.

Meanwhile crises of another kind often occurred. Sometimes, for example, the bride (or groom, or both) developed second (or third, or fourth, etc.) thoughts about the match, thereby producing flurries of speculation throughout the community and reports of parental pressure being applied. Sometimes a disappointed suitor or a jilted mistress would spread malicious stories about the affianced pair, thereby enlivening local gossip and even provoking quarrels and fights. I recorded reports of some intended weddings that had to be called off because of those and other kinds of events, including one in which the bride eloped with a former suitor and one in which the groom did the reverse. (In this connection, a more usual outcome was for the couple to separate soon after their wedding, but that is another matter discussed below.)

The wedding day itself began with the civil rite—after, of course, hours spent by the bride and her attendants costuming themselves. The civil rite was conducted by the chief (*tāvana*) in the schoolhouse and was usually attended by only the bride and groom and their next of kin. Then to the flower-bedecked church, where the religious rite was performed by the pastor and witnessed by much of the congregation. Following this came the procession—a sight to behold!—made up of the bridal couple, their attendants, and nearest of kin, who all trudged slowly and perspiringly and with deadly serious formality along the rough paths to the banquet pavilion, between lines of onlookers who expressed their reactions to the bizarre sight—for such it was even to Te Pitians—with titters or with ribald or mordant comment.

The ensuing banquet was conventionally a socially stratified affair. At the head table sat the bride and groom, their principal attendants, and their parents. Next to this was the table reserved for the *invités*—i.e., the official "guests," those specially invited by letter, including chief, schoolteacher, pastor, and distinguished outsiders (e.g., pastors from other places, Administration officials, nearby European planters—and ethnographers!). Next were the tables occupied by other visitors and by the closer kinfolk of the bridal couple. And outside was the usual throng of children, and the friends and other relatives occupied in cooking and serving. (In Atea, the local Chinese storekeepers usually attended the wedding banquets and were seated at the third-place tables; in Fatata, they were seldom invited.)

The *invités* conventionally deposited their gifts upon entry—almost, it seemed, like a ticket of admission.

The menu invariably included large numbers of store-bought dishes—canned meats and fish, canned vegetables and fruit, etc., and Chinese specialties—along with such local delicacies as roast pork and sweet puddings. At the banquets I attended, the most valued dishes were placed first on the two top tables and passed to the other tables only after the occupants of the former had had their fill. Usually, also, the best chinaware and cutlery was reserved for the two top tables, as was the champagne when it was served, the third tables having to be satisfied with ordinary red wine and beer.

Speeches were of course delivered by the pastor, chief, and other distinguished guests, and homily was the theme of the day—long life, many children, sexual fidelity, sobriety, piety, etc.—homilies of such duration, repetition, and banality that, on the occasions I witnessed, even these sermon-hardened stoics became restive (encouraged, of course, by alcohol). The one speech that was followed with interest was that announcing the "marriage name" (*i'oa ha'aipoipo*) chosen for the newlyweds, a name usually decided upon by the pastor in consultation with the parents, and one formerly held by some notable ancestor of the bride or (more often) groom.

After this ceremonious climax the banquet invariably turned into a merrier mood, with guitar playing and singing and relentless drinking, by which time the pastors and others of the more sedate *invités* would have left. Some of these parties went on all night and became very drunken affairs. And at the ones that I witnessed the bridal couples remained to the end. (My description of the American custom wherein the bridal couple "escapes" from their wedding reception before it actually ends struck my informants as a ridiculous waste of a good party.)

As noted earlier, a full veiled-wedding celebration usually lasted three days, but the more distinctive and significant events took place on the first day, as just described hence I will omit further details about days two and three and turn to a summary and analysis of the transactions that customarily constituted or accompanied this important Te Pitian ceremony. But first, a digression on marital and other kinds of Te Pitian personal names.

Names

At birth every Te Pitian received a "calling name" (*i'oa pi'i*) and a "surname" (*i'oa pa'era'a*). These were the ones that were recorded in the civil register and that were thenceforth used for all official purposes, except and until the surname was changed by legal adoption (which did not take place in Te Piti). When written, the two were joined by the particle *a*, thus: *Jean a Taro'o, Teri'i a Teihotu*, etc.

Most "calling" names in Te Piti were Tahitian, but judging from genealogical records there was an increasing tendency to select European ones, such as *Tihoni* (i.e., *John*) or *Marianne*—or such gems as *Ero-firene* (i.e., *Errol Flynn*) or *Paronti* (i.e., *Blondie*). All those names of European origin were sex-linked, but some of the Tahitian ones were used for both sexes. The "calling" name was the one most commonly used in ordinary conversation for both address and reference, though it was often abbreviated in usage, e.g., *Rosina* became *Sina*, *Viriamu* (i.e., *William*) became *Viri*. But nearly as common in conversation was the use of nicknames (*i'oa ha'uti*, name play), which were usually apt and occasionally unsparingly so; e.g., a dark-skinned person became *Blackie*, a fleshy one *Fatty*, a crippled one *Crab-foot*, and, by inversion, a lazy one usually seated or lying down became *Stand-up*. Play-names were of course not sanctioned by official action and hence were subject to change, but it was my impression that once hit upon they seldom changed, as witnessed by the persistent application of *Baby* or *Crybaby* or *Little-one* to decrepit old men and women.

The surname (*pa'era'a*) given to an individual was that of the person officially acknowledging parenthood—the "father" if his identity be acknowledged by himself (otherwise someone agreeing to act as "father") and/or the mother.

Next in sequence was the name used by the pastor in baptizing the child. In most cases, that was the child's official name, "calling" and "surname," but occasionally a different "calling" name was used for this ritual, selected from among the names, of whatever type, associated with one of the child's ascendants, maternal or paternal, remembered for some special virtue or deed. From my cursory researches, separate baptismal names (*i'oa papatito*), which were usually Tahitian, were bestowed mostly upon children whose "calling" names were European and hence may have been done to "re-Tahitianize" the child (although no one acknowledged that to be the purpose). If the two names were different, the baptismal name thenceforth tended to supplant the original "calling" name in parish contexts and sometimes in popular usage as well.

Next was the "married" name (*i'oa ha'aipoipo*) referred to earlier, the one bestowed on most couples united by civil and church ceremonies. It was ordinarily selected from among the surnames associated with one of the spouses', most usually the husband's, ascendants. Thereafter it was used on occasions calling for some formality in address or in reference, as when introducing or discussing people at church or when recording their contributions to religious or semireligious collections. The form was standard, thus: *Hanere tane* (Henry-husband) or *Hanere vahine* (Henry-wife).[11] In Te Piti, the parents' "marriage" name was not passed on to their offspring, although the child of a couple may in time have received the same marriage name as its parents'.

Another kind of "marriage" name was occasionally used in Te Piti, especially in conversations in French with Europeans and when addressing or referring to Tahitians holding some official position. This involved calling a husband or his wife by his surname, introduced with "Monsieur" or "Madame"—obviously an effort to adjust to European nomenclature, appropriate enough in the case of the husband but unsuited to Te Piti practice in the case of the wife.

In some cases an individual's official surname, baptismal, and even marriage name were the same, thus: *Jean a Amaru* (official), *Amaru a Amaru* (baptismal), and *Amaru tane* (marriage). But much more often, one found something like the following (say, of a hypothetical married, female schoolteacher):

Césarine a Nohotua: calling and surname (official)
Tera'i a Nohotua: baptismal
Manea vahine: marital

---

[11]The nearest analogy I know of is the "Brother" or "Sister" Smith kind of name used in some American Protestant congregations, although in these latter the "Smith" is of course the official surname of both spouses.

Madame Marama: her husband's surname;

but, as like as not, the name most often used for her would be "Ignorant" (because she was so intelligent), or perhaps "Quiet" (because she was so loud)!

Numerous residents of Te Piti held elective or appointed offices, but the only *status names* of this kind that were consistently used in ordinary address and reference were: *'orometua* (pastor), *tāvana* (chief, from English "governor"), and *taote* (doctor, infirmier). *Muto'i* (constable) was also occasionally used in address, with a shade more of good-natured contempt than of respect. Deacon, deputy chief, counsellor, schoolteacher, and veteran also figured in public oratory, but in daily discourse the Te Pitians cut down these worthies to the size of their respective calling names or nicknames. The use of such honorifics as "Great-chief-power-filling-the-heavens," "Mighty-warrior-devastating-the-lands," or "Sure-handed-craftsman-builder-of-ocean-sweeping-canoes" seems to have ended with the final crumbling of the old polity.

As noted above, marriage names were used mainly in formal situations more or less connected with parish activities; I have never heard a couple refer to each other or even address each other by such names. In fact, the only terms of address I heard married couples use for each other were "calling" names and nicknames "You" (Hey, you there seawards), or occasionally "Mother" (Mama) or "Father" (Papa)—in the sense of "family mother or father" (and most definitely not in the sense of "you who mothers or fathers me").

Te Pitians usually referred to their own spouses as *nou vahine* (my woman) or *nou tane* (my man), and people normally also referred to others' spouses (as such) in those terms, although I was cautioned by some of my older neighbors that this was not "correct." The correct term, I was told, was *hoa* (friend, companion, helpmate); and the occasions on which I heard *hoa* used in this context did indeed reek of respectability.

Outside of church contexts, the only collective term I heard used to refer to a married couple was, say, *Teri'i* (or whatever happened to be the husband's calling name, nickname, or title) *ma*, i.e., Teri'i-and-company, which, according to context, could also have referred to Teri'i and his whole family or to any other social unit being identified by reference to him, e.g., "Here come *Teri'i ma* (Teri'i and some friends of his)."

Te Pitians also made the distinction, in reference, between a man's regular spouse (*vahine metua*, woman, [co]parent) and his casual lover (*vahine tai'ata*, dissolute woman; *vahine purūmu*, street woman), but the only times I heard this distinction implied in address were in street quarrels between women. When addressing their spouses or mistresses, men were presumably wise enough to leave unuttered the implications of this latter usage.

Wedding Transactions

The basic normative principle governing contributions of money, objects, and services used for a veiled-bride wedding celebration was symmetrical bilaterality: the relatives and friends of the groom, "the upper side" (*te pae i ni'a*), should contribute the same amount as relatives and friends of the bride, "the under side" (*te pae i raro*). (These were the same terms used in ancient Tahiti.) Each side was required to contribute "half," every informant categorically stated; but it sometimes happened—many of them would add—that one side gave a larger "half" than the other.

On several occasions, when I tallied up the costs of these events and pointed out inequalities in contributions—not just in total contributions of services and objects and money, but of money alone—the surprised reaction was invariably: "Ah, yes. Perhaps not in this case; and that's because . . . . But the real Tahitian way of conducting a wedding is for each side to pay half the costs." (What is meant by "costs" will become clear as I proceed.)

The principle of bilaterality began to operate prior to the wedding itself. If there were an engagement celebration, one side was mainly responsible for arranging and financing it, leaving to the other side the main responsibility for organizing and conducting the wedding feast. That this was not an equitable division of labor was widely recognized. Engagement parties were at most very modest affairs, rarely costing more than 500 to 1,000 francs (for cakes and lemonade and perhaps a few litres of wine), whereas the job of producing a wedding feast involved hundreds of man- (and woman-) hours of work. At one level of discourse, informants not only acknowledged the discrepancy but commented on it cynically; yet those same informants, when talking in generalities, pointed with pride to the principle of "engagement party by one side; wedding feast by the other" as epitomizing the sensible and truly *Tahitian* ideal of perfect bilaterality.

This ideal also suffered some neglect with respect to the groom's engagement gift to the bride, which was not reciprocated in any form as far as I could discover. When I drew attention to this asymmetry, most Te Pitians I queried indicated by their reactions that they had not thought about the matter previously and usually offered the ad hoc explanation that it was probably a European custom—as indeed it could well have been.

Somewhat different was the case with another "gift" presented by the groom or the groom's parents to the bride in preparation for the wedding: this was the money given towards the cost of the bridal costume. This costume—wedding gown, veil, and shoes—was acquired just for the occasion and, except for the shoes, was not worn again. Usually from Pape'ete or Uturoa, its cost was high, representing the income from weeks of working for wages or producing cash crops. In Te Pitians' calculations, it was therefore entirely proper for the groom to bear about half the cost of this outlay, which after all was as much a part of the wedding program as the food and the drink itself.

When a Te Pitian was asked "how big was such and such a (veiled-bride) wedding?" he would almost invariably give as his reply the amount of money spent by the organizers in buying or renting materials for the feast, for buying or renting materials for the wedding pavilion, and for hiring vehicles to transport guests; this basic expense was known in Te Piti as the *moni tumu* ("foundation money," a term applied also to the basic donations to the May Collection of Fatata). Numerous other costs, although not usually listed in these recitals, would nevertheless figure in the calculations of participants if subsequently there happened to be any trouble between the sides; such additional costs included vegetables and seafood donated rather than purchased, borrowed cooking and eating utensils, and the large amounts and various kinds of services contributed by relatives and friends in preparing and conducting the festivities. And finally there were such items as the bridesmaids' costumes, (sometimes) the groom's and his aides' new clothes, and the boat or truck fares paid by guests not brought in specially chartered vehicles. Actually, although all these required money, it is unlikely that the Te Pitians considered such expenditures as part of the "costs" of the wedding itself.

The sum of the first kind of cost, the *moni tumu*, was always agreed upon in advance by the parents of bride and groom; for the weddings I had information on, the amount ranged from 10,000 to 130,000 francs, the mode having been 15,000 to 20,000. In principle, each side was required to contribute exactly half this amount. Many informants went a step further and added that the money contributed by each side should be borne in equal amounts by relatives of the father and of the mother, respectively, of bride and groom.

Another rule stated was to the effect that the contribution of the side of, say, the groom's father should be borne equally by relatives of *his* birth-father (*papa fānau*) and, if he had one, of his foster-father (*papa faʻaʻamu*).

Some relatives volunteered their contributions to the *moni tumu* as soon as they heard about the wedding. Others living nearby were visited by one of the parents or by some other relative possessing influence and willing to assist. In some rare instances, letters were written to relatives living farther away, but no effort was usually made to communicate with those—except perhaps primary and secondary kinfolk—at different ends of the archipelago (i.e., people on Tahiti and Moʻorea would intercommunicate quite readily on such occasions, as would those on, say, Huahine and Raʻaiatea; but a writer on Moʻorea would characteristically conclude that Maupiti and Borabora were "too far away").

A written record was kept of these contributions, but even without it I came across individuals who could reproduce the names and amounts of each donor several years after the event. Analysis of *moni tumu* contributions to each of the veiled-bride weddings on which I possess credible records reveals the following tendencies:

1. While the principle of bilateral symmetry was always considered most desirable, realistic allowances were usually made for the abilities of the respective sides to contribute. (And according to my observations, many Te Pitians possessed remarkably detailed and largely accurate knowledge of their kinfolks' and neighbors' economic assets and liabilities, and if necessary could obtain similar information about other Tahitians residing elsewhere.)

2. Within a side, while many informants tended to agree with the principle that the costs ought to be levied equally between relatives of the father and of the mother of bride or groom, the same kind of allowance, for ability to pay, was made when a contribution was requested or received.

3. As for the rule regarding equality of payments between birth- and foster parents, it usually did transpire that the latter—and sometimes even their kinfolk—contributed to the *moni tumu* fund, but the actual proportions of such contributions appeared to follow no set formula.

4. Otherwise, while those who had thought about it (and these were not numerous) expressed the view that contributions ought to be graduated in terms of kinship distance, and while in fact that principle was usually honored in a general sort of way, no one proposed any kind of fractional formula for it. Here again, ability to pay was taken into account.

5. With respect to "ability to pay," however, judgments about that were influenced also by what was considered to be an individual's moral qualities. If, for example, an otherwise industrious father or a father's brother were unable to contribute a substantial amount because of his poverty in capital assets, or because of a large brood of dependent children, or an illness, or a run of fishing failures, etc., he was subject to little or no criticism. But if his inability to pay were due to notorious laziness or prodigality (especially regarding alcohol), his kinfolk would have been certain to complain and his neighbors to criticize.

The supplementary costs of a *veiled-bride* wedding included the services of the organizers and helpers in erecting and taking down the banquet pavilion; collecting, cooking, and serving the meals; and preparing bouquets for the bride and floral leis for the guests. If such had been hired, the cost would on some occasions have exceeded the amount of the *moni tumu* spent. Actually, nothing was paid to the workers, unless coffee and bread and feast leftovers can count as payment; and none of the workers would normally have expected any other immediate and tangible remuneration. There was, however, a rough calculation made of such services by some participants, and it entered into subsequent events in two ways. First, if troubles had developed between the two sides—say, domestic quarrels between bride and groom or some property dispute between their parents—the party whose side worked harder for the wedding could have been counted upon to air this as a grievance. And secondly, if people had worked especially hard at another's wedding they would usually have expected reciprocation later on, when they themselves needed help on some project requiring unpaid services. And if such help were not forthcoming, one can be certain that neighbors would hear of it, and it sometimes resulted in "coolness" that persisted for years.

The same considerations governed donations of food not ordinarily purchased for money, e.g., breadfruit, eating bananas, mangoes, limes, coconuts in small quantities, and sometimes root crops and seafood as well. As for the cooking and eating utensils borrowed for the feasts from relatives and neighbors, I never heard them discussed in anyone's calculations of reciprocities except when one was spoiled or broken, in which case it was usually replaced by means of the *moni tumu*.

A wholly different kind of transaction was involved in things given to the bride and groom, usually for their joint use, by their parents or other close relatives. These included house furnishings or money to buy them with, and occasionally even a house. Such gifts were not invariably given, and they ranged very widely in value from wedding to wedding. They did not enter directly into Te Pitians' calculations of the costs of the wedding celebrations; and although it was said that "the gifts of the bride's parents should more or less equal those of the groom's," I heard no recrimination when actions did not follow the rule. People usually knew the economic circumstances of the individual donors of these gifts, and their gifts were measured more in terms of the donors' own resources. On the other hand, the seemingly limitless ramifications of a *"pae feti'i"* seemed to make it reasonable to expect a closer matching of contributions for the fundamental *moni tumu*.

Finally, there are to be considered the gifts that appeared to involve no element of equality between sides, and in conventional discourse, at least, no expectation of return. These were the gifts given to the couple by the *invités*, persons specifically invited to the main banquet held immediately after the civil and church ceremonies. Such gifts were usually in the form of linens, cooking and eating utensils, bedspreads and the like. At some weddings they were placed on display in true European fashion. It was well understood that each *invité*—or every invited couple, since most invitations were so addressed—would bring a gift; and inasmuch as the name of each donor was widely known there was some social pressure to give something not too inconsequential. (In cases I witnessed, fewer, say, than four glasses or plates would have been regarded as too little while more than a dozen would have brought exclamations of praise for the donor's generosity.)

In many instances, the value of the *invité*'s gift was less than the money cost—not to mention the "total" cost—of the food and drink consumed by the donor. When with my customary disregard for the conventions I would point out such discrepancies to one of the hosts, the first reaction would be reluctance to discuss such delicate issues in such crass terms. A little more prodding along these lines would, however, nearly always induce the host to drop his pose and say things about "tight-fisted guests"—which convinced me that despite their polite disclaimers, the Te Pitians did not close their mental account books just because the transaction was called a wedding "gift."

Parish Weddings

I have already described how parish weddings differed from veiled-bride ones (pages 265–66). I did not witness a parish wedding during my visits but received detailed accounts of several of them that had taken place in the near past. As already stated, they provided church and civil sanctions to unions already established, and the stated reason given for performing them was to make the principals eligible to become Communicant members of the Protestant Church.

Some parish weddings involved a single couple, others two or more. The largest I heard about was one held at Atea, where the event took place in connection with the dedication of the new parish meeting house, described above (page 266).

Some such weddings were literally "parish" affairs, sponsored by all of the postchildhood members of the parish, who financed and attended the accompanying feast in a body. Others were the concern of a single sodality, while still others were sponsored and financed by a single sodality but included marrying couples from others.

The costs of such celebrations were modest in comparison with veiled-bride feasts, rarely exceeding 5,000 to 6,000 francs; this money was either taken from existing treasuries or was raised by assessing more or less equally each member of the parish or sodality.

Because of the nature of the sponsorship and the religious setting, alcoholic beverages were not served at the accompanying feast; and this meal was usually followed by a lively *tūaro'i* session instead of a secular and usually drunken fête.

As noted earlier (page 264), with respect to the marital unions extant in Te Piti during 1954–55, relatively more of them had been instituted by parish weddings in Atea (28 percent) than in Fatata (18 percent).

The Fidelity Pledge

As mentioned earlier (page 263), a ceremony not unlike parts of a church wedding in its intent was performed occasionally in Te Piti for legally "unmarried" couples. If a couple could not or would not engage in a civil wedding (and hence were not eligible for a proper religious ceremony), they could nevertheless appear before their pastor and sign a written pledge (*hamani i te sinie*) that they would remain faithful, sexually, to each other. Sometimes couples signed this pledge as a result of admonitions of their pastor; but just as often they did so voluntarily or, as more usually happened, as a result of the woman's insistence. One sanction behind the pledge was parish opinion, epitomized by the pastor's publicly expressed disapproval, and this was effective enough in the cases I knew. In addition, some informants reported that there was a supernatural sanction involved—one that brought sickness to the pledge-breaker—but the agency and mechanism of that sanction was not specified. (Undoubtedly I could have elicited "explanations" had I tried; and while this would have cast some light on Te Pitians' reasoning processes, the explanations would probably have been ad hoc.)

A couple could also terminate their pledge by appearing together before the pastor, and this occasionally happened. Temporary relaxations were, however, not permitted. One pastor confided to me that men occasionally asked him to "unsign" them for short periods when they had to travel, say, to Pape'ete, but his personal policy was: "Sign altogether, or unsign altogether." Technically, only the pastor who performed the pledge-signing could void it.

The pledge regarding sexual fidelity was, in some cases, undertaken in conjunction with that regarding alcoholic consumption, but in other cases quite on its own. And, as noted earlier, pledging of both kinds was engaged in more frequently in Atea than in Fatata.

Marital Residence

"Why did the couple leave their wedding feast and go away just when the party was beginning?"—thus did one Te Pitian youth react to a Hollywood romance shown at the local cinema.

The nearest Te Pitian approach to the western "honeymoon" institution was to move into the nearest available vacant house for unremitting lovemaking, until the novelty wore off. In my observation this period seldom lasted more than a week and involved only young couples who had not enjoyed many such opportunities with each other before marriage. Older couples not already residing together at the time of their wedding (or decision to "wed") combined their households immediately thereafter, but younger ones tended to remain together in or near one of the parental homes for periods lasting from weeks to years.

With which vast oversimplification I introduce the complex topic of Te Pitian marital-residence patterns.

First to be considered is what the Te Pitians themselves had to say about where married couples *ought* to reside. "Young couples ought to live with their parents and help them out," said most older people questioned (not, however, specifying which set of parents). "Young couples ought to have a house of their own. They ought to help out their parents, but living with them results in *pe'ape'a* [conflict, tension]." Such was the sentiment expressed by most of the young people, married or unmarried, I questioned on this point.

Opinions opposing these were occasionally offered by both older and younger people. Toni's second (and middle-aged) wife, for example, did everything possible to force her married stepdaughter and the latter's husband into moving elsewhere, even at the risk of incurring her own husband's wrath; she and the younger woman quarrelled continually over the latter's notorious laziness and caustic tongue. In contrast, young Hama and his new wife described it as a "right" (*mea tano*) to reside with Hama's parents: "We divide the work," they explained.

When my question was rephrased in terms of who made the choice about where to reside, nearly all the males I queried, and most of the females, laid down the definitive rule that ". . . a woman lives where her man wants her to live," (which, incidentally, was in [unknowing] accord with the French *Code Civil* on family domicile until 1969, when the *Code* was revised in this respect).

"Then why don't all couples live near the man's parents?" I usually countered—to which was given the reply, after some hesitation in an obviously painful search for explanation: "Because lots of Tahitians do not think right."—And that was about as far as I got in eliciting general replies in my too-general enquiries about marital residence norms.

Turning to where Te Piti's married couples actually resided, with reference to where they had lived before marriage, it becomes necessary to specify the locus of reference, there having been three distinguishable locales: household, neighborhood, and village. Neighborhoods had less clear boundaries than households but were nevertheless distinguishable in geographic, interactional, and occasionally even in symbolic terms (page 223).

With respect to these three locuses, a married couple had a number of residential options:

   —*same*: they could reside in the locus where both of them had previously resided; or

—*virilocal*: the woman could move to the locus where the man was already living; or

—*uxorilocal*: the man could move to the locus where the woman was already living; or

—*neolocal*: they could reside in a local where neither had previously resided and which was not identified with either of them in other ways; or

—*bilocal*: they could alternate residence, more or less equally, between the two (separate) locuses where each of them had previously resided.

(There was in addition a small number of couples, mainly very recently wed ones, who alternated for a while between neolocal and either uxori- or virilocal residence, but after a while these settled down into one or another of the residential patterns listed above.)

The first noteworthy finding to emerge from my inquiries about actual marital residence was that in all but four cases (out of the total of 130 unions extant in 1954–55) one at least of each couple had resided in the village (Atea or Fatata) prior to the marriage; and in fifty-eight cases both spouses had resided there. Of the four couples who had moved to Atea (or Fatata) after their marriage, only one is strictly relevant to the present discussion; the other three couples were public servants (two schoolteachers and their wives and a public works supervisor and his) who were posted there by the Administration. (Because of their special circumstances, these three couples are excluded from the following summary of findings.)

A second finding was that in neither Atea nor Fatata did any couple reside in the household where both of them had been residing before. This is a consequence of kin-based incest rules, but only in part; there were, in fact, a few instances of otherwise unrelated and maritally unproscribed young people residing in the same household.

A third finding was that, out of a total of 127 unions, twenty-seven of the couples had continued to reside in the same neighborhood where both of them had resided before (clear proof of the operation of the "conservation of energy" principle mentioned above!).

Two other findings, much more noteworthy than the above, concern neolocal residence and, conversely, husbandly versus wifely "pull."

Forty-six percent of all extant couples resided in households identified with neither of them (nor their respective relatives) before their marriage. Of the remaining sixty-eight unions (i.e., 54 percent of all unions), thirty-seven of the couples resided full-time in a household previously resided in by the husband, twenty-six in one previously resided in by the wife, and five spent about equal amounts of time in the previous households of both.

Thus, the sentiment about marital residence expressed mainly by older people remained weightier than that held by most young people, but only slightly so. As for husbandly versus wifely "pull," the former clearly exercised a stronger one than the latter.

The stronger pull exercised by a husband was also revealed with respect to neighborhood. In the cases in which the couple resided in a neighborhood where only one of them had resided prior to marriage, fifty-two resided in that of the husband and only thirty-one in that of the wife.

In terms of the village as a locus, however, the "pull" exercised by husbands or wives differed less, i.e., in the sixty-three cases (excluding the five bilocal unions referred to below) in which one of the spouses had married into Atea or Fatata from elsewhere, the in-marrying spouses were females in thirty-three cases, as against thirty for males.

Explanations for residential arrangements just described must take account of a number of factors.[12] To begin with, I believe that the sentiment of most young people to live in a household of their own, not for privacy per se but for autonomy in managing their own affairs, was more widespread than the residential statistics indicate and that it would have been even weightier had other circumstances (e.g., economic dependency, invalided parents) not intervened.

As for differences in "pull" between husband and wife, I believe again that the value about male "superiority" was overriding except where economic factors intervened. Thus it was mainly in cases where the wife's economic assets, including those of her parents, were greater that the husband moved to her locus, especially to her household and especially to her village (if he had lived elsewhere), but even to her neighborhood as well (if, for example, she had readier access to a house or building-site there).

Finally, there were four cases (in Atea only) in which couples moved regularly back and forth between Atea and the other spouse's village elsewhere. In all such cases but one, the couples resided (when in Atea) in the household of the resident spouse's parents or other close relatives. And in all these cases, the direct cause of the bilocality was economic, i.e., each of the spouses owned cash crops in his or her respective village.

I cannot, of course, hope to know or describe all of the other more individual and situational factors that went into Te Pitians' choice (or nonchoice!) of where to reside after marriage, but the ones I have listed were the more general and more underlying ones shared by people in both Atea and Fatata. But what about differences, if any, between Atea and Fatata in this regard?

---

[12]This inquiry would have provided an opportunity to apply decision-theory procedures *if* I had been able to collect all the relevant historical facts, or *if* ex post facto explanations by the principals could have been relied upon, neither of which was the case.

The most noteworthy differences between the two villages with respect to marital residence patterns had to do with neolocality and spouse "pull."

In Atea, thirty of all couples (i.e., 54 percent of all extant Atea unions) resided in households of their own where neither had resided previously; in Fatata the number was twenty-nine, or only 41 percent of all these unions. This difference might appear surprising in one respect, i.e., the desire of a young couple for a separate household could be put down to European modernism, but only up to a point,[13] and Fatata was undoubtedly more Europeanized than Atea in several ways. Moreover, it may well be that Fatata's young people were indeed more strongly inclined, in motive, towards neolocal residence than were those of Atea. The housing situation, however, worked against the wishes of the former in this regard, or rather, the housing situation in Atea worked against coresidence with parents more than it did so in Fatata. That is to say, Atea's houses were on the whole smaller than those of Fatata and hence less capable of accommodating—or rather, less conducive to encouraging—the addition of an extra family. (This may strike the reader as a ridiculously simplistic explanation for a situation as potentially complex as marital-residence choice, but I think that this reason was one of the weightiest ones, if not the only one, that led some married couples to reside where they did.)

With respect to the second notable difference between the two villages, namely "spouse pull," in the households where one of the spouses had resided prior to marriage (twenty-one in Atea, forty-two in Fatata), 71 percent of Atea's unions of this kind were virilocal, as against 52 percent of Fatata's. (The five bilocal unions are excluded from this numeration as discussed in the following paragraphs.) I do not know the various factors that influenced all those specific decisions as to where to reside, but the above outcomes suggest that, relatively speaking, Ateans subscribed even more strongly than Fatatans to the popular rule that "a woman lives where her man wants her to live."

In the neighborhoods where only one of the spouses had resided previously (thirty-one in Atea and fifty-two in Fatata) 68 percent of Atea's unions of this kind were virilocal as against 60 percent of Fatata's—a difference, but probably not wide enough to pursue. Also, in the cases where one of the spouses had lived in a different village prior to marriage and residence in Te Piti (of which there were twenty-seven in Atea and thirty-six in Fatata), 56 percent of such cases in Atea were virilocal, as were 50 percent

---

[13]This is, however, a more complicated matter, historically, than might be supposed. For, while large extended-family households seem to have been the more usual pattern in ancient Tahiti, the early English missionaries actively encouraged nuclear-family separateness a century and a half ago, with what seems to have been considerable success.

of Fatata's—again, a difference, but not a wide enough one to invite explanation.

The above has to do with all of Te Piti's "local" married couples, regardless of the chronological ages of the spouses and regardless of the age of the union. As reported earlier, even those couples which eventually lived on their own tended to remain for a while, from a few weeks to several years, in the household of the parents of one of them, and in this respect legalized unions did not differ markedly from nonlegalized ones, nor did Atea differ markedly from Fatata. Conversely, in both villages, in new unions between older (and in nearly all such cases, previously married) persons, the couple usually resided from the start in the household of one of them, and in the household of the husband more frequently than in that of the wife.

Separation

Te Pitian marital unions entered into before the age of about twenty-five for males and about twenty-two for females were rather fragile affairs, but once both spouses were past those ages, old as well as new unions tended to be stable. Unlike couples in some societies, it did not take Te Pitians very long to discover and resolve their intolerable incompatibilities.

Official statistics on divorce rate and duration of union are of limited usefulness because of the narrowness of the legal definition of marriage. My own figures are more comprehensive but not as precise as I would wish, because many Te Pitians could not give exact dates for their nonlegal unions. One thing, however, can be depended upon in the case of younger people at least: there was usually little or no time lapse between the termination of an old union and the beginning of a new one. In fact, there was sometimes a period of overlap, when neighbors may not have been certain about who was living with whom.

I arrived at the above threshold ages of twenty-five and twenty-two in two ways: by noting the numerical infrequency of separations by people beyond those ages, and by recognizing in contemporary unions of people over twenty-five (and twenty-two) what appeared to be some telling signs of firm marital stability, i.e., a duration of the union for five years or more, the presence of two or more offspring, the abandonment of *taure'are'a* activities by both spouses, and their deep involvement in parish affairs. This is not to say that couples did not separate once having embarked upon that mode of life, but such separations were relatively infrequent.

Divorce in the legal sense, the dissolution of a legalized marriage, was for Te Pitians a difficult and costly action. It usually involved visits to Pape'ete or Uturoa, the hiring of a lawyer, and personal appearance before various officials. At best it was a troublesome experience, and for many it was too complicated and costly to contemplate. Presumably the official rationale for making divorce difficult was that it would help stabilize marriages. Far from accomplishing that, among Te Pitians, it served rather to discourage legal marriage, i.e., one of the chief reasons given by them for not going through with a civil ceremony was the difficulty, later on, of legally dissolving the union.

In actuality, the legal divorce procedures had been exceedingly simplified in these islands: one simply placed the matter in the hands of a lawyer, of which there were several, mainly Europeans, and he did almost all the rest. The cost, however, was great in terms of Te Pitians' earning power; the average was about 14,000 francs, which represented an unskilled laborer's wages for about one hundred days and which was larger than the yearly cash income of many families.

In any case, only a very small percentage of the terminated legalized marriages I knew about had ended "legally"; in the other cases, the estranged spouses had simply begun living with other mates without much concern about the legality of their action. Concern usually came only later when problems of legal paternity arose in connection with inheritance and "paternal authority," but that was too distant in time to worry most remarrying Te Pitians I knew. (It was this circumstance that accounted for the action, curious to some observers, of Tahitians occasionally securing legal divorces twenty or more years, and sometimes two or three "marriages," after separation from the legal spouse.)

By French law (*Code Civil*, Articles 229–232), the grounds for divorce were, on the part of either spouse, adultery and any action causing the other "painful or degrading injury or anguish."

Needless to say, with specifications as broad as these it would not have been difficult for most Te Pitians to adduce sufficient grounds for divorce from any but the most faithful and angelic spouse, and particularly was this true of the woman wishing a legal divorce from her husband—which, incidentally, was the sequence in most legal divorce proceedings I knew about. But, as already noted, most of Te Piti's "divorces" were accomplished Tahitian-style.

Tahitian-style "divorce" usually consisted merely of leaving one spouse and moving in with another. In only two kinds of cases did I hear of any angry or evidently deep-felt moral disapproval of such a breakup on the part of kinfolk and neighbors. One of these occurred when newlyweds separated only a short time after an expensive veiled-bride wedding; in this case, some of the kinfolk appeared thoroughly angered that all their money and efforts had been "wasted." The second kind of situation that provoked widespread indignation was that in which one spouse abandoned the other along with helplessly dependent offspring, and women did this almost as frequently as men. In most other cases, when one spouse left the other, everyone except for the most partisan of their kinfolk and neighbors appeared to accept the announced reasons for the separation to be sufficient. If the separation was mutual, there appeared to be little or no disapproval at all, and, unless one was closely attached to one of the principals by ties of kinship or friendship, little interest in discovering the causes.

In fact, when I inquired of other persons about the grounds for any particular separation, the answer was usually, "They (or he, or she) were *fiu* (fed up, *dégouté*)." Any further probing into the basis of the *fiu* usually turned up one of two situations: either the informant did not know and was not interested in finding out about any more fundamental causes; or, he did not consider what Europeans might call "efficient" causes to be decisive. *Fiu* (like the equally broad and in one sense equally unexplanatory "*ma'i*," ailing) was for Te Pitians an adequate summary for motivation and cause in matters of this kind.

What then were the "efficient" causes of marital breakup? And what accounted for the fragility of younger people's unions and the greater stability of the unions of the older?

In the first place, there was a general expectation among Te Pitians that unions of the young would be short-lived; in fact, this expectation was occasionally expressed as a species of norm: "Youth is the time for trying out (sexual) mates; and that is the Tahitian way of life" (i.e., the normal kind of life for Tahitians).

But what about more explicit causes such as, say, adultery?

Adultery was the most common cause cited in the legal divorces I knew about, and flagrant occurrences of it were occasionally given as the main cause for dissolving a nonlegalized union. But even when it was flagrant, Te Pitians generally did not discard an otherwise satisfactory spouse because of adultery alone. Nearly all those I questioned assumed as a matter of course that most married men, including the church-wed or pastor-pledged, would avail themselves of any and all sexual opportunities, even though some would not have made much effort to create such opportunities. Many males also stated, with what accuracy I cannot judge, that almost any woman, married or not, would acquiesce if her seducer was not ill-favored and if the chance for discovery was slight. And as for age, I have some reason to believe that spouses in their thirties and forties committed adultery more often than those in their twenties and teens.

Wife-beating was something like adultery in one respect: a certain amount of it was expected although it was not strictly *tano* (on the mark; proper); but it was probably more decisive than infidelity in influencing a woman to leave her spouse.

An even more decisive cause for leaving a husband was his failure as a provider. Infidelities and beatings could be tolerated within limits, but hunger—especially a child's hunger—would seldom be patiently borne by its mother.

Chronic drunkenness was also cited as a cause for separation, but on inquiry it usually turned out that it was not the drunkenness itself but the improvidence or too-frequent beatings that accompanied it.

And finally, some people—and especially young ones—terminated their unions simply because a more attractive person had turned up. Older people, having more ties to buttress their marital ones and greater consensus around them that their unions ought to last, did indeed go adventuring but were more likely to return home after a time.

In all these actions, one tendency was quite clear: it was more frequently the woman who took the initiative in ending a union, just as it was the woman who usually decided when a nonarranged union was to begin.

Size for size, Fatata exceeded Atea in (legal) divorce rate during the period 1950–60, but the two villages were much alike in rates of separations, both between legally wed and nonlegally wed spouses. The divorces, which were so exceptional as to be well known, numbered five for Fatatans, and only one (plus one pending) for Ateans. The separations, which I recorded as numbering about thirty-four in Fatata and about twenty-three in Atea, were so commonplace as to escape widespread public interest and hence awareness, but I believe that I succeeded in uncovering a large enough proportion of them in both Atea and Fatata to indicate, as reported, that the two villages did not differ markedly in this regard.

Husband-Wife Relations

Having described how marital unions were established in Te Piti, I now turn to the social relations that obtained between husband and wife. Such a description is inevitably incomplete, because a man's wife was also usually the mother of his coresident children (and vice versa), and this circumstance invariably complicated the more direct aspect of the relationship between spouses. Also, the fact that many married couples in Te Piti resided in households shared with other relatives, including other married couples, served to complicate their mutual relationships even further. Some of these complications will be mentioned in the next chapter, when describing relations among members of those larger households, but the inadequacies of my data rule out the possibility of determining precisely how all those variables influenced the husband-wife relationship itself.

Normatively, and in most actual cases, except when a husband's job required otherwise, all Te Pitian couples resided in the same household, cooperated in obtaining and preparing food, partook of a common meal, and shared in the nurturing and socializing of any children they had living with them. Not all married couples slept in the same bed all or even most of the time, but except for the very old, I heard of no coresiding couples deliberately ceasing to cohabit sexually for any length of time. (When a married Te Pitian wished to break off the relationship, she [or less frequently he] would move out of the household rather than, figuratively, "lock the bedroom door.")

Such were the shared activities of all nonsenile married couples. In addition, most couples in both villages took part in building or maintaining their common residence. Many others also worked together in their gardens (growing the vegetables they consumed) and some even worked together in money-earning enterprises, but in these two kinds of activities there were noteworthy differences between Atea and Fatata.

Out of the total of fifty-six married couples living together in Atea at the time of my first visit, twenty-eight (50 percent) cooperated actively in subsistence gardening and twenty-three (41 percent) worked together in producing things for money. The corresponding figures for Fatata's seventy-one married couples were much smaller, namely, eighteen percent and fifteen percent.

At one end of this "togetherness" range was Tihoni, a man who spent most weekday daylight hours working for wages at a nearby European plantation. At the other end was Manea who, with the exception of the few hours weekly spent in fishing, was, literally, with his wife and preschool children all of the time—in the garden, the coconut grove, the vanilla patch, or the home. Te Pitian couples were on the average closer to Tihoni than to Manea in this aspect of marital life, but there was a noteworthy difference between Atea and Fatata in this regard. As the above figures reveal, the smaller amount of cooperation in subsistence and money-earning activities engaged in by Fatatan couples meant, among other things, that such couples spent less time together than did their Atean counterparts.

French law in force during my visits required that a wife reside at the marital residence fixed by her husband but did not specify the amount of time the spouses should be together. Te Pitian norms were not much more explicit on this point, but it was generally held that if one spouse was absent for more than a few weeks the other was not solely blamed for seeking sexual solace elsewhere. I even heard an erring wife defended in these terms: "What can you expect if her husband stays away all the time?" (His wage job kept him away from home most days and alternate nights.)

In Fatata I was cautioned not to employ young married women for domestic services "because they don't want to be away from their husbands all the time." Nor did young husbands approve of their young wives being away from home, but I suspect that this was due as much to jealous suspicion as to a desire for constant companionship. In any case, whatever the basis, this attitude appeared to lose weight as marriages mellowed and became "firm" (*tāmau*).

From the opposite tack, not once did I hear a man criticized by his wife or by anyone else for staying home all the time—unless in doing so he was failing to do his job as family provider. Te Pitians had not yet begun to value activity for activity's sake; and being home with wife and children was regarded as the "natural" place to be unless making a living required a man to be elsewhere.

Interactions between spouses had their spatial as well as their temporal aspect. I noted earlier that at the time of weddings the kin of the groom were known as the upper side (*pae i ni'a*), those of the bride the underside (*pae i raro*): this metaphor served throughout their married life to distinguish their respective kindreds. And despite the emphasis on bilaterality in some transactions (see page 293), there is no doubt that this "upper-under" expression faithfully reflected the privileged position of the husband with respect to, e.g., choice of the couple's marital name, the name of their firstborn, etc.;[14] and this inequality was reinforced by the patriarchal bias of French law.

Mua-muri (front-behind) reflects a similar spatial ordering of spouses. The women of Te Piti often sat on their front steps or verandahs along with their husbands and children—except when some unrelated male of important position arrived for a visit. Then the wife and children would retire *i muri* (to the back [of house]) leaving the lords of creation to discuss their weighty matters *i mua* (in front)—or, at least, this is what Te Pitians said *ought* to happen (and what did, in fact, happen in most such situations I saw). This rule was nearly always applied when food was served on such occasions, the husband and his guests having eaten alone, served by his wife. At other times, however, in the households I knew and inquired about, the husband and wife nearly always ate together, along with their older children—although some measure of male precedence was preserved even at those times, inasmuch as the husband usually ate at the "head" of the table (a European borrowing) and ordinarily helped himself first to food.

Most of Te Piti's sleeping houses contained at least one large double bed, but use of it was not reserved for the household's most lordly male. More often than not, it was the wife who chose to sleep on it, her husband having usually preferred a harder but cooler cot or even a mat on the floor.

---

[14]The metaphor might in the past have referred also, or primarily, to positions during sexual intercourse, but I did not succeed in eliciting that explanation from anyone.

Nor could I discover any explicit rules regarding precedence in walking. When walking "with" his wife, the husband sometimes strode out ahead because he could walk faster or carried a heavier load to be rid of; but almost as often he would lag behind to talk to friends or, for example, to size up breadfruit growing along the way.

In any case, when married couples did appear together in public, they nearly always positioned themselves somewhat apart. They were rarely to be seen walking side by side; and when sitting or standing in public view, e.g., in church or cinema theater, they usually separated and sat with others of the same sex. One of the unforgettable sights in late afternoon was that of older married couples taking their postprandial ease, sitting in yards or on verandahs usually a wide distance apart and audibly digesting their heavy meal while now and then exchanging a labored word or two.

I could detect little or no squeamishness in Tahitians in general about close physical contact with their fellow mortals—in crowded buses or launches, in packed cinemas, or in the throngs crushed together to witness a cockfight. Nevertheless, in Te Piti, at least, it was considered somewhat unseemly for a husband and his wife to be close together in public.

The foregoing description of the spatial dimension of spouse's interactions apply equally to Atea and Fatata—in other words, I could detect no noteworthy differences between the two villages in this regard.

The norms operative in Te Piti—official, ecclesiastical, and "indigenous"—placed initiative and authority decisively in the hands of husbands *vis-à-vis* their wives, and my informants expressed the opinion that such indeed was the prevalent state of affairs with most married couples there. In fact, those norms and suppositions of theirs appear to have been borne out in actuality, at least in the situations where initiative was called for or where alternative courses of action were open. On the other hand, most of the kinds of activities in which spouses interacted involved action-sequences so standardized as to require little or no making of decisions or issuing of commands. In connection with gardening, for example, the husband usually decided where and when to begin planting, but thenceforth he did not ordinarily tell his wife how or when her cooperation was required. Again, on Saturdays in most families, the work routines were so firmly established that no supervision or coordination was required: the man went fishing, for example, while his wife prepared other foods for the Sunday meal and readied their clothes for church. In response to my question, "who supervises (*fa'atere*) the work of households?" one man summed up the matter by reference to his own: "When there is no 'relish' and I have other work to do, it is my wife who takes out the canoe. I do not tell her to do so; she is an industrious woman."

A factor perhaps contributing to this unobtrusiveness of "authority" in ordinary domestic activities was the age similarity of most couples and the implications of that fact. At no stage in their lives did girls behave deferentially towards boys of their own age, and when to this general conditioning was added the circumstance that many married couples had grown up together as playmates or schoolmates, it is not surprising that initiative was not markedly one-sided in the everyday interactions of most of them.

Still, in situations requiring decision and supervision of coordination, most women I knew about were more or less content to follow their husbands' leads. Perhaps the most important of such situations were those concerned with the acquisition and expenditure of money. A woman's voiced needs or wants might have stimulated her husband to acquire more money, but it was usually he who decided how much to work for and how to get it. Even when it involved exploiting the resources of her (local) land, it was usually the man who decided what and when. Nena's case was fairly typical. Born in another island, he had no land of his own in Fatata, but his wife owned sole title to one good valley plot and to a small grove of coconut palms. In addition, she owned part-title to a large grove of producing palms in a neighboring district. Nena produced food crops and vanilla on the valley plot. His wife helped him cultivate the garden and to pollinate the vanilla, but he directed both these enterprises from start to finish. He used some of the vanilla profits for domestic expenses but spent most of the rest on goods for himself. On the other hand, he had no voice in managing the distant palm grove, which was worked by his wife's nephew; and he did not attempt to instruct her how she should use the annual income she received from it. (In fact, she spent it for luxury goods, mainly for their children and herself.)

There were of course exceptions to these modes. There were men who officiously intruded with advice and instructions into nearly every sphere of domestic activity. And there were women who exercised much initiative in family cash-income enterprises, sometimes in spite of and sometimes in accord with their husbands' wishes. This last situation most frequently prevailed in families where women owned most of the land.

One of the most henpecked men in Te Piti was Vari, about whose wife the neighbors said: "She is his head" (*Ona te upo'o o te tane*) meaning she is as continually "over" him as is his head. Neighbors retailed with evident disapproval how Vari had to spend most of his days working hard in his groves and gardens and then did most of the domestic chores when he returned home, while his enormously fat wife sat around most of the day gossiping. They even related with amused incredibility how Vari's wife forced him to give up even his occasional drink of beer by leaving him and remaining away until he promised to "reform."

Tumu was as firmly under the "head" of his wife as was Vari, but due to the newness of their marriage the nature of their relationship had not yet become gossiped about. Tumu was described as being merely "easygoing" (*marū*) but it was widely predicted that he would become as henpecked as Vari in time.

At the other extreme were Natua, Nini, and Temo. The former busied himself in everything going on in his household, including directing the preparation of meals, the dressing of children, and even the sweeping of rooms—sometimes with his wife's grateful approval but at other times to her evident annoyance. Most of his male neighbors considered Natua's aberrance with amused contempt, believing it to be the result of a congenital tendency to do inexplicable things ("insanity runs in his family").

Nini intervened in domestic affairs almost as often as Natua, but the public reactions to this was one of approval, his wife having been considered too stupid to manage by herself.

Temo's case was quite different. He did not meddle with ordinary domestic activities of his wife, but on other occasions he was so unnecessarily and brutally dictatorial that even male neighbors expressed pity for his wife and occasionally intervened when he beat her beyond the normal range of marital life.

Between these extremes were most other couples, who worked out apparently successful adjustments in deciding and managing common affairs. A few examples will illustrate the extent of give and take that prevailed.

Tane was unquestioned master of his household. He did not interfere in his wife's sphere of activities, but he made all decisions concerning exploitation of her land. Moreover, he forbade his wife to exchange visits with certain notorious gossipers ("gossip leads to trouble"), and his credit arrangement with the Chinese storekeeper included a proviso that no member of his household could obtain goods on credit without a note from him. Tane was intelligent, resourceful, and energetic, one of the most enterprising and financially successful men in Te Piti. He drank heavily on occasion but was able to sober up and get back to heavy work a few hours later. He occasionally chastised his wife and children, and they all appear to have had a healthy respect for his authority but seemed also to be fond of him and to take pride in his accomplishments. Notwithstanding all this, it was not a peaceful household, mainly because of the mutual dislike of Tane's wife and his daughter by a previous marriage. The daughter lived there with her husband, against her own wishes and those of her stepmother. The latter urged Tane to set up the young couple in another house of his, but he at first refused ("the place for children is with the parents"). When his wife became insistent, he threatened her with beating, but after about two weeks of bickering, he finally gave in. ("She kept at me all the time. Even when I hit her she kept at it, so I finally gave in. One can't live in continuous bickering like that.")

Toru's control over his household was no less complete than Tane's, although accomplished more quietly and with much less physical chastisement. Nevertheless, when he decided to recall his daughter from a Pape'ete school because of the increased cost of maintaining her there, his usually cooperative spouse balked—quietly, but firmly and successfully. Later Toru confided somewhat sheepishly: "There would have been trouble (*pe'ape'a*) in the household if I hadn't agreed."

No couple living in Te Piti at the time of my visits resolved all their differences peacefully, and some were notoriously quarrelsome. Of these, Mara and his spouse were among the worst. Sometimes they physically fought but more often they wrangled verbally. ("They start in the morning and stop only to sleep at night.") The main subject of their quarrels was over the shortcomings of each other's children born of previous marriages, but they also bickered over Mara's improvidence and his spouse's slatternly housekeeping. Neighbors complained of their noise but agreed that nothing was to be done about it, since neither spouse had the personal attributes nor other resources for living separately or for finding new mates.

Quarrels between spouses touched upon countless subjects, but the most frequent points of difference were—successively, as the marriage aged—one another's real or imagined extramarital sexual relations, the man's improvidence or the woman's laziness, and the man's drunkenness. In one sense, some of that quarreling can be looked upon as a kind of discussion leading up to decision-making, an indication that the locus of authority was not always predetermined. Or it could serve as an indication that many couples did not abide by the rules. Whatever the interpretation, it was a matter of observation that chronically quarrelsome couples fared poorly in nearly every task conventionally allocated to married pairs, hence one may conclude that their quarreling seldom produced workable decisions.

The exercise of comparing Atea and Fatata with respect to the management aspect of marital relations, just described, presents problems I am unable to solve. Asking informants directly about this matter usually elicited the conventional reply that, "it is he [the husband] who decides"—except for some notorious cases of the reverse. And based on such "information," there was no marked statistical difference between Atea and Fatata in this respect. Against this, however, was the fact that Atea's wives, on the average, exceeded those of Fatata in the number of them contributing food-producing labor and self-earned money to the common household pool,[15]

---

[15]There were a few Fatatan women who earned more money than did any women of Atea, but most of them were widows.

hence might be expected (i.e., according to Te Pitian expectations) to have had more important voice in domestic decision-making and may indeed have done so. (On the other hand, I formed the impression that, in public at least, Fatata's wives were markedly less diffident than were those of Atea, *vis-à-vis* their husbands in particular and males in general.) I did manage to make fairly direct and lengthy observations in a few households in both villages, and on this basis the two villages could be said to be much alike with regard to this aspect of marital relations; but my samples were too small to justify extension of this finding to the villages as wholes.

In an earlier draft of this chapter, I devoted several pages to a description of the different types of "emotion" Te Piti's spouses were said to feel and express toward each other. Fortunately for me (and for the reader!) my amateur efforts with this subject matter have been rendered unnecessary by the subsequent publication of Robert Levy's treatment of this phase of Tahitian social relationship—which, in any case, is only marginally relevant to the "economic" focus of this study. For the record, however, it may be useful to list the main terms used by Te Pitians to classify this "emotional" dimension of marital (and other kinds of) relationships: *hina'aro* (desire, i.e., in the present context, *sexual* desire); *here* (affection, i.e., said to be more characteristically felt for one's children than for one's spouse); *pohehae* (jealousy); *fiu* (boredom, fed-up-ness); *riri* (anger) *fe'i'i* (coolness); *faufau* (repugnance); and that most revealing of terms, *mātua*, which meant in this context "amity based on being acquainted with and hence accustomed to" and which was used to characterize and to explain long-established and continuing relationships of spouses as well as of friendly acquaintances.

Turning now to the more "economic" aspect of marital relations: the transactions between spouses may be said to have consisted of pool-sharing (*tāhō'e*), direct exchange, and non-reciprocable giving. Of these, the first was by far most important in numbers of transactions and in total "value" of objects and services circulated. Inasmuch as married couples also formed the nuclei of most households, the objects and services contributed by a man and his wife for common consumption included most of the goods needed for subsistence.

First of all was food. Generally speaking, a man and his wife had—or came to have—about the same tastes in these matters, although I heard occasional complaints to the effect that when one spouse disliked a certain food the other had to do without it in consequence. (This was voiced most frequently in connection with *fāfaru*, a relish made of fermented fish.)

The general rule was that the man was chiefly responsible for providing the food itself, while the wife was chiefly responsible for preparing and serving it and wholly responsible for cleaning up afterwards; this, however, did not exempt either one from assisting the other in any of these chores. Te Pitians asserted that a woman ought to help her husband with some phases of gardening and collecting and that a man ought to provide the fuel for cooking and to at least assist in oven-baking. Butchering was also a man's job, but so seldom was an animal butchered for household consumption that it was rarely mentioned by informants when describing the division of labor between spouses.

Next came the household buildings and their utilities and furnishings. It was the husband who was held chiefly responsible for providing these things and keeping them in repair, while the wife was expected to keep them tidy and clean. Again, however, most informants asserted that husband and wife ought to assist one another when possible and appropriate, such as in the making of roof thatch (by the wife) and the cutting of heavy grass (by the husband).

The husband was also held mainly responsible for providing the land on which to build the house and to produce food and cash crops, but there was less emphasis on this obligation than on those concerning food and shelter. Te Pitians expected that any able-bodied man could and should provide food and build and maintain a house, but they stated or implied that acquiring land by one's own efforts was not only very costly but often quite impossible (because, e.g., there may have been none to buy); consequently, no criticism was voiced of a man using land belonging to his wife for their common use.

Te Pitians also held the man mainly responsible for providing money for cloth and sewing materials, but his wife was expected to make most of her own and her children's clothes and to keep all the family's clothes clean and in repair. Moreover, the obligations of the husband in this sphere were held to be quite limited, i.e., enough material for two or three everyday work garments and one churchgoing dress for his wife and an extra school and church outfit for each child. No adult I spoke with about this matter expected a man to satisfy fully his wife's wish for a large wardrobe of dresses, and the most demanding wives appeared to recognize the limits of their rights here. The same was true of false teeth: women may have hoped but few seemed to expect that their husband would pay for such luxury goods as these.

A man known to have money was apt to be criticized if he did not make an appropriate family contribution to the annual May Collection, but if his wife had the ready money and he did not, then the obligation was considered to rest with her.

Some women and perhaps all children expected the husband to provide for an occasional visit to the cinema and for an occasional treat at the store, but the only times I heard complaints or criticism about nonperformance was against men who selfishly used all such "surplus" cash for themselves or wine or beer.

The case with family health was more complicated. The condition of a thin and exhausted woman was usually blamed on her husband, and the same was true of sickly, undernourished children. With specific maladies, either acute or chronic, the case was, however, somewhat different. First of all, the causes of some sickness were considered either unknowable or beyond the powers of either spouse or parent to prevent. And secondly, the cures of many sicknesses were believed to be either impossible or exclusively within the domain of specialists. Regarding the latter, a man, more so than his wife, was expected to make some effort to secure medical aid on behalf of his family, but this usually consisted of searching for some native remedy or eventually turning over the case to an Administration medical aide. None of these expediencies required much effort, so that the responsibility was not costly; and after the case was in the hands of the specialist, then all responsibility rested there too. I often heard the Administration blamed for not curing an ailment—under circumstances so impossible as to be amusing, if they were not also tragic—but only those husbands and fathers were blamed who were known to avoid seeking aid purposely out of stubborness or pique.

Such was the case of Kara, who threw away antifilariasis pills provided by the Administration because of his sullen discontent with the Administration and all its agents; his neighbors blamed this action of his for his own and his wife's advanced cases of elephantiasis. In another instance, people criticized Ara for the stillbirth of his wife's third child; he had refused to call the Administration's midwife (through anger against a recent court ruling against his claim for some land). On the other hand, no criticism was voiced at either Fira or his wife when their month-old daughter died while they were celebrating a neighbor's wedding; the child simply "became sick and died." And in another case, neither parent was censured when nothing was done to set the arm broken by their young son when he fell from a tree: "Children are always playing like that and hurting themselves; that's what Tahitian children are like." Had a medical aide been posted in the village at that time they would undoubtedly have taken the boy to him, but no one really expected them to pay for charter of a launch to take the boy to the hospital four miles away.

The daily care of children was considered to be the responsibility mainly of their mother—although there was some variation in this expectation, and most fathers of young children seemed to take delight in sharing this responsibility when the nature of their work permitted. I did, however, sometimes hear women criticized for child neglect but never the same charge levelled at men—except of course for failure to provide food and clothing. Schoolteachers sometimes criticized men for taking their children out of school prematurely and putting them to work, but most other Te Pitians either approved of this action or considered it none of their concern—nor of the schoolteachers' either.

And finally there was the service involved in *reproducing* offspring. Te Pitians knew that it requires the man as well as the woman to procreate; but did they tend in any way to fix chief responsibility for infertility upon either one of the pair? I found that they did so but that such responsibility fixing varied with circumstance. Inability to conceive or to bear a living infant was usually, though not always, associated with the woman, but the blame for this inability was not always thought to be hers. Sometimes the responsibility was laid at her door with the charge that she had done so deliberately or that she rendered herself infertile through repeated abortions or through some improper action that had induced a spirit to place upon her a curse. Almost as often, however, a woman's barrenness would be laid at the door of her husband if, for example, the latter were known to beat her too frequently or if his improvidence compelled her to work too hard.

There were certain situations that were widely acknowledged to permit or even require relaxation of the rules regarding division of labor I have just described. This was the case, for example, with women either pregnant or occupied with nursing an infant, such women having been excused from much of the heavier domestic work. As Te Pitians saw it, this lowered expectation represented not a decrease in her total contribution to family welfare but rather a shift in the nature of her contribution or, as one might phrase it, her let-up in domestic services was compensated by her increase in reproductive services. In fact, the rules I have listed admitted of considerable variation of this sort. If, for example, a woman were to use her own cash income to buy some of the family food, her husband would have been more willing to help with household chores, or at least some Te Pitians asserted that he should have done so.

Another situation that permitted relaxation of division-of-labor rules (or rather, application of an alternative rule) concerned sick spouses. Generally speaking, a person's sickness seemed to justify his or her inaction—but only up to a point, it having been my observation that the signs of an illness or infirmity had to be plainly visible to invoke sympathy over a long period. Otherwise, murmurs of malingering would begin to spread, and if such suspicions were shared by the subject's spouse, they could precipitate a quarrel or even a separation.

How were these rules regarding sharing enforced, i.e., what sanctions helped to maintain the proper proportion between contribution and consumption in the "economic" sphere of married life? Public censure was undoubtedly one powerful sanction, particularly in the trenchant gossiping of Te Piti's women! In addition, many of these norms were presumably "internalized"; but how effective these would have been unless backed by other forms of sanction it is difficult to say. Probably most effective of all were the tangible measures taken by the aggrieved spouse, namely, beatings by the husband; slow-downs, desertion, and separation by the wife.

Te Pitians saw marriage not as an alliance between groups nor as a convenience for one of the spouses, but rather as a partnership of individuals. In the view of most of my informants, both spouses were obligated to contribute to the partnership in order to maintain it, and it was implied that their contributions ought to balance over time. This attitude was in fact rendered quite explicit on some occasions, for example, in homilies from the pulpit or in morals drawn from marriage failures. Thus, comparing contributions of the spouses to their commonly used pool of resources should throw some light upon the relative valuation Te Pitians attached to them.

Such a comparison is not without complications. For example, there were differences in the length of the time-units within which contributions were measured. For most women, that unit was usually the week; food had to be prepared every day, but no woman was criticized for slighting her cooking on those days when a heavy laundry had to be done or a large batch of roof thatch made. At times that time-unit was even longer, as for example when she helped her husband with gardening or with pollinating vanilla; several days of such heavy work could be followed by a week or more of the barest minimum of domestic work chores without arousing criticism.

In the case of men, on the other hand, the week was considered to be an important work unit only for those engaged steadily in wage labor; only in such cases did Te Pitians implicitly "balance the books" of marital obligations within the same unit of time. For most men, the time unit for comparison was much longer—as long as a year in the case of the full-time fisherman or farmer, whose periods of daily work alternated with periods of almost no work at all. This discrepancy accounts for the seeming paradox wherein a woman would be criticized for shirking her domestic duties for a single day by a husband who did nothing productive for a week or more.

Another factor complicating this comparison was the difference in the nature of the goods, both objects and services, contributed by the respective spouses. Such and such amounts of cash, usually brought home by the husband, had to be measured against such and such domestic services contributed by the wife. So many hours spent fishing or planting taro by the husband had to be compared with time spent by the wife washing or mending clothes.

But however complicated the "bookkeeping" may have been, the principle that clearly emerges from this comparison is that a man's services, time for time, received a higher valuation than his wife's in the transaction formula of domestic pool-sharing. A woman had to work longer than her husband to fulfill her obligations, and judging by my rough measures this time ratio was about three to two—which raises the question of how to account for this discrepancy in a society so traditionally bilateral in other familial respects.

Although they made no precise calculations in this respect, Te Pitians themselves acknowledged and rationalized the discrepancy with such stereotypes as, "Man's work is harder than woman's." It was certainly true that some male tasks required greater bursts of effort or exposure to more discomfort, but then, most men were somewhat stronger and hardier than their wives to begin with. Also, it was some of those "harder" tasks that appeared to give men most pleasure, having been regarded more like sport than work. Another such stereotype was, "A man's jobs require more skill than women's." This of course would have been a difficult proposition to support unless it could have been demonstrated, say, that spearing a fish required more skill than sewing a dress. But insofar as these stereotypes were believed by Te Pitians, they did indeed explain and justify the discrepancy. In any case, whether those particular stereotypes were believed or not, there was that other more general belief expressed by both men and women that "men are in general more intelligent than women." No Te Pitian I knew indicated any necessity to document a postulate as basic as that!

The strength of that more basic postulate shows up in connection with one attitude regarding the source of money income. As was shown, many women in Te Piti earned some of their own money—by growing vanilla, sewing, making thatch-plates, or working for wages. Ordinarily these earnings were small and were usually spent by the women on luxury items for themselves or their children. In some cases, however, these earnings were quite regular and were used in whole or in part to augment the husband's income for buying food. In other words, such women played in part the roles normally played by men in this phase of domestic pool-sharing. Yet, despite the fact that a *tārā* (five francs) earned by such a woman would buy as much bread or tinned meat as the one earned by her husband, it was not usually evaluated as highly as the latter, i.e., it did not reduce the woman's other domestic obligations to the extent that it reduced those of her husband. A man working steadily for wages was excused from carrying out many other domestic tasks ordinarily carried out by men, whereas a woman income-earner simply had to work longer. (Even though she helped to "bring home the bacon," she still had to cook it!) Some men with whom I discussed this situation remarked tentatively that it was, "possibly, not quite fair," but they probably did so because I, a European, had raised the question, and they knew that some Europeans felt differently about such matters.

Atea: Wedding procession—"Veiled Bride" style

Atea: Sunday afternoon meeting on the plaza

Ritz Bar—Fatata style

Atea: Beginning (!) of New Year Parade

So far I have been describing the "economic" relationship of Te Piti's married couples in terms of their respective contributions of objects and services pooled for their common consumption. I turn now to those transactions between husband and wife that involved a direct exchange of goods between them, for more or less separate consumption.

One such type of goods exchanged between spouses was sexual services (as distinct from reproductive services); there were at least two different sets of rules governing this exchange. One set was the one enunciated in civil law and in church doctrine: it called for exclusiveness and provided severe sanctions against the adulterous spouse—civil divorce or prohibition against church communion-taking. The other set was that expressed in public opinion and sanctioned by public censure; it permitted some deviation from exclusiveness, especially for the husband.

The first set of rules applied, of course, only to couples married in civil and church ceremonies. It was, however, only implied in the terms of the civil contract, and thereafter the civil authorities did not exercise initiative in enforcing it. In fact, during my visits the civil authorities, the French gendarme and the *tāvana* and *mūto'i*, acted to enforce the rules against adultery only when a complaint was lodged (usually by a woman against her legally wed spouse). And in the cases I heard about, the official was more concerned with reuniting the couple than with punishing the erring spouse.

Not so with the church. The pastors of both parishes unambiguously declared against adultery during the church wedding ceremony and thereafter frequently reinforced the declaration in sermon and in prayer. In this context, adultery was termed a "sin" (*hara*), subject not only to expulsion from the ranks of church Communicants but to (undefined) supernatural punishment as well. During my visits, no married Communicants were openly accused of committing adultery, but I collected well-documented case histories of men having been so expelled in the past, their extramarital affairs having become too notorious to be ignored.

Moreover, in contrast to the civil authorities, the pastors showed concern over the sexual relations of common-law spouses as well. In the first place, although they continuously advocated civil and church marriages, I did not once hear them describe common-law marriage as "sinful"; in fact they accorded such marriages a kind of recognition by urging mutual fidelity upon common-law spouses, institutionalized in some cases in the Fidelity Pledge (page 298).

The "popular," more prevalent "Tahitian" set of rules governing exchange of sexual services involved little or no distinction between legalized and nonlegalized unions, once the latter had become "firm" (*tāmau*). In both cases, the man was permitted considerable extramarital freedom, and even the woman some—the amounts having tended to vary with factors that I shall presently describe.

It was generally assumed that most men would avail themselves of sexual opportunities outside "marriage," and little or no public censure was aroused by this form of adultery except when the man in question was a civil or church official, and even then he was blamed more for his hypocrisy than for the infidelity itself.

Wives differed in their reactions to their husbands' extramarital affairs. From the numerous case histories I recorded, I gained the impression that a woman would terminate her union in the event of her husband's adultery only if she was much younger or wealthier than he and hence in a position to attract another desirable husband, or only if she was already preoccupied with another man and chose to use her husband's infidelity as an excuse for leaving him. More typically, an aggrieved wife would "punish" her erring husband by going away to stay with relatives until he relented and begged her to return home. But most frequently of all, such a woman would remain at home and either quietly accept the situation as inescapable or settle into the violent *modus vivendi in bellum* that characterized several of Te Piti's marital unions while I was there.

The general public was less tolerant of the erring wife than of the unfaithful husband. Other women could be counted upon to see that her transgressions were well publicized and usually harshly condemned. Men would usually laugh over the spectacle of the cuckolded husband and indicate willingness to join in the sport. (In their more serious moments, however, some men revealed uneasiness over another husband's discomfiture: it could happen also to themselves!) As for the aggrieved husbands themselves, most of them I heard took immediate satisfaction by beating their guilty wives into numb and bruised submission, a measure that usually met with wide public approval. Some men would also go after the lover and provoke him into a fight; but more characteristically such grievances remained latent until released by alcohol, i.e., on nearly every large occasion where wine or beer flowed there used to develop two or three such battles. In fact, some men would nourish for years a bitter grievance against their wives' one-time lovers, long after they had made peace with their wives—another instance of a conventional notion that men were the active initiating agents in social relations and women the compliant irresponsibles.

During my enquiries into marital histories, I came across several episodes in which women were said to have had extramarital affairs without arousing their husbands' ire. The explanation usually given for this was: "She was much younger and better looking than her husband"; or "Hers was the wealth." In other words, in this marital exchange of sexual services, contributions short of the customary measure of exclusiveness and "balance" could be compensated—either directly (by factors of quality of the service) or indirectly (by increased contributions to other parts of the couple's "total economy"). With respect to the first, it was a matter of widespread opinion that older men marrying young and pretty women got just what they deserved, i.e., less than exclusive enjoyment of their wife's sexual services. (The same was true, to an even greater degree, of older women marrying younger men.) And with respect to the second explanation, my informants agreed that no man of sense would throw out an unfaithful spouse if their domestic economy depended mainly upon her economic resources. Beat her, perhaps, but not abandon such a source of material satisfaction. In fact, Te Pitians were quite explicit about the compensatory effects of one-sided wealth or sexual desirability in serving to maintain the proper "balance" in marital sexual exchange.

Other types of goods that circulated between spouses by direct exchange included money (in the form of no-interest loans), fishing gear (which was usually individually owned), and bicycles (in Fatata). Otherwise, nearly all instances of the circulation of those and other objects (and services) took place within the context of pool-sharing, either explicitly or implicitly. In other words, a husband did not, for example, borrow land from his wife to garden on, or even to earn money on for his own exclusive use. Instead, he made use of it as of his right as a partner in the pool-share formula on which marriages were mainly based.

Next we come to the question of non-reciprocable giving. Did Te Piti's spouses perform services or give objects to one another outside the context of pool-sharing or sexual exchange and without apparent expectation of return? With respect to gifts of large-size objects, the answer to this question is quite clear. I heard of only one instance of a person making such an outright gift to a spouse, and that was the testamentary gift of land made by a dying wife to her husband; and even this transaction had something of the nature of an exchange, since she imposed the qualification that he was to possess the land only so long as he did not legally remarry. (The man in question valued this land so highly that he would not legally marry his common-law wife despite her wishes and his own desire to become a church Communicant, for which they were of course disqualified.)

There were undoubtedly countless occasions on which married couples gave objects to and performed services for each other without expectation of specific retu*.s. Such transactions were, I expect, part of the cement that kept most marriages intact—not everything that passed between spouses did so according to formulae requiring "balance" according to fixed conventions of "Who Does What." On the other hand, no Te Pitian I talked to about such matters specified this kind of giving as being *appropriate* to marriage. And when I gave hypothetical examples of it in order to learn about its prevalence, the most usual response was, "That's what we do for our children."

Finally, there are the transaction categories of *coercive giving* and *competitive giving* to be considered.

By coercive giving, I refer to the unsolicited, gratuitous "giving" of objects or services for the more or less tacit purpose of building up a credit with the recipient against the day when the donor wishes something in return. Te Pitians utilized this kind of transaction in several contexts and particularly in their relations with Europeans, but not, I believe, with a spouse.

Under the heading of competitive giving, I include all those transactions in which the donor hands over objects or performs services for another with the expressed or implied hope that the recipient will be *unable* to make an equivalent return. Instead, the anticipated return will be in the form of enhanced status *vis-à-vis* the recipient, acknowledged either by the public at large or by the recipient alone. This kind of transaction is familiar to anthropologists who have worked in "pot latching" societies of Melanesia, the Northwest Coast of North America, and elsewhere, but it is also characteristic of smaller scale and less dramatic interaction in many other societies, including our own, where it occurs, for example, between spouses whose pool-sharing obligations are not well defined.

In Te Piti, there was an element of competitive giving in many transaction episodes, e.g., in certain forms of "hospitality," but I could detect no evidence of it in the relations of spouse to spouse. This may be due to the superficiality of much of my data on marital relations, but I believe not entirely so. In their marital relations, the Te Pitians possessed more direct, forthright means for emphasizing status differences and for expressing aggression, for which competitive giving was elsewhere often employed.

Finally, any description of "economic" relations between spouses must include mention of the disposition of the possessions of the first one of them to die.

French laws regarding inheritance were comprehensive and detailed, but the only ones that concerned Te Pitians or, to put it more accurately, the only ones that Te Pitians knew about and considered relevant and locally applicable, had to do with land (and in a few instances, with "permanent" buildings).

Te Pitians knew, for example, that unless otherwise devised by an officially approved testament, a deceased's rights in land passed not to his or her spouse, even if legally wed, but to those children to whom he or she was the legally registered "parent"—or, lacking any children, to other consanguines, according to a precise formula set forth in the *Code Civil*.[16] (What constituted legal parenthood will be described in the next chapter.) A few Te Pitians did indeed possess land rights obtained from a foster parent by testament, and some others had expectations of acquiring rights in the future in this way, usually on the basis of a promise from a foster parent. Most of them, however, considered testamentary disposition to be, like legal divorce, a mysterious procedure that was too difficult and presumably too costly to undertake. As for testamentary inheritance from a spouse, instances of this were exceedingly rare.

In this connection, I recorded no instances of an existing or recent Te Piti marriage contract having been accompanied by any legal arrangement regarding the spouses' respective estates. As for any goods acquired by them jointly, these were either too trivial or impermanent to raise issue over, or they were simply utilized by the widow or widower during the latter's lifetime and then shared equally by their "legal" offspring.

What differences can be discerned between Atea and Fatata regarding the "economic" aspects of a married couple's relationship? Consider first the parts played by wives in domestic pool-sharing.

I have implied that Atean women on the average contributed more self-earned money and more food-producing labor into their family "pools" than did their Fatatan counterparts. Relatively more Fatatan wives contributed land for their husbands' money-earning enterprises (see below), but not enough more to offset the overall superiority of Atea's wives as contributors.

If there were any differences between Atean and Fatatan wives with respect to their contributions to housing and clothing, I must confess that they escaped me. I suppose that, being at home on the average more than their Atean counterparts, the wives of Fatata contributed more labor to such pool-sharing family jobs as food preparation, housecleaning, and child care, but I did not make any systematic observations of these activities and have the impression that such differences, if they existed, were slight and socially inconsequential.

How, then, were Fatatan wives able to maintain the fiction of "economic balance" (which I imagine to have been a normative model for all Tahitian rural marriages) by contributing less to their domestic "pools" than did their Atean counterparts?

That they did contribute less was confirmed by observers from the Leeward Islands then resident in Fatata and by Fatata-born men and women

---

[16]The details of which were, however, unknown by and of no evident interest to Te Pitians, for whom the problem did not arise.

who had resided in the Leeward Islands. Their judgments were, without exception, that Leeward women (including those of Huahine) worked much harder than those of Mo'orea and Tahiti. (Moreover, the same opinions were expressed by all the Atean men I subsequently discussed the subject with,[17] hence it cannot be put down entirely to sour grapes on the part of the Fatatan men.)

Evidently, Fatata's husbands expected less food and money-earning work from their wives than did their Atean counterparts; otherwise there would have been more tension between Fatatan couples than there appeared to be. And the most plausible explanation I can offer for that lower expectation is that the Fatatan husbands viewed their wives as possessing, and contributing, other resources of sufficient value to offset the latters' "shortfall" in food and money-earning work. What those other resources were is obscure, but I suggest that Fatatan women's better formal education (relative to Ateans') and their somewhat more urbane, westernized social deportment were positive components in the equation. (After all, such intangibles figure in marital balances in other societies, e.g., in those in which a poor but high-born woman can be matched with a rich but low-born man.)

If this suggestion is true, then it does not really matter where, analytically, in the formulae of marriage, the Fatatan women's extra resource should be added. In one sense, it might be viewed as adding value to a wife's attractiveness in her direct sexual and sex-colored social exchanges with her husband. Or, it could also be viewed as an added component in the pool-share equation of the conjugal family as a whole. Or, what is more reasonable, it might be both.

Summary of Differences

1. With respect to the marital unions extant in Te Piti during my 1954–55 visits, the two villages contained about the same number, proportionately, of the nonlegalized "temporary" type but differed in their percentages of nonlegalized "firm" types, Fatata having contained more of those whose legalization was prevented by "technical" considerations. Of the legalized unions that prevailed, Fatata contained many more, proportionately, of those that had been sponsored by the couples' kinfolk and ceremonialized in veiled-bride weddings, Atea proportionately more of those

---

[17] When I informed Ateans of my plan to pursue my research on Mo'orea, I was warned by them against two things: drinking open-bottled beer and employing local women. Mo'orean men, I was told, were notorious for inflicting elephantiasis upon their guests by urinating in their beer. And Mo'orean women were spoiled by their men and too lazy to work—except in bed!

that had been promoted by the couples' pastor or sponsored and ceremonialized by their sodality associates.

2. Comparison revealed a higher incidence of Fidelity Pledging in Atea than in Fatata.

3. Two noteworthy differences between Atea and Fatata were also manifested in the criteria used for choosing a spouse. First, age discrepancy between spouses (mainly between older women and younger men) was more marked and more widely prevalent in Fatata than in Atea. And second, the factor of social class weighed more heavily in Fatata than in Atea when parents had voices in choosing spouses for their children.

4. The most noteworthy difference between the two villages with respect to marital residence patterns concerned the locus of the household chosen to live in. In this sense, 54 percent of all Atean married couples resided neolocally, as contrasted with only 41 percent of Fatata's. In cases where the couple did not set up a new household of their own, they tended in both villages to live in the household where the husband had previously lived, and this tendency was even stronger in Atea than in Fatata.

5. Differences between the two villages were also manifest in terms of the contributions made by spouses to their households' "economic" resource pools. In Atea, relatively more wives contributed self-earned (in contrast to inherited) money to the "pool," and more of them contributed their labor in subsistence gardening and to husbands' money-earning enterprises. In Fatata, more wives contributed their own land to their husbands' gardening and money-earning enterprises.

6. And finally, although marital unions were terminated at about the same level of frequency in both villages, those terminations finalized by legal divorce were considerably more numerous, proportionately, in Fatata, a difference that may be seen to be even wider, inasmuch as Atea contained proportionately more legally wed couples than Fatata (63 percent to 54 percent).

CHAPTER IX

PASSING THROUGH LIFE

Having Children

I talked with no married person in Te Piti who did not want some children, preferably one's own but, if that was not possible, then someone else's. It occasionally happened that a woman and perhaps even her husband wished to space their offspring more widely, or for the sake of her health even cease having them at all, but only after some had been born.

To the question of how many offspring married people wanted to have, I met with various responses. The stock answer, which usually came quickly and with a smile, was: "Many. Tahitians like lots of children," and this indeed may have been the sincere wish of a large number of couples. On the other hand, I gained from other evidence the impression that most women considered seven or eight the extreme limit and four or five the optimum; and some of the younger ones expressed the opinion that two would be quite sufficient.

Under special circumstances, some women expressed a wish to stop childbearing altogether, quite apart from their notions about the optimum number. Occasionally this happened when a woman in poor health believed that more pregnancies or a child to nurse would harm her still more. In some of these instances, a considerate husband appeared to share his spouse's concern, going so far as to express the wish to avoid pregnancies, but such a wish was seldom put into practice as far as I could learn.

Te Pitian attitudes about contraception ranged from insouciance to strongly expressed opinions for or against. Those expressing opposition usually did so on religious grounds. I did not inquire about the Protestant Church's "official" stand on the matter, but the "anticontraception" residents I questioned seemed to assume that their view had church backing. Most of those favoring contraception did so not as a measure for insuring general population control but as a specific one for, say, sparing a sickly, child-burdened woman. In addition, a few young unmarried women spoke in favor of it as a means of sparing themselves unwanted pregnancies, and a few (a very few) young married ones—typically, the better educated ones and largely in Fatata—supported contraception as a means of keeping their families small.[1]

Not that any of the favoring attitudes were implemented by practice: some Te Pitians knew of the existence of contraceptive devices (mainly condoms) but I doubt that any of them used them regularly and consistently.

One such situation was described by Amo, a relatively well-educated and cosmopolitanized man, who decided along with his wife that they had had enough children—8 in 18 years—especially in view of his wife's excessive thinness and chronic fatigue. They consulted a European doctor Amo was acquainted with (it is unlikely that they would have gone to a stranger, on a professional basis alone). "He told us about sterilization and some other things we could do. I wouldn't mind being sterilized [probably an untruth!], but my wife is afraid to be." And so they continued to have babies, about one every eighteen months. Apparently the doctor's advice about cyclic timing of intercourse made as little impression upon their comprehension as his suggestion about prophylactics or *interruptus* did upon their volition.

More typically, a married woman's wish to cease having children originated in some quarrel with her husband or some chronic discontent with her married life. When this wish seized her, she could either have refused to have intercourse or, if already pregnant, resort to abortion.

The standard abortificant was a bitter brew made of the juices of green pineapple and lemon; in each village, certain older women specialized in its preparation and administration. It was held to be highly effective and to take effect about two months after imbibing.

Attitudes towards abortion varied. In general, men opposed it more than women but opinions differed according to context.

When speaking as parishioners, more or less "for the record," Te Pitians invariably said that abortion was sinful (*mea hara*), subject to divine punishment, e.g., sterility, premature aging, generally poor health. (Paradoxically, the women known to be experts in preparing the brew were respected pillars of the church and were not criticized for practicing their craft.) On the conversational plane of give-and-take informality, however, most residents I

---

[1]In this connection, the percentage of children in the under-five-year-old cohort was smaller in Fatata (16.9 percent) than in Atea (20.2 percent), but whether the difference in attitudes towards contraception had any influence on this demographic difference I am unable to say.

talked with about the matter—young and old, male and female—verbally expressed the attitude that abortion in general was "perhaps wrong but not really a matter for public concern," an attitude which individual reactions to specific abortion events tended to confirm.[2]

In the fairly typical case of one young married woman whose frequent miscarriages were suspected of having been self-induced, some people censured her ("she doesn't want to settle down") and others sympathized with her ("her man is brutal" or "he is a good-for-nothing who doesn't provide for his family"), but most others considered the matter to be either wholly unimportant or of concern to no one but the principals themselves. Usually, in instances of more positive reaction, men were disposed to censure the woman and women to sympathize with her, but sentiment was also influenced by the reputations of the principals and by one's kinship ties with them. In any case, the emphasis was nearly always on the loss or gain to the parents; I heard no expression of concern for any "rights" of the embryo itself.

This was also true of cases of alleged malicious abortion. When miscarriages were suspected of having been caused magically by third persons— typically by some thwarted suitor or jealous rival—public indignation against the unknown or suspected culprit was outspoken, but sympathy was for the mother, and perhaps also for the father, and not for the unborn.

In the case of an unmarried woman suspected of aborting her unwanted "mistakes," criticism was directed at the woman for her notorious promiscuity and not directly at the act itself as destruction of life.

But to return to the wish for children—the wide consensus of that wish, and the sincerity of it, was to be seen in the evident pleasure with which most married, and many unmarried, females greeted the birth of babies of their own. (I knew two young unmarried women who, unable or unwilling to produce their own babies, were eager even to acquire them by fosterage.) Moreover, most married men I knew about took as much, or about as much, pleasure in the birth of their wives' children as did the women themselves.

Thus it is fairly safe to conclude that in general most Te Pitian adults welcomed having children and, I adduce from many statements and observed reactions, *lots* of children. Why was that so? The motives within my range of scrutiny—and these may not have been the most decisive—were of various kinds.

---

[2]According to the *Code Penal* (Article 317), all acts of willful abortion, unless established as necessary to preserve the life of the mother, were punishable by imprisonment and fine. No Te Pitian I talked with on the subject knew about this statute, nor, I suspect, would have given much heed to it if he had known.

First of all, the conditions of Te Pitian subsistence life did not directly *discourage* having children. One more child in a household did not usually place an additional burden on the parents' labor or material resources—and I heard only a few, i.e., the young married women referred to above, object to children on that basis. (Nor, for that matter, did I hear anyone rationalize the *having* of children on these terms.) There were always other people around to share the chores of nurturance, and, except for canned milk, which only the poorest of families could not purchase in the quantities required, the extra food needed to feed one more mouth was fairly easy to obtain. Moreover, if the child had been viewed as a burden, there were sure to be relatives or other neighbors eager to foster it, and Te Pitian parents were well conditioned to permit their doing so. A few European social-class attitudes had indeed penetrated Te Pitian society, but I found no evidence of the notion that "only uncouth peasants have litters of children."

Conversely, I could discover no influential economic factors that might have directly *encouraged* the desire for children, including, in most cases, lots of children.

Throughout the Society Islands, schoolteachers did, it is true, receive an allowance from the Administration for each offspring,[3] and employed women in general were qualified to receive extra wages for a few months before and after they gave birth, but those in Te Piti so affected were few in number, and even for such persons the amounts were not likely to have served as positive incentives to procreate.

Nor does the image of farmers and fishermen producing large families to work their crops and tend their nets apply here. Te Piti's children did indeed help their parents with household chores and gardening and fishing, but they did not add much, if anything, to any household's surplus while children, nor did their parents explicitly evaluate them in such terms. Men with large vanilla or coconut plantations and those with large fishnets evidently did welcome the assistance of their older sons, but I am firmly convinced that Te Pitians did not procreate with this distant objective consciously in mind.[4]

---

[3]Allowances to children whose legal guardians were schoolteachers or other types of civil servants depended upon the guardians' salaries and the number of children. The three recipient families in Te Piti received per month respectively, 1,200, 6,220, and 8,720 francs. Child allowances to certified workers in the private sector were calculated at a much larger rate, namely, 300 francs per month; only one family in Te Piti received such an allowance there during the years of my visits.

[4]A rash statement, I acknowledge, and one for which I have little positive evidence—and none of the kind of systematic questionnaire-based data used to discover such motivation, or lack of it, elsewhere (compare Nag 1972; Nag, Peet, and White 1978; White 1975).

In summary, I shall have to leave the matter with an assertion that most Te Pitian parents appeared to want lots of children. Aside from biblical discourse, I did not hear offspring characterized as a "blessing," but I often heard childlessness characterized as a deprivation or even a curse. With regard to the former, the shrewishness of some women was explained as having developed as a result of childlessness. And with regard to the latter, childlessness itself was thought to come about as a result of some transgression, such as a deliberate abortion, petty though chronic thievery, or disobedience to parents. (In connection with some filial disobedience, parents were believed to utter such curses, deliberately and explicitly.) The woman was usually considered the responsible party in childlessness, but occasionally blame was attributed to the man if, for example, he was a notorious filcher of his neighbors' vanilla.[5]

For women unable to conceive, there were native medicines (*ra'au huero*, medicine-egg), and women expert in such matters. Recipes differed: the most common I heard about consisted of hibiscus and the liquid of a green coconut. If these measures did not work, some nonconceiving women either reconstructed explanations from memories of past errors, or sought the reason through a diviner, or, more rarely and usually as a last resort, consulted a physician or bona-fide midwife.

An interesting and perhaps socially relevant belief concerning child conception was that held by some that frequent intercourse over a period of a year was required for first impregnation of a woman by any particular man. Some persons I questioned held tenaciously to this belief—or so they claimed—despite widely stated contrasting "evidence" (e.g., statements about some child having been sired by a certain man during his brief visit or during the mother's short visit elsewhere—European- and Chinese-looking children having been usually accounted for in this way). But this latter kind of "evidence" was apparently less decisive in theorizing than the other "evidence" they cited, namely, that "most women do not conceive for a year or more after first settling down with any particular man."

With so many women pregnant so much of the time, it was surprising to me how unelaborated were the beliefs and practices I was able to discover about this condition of life. There was a widespread saying that pregnant women who ate crabs would give birth to "crab-footed" or "crab-handed"

---

[5]One highly Europeanized informant attributed one woman's inability to conceive to the fact that she made a "*culte*" (the word used was French) of hard work. I doubt that the most supinely inactive Te Pitian would have gone so far as to consider continuous hard work an error punishable by supernatural intercession, but it was undoubtedly something that should not be overdone!

children, and a few other magical similes of this sort; but most abnor-
malities—miscarriages, stillbirths, double deaths, and malformed infants—
were attributed to sorcery (*pífao*), to the malevolence of ghosts, or to over-
work. The emaciated and prematurely aged appearance of some women
was often explained to be the result of their having worked too hard and
too far along in pregnancy because, it was usually added, of a lazy and in-
considerate husband.[6] In this connection, there appeared to be no slack-
ening of sexual activity until very late in pregnancy and no widespread belief that any harm was thus done.

In connection with the above, there was, however, a widespread belief in
a connection between the life of the newborn and his umbilicus and associated placenta. In the case of babies born at home (I neglected to inquire
about those born in hospital), the placenta (*pūfenua*) was usually buried under or nearby the house; had it been thrown away (it was stated), the child
would soon die. As for the umbilicus cord (*pito*), it was usually allowed to remain attached until it rotted and fell away, the explanation having been
that the longer it remained attached the longer the child would live. (Then,
I was told, the ideal practice was to place the cord in a container and throw
it into the depths of the sea, thereby assuring an unusually long life for the
individual. However, I heard of no instance of this having been done during
my visits.)

Fatata contained an infirmary, staffed by a trained medical technician.
In addition, the village was regularly and frequently visited by a medically
trained midwife and was within easy reach by the daily three-hour boat trip
of Pape'ete's large and expertly staffed public lying-in hospital. All of these
services were virtually free, and many Fatatan women utilized them. On the
other hand, numbers of other Fatatan women preferred to be delivered at
home, with assistance of one of the local "amateur" midwives (*vahine
fa'afānua*). The latter were usually themselves mothers of large families and
were characterized as having been not afraid of the blood; they served without recompense.

Atean women also had access to an infirmary, a small one at Fare, and
were visited—but more infrequently—by the infirmary's medical technician,
who, however, was male and hence less acceptable to Atea's pregnant wom-
en. Partly in consequence of this, and partly in consequence of deep-seated
anxieties about European hospitals and being ill away from home—
attitudes that were represented also in Fatata, but in smaller measure—most
Atean women went through childbirth at home, with the assistance of their
local, unpaid midwives.

---

[6]The "scientific" explanation for this offered by one enlightened informant was that the
"womb will 'turn over' and the fetus usually die."

Thus, although the two villages differed somewhat with respect to where their children were born, the difference counted for little in terms of direct money costs. Ateans' predilection for home deliveries may have resulted in some higher costs (e.g., the cost of home-feeding versus free hospital meals, etc.) but these, if any, could be offset against savings (e.g., having a husband at home and hence more continually productive rather than waiting, idle, and unproductive at the hospital). Also, the Fatatans' preference for hospital deliveries may, over the long run, have resulted in fewer fatalities and hence lower costs in terms of the basic economic asset that human life and labor constitutes, but I have no figures with which to document this potentially important contrast.

Nor can I offer any relevant figures concerning how many children Te Piti's couples had produced, although I tried in several ways to discover such figures.

One way was to try to discover the total number of live offspring that had been borne by married females resident in Te Piti in 1954–55. To the extent that answers to this question were reliable, and in the case of some women I doubt that they were, the numbers ranged from none to sixteen and averaged about 3.5 (there having been no noteworthy difference between Atea and Fatata in this respect).

Another way was to limit the enquiry to 1954–55 female residents past childbearing age (or, at least, past active childbearing). This produced the same range of zero to sixteen, and an average of about five, but was of even more dubious reliability. (Many such women had clearly "forgotten" and had to be reminded of some birth by older kinfolk.)

Nor did the civil registers, with all their semblance of completeness and authenticity, turn out to be so in fact. For example, I learned with near certainty that some births had not been recorded (e.g., of infants expiring a day or two after birth) and that some of the offspring of locally resident women had been registered elsewhere (e.g., in Pape'ete or Uturoa, where they had been delivered). And, of course, the registers included births by women who no longer resided permanently in Te Piti or who were "temporarily" away during 1954–55.

Which raised the question in my mind: Why limit the enquiry to women who happened to be residing in Te Piti in 1954–55? Why not include others "temporarily" away (and how long is "temporary"?), or those who had resided there, "permanently," during the last decade or so?

And so on, and so on. Finally, I reached the conclusion (or sought refuge in the excuse!) that, while demographic statistics of the kind being sought after may be feasible, and perhaps more reliable and credible, for stationary (and preferably large) populations, they are inevitably incomplete or irrelevant, or both, for communities as small as and for residents as mobile as those of Atea and Fatata.

Stillbirths were buried without ceremony, but those dying after birth—even within minutes of delivery—were usually placed in a coffin and buried like anyone else. And if the mother also died in childbirth, she and the dead infant were ordinarily placed in the same coffin. In none of these customs could I discover any differences between Atea and Fatata.

In both villages, women flocked around new babies, petting them and detecting likenesses with relatives. Younger mothers displayed their infants with all the earmarks of immense pride, whether they were the product of veiled-bride wedlock or of a one-night encounter. Young fathers were also not above displaying pleasure in their new offspring, but for most other men—except perhaps grandfathers—a new baby in the village or even in the household was greeted with indifference, either genuine or pretended, such matters having been described as the concern of women.

The males I questioned stated that there was no general time restriction on the resumption of sexual intercourse after a birth: "They begin again as soon as the woman feels like it." ("Is a month afterwards too soon?" "No, but a week probably is.") In many cases, the time lapse between births was very short by some European standards, but the only negative reaction to close-order births that I heard was in reference to women evidently overburdened by too many children born in close succession: "Their husbands should sleep elsewhere for a while." On the other hand, the robust fast-producing woman was for some husbands a matter of pride.

The offspring of Protestant parents were invariably baptized in their parish church. The services were generally held on the first Sunday of each month, directly after the main service and before communion, except in Atea, where those children born during the later months of the year had their baptisms postponed until New Year's Eve, when a special midnight baptismal service was held.

The rite itself followed a standard Protestant pattern: the child, accompanied by its parents but usually presented by a godparent (*paren*), was christened "in the name of the Father, etc." If the child's mother was not legally wed, a Communicant acting as *paren* was required by church rule to make the presentation. (The practice of *paren* probably originated with this requirement and later became extended to include all babies, whether their mothers were legally wed or not.) Beyond this occasion, the *paren* played no further role, as such, in the child's life.

In both villages, a small feast was usually given by a child's parents to celebrate its baptism; to it were invited the pastor, a deacon or two, close and locally resident kinfolk of the parents, and perhaps a few local friends. (In Atea, however, the family's own celebration tended to be merged with the larger New Year festivities for babies baptized at that time.) In addition to the costs of such celebrations, usually for food, considerable amounts of money were spent in both villages by the parents on the garments in which the infants were invariably clothed for the church services: bonnets, gowns, booties—the lot!

Some Bible-versed Te Pitian asserted that "God watches over the fall of every sparrow," and a few of them extended this analogy to humans, whatever the age. In fact, I collected several sanctimonious declarations to the effect that every living human, however young or old, was a child of *Te Atua* and hence deserving of full recognition as a member of God's community; but most informants—including pastors and deacons—concurred in the opinion that a newborn infant gained a significant measure of (Christian) humanity only through the ritual of baptism.

Meanwhile, in both villages and for all babies there had to be performed another ritual which had nothing to do with the child's soul but was of crucial importance to his legal rights and responsibilities. This was the act of entering the child's name in the local civil register.

The civil register (*état civil*; *eita tivira*) maintained in every district and municipality of the Society Islands was mentioned earlier (pages 232–34). In addition to acts of civil marriage, it was required that those concerning birth, filiation, and decease also be recorded therein (*Code,* Art. 34). The facts of birth, which had to be recorded within three days of delivery, included the place, date, and hour of birth; sex and *prénom* ("calling name") of infant; and name, age, profession, and place of domicile of mother and father (Art. 57). If the mother was legally wed and her husband did not disavow paternity, then the latter was ipso facto the child's father for this purpose—all very neat and straightforward except for settlements like Atea and Fatata, where numbers of children were born out of legal wedlock. Fortunately, the French *Code Civil* was comprehensive enough to accommodate the complexities of Tahitian filiation in letter at least, if not in spirit.

According to the *Code,* a woman's legal spouse could disavow her offspring under the following conditions:
—if he could prove the physical impossibility of his having cohabited with her during the legally defined period of conception (i.e., from the 300th to the 180th day before birth);
—if the infant had been conceived before the marriage (provided that the husband was not aware of the pregnancy at the time of the marriage, that he did not assist at its birth, and that he did not register himself as the infant's father in the civil register);
—if he could prove to the satisfaction of the court that the infant was conceived in adultery.

In terms of the first two conditions, I knew of several cases where husbands would have been thus enabled to disavow their wife's offspring, but in none of these were such rights exercised even though the men were informed of their rights. In two of these, the wife owned much more land than the husband (or, so my informants explained the husband's acceptance); in the other instance the husband was characterized as "stupid" (*mā'au*) or "lazy" (*hupehupe*).

Recognition (*reconnaissance*, *'ite*) was a civil act that established the legal paternity or maternity of a child born out of wedlock, the legal presumption having been that those parents were the child's biological parents. It could be performed voluntarily by the parents themselves or by judicial determination. The mother could be of any age to perform the act of recognition, but the father had to be twenty-one or over.

In the decade of 1945–54, 63 percent of all children born and registered in Te Piti were illegitimate in the legal sense; of these latter, 12 percent were accorded maternal recognition only, the rest having been recognized by the presumed genitor as well (all more or less voluntary, there having been no cases of judicial determination). Comparatively, Atea and Fatata were about the same in their percentages of "illegitimate" births during that decade (i.e., 61 percent and 64 percent, respectively), but Atea's percentages of mother-only recognition (16.6 percent) outnumbered Fatata's (9.7 percent).

Inasmuch as recognition bestowed certain mutual rights and obligations upon the parent and offspring, its existence or nonexistence could conceivably have had important social-relational consequences. Let me list these rights, etc., and then see how this alien code applied in Te Piti.

To begin with, the *Code* distinguished three types of illegitimate but recognized offspring: (1) those ultimately legitimatized; (2) those born of adulterous or "incestuous" unions and not subsequently legitimatized (for legal definition of "incestuous union" see Art. 161); (3) all others.

If the acknowledged parents subsequently married and recognized the child, these acts fully legitimatized the child and placed it in the same legal position as other (legitimate) offspring of the union with respect to paternal authority and inheritance. In fact, most of the illegitimate children born in Te Piti between 1940 and 1950, and recognized by both parents at about the time of birth, had become subsequently legitimatized in this way by 1955. (As stated earlier, one of the reasons given by some couples for eventually marrying legally was to legitimatize their offspring.)[7]

Some actual cases involving living Te Pitians will serve as illustrations of the bizarre consequences of the application of French paternity laws to this Polynesian kinship system.

---

[7]In case a person's legitimacy could not be established by means of facts recorded in the civil register, there were other kinds of evidence that could be cited to establish it (before a civil tribunal): i.e., proof that the child had been treated as a legitimate offspring by the claimed "father" and that it had been considered as such by the family and by society at large.

Hera and Tina, both in their fifties, had been living together for over twenty-five years and had produced numerous offspring, some of them (in 1955) with children of their own. Hera was an affectionate and indulgent parent and was troubled by the circumstance that his children were, according to French law, not his own. Prior to her life with Hera, Tina had been legally wed to a man who subsequently moved away and who was unwilling, for reasons of spite more than of cost, said Hera, to cooperate in obtaining a divorce. (A neighbor of Hera who knew the man said that he refused the divorce in order not to have to marry any of the other women he had been living with.) As a consequence, Tina's legal husband was the legal "father" of all of Tina's offspring. Hera "supposed" that he would be able to transmit his property, such as it was, to his offspring by making a will, but that, according to him, was a "very difficult and costly" thing to do. And so the matter rested.

Timi, a youth of about twenty, who lived in the house of his mother and her (legal) husband, Toma, believed that he was actually sired by a local man named Tave (a belief evidently shared by the latter himself) who, however, did not (and could not, because he was a minor at the time) recognize the child. Instead, Timi was legally recognized by the husband of his mother's sister ("because of sympathy," Timi explained). Later on, Timi's mother became legally married to Homa who, Timi supposed, was consequently also a "kind of father" to him. Meanwhile, Tave had ceased all contacts with Timi (he used to give him presents) because of the "jealousy" of Tave's current wife. (After which recital, Timi turned the question to me, the reported "expert" on such matters, with: "Who then is my father [*pāpā*]?")

Despite his quandry, Timi could at least point not to one but to three kinds of father. Some Te Pitians could point only to one, i.e., to someone believed to have sired them but who did not—or could not (because of age)—actually recognize them; and a few others could point to none (their mothers having been so promiscuous that they themselves had not known who their begetters had been).

Those unfortunates in the *Code Civil*'s second category, i.e., those born of an adulterous or incestuous union and not subsequently legitimatized, received the surname of the recognizing parent and were subject to his or her parental authority but could lay claim only to *aliments* from that parent, and that only during minority. Such illegitimates could not receive any property from their parents by act of "donation," nor could they receive legacies from them or share in their inheritance. There were no individuals of this category in Te Piti during my visits, or at least the Te Pitians did not recognize any as such.

According to the *Code,* all other recognized (but not legitimatized) off-spring were subject to parental authority of the recognizing parent, but their rights with respect to transactions were somewhat limited by law. In the first place, the relationship legally created by recognition was limited to the parent and child only, i.e., it created no legally valid ties of kinship between the recognized offspring and other relatives of the parent.

The *Code* also laid down very precise rules concerning the size of the portion inheritable from the parent.[8] If the parent had left any legitimate descendants, then the illegitimate but recognized offspring would receive one-half of the inheritance portion that it would have received had he been legitimate (758). If the parent had had no legitimate descendants but did have other relatives in line of succession, then the portion due the illegitimate but recognized offspring was raised to three-fourths of what it would have been had he been legitimate. If there were no other relatives in line to succeed the parent, then his illegitimate but recognized offspring could receive an inheritance portion equal to that due a legitimate offspring. Conversely, the succession of an illegitimate offspring without posterity devolved upon the parent or parents that recognized him.

While alive, a parent could not transfer to his recognized but illegitimate offspring any property coming under the heading of "donation," but he could will property to the offspring to an amount where it and the inheritance portion received by the offspring did not exceed the total amount inherited by any of the parent's legitimate offspring.

Most of the nuances of the French laws just cited were either unknown to or ignored by Te Pitians in their daily interactions with the individuals subject to such legal disabilities. In fact, it was only in matters of legal inheritance, which usually meant land, that such individuals were ever disadvantaged, and only then when land was legally divided. In all other respects such individuals were treated (or mistreated!) like other kinfolk.

In contrast with state- and church-regulated behavior, with their rituals of civil registrations or baptism, native Te Pitian ideology did not recognize any sharp threshold marking an infant's social *début* into community life. The relative influence of these differing ideologies can be tested by reference to burial rites.

It was customary for the pastor to officiate at the funeral of infants who died after baptism, or, if not yet baptized, after the first two or three weeks of life. For those dying before baptism and after only a week or so of life, it

---

[8]An exception being the recognition made during a marriage by one spouse in favor of an illegitimate offspring born before the marriage and of someone other than the (present) spouse, had no effects on the rights of the spouse nor of their legitimate children (337).

was more usual for the deacon of the mother's sodality to officiate. Christian prayers accompanied the burial of nearly all babies born alive but, in the case of those dying within a few days after birth, the rites were more usually performed by a close relative who was not necessarily a church official.

Noteworthy about the above is that the timing of the infant's listing in the civil register did not influence the type of officiation at its funeral rites.

The relative weightiness of these three ideologies may also be tested in the treatment of sick or otherwise abnormal infants. According to state (and to a slightly less degree, church) norms, every infant, whatever its age, should have received the fullest medical attention available. In contrast, most Te Pitian parents (who were more "native" in their attitudes about infancy) did not seek expert medical assistance, native or European, for their sick children until they were several weeks, or even months, old.

Infancy and Childhood

In official governmental terms, a newly born individual received its civil identity upon listing in the civil register but it was regarded as a social person from birth onwards, e.g., it received state protection from physical harm by another person (from conception onwards, actually, as acknowledged in laws against abortion). Then, during the period from birth (*naissance*) to "majority" (*émancipation,* age twenty-one except as noted below), the individual was deemed to remain in a legal condition of childhood, of "minority" (*minorité*), subject to certain restrictions and protected by certain measures. The more important of the restrictions related to "parental authority" and to limitations on entering into legal contracts, including the marriage contract, for example:

(a) children of all ages owed "respect" and "honor" to mother and father (Art. 371);

(b) minors were in general subject to parental authority[9] (*la puissance paternelle*): he (or she) could not reside away from the parental home without permission—except, in the case of boys eighteen and over, to enroll voluntarily in the armed services (Art. 374); parents or guardians were empowered to request the courts to apply correctional measures, including placement in a special "educational" institution, in the case of an infractious minor.

---

[9]"Parental authority" (*puissance paternelle*) was exercised primarily by the father unless he had been relieved of this duty-right by law.

Protective measures could take two forms: more severe sanctions for offenses committed against minors and less severe sanctions for offenses committed by minors.

Within this extended period of minority, French law also drew certain other age-behavior distinctions:

(a) Material goods to which a minor under eighteen held title were controlled by parent or guardian, except for goods acquired by the minor through his own independent efforts or through legacy or gift specifying sole enjoyment (Arts. 903ff). (Such management must, of course, have been for the welfare of the minor [Arts. 384–5].)

(b) Minors aged thirteen and under were ordinarily to be turned over to their parents or guardian upon conviction for a legal infraction. Those aged fourteen and over could, if judged appropriate, be subject to penal sanctions, though of reduced stringency, except in the case of those who had reached age sixteen, against whom the defense of minority could be entirely disregarded.

(c) For certain purposes, a "child" was classed with invalids: "Any person who, at an isolated place, leaves or causes to be abandoned, a child or invalid, incapable of protecting himself for physical or mental reasons, shall be punished for such conduct by jailing from one to three years and by fine of 50,000 to 450,000 francs" (*Code Penal* Art. 349). (This law does not specify the age of such a "child," but an earlier version set it at six and under.)

(d) In general, more severe sanctions were applied against persons causing harm to minors, and if the minor were under fifteen to sixteen years of age the penalties were usually doubled (Arts. 331, 332, 354, 355, 356).

(e) Individuals between six and fourteen were "required" to attend school.

Youths of eighteen and over could enlist voluntarily in the armed forces and without parental consent; and at age twenty they became eligible for conscription.

Full "majority," achieved automatically at twenty-one (except in cases of imbecility or insanity), or earlier through legally bestowed *émancipation*, qualified the citizen to engage in all acts of civil life,[10] except to hold certain elective offices and to adopt children. For the latter, the adopting parent had to be at least forty years old.

---

[10]However, the state also had the judicial power to extinguish some of a citizen's rights, for limited times or in perpetuity, as penalty for certain crimes.

In Protestant Church terms, like those of the state, the individual was re-garded as a social person from conception onwards, but for church purposes the person's advances in life took place in several distinct steps. As described earlier, neonates were treated as something less than full parishioners until baptized, and even after that no official church cognizance was taken of their existence—except to officiate at their funerals—until they began to at-tend Sunday School. Before that, they were regularly taken to church and sodality meetings, but that was all.

Once enrolled in Sunday School, they were labelled *tamari'i,* which they remained until "graduation" or dropout, as was previously mentioned.

Te Pitian "native" labels and practice conceptualized an individual's ad-vance in life and his progressive involvement in community affairs in ways quite different from those defined by state and church norms and practice. To begin with, the stages comprising that progression were not divided by such sharp thresholds. In the contexts of everyday living, the transitions from one life stage to another—infancy to childhood to youth, etc.—were treated as gradual movements, as cumulations of numerous small changes in the individual's behavior, this having been true not only of actual events but of ideas about such events as well.

My queries about the beginning and end of the first stage, *'aiura'a,* brought various responses. Some of the more literal-minded replied that *'aiura'a* began at the moment of birth, or even before, while the baby was *'ōteo,* an embryo, in the womb (*i roto*). Most others said that the being was not fully alive (*ora*) until it had survived the first few hours; and some in-formants, particularly males, implied that it was not "truly alive" until it had outlasted the first few precarious days after parturition.

'Aiura'a literally means "eat-milk-hood," and some informants stated that a person was an *'aiu* for as long as it nursed, from breast or bottle; but just as many insisted that a person was an *'aiu* until it walked unaided. Neither of these characterizations was specific in terms of chronological age: some babies breast-fed until over two or were given bottles even longer; and walking unaided began from about one year old to over two. Both such characterizations were typical of native age grading in general; even after more than a century of familiarity with European time concepts, the Te Pi-tians continued to measure life progress in behavioral terms, at least outside the context of state and church affairs. After a thoughtful pause for calcu-lation, one male informant stated that infancy lasted "one year," plainly as an accommodation to a naive European asking a rather foolish question.

Rephrasing the matter in native terms, it became a question of how soon it was believed normal or desirable for babies to leave off nursing or to begin walking alone. Here again, these transitions were defined variously and in terms of situational rather than strictly chronological terms.

Of the many nursing mothers I knew, some seemed intent on breast-feeding their babies for as long as possible; this was especially true of many young mothers with their first babies. In contrast, there were some women who hastened to wean their babies, either in their eagerness to resume other activities or because of harassment by domestic pressures. In this con-nection, I never heard a woman censured or even discussed for drawing out the nursing period; on the other hand, young women who hurried the pro-cess for reasons considered selfish were reproached by both women and men. (In the case of the harried housewife, neighbors were more apt to blame her husband for burdening her with too many children or too much work.)

Another indirect criterion for demarcating this first major life stage was the native view of "the right time" for fostering.

If a census were made of Atea or Fatata on any one day, there would be found eating and sleeping in many households one or more persons whose presence would be accounted for by the statement that he or she was "fed" by some older member of the household (*fa'a'amu*, to cause to eat). Put an-other way, the collecting of pedigrees in Te Piti turned up the statistic that two in five persons could claim to have one or more "feeding parents" (sing., *metua fa'a'amu*), in addition to birth-parents (sing., *metua fānau*). In fact, when collecting pedigrees I quickly learned the necessity of specifying which kind of parent I wanted to know about, and exchanges like the following were quite typical:

"Who is your father (*pāpā*)?"
"Tetuanui is my father."
"Your *procreative* father or your *feeding* father?"
"My feeding father."
"Then who is your procreative father?"
"He is Tera'i." (Or, not infrequently, "I don't know.")

(Experience also taught me that the first response tended to be the name of the parent with whom the person was living at the time.)

The institution of "feeding parent" (or "fed child") has intrigued and be-wildered visitors to Tahiti for a century and a half. Today many Europeans use the words *fa'a'amu* and *adopt* (or *adopter*) interchangeably, and Tahitians speaking French tend to translate *fa'a'amu* as *adopter*. The Davies Dictionary, published in 1851, does not even list the term *fa'a'amu*. Instead, it dis-tinguishes two other terms: *fa'a'ai* (from *'ai*, to eat, and *fa'a-*, the causative prefix), "foster, feeding" (p. 61), and *tāvai*, "adoption of another's child; adopted, *tamaiti tāvai*, an adopted son" (p. 262). In Te Piti, by 1954-55, *fa'a'amu* had almost completely replaced *fa'a'ai* and also largely absorbed the meaning formerly expressed by *tāvai*, which was used very rarely and then interchangeably with *fa'a'amu*.[11]

Some Te Pitians used the word *fa'a'amu* very broadly, even to include situations in which a child visited relatives for a year or so—say, while a parent was ill, or while attending school in Pape'ete. Others, desirous that the ethnographer learn the "correct" meanings of words, insisted that a person became a *tamaiti fa'a'amu*, the fed son or daughter of another, only when the relationship had been established during childhood (i.e., before about the age of fourteen to fifteen) and when it was understood to be a permanent one and not just a matter of expediency during a critical period. Moreover, these same purists insisted that after the relationship was established the ties with the feeding parent more or less displaced, though never totally replaced, those with the birth-parent in terms of place of residence, nurturance, and parental authority. This "clarification" did not, however, simplify matters for the ethnographer in search of clear-cut definitions; the fact is, there was a continuum of situations involving children in households other than those of their birth- (or recognizing-) parents. At one extreme was the case of Tiona.

When Tiona was a child of five or six, she spent almost as much time at the home of Teuru, who was a distant cousin of her father, as she did at home, although in retrospect not even Teuru claimed that she had been handed over to him to feed and educate at that time. Later, Teuru moved to Pape'ete; in due course Tiona also went to Pape'ete to school and while there she was housed and fed by Teuru for several years, and Teuru subsequently claimed that this made him her "*pāpā fa'a'amu.*" Evidently the two were very fond of each other, for when Teuru moved back to the village Tiona wrote to him more often than to her own parents; and when Tiona returned to the village for vacations she spent as much time in Teuru's household as in her parents'. But the time came when Tiona's own father and Teuru had a violent quarrel (see above, page 222), whereupon the former asserted that Tiona was to stay in Teuru's household no longer. (Teuru appealed to me to patch up the matter, saying that he had great affection for Tiona as proved by the fact that he had fed her so long. Moreover, it was "while staying with him at Pape'ete and consuming twelve cases of canned milk that she had learned French, English *and* American.")

---

[11]The Davies Dictionary's *tāvai* was in 1954–55 more commonly used in church parlance in the sense of "anoint," which suggests that there was a distinction between the two kinds of fosterage in ancient Tahiti: the one, *fa'a'ai* characterized simply by nurturance, the other, *tāvai,* by a more formal relationship that was instituted by ritual (including some form of "anointing").

At another extreme was the case of thirty-year-old Poni, who was *fa'a'amu*-ed to his father's full brother at the age of six months, having been asked for by the latter even before birth. (The brother's wife had not borne any children during six years of marriage, while Poni's own mother had successfully borne six.) Poni lived with his uncle and uncle's wife until their deaths a few years prior to my visit, rarely seeing his birth-parents, who lived on another island. His *fa'a'amu* parents neither recognized nor legally adopted Poni but did will him in a written testament all their property, an action not contested by their own relatives, who in fact considered the transaction entirely proper. (Poni reported that he had also inherited some land from his birth-parents, but hadn't yet bothered to collect any income from it.)

True adoption, ie., legally valid adoption in terms of the French *Code Civil,* was a process heard about but only vaguely understood by Te Pitians. No one living there during my visits had been a party to an adoption contract; and they considered it a mysterious, difficult, and "probably costly" process, a typical example of the working of an arbitrary Administration.

Between the extremes represented by the "feeding" relationships listed above were to be found cases all along the continuum, or rather continua. At one point in my research, I believed it might be possible to construct a kind of "adhesion index" indicating more precisely the degree to which the child had become identified with the foster family and using such criteria as relative amounts of time spent with the two parental households; relative parental contributions to nurturance and education; participation of child in the inheritance of foster parents; etc. But the cases I knew did not fit neatly into any such scheme. For one thing, the variables did not vary dependently, and there was no objective formula for weighting them.

As in the case of marital unions, Te Pitians used the word *tāmau*—"firmly established, or tied"—to describe some "feeding" relationships. Everyone I questioned agreed that such a relationship was *tāmau* when the feeding parents had announced their intention of making a property settlement, mainly land, upon the child; but in most opinions on this matter the relative amounts of time spent in the two parental households was not decisive, nor was the question of who had nurtured the child and directed its actions (i.e., a man should feed and supervise *everyone* staying in his household).

The subject of incest boundaries was not volunteered by informants as an index of "firmness," but when I raised the question people agreed that when a "feeding" relationship was firm the child should not have sexual relations with any of his new "siblings," even if they were fed-children like himself. According to some, this proscription should also apply to descendants of those "siblings" but not necessarily to collateral relatives of the feeding parents. However, the question was more often than not academic, since most "feeding" relationships were between consanguines, who were already sexually proscribed to one another.

It is, of course, significant that the Te Pitians considered property to be the decisive factor in identifying with a family, and in some instances this may well have been so. On the other hand, I recorded some episodes that cast a different light on how and why "feeding" relationships became "firm"; one such involved a fourteen-year-old girl, Mona.

Mona was the eleventh and last offspring of Mara and his (legal) wife. When Mona was only six months old, the family house caught fire and her mother was badly burned. Being unable to cope with all the reconstruction work that had to be done, she and her husband had gratefully acceded to the request of Tani that Mona be "fed" by him and his wife as "their other children were much older and they longed for a baby around the house." So Mona was raised in Tani's house, about 200 meters from that of Mara. When she was about eight years old, there developed a serious quarrel between Tani and Mara as a result of a business rivalry, and the latter wanted to recover Mona. ("That's the way it is with some parents," interpolated my informant. "They will hand over a child to someone for feeding, and then when the child is older and more useful they try to get it back.") But Tani would not relinquish her: "He loved her very much." ("Couldn't Mara have taken her away?" "Yes, but that wouldn't have been right.") The active quarrel between the families subsided when the business rivalry ceased, but the coolness between them had persisted ever since. And Mona had remained with Tani. During my visits, she occasionally stopped by to chat with her mother and siblings but did not stay there overnight. ("Tani forbade her to be away from home at night.") During my second visit, when Mara's widow (Mona's birth-mother) suffered a stroke and was taken by boat to Papeʻete for treatment, all her other children and many neighbors and friends were on hand to provide an emotional departure; Mona, however, only heard of the illness (from me) later on and even then did not display great concern.

Paura and Nirai had been *faʻaʻamu*-ed by the same "mother": Paura and her husband, Para, had produced nine children; Nirai and her husband, Nani, none. Three of Paura's children had been "fed" by Nani and Nirai, but only Fereti's (aged nine) relationship with them appeared to be firm: he spent some time at Para's but was mostly at Nani's some 100 meters away, where he was very frequently to be seen in company with Nirai's aged and almost houseridden parents. Nirai was notorious for her bad temper ("Because she has never been able to have children of her own"), and her behavior to Fereti seemed to alternate between severe scoldings and canings and affectionate displays. One day she stalked by my house toward Para's with stick in hand and soon returned with Fereti, beating him before her. ("He had gone there without asking her permission," she screamed to people who stood and watched disapprovingly as they went by.) An hour later Para returned home from work and, learning of the affair, marched to Nani's to protest the beatings and take Fereti home. There ensued a characteristic "street battle" (*tama'i purūmu*) between Nirai and Para, she hysterically shrill and obscene, he reasonable and calm; he saying she had gone too far in continually beating the boy, she retorting that the boy was disobedient and that, besides, it was her business anyway. ("If Nani had been home, he would have beaten Nirai," onlookers told me.) At one point the constable tried to intervene and quiet the woman, but she easily shouted him down and he retired with injured dignity to compose a complaint to the gendarme. After some twenty minutes, Para called the boy to him and led him home, leaving Narai weeping and screaming after him. ("This is the end," everyone said. "He won't return there.") Next day, however, Fereti was back at Nani's, helping his "feeding" mother prepare the afternoon meal, and remained there throughout the rest of my stay.

The sequel occurred two months later when I was taking photographs of the occupants of each household, as a present for them and as a record for myself. In the group assembled before Para's house, Fereti was conspicuously absent. ("Don't you want your son Fereti in the picture too?" "Oh, he'll be at Nani's; that's where he stays." "Why? Has Nani willed him property?" "No. They have no property to will; it's a question of affection (*e mea here*)." And then the inevitable: "That's the way it is with us Tahitians.")

The initiative in establishing a *fa'a'amu* relationship was usually but not always taken by the would-be feeding parent; birth parents would, it was said, feel "shame" to request someone else to bring up their child. (Once when I commented to an informant on the undernourished and unkempt appearance of a neighbor's numerous small children, his reply was: "Yes. Other people ought to 'feed' some of them, but they don't. This is a hard-hearted place." "Couldn't they ask relatives to feed them?" "They could, but they wouldn't like to; they would feel shame.") Nevertheless, if parents did wish to "feed" out their offspring for some reason or other, they usually had only to drop a hint and there would always be others willing and eager to take them.

In the course of my "official" household surveys, I found eighty-seven persons (out of a total Te Piti population of 665 at that time) residing in the same household as some older person who was described as his or her feeding parent. But had I carried out the surveys a week later, or earlier, I am certain that the numbers would have been somewhat different, such were the comings and goings of young Te Pitians between the residences of their birth- and feeding parents. Moreover, the eighty-seven individuals (plus or minus) actually living with their feeding parents constituted only part of the total number of relationships identified by Te Pitians as the "feeding" kind, including adult fed "sons" or "daughters" who had long since established their own households independent of both birth- and feeding parents. In fact, virtually every adult Te Pitian was, or had been at some time, involved in one or more "feeding" relationships of some degree of firmness, but the protean nature of the practice ruled out any reliable statistical statement about it. Some generalities about it are, however, possible.

One such is that, while most "feeding" was undertaken by married couples, there were some intriguing exceptions. Among the scores of sets of feeding relationships among Te Piti people in 1955, several of them had been instituted by spinsters or widowed women and two at least by bachelors. One spinster had reared two children in this way and one bachelor three. One young woman described her efforts to me (she had up to that time not lived with a man and said she did not wish to do so with a Tahitian because "they beat their women"): "I would like to have a baby to feed. Three years ago when my sister had a new baby I was going to take it but it died; and then when the next one was born she wanted to keep it herself."[12]

Again, although most feeding relationships were established between relatives, mainly consanguines, friendship or even mere acquaintanceship was not infrequently the basis.

The eighty-seven "active" feeding-relationship sets I encountered in my household surveys were distributed in the following order of frequency, in terms, that is, of the relationship of the feeding parent socially "closest" to the fed child's birth-parents:

> —sibling of mother
> —sibling of father
> —affine of mother or father
> —close friendship with mother or father
> —other

The "other" category contained some dyads that might appear bizarre in some societies but occasioned no surprise at all in Te Piti. One, for example, was that of Mari Vahine. Mari Vahine and her present husband had no children of their own but residing with them was a child who was, in fact, the offspring of Mari Vahine's daughter (by a former marriage) and of Mari Vahine's present husband. The child, whom Mari Vahine doted on, was unequivocally described as Mari Vahine's feeding child (and

---

[12]Under French law, such a person, having been under forty years of age, could not have legally adopted a child, but, as previously stated, Te Pitian fosterage did not involve legal adoption.

expressly not her grandchild), which may have been a way of getting around the ambiguities of Mari Vahine's other link with it but which was well within the range of meanings, as Europeans would perceive them, comprehended by the term *fa'a'amu.*

Some of the reasons given for taking or releasing children for feeding have been mentioned in passing. In going over other cases, the following immediate (i.e., "efficient") reasons seem to have been most decisive, listed in order of frequency. First, on the part of the releasing parent(s):

1. Inability to nurture a child properly because of inadequate material resources or because of sickness or the death of one spouse.
2. Sympathy for relatives or friends without children at home.
3. Desire to place a child beyond the reach of a bad-tempered or drunken spouse (who was usually, but not always, the child's stepparent).
4. Wish to avoid being tied down by parenthood. (This occurred mainly in the case of some young women who wanted to retain their freedom of movement.)
5. Desire to have the child educated in Pape'ete, which in most instances required placing the child with a relative there.

On the part of the taking parents, the first three factors may have operated reciprocally, but there was in addition nearly always the predisposing factor of the deeply felt wish for children, preferably one's own progeny but not exclusively so.

I recorded some instances wherein the feeding parents "explained" their action as based mainly on the desire to have progeny to leave property to. I also recorded instances of people taking from or releasing a child to relatives or friends expressly in order to cement relations with them; sometimes this even involved an exchange of children. And finally, my queries sometimes elicited the reply: "I asked so-and-so's parents for the child because I saw him (or her) and wanted him."

In this connection, it is necessary to state that, in this monograph, which designedly focuses on economic matters, I found no evidence that Te Pitians consciously released or took children for "feeding" primarily, or even weightily, for their present or potential labor in food- or money-producing enterprises. In the broader usage of "economic," of course, some children were released to and accepted by adults for, among other things, the domestic services they could perform for the latter, or on account of the reduction in work that their release provided for the former. Also, the pleasure anticipated by taking a fed-child contained an "economic" dimension in the sense that similar pleasures, derived from socializing, were deemed valuable enough to pay for, say, in terms of hospitality and drink. However, I doubt that many, if indeed any, Te Pitians would have agreed to an analysis of the feeding relationship in anything approaching monetary terms.[13]

Finally, when using "economic" in the broader sense, I suggest that the pervasiveness in Te Piti of the feeding relationship indicates something about the residents' attitude toward their own progeny as "property." That is to say, while they displayed towards them many signs that Europeans would label "love" and "affection," they tended not to cling to them as possessively as parents in many European subsocieties do.

Because of its multiformity in kinds and degrees of firmness, and because of the practical difficulty in categorizing those various forms, I am unable to compare Atea with Fatata, quantitatively, in terms of the feeding relationship. So, once again I am reduced to falling back upon the familiar conclusion that, according to my *impressions* the two villages revealed no large or important differences in this aspect of their social structures. With respect to the eighty-seven instances of "active" coresident feeding turned up in my household surveys, the numbers for each village were closely the same, proportionate to each village's total population. And with respect to the explanations given for releasing and taking children for feeding, the percentages were also much the same in both places[14]—except for one. In line with Fatata's deeper commitment to formal education, more of its children were sent to secondary schools in Pape'ete and hence more of them were fed for this reason—boarded, actually, but with Pape'ete relatives and thus described as fed—than occurred with Ateans.[15]

Returning now to the question that served to introduce this digression on fosterage, namely, what were the Te Pitians' view about the "right time" for releasing a child to its feeding parents, I did not ask the direct question: "How old must a baby be before it may be transferred in fosterage" (realizing full well that the question would be naîve); but some recorded reactions to actual instances indicated a popular preference that the baby ought to be kept with its own mother while it was still mainly dependent on nursing, from breast or bottle.

---

[13]Also, other writers have speculated about the effects of Polynesian-style adoption upon personality development, in the sense of its creation of alternate families for many individuals. For discussion of this and other psychological aspects of Tahitian filiation, including feeding, see Levy 1973:473 ff.

[14]If purely economic motives had been weightier in decisions made by Te Pitians for taking children to be fed, one might expect that Ateans would have outnumbered Fatatans among those wishing to take children, i.e., for labor, since Atean children tended to engage more in subsistence and even cash-cropping activities than their Fatatan counterparts. On the other hand, this fact would also have served to make the child-releasers less willing to lose that labor, so that in the end the weight of this motive would have been neutralized.

[15]For more on fosterage in rural Tahiti, see Hooper 1970A.

As in the case of weaning and walking, there were some marked differences among parents with respect to the time of beginning positive efforts to toilet-train their offspring. I saw some mothers whack three- and four-month-old infants for soiling them; others expressed only slight annoyance at two-year-olds for doing the same thing. In any case, although some adults verbally linked elimination with *aiūra'a,* no one volunteered general opinions about when toilet habits ought to be under control.

Crying was a somewhat different matter. It was regarded as "natural" that proper elimination habits come only with aging and some measure of training, but even the youngest baby whose crying could not be stilled by feeding was considered to be ill or otherwise abnormal. If the behavior persisted for several months without visible signs of illness, sympathy was usually replaced by annoyance, and the annoyance became general and sharply vocal against a whimpering toddler. As for a whining, crying walker, playmates could be counted on to jeer and older relations to punish. In other words, "unwarranted" crying was not considered "natural" at any time of life, but tolerance for it did decrease with age.

And finally there was the faculty for speech. As elsewhere in Polynesia, Te Pitians took great pleasure in talking and rewarded oratorical excellence with attention and praise. Individuals past early childhood who spoke with awkwardness were often labelled *ma'au,* which also included the meaning of simplemindedness and even idiocy. In fact, in both Sunday and secular schools much time was spent on development of verbal skills. Yet I found no evidence in native belief or preference that would directly link talking with aging. Silence or speech-awkwardness was not considered to be a mark of general age retardation per se, nor verbal facility a mark of general precocity.

As described above, in terms of state-defined rules and practices a Te Pitian's life-progression proceeded by clearly demarcated stages: first, the period between conception and birth (or registration); second, a lengthy period of minority, which was terminated by attainment of age twenty-one (or in some cases, prior to twenty-one in consequence of certain actions deemed by law to emancipate); and third, a period of full majority which was terminated by biological death. The stage of minority also consisted of a series of substages defined in terms of chronological age and characterized by smaller gradations in rights and responsibilities regarding material welfare, school attendance, and legal culpability.

The Te Pitians I questioned about these matters were aware of state rules about school attendance and about the crucial twenty-one-year age threshold, but except for the parental-consent requirement attached to early marriages they were largely ignorant of and unconcerned with the other aspects of minority, as defined by the state.[16]

The Protestant Church's conceptualization of membership stages located the boundary between *tamari'i* and *taure'are'a* at the end of regular Sunday School attendance, which occurred at about age fifteen to sixteen for girls, somewhat earlier in the case of most boys. A parishioner became potentially eligible to be an *'ētāretia,* a Communicant, at age fifteen, but no Te Pitian had actually done so within memory. In fact, during the times of my visits there were no Communicants in either parish under age twenty-five. Earlier than that (I was informed by both pastors), no Tahitian settles down suffi- ciently to acquire the other qualifications deemed essential for Commu- nicant status. And, as already mentioned, until a post-Sunday Schooler did become a Communicant he (or she) was labelled *taure'are'a,* whatever his or her age.

Fifteen was also the minimum age for joining a sodality, and most Te Pi- tians did such at this age, or after leaving Sunday School if that occurred later.

Turning now to Te Pitians' everyday "native" conceptualization of life progression, the major stages after *'aiūra'a* were *tamari'ira'a, taure'are'a, pa'arira'a* (maturity), and *rū'aura'a* (old age). In addition, as mentioned in Chapter VII, all Tahitian residents over age fourteen (or school-leaving, whichever came later) were labeled *hui ra'atira* and as such were, unless aged (i.e., sixty and over) or otherwise physically incapacitated, required to con- tribute (usually in the form of services) to community enterprises such as road building and wharf repair (in the case of males; females were usually exempt from all such services).

In some everyday contexts, the word *tamari'i* meant "the children (de- scendant or "fed") of so-and-so" but when suffixed with *-ra'a* (particle in- dicating time or place of an event) it carried the meaning of *childhood,* a life stage between *'aiūra'a* and *taure'are'a* and one which Te Pitians conceived of in terms of some fairly definite behavior patterns, however hazy their ideas concerning the "natural" or "proper" age such behavior begins and ends.

Childhood was considered to be the most "natural" age of *ha'uti,* or play (*te ha'uti te huru ta te mau tamari'i*). And closely associated with this expecta- tion that children were incessantly playful was the notion that they pos- sessed no knowledge about the more deeply "profound" or "serious" (*hohonu*) matters of life and that they were almost wholly lacking in good judgment about such matters. (Playfulness in adults was not regarded in all instances

---

[16]Although an inexpensive edition of the *Code Civil* was on sale in Pape'ete, to the best of my knowledge no Te Pitian owned one—or had even seen one.

as necessarily linked with ignorance and irresponsibility but there was undoubtedly believed to be some connection.) What constituted "profound" was, of course, subject to local definition. Some European parents are fearfully reluctant to let their children wander freely about the countryside, while encouraging them to learn how to use money. Most Te Pitian parents I knew about gave scarcely a thought to their children's roamings, including places Europeans would call dangerous, but considered money too "profound" a concern for children to be entrusted with or even learn about.

This does not mean that positive efforts were not made to teach children any technical skills. Parents were to be seen actively, and often pleasurably, engaged in instructing even four- and five-year-olds in such special skills as canoe paddling, line or cast-net fishing, sewing, plaiting, dancing, etc., and evidently took pride in their accomplishments. Most such activities will be seen to be physical, or mainly so. In contrast, however, most adults considered some things to be too "profound" for children to begin to grasp, e.g., such intellectual subjects as Tahiti's past and contemporary politics or the meanings of Biblical passages. And the actions most parents did not expect, or one might conclude did not even desire, their children to perform were those requiring mental decisions between alternate courses, especially those involving transactions of money or of goods convertible into money.

The kinds of knowledge and skill gained in school were in a somewhat different category. As previously described, very few adults considered these in themselves to be desirable ends; most looked upon them as means to ends, either desirable or dispensable according to individual evaluation. In any event, knowledge acquired in school referred mostly to the world beyond Te Piti; it was not a prerequisite to local authority or wealth or salvation or, except to a minor degree, local prestige. For those few who were oriented beyond life in the village, schooling was one means of starting off on that quest. But even for these few, the very fact that only children attended school served to devalue schooling; it was an activity of "mere" children. A few parents took pride in their children's accomplishments in school, but usually as means to some end and not because of the intrinsic value of the things learned. And even such parents as these did not consider themselves to be any less superior to their better-schooled offspring in judgment or in knowledge of the more "serious" matters of life.

In addition to the special skills that parents encouraged their children to learn, by explicit instruction and verbal reward, there were some other activities expected of children. A parent would take delight in watching a small child propel a canoe or plait a leaf container but would rarely punish one for ignorance or failure in such matters. On the other hand, many parents—not all of them, however—voiced the expectation that "children *ought* to help" at such tasks as fetching and carrying, pig feeding, rubbish clearing, baby tending, and, for girls, dishwashing and laundering. In terms of norms, there was virtually no age limit for beginning such work; and in the opinion of many parents, children ought to share in domestic work to the limit of their physical strength.

Parents also indicated by word and action that children ought to be well embarked on the route to social sex-differentiation by school age but opinions and practices differed as to when this process should actually begin.

One important aspect of sex differentiation had to do with clothing, which was also differentiated according to stage of life. This subject was discussed in an earlier chapter (pages 88–90), hence will not be described again here, but the reader is invited to review that discussion inasmuch as body-grooming in general, and clothing in particular, were so definitely, even definitively, associated with life stage.

Te Pitian native opinions concerning when in life one may or should commence sexual intercourse were somewhat mixed. Sexual intercourse was no mystery to Te Piti's children; nor in everyday life was it presented to them as something wicked. Sound sleepers though they were, they could not avoid now and then witnessing their elders' lovemaking; and most adults made little or no effort to inhibit their conversation about sexual matters within hearing of children. Copulating dogs produced vast amusement before old and young, males and females, separately or together; and the reactions I noted from adults walking by a place where some seven- and eight-year-olds were playing at copulation was laughter and good-natured derision.

Boys and girls played together until thirteen or fourteen, and much of this play was rough—shoving, hitting, ducking under water, etc.; girls, about as strong and agile as boys, asked and received no quarter because of their sex. Among the older ones, some of this play had sexual content—grabbing at each other's clothes or genitals. The only parental reaction I noted to such horseplay was an occasional mild "you're too old for that sort of play," from the older relatives of a girl.

Among younger children, mixed play included some earnest attempts at copulation. The older people who provided this information—no great revelation to me!—seemed highly diverted by such antics, even when their own daughters and sons were involved.

Then—the age is difficult to fix—mixed play began to decrease. Boys tended to drop out of these groups earlier than girls; it was not unusual to see girls of sixteen and seventeen—or even older—playing or roughhousing with younger girls and boys, but a boy past about fifteen who continued in these mixed events was likely to become known as a "sissy" (*māhū*).[17]

---

[17]As noted earlier, *māhū* was a very complex term, but "sissy" is an apt gloss in this context.

Meanwhile, sex "play" tended to become less innocent, it having been generally assumed that all boys and most girls past about eleven would fornicate, or at least try to do so, if opportunity were there. The question arises: how did Te Piti's adults adjudge these real or suspected actions?

For nearly two hundred years, the natives of these Polynesian Islands have been stereotyped as sex "libertarians," and there is much historical evidence to support this popular European judgment. Even a century and a half of missionary puritanism had not translated sex into a sullying pastime. Yet the fact remains that most Te Pitian parents and other older relatives of girls past about eleven firmly objected to extramarital fornication on their part. (I use the word "marital" in the relatively loose sense defined earlier) Parental reaction to infraction ranged from angry denunciation and savage beatings to mild lectures, but it was virtually universal (that is to say, there may have been exceptions, although I did not hear of one). Moreover, this parental attitude persisted until the girl reached about twenty, or until she became more or less "married," and it was expressed most clearly in the very high value attached to veiled-bride weddings, as already described.

Thus, alongside a popular set of attitudes about sex, which can only be described as matter-of-fact and nonprudish, there was an alternative but distinctly preferred norm to the effect that young females should not engage in actual sexual intercourse until they were "married." Attitudes about how females should conduct their sexual relations for the remainder of their lives after "marriage," which usually meant after 20 or so, were based largely on social factors other than age.

With respect to males, chastity in general, and youthful virginity in particular, were not normatively defined in native attitudes. One occasionally heard about a father berating his sons for playing around with young girls, but mainly on account of the troubles that might be stirred up with the girls' relatives.[18]

The only native rule regarding when a male should commence sexual activity was the one implicit in the pattern of supercision (*tehe*). Sometime between the ages of about ten and fourteen, Te Piti's boys underwent this operation. It was a minor one and was carried out in relative secrecy but without ceremony and performed by some older male noted for his deftness with a razor blade. The widespread attitude was that a male should not begin the regime of regular and frequent sexual intercourse until he had been supercised—otherwise, it was said, his sexual partners would ridicule him for

---

[18]Also, older relatives would occasionally warn a boy against copulating with promiscuous females because of infection; and there were a few parents, especially in Fatata, who frowned on liaisons because of the possibility of their developing into socially unsuitable marriages.

being a mere child or might even refuse their favors, contemptuously chid-
ing him for being "like a dog; unsupercised." And, like all personal shortcomings in Te Piti, the knowledge of this one soon became public information and the basis for widespread ridicule. The weight of this ridicule was
not that "so and so had not yet been supercised"; that information will
have already been available and did not provoke much adverse criticism.
Rather, it was aimed at the boy's pretensions to sexual adequacy while still
bearing the physical sign of childhood. (For more on the psychological significance of supercision see Levy, 1973.)

Relations between Parents and Children

In line with the "economic" focus of this study, that aspect of parent-
child relations will be accented here, although a few observations on other
dimensions of the relationship will be given as background.

To begin with, "parent" should be read to mean anyone performing that
role—actual biological parent, stepparent, foster parent, etc. And "children"
means in this context those under the *taure'are'a* stage. Also, it should be kept
in mind that many of Te Piti's domestic households were multifamily or
contained relatives in addition to parent-child units, some of them acting
like parents, thereby complicating, e.g., in some cases "spreading," the
parent-child relationship itself.

Except to accompany their parents elsewhere, Te Piti's children were seldom away from a "parental" home or its close environs for more than a few
hours at a time. Older children spent part of their lives at school and at the
villages' favorite play sites (e.g., plazas, beaches, lagoon shallows, boat land-
ings) but younger ones were seldom outside their own houses or house yards
(which were fairly capacious in Fatata but very narrow in most of Atea).
This difference meant that Atea's parents were literally *closer* to their younger children than were those of Fatata, but I do not know what effects, if
any, this circumstance had on other aspects of their relationships.

Because of their architecture and generally small size, few of Te Piti's
houses permitted their residents much "privacy" (not that privacy was necessarily desired or sought after). Asleep as well as awake, Te Pitians were accustomed to being in a proximity to one another that most middle-class
Americans would consider intolerably congested. Beginning with the appearance of signs of physical puberty, boys and girls slept as far removed
from each other as space would permit, and in a one-room sleeping house
that could not have been very far. But even so I heard of no Te Pitian who
regretted the size of his house or who expressed a wish to enlarge it to meet
this particular requirement or to accommodate additional children or other
residents.

The situation just described has implications for many aspects of interpersonal relationships, but it is the "economic" ones that concern us here. And those, I suggest, consisted mainly of their effects, or rather noneffects, upon Te Pitians' perceived housing needs which, had they been expansive, would have required labor and money to fulfill. I cannot say which preceded the other, the toleration of social "crowding" or the smallness of houses, but in Te Piti of 1954–55 the two circumstances coexisted in what appeared to be a mutually supporting way. That situation was already well established by the time Europeans first arrived on the scene and has persisted ever since, despite the efforts of missionaries and others to introduce more "civilized" standards of social space. For a time, the reformers appear to have succeeded to some extent—in Fatata, at least, as witnessed by the presence there of several ancient, relatively large and multiroomed "vanilla houses." (Even the "vanilla houses" were smaller in Atea.) However, most of the houses that had been constructed since the "vanilla-house" era, including the very recent fashionable "Pape'ete suburban'" types described above (page 93), were much smaller in actual floor space.

Te Pitians were in general agreement that parents ought to exercise authority over their children, and most parents did in fact do so, although with varying degrees of application, consistency, and effectiveness. Some parents were comprehensively and consistently strict and relentless in applying punitive sanctions. Others were haphazard, inconsistent, and lax in follow-through. Also, there were differences regarding the locus of authority; in some families it was the father, in others mainly the mother, and in still others both. Alongside this variability there were two other situations that obtained more universally and that contained more specifically "economic" implications: one had to do with the nature of parental sanctions, the other with the kinds of economic matters reserved for parental decision-making.

Regarding the sanctions parents applied to enforce their authority, those rarely if ever included objects or things that cost money. Parents neither rewarded good behavior with, say, special foods or store-bought sweets or cinema tickets, nor did they punish bad behavior by withholding material things. (As will be mentioned in another section, the threat of deprivation, specifically of land inheritance, was sometimes used *vis-à-vis* older offspring, but I did not once hear it mentioned or implied towards the young children now being discussed.[19]

---

[19]Though having little direct "economic" relevance, I can note that the most palpable form of punitive sanction I saw parents applying to their children was physical chastisement or the threat thereof—slapping, hitting with a stick, etc., and often very hard. I mention this for two reasons. First, because it evidently reinforced, and quite effectively, all the other behavior, of

Regarding the kinds of matters reserved for parental decision-making, those included almost everything having to do with money. When children were given money to spend, a rare occurrence, it was for specific things. "Allowances" were practically unheard of; even on those few occasions when children earned money (mainly by harvesting vanilla), they were not allowed to spend it entirely as they pleased. As a consequence of these constraints, the frequently voiced assertion by adults that "money matters are the domain of adults" was in fact very nearly true.

The kinds of transactions normatively and actually characteristic of parent-child relations consisted mainly of pool-sharing and of altruistic (i.e., nonreciprocable) giving by parent to child. The expectations regarding pool-sharing have been described above, i.e., parents were expected to provide their children with the material essentials for living but the latter were also expected to contribute their services to the domestic economy up to the limits of their physical abilities, except during the time required by school (in school) and except for some time devoted to play. School time was set by law. Some parents considered that time to be excessive, as a detraction from time that should have been spent in domestic work. A few others, mainly in Fatata, considered schooling important enough (as an investment for future earning power) to justify even longer absences from work. Beyond those there were, of course, other wide differences in the amounts of time children were required to work and were permitted to play and differences also in parents' expectations concerning the kinds of work their children should do, including children of about the same age. The whole range of such parental attitudes was to be found in both villages, but I gained the impression—I did not inquire systematically about the matter—that, corresponding to their views about schooling, the parents of Fatata on the average demanded somewhat less domestic and other subsistence work from their children than did those of Atea.

Altruistic giving, by parents to children, was also characteristic of the relationship, both normatively and actually, and in both objects and services. It was, in fact, the main example people gave when called on to define the affect-word *here*—which, incidentally, was most typically applied to the feelings said to exist between parent and child.

There were differences, sometimes wide ones, between individual parents with respect to the stages of growth of their children when altruistic giving began to be replaced by expectations of pool-share work, and not only

---

parents and others, which served to make Te Pitians, old and young, generally obedient to "official" authority. And secondly, because my observations in this matter appear to differ from those of some other writers who have emphasized the noncorporal side of child punishment in Tahiti.

differences between one parent and another but sometimes differences displayed by one parent towards his or her separate children. Again, I made no systematic observations of these behaviors but I saw enough of them to learn that the range of differences was quite wide. I saw families in which four-year-olds were given fairly exacting household chores and others in which five- and six-year-olds continued to be treated as helpless toddlers. And I saw families in which a three-year-old was indulged in every whim while its four-year-old sibling was made to fetch and carry.

In view of Fatatan parents' (on the average) more indulgent attitude towards the quantity of work expected of their children, it is logical to suppose that they were more indulgent about the age of beginning that work as well, but concerning that I cannot judge with any certainty.

Finally, it is possible that some of Te Piti's parents viewed some of their contributions towards their children's welfare as a form of direct exchange—specifically, as a long-term loan. I never heard the parents of young children characterize any part of their contributions in such terms, but I did hear, and not infrequently, aged individuals imply as much when complaining that their now-adult offspring were not assisting them economically, "despite all they had done for" the latter during their infancy and childhood.

Youth

In terms of Te Piti's native rules and expectations, *taure'are'a* was perhaps the most clearly defined life stage in behavioral attributes, if not in chronological age boundaries. As its label may indicate, it was the stage for pleasure-seeking; but it was also the time for hard work. In other words, it was a time for unremitting physical activity, for hard work relieved by bursts of equally energetic play, the assumption having been that bodily strength and vitality (including sexuality) reached their peak at this stage of life.

There was something quite fascinating about Te Piti's young men behaving as young men were expected to behave; one of the clearest expressions of this occurred regularly out of Atea, when the local launches were taken to Fare, the islands' overseas port, to meet the weekly schooner from Pape'ete. During the chilly hour-long predawn trip to Fare, the mood of crew and passengers would be quietly subdued, still drowsy and shivering. On arrival, people would warm up and liven up on coffee, and the crew of young men would unload their produce and load up the Pape'ete goods destined for the village stores—heavy work carried out with vigor and spirit. As the launch pulled away from the wharf headed for home, the youths would sprawl out for a moment to catch their breaths and then plunge into *'arearea*—"enjoyment." Someone would begin by knocking off the cap of a bottle and passing the beer around, someone else would begin strumming a ukulele or guitar, and they would all fall to: singing, yelping, jostling together, behaving drunkenly long before the mild beer could have begun to act; announcing to themselves and the world at large that "youth is now youthing," that it is now, conventionally and relentlessly, having a wild, good time. Meanwhile, younger passengers would look on in appreciation and envy and most older ones would smile tolerantly and probably nostalgically. Even the frowns of the more sedate adults could not disguise their attitude that, "silly and annoying as it is, youths are necessarily youthful."

A milder and more frequent expression of youthful amusement used to take place in both villages three or four evenings a week. After finishing the day's work and the evening meal of coffee and bread, several youths, and occasionally two or three young women, would gather outside someone's house to talk and make music and sometimes dance. Older villagers would often sit near the group and join in their talk, but the occasion was unquestionably not theirs. (And some patronizing elder would invariably explain to the watching ethnographer: "The young people are at it again.")

Most adults occasionally set aside the serious business of making a living, or practicing Christianity, for periods of just as deliberate pleasuremaking. In contrast, with youths the proportions between pleasuremaking and other activities were conventionally reversed—if, that is, one includes the "pleasure" youths were expected to derive from work itself.

Te Pitians did not, normatively, link work jobs directly with stage of life. As noted above, even children were expected to perform domestic jobs to the limit of their physical abilities; and most adults insisted (and most younger people in principle agreed) that by fourteen or fifteen at latest an individual should be working like an adult, it having been assumed that by this time he or she will have acquired the requisite physical strength, the stamina, and the manual skills. And to anticipate a later discussion, advancing age did not merit the privilege of lighter work except insofar as it was accompanied by physical incapacity or, in rare cases, supervisory authority. (Reference here is to such common jobs as clearing, digging, carrying, canoe-paddling, tree-felling, sewing, plaiting, roofing, etc., and not to special skills like spearfishing under water, canoe fishing, fishnet knotting, and hat-making.) The application of these norms was to be observed at almost any large cooperative task such as houseroofing or feast preparation, where, except for the very young or the decrepitly old, people worked together at identical tasks regardless of age. Indeed, the main difference in native ideology between the working habits of young and old (specifically of young and old males) was the expectation that young men *would* enjoy, one could even say *should* enjoy, their work more, which was not unconnected with the expectation and the actual observable fact that young men tended to work in groups whenever feasible. It was this allegedly greater pleasure in work, expressed by playful exuberance, which added even more substance to the meaning of *taure'are'a* as the time of pleasure-seeking.

While expecting from "young" people a full share of work, most adults continued to regard them somewhat as children in matters concerning "profound" knowledge or in transactions involving valuable family resources. Young people were considered to be "too ignorant," for example, to provide the ethnographer with "true" information about political issues; or they were "too irresponsible" to have a voice in managing household expenditures—even, in many instances, though they contributed large shares to family income. (Needless to say, many young people disagreed with this evaluation.)

The contrast between school-acquired knowledge and native wisdom concerned with socially more relevant aspects of life shows up sharply here. In neither village was the achiever of a primary school diploma (*certificat*) accorded greater voice in household or village-wide councils than was the youth who could barely read.

The postulates and norms just listed about behavior during "youth" refer to females as well as males, except for the nature of the "pleasures" that females could with impunity indulge in. In addition to the double standards in sexuality, which have already been noted, young women were expected to express their youthful exuberance in much less boisterous accents. And whereas drinking and drunkenness was fairly "natural" with young males, it was universally deplored for young females.

And finally, in the matter of youthful "ignorance" and "irresponsibility," young women faced a double prejudice, against both their youth and their femaleness; in this respect, they were considered even more childlike than were young males.

As we saw, Te Pitians remained with their parents—some "parents"—throughout their stage of childhood. Then upon reaching youthhood, some of them began to leave their parental homes and their home villages, temporarily or even permanently. A few left for secondary schooling. Others left to see the world, or to earn money, or to visit kinfolk, or to seek a spouse, or to escape an intolerable home situation—or some combination of these. At the time of my 1954–55 visits, twenty-three of Te Piti's ninety-nine usually resident unmarried young people were living elsewhere, for one reason or another. Of these, sixteen were males and seven were females. And of the total, Fatata showed relatively more absentees than Atea (i.e., 28 percent of all Fatata's unmarried *taure'are'a* and 17 percent of Atea's)—a difference to be explained mainly by the larger number of the former attending secondary schools in Pape'ete and by Pape'ete's generally easier access.

In any case, the figures also reveal that most of Te Piti's unmarried *taure'are'a* remained in their parental homes until they married[20]—a circumstance that raises questions concerning the "economic" aspects of relationships between parents and their coresident progeny of this life-stage.

As described earlier, offspring of childhood age were expected by their parents to contribute their services to the household pool-share economy; parents differed somewhat in the extent of their expectations but the most common standard was "up to the limits of the child's physical abilities." The same standard was applied to youthhood male offspring, although regarding these it was commonly assumed that at this stage of life the individual's physical abilities, or at least physical strength and stamina, had reached the peak. Thus, youthhood males were expected to work physically as hard as or harder than persons of any other age. Also, whereas most parents were at times insouciant and pliant in the mental account they kept of their childhood progeny's contributions to the household pool, they tended to be exact and exacting in this regard *vis-à-vis* those of their youthhood ones. But only up to a point.

Although most youthhood males continued to work with their fathers, producing food and cash crops, many of them also began to earn separate "incomes." Some of that income consisted of the fish that was consumed by the household and that was viewed as partial substitute for other kinds of contributions. And some consisted of money, part of which was used to buy food and other goods for the household—but not all. For, most unmarried youths kept some of their money earnings for their own individual uses, and most older Te Pitians with whom I discussed this situation considered it to be "right," although there were some fairly diverse opinions regarding the percentage that could rightfully be retained in this way.

Youthhood home-residing females were also expected to contribute more services to their household pools than their younger sisters, but for those few who earned any money, such earnings were usually regarded as being exclusively their own. (Even some parents I questioned who were directly affected by these arrangements seemed to consider them just.)

What of those unmarried *taure'are'a* who had left their home villages and were residing elsewhere: did they remit any of their earnings to their parents to help maintain the home household? According to my inquiries, very few of them did so. In fact, some of them were receiving some money allowances from their parents which, as far as I could discover, were not usually "debited to their accounts" when they finally returned home. (An exception to

---

[20]And, as was pointed out earlier (pages 299–303), many of them continued to reside in or very close to their parents' homes after marriage as well.

this did, however, occasionally occur with respect to an absentee's customary share of profits from jointly held land. See page 111.)

One should not assume from the above generalities that household pool-sharing involving youthhood and unmarried males and females was all cut and dried. In some such households I knew, the pooling and sharing appeared to work smoothly—either by means of contented consensus or strong paternal management. But there were other such households in which pool-share equity (as, of course, locally defined) was maintained at a cost of considerable stress or was not maintained at all. An attempt to measure this facet of household economy will be presented in Chapter X. To anticipate some of those findings: the presence of an unmarried youth in a household evidently served in some cases to challenge or even to reduce paternal authority over management of the household economy—but only to a limited extent.

As related earlier, the French *Code Civil* specified that an individual remained a "minor" until he or she reached age twenty-one, or until *émancipation*. And while a "minor," the individual remained under "paternal authority" (*la puissance paternelle*) with respect to freedom of movement and contract-making, application of coercive sanctions, etc. Few Te Pitians were even aware of the Administration's rules on such matters, which, however, mattered little, since they were in many respects quite similar to their own traditional views about family governance.

I found few dissenters in Te Piti to the proposition that parents, more specifically fathers, possessed the right to make most decisions that concerned their unmarried offspring, whatever the latter's ages. Even those *taure'are'a* and their sympathizers who objected, silently or loudly, to their own parents' treatment of themselves would qualify their objections by pointing to parental *excesses* in this regard, e.g., to a father who was *frequently* drunk and abusive or who contributed virtually *nothing* to the household larder, or to a mother who required her daughter to do nearly all the domestic chores.

There were, however, some wide differences in parents' modes of asserting and enforcing their rightful authority, and parents differed with respect to the amount of latitude they allowed their unmarried offspring in decision-making. But in matters of household management, parental authority tended to be undelegated, firm, and fairly effective in most families.

Some parents probably continued giving goods altruistically to their sons and daughters throughout the latters' *taure'are'a* stage of life and even beyond. I recorded a few instances of transactions that can be classified as such and others that involved such gift-giving from *taure'are'a* to parent. I also recorded a few instances of direct exchange, in the form of (interest-free) loans of money or other things, between parent and *taure'are'a* son or daughter. Also, I recorded a few instances of what the principals themselves described as "loan repayment." Typical of these was the solicitous support which one youth gave to his elderly and ailing parents "because they helped me when I was a child." In fact, the *Code Civil* itself specified that "*les infants doivent des aliments à leur père et mère ou autres ascendants qui sont dans le besoin*" (Article 205)—but, needless to say, Te Pitians were unaware of this prescript. However, by far the largest amount of goods that circulated between family members of this kind did so according to the equation underlying pool-sharing.

Siblings and Alternate Generations

During their progression towards adulthood, most Te Pitians resided in households containing siblings, actual and/or foster, and some of them in households containing other kinfolk as well, e.g., "cousins," aunts and uncles (consanguineal or affinal), nieces and nephews, grandparents, etc. Since this study is not intended to be an exhausting sociological description of the whole domain of kinship, I will offer only a few observations on the subject—those directly pertinent to the "economic" aspects of kin relationship—and will not attempt a systematic account of all specific dyads, as is customarily done in many general ethnographies.

In pursuing this limited objective, I am, however, not far removed from the way the Te Pitians themselves practiced kinship. In the first place, they, like other Polynesians utilizing the so-called Hawaiian system of kin terminology, made use of a relatively small number of kin terms. This does not imply, necessarily, that they thought about or acted towards all relatives bearing the same kin-term label in identical ways, but the prevalence of such labelling must surely have had *some* correspondence with nonverbal thought and action.

The kin terms that I elicited from them by direct questioning were as follows:

tupuna—"ancestor/ress." This term was used, as reference and address, for all consanguines of second or higher genealogical levels and occasionally for affines of those levels as well.

metua—"parent." A term of reference for "mother" (i.e., *metua vahine*), "father" (i.e., *metua tane*), and their siblings and other same-genealogical-level collaterals.

ho'ovai—"father" or "mother" of spouse. Used mainly as a term of reference, usually for the spouse's own parents, actual, step-, or foster.

tua'ana—older same-sex sibling or cousin (mostly reference).

teina—younger same-sex sibling or cousin (mostly reference).

tu'āne—brother or male cousin of a female (mostly reference).

tuahine—sister or female cousin of a male (mostly reference).

tane—"husband"; occasionally "husband's brother" (address and reference).

vahine—"wife"; occasionally "wife's sister" (address and reference).

tao'ete—"wife's brother," "husband's sister" (mainly reference).

tamaiti—"son" or "nephew" (address and reference).

tamāhine—"daughter" or "niece" (address and reference).

mo'otua—"grandchild" and all consanguines of second descending genealogical level (address and reference).

hina—"great-grandchild" and all consanguines of third descending genealogical level (address and reference).

hinarere—"great-great-grandchild" and all consanguines of fourth descending genealogical level (reference).

In addition, *taea'e* was occasionally used, mainly from the pulpit, to refer to "brothers and sisters," and *hoa*, the usual word for "friend," was sometimes used as a more "respectable" term for a person's spouse, like English "helpmate."

Considered comparatively in a universal sense, the most salient features of this set of terms are its emphasis throughout on genealogical level and on consanguinity (in contrast to affinity) and its disregard for distinctions between lineality and collaterality among consanguines. Sex differences are also denoted, but only in one's own genealogical level and in those of one's parents and offspring. And birth order is denoted in one's own genealogical level alone.

Such were the normative definitions; actual usage of these terms (within my hearing) was more flexible. For example, the (French-derived?) terms *māmā* and *pāpā* were used much more frequently than *metua* (*tane, vahine*) for both address and reference, and were extended not only to parents' same-genealogical-level collaterals but to affines (including spouse's parents) and other acquaintances of corresponding age. Moreover, in combination with *ru'au* (aged), *māmā* and *pāpā* were used for grandparents and for many other elderly persons, whether kinfolk or not. Another example: *mo'otua* served as a general term, not only for consanguines of second descending genealogical level but for those of third and fourth, etc., levels as well.

As for any patterns of interpersonal behavior normatively associated with the above terms, I managed to elicit only a few such statements, and most of those were diffuse and obviously ad hoc. (For example, "a person ought to show respect for his *metua*." "And what about his *tupuna* [or *tua'ana*? or *ho'ovai*?]?" "Yes, to them, too.")

In other words, while kinship enveloped the Te Pitians in their everyday lives, its parameters were to be sought more in actual situations than in categories defined by "authoritative" kin terms. Such situations included household coresidence, co-ownership of land, and cooperation on ceremonial occasions. Some generalizations about those and other kin-involved situations are presented elsewhere in this study; here I will mention only those most ubiquitous kinds of kin relationships (other than that of parent and child) in which preadult Te Pitians participated as members of households, namely, their relationships with siblings and with grandparents.

Nearly every Te Pitian lived his preadult years residing in a household containing at least one sibling—full, step-, or foster (*fa'a'amu*). Interactions between such siblings were, of course, complicated by the exact genealogical nature of the relationship, but there were two other factors that influenced all of them, namely, sex and relative age.

The most conspicuous things about the relationship between brother and sister were their avoidance of sexual or sex-colored interactions, and the advantage possessed by the brother in command and decision-making. The sexual taboo commenced with puberty and consisted of avoidance of proximity during sleep, of seeing or touching one another's genitals, of discussing sex-related subjects in one another's presence, etc. Some informants said that the two ought not to sleep even in the same room but agreed that this rule was sometimes impossible to abide by.

According to many Te Pitians, the avoidance rule applied not only between siblings and cousins but between all male and female consanguines of similar age, regardless of their relative genealogical levels. In fact, according to my observations, relative age was more important than genealogical level in defining an avoidance relationship among collaterals. I saw much evidence in support of the statements just mentioned, and in addition, I saw siblings of widely discrepant ages, e.g., a forty-year-old woman and her twenty-year-old stepbrother, behaving towards one another in the freest of ways (e.g., joking about each other's sex life).

As for a brother's authority over his sister, this usually tended to be effective only if he was older (and such authority was, in fact, simply a specific application of the generic superiority accorded males over females). According to my observations, a brother's authority over his unmarried and co-resident sister in household economics (e.g., in pool-sharing) was exercised mainly in loco parentis, when the father was absent or dead. Brothers also tended to outweigh their sisters in decision-making related to the use or disposal of jointly owned land—although there were instances, some of them marked by high drama, when strong-willed sisters managed to prevail.

I will not even attempt to list the many incidents I observed pertaining to the goods that passed between brothers and sisters, both "altruistically" and in direct exchange, but cannot neglect mention of the countless hours that many sisters spent nursemaiding their younger brothers (far more so than the reverse). Part of those services was in fulfillment of a daughter's prescribed contribution to her family's pool-sharing economy, but, I am convinced, some of them can be credited to the sisters' unselfish affection for their younger charges.

Interaction between same-sex siblings was influenced weightily by the rule that "the older ought to take care of the younger, and the younger ought to obey the older"—but mainly during the younger's preadult (pre-*pa'ari*) years. (The same norm applied as well to different-sex siblings, extenuated somewhat by the generic authority assigned to males over females.)

The "taking care of" part of this formula was manifested most actively during the younger's late infancy and early childhood, when its older siblings, and especially its older sisters, served as part- or full-time nurses (typically, as substitute for the mother, who was by that time nursing a later child). Undoubtedly, many of those services were performed willingly and affectionately—but many others of them were carried out under parental duress. (And some children I knew had adopted ingenious ways of penalizing their troublesome charges, e.g., by walking faster than the younger could manage when jointly carrying heavy loads or by handing the younger a burning hot piece of food).

In a few instances, pairs of siblings continued or resumed residing together even after the younger one had become adult—which, of course, implicated them in continuous pool-sharing and other transactions characteristic of co-residence. But transactions between siblings did not always cease when they resided separately—nor did those transactions always conform to the standard rule that "consanguines (*fēti'i*) in general, and siblings in particular, ought to help one another" (i.e., give objects and services to one another nonreciprocably, or at least in the form of long-term, interest-free loans). Some adult siblings I knew did, in fact, engage continuously in such transactions, accompanied by affection and mutual concern. But there were others who, while maintaining friendly demeanors towards one another, conducted their transactions "commercially," i.e., on the basis of sale, barter, and interest-bearing loans. And there were still other pairs of siblings who had become estranged to the point of mutual avoidance or feud. Several kinds of reasons can be pointed to to account for those wide differences in sibling relationships, e.g., the friendship or quarrels of their respective spouses or children, church or political issues, etc., but the most influential had to do with jointly owned property, mostly land, as will be described later on.

The extent of an older sibling's authority over a younger varied from family to family. I saw instances of teenagers beating younger siblings within the unconcerned, or even approving, view of their parents, and other instances of parents forbidding an older child even to reprimand an obviously troublesome younger one. Some of the latter instances occurred, characteristically, in mixed families, e.g., when a stepmother sought to shield one of her own children from one of her husband's, but differences in family size, parental temperament, etc., were also factors in bringing about such differences.

In any case, an older sibling's authority was usually limited to younger ones living in the same household and became reduced nearly to the point of absence when the latter became adults. Thereafter, the principal, and in most cases the only, form of authority exercised by an older sibling over a younger one had to do with the use or disposal of their jointly owned property, mainly land. And, in such matters it was not strictly a situation of an older sibling's decision being weightier than a younger one's, but rather of an *eldest's* (and usually an eldest male's) decision being weightier than those of all younger siblings.

I turn now to relationships between preadults and their grandparents. (There were a few instances of adults having grandparents still alive, but in most of these the latter were almost vegetably senile.)

In 1954–55, there were twenty-six households in Te Piti—seven in Atea and nineteen in Fatata—that contained parents and their children plus one or two of the parents' parents. (There were, in addition, several households containing children and one or more grandparents but no parents as such, but these units were so similar, economically, to parent-child ones that I have classed them with the latter for the purposes of this study. Page 392ff.)

It was easy enough to elicit statements from Te Pitians concerning how grandparents and grandchildren *should* behave towards one another, and at the core of all such statements was the generality that the former ought to "help" the latter, and the latter to "help," "obey," and "respect" the former.

Other, less sententious, expressions concerning this relationship can be extracted from remarks about episodes involving particular grandparent-grandchild pairs, but the norms thus educed are identical with and no more specific than the generality just mentioned.

The "help" provided by grandparents comprised a wide range of objects and services. At a minimum, it consisted of occasional nursemaiding and small presents (e.g., cinema tickets, treats at the store); at the maximum, it included full parental nurturance for days or weeks at a time while the parents were absent or disabled. Also, there were a few cases in which grandchildren, normally resident in their parents' households, spent weeks or months at a time "visiting" their grandparents. Some informants asserted that in all such transactions, grandparents tended to be more "generous" than parents (i.e., to indulge in more altruistic giving), and that may well have been so, although I did not inquire systematically into the matter.

As for "help" from grandchild to grandparent, that differed not only with individual inclination but in large measure with the ages of each pair. Some grandparents directly extracted more services from their grandchildren than the latters' own parents tried to do, while others asked for or received almost none. Similarly with objects, some *taure'are'a* made a point of sharing their windfalls, e.g., of cash, fish, pork, with grandparents, coresident or otherwise, while others were notoriously selfish in this regard.

"Obedience" and "respect" also varied with grandparent-grandchild pairs. Some of the former were arrantly dictatorial (and effective—or ineffective); others were *marū* (easygoing, benign) and were either disregarded or treated with affection and respectful solicitude. It is possible that differences in, for example, household size or composition, or grandparental affluence, had something to do with the effectiveness of the latters' authority, but I feel certain that personality differences—that unexplainable explain-all—were also implicated.

In any case, before becoming what they called "adult," most Te Pitians lived for twenty or more years in coresidential proximity with persons of various kinds—differentiated in terms of kin linkage, age, sex, and personality. And while a few patterns, some of them having many exemplars, can be educed from the compositions of those households, no two of them were identical in all those componental aspects.

Adulthood

State and church norms regarding the attainment of "adulthood" have already been described, i.e., *majority* in the case of the former, Communicant (*'ētāretia*) in the case of the latter. In the Te Pitians' "native" conceptualization of life stages, the closest equivalent to those categories was *pa'arira'a*. When asked to list the major life stages, Te Pitians did not hesitate to place *pa'arira'a* after *taure'are'a* and before *rū'aura'a*, but it was not clear from that usage whether *pa'ari* referred exclusively to physiological phenomena, to social-behavioral attributes, or to both.

Fruit was *pa'ari* when it was ripe, ready for eating; an animal was *pa'ari* when fully grown and sexually mature; some wood was *pa'ari*, "hard" in opposition to soft and more easily worked. On the other hand, *pa'ari* also referred to behavioral attributes ranging (in terms of English) from "hard bargaining" to "admirable judiciousness."[21] In the first of those current glosses, a "hard" man was one who was cautious and calculating in

---

[21]The Davies Dictionary defines *pa'ari* as: (1) wisdom, knowledge, skill, cunning; (2) wise, knowing, skillful, cunning; (3) mature, old, ripe, hard.

exchange—"like a Chinese"; in the second, he was one who was knowledgeable, serious-minded, careful in judgment, calm, "firm."

From the above, it seems quite clear that Te Pitian usage of *pa'ari* implied a conceptual correlation of what English-speakers would call physical *and* behavioral attributes. (I feel quite certain that we are dealing here with shades of meaning rather than with distinct though homonymous words.) That the correlation appears imperfect is due in part to the inevitable dilemma of translation and in part to the fact that, even within a small language community like this, verbal labels for complex phenomena are seldom unequivocal.

Fortunately (for this ethnographer), there was a more direct method for investigating "meaning," i.e., by learning, in this instance, whom Te Pitians called *pa'ari* in explicit opposition to *taure'are'a* or to *rū'au*. And despite some disagreement about a few borderline cases, which served in fact to encourage discussion of the distinctions, there was enough consensus to provide the following definition: a full *pa'ari* individual was one who:

(1) had discontinued more or less overt sexual promiscuity and settled down with a mate in a seemingly "permanent" marital union and with one—or better two or more—children (whether own offspring or foster children was not important);

(2) had established a large degree of autonomy in subsistence economy, i.e., either by setting up and maintaining a separate household or by contributing heavily to a composite household and exercising a decisive voice in managing and expending its resources;

(3) had given up direct participation in the conventional pleasure-making sessions characteristic of *taure'are'a*.

These transformations were in many respects complementary and tended to take place concurrently. In many cases, they occupied several years and were usually completed by about age twenty-five for males and three to four years younger for females. (Or, such at least was my own observation.) And those, said several informants, were indeed the *appropriate* ages for *taure'are'a* to become *pa'ari*.[22] (But whether they held such opinions before I posed the question and thereby led them to their calculations is, of course, another matter.)

In any event, by the time people had reached a state of physical maturation which I myself judged to be about thirty in males and twenty-five in females, Te Pitians expected them to be "old enough" to conform to the three standards listed above and to bear all the privileges and responsibilities of full community membership, namely:

---

[22]The statement, by some informants, that people became *pa'ari* at age twenty-one was obviously derived from the *Code Civil*.

(1) a full[23] voice in those community-wide decisions not explicitly re-
    served to privileged statuses in church and district government;
(2) full claims on respectful treatment by peers and somewhat deferential
    treatment by children and *taure'are'a*;
(3) full rights to freedom of action—insofar as such "freedom" was locally
    delimited; and
(4) full responsibility for their own acts in violation of local norms.[24]

Old Age

The only state-associated norms regarding old age that had much relevance to Te Piti were those related to eligibility for public office and old-
age welfare. People over sixty-five were no longer eligible for holding the
position of *muto'i* (constable), but age restrictions did not apply to a *tāvana*
(chief). During my 1954–55 visits, there were several persons aged seventy
and over but only three, and those in Fatata, who were receiving such pensions. In Atea, there were several persons who may have been eligible, but
none was actually pensioned. Ateans knew vaguely about the existence of
pensions, but no one had troubled to apply for one.

Another state-associated norm that might conceivably have affected Te
Pitians was the one that reduced the severity of penal sanctions in the cases
of violators aged sixty and over. As far as I could discover, however, no Te
Pitian was aware of this measure—nor was there any immediate likelihood
of any of them being affected by it anyway.

In Protestant Church terms, chronic feebleness (*paruparu*) rather than
chronological age served to define an individual's rights and duties in parish
affairs. That is to say, a parishioner was excused from the usual levies in
money and services when he (or she) became chronically infirm, regardless
of age. There were several clear cases in this category in both parishes—and
a few more cases in which, it was sometimes charged, the individual was
laying claim to *paruparu* falsely and in extenuation of meanness and
indolence.

In "native" conceptualization, *rū'au* primarily meant "old person," and
the reference had to do mainly with chronological aging. Answers to my
query as to the age of becoming *rū'au* varied from fifty to sixty to seventy—a
clear indication that the answers were no better than my naïve question deserved. However, queries about specific individuals did produce much (but

---

[23]"Full," that is, within the limits of sex-based prerogatives.

[24]It should be noted that *pa'arira'a* began several years later than the status of "responsible
citizenship" that Te Pitians labelled *ra'atira* (see Chapter 7).

not total) consensus to the effect that anyone past about sixty was labelled *rū'au* regardless of physical or mental condition.

In this sense, the label *rū'au* also carried the implication that the person in question had begun to experience a marked decrease in physical vitality and in mental alertness. These conclusions found verbal expression in norms to the effect that "old" people should not be required to work as hard as younger ones—they should be excused from participation in community work levees and ought to be supported, in part at least, by their younger relatives. Those few *rū'au* who voluntarily continued active work received praise, and those forced to fend for themselves were widely pitied. Those same sentiments applied also to people who were more or less invalid—but only provided they were within five or ten years of "old age." It was only in cases of palpable infirmity—grossly enlarged elephantiasis, emaciated tuberculosis, and the like—that individuals under about fifty were considered justifiably exempt from normal work load; less obvious cases nearly always aroused charges of malingering.

The statement that Te Pitians believed mental alertness to be impaired by old age requires some qualification. In fact, old age was widely believed to enhance certain kinds of mental activity—principally the recall of events long past and "wisdom" born of those greater perspectives. This belief was based not only on the perfectly obvious fact that only aged individuals had been alive to experience those remote events but also, I suggest, on an uncrystallized assumption to the effect that younger people, still actively engaged in everyday affairs of the contemporary world, did not have much room for thought about past events, i.e., that retirement from everyday preoccupation provided such room.[25]

In addition to recall of ancient events, the wisdom of the aged was believed to be superior with respect to matters contained in the Bible, and this assumption was based on the common observation that some old people did, in fact, spend several hours every week, or even every day, reading the Word of God.

In contrast, the kind of mental activity that was widely believed to be impaired with advancing age concerned such matters as the working of machines, buying and selling, and politics, i.e., with the tactics of everyday living as well as with the strategies for attaining worldly goals. I heard no explicit verbal assertions that "old people ought not to have a voice in contemporary affairs," but inferences to that effect are not unjustified from other remarks made by Te Pitians. Those old people who did occasionally speak up at large political or administrative gatherings were either praised,

---

[25]This metaphor is English, not Tahitian; I know of no Tahitian way of expressing this general proposition.

patronizingly, for "saying such appropriate things despite their age" or politely ignored because of their "obvious" incompetence in such matters.

The first of these kinds of public reactions to "age speaking out of turn" seems to have helped encourage some old people to take delight in asserting, or in otherwise expressing "how clever and agile I am despite my age." But when this reached the extreme—which it occasionally did—of repeated exhibitions of silly boastfulness, younger adults were likely to show their impatience with more than usual gruffness. In fact, most Te Pitians appeared to regard a kind of ponderous dignity to be the most appropriate cloak of old age, although there were occasions when it was shed with impunity, as for example in verbal or other horseplay about sex.

My notes contain only the most indirect evidence about sexual activity in old age. A few men did inquire about European remedies for sexual juvenescence, but I also heard sharp criticisms of several liaisons between old males and young females, most of which, by the way, involved a European or Chinese male. Boasting about sexual vitality was characteristic of talk among youths but tended to drop out of conversation with increasing age, except under the influence of alcohol and *are'are'a*. In fact, although "prudery" is far too strong a word to apply, it did appear that most Te Pitians considered middle-aged sexuality a matter for private pursuit rather than public discussion. On the other hand, save perhaps for pratfall accidents, few things seemed to amuse a Te Pitian so much as ribald sexual allusions from the aged. Let an aged old dame jokingly offer her services to a much younger man and her audience's appreciative laughter would know no bounds. Or, move a decrepit old man to burlesque the sex-colored movements of the Tahitian dance, and public reaction would be nearly convulsive. Far from being berated for senile silliness, such old folk were admired for their wittiness and lost no dignity in the process.

But all that pleasurable cynosure was a far cry from the fate experienced by the more decrepitly aged which, up to a point, was an echo, faint but recognizable, of the way their counterparts were customarily treated in ancient Tahiti (Oliver 1975:466 ff.). In all such cases in Te Piti, the helpless or near-helpless aged were provided by relatives with food and shelter, but in some instances the food appeared to be minimal in quantity and quality; and in most of the instances that I knew of, the support seemed to be tendered, if not grudgingly, then at least impatiently—nothing like the *aroha*, the emotion of compassion, which the local pastors and other moralizers prescribed.

To a European accustomed to encountering the *decrepitly* aged only rarely in public, and then usually within the protective shell of wheelchairs and solicitous attendants, it was always something of a shock to witness aged and infirm Te Pitians trying to move and even trying to carry heavy things around the village, assisted only occasionally and otherwise ignored (except perhaps by someone remarking sententiously, that "the *rū'au*'s relatives ought to look after him better.")

An even later stage of agedness was attained by some Te Pitians who, unable even to move about outside their houses, spent their final months or years in what even by minimal local standards of comfort and social ambience can only be described as squalor and inert solitude. (Regarding the latter, when I conducted my first census, there were two households in each village whose spokesmen did not include in their lists their aged and roombound occupants. In fact, it was only near the end of my stay in one village when I discovered, quite by accident, that one house near mine, whose occupants I knew well, contained also an ancient couple.)

Death

French laws doubtless embodied many views and official procedures concerning death, but the only ones that directly affected Te Piti had to do with its registration, with place of burial, and with disposal of the deceased's possessions. Regarding the first, every death had to be recorded in the district civil register. Regarding the second, bodies were required to be buried in a common cemetery located at what was probably intended to be a hygienic distance from dwellings. And regarding the third, a deceased's possessions were required to be distributed according to the (exceedingly complex and detailed) official principles of inheritance set forth in the *Code Civil.*

The only instance I encountered of deaths not being registered concerned a few—but not all—infants who had died before registration of their births. In the official view, it would seem, such persons had never existed at all—a view also shared by most Te Pitians.

According to Te Piti's most "officially" expounded Protestant beliefs, an individual's soul survived the death of his body and ended up in either heaven or hell. (This, however, was not a universal view; even some otherwise practicing Protestants stated to me that every part and aspect of an individual ceased at death.) Also, the "threescore years and ten" lifespan mentioned in the Bible led some Te Pitians to conclude that anyone dying before attainment of that age was subject to pity—presumably for having been deprived, unless otherwise rescinded, of a God-given right. (I did not witness a funeral of anyone dying past seventy so cannot report whether the corollary of this view also obtained!) Moreover, the more-or-less churchbacked practice of keeping graves tidy and periodically flower-decorated can be taken to imply a belief that the soul maintained some kind of link with the decaying body for a considerable time. On the other hand, I could not elicit any but extempore explanations for such practices, or even for the practice of conducting funerals with religious rites. Some said that they were "possibly" done to help the departed soul, some that they were "possibly" done to maintain the soul's good will, and some that it was done "because it had always been done." The same explanations were given for the practice of making up memorial funds for deceased persons on May Collection Day—plus another one to the effect that such donations served to remind the deceased's former neighbors of his virtues—for whatever purposes I could not discover.

It would be difficult, and beyond the scope of this study, to try to separate all "native" from specifically Protestant beliefs and practices regarding death, but two deserve mention. One had to do with ghosts, another with age at death.

Te Pitians' belief in ghosts—in a spirit aspect of an individual that survived physical death and was somewhat different from "official" Christian notions of soul—was clearly a survival of pre-Christian ideas. My informants were not agreed on how distinct, if at all, ghosts were from souls, but a few who had formed opinions on the matter—most had evidently not done so—stated that they were nevertheless different (*mea 'ē*).[26]

Regarding age at death, although both pastors and several deacons stated, more or less "officially," that a person's age at death should not influence public reaction to the death—every individual being "a child of God and equal in His eyes," this view was implicitly contravened by other views and practices, including some by the pastors themselves, which indicated that the death of the very young warranted less parish-wide concern than that of older people. In Fatata, this view was in fact institutionalized in the workings of the local funeral fund (see below).

Several other "native" beliefs had to do with both ghosts and age. While there did not seem to have been a clearly formulated community-wide consensus on the matter, the people I queried "supposed" that ghosts behaved ever after as they had behaved, in terms of age, at the time of death. This view was borne out in the few cases of ghostly intervention that occurred during my visits or that remained fresh in the minds of my informants— except that the behaviors attributed to some infant ghosts were "older" than thus warranted.

A more significant inference is the one suggested by the circumstance that ghosts of people dying during old age seldom materialized actively. It was mainly those who had not yet lived out their "natural" span—or so the data imply—who intervened in mundane daily affairs; and the nature of that intervention usually ranged from mildly petulant to viciously malevolent,

---

[26]For more on contemporary Tahitian eschatology see above, page 376, and Levy 1973.

indicating what might be interpreted as angry frustration for their premature demise.[27]

"Native" values and practices not only differed from but in some cases sharply conflicted with one view of the Administration, namely, the one expressed in the regulation that bodies should be buried at some distance from residences. Prior to that ruling, Te Pitians buried their deceased relatives very close to their dwellings. Many of those in Atea continued to do so up to the time of my visits, or, as a compromise, they buried them on family agricultural lands outside the village. In Fatata, however, all recent burials were located in the Administration-approved cemetery, as described above; but Fatatans did so, they said, to escape the penalties they believed they would otherwise incur and not because they shared the Administration's concerns behind the regulation.

Funerals, even more than May Collections, served to express community-wide society principles within a religious context, and some important social differences between Atea and Fatata were exemplified in the ways that funerals were sponsored and financed.

In both villages, the burials of live-born infants dying shortly after birth and before baptism were attended only by close relatives, one of whom usually presided at the graveside rites (pages 334–35). In the case of other pre-Sunday School children, in both villages, the pastor or a deacon usually officiated at the graveside rites, but the wakes were mainly family affairs. With the deaths of persons older than that, however, Atea and Fatata differed in the ways that wakes were conducted and funeral costs distributed.

In Atea, the wakes for such persons varied in attendance size, I was told, according to the deceased's social importance and number of nearby kin. (For example, a deacon or district councilor, or their wives, would have attracted more mourners than a nonofficial; and someone with many local or nearby kinfolk more than someone with a few.) All of a deceased's sodality mates would usually attend but would not participate as a distinct group. Also, in Atea, the deceased's closest kin relatives—say, a husband in the case of a deceased woman, or the parents in the case of a deceased child—paid most of the funeral costs, i.e., for the coffin and for the meal shared by the mourners after the funeral. In wakes involving large gatherings—and hence large feasts—other kinfolk of the deceased, and perhaps a few sodality mates, sometimes contributed, voluntarily, small sums to cover the costs (especially if the principal sponsors were very poor), but the major expense was conventionally borne by the deceased's principal kin.[28]

---

[27]The principal exception to this belief was one that identified some porpoises, those most friendly and nonmalicious of creatures, as being the ghosts of stillborn infants.

[28]For an eyewitness account of a large Atea-like funeral, see Levy 1973:291–301.

In Fatata, the sodalities participated more corporately and actively in the wakes for persons of Sunday School age and older, i.e., the sodality of the deceased in the case of an older person, that of the parents in the case of a nonmember; and the village as a whole helped to finance funeral costs. Just prior to my visits, the method of financing had been institutionalized in the shape of a mutual assistance arrangement called the *Taiete Firarefia* (which term, when I first heard it mentioned, excited me to think, "At last; something exotic!" but which turned out to be nothing more outlandish than *Philadelphia Society*).

According to some of its founders, the *Taiete Firarefia* had its beginning in the early 1930s, when several members of one of the parishes' two sodalities started actively canvassing all their relatives for funeral-expense contributions when one of those relatives died; mainly, it was explained, to assist family survivors who were relatively poor. In time, the canvassing was extended to include nonrelatives of a deceased person, and by 1939 the list of regular subscribers numbered over a hundred. Five years later, the list became established as a village-wide one and sponsorship of it was assumed by the pastor, who "invented" its name, which he translated to be: *Taiete no te 'oire no te here taea'e* (Society of the City of Love [Among] Siblings). (Fatatan informants claimed that the *Taiete* was the only one of its kind in French Polynesia and that its name had, in fact, been "invented" by their pastor. Regrettably, I did not check the accuracy of either claim.)

The *Taiete Firarefia* operated as follows. When a person died, his family managed the funeral as usual, including the meal given the mourners. The family then reported their costs—for coffin and food—to the leaders of the *Taiete*, who canvassed all *hui ra'atira*, i.e., all village residents past school age and under sixty, for equal fractions of the funeral costs. (Reportedly, all coffins cost about the same; food costs varied with numbers of mourners fed but seldom exceeded 2,500 francs.) If, however, a resident died while "abroad" (*i rāpae*)—say, in Pape'ete—his family was given an amount based on the sum collected for the immediately preceding funeral held in Fatata, i.e., an identical sum if the deceased was of *hui ra'atira* or older age, one-half of that sum if the deceased was younger.

Evidently the arrangements worked well for a while. Then, as was inevitable with Te Piti's "cooperatives," it began to break down on account of default by some members. A few members held back their contributions because of their dissatisfaction with what they considered the inequity of giving parents of a child dying abroad only one-half the sum given on behalf of older persons. But most defaulters held back their contributions because of their dissatisfaction with having to continue to pay for other people's funerals without receiving money in return. No one, it was explained to me, objected to the fact that some funerals cost more than others (since, in the role of mourners most contributors had joined in eating the food), but several members whose families had suffered no recent bereavements objected to having to pay for what they considered to be the inordinate numbers of deaths taking place in other families! ("Why should we, who seldom die, continue to pay for others, who are always dying?")

In any event, other members also began to default, because of the defaults just described, so that by the time of my visit in 1955 the *Taiete* was no longer functioning—much to the regret of some of the village's leaders, who described it as "an excellent institution" (*'ohipa nehenehe roa*) and who were considering resurrecting the idea of mutual assistance in a somewhat different form, modelled after a plan used by the RDPT (i.e., the Pouvana'aist political party) branch in a nearby district. Following that plan, when a death occurred, members of the party went around the district soliciting voluntary contributions from all residents, and the money collected was then presented to the deceased's family at the graveside. No attempt was made to match the cost of the funeral and no specific assessment was set. The advantage of this plan over that of the *Taiete Firarefia*, I was informed, lay in its *voluntary* nature, i.e., it avoided *pe'ape'a* (disturbance) by removing the source of individual grievances. (Except, one can be certain, those generated among survivors whose previous contributions were not reciprocated when their turns came to be recipients!) "But what happens," I asked, "if the collecting does not cover the cost of the funeral and if the family in question is very poor?" To which was answered: "In that case, we would extend *aroha* (sympathy) to the survivors." (But not, it would appear, in the form of money.)

I began this discussion of funerals with the statement that they exemplified some important social differences between Atea and Fatata. Thus, Atea's emphasis on kinship (as a basis of financing funerals) was in sharp contrast to Fatata's emphasis, formerly, on the *Taiete Firarefia*-based assumption of village-wide responsibility, later, in process of introduction—on a system of financing based on individual volition and political party sponsorship. It would be a mistake to make too much of or to generalize too extensively from those differences: kinship (as will be seen) continued to exercise a very weighty influence in Fatata, and both common residence (i.e., the basis of community) and politics did likewise in Atea. However, the different emphasis exercised by those different modes of relationship in connection with such a crucial social event as a funeral constitutes a noteworthy enough contrast per se.

Summary of Differences

1. Relatively more of Fatatan children than Atean were born in infirmaries, rather than at home, but this difference appears to have counted for little in terms of direct money costs.

2. More important in economic terms was the difference between the two villages in their attitudes towards childhood. Fatatan parents tended to view this "consumption" period of their children's lives as more strictly so, and as lasting longer, than did their Atean counterparts—an attitude that resulted in Fatatan children remaining more years in school and engaging less actively in productive work. (As a corollary, more Fatatan children were fostered out for schooling purposes, and more of Fatata's unmarried residents were living elsewhere—mainly for schooling.)

3. The only other noteworthy difference between Ateans and Fatatans in the subject matter of this chapter had to do with their behavior towards their dead. In Atea, a deceased's body was interred in places associated with its close kinfolk and its funeral was financed largely by the latter as well. In Fatata, all deceased residents were interred in a common cemetery and their funerals were, until very recently, financed by a community-wide self-imposed tax.

Epilogue: Life-Cycling in Te Piti

It should be evident that one cannot label the ideas and events described in this chapter as *the* life cycle of Te Piti.[29] Even on the conceptual normative level, there were in existence *three* more or less authoritative and somewhat different time scales for defining individuals' attributes and for assigning rights and obligations; those of the state, those of the Protestant Church, and those that were not explicitly codified by state or church but were shared by most of the two villages' residents past the age of puberty (i.e., those norms that I call "native"). In addition, it was a matter of observation that not all Te Pitians held identical views about the facts and meanings of all the state and church life-cycle rules. And there were some sharp individual disagreements about some of the more authoritative "native" precepts, e.g., some *taure'are'a* held that they were as well qualified in money matters as their elders. Nevertheless, there were widespread agreements about most

---

[29]Writing literally, one should not even summarize these behaviors under the label of "life cycle," inasmuch as their conceptual frames did not posit a rebirth after death, an actual cycling of an individual's life. Nevertheless, I stay with the label because of its widespread usage for the matters under discussion.

of the criteria used in defining life stage, enough to warrant the generalizations that were presented above and that I shall now attempt to summarize.

The following table compares the three most authoritative time scales in terms of the labels customarily attached to their respective phases.

Table 9. Life Stages

	State	Church	"Native"
Conception	—embryo, under State protection	—a body and soul, protected by God	'OTEO
Birth 0	—registration: a person	—baptism	
3			AIURA'A
6	—school beginning	—Sunday School joining	
9			T A M A R I 'I R A 'A
12			
	—school leaving —female marriage	—Sunday School leaving	—male supercision
15	w/out parental consent	—sodality joining	
	—male marriage		R A 'A T I R A
18	w/out parental consent		
	—male conscription		T A U R E 'A R E 'A R A 'A A
21	—emancipation		
24			
27		—full membership	
30			
33			

(State column bracketed: M I N O R I T Y)

Table 9. Life Stages (continued)

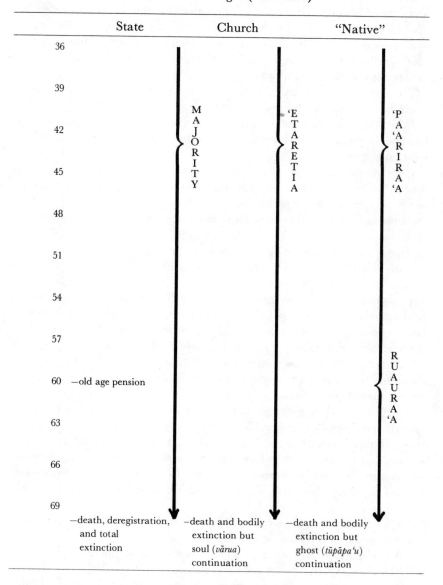

State	Church	"Native"
36		
39		
42 MAJORITY	'ETARETIA	'PA'ARIRA'A
45		
48		
51		
54		
57		RUAURA'A
60 —old age pension		
63		
66		
69		
—death, deregistration, and total extinction	—death and bodily extinction but soul (*vārua*) continuation	—death and bodily extinction but ghost (*tūpāpa'u*) continuation

Except for the ineluctable events of birth and death, it will be noted that these three scales differed, in parts quite markedly, with respect to which attributes of an individual they measured and, consequently, as to when the bounds in time should be.

The state scale defined an individual's life-cycle changes almost entirely in terms of chronological age, as measured by the Gregorian calendar. (Even its definitions of "precocity," i.e., early attainment of *émancipation*— were limited by minimums in terms of calendar-year age!) However, that scale synchronized with individuals' physiological and mental age changes in only the broadest kind of way.

The church scale was based in part on chronological age, but much more so on the individual's adherence to church precepts.

As for the "native" scale, it was based largely on the individual's behavior, mainly physical and mental, and on customary assessments of behavioral capacities.

It should be noted that of all three of these scales, the "native" one was least arbitrary, i.e., it was based more directly on observed (and hence *expected*) age changes in behavior. But even those behaviors were arbitrary in the sense of their having been in large measure culturally shaped—as indeed is the case with every human society's life-cycle scale, including of course the European calendrical method of measuring chronological age.

Table 9 also serves to accentuate inconformities among the scales. As can be seen, these occurred mainly with respect to individuals (chronologically) aged between about thirteen and twenty-five. Conceivably, these inconformities in age status could subject individuals in that cohort to considerable amounts of role conflict, which would inevitably affect the communities at large. Fortunately, i.e., "fortunately" in the eyes of those who value social tranquility over social tension, Te Pitians' "native" behavior standards for that age span were so much weightier than those of state and church that the potential for role conflict seldom, if ever, eventuated.

The three life-cycle scales prevalent in Te Piti can be looked at from several viewpoints (e.g., their specific inconformities with each other; their relevance to physiological, mental, and emotional aging; their influence upon social grouping, etc.); but in line with the emphasis of this study, they will be discussed here mainly in economic terms. In this sense, I will inquire how each of the three normative scales sized up an individual at each life stage as:

(1) a bundle of resources convertible into circulatable economic services;

(2) a producer of economic objects;

(3) a circulator of economic services and objects (including decision-making regarding that circulation); and

(4) a consumer of economic services and objects, produced by himself and others.

The state-sanctioned norms described in this chapter contained several assumptions about these economic aspects of an individual. To begin with, the *Code* implied that the early years of an individual's life are a period for "resource development." The individual consists of a combination of behavioral potentialities that increase in kind and in quantity with the passage of time, and it is the responsibility of the parents and the state to nurture and mold those potentialities. Parents must to the limits of their abilities provide the services and objects involved in that nurturance: food, shelter, formative socialization, etc. And it was up to the state to provide the services and objects involved in formal schooling, corrective socialization, protection from bodily and economic harm, and, in default of parental provision, with nurturance as well. By age twenty-one, most of the individual's behavioral resources were deemed by the state *Code* to be fully developed and ready for "circulation"—except for the individual's abilities to be an adoptive parent or to perform in certain elective offices, which were held to be developed somewhat later on in life. (Inversely, the *Code* implied that under certain circumstances an individual could "mature" somewhat earlier in life, if, for example, he served in the armed services or married earlier or was deemed mature by the parental decision to emancipate him.)

Throughout that *minority* phase of an individual's life, the state *Code* implied that he was mainly a consumer of objects and services provided by parents and state, but back of this assumption were other implicit ones that could be viewed as defining this transaction not as an outright gift but as a long-term loan. That is to say, it was implicitly expected that the young consumer would eventually repay what he had received—in the form of taxes to the state (including the conscriptee's *impôt de sang*) and of economic help to aging parents. Or, some of the "nurturance" received from parents might be viewed as having been reciprocated at the time by the "obedience, honor, and respect" that the children were required to display, thereby constituting a transaction of more direct exchange. (Among adults, "honor and respect" were ofttimes concretely negotiable—as for example in the case of "votes." Such services from one's child may have had lower social value than an adult's votes but presumably contained *something* of value to the recipients.)

Another way of viewing the state-defined "consumer" phase of an individual's life is as an example of pool-sharing (rather than of exchange). In this light, all citizens would be seen as belonging to a comprehensive *French* societal unit, which was modeled on the ideal family unit and which operated on the principle of "to each according to his needs, from each according to his capacities." According to this model, the Administration would not constitute a party having an exchange relationship with an individual but a manager of certain of the society's pool-sharing transactions.[30] But,

---

[30]I do not for a moment believe that the legislators who drew up the *Code* consciously thought about them in these "economic" terms, but that does not weigh against the validity of phrasing the underlying assumptions of the *Code* in such terms.

needless to say, the Te Pitians themselves did not view the situation in these terms. To them, their relationship with the Administration was one of exchange—in which a very rich and powerful Administration took objects and services from them and gave them very little in return. To most Te Pitians, in fact, the government should give to them, nonreciprocably, in keeping with its wealth and power over them.

Corollary to these ideas about the "economic" behaviors natural and desirable during an individual's age of (consumer) minority were the *Code*'s assumptions about his rationality. That is to say, limitations were imposed on his freedom to dispose of his goods (partly to protect him and partly to protect his successors) and upon his freedom to enter into exchanges, both commercial and noncommercial. Moreover, until an individual had reached age eighteen he himself was not held fully responsible for many of his actions, "economic" or otherwise.

Then, from age twenty-one, or *émancipation* if that was bestowed earlier, until extinction of his civil rights (resulting either from biological death or court ruling) the individual was deemed by the state to be fully "mature" (except for those office-holding and adopting rights mentioned above). As a "mature" individual, he was enabled to enter into all kinds of transactions permitted by law and was fully responsible for all of his acts. If he kept within certain limits and abided by certain procedural rules, he was free to create, destroy, dispose of, receive, share, exchange, or even appropriate a wide assortment of goods and services. In addition, he possessed many state-protected rights as a consumer, e.g., if married, to his wife's sexual services, or, if indigent, to familial or state support. But at the same time, he was obligated to share some of his goods with his family and with the state.

And finally, according to assumptions contained in the *Code* and other state rules, an individual resumed some of the attributes and rights of a pre-adult consumer upon reaching age sixty, i.e., at that point he was deemed no longer capable of complete material self-support and, unless otherwise provisioned, was assisted materially by the state. As described earlier, the elderly citizen was also subjected to less severe penal sanctions than those of younger majority status, but the assumption underlying this legal convention was, I suggest, not to the effect that the older individual was any less rational and hence (like a child) less responsible for his actions but that any imprisonment coming at that stage of life constituted an inequitably larger portion of an elderly malefactor's remaining lifespan.

Compare this state-sanctioned view of age-based "economic" behavior with that implicit in church and parish rules. In the first place, the assumptions underlying state and church norms differed markedly regarding the boundaries of the relevant social universes. For the state, the social unit in question consisted of all French citizens but only those alive (i.e., from conception to biological or legal death). For Te Piti's parishioners, as such, the relevant social unit consisted of all living persons associated with the Protestant Church of French Polynesia, plus certain spiritual beings (e.g., God, Jesus, etc., and the souls of former Protestant associates). In this light, one view of the structure of that encompassing Protestant social unit (the one voiced occasionally by the pastors and other moralizers) held that God (*Te Atua*) was the ultimate provider of all goods and of all resources convertible into such goods, including an individual's physical and mental resources. And, this view held, although He gives many of these things quite altruistically, there is also an obligation upon the individual to give what he can in return. (This view was exemplified in the locally well-known, but rarely practiced, custom of tithing.)

Another more mundane view of the church's "economic" structure—the view voiced by most adult parishioners of Te Piti—agreed with the above conception in viewing their parish as a subdivision of the whole French Polynesian Protestant Church, fraternally coordinate with all other parishes, and in regarding the church officials in Pape'ete as leaders of the whole. But it differed from the orthodox conception by regarding *Te Atua* and other spiritual beings as somewhat outside the organization and by regarding the church's Pape'ete officials (who were mostly metropolitan French) as "colonial" representatives not very different from those in the civil Administration.

According to this view, the individual parishioners engaged in three circuits of exchanges. The first and most important of these was the parish itself, in which the dominant kind of transaction was pool-sharing. The second was the exchanging, phrased as altruistic "giving" but implicitly reciprocal, that went on between parishes. And the third was the exchanging of money for services that went on between parish and church officials. Although (in view of many parishioners) this exchange ought to have been balanced, or more open-handed on the part of the church officials (because of the church's greater wealth), the parish actually gave more than it received.

Like the assumptions discernible in the *Code,* church rules implied that the early years of an individual's life were mainly a period for consumption, while resources were being developed. Nevertheless, Sunday School children were urged, as part of their training, to put at least token contributions into the collection box, even if the money came from their parents.

For the state, the period of consumption accompanying immaturity ended at age twenty-one (or at *émancipation*). For the church, full maturity, as represented by *'ētāretia*-hood, could conceivably have begun at about age

fifteen (i.e., upon graduation from Sunday School) but in fact, as was generally recognized, rarely did begin before age twenty-five—and in many cases
never did take place. And because *'ētāretia* (Communicants) received more
services than *taure'are'a* (e.g., in the form of participation in Communion
and in respect-receiving status), and had more decision-making authority
than the latter, they were expected to contribute more money and services
to parish projects.

Like the elderly citizen of the state, the elderly parishioner was permitted
some reversion to childlike nonproducer (i.e., consumer) status, but whereas
the criterion for such was chronological age in the case of the citizen, it was
physical infirmity and decrepitude in the case of the parishioner. Meanwhile, neither of these life-cycle scales contained an assumption that decision-making power necessarily declines with increasing age (in the case of
state norms) or increasing decrepitude (in the case of church-parish norms).
In fact, according to the latter viewpoint, an individual's knowledge and
judgment about profound matters (including religion) actually tended to
increase with the passage of time.

We can turn now to "native" views about the economic aspects of individuals as they pass through life. To begin with, Te Pitians produced, trans-
acted, and consumed valued objects and services not only within the context of state and church relationships just described but also with all other
residents of their respective villages, *qua* coresidents, and with: (1) kinfolk residing outside the village, (2) other persons living outside the village, such as
produce-buyers, retailers, sport team rivals, etc. For Ateans, the social
boundaries of "village" were virtually the same as their district and parish,
but for the Fatatans, their village was only a part of the larger Toerau District and Parish.

The "native" social universes of Ateans and Fatatans also included ghosts
of former neighbors, etc., but their supposed transactions with those ghosts
were mediated through living specialists except for the times when those
ghosts intervened directly in their lives (which was usually in the form of
deprivation).

Several kinds of valued goods circulated within the sets of relationships
comprising this part of Te Piti life. First, there were the various sorts of labor employed for subsistence and money-earning purposes, and the objects
produced by that labor (e.g., food, shelter, money, and the objects purchased with money). Second, there was the labor expended by the *hui
ra'atira* in village projects (e.g., road building, cemetery maintenance, visitor
reception) Next, were the special kinds of services performed by midwives,
herbalists, spirit mediums, and other experts; most of these were performed
gratis, except for the expectation (which may not have been explicit) that

the donee would reciprocate with something of equivalent value if the need were to arise. (The sexual services that were dispensed by some women for consideration should also be mentioned but were an infrequent kind of exchange.)

No less "economic" than the above were the verbal services, usually uttered in the form of praise and votes for office, that enhanced a recipient's social capital. (If anyone doubts the "economic" value of this kind of service, he should recall the efforts made by some, but not all, individuals seeking it in the form of hospitality, gardening labor, etc., as the basis for such an exchange.)

And finally, to this list of "economic" goods and transactions must be added the actions, i.e., "disservices," that resulted in *depriving* an individual of something of value, including such actions as thieving and malicious destruction of objects and verbal slander and belittlement.

Te Piti's "native" ideology contained several postulates, explicit and implicit, that linked the above services, or capacities for such services, with an individual's age. Community service, for example, was required of (and hence considered "natural" and appropriate to) individuals of *hui ra'atira* age (i.e., fourteen to sixty) with the addition that children were also called upon on occasion to entertain official visitors with singing. Age also figured in the value (or disvalue) attached to the kinds of verbal services listed, i.e., praise and detraction were weightier when uttered by someone *mature* (*pa'ari*) than by someone younger or very old.

With regard to subsistence labor, Te Piti's "native" norms differed from those of the state. Whereas the latter assigned productive obligations and consumer rights to individuals on the basis of chronological age (e.g., school-leaving age, majority, old-age-pension age), the "native" norms assigned such obligations and rights on the basis of physical abilities. The physical abilities in question were roughly coincidental with age-phase in "native" expectations but not with calendrical age. Thus, while childhood was viewed as a period mainly of consumption, a child was also encouraged, and often expected, to embark on productive labor as soon as he was physically capable. And the end of childhood was signalled more by the individual's productive (and recreational) activities than by his number of years. (Similar considerations obtained, though inversely, for the other end of an individual's life.)

There was also some tendency in both Atea and Fatata to associate *taure'are'a* with the more strenuous forms of labor, e.g., digging, heavy carrying, underwater spearfishing, etc., but not to the extent that such work was conventionally assigned (as, for example, in Samoa).

Some of the special kinds of services referred to earlier were also viewed as being linked with age-phase, specifically with late maturity and old age, the main ones having been midwifery and spirit mediumship. The former was regarded as requiring expertise attainable only with long experience, the latter as requiring knowledge of "profound" matters attainable only with long life and retirement from more active pursuits.

Finally, in the "native" view of human development most widely current in Te Piti, individuals possessed the knowledge and judgment essential for making decisions about important economic transactions, especially those involving money, only during the maturity phase of their lives—which usually lasted from about ages twenty-five to sixty but which was not specifically defined by those (calendrical) years.[31]

The only noteworthy difference between Atea and Fatata with respect to the matters discussed in this Epilogue had to do with concepts and practices concerning time of transition from childhood (the mainly consuming phase of life) to the *youthing,* more productive one. That is to say, there were proportionately more parents in Fatata than in Atea who appeared content, even eager, to maintain their children's formal schooling past the official minimum school-leaving age—a sentiment that seems to have been based mainly on the assumption that the additional schooling would add value to their future money-earning abilities more than sufficient to compensate for that lost by deferring the children's productive labor for a while.[32]

---

[31]As in many other societies, e.g., the Tallensi (Fortes 1949), the making of important economic decisions, and especially those regarding land, was sometimes influenced by whether one's parent(s) were still alive and regardless of one's age-phase, but the weightiness of this factor in Te Piti varied so widely with family structure and personality that it eludes generalization.

[32]A quantitative comparison of Atea and Fatata, with respect to their human resources in these service-defined terms, will be given in the Appendix.

CHAPTER X

HOUSEHOLDS

The Nature of Households

Throughout the preceding chapters, I have described and endeavored to compare several kinds of social groups and dyads that were found in both Atea and Fatata: district (i.e., governmental), political party, parish, parish sodality, stores and their customers, work groups, conjugal units, sibling pairs, etc. In addition, there were in both villages two other kinds of groups, which have been mentioned several times in passing but which require more detailed treatment, namely, households and land-owning units.

Te Piti's households, the subject of this chapter, deserve special attention in this work devoted pointedly to comparison and will be examined more systematically than it has been possible to do in the cases of the other kinds of social groups thus far described.

Household groups, *'utuāfare,* were the most palpable of Te Piti's social units. Minimally, they were the units made up of people who regularly and frequently ate together and who usually slept under the same or closely adjoining roofs. Every Tahitian resident in Te Piti during my visits belonged to one of them more or less exclusively; although some individuals changed households from time to time, no one made a practice of drifting from one to another. Moreover, the activities I designate in characterizing households—commensality and sleeping together—were regarded as definitive not only by myself but by the Te Pitians themselves.

Of all the criteria employed in the Society Islands to identify people ethnically, cuisine and style of eating were perhaps the most decisive. Some informants used this as the sole criterion when asked to clarify otherwise ambiguous identities, e.g.: "They are Chinese [or *Demi* or *true* Tahitians]; they

401

eat Chinese [or European, or Tahitian]-style." Many ethnically mixed households in the Society Islands maintained two separate food regimes: thus, a Chinese merchant ordinarily ate his customary food with chopsticks, etc., in one room of the store, while his Tahitian spouse and younger off-spring and whichever of his spouse's relatives were currently—and inevitably!—there, ordinarily ate their taro, etc., at the back. Again, in many affluent French-Tahitian households in and near Pape'ete, the members ate Tahitian-style most of the time but repaired to a formal dining room to eat European foods when entertaining guests of their own station in life.[1]

Another indication of the importance of eating in general, and of commensality in particular, was the relative amount of time used in producing food for home consumption, or the relative amount of money incomes spent in purchasing food.

While it would be an oversimplification to say that Te Pitians lived mainly to eat, it would be entirely inaccurate to assert that they ate only to live. The pleasure they derived from eating—and eating large amounts—was obvious. The shouted *"Haere mai tāmā'a"*—Come in and eat—was the standard formula for greeting a passerby. Moreover, as noted earlier, the conventional word for fosterage was *fa'a'amu*—to feed (thus, a foster child was a *tama'iti fa'a'amu*). When asking Te Pitians about their foreign travels, I was told mainly what and how they ate. And when inquiring about local history, I often had it described to me as, for example, "The era before (or after) coffee and bread."

Finally, as in most human societies but perhaps to a greater-than-average degree, food and eating accompanied numerous kinds of rituals and had many other symbolic usages besides.

Turning now to *sleeping,* having characterized Te Piti's households also as co-sleeping groups, I should add that how and where they slept was of perhaps less concern to them than what and where they ate.[2] It was a matter of observation that they slept a lot! By European, bed-bound, quiet-demanding, darkness-needing, eight-hour standards, however, they were remarkably flexible in their requirements, seemingly able to drop off

---

[1]When a Tahitian public works supervisor moved to Fatata from Noumea with his Wallis Islander wife, the latter was described by her neighbors as having been at first very unhappy. After a while, however, she settled down to being contentedly "Tahitian," i.e., she learned to eat and enjoy Tahitian food.

[2]The European-style beds, huge and colorfully coverleted, which occupied such dominating and usually public positions in many of Te Piti's houses, may have represented deliberate efforts to symbolize the householder's affluence, or the women's skill in appliqué needlework, but I do not believe that they were meant to signify, "This is our household, the place where we *sleep.*"

anywhere and any time. Nevertheless, Te Pitians did indulge in most of their sleeping in or near the houses where they did most of their eating, and hence I am led to define their "households" as commensual *and* co-sleeping groups.

There were, however, some marked differences among Te Piti's households: in size, in composition, in internal economy, in governance, etc.; and what is particularly relevant for this exercise in comparison is that *the full range of these several kinds of differences prevailed in both Atea and Fatata.* On the other hand (and of focal importance to this exercise), there were differences between Atea and Fatata with respect to local percentages of this or that type of household in terms of composition, economy, etc., and the principal task of this chapter will be to quantify those differences and attempt to explain them. Quite frankly, the expectation behind this exercise was that the percentage differences could be accounted for by factors exogenous to the households themselves—and hence would yield some evidence of the scientific validity of the method of "controlled comparison."

Size and Composition

The aspects of household composition I select as criteria for classification concern the number of their respective members and the latters' ages and kinship ties.

As reported earlier, at the time of my first household census in Atea the total population then in residence was 217. Fatata's population at the corresponding time was more difficult to pin down, because of more frequent comings and goings, but was near enough to 348. Combining these populations (i.e., 565), there were in all 104 households, two of which had only one member each. One of these one-member households consisted of an elderly and virtually houseridden widow. She lived alone most of the time but was visited by neighbors, who kept her well supplied with cooked food and helped keep her house in order. The other one-member household consisted of a middle-aged man, never married, who spent most of his days roaming around the countryside—"hunting wild pigs" he claimed; "stealing from our gardens" his neighbors said. He was always dirty and unkempt and clothed in rags. Even his closest local kinfolk had long since given up trying to befriend and socialize him.

Neither of these two one-member households will figure in the following comparisons, which will consequently be reduced to 102: forty of them in Atea, sixty-two in Fatata. The total sizes of these were distributed as follows:

Table 10A. Total Household Size

Number in Household	Percentage of Households in Atea and Fatata (N = 102)	Percentage of Households		Percentage Difference between Atea and Fatata
		Atea (N = 40)	Fatata (N = 62)	
2	9.8	15.0	6.4	8.6
3	16.6	20.0	14.5	5.5
4	12.7	12.5	12.9	0.4
5	19.6	12.5	24.1	11.6
6	12.7	7.5	16.1	8.6
7	8.8	10.0	8.1	1.9
8	5.8	10.0	3.2	6.8
9	2.9	2.5	3.2	0.7
10	4.9	0.0	8.0	8.0
11	1.9	2.5	1.6	0.9
12	1.9	5.0	0.0	5.0
13	0.9	2.5	0.0	2.5
14	0.0	0.0	0.0	0.0
15	0.9	0.0	1.6	1.6

Evidently, the smaller the household the more there were of them, except that households containing three and five members, respectively, outnumbered those containing two or four.

To anticipate some findings that will be reported below, I found that for most purposes of comparison the number of postchildhood residents in a household was a more significant criterion than the household's total size.

One of the four single-adult households consisted of a middle-aged widow and her young children: it was assumed by her neighbors that she would eventually rewed (she owned fairly large land holdings in a neighboring district). The other three single-adult households consisted of late-middle-aged males; all of these had been previously married and divorced (because of their various shortcomings: frequent drunkenness, bad tempers, filthy personal habits, etc.). It was generally accepted that no woman in her right mind would consent to live with any of them again.

Most of the two-adult households consisted of a married couple, with or without children. One notable exception, however, was a Fatata household occupied solely by two middle-aged men, a local widower and his (permanent) visitor-friend. This pair worked mainly at commercial fishing and

Table 10-B. Adults in Household
(Members of post-childhood age)

Number of Adults in Household	Percentage of Households in Atea and Fatata (N=102)	Percentage of Households		Percentage Difference between Atea and Fatata
		Atea (N=40)	Fatata (N=62)	
1	3.9	7.5	1.6	5.9
2	50.0	47.5	51.6	4.1
3	20.6	22.5	19.3	3.2
4	9.8	7.5	11.3	3.8
5	7.8	7.5	8.0	0.5
6	4.9	7.5	3.2	4.3
7	1.0	0.0	1.6	1.6
8	1.0	0.0	1.6	1.6
9	1.0	0.0	1.6	1.6

purchased most of their other food. They shared domestic duties, even to laundering their clothes, and spent all their extra money on beer and wine. (No one voiced surprise or disapproval for their womanless life—there was evidently nothing sexual about their relationship; in fact, some of their male neighbors expressed envy of their independence and way of life.)

Such special cases aside, all other households in Te Piti were composed of individuals sharing real or simulated kinship ties. And looking at households from this perspective, I have found it most useful to distinguish three major types, which will now be identified.

I. **Single-family household, i.e., that comprising a "married" couple with or without their children or a sole "parent" (widowed or "divorced") along with his or her coresident children.**

In this connection, the reader should recall three points about Te Piti's ethnography. First, a couple could enter into a "marriage" relationship without having to go through a civil or religious ritual, and the same held for "divorces." Second, in Te Piti terms an adult could serve and be known as a "parent" to a younger person through the custom of fosterage (*fa'a'amura'a*) without regard to genealogical connection. And third, those units I label "skip-generation" households, i.e., those consisting of "grandparent(s)" and "grandchild(ren)" only, were similar enough to the (true) parent-child units, in Te Pitians' conceptualization and in many behavioral respects as well, to include within the single-family type. Events producing skip-generation households were of various kinds, the two most typical having been as follows:

—both "parents" were either dead or permanently resident, more or less, in other villages, or,

—one or both of the "parents" resided locally, in other households, and their children resided with the grandparent(s) in order either to "help" the latter or to escape or relieve stressful situations in the parental household.

The age and sex-composition of skip-generation households varied so widely that it is not practicable to generalize about them except in very broad terms. For example, one of them consisted of a decrepit old man and two of his unmarried grandchildren, a youth of twenty-eight and a girl of twenty-two. By contrast, another such household consisted of a still-active woman of fifty-five and two grandsons, aged ten and seven. The first of these two households was wholly autonomous, economically; the second was dependent for some of its material requirements upon contributions from other households, mainly from the boys' parents who dwelt a few houses distant.

Thus for these and other ethnographically based reasons, I find it sensible to lump together all of the following kin constellations into the same single-family household type:

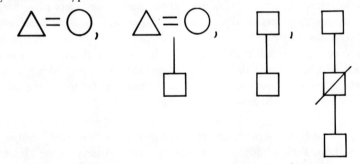

At the same time, I find it necessary to draw a distinction for some purposes among single-family households on the basis of the age of their children (if any), i.e., between those with and those without resident children older than the life-stage the Te Pitians called "childhood."

As described earlier, sooner or later nearly all Te Pitians married and reproduced, or otherwise acquired, offspring of their own. And as was also described earlier, with regard to their immediate household of residence, a newly married couple had three kinds of options (which, however, were not equally "free"):

a. they could reside in the established household where one of them previously resided;

b. they could move into another already established household where neither had previously resided; or

c. they could set up a new household of their own. (I know of no instance in Te Piti where two or more newly married couples set up a new joint household together.)

My data indicate that options (b) and (c) were selected very rarely. In most instances, newly married couples began their conjugal life in the household previously resided in by one of them. After that, some of these remained more or less permanently in the household where their conjugal life began, while others eventually established separate households of their own. But even in these latter instances, there came into being, for a while, some households containing nuclear families one or more generations apart.

At one stage of my census-taking, I was seized with the notion that many Te Pitians had made their residential choices deliberately to frustrate attempts to classify household compositions![3] Nevertheless, some patterns can be educed even from the more heterogeneous ones. Most of the latter consisted mainly of an older married couple and their child(ren), one at least of whom coresided with his or her spouse and child(ren), if there were any, or with his or her child(ren) only, if there was no longer a spouse present. Clearly, these criteria admit of several different subpatterns, most of which were, in fact, present in Te Piti in 1954–55,[4] but I have lumped all of them together into a second major type, which I label:

II. Extended-family household, i.e., one comprising two or more nuclear families linked by ties of filiation (plus, in some cases, siblinghood).

The genealogical patterns included in this category are numerous, logically and in fact, e.g.,

---

[3]Speaking of "choices," I am aware that the topic of household composition might also be approached in such terms, i.e., through the method of "decision-making." Indeed, much useful information about Te Piti's culture could be presented through use of this method (compare Ross 1973), but for present purposes I am concerned more with who lived together than with why particular individuals lived where they did—although focus on the former inevitably reveals some information about the latter as well.

[4]As with the decision-making approach to coresidence, some interesting insights into Te Pitians' social relations might be revealed by a detailed examination of all those variations actually present at the time of my study, but no ethnography can be exhaustive, and the purposes, mainly comparative, of this study do not require such detail.

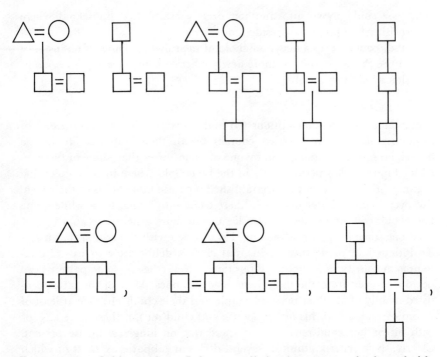

For purposes of this typology, I draw no distinction among the households exemplifying any of these patterns, provided that at least one of the "grand-parents" was not wholly senile. Where both grandparents (or the surviving one) were senile, the household in question resembled a single-family one in many behavioral aspects but will be classified separately:

III. **Joint-sibling household—one made up of two or more nuclear families linked only by ties of sibship. The logical genealogical patterns included in this category are:**

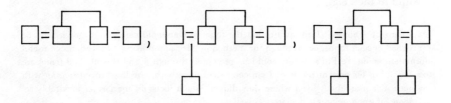

Te Piti also contained households that consisted of a married couple and the unmarried sibling of one of the spouses (or if married, not living with his or her spouse), thus:

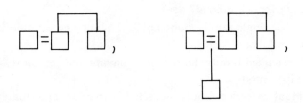

In cases where the sibling in question was still a "child" or "infant," the constellations differed only slightly or not at all from single-family units, and I have classified them as such. There were, however, a few households where the "unspoused" sibling was of the lifestage called *youth*, and where the social relations between him (or her) and his married sibling and sibling-in-law differed enough from single-family intrarelations to warrant placing them in a distinctive category.

Here then are the numbers of each type of household found in Te Piti in 1954–55. It should be noted that, with the exception of the two aged-widow households just mentioned, examples of every type were found in both places.

Table 10C. Household Kin-Type

Kin-Type	Percentage of Households in Atea and Fatata (N = 102)	Percentage of Households Atea (N = 40)	Fatata (N = 62)	Percentage Difference between Atea and Fatata
I. Single Family				
IA. Simple	50.0	52.5	48.4	4.1
IB. Complex	9.8	12.5	8.0	4.5
II. Extended Family				
IIA. Full	25.4	17.5	30.6	13.1
IIB. Residual	5.8	12.5	1.6	10.9
III. Joint-Sib Family				
IIIA. Complete	1.9	2.5	1.6	0.9
IIIB. Partial	6.8	2.5	9.7	7.2

IA. Simple single-family households (having no offspring or parent's sibling over "childhood" age)

IB. Complex single-family households (having one or more offspring over "childhood" age)

IIA. Full extended-family households (having one or more nonsenile grandparent(s))

IIB. Residual extended-family households (having grandparent(s) but only senile one(s))

IIIA. Full joint-sib-family households (comprising two or more nuclear families linked by sibling ties)

IIIB. Partial joint-sib-family households (comprising a nuclear family and the postchildhood unspoused sibling(s) of one of the spouses)

It would be possible to subdivide these types according to certain other criteria, e.g., the absolute and relative ages of spouses, but the classification just given will be sufficient for present purposes.

Household Economics

The next features of Te Piti's households to be compared are certain aspects of their "economics" that were related to the pool-sharing of goods among their respective members—pool-sharing having been the most important of all whole-household transactions both in terms of frequency and volume of goods. The aspects singled out for comparison are as follows:

1. Unity—the degree to which most goods (objects and services) used by members of a household were pooled and redistributed among them.

2. Equity—the degree to which all members of a household conformed to conventional Te Pitian norms of "redistributive" justice, i.e., to ideals regarding the proper balance between what they put into the common pool (in the form of labor, objects, money) and what they took out (ate or otherwise utilized).

3. Monetization—the proportion of money or money-bought objects to other forms of contributions (e.g., labor, self-grown vegetables, self-caught fish) that went into the common household pool).

It now remains to classify Te Piti's households according to these three variable, and inquire into the degree to which those variables were independent of one another.

With respect to *unity* the households may be divided into two types:

Type 1. Those where virtually all the goods used by household members were pooled and redistributed through the network comprising all members of the household.

Type 2. Those where virtually all food used by household members were pooled and redistributed through the whole network but where considerable amounts of nonfood objects were pooled and redistributed through sub-household units.

Words like "virtually" and "considerable amounts" reflect the circumstance that I find it impossible to be more precise and quantitative in this exercise. Nevertheless, according to my observations and the reports of knowledgeable informants, Te Piti's households did in fact polarize, and quite distinctly, in this domain.[5]

Although every Te Piti household, large or small, single or multifamily, acted as a single unit with respect to the preparation and consumption of its members' principal meals,[6] there were some noteworthy differences among them respecting the *supply* of the food they ate and of other material items they consumed or made use of.

At one pole were several households that operated as a single economic unit in every respect. One such was that headed by Teuru which at the beginning of my 1954–55 visit was constituted as follows:

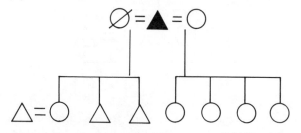

The sons and son-in-law worked with Teuru producing vegetable food for their common consumption; and all the fish they caught, jointly or separately, were pooled and eaten together. Teuru, Atea's most energetic producer, had extensive coconut groves and vanilla plantings and owned and operated the village's principal commercial launch. In all these enterprises, his sons and son-in-law worked with him without pay. The father received all the money income and paid for all household purchases for all

[5]If this report were extended to the two more urbanized settlements studied by my colleagues as part of our eight-community research program, it would be necessary to add a third category to typify those households in which virtually all goods (except shelter) used by household members were pooled and redistributed through subhousehold social units—including sole individuals. However, this extreme was not exemplified by any of Te Piti's households during my visits to them.

[6]My questions as to whether nuclear family or other subunits of a family prepared or ate their food separately were met with amused denials. "What would be the point?" people said. In special circumstances, individuals occasionally ate at times other than the main household meal but not deliberately as members of distinct subunits.

members—including clothes, tobacco, cinema tickets, etc. He was a lavish spender and a generous husband and father, but not even his son-in-law received any money except on request for specific purchases. The two sons were apparently dissatisfied with the arrangement—the older had previously "run away" to Pape'ete and had returned home only after Teuru had followed and pleaded with him—but they appeared to feel respect and warm affection for their father, and were, moreover, conscious of his ability to reduce their heritable shares of his properties, which were considerable. As for the daughter and her husband, they both wanted to set up separate residence elsewhere (a wish shared by the girl's stepmother!) but the young husband had neither the resources nor, evidently, the initiative to do so on his own. Eventually the young couple did move away, but throughout the first months of my stay, and during the preceding two years, the arrangements were as described.

At the other pole was the extended family of Hamu.

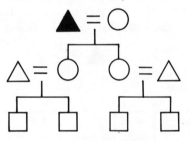

Hamu produced vegetables, unaided, for common household consumption, and his two sons-in-law fished for the household table, sometimes together, sometimes separately. In money-earning, however, all three earned separate incomes from entirely separate copra and vanilla enterprises, and each paid a more or less equal amount from his earnings to purchase food for their common consumption, retaining the rest for clothes, etc., for their respective wives (and children).

A somewhat different pattern of transactions obtained in extended-family households where only one of the senior "parents" resided. In general, such households tended to be more unified, economically, than those with both senior parents in residence. In both kinds of extended-family households, however, the physical conditions of the senior parents were differentiating factors, i.e., with increasing decrepitude the latter played smaller and smaller roles as contributors, until they finally reverted to being consumers only.

Summarizing, of the 102 households contained in Te Piti at the times of my visits in 1954–55, ninety-one may be classed as Type 1 (i.e., 89.8 percent) and eleven (or 10.8 percent) as Type 2 with respect to their redistributive unity.

Comparing the two villages in this characteristic, there were thirty-eight (95 percent) of Atea's households were "unified" as against fifty-three (85 percent) of Fatata's—a difference of 10 percent.

The reader will have noted that house space and child tending were not included among the "goods" customarily pooled and shared by some or all members of any household. The reason for this exclusion is the difficulty I experienced in grading the behavior related to those two items.

Regarding individuals' use of house space, I found it next to impossible to map people's daytime movements around their houses. I gained the impression that all the space was usually common to all but cannot back that up with any systematic observations. Nighttime use, for sleeping, was more mappable, but even that fell short of the kind of spatial exclusiveness met with, say, in middle-class American households. Newlyweds usually occupied rooms or adjacent shelters by themselves, but for only a year or so after marrying. After a while, the husband tended to sleep often on a cot or mat placed elsewhere, typically on an open verandah ("where it is cooler"). With the birth of a child, the latter slept near its mother in a separate room (if there were one), and the father tended to sleep more regularly elsewhere. Then, when the child reached toddling stage it also became accustomed to sleeping some nights outside its parents' separate room, nearer the father or some other household member. This tendency increased with a child's age, so that by adolescence it was uncommon for a girl—and highly unusual for a boy—to sleep in the parental room. Finally, in the case of middle-aged or elderly couples, the sleeping locations of themselves or of their offspring provided few or no clues as to their familial separateness in the larger households.

As for the tending of older children, an important kind of service performed in most households, this was spread around among a household's older members to a degree that frustrated all my efforts to educe regularities. During a child's infancy, its own mother and father and older siblings were more actively concerned with its welfare, but usually by toddling time the child had become the charge, or toy, of all older household members (a circumstance, by the way, that was reflected in part in terminology[7]).

With respect to equity, Te Piti's households may be typed as follows:

Type 1. With only occasional lapse by a minority, all members conformed fairly strictly to Te Pitian norms of "redistributive justice."

---

[7]In most households I knew, the younger children tended to address or refer to their parents and all other household members of the latter's age, or older, as *pāpā or māmā*, regardless of the specific kin tie involved.

Type 2. While most members conformed fairly strictly to such norms, others flouted them frequently or even chronically.[8]

Needless to say, the Te Pitians' expectations concerning what and how much an individual ought to put into the household pool took into account the latter's sex, age, and state of health, the standards for which were described in various places above. They also allowed for other special circumstances, as exemplified in the case of "grandparents."

While contributions to a household's pool-share economy were made, and evaluated, mainly in terms of labor and of money, food and other material objects as well as houses and productive land also constituted credit-worthy benefactions. As mentioned earlier, several of Te Piti's households consisted of one or more nuclear families plus one "grandparent," male or female. In some instances, the latter was the survivor of a marital union that had occupied the house before; in other instances, the grandparent was usually a "parent" of one of the house owners and had moved into the house upon becoming widowed or divorced elsewhere. Prior residence (and hence some measure of house ownership) provided a "grandparent" with some *credit* with respect to the household's pool-share economy. Also a "grandparent's" credit was enhanced if he or she held title to any of the land used by other household members for subsistence or cash-cropping (although in some cases the credit was rendered more tangible in the form of money obtained by receiving and selling part of the cash crop). However, such special, less tangible contributions as house and land ownership did not usually serve to relieve the "grandparent" of making *some* contribution in the form of labor or money or other more tangible objects. A lazy or selfish "grandparent" was criticized, however large his or her contribution in housing or land.

As with the variable of *unity,* I found that Te Piti's households polarized quite distinctly in the *equity* domain. Combining the two villages, seventy-nine (77.4 percent) of their 102 households of 1954–55 may be classed as Type 1 and the remaining twenty-three (22.5 percent) as Type 2, with regard to the "redistributive justice" obtaining among their respective members.

A comparison of the two villages reveals some difference in this respect. Thirty-three (82.5 percent) of Atea's forty households were "equitable" as against forty-six (74.2 percent) of Fatata's.

---

[8]Again, if this survey were to include the more urbanized settlements studied by my colleagues, it would be necessary to add a third category to exemplify certain households in which most of the productive members chronically behaved contrary to the more "rural" norms characteristic of Te Piti.

Turning now to the monetization variable, the limiting cases in this kind of scaling were represented, at one extreme, by the (hypothetical) household whose pool-shared objects included *none* purchased by money and at the other extreme by households virtually *all* of whose pool-shared objects were purchased by money. However, no such households as these were to be found in Fatata and Atea.[9]

All Te Pitians, occasionally or regularly, acquired the following kinds of pool-shared objects by purchase: bread, flour, sugar, tea, canned milk, kerosene, lamps, soap, clothing and sewing materials, cooking and eating utensils, and a few other imported items. Also, all households acquired some or all of their supplies of breadfruit, eating coconuts, building materials, cordage, and such, by nonpurchase, i.e., by collection from their own or neighbors' lands. Within these limits, however, it is feasible to type Te Piti's households in terms of the proportions of pool-shared objects acquired by purchase, but it has not proved feasible to type them all according to a single scale. There were, it is true, two households where all building materials and cordage and such and nearly all foodstuffs were purchased, but others were to be found in which, say, all starchy foods were self-produced but most building materials purchased. Thus it will be necessary to set up two monetization scales—one for starchy vegetables (other than breadfruit) and one for building materials and cordage, etc.

Food scale:

Type I. Households that self-produced virtually all their pool-shared starchy vegetables and usually large proportions of their pool-shared meat and/or fish.

Type II. Households that self-produced somewhat less than one-half of their pool-shared starchy vegetables.

Type III. Households that self-produced none of the above.

Building materials scale:

Type I. Households that self-produced most of the materials used in repair and enlargement of their buildings.

Type II. Households that purchased most of the above.

Had it been feasible to extend the time span for behaviors covered in these comparisons, another item could and should have been included, namely, the labor involved in building and repairing houses. I have indicated elsewhere that the two villages differed markedly in this respect

---

[9]For the definition of this method of scaling, I am indebted to my survey colleagues—and particularly to Paul Kay, much of whose wording I have used in the following paragraphs.

during the time span of my visits and for one or two years prior thereto. In a word, most Ateans tended to build and repair their houses by means of labor supplied on a quid pro quo basis (including the use of reciprocating construction and repair work groups), whereas most Fatatans relied on paid labor for the building and major repairing of their houses. However, most of the houses in both villages had been built long before my visit, and what information I was able to gather about the labor arrangements that went into their construction is too sparse and ambiguous to rely upon.

Finally, if this survey were to be extended to the more urbanized Tahiti (Island) communities studied by my colleagues, it would be useful to set up a scale that would describe the amount of paid labor employed by the households to help with domestic work. In fact, the number of Te Piti's households employing domestic labor was so few—two in Atea and one in Fatata—that I am persuaded to disregard this variable. The sole household in Fatata that employed a domestic was headed by a middle-aged, widowed schoolteacher and contained no younger female to help with household chores. Moreover, the woman in question received a regular salary large enough to accommodate this luxury with ease. One of the two Atean cases was similar in that its head earned nearly all of the household's ample income as a teacher. In addition, he and his wife derived from affluent and well-educated Tahiti families and evidently thought that having a servant was appropriate for persons like themselves. The other Atean case was that of a large extended family whose male head earned an ample enough cash income to hire a household domestic, whose services his wife obviously needed on account of the large ménage and her spouse's expansive hospitality.

We are left, then, with the two scales for which my data are more dependable, and more relevant to Te Piti life. The findings regarding these are given in Table 10D.

Summary of Intervillage Differences

As pointed out earlier, all the variables singled out for comparison in this exercise were found to be represented in both Atea and Fatata. On the other hand, the comparisons show that in the case of each and every one of those variables the two villages were found to differ with respect to the percentage represented. The question is, what degree of difference should be regarded as wide enough to be "significant"?

For some purposes, e.g., for the study of "sibling solidarity," it might turn out to be "significant" that Atea had even a slightly higher percentage of "complete joint-sibling family" households than Fatata (i.e., 2.5 percent against 1.6 percent), but for present purposes that difference does not seem wide enough to warrant further consideration. And in terms of the nature of

Table 10D. Households Classified According to Degree of Monetization

Household Type	Percentage of Households in Atea and Fatata	Percentage of Households		Percentage Difference between Atea and Fatata
		Atea (N=40)	Fatata (N=62)	
FOOD				
1	41.2	65.0	25.8	39.2
2	28.4	32.5	25.8	6.7
3	30.4	2.5	48.4	45.9
MATERIALS				
1	41.2	65.0	25.8	39.2
2	58.8	35.0	74.2	39.2

the data, which are small in size of sample and in some instances only roughly quantifiable, an attempt to define precise levels of significance for all the comparisons would be rather spurious. Consequently, I will proceed to mention only those differences that, on the basis of visual inspection and impression, strike me as being wide enough to warrant further consideration. (If any reader wishes to explore some other differences revealed in the tables, he can probably find enough data throughout this publication to pursue that praiseworthy but tedious endeavor.)

In the sense of the above, the households of Atea and Fatata differed "significantly" from one another in the following aspects:

1. There were some wide differences between Atea and Fatata with respect to total household size (i.e., counting all of a household's residents regardless of age) but I consider such differences to be less relevant to this study than those derived from counting adults only (i.e., individuals who were older than "children"). In this sense, Atea had a much larger percentage of single-adult (widowed or "divorced") households than Fatata and a slightly larger percentage of households with three adult members. In contrast, Fatata had slightly larger percentages of households containing two or four adults. (With respect to households containing five or more adults, the percentages of the two villages were virtually the same.)

2. In the matter of kin-age composition, Atea's percentages were somewhat larger in Type IA and Type IB (simple and complex single-family), and much larger in Type IIB ("residual" extended-family), whereas Fatata

exceeded Atea greatly in Types IIA (full extended-family) and IIIB (partial sib).

3. In terms of transactional *unity* and distributive *equity*, Atea exceeded Fatata on both counts: 95 percent against 85 percent with regard to *unity* and 82.5 percent against 74.2 percent with regard to *equity.*

4. Finally, a significantly higher percentage of Fatata's households acquired relatively large amounts of their food and building materials by purchase than was the case in Atea.

An initial reaction to these intervillage differences might suggest a necessary relation between some of these variables—say, between transactional unity (or distributive equity) and monetization, but is that in fact so? To answer this question, I applied tests of association to the several variables for Atea and Fatata combined and discovered a fairly high and unambiguous association to exist only between the variables of adult household size and kin-age composition—not a surprising finding in view of the large preponderance of simple nuclear-family households in both villages. Some association was also found to exist between size of household and monetization—viz., with respect to starchy foods and building materials, the larger the total (adults and children) household size, the smaller the percentage of those items that were purchased; but in terms of a household's adult membership, the opposite tendency prevailed.

In other instances, the degrees of association between variables were too low or equivocal to indicate necessary interrelations, causal or otherwise, for the combined series. For example, although seventy-eight of the 102 households in the combined series were both *unified* and *equitable,* and another ten were neither, the fourteen mixed cases represented a large enough proportion of the whole to rule out a necessary association between these variables.

The tests did, however, reveal some partial conformations. For example, *unity* and *equity* were more prevalent in the simple single-family households (which were, of course, those with fewest adults). On the other hand, the two households in the series that contained the largest number of adults (both of them in Fatata) were also *unified* and *equitable,* but perhaps significance should not be attached to a finding based on only two cases. More noteworthy was the high prevalence of *disunity* and *nonequity* found to prevail in three- and five-adult households, a situation possibly due to the unmarried condition of at least one adult of all such households.

Household Governance and Harmony

There are two other aspects of Te Piti's households yet to be touched on: their internal authority structure and the degree to which social harmony prevailed among each one's members. Surely, these are aspects of any social group important enough to warrant attention. And it is logical to propose that the households might be found to vary (e.g., in authority central-ization, in amount of interpersonal conflict, etc.) with such other household characteristics as pool-share *unity* and *equity*, with age profile, etc. More-over, in communities as small and "open" as these, information about dis-harmony and bossiness is readily available to an interested observer—or at least this is the case with the noisier expressions of such behaviors.

Unfortunately for this exercise, I found it impossible to identify any cri-teria that would permit me to type and thus compare all of Te Piti's house-holds in these respects. There were, for example, some notorious cases of disharmony—households whose members could be overheard quarrelling long into the night nearly every night. And there were households from which such sounds never issued and about which neighbors were ignorant of any dissent. On the other hand, there were many other households about whose "harmony" neighbors disagreed or about which they confessed igno-rance (though not disinterest!).

Similarly, some households were widely known for the strict, even tyran-nical, control exercised by their heads, and there were others that appeared to operate with little supervision at all. However, as far as I could ascertain, in most of Te Piti's households, authority was too diffuse and episodic to permit any neat classifying.

In view of these circumstances, and at the risk of disappointing more precision-minded readers, I shall content myself with the recording of a few general impressions and refer the reader to previous chapters for other infor-mation bearing on these matters.

Earlier, when discussing husband-wife relations, I asserted that, norma-tively, the husband-father was the final-decision maker and coordinator on certain special occasions requiring such, but that in fact such occasions were rare inasmuch as most everyday activities affecting a household were car-ried out following conventional patterns of divisions of labor. I went on to report that perhaps the most important of those special occasions left nor-matively to the husband-father for decision and supervision were those con-cerned with the acquisition and expenditure of money; but even here some exceptions to the stated rules occurred.

The same stated norms and conventions were evident in extended-family households, and some of the same kinds of exceptions thereto. For example, in the household of Teuru referred to earlier, Teuru himself exercised his firm and comprehensive authority not only over his wife and unmarried children but over his married daughter and her husband as well; and not only concerning matters involving money but over many of their other activities—their deportment around the house, their comings and goings, and their amusements. By contrast, the extended-family household of

Hamu (also referred to earlier) lacked any palpable sign of overall governance. Each nuclear-family component seemed to decide on its own contribution and to set its own pace.

Nor was the centralization of household authority invariably correlated
with the degree of unity of household economy. Some tendency of that kind
did prevail, but there were some notable exceptions, in both directions, i.e.,
there were some households characterized by a high degree of economic
unity but dispersed authority and some just the reverse. In other words, as
in some other domains of Te Piti's social life, personality and certain other
factors too numerous or too uniquely situational to be epitomized exercised
differentiating effects upon the ways extended-family households were governed and economically organized.

In discussing the "emotional" dimension of interaction among members
of nuclear families, I first listed the Te Pitians' stated rules for such relations, e.g., the *here* (affection, fondness) deemed proper between parents and
their own children; the respect required of children for their parents; etc.
The questions now addressed are, first, whether Te Pitians believed such
norms to be applicable in extended families as well—whether, for example,
the feeling of *mātau* (amity based on adjustment) deemed proper among nuclear-family members was considered equally requisite among all members
of an extended family—and, second, what the feelings among the members
of particular households actually were.

The answer to the first question is definitely "yes"—at least if one can
credit the Te Pitians' more formal verbal statements on this matter. Less
formally, several individuals acknowledged, e.g., that a person could not be
criticized for displaying more *here* for his own child than for the nephews
and nieces in his household, but some *here* was appropriate towards all.

Needless to say, the ideal of comprehensive loving-kindness, etc., was not
always and everywhere attained—which raises still another question, namely, what part did nuclear-family boundaries play in contravening the ideal?
Regrettably, a definitive answer to this question requires more information
than I possess. On the one hand, episodic coolness and quarrelling did tend
to reinforce nuclear-family boundaries in some households I knew, but the
most rancorous and chronic intrahousehold conflicts I knew about occurred
between spouses, or between parents and one or more of their offspring.
(Moreover, when conflict between whole nuclear families reached such a
level, it was more usual for all of the members of one of them to move elsewhere.) The fact that many such conflicts had their sources in "economic"
matters, e.g., in pool-sharing inequities, is, of course, relevant to the comparisons just carried out, but I am quite certain that not all such conflicts
had "economic" sources.

Relations between Households

Individual Te Pitians spent much time interacting with other members of their households, as previous sections of this chapter recorded. They also interacted, some of them frequently, with other Te Pitians—in church, in sodalities, at stores, in work groups, etc., and randomly, as they walked along the village paths. The more institutionalized of those interactions have been described elsewhere; here in this section I will be concerned with interactions between members of separate households on the occasions when they acted as whole households, more or less, or as representatives of whole households. A couple of examples will serve to indicate what I do and do not intend to concern myself with here.

In both Atea and Fatata, children living in neighboring houses tended to interact more often than those living farther apart, and the same was true of older neighbors, who typically exchanged messages like "What relish did you have for dinner?" or "Where did you work today?" There were exceptions, in both villages, where strained relations between individual members of separate households tended to interrupt interaction between the whole households, including even immediately adjacent ones, but the tendency was for neighbors to exchange talk whenever they were near enough to do so. However, this kind of interaction is not what I am concerned with here. Rather, I want to consider the class of events exemplified, e.g., when the head of one household passed on some of his household's food to the head of another, or when all or most members of one household visited another for a meal, or when whole households ceased interacting with each other deliberately because of animosity between one or more of their respective members.

To begin with, Te Pitians held views regarding how close to one another their household buildings should be, and there were some differences between the two villages in this regard.

In Atea, the houses were generally much closer together than they were in Fatata—most of Atea's forty-two households were concentrated within a residential area of about 0.65 square km, where most of Fatata's sixty-one were scattered over an area of about four square km. Moreover, most of the Te Pitians I talked with about this matter expressed preference for their own village's household spacing, the Ateans saying, in effect, that their close-togetherness was a friendlier, more pleasant way to live and the Fatatans asserting that closeness usually resulted in *pe'ape'a* (trouble, conflict). To some degree, these opposing preferences may have been rationalizations of each community's historically given residential patterns, but even so, they were nevertheless strong enough to influence current choice, i.e., many Ateans had the means of residing farther apart from their neighbors and many Fatatans of moving closer together, but few, in fact, had done so. Indeed, several of the former owned two houses, one in the village and one near its gardens and groves, and there were times during the year (regularly during the weeks after New Year) when they resided for days at a time in their "country" houses in order to be nearer their current work locations; but they all returned to their village houses for weekends and sometimes for cinema, etc., during the week as well.

There were individuals, even in Atea, who complained that the houses were too close together,[10] with resulting noisiness and potential for *pe'ape'a*, and at least three men reported that they had located their houses, which were relatively isolated, on account of their preference for spaciousness, quiet, and reduction of risk of *pe'ape'a*. However, two of these houses were separated from all others by thirty and forty-five meters, and the third by only eighty.

Also, there were parallel views, with social-class overtones, held in both villages associating residential crowdedness with "lower" status (see above), but what the "upper-class" Fatatans regarded as crowding would have been considered by their Atean counterparts to be quite far enough apart.

Transactions between Te Piti's households comprised the following kinds of objects and services: food—both comestibles and whole meals; utensils (cooking pots, dishes, etc.); furniture; tools; services of various kinds (e.g., house-building and repairing labor, laundering, childcare, invalid nursing); and some mutual help with gardening and food processing. Between specific pairs of households, these exchanges ranged widely in frequency and value—from weekly "gifts" of, say, a surplus fish or a helping hand with an infant, to an interdependency approximating symbiosis.

A typical example of the former was the exchange of *po'e,* which many households gave to one another on Sundays and other special occasions (not both of them, however, on the same day). *Po'e,* it may be recalled, is a sweet and chewy pudding made of cassava starch and fruit. It is laborious to prepare and is considered a delicacy (even by myself, who am not altogether enamoured of most kinds of everyday Te Piti food). *Po'e* was usually concocted only in fairly large quantities—partly perhaps because of the difficulty of preparation—and typically larger than many households could or would consume at the time. Hence it was common practice for the surpluses to be sent to certain other households which, in due course, would usually reciprocate in kind. Not all households made *po'e,* and not all those that

---

[10]In one instance, a rift developed between two friends when one of them laid the foundation for his new cement house "too close" to the other's wooden one, and friendship was restored only after the former financed the moving of the wooden structure (his own cement foundation being immovable) five (!) meters from the new one.

made it prepared enough to send outside. (It was unusual for two- and three-member households to make it and for very large ones to make more than they themselves consumed.) However, many of Te Piti's households were actively engaged in *po'e* exchanging, in networks ranging in size from two to five households each.

Full meals were also occasionally exchanged among some households, but most of this kind of exchanging was reserved for ceremonious occasions and such "dinner parties" usually included other guests, especially the *tāvana* and pastor (and even the ethnographer as well, with notebook and antacid tablets on the ready!).

Other objects regularly exchanged between some households were fish, pork, utensils, and tools (including rent-free use of another's copra dryer). Not all of these types of goods circulated through all of the networks (e.g., some small households exchanged fish and tools but not *po'e* or whole meals) and the exchanges were not in all cases of the same kind (e.g., one household regularly gave fish to its exchange partners and received other kinds of objects in return).

It also happened sometimes that a household acquiring a windfall—say, a very large catch of fish—gave (not sold) some of its surplus to households outside their usual exchange networks, but such donations were generally discrete enough, in terms of frequency (rare) and volume (small), to be described as such by donors and donees as well.

The most common kinds of *services* exchanged between household groups were child-tending, invalid-nursing, house-repairing, and oven-baking. (Concerning the last, some households occasionally baked their breadfruit, etc., in another's earth oven when it was not possible or convenient to carry out that lengthy and laborious chore on their own.) Also, in Atea, the women of one household regularly did the laundry, gratis, for a widower's household nearby. And in Atea there were several cases wherein members of two households took turns feeding one another's pigs maintained on distant (and usually adjoining) tracts of land, a service that involved canoe trips across the bay. In addition, in both villages there were a few cases of households making purchases for one another when a member of either of them visited *Te Oire* (i.e., "The Town"—Fare or Uturoa in the case of Atea, Pape'ete in the case of Fatata).

Two questions arise concerning the more established of these exchange networks: first, on what basis were they instituted and maintained? and second, in which of the two villages were they most numerous and active—and why?

Of the eighty regular linkages comprising both villages' interhousehold exchange networks, thirty-two involved household heads (male, female, or male and female) that were connected by some purported tie of kinship (consanguineous or affinal) of primary or secondary degree (i.e., with, say, a sibling or parent's sibling but not with a parent's sibling's child), while the other forty-eight involved more distant kin pairs or those with no purported kin tie at all. Examining the latter more closely: the usual explanation for such exchanges was simply, *mea au* (a matter of friendship) or, in the case of links between close neighbors, *mea au; fātata te fare* (a matter of friendship based on the proximity of houses). (Be it noted, however, that Te Piti also contained pairs of adult friends, including some who were heads of their respective households, whose households did not engage in regular exchanges with each other.)

A noteworthy aspect of interhousehold exchanges was the part played by fosterage in initiating or reinforcing them. Several of the linkages in both villages involved households whose connections included a fosterage tie. I came across no linkage that was explained by the fosterage tie alone, however; in fact, in all such cases the fosterage appears to have been preceded by a linkage based on kinship or friendship and served in part to reinforce that linkage, an explanation actually volunteered by the principals of some of those linkages. No one agreed verbally to my suggestion that parents might have given a child in fosterage in order to initiate such a linkage with another household, but I do believe that to have been the case in two or three instances. And while no one I questioned agreed with my semiserious suggestion that children served as goods in interhousehold exchanges ("like *po'e* or fish"), no one appeared scandalized by the suggestion, and all agreed to the relevance of the suggestion when I drew their attention to some cases of reciprocal fosterage—for such there were.

Earlier in this section, I characterized some interhousehold linkages as approximating symbiosis. In fact, there were cases in both villages wherein the exchanges of objects and services between separate residential units were so frequent and copious that I wavered before identifying them as separate households when carrying out the comparisons summarized earlier in this chapter.

One such case involved a pair of residential units—one occupied by a man, his wife and two of their children, and the other by the wife's mother and two of the couple's older children. Although there was continuous coming and going between the two houses and frequent common meals, each unit prepared and ate most of its meals separately and the members slept most nights in their separate houses. With respect to income, the man provided his mother-in-law with vegetables from a garden that was located on the latter's land and paid her half of the profits from the vanilla grown by him on land that belonged to her. On her part, the older woman bought all the store food used in her unit and much of that consumed in the other unit as well. Also, she used much of her money to buy clothes for her grand-children in both houses. Clearly, a very close interdependency but each unit still autonomous enough to qualify as separate households (mainly because of the mother-in-law's separate land, which could have earned a sufficient living income from another sharecropping tenant if her son-in-law had not himself chosen to work it).

Another borderline case was that of Old Nai, his elderly wife, their middle-aged adopted son, and the latter's wife and several children. Old Nai and wife slept in one house, the son and his family in a separate house a few meters away. Each sleeping house had its own cookhouse where each unit sometimes ate alone, but much of the cooking was done in that of the son, using food contributed about equally by both couples—from separate gardens and from separate cash-crop incomes (Old Nai's from copra pro-duced by him from his own land, the son's from vanilla grown by him on his wife's land). Sometimes the son and his wife and preschool children went to live in their country house for a few days in order to weed and pollinate their vanilla. When this occurred, Old Nai and his wife remained in the vil-lage and took over the care and feeding of the older children, who had to attend school, and it was this arrangement, along with the fact of the two families' frequent meal-sharing, that persuaded me to classify them as a single household for purposes of my survey.[11]

The phenomenon of interhousehold dependency (and hence the method-ological problem of defining household boundaries) is well typified in in-stances of extended families in process of segmenting or of coming together again. An example of the former was that of a certain man and his married son. At the beginning of my stay, the two men and their spouses and off-spring lived together in the older man's house and constituted a tightly or-ganized economic unit. Six months later, the two families lived in separate houses and constituted entirely separate economic units, but the transition had been a gradual, piecemeal one, both residentially and economically; I would have been hard put to decide when to count them as separate enough with respect to my survey criteria. In contrast, the separation of young Timi and his wife and child from the household of his father-in-law took place in one decisive move, having been preceded by a lengthy period of tension between the two families and accompanied by sharp recrimina-tion on both sides.

---

[11]The two cases just cited point up the arbitrariness of much of the classifying and labelling involved in quantitative survey-type ethnographic reporting, although I should add that most of the units I labelled "households" in the survey had much sharper boundaries than those just described.

The other end of the process was exemplified by the case of Old Toni and his wife. At the beginning of my stay in Atea, this senile couple lived in squalor in a house about 600 meters distant from that of their married daughter. They received some food and services from their daughter's household but evidently not enough to keep them well-fed. Yet, they were determined to live alone—"because of the *pe'ape'a* in their daughter's household." Six months later they had become wholly integrated into their daughter's household and their own household left unoccupied. Again, I would have found it difficult to decide at what point the two households had become one.

At the beginning of this section, I referred to instances of whole households having deliberately avoided interaction with all members of other households. Here again, a range of such "antilinkages" could be discerned. Near one extreme was the situation that prevailed between the household of Ama and that of his older brother Mani. The two brothers had fallen out years previously over a question of inheritance and had maintained their "coolness" (*fe'i'i*) ever since; they and their wives spoke to one another occasionally but never visited or exchanged things.

Another instance of interhousehold "coolness" occurred in Fatata, when a young woman nearly lost her own life and that of her baby through lack of assistance during labor. When her pains began, her husband went in search of a midwife, but while he was away, the woman's condition became acutely and inexplicably worse, so that she sent one of her children to her neighbors for aid. Two of the latter refused to attend her because, they said, of their "fear of blood." A third woman stayed away because, she explained, she wished to avoid blame should anything go wrong. And a fourth refused to go because of "coolness" occasioned by a quarrel over inheritance. In due course, the husband returned with the Administration midwife, who managed to save mother and infant. (So much for the widely advertised *aroha* of these "Happy Isles"!)

The most extreme instance of this kind of relationship prevailed between the households of Teuru and Vani. Here, I was instructed, it was not a case of mere "coolness," but of *enemi*. The two men deliberately avoided all interaction, except on one or two occasions when they exchanged threats and insults and had to be constrained from fighting.[12] Moreover, their relationship was also expressed in an economic rivalry; as Atea's only transport-boat owners, they engaged in active and sometimes cutthroat competition for passengers and freight between Atea and Fare. Some of their neighbors

---

[12]The insults included the ultimate contempt gesture of buttocks-baring in each other's direction, and the threats culminated in Teuru's brandishing his shotgun, for which he was subsequently fined and briefly incarcerated by the island's gendarme.

attributed their *enemi* to their transport rivalry, but those with longer memories said that it had begun many years previously with Vani's seduction of Teuru's wife. In any case, the antagonism between the two men embraced their respective households, whether voluntarily or by fiat I was unable to discover. (In this connection, when his daughter and son-in-law broke away from Teuru's household, as just reported, the daughter engaged in what seemed to be a deliberate and publicly symbolic effort to become friendly with Vani's wife.)

One of the most common causes of "anger" was some abuse of a child or young person by an older member of another household. When this occurred—and it could be either verbal abuse or reprimand or a physical blow—the mother of the victim could usually be relied upon to rush to the defense or to throw herself into revenging the foul deed. A typical example of this kind of episode took place in Atea. It began with two teenage girls of one household teasing another slightly younger one about her practice of wearing neither panties nor bra. When the mother of the victim heard about the matter, she rushed to the house of the teasers, all flags flying, and began a loud tirade against them. Thereupon, the mother of the teasers emerged and replied in kind at the top of her impressively loud voice. The two gladiatrixes carried on their vituperative contest—a good example of the custom of "street battling" (*tama'i purūmu*) mentioned in Chapter IX— standing about fifteen meters apart and in the midst of a large crowd of onlookers who seemed both amused and apprehensive. After some twenty minutes of this, the attacking mother left off and returned home, having evidently run out of voice and steam. Following this episode, the whole households of the principals remained "angry" with one another for several weeks but finally resumed their previous relationship (which had been mutually amicable but which had not included regular exchanges). In several other such instances of quarrels between wives, their "anger" remained limited to the principals themselves—their husbands, especially, having refused to become involved.

Specific instances of interhousehold "anger" (and even longer-enduring "coolness") were also caused, or detonated, by quarrels between parish sodalities—usually over "song stealing," disagreements over land boundaries, and crop destruction by another's pigs. In general, however, I was surprised and impressed during my 1954–55 visits by the infrequency of overt interhousehold disharmonies. (This impression perhaps reveals as much about my personal views on social relations as it does about actual conditions in Te Piti, and it may overlook less overt antagonisms, but it is nevertheless worth recording.) The question that arises in this deliberately comparative study is what differences, if any, there were between Atea and Fatata with respect to the prevalence of interhousehold interactions, both "positive," i.e., those comprising regular exchanges of mutually beneficial objects and services, and "negative," i.e., those comprising deliberate avoidance or mutually detrimental acts. First, the "positive" linkages.

I recorded fifty-two well-established and mutually acknowledged "positive" linkages among Atea's forty multimember households, in contrast to the twenty-eight recorded among Fatata's sixty-two, i.e., roughly three times as many per household. And of Atea's fifty-two "positive" linkages, twenty-four were between household heads who were "close" kin, whereas only eight of Fatata's linkages were so.

"Negative" interhousehold relations were not nearly so amenable to identification as were the "positive" ones. A couple of instances of longstanding _enemi_ relationships were identifiable in each village, and several instances of interhousehold "anger" were publicly displayed in Atea while I was there; but instances of longstanding interhousehold "coolness" were less accessible to inquiry in both villages, and I witnessed no episode of verbal street battling during my two visits to Fatata. (They may have occurred out of my hearing, but informants in Fatata disavowed their occurrence and reacted to my account of Atean occurrences with amusement.) In general, I can only report my impression that, however deep and widespread their interpersonal, specifically interhousehold, antagonisms may have been, the Fatatans were less given to expressing them in public than were the Ateans.

CHAPTER XI

KINSHIP AND LAND TENURE

Kin Networks

Both Atea and Fatata contained numerous kin networks that linked households with one another genealogically. These ranged in size and complexity from a few otherwise unlinked ones consisting of one pair of household heads who were siblings, or parent and child, to several large and unique constellations, such as the following:

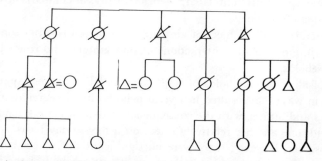

(This particular network can also be shown to have been interlinked with other local networks through kin links of the spouses of the household heads represented in the above diagram.)

Unfortunately—for the tidy-minded ethnographer, that is—Te Piti's larger interhousehold kin networks varied so widely in genealogical shape that it is not feasible to classify them for purposes of comparison. Each village, it is true, contained several clusters of consanguines to which were applied the generic label of 'ōpū fēti'i (kinfolk from the same "belly," i.e., a cognatic stock), and some of those bore names of one of their local ancestors.

However, there was widespread ignorance, or disagreement, about the boundaries of those clusters.

A similar difficulty is presented by my data relevant to classification of kin links between households (for example, with respect to the percentages of household heads related by primary consanguineal ties). And although some 'ōpū fēti'i were described as having had local origins, in no case in 1954–55 were all of their living members residing locally nor did any of those clusters function as distinct social units in any way except for land ownership, which will be described below.[1]

With more time than I care to devote to the matter (and with more ingenuity than I possess), it might be possible to devise algebraic formulas for comparing Atea and Fatata in terms of interhousehold kin links (for example, with respect to the proportions of cases in which households were linked by their heads' primary, secondary, tertiary, etc., kin ties). However, after experimenting with various indices based on such links, to no satisfying effect, I will base the comparisons on one negative criterion, namely, the percentage of household heads, male and/or female, who had *no* ascendant or collateral kin ties with members of other local households. In this respect, one would have to conclude that Fatata was much less interlinked than Atea, since thirty-three of Fatata's sixty-three household heads, male and female, were thus "unrelated," genealogically, in comparison with only nine of Atea's forty-one.[2]

I will return to the subject of kin categories presently, after some review and description of actual interactions among kinfolk who resided in separate households.

First of all, the households of both Atea and Fatata were spatially distributed in ways that resulted in several neighborhood aggregations of consanguines and affines, with the consequence that such kinfolk tended to interact with one another relatively often, on a day-to-day basis. As far as I could discover, however, there were no significant differences between the two villages in this respect; in both places, about one-half of the residences were situated in such neighborhoods.[3]

---

[1]See above, pages 272–73, for discussion of the term *fēti'i*, and see Hooper 1970, p. 6, for further information about the category *'ōpū fēti'i*.

[2]Included within these numbers are the two live-alone adults, one in each village, that were excluded in the comparisons of Chapter X.

[3]One of the clearest examples of a consanguineal household neighborhood was the cluster of four of them in Fatata, comprising a single extended family, located in a valley about one-third mile from all other houses. Even more distinct was the one (not included in this study) residing on a large tract located about one-half mile southeast of Fatata. Although this tract was within the Toerau Administrative District and Parish, its residents, numbering some forty-seven divided into nine households, comprised one large extended family, the nucleus of which

A second, more institutionalized form of kin interaction was exemplified in the interhousehold exchanges described in Chapter X. (The deliberate avoidance relationship based on "coolness" was also relevant in this context.)

A third form of kin interaction, also somewhat institutionalized, took place on certain ceremonial occasions, mainly weddings, funerals, and New Year celebrations. The parts played by kinfolk at weddings and funerals have already been described; a further word should be said here about the highly organized and costly New Year celebrations, which constituted, among other things, annual reunions of kinfolk.

For some Te Pitians, "New Year" (*Matahiti 'āpī*) was a time for daily church attendance, for others a time for drinking parties and dancing. And for nearly everyone it was a time for visiting among local households and by kinfolk from afar. The most numerous of the latter were individuals returning home from Pape'ete or other places where they had been working or attending school, but some of the visitors comprised whole families of close relatives with their permanent residences elsewhere.

Providing sleeping places for the visitors was not difficult, but feeding, and in some cases beveraging, the visitors for a week or two—the usual duration of such visits—was no easy matter, particularly since it usually included such delicacies as pork and more than normal amounts of store-bought food (and in some cases a steady supply of wine and beer). In many instances, the visitors contributed in money or in kind to their keep (this was more typical of young adults visiting their parents or siblings), but in other instances the material hospitality was provided on the tacit, but strictly unstated, assumption that it would be reciprocated on some future occasion. It was the supplying of the food and drink included in this "reciprocal" hospitality that is of present concern.

When I made my first roundabout inquiries about how households met the increased demands of entertaining New Year visitors, I received the usual: "They are *fēti'i* we simply share with them what we have"; (i.e., "there is no difficulty in feeding *fēti'i*, and of course not even a thought about eventual repayment"). With this ritualistic reply disposed of, however, several informants were quite willing, even eager, to describe the costs and financing of such entertaining and, in a few instances, the unlikelihood of any future reciprocation.

---

were the fourth- and fifth-generation descendants of a European planter and his Tahitian wives. These people visited Fatata infrequently, only to patronize the stores or to attend church services or sodality meetings. Otherwise, they were a community unto themselves—even sexually, according to some Fatatans, who described them as being "disgustingly" incestuous.

In the event that the expected visitors were kin-related to the host household only, the entire expense had to be borne by that household—by setting aside some of its own pigs for butchering, by extra money-earning work during the month or so preceding the visit, by obtaining assurances of increased credit or even money loans from the storekeepers, etc. In most instances, however, the expected visitors would have had kin ties with two or more local households, and when this occurred the heads of the latter usually arranged some sharing of costs, most typically by taking turns in feeding the visitors (and not by contributing food or money to the visitors' principal household host). In one case—the only one I uncovered—three brother-linked households in Atea regularized such arrangements by establishing a joint "household bank" ('āfata 'utuāfare), which—amazing to relate!—was still in operation when I revisited the village five years later.

New Year was undoubtedly the most favored occasion for kinfolk residing in different communities to visit one another, but it was not the only one. When Te Pitians, individuals or families, travelled to Pape'ete or Uturoa for medical or other special reasons, they usually camped with kinfolk, if they had any, while there. (Hotels were considered places for Europeans; no Te Pitian I knew about would have spent money willingly for a place merely to sleep in.) On occasions such as those just mentioned, when the main reason for the trip was other than a social visit itself, the visitors customarily took along some food, or even insisted on contributing money towards the hosts' food expenditures while there. In addition, there was some intervillage visiting by kinfolk on the occasion of weddings and funerals, as well as at times when no reason for the visit was summoned save for the desire to see long-separated kin.

A comparison of Atea and Fatata in terms of kin relations as exemplified by the organization of weddings reveals no noteworthy differences with respect to the large veiled-bride affairs. In both places, the ones I witnessed, or collected seemingly reliable accounts about, were managed and financed, ideally, according to the standard Tahitian (i.e., not uniquely Te Pitian) practice whereby the respective sides (pae) of the bride and groom had more or less equal voices in planning and contributed more or less equally, in services and in money or other objects, to the celebrations.[4] Also, although the participants in the church services and in the banquets that followed them included many other persons (particularly all the local officials of both

---

[4]The fact that 22.5 percent of Fatata's marital unions in existence during my first visit had been celebrated with veiled-bride nuptials, as against only 8.9 percent of those in Atea, means, of course, that the constituent kin ties of the former had been activated more often than those of the latter through this particular kind of ceremony, but this quantifiable difference must be considered in relation to the other kinds of nuptials about to be discussed.

parish and district), kinfolk of the brides and grooms always predominated, including some from distant places.

Judging from the marital unions extant in Te Piti in 1954–55, parish-type weddings had been considerably more popular in Atea than in Fatata during the preceding decades—i.e., 28.6 percent to 18.3 percent. Such unions, it will be recalled, were those that had been sanctioned by civil and church rites and by whole parish or sodality wedding feasts. In other words, the principal arrangers, participants, and contributors on such occasions were the principals' church or sodality associates and not their respective kinfolk as such (although some of those kinfolk were inevitably included among the sponsors). Thus, with respect to this kind of wedding celebration, Ateans tended to place more emphasis than Fatatans on relationships that were not explicitly based on kinship.

Turning however to other kinds of unions listed above (Chapter VIII, pages 263-69), both legalized (*ha'aipoipo*) and nonlegalized (*fa'a'aea noa*), from the information I gathered it appeared that kinfolk per se in Atea played much larger roles in ceremonially initiating such unions than did their counterparts in Fatata. In fact, even some of the most "temporary" of nonlegalized unions I knew about in Atea had been formalized by small-scale but special feasts held jointly by kinfolk of both principals. In Fatata, on the other hand, those and other nonlegalized unions were rarely celebrated by any kind of gathering, and even an official union performed by the local pastor for his own daughter and the latter's long-standing paramour received no celebration of any kind.

Another difference between the two villages in the domain of "kinship" was to be seen in the burial of the dead and in the financing of funerals. As was described in Chapter IX, in Fatata bodies were interred in a common district cemetery, in obedience to Administration regulations, and funerals were until recently financed by a village-wide levy. In Atea, funerals were financed by the deceased's close kinfolk and, despite Administration regulations, bodies were also interred in places associated with kinfolk (see pages 374-75).

In summary, beyond the boundaries of individual households, kinship ties served not only to link pairs of households in fairly regular bilateral exchanges, as described in Chapter X, but they served also as an important basis for association in other kinds of social units or aggregations as well—in sodalities, in neighborhoods, in weddings, in funerals, in New Year reunions, and in visits elsewhere. Comparing Atea and Fatata in this respect, kinship exercised about the same weight of influence in both villages with respect to neighborhood affiliation (or rather, placement of residence), to membership in the separate sodality units, to participation in New Year reunions, and in visits away from home. On the other hand, it was weightier in Fatata than in Atea with respect to the sponsorship of weddings—and quite the reverse with respect to funerals.

The above has to do with only one aspect of extrahousehold interaction among kinfolk, namely, with the frequency and amounts of time spent by kinfolk, *qua* kinfolk with one another in the activities listed. Another aspect of such interaction concerns the value of the goods included therein.

At least three kinds of goods were involved in those interactions: services (including a person's mere presence at, say, a wedding or funeral); food and other objects; and money. Of these three, I can provide "hard" data only for the last, and this has to do, first, with Te Pitians' reported money expenditures on *ohipa fēti'i* during 1954–55.[5] I cannot, of course, vouch for the accuracy of all the answers received, but, for whatever their worth, they indicate that Ateans spent more money, per capita, on such events than Fatatans, i.e., 406 francs against the latters' 367. Figure for figure, this difference is not a very wide one, but its significance is increased when it is viewed as representing 5 percent of all money expenditures by the Ateans during the period in question, as against only 3.6 percent of those of the Fatatans.

I turn now to a consideration of kinship as a basis of joint ownership, which among contemporary Te Pitians had to do mainly with land. A few of the older, more permanently fixed houses were owned jointly by siblings, or by collateral sets of siblings, etc., but those too were for the most part held in association with land, as will be described.

Before embarking on a description of current Te Pitian land tenure, it may be useful, however, to summarize its historical and prehistorical background.

Land Tenure in Ancient Tahiti[6]

The subject of land tenure in Ancient Tahiti[7] is obscure, to say the least. As a system of overlapping rights, etc., it was probably no more complex

---

[5]In preparing and administering the questionnaire whose findings were summarized on Table 3, all contributions and expenditures on the weddings, illnesses, funerals, New Year hospitality, etc., of extrahousehold kinfolk were so categorized.

[6]The contents of this and of the following two sections were first published in *The Changing Pacific: Essays in Honour of H. E. Maude*, edited by Niel Gunson (Melbourne: Oxford University Press, 1978), under the title of "Norms of Tahitian Land Tenure: Ancient and Modern." Grateful acknowledgment is hereby made to the editor and publisher for permission to reprint them here.

[7]By "ancient" Tahiti I mean the era from about 1750 to about 1800, i.e., that immediately preceding and during the period of the first European visits and before those visits had, directly or indirectly, brought about radical changes in the indigenous society. And by "Tahiti" I include all of the islands that have come to be known as the Society Islands. The customs I attribute to that era may have been, and indeed probably were, prevalent before then, but about that there is no reliable evidence.

than the European systems prevailing at that time, but the European observers who reported anything about it—and not many did—either misunderstood or oversimplified its actual workings. In addition, most subsequent attempts to delineate it—the system having undergone far-reaching changes under early European influence and later under European political control—have been obfuscated by application of terms like "feudal" and rendered suspect by their authors' tendency to fill in the gaps in the Tahitian data with data from other Polynesian societies (an expedient that might be warranted in some instances but could be partly or wholly fallacious).

The two kinds of social units in ancient Tahiti with which territory was most universally and exclusively associated were kin-congregations and tribes. I apply the former label to residential, co-worshipping groups of people that consisted of a core of consanguines along with a fringe of other individuals who had become attached to them as spouses, refugees, bond-friends, etc. The focus of such a group was a *marae,* or temple, at which the members (usually only the adult males or their priestly representatives) communicated—including presentation of offerings—with their tutelar spirits, who included, typically, one or more ancestral ghosts. Kin-congregation temples varied widely in size, in architecture, and in accessories, but they all included these features: a stone rest for the spirit(s) during the religious service, a fixed place for the principal officient(s), an altar for offerings, and a space for the worshippers. The spirits' place ranged in size and form from a single slab to huge platforms or multistepped pyramids; the officients' place consisted usually of one or more basalt uprights. In addition, each temple had associated with it, more or less exclusively, one or more tracts of clearly demarcated land, and in some cases adjacent portions of lagoon or sea. And anyone who was acknowledged by the congregation's leaders to be a fellow member, either by birth from a prior member or by "adoption,"[8] was entitled to use-rights in its temple-associated territory. Also, any non-member married to a kin-congregation's member enjoyed use-rights in such territory—rights that continued after the member-spouse's decease, provided the survivor did not marry and live with a nonmember elsewhere. However, in keeping with the pervasively hierarchic ordering of ancient Tahitian society, the territorial use-rights of a kin-congregation's members were markedly differentiated, e.g., those of an eldest sibling (especially if male) enjoyed precedence over those of younger ones, and those of the head member of a senior line over those of the head of a cadet line.[9]

---

[8] There appears to have existed a nuptiallike rite that was performed for validating an outsider's "adoption" to congregation membership.

[9] There is some evidence to suggest that a male's use-rights outweighed those of his sisters and that this inequality extended to the latters' progeny, but this is not altogether certain.

When in the course of time a kin-congregation proliferated, the additional residences built to accommodate the increase were usually located quite widely apart and at some considerable distance from the "ancestral" ones—in other words, the most typical settlement pattern of that era was of the type now called "dispersed." This residential movement was usually accompanied (or preceded?) by dispersion of the emigrés' gardens and groves, to which they thus came to acquire distinctive use-rights. Indeed, it seems likely that continual and uncontested use by a subunit of any portion of a kin-congregation's territory served to enhance its rights over it, with or without a shift in residence.

After a few generations of this kind of differentiation, the territory of a kin-congregation, like the group itself, would have become segmented into numerous subdivisions, each with its own temple and fairly exclusive land boundaries. However, in the ordinary course of events, the kin-congregation as a whole, represented by the head of its senior subgroup (in effect, the kin-congregation's "chief") continued to have residual rights in all the kin-congregation's territory—rights that were periodically acknowledged by the subunits in the form of firstfruits presented to that chief at the "ancestral" temple, partly for token redistribution and partly for offerings to the group's tutelar spirits (who were concerned with the productivity of the kin-congregation territory as a whole). In addition, the chief of a kin-congregation was entitled to impose a *rahui* over resources of· its territory from time to time, i.e., a prohibition against, say, the eating of its coconuts or the catching of its fish. (It seems likely that the senior member of each subunit of a kin-congregation possessed similar rights over his unit's territorial subdivision, but about that the sources are silent.)

In addition to the process of *internal* differentiation just described, some kin-congregations underwent dispersion and differentiation through "colonial" expansion. That is to say, it sometimes happened that one or more members of a kin-congregation left the home territory altogether and established a new settlement elsewhere, say, by migration into an uninhabited and unclaimed area or by successful conquest. When that occurred, and if communication with the homeland could be maintained, the "colonials" usually continued to acknowledge their ties with the homeland by rendering firstfruits to the kin-congregation chief at the ancestral temple. Moreover, their derivation from and allegiance to the larger unit were concretely symbolized in their own temple, into which was built a cornerstone taken from the ancestral temple.

It goes without saying that, among the many kin-congregations into which ancient Tahitian society was divided, the potency of the residual territorial entitlements just mentioned must have varied quite widely, e.g., according to the size and scatter of each one's subunits, the degree of amity or enmity among its subunit heads, the personality of its current senior chief. Nevertheless, the ideological model just summarized remained available, to be followed or ignored as circumstances or ambitions decreed.

In listing the criteria for membership in a kin-congregation, I mentioned the rights accruing to a member's spouse, the reference having been to a spouse from elsewhere. It should be noted that in many, if not most, marriages, and particularly between persons of the lower social classes (above, page 37–38), both spouses were likely to have belonged to the same kin-congregation—that is to say, except for upper-class persons, some of whom married "close in" in order to preserve "purity" of line, most other persons were at pains to avoid reproductive matings with consanguines. (In other words, kin-congregations were not exogamous per se, and most of them were probably wide enough in span, and localized enough in distribution, to permit and encourage matings between fellow members.) When, however, a husband and wife did belong to distinct kin-congregations, their progeny acquired entitlements in the kin-congregations of both. Thus individuals could, and evidently did, inherit entitlements in the territories of numerous kin-congregations—but the potency of such rights would of course have depended upon the claimants' ability to validate them genealogically and upon the uses actually made of them. In most cases, probably, an individual of middle- or lower-class status maintained effective inherited use-rights only in the territory of his or her residence, or if married elsewhere, only in that of his birth. Some high-ranking *ari'i* made a practice of revisiting the various kin-congregation territories in which they possessed entitlements in order to revalidate them there, but there seems not to have been any formal procedure whereby lowlier persons could keep their claims "warm."

The second kind of ancient Tahitian social unit possessing important territorial domains was, for want of a distinctive native label, what I call a tribe, i.e., a unit all of whose members resided contiguously[10] and under the leadership of someone—a chief—who himself was not under the leadership of another chief (see above, page 36). Leadership of the kind I refer to embraced acknowledged and effective command over the goods and services of people, including war-making and periodic levies of objects and labor. The comprehensiveness and absoluteness of that command varied not only with the character of the tribal chiefs but also with the strength of subtribal units and even, it appears, with regional differences in opinion about chiefs' rights. That is to say, some tribes were ruled totally and despotically and others only partially and with laxity.

---

[10]That is, except for two parts of a subtribal division in Tahiti's southern peninsula, which were separated by a separate subtribe.

There may have been periods during the era of Tahiti's initial settlement when each kin-congregation was an autonomous tribe, but by the time Europeans arrived on the scene none of the tribes then extant comprised less than three or four distinct kin-congregations, with the result that each of them contained two or more levels of administrative leadership, to which corresponded a like number of levels of territorial rights. A tribal chief's authority over the territories of other kin-congregations within his domain may not have been as direct or as priestly or as supernaturally sanctioned as over his own, but at the very least he received tribute, through their own chiefs, in the form of food and other objects produced in those territories, and, through their own chiefs, was able to impose *rahui* over them. Morever, each tribe also had *its* temple, which on occasion served as a religious center for the tribe as a whole. (In some cases the kin-congregation temple of the tribal chief doubled as a tribal temple as well; in others a separate and distinct tribal temple was constructed for this purpose.)

All the territorial entitlements so far mentioned pertained to social groups, or to individuals as heads of such groups. It should also be added that some ancient Tahitians, notably some tribal chiefs and members of their immediate families, individually possessed full, undivided rights over certain tracts of land, from which each obtained some or most of his daily food. Most of these chiefly lands constituted those parts of a chief's kin-congregation land that had become identified with his lineal ascendants by use over time, but some of them had been acquired by extratribal conquest, or by dispossession of former intratribal members as punishment for some misdeed (most typically, for *lèse-majesté*).

The above reconstruction of ancient Tahitian land tenure is not in accord with one put forward by some ethnologists, who viewed that society as having been stratified more discontinuously and along more ethnic lines. Those writers, having accepted certain liturgical myths more historically and literally than I am inclined to do, perceived the three major social classes into which the society was stratified as having been different and distinctive with respect to land ownership as well, namely:

—the aristocratic *Hui Ari'i*, a race of immigrant conquerors, who owned the most favored coastal lands and lagoons;
—the yeomen *Pue Ra'atira*, who owned the less favored but still productive lands bordering those of the *Hui Ari'i*; and
—the common *Manahune*, survivors of the islands' original, conquered inhabitants, who lived inland and who "owned no land."

Ancient Tahitian society was indeed stratified, but not, I believe on this basis and not with the kind of land-tenure attributions just reported. In my view, most of the larger widely ramified kin-congregations would have included *ari'i, ra'atira,* and *manahune* members. And although the *hui ari'i* of a kin-congregation might, had they wished, have enjoyed more preemptive rights than lower-class members over their jointly-owned territory, the difference in entitlements was a matter of degree and not of kind. Moreover, although it occasionally transpired that an individual was banished from his tribal territory for some offense or other and was hence "landless"—at least temporarily—in that particular area, an ancient Tahitian's kin ties (and hence land-use rights) were so widely ramified that it would in my opinion have been quite exceptional for an exile to have had no rights to any land anywhere.

Land Tenure Changes under Colonial Rule

Needless to say, the land tenure regime I have just summarized has undergone some major transformations since Europeans appeared on the scene—first, as result of unification of the islands' twenty or more eighteenth-century tribes into four European-style "kingdoms" (Tahiti-Mo'orea-Tetiaroa-Me'etia, Huahine-Mai'ao, Rai'atea-Taha'a, and Porapora-Maupiti); later, as an aspect of French colonial control. A full historical account of the land tenure changes accompanying these developments would require a whole volume (and one well worth compiling[11]) but I shall sketch only enough of it to provide a background for the situation that prevailed in 1954–55, during my first visits to Te Piti.

The Windward Islands (Tahiti, Mo'orea, Me'etia, and Tetiaroa) became a French Protectorate in 1842. By then, some of their lands had already been acquired by Europeans, and those remaining in Tahitians' hands had become, de facto, identified fairly exclusively with coresidential kin groups that were much narrower in span than the earlier pagan kin-congregations had been. Meanwhile, the kind of "citizenship" estate earlier associated with tribal membership had become attenuated nearly to the point of nonexistence through the coalescence of the former tribes into the larger and less functional political units represented by the new kingdoms. In connection with the latter change, the "chiefly lands" referred to above had become appanages (*fari'i hau*) of the offices of the district chiefs (*tāvana*), who by 1842 had come to be representatives and subordinates of the monarch. Also, by this time the land rights of the monarch (Aimata, Queen Pomare IV) had become reduced to those pertaining to a few explicitly royal appanages and to a small number of her kin units.

French officials exerted first their influence and then their authority in an effort to westernize land tenure in the Windward Islands. The process began in 1852 with a law of the Tahitian Kingdom that ordered the registration,

---

[11]Newbury 1956.

by district,[12] of every distinct land parcel (French *terre*; Tahitian *fenua*) according to its native name, its geographic boundaries, its approximate area, and the name(s) of its principal owner(s). Separate registers were to be kept for privately owned and official appanage lands. With respect to the former, an owner was evidently identified with the head, usually male, of the household having most active locally acknowledged household rights in the parcel in question. (No provision was made at that time for the rights, if any, of absent, co-owning collaterals, nor for minors for whom the parcel might have been held in trust.) With respect to the appanages—the parcels known as *fari'i hau*—these were intended to provide for the subsistence of the district chiefs and their families—in amounts "in keeping with their superior social status"—and were declared to be subject to alienation only after approval by the Protectorate's legislative assembly.[13]

Once recorded (presumably by each district's local officials), the lists were required to be checked for accuracy and authenticity by a commission consisting of the Protectorate's official interpreter, a member of the Protectorate High Court, the district's chief local judge, and its oldest Tahitian citizen. After approval by this commission, one copy of each list (in Tahitian) was deposited with the Tahitian High Court (*To'ohitu*) and another (in French) with the Protectorate Lands Office (*Service des Domaines*). Thereafter, all changes in a parcel's boundaries and ownership were required to be recorded in a separate register lodged with the High Court.

All very sensible and orderly, from the colonizers' point of view. Notwithstanding, many of the Tahitians of that time failed to register their land holdings, either from negligence or ignorance of the law. In fact, many had still not done so by 1880 (when the Windward Islands were formally annexed), so that the French authorities issued another decree (24 August 1887) which revised the registration procedure somewhat and contained sanctions against nonregistration. By this decree, all lands in the colony were initially viewed as if belonging to the Lands Office. Thereupon a title deed was handed over to each officially acknowledged owner, and all parcels not so allocated were classified temporarily as "district lands."

In the case of the latter, the decree allowed the claimants to them a year in which to lodge their claims, failing which these lands were to become *domaines*. To lodge a claim, the claimant(s) were required to state their officially

---

[12]The colonial administrative districts (Tahitian *mata'eina'a*) into which the islands were and are subdivided (at that time Tahiti had seventeen, Mo'orea four) were in most cases perpetuations of ancient tribal or subtribal divisions.

[13]The clause in quotes is taken (in translation) from Pambrun 1958, upon which much of the historical summary of this and following paragraphs is based. The other secondary source I have used extensively in this historical *précis* is Colin Newbury's excellent Ph.D. dissertation (Newbury 1956), which, most unfortunately, was not published until 1980, i.e., after the present work was completed. See Newbury 1980.

registered names, the name and area of the parcel, and the names of all parcels bordering it. This information had to be presented at a meeting of the district's council and inscribed on a public notice. If after three months no opposition to the claim had been lodged with the Lands Office, it was declared to be authentic, the claimant(s) was given a title deed, and the parcel was registered in the Lands Office. On the other hand, if an opposing claim was lodged within the specified period the district council in question was empowered to decide between the rival claimants—which they did, it would appear, mainly on the basis of genealogical evidence.

Titles to the traditional *fari'i hau* parcels were handled in the same manner. In addition, all those areas on which had been built public structures, such as churches, schools, and Administration offices, were declared to belong to the colonial Administration or to the district in question.

And finally, all parcels unclaimed or otherwise unattributed were declared to be Territory *domaine*. The decree of 1887 also established the principle that, after a specified lapse of time, all future claims and counterclaims would have to be considered according to standard civil-law procedures.

In the Leeward Islands, the history of land registration followed a different course, inasmuch as these islands did not come under direct French rule until later. During the preceding eight decades, each of the petty kingdoms comprising these islands had its own law codes (inspired mainly by missionaries of the London Missionary Society) and these served to formalize land tenure regimes that incorporated elements of ancient Tahitian ideas about kin-communality and social hierarchy, along with European ones about individual private ownership, land buying and selling, and church property.

One of France's first official acts in the Leeward Islands was to issue a decree (22 December 1898) establishing a procedure for attributing and registering land ownership. By it, the authorities appointed a commission in each of the Leewards' major subdivisions (*arrondisements*) to receive and review land claims.[14] As a first step, each claimant declared his claim before the commission, which caused it to be published in the *Journal Official*. After that, a period of six months was allowed to permit other parties to submit counterclaims. If none was submitted, the commission nevertheless inquired closely into the bases of the claim and approved it only if they considered it to be justified (presumably on the basis of genealogy or clear proof of purchase or gift). If a counterclaim was submitted, the commission scrutinized that in the same manner and either decided in favor of one of the claimants

---

[14]Each commission was composed of five or more Tahitian residents of the subdivision, including one or two judges and district chiefs.

or, if neither claim was strong enough, declared the parcel to be Administration *domaine*. As a further safeguard, the commission's decisions were permitted to be appealed against before a special court, consisting of judges and chiefs, before final approval and registration.

Eventually, both Windward and Leeward islands were mapped to show the boundaries, place-names, area (in hectares), and current owner(s) of each tract of land[15] recognized as being a separately owned *parcel* (French, *terre*; Tahitian, *fenua*); and new boundary markers were set up when necessary.[16]

According to the principles that seem to have governed these initial attributions, the listed owner(s) (*proprietaire*) of a parcel, or fraction thereof, was the head, usually the oldest male, of the household currently exercising uncontested use-rights over it—or the "heirs" of that head if he were but recently deceased. Obviously, this definition of land ownership constituted some narrowing of the usages that prevailed in pre-European times. It did not, for example, take into account any residual rights of more-senior-line collaterals, nor any joint-use rights of absent siblings. As such, however, it reflected realistically the changes in land-use practice that had come about during the previous decades of depopulation and European influence.

Also, in identifying parcels with specific households the commissioner and judges seem to have given much weight to the presence of the burial sites of the claimants' ancestors. In instances of disagreement and challenges, where all the parties were able to provide equally persuasive "proofs" of ownership, the issues seem to have been settled by adopting one of three solutions:

—by dividing the parcel among the claimants (in some cases into minute fractions of the original tracts);

—by awarding ownership to the oldest surviving "heir" of an agreed-upon "original" owner, in the terms governing inheritance set forth in the *Code Civil*; or

—by attributing equal-part ownership to two or more claimants or sets of claimants, who thereafter constituted a *tōmite* (from English "committee").

---

[15]By French law, lagoon and sea areas were no longer subject to private ownership.

[16]The type of real property systems thus applied goes under the label of *Régime Hypothécaire du Code Civil*, to distinguish it from the *Régime de l'Immatriculation ou du Livre Foncier*. In 1955, the former operated in metropolitan France, Martinique, Guadeloupe, Réunion, New Caledonia, in parts of Sénégal, and in French dependencies elsewhere. The principal difference between the two *régimes* lies in the form in which lands are identified and registered in the official records—the former being done so by name(s) of the owner(s), the second by the name of each land parcel (Pambrun 1958).

Regarding these latter, many parcels were also attributed to two or more *tōmite*, not as a result of contesting claims but by mutual agreement of the parties themselves—in cases, for example, where two or more households had been peacefully sharing the use of a parcel and did not wish to divide it.

From this distance in time, it is impossible to reconstruct all the specific changes the initial land registrations served to introduce or perpetuate, but two general ones can be listed.

By defining "ownership" more narrowly and more exclusively than the traditional principles had done, the registration focussed people's land-use rights upon smaller geographic areas and reduced or extinguished their rights elsewhere. (In doing so, the registration served to decrease the size and sharpen the boundaries of their kin-corporations.)

By attributing ownership principally to specific individuals or heirs of individuals, the registration *could* have disenfranchised altogether some other persons who possessed rights according to older usages.[17] It may, in fact, have done so in some instances; however, in view of the principle, traditionally practiced and now officially recognized, whereby children inherited from both parents, this disability would not necessarily have led to the foundation of perpetually landless family lines.

One ancient feature of Tahitian land tenure, which neither time nor European influence and legislation has altered, is the Tahitians' respect for the boundary stones (*'ofa'i 'oti'a*) that anciently served to mark land-parcel boundaries not otherwise delimited, e.g., by streams or cliffs or conspicuous trees. Stones—low stone posts—were also set up to mark the new boundaries delimited during the initial colonial land registrations, and these, like the ancient ones, were sacrosanct to all of the Tahitians I queried on the subject. Many of these informants knew some of the stones to be venerable (i.e., those from heathen times, *tau 'etene*) and others more recent, but all of them considered both kinds of boundary stones to possess (or *be?*) *mana* (power)— whether derived from the ancient gods (now collectively identified as Satan, *Tatani*) or from more recent but deceased (and potentially vengeful) chiefs and judges. I discovered no Tahitian who would have had the audacity to move a boundary stone. And I was cited examples, even by the best educated of my informants (including those who disavowed Satan's role in the matter), of individuals who had become ill or crippled through having accidentally moved or damaged one of them.

---

[17]During the drafting of the 1887 decree, referred to earlier, a suggestion was made in Privy Council that attributions be recorded in the names of whole land-using groups, but this was turned down on the grounds that it would perpetuate land indivisibility (Newbury 1956).

Meanwhile, the French *Code Civil* was applied to govern the ways in which full ownership of a parcel could be transferred, namely, by inheritance (*succession*), testament, gift, purchase or barter, "prescription acquisitive," and uncontested occupation of thirty or more years.

French laws governing inheritance were (and are) precise, detailed, and—for metropolitan French society, at least—exhaustive. Among other things, they defined filiation more narrowly than the traditional Tahitian usages (e.g., by reducing the inheritance rights of illegitimate and "unrecognized" offspring); and in the absence of offspring, they specified with mathematical precision the fractional residual rights of ascendants, of collaterals, of spouses, etc. Fortunately (for the ethnographer!), the nearly endless possibilities envisaged by the *Code* had very little real relevance for the communities I studied, where virtually every landowner since the initial registration has had either offspring or siblings to whom his or her land titles did or could devolve. (And in the few instances I knew about where that was not the case, the owner in question usually purposely avoided wider distribution by making a will.)[18]

With respect to land transaction by "gift," the *Code* served to substantiate and formalize some previous ceremonial transactions to a degree beyond the intent of the original donors (and at the same time it perpetuated an aspect of class stratification in a society that had otherwise become more egalitarian in its official ideals). I refer here to a situation that prevailed—and still does—in some districts including Te Piti, namely, the ownership of large parcels of prime land by absentee descendants of former *ari'i*. With the egalitarianizing of Tahitian colonial society, the traditional *ari'i* lost even their symbolic, residual proprietorship over their former subjects' lands and would have retained rights only over their own family lands but for the rhetoric of some of their former subjects or others of like class. That is to say, even well into the colonial era, it often happened that when a member of the disappearing but still respected *ari'i* class went visiting, his local host, if of inferior social status, conventionally greeted him (or her) with traditional, hyperbolic phrases of hospitality, including the invitation to "consider all my lands to be your own"—and some of the visitors did just that when colonial land registration took place. (Something similar occurred with respect

---

[18]There were some parcels of land in Te Piti whose post-registration ownership histories I was unable to trace, on account of their owners, or joint owners, having left the community and lost contact with their former lands and neighbors. In some of these cases, in which actual transfer of ownership had not been recorded in the Lands Office, it could be that ownership rights had devolved along more unusual lines, e.g., from owner to distant collaterals, but the inheritances I knew about followed the paths just noted.

to some early European visitors, but fewer of these ceremonial transfers seem to have been perpetuated.)

The purchasing (and bartering) of land that was sanctioned by the *Code* was probably unknown in pre-European Tahiti but had become a common transaction by the time the *Code* began to be applied. It is highly likely that in many of the instances of "purchase" (by Europeans and Chinese especially) the initial registrations recorded—and hence officially sanctioned—were never intended by their Tahitian "sellers" to be such, or were "sold" under duress of one kind or another (e.g., while drunk, or under threat of arrest for nonpayment of debt).[19] In any case, the purchase of land had by 1954–55 become commonplace in Te Piti, but the sellers were no longer gullible, open-handed marks.

The French Administration also set up procedures for dividing a parcel into two or more separate ones.

"To divide or not to divide" is an issue that probably all adult Tahitians are conscious of, and most of those with whom I discussed it held strong views favoring one solution or the other. Some more general reasons given for these views are "moral," i.e., "it is better, more *Tahitian,* for kinfolk to keep together and share their land" versus "every (nuclear) family ought to have separate land, in order to avoid conflict and quarrels." Other general reasons for taking this or that stand were economic, i.e., "people produce more by cooperating," versus "a man is more certain of his earnings if he does not have to depend upon others." Informants also volunteered more specific, situational reasons for wanting to divide or not divide, e.g., a desire to cease trying to work with an uncongenial brother or sister's husband; a wish to continue working with a congenial and industrious cousin.

In addition, there were certain technological factors that influenced peoples' decisions to divide or not to divide. One such was vanilla-growing; in Te Piti it was rare for two or more adults from different households to cooperate in growing vanilla beans in the same garden. And since a vanilla production lasted six or more years—from planting to depletion—a person wishing to grow the crop could expect to be met with reluctance or outright refusal from his co-proprietors when proposing such a long-term tie-up of what in most such instances was the most fertile part of their jointly owned land. Hence, the impulse in this kind of situation was to divide.

---

[19]In fact, when I was inquiring into the histories of specific land parcels and came to those owned by Europeans or by descendants of Europeans, the standard explanation given me by my Tahitian informants (including, in one case, a mixed-blood descendant of one of them!) was that the land in question had been acquired for a pittance and usually by guile, lubricated with alcohol. Such may in fact have been the case, although I cannot document it one way or another.

With copra production it was usually the reverse, especially with respect to already producing groves (which, at the time of my visits, was the state of most of them). With such groves, the original investment in labor, in ground-clearing and planting, had long since been made, and current production consisted only of keeping the ground vegetation reasonably low and harvesting the nuts as they ripened. (In other words, no current producer was impelled to control a specific piece of land continuously for a long period of time in order to obtain returns for his own original investment of labor, etc.) Thus, the co-proprietors of such a parcel found it feasible and reasonable to divide harvest rights on a time basis (*'opu i te faufa'a*) rather than divide the land (*vavahi i te fenua*); and in the absence of other, noneconomic, reasons for dividing they found it less of a bother, and hence highly preferable, to leave things as they were.

Dividing land not only involved negotiation and initiative, e.g., bargaining sessions with co-proprietors and trips to Administration centers, but was expensive as well. The services of a surveyor were required to lay out and map the new boundaries, and those of a notary—and sometimes a lawyer— to legalize the transaction.

The *Code* also sanctioned various kinds of arrangements for the temporary transfer of use-rights in land and in objects associated with land, e.g., houses, trees, etc. Many of these arrangements were not practiced—had no relevance—in Te Piti during my visits, and some of the local transactions of this nature were without exact parallels in the *Code*. There follows a brief description of the more tangible kinds of arrangements I found in operation there.

Land Rights and Transactions in Te Piti[20]

Fixed-rate lease. When applied to land (i.e., territory), this transaction involved different types of rights—some explicit, some implicit—according to context. For example, when land was leased for vanilla-growing, the lease-time was usually for an explicitly stated period of nine years; and although the contract, which was usually a written one, did not specify such, the lessee was understood to have the right of subleasing and of using the fruit of trees already growing there. On the other hand, it was questionable that he had the right to cut down, say, a breadfruit tree or coconut palm without explicit permission of the lessor. As for growing other cash crops, I know of only one instance of land having been leased for such purposes—in this case,

---

[20]In this section, I have repeated some matter given in previous chapters, in order to spare the reader the task of rereading or recall.

pineapples—and the period was also nine years. To the best of my knowledge, no one in Te Piti had ever leased land for growing coconuts, the growing and producing cycle having been considered too long (i.e., up to fifty or sixty years). Nor did I hear of any instance of leasing land for money for growing food crops—a scandalous suggestion to my informants.

Atea contained two parcels of Administration *domaines*. One was leased by the current *tāvana*, the other by his predecessor (in both cases at low rents—transparently, a perquisite of office). Rents were paid yearly and the agreements were evidently for unspecified and indefinite donations and entailed no restrictions on use, either of soil or of trees already growing there. In Fatata, a parcel of *domaine* (and its Administration-owned house) was lived in by a public works official; I was unable to discover whether he paid rent.

In Atea, most houses were built on lots comprising a parcel owned by a Chinese living on Ra'itea, who charged a token rental of ten francs per lot per annum. The houses themselves were owned either by residents themselves or by absent kinsmen (who usually charged no money rent).

Share-crop lease. This type of transaction took place mainly in connection with coconut- and vanilla-growing. For coconuts, the conventional arrangement was for the lessee to acquire the right to harvest the nuts (for a specified or indefinite period of time), (sometimes) process them into dried copra, sell the copra (dried or green), and pay the lessor one-half of his net profits (i.e., after deducting out-of-pocket costs of drying, bagging, and transporting—but not of the labor expended of himself or his unpaid, i.e., usually household, helpers.)[21] For vanilla sharecropping, two kinds of arrangements obtained. By one of them, the lessee took over uncleared land—usually by written contract and for a period of nine years—cleared, planted, and harvested it, and paid the lessor a specified percentage (typically, 20 percent) of the price received for the ripe beans. The other arrangement was for the lessee to lease an already planted garden and thereafter keep it weeded, pollinate the plants, and harvest the beans—again, for a specified or indefinite period of time. The rent paid for this kind of leasing was a fraction of the price received for the beans (50 percent in Atea, 30 percent in Fatata) with no deductions allowed—or in fact claimed—for labor or other production "costs."

Crop purchase. This somewhat anomalous type of transaction involved outright sale, at a price fixed in advance, of harvesting rights of a crop for a specified time period. It was applied mainly to coconuts—only rarely to vanilla—and the price was usually based on that received for the previous harvest.

---

[21] I failed to inquire whether the lessee deducted any if he dried the crop in his own dryer.

Food-growing "lease." As implied above, it was a conventional practice in Te Piti for landowners to permit others to grow food crops on their land, in return for the planting, by the users, of a few coconut palms (which was viewed as a "permanent" improvement of the land). The assumption behind this practice was that taro and other food crops produced would be eaten by the growers themselves. I heard of no instance where any part of such harvests was sold by the grower but failed to inquire whether that would have altered the arrangement, had it occurred.

In addition to these more or less explicit and formalized lease transactions, the Te Pitians practiced and concurred in various informal and more or less implicit arrangements respecting use of land and its resources by persons other than the owners themselves.

First, there was the right of *transit,* which owners usually permitted neighbors to exercise. The only situations I heard of in which this right was limited were during vanilla-harvest seasons, when some growers tried to discourage passage through their gardens on the assumption that the passer-by might steal some beans. Some of the more anxious vanilla growers went so far as to put "keep-out" marks at the entrance to trails leading through their gardens, but this action was popularly considered to be either unnecessarily hard and selfish or ridiculous.

Second was the right whereby most owners permitted their fellow villagers to take a few coconuts, breadfruit, or mangoes (but not bananas or coffee beans) from their land for home use (but, emphatically, *not* for sale); and the same degree of permissiveness extended to firewood and palm fronds (used for thatch). If an owner wished to restrict such rights, he put up keep-out marks (e.g., a strip of frond tied around the trunk of the tree in question); but as in the case of transit-blocking such measures were unpopular—and in fact not often required or resorted to.

Large trees to be used for house construction or for canoe hulls were a different matter. Before obtaining such as these it was necessary for the taker to obtain consent of the landowner and sometimes to pay a price, which—again—was usually higher if the end-product was intended for sale.

Most owners were anything but permissive about allowing neighbors' pigs or cattle access to their lands. Cattle were in fact no great problem; their owners usually kept them tied up or fenced in. But some residents allowed their pigs free range, or found it difficult to confine them, and these animals often played havoc with garden crops. When that occurred, the garden owners either killed them or brought suit against their owners, or both—usually to the accompaniment of mutual ill-feeling.

Next, there was the kind of land-use right practiced in connection with the hunting of wild pigs. It was customary, I was told, for the successful hunter to give some of the animal's flesh to the owner of the land on which it was killed. (And just as customary, it was added, for the hunter to forego doing so unless the landowner could prove that the killing had taken place on his land!)

Finally, there remains the question of use-rights in waterways. In the communities studied, when a stream flowed through a land parcel it was generally considered to be part of the parcel, and its resources, if any—mainly crayfish and shrimps—were held to belong to the parcel's owner and to require his permission before fishing there. (Also, it was considered necessary to share the catch with the owner if it were "large" enough—how large I could not discover.) With streams forming boundaries between parcels, the matter of ownership was open to question—and to some argument, I was informed, when large catches of crayfish were made. However, this latter situation occurred too infrequently, it would appear, for any consensus to have developed concerning its rights and wrongs.[22]

Now to summarize the types of rights and transactions exercised by the Te Pitians with respect to private lands and its appurtenances.[23]

Proprietary rights. Parcels of land were officially owned either by a *sole proprietor* or the heirs of a sole proprietor, or by two or more name-specified *joint proprietors* and their respective heirs. A sole proprietor was empowered to lease all or part of his parcel or to dispose of it by sale or (within limits) by gift. A joint proprietor possessed similar rights of lease and disposal over his fraction of a parcel—normatively, but not always in practice—after agreement with the other joint owner(s). With respect to the heirs of a deceased sole or joint proprietor, their respective proprietary rights in the parcel, or fraction of the parcel, were proportional to their number—for example, each of three heirs held a one-third proprietary interest in the parcel, or fraction of the parcel—and each had rights of lease or disposal over his portion.

In the case of parcels held by two or more proprietors, they could make use of its soil and other resources either by serial allotment of time (as with coconut-harvesting) or by informal territorial subdivision.

---

[22]As noted earlier, with the application of French law private ownership of lagoon and ocean water areas was abolished. And although the Tahitians I knew respected this ruling with regard to fishing rights—indeed, they were no longer aware that the land tenure practices of their pre-European ancestors included lagoon fishing rights as well—they were uninformed or unpersuaded about some other aspects of this law.

[23]In what follows, I employ some familiar labels in ways that may be unfamiliar to many readers. I regret having to resort to this inconvenient practice but have had to do so in order to clarify my own ideas about this complex subject. Hopefully it will add clarity to my written description of it as well.

By following official procedures, a parcel could be territorially divided into two or more separate parcels, either by its sole proprietor, or by agreement among all its coproprietors, or by judicial order.

Inheritance rights. These refer to the rights to a whole parcel, or fraction thereof, held by all the heirs of a living proprietor (sole or co-), as identified and defined by French laws of succession. They entailed rights of use and lease but not of disposal, and even their use and lease rights were subject to consent of the parcel's proprietor. The French *Code* also extended inheritance rights to spouses, to ascendants, and to collaterals of various degrees of kinship, but since land registration was first instituted in Te Piti, inheritance rights were in practice exercised or claimed by only the offspring (legitimate, or illegitimate and "recognized") and siblings of a proprietor; and it is in this limited, but ethnographically relevant, sense that I use the term. Some Te Pitians I knew were aware of some of the ramifications of inheritance contained in the *Code* but considered them irrelevant, or even inapplicable to themselves. Indeed, many of them were so uninformed about the inclusion of spouses among an individual's potential heirs that they complained about their supposed exclusion.

In this connection, the word *tōmite,* as used by Te Pitians, was the social unit comprising all persons holding proprietary or inheritance rights to that fraction of a parcel that had been apportioned, by either official or unofficial agreement, among a parcel's coproprietors.

Familial rights. I have invented this label to apply to a category of land-use rights that were not explicitly defined in the *Code* but that were distinctively conceptualized and practiced in Te Piti. I refer to the special and more or less exclusive uses made of a proprietor's land by *all* members of his or her household—including spouse, offspring (legitimate, illegitimate, and foster), ascendants, and any other persons—kin or not—residing more or less permanently in the household. Familial rights did not include rights of lease or disposal, but they served to empower the holder to freer use of the land and its resources than was permitted, say, to the proprietor's siblings residing elsewhere. (In other words, familial rights superseded inheritance rights under some circumstances.) Moreover, even for those few of my informants who knew about a spouse's legal rights as a potential heir, it was her (or his) identity as a familial-rights holder that effectively defined her (or his) use of the proprietor's land.

There was, of course, some differentiation of land-use rights among familial rights-holders, e.g., a spouse's having usually been "stronger" than, say, an unmarried offspring—although instances of disagreement did occasionally occur; but the kinds of common-use rights possessed by all its resident members set each household off from all others in this respect.

Lease rights. These refer to the types of rights that a proprietor transferred to someone for temporary periods and limited kinds of use in return for some material kind of consideration (i.e., "rent").[24] The period could be for a few months, a whole year, several years (nine being the usual term), the time it took to plant and harvest a food garden or specific cash crop, or indefinitely. The kinds of use included planting and harvesting gardens or cash crops, harvesting already growing coconuts, pollinating and harvesting already planted vanilla, and residing—either in houses already built or in those built by the lessee. The rents paid for lease rights were in the form of money (either a fixed amount of it or a specified sharing of profits) or of food-bearing trees planted on the leasehold by the lessee.

Neighbor rights. Finally, I found it to be the practice in both Atea and Fatata for proprietors and tenants to extend certain land-use rights to their community-mates with a degree of permissiveness beyond that offered to outsiders (except, of course, to outsiders who were kinsmen or friends). These included rights of transit; of occasional collection of coconuts, breadfruit, mangoes, firewood, and some building material; of hunting; and of fishing. The successful hunter or fisherman was expected to pay some "rent" in the form of part of the catch, but the only "rent" charged for use of the other rights was the implicit expectation of reciprocity should the need arise—all of which may sound very nebulous but which was shown to be solidly tangible by the angry reactions I witnessed to some instances when *outsiders* were known or suspected of making use of such rights.

Except for the brief references to the Administration *domaines* that were leased by some residents, all the above description applies to privately owned land. In Te Piti, there were also to be found parcels owned by other social units: by the Administration (e.g., the lots on which the schools were built), by the Protestant mission, and by the local Protestant parish. During my visits, questions arose among the local residents concerning the appropriate allocation of use rights to all of these, but opinion differed so widely that, in the absence of judicial determination or Administration fiat, no consensus was ever obtained.

Land Holdings in Te Piti

Against this background, I can now compare and contrast Atea and Fatata with respect to their residents' local land holdings.

---

[24]Lessees were also empowered by local convention to sublet their leaseholds, and in Te Piti they occasionally did so.

As described earlier, the two villages have had markedly different histories, colonial and precolonial, and this is reflected in the sizes and title distributions of local parcels of land. Fatata, it will be recalled, was a populous and important political and religious center in pre-European times, an early site of mission activity, and until recently the headquarters of Mo'orea's colonial Administration. Atea, in contrast, consisted of only a scattering of socially undistinguished residents in pre-European times, and its postcolonial history as a unified community has been brief and uneventful. Moreover, in 1954 Fatata was immediately adjacent to some large European plantations and within easy reach of Pape'ete, whereas Atea was flanked by communities as rural and nondescript as itself and far away from large centers of population, production, and commerce.

As the basis for comparing land tenure in these two villages, I have restricted my enquiry to the areas within whose boundaries their residents owned most of their land, or over which they exercised most use rights, or both. For Ateans, these boundaries happened to be conterminous with the official boundaries of Atea District itself, except in the south, where a narrow strip of Ateans' lands extended into another district. For the Fatatans, the boundaries of their "land-tenure" area coincided with the "Toerau" District's administrative boundary in the west but extended only to a bloc of large outsider-owned (and mainly European-owned) holdings in the east. Thus defined, the two areas turn out to have been almost identical in size, there having been about 695 hectares in Fatata and about 680 in Atea, thereby providing a convenient basis for direct, unweighted comparison.[25]

The data on which I base my statements about the two villages' land tenure included cadastral maps provided by the Administration Lands Office, official records of registration and transfer, and my own inquiries in Atea and Fatata. The cadastral maps in question were drawn by the Lands Office and were based on field surveys carried out in 1945–46 in Atea and in 1941 in Fatata. In making the survey, each parcel was given a number and the names of its current recorded owners. In addition, the Lands Office maintained a record of all legal transactions relating to each parcel from the time of its original registration. Thus, for Parcel 19 in Fatata the following is recorded:

---

[25]Unweighted, that is, in terms of total land area; when weighted in terms of population, the area identified with the Ateans (who numbered 217) results in a per capita amount of 3.13 hectares, and that identified with the Fatatans about 2 hectares—a circumstance that should be kept in mind during the discussion of unweighted area-for-area comparisons presented below.

19. TIAPATETE-2. Attributed in 1888 by [unchallenged] declaration of ownership to (1) Tetutaata a Teamo and (2) Manoi a Apa. By testament of 1918 Manoi a Apa left his [interest in this parcel] to his legitimate daughter, Eliza Orzay, who was issue of his [first] marriage. Eliza Orzay, deceased 1924, left as her successors her ten offspring: Hitoto a Tetauira, Ariitaata a Tetauira, Taaroa a Tetauira, Mona a Tetauira, Mouyot *dit* Amaru a Tetauira, Eliza a Tetuaira, Vahineroo a Tetauira, Raita a Tetuaira, Louis Orzay, Meza Corsica a Noho (wife of F. Maraeauna *dit* Herault).

By act of sale of 1929 Hitoto a Tetauira transferred his rights to Tauraa a Mauiui.

Armed with these official records, I then endeavored to learn by questioning about the subsequent unrecorded, i.e., "unofficial," changes that had taken place with respect to each parcel, along with its current status, including the names and whereabouts of its de facto owners, the use being made of it, etc.—admittedly, a long and tedious search (involving as it did 321 parcels) and one that in some instances fell short of success. It was, however, a necessary chore and one that provided insights not only about Te Piti's land tenure but about many other aspects of Te Pitians' behavior as well. Moreover, the focus of the inquiry was of keen interest to most adult Te Pitians and one about which many of them were extremely well informed.

Returning to Parcel 19, as an example: since the official records revealed no subsequent legal dividing of this property, I was justified in assuming, until facts proved otherwise, that its resources were shared equally by two *tōmite* (committee, see above, p. 429) consisting respectively of the heirs of Tetutaata a Teamo and by the heirs of the listed offspring of Eliza Orzay (except for Hitoto), plus the heirs of Tauraa a Mauiui. Based on this assumption, I sought to learn the names and whereabouts of those heirs and the actual part played by them, if any, in sharing the use or the produce of the parcel.

I begin this account of Te Piti's land tenure with a comparison of the degree to which the lands of the two villages were subdivided, by size of area and by numbers of co-owners per parcel.

At the beginning of 1955, Atea's 680 hectares were divided into seventy-three distinct parcels and Fatata's 695 hectares into 248. Thus, in average size of parcel, the figure for Atea was 9.32 hectares and for Fatata only 2.78. The difference between these averages is in itself interesting, but much more informative is the comparison of parcel-size frequencies:

Table 11-A

Size of Parcel	Atea		Fatata	
(in hectares)	Number	Percentage	Number	Percentage
under 1	4	5.47	160	64.51
1 to under 2	5	6.84	34	13.71
2 to under 3	9	12.32	13	5.24
3 to under 4	4	5.47	8	3.22
4 to under 5	9	12.32	4	1.61
5 to under 6	6	8.21	4	1.61
6 to under 7	5	6.84	2	0.80
7 to under 8	1	1.36	1	0.40
8 to under 9	5	6.84	1	0.40
9 to under 10	0	0	2	0.80
10 to under 15	9	12.32	7	2.82
15 to under 25	11	15.06	6	2.42
25 and over	5	6.84	6	2.42
Total	73	99.89	248	99.96

The very wide differences that existed between Atea and Fatata exemplified in this comparison of parcel size are emphasized in the statistics concerning parcels under one hectare in area. In Atea the four such parcels measured ten, twenty-five, sixty, and seventy *are* (i.e., 100 sq. meters) respectively, whereas in Fatata fifty such parcels measured less than twenty-five *are* each, and of these twenty-three measured less than ten *are* each.

One explanation for Fatata's very large number of small and very small parcels may lie in the nature of most of the latter, i.e., about 150 of them were separately owned house lots concentrated in the main residential area near the shore and along the lower reaches of the main valley. That situation may possibly be attributed to Fatata's long history as a populous center and its long and close association with Europeans, including many who actually resided there. In contrast, all of Atea's residences were located on only eight distinct parcels, and most of these on a single parcel (which belonged to a Chinese storekeeper residing on Rai'atea, who charged—but seldom collected—an annual rent of ten francs per house lot).[26]

---

[26]I had the impression that most Atean household heads living on rented land would have preferred to own their own house lots but were dissuaded from attempting to do so by their fantasies about the vast sums they would cost and by the acknowledged minuteness of their rents.

But house lots aside, even the "agricultural" portions of the Fatata area, i.e., the lands exploited or exploitable in terms of producing or collecting food or cash crops, or animals, or building materials, etc., were on the average subdivided into smaller parcels than were those of Atea.[27] (For example, 67 percent of Atea's "agricultural" parcels were over five hectares in area, as against only 30 percent of Fatata's.)

The marked difference between Atea and Fatata in size of "agricultural" parcel cannot be attributed solely, or even weightily, to topography. Nor can it be explained by technical differences in agricultural use—quite the contrary, since Ateans were and had been more extensively engaged in vanilla growing (which, it will be recalled, encouraged subdivision) than their Fatatan counterparts. Nor can the difference be attributed more than marginally to the Fatatans' larger money resources for paying the cost of division, nor their readier access to Administration personnel to carry out the surveying and other services required in land-dividing.[28] Hence, explanations for the differences must be sought in other directions.

For one thing, the larger population that had existed in Fatata over a longer period of time probably provided, indirectly, more pressure for subdivision than was present in Atea, and this pressure was probably reinforced by the Fatatans' longer and more frequent contacts with the Europeans, who indirectly contributed to subdivision by their local land purchases.

Another explanation, however, may be sought in historic differences in mental attitude between Fatatans and Ateans in connection not only with land ownership but with other social-relational matters as well. (For land ownership is not simply a direct relation between people and land but *between people and other people with respect to land*.) My suggestion is that the Ateans I knew, and their forebears during the past century or so, have been less desirous of dividing (including individualizing) their jointly held land parcels than were their counterparts in Fatata. Some of this difference in attitude may be accounted for by the Fatatans' longer, more frequent, and more direct contact with Europeans, who typically have tended to proselytize in favor of individuation. But I suggest that much of this difference in

---

[27]Some breadfruit, coconuts, and bananas also grew on house lots, as did some coffee and kapok trees, but I saw only one instance of vanilla planting on a house lot and none of root crops.

[28]It could, of course, be reasoned that the circumstance of the Fatatans having had not only *more* money but also alternative sources of money might have reduced, comparatively, their demand for, and hence the further fragmentation of land—but this factor (if, in fact, it had been operative) evidently had not been influential enough to outweigh those contributing to fragmentation. In this connection, the absence of this category of money expenditure on Table 3H simply reflects the fact that, according to their answers to my enquiries, no Te Pitian had in fact spent any money for that purpose during 1954.

attitude derives from, or is a component of, the respective Ateans' and Fatatans' views about cooperation among Tahitians in general and among
neighbors and kinsmen in particular. In a word, Ateans were (and probably
had been for decades) more disposed to *share* labor and goods with each
other, unless and until *pe'ape'a* reached an intolerable intensity; whereas
Fatatans felt more inclined to do and own things on their own unless and
until tangible advantages were perceived in cooperation and sharing. Admittedly, a conclusion as comprehensive and positive as this requires more
proof than mere assertion, but I expect to be able to document it in pages to
come.

Having touched upon more "generic" factors influencing the statistical
results of land subdivision, I turn now to the kinds of "efficient" causes that
have operated during recent decades to promote it—or, conversely, to pre-
clude it.

Whatever may have been the "real" causes behind any particular subdivision, the verbal explanation that was given for most cases within memory was "*pe'ape'a fenua,*" i.e., disagreement and tension among co-owners concerning appropriate sharing of a parcel's resources. I recorded instances in
which subdivision had followed conflict between co-owners on other
grounds, e.g., wife-stealing, child mistreatment, or chronic incompatibility,
but the usual rationalization was "conflict over land."

Several subdivisions were indeed occasioned specifically and principally,
or perhaps even solely, by *pe'ape'a fenua.* Three such that I knew about resulted from disagreement between their respective *tōmite*—distant collaterals
in these cases—over the size and location of proposed vanilla plantings,
there having been not enough appropriate sites to accommodate all the co-
owners' aims. (As noted earlier, sites for growing vanilla were more apt to be
subdivided than were those containing coconut palms.) Another subdivision
I knew about resulted directly—and so far as I could learn, solely—from conflict between the two co-owners over the depredation caused by the pigs of
one of them in the food garden of the other.

Instances of land subdivision resulting from specific conflicts of other
kinds were more numerous. For example, I recorded three in which the co-
owners parted company and divided their land after one of each pair had
"stolen" the wife of the other—in one case the "stealing" was a one-time seduction, in the others a permanent confiscation. In each of two other instances, coolness between the co-owners had begun when one of them recalled his natural child from the fosterage of the other as result of alleged
mistreatment by the latter. And in at least four other instances that I was
able to document, land subdivision was the culmination of long series of
conflicts and incompatibilities over other matters—commercial rivalry,
drunkenness, one-sided "sponging," etc.

A more "structural" kind of subdivision stimulus sometimes occurred when one of a parcel's co-owning committees consisted entirely of members residing permanently elsewhere. In most such situations the principal member of the local resident committee managed the land's production in return for one-half of the profits ordinarily due the absentee co-owners, but I recorded other instances in which the absentees had caused the land to be divided in order to sell their portion to a third party—either because of an urgent need for cash or because of dissatisfaction with their income from the parcel. I also recorded instances—two of them very recent—in which the absentee co-owners had returned from long residence elsewhere (three generations long in one case) and had insisted on subdividing, "to avoid *peʻapeʻa*" it was said, but also probably because of acquired ideas about the more "civilized" nature of individual proprietorship.

Long absence sometimes produced other kinds of solutions. There were several instances—all, by the way, in Fatata—where one committee of co-owners had been away from the community for so long a time and without communication that their whereabouts, indeed their very existence, had become unknown. In these cases the local co-owners acted as if they themselves were sole owners—even, in one case, in a proposed sale. In yet another instance, in which a set of collaterals had jointly owned parcels in both Fatata and on Tahiti, they agreed to transfer all rights in the Fatatan parcel to the branch living there, and vice versa—thereby substantiating, and probably finalizing, the fission of that social unit—that cognatic stock—as well.[29]

A generalization about certain instances of a subdivision that applies to both communities, but more emphatically to Fatata than to Atea, concerns the accessibility, i.e., mainly proximity, of the parcels in question to each community's residential areas. The land maps of both areas revealed that the agricultural lands nearer the residences tended to be smaller than those farther away. A similar tendency was apparent with respect to a parcel's productive potential—its soil, drainage, slope, etc.; that is to say, the greater its potential, the smaller it tended to be. But of the two variables, proximity was clearly the more decisive one. In this matter at least, Te Pitians appear to have coveted nearby assets more avidly than they did potentially more valuable ones farther away.

Legal subdivision represented the extreme and final partitioning of a land parcel's assets among its co-owners. More frequently, the co-owners resorted to unofficial "sharing of its assets" (*ʻōpū i te faufaʻa*), often but not

---

[29]Just prior to my visit there was enacted a new law that had the effect of limiting testamentary disposition to a much narrower range of kinfolk. And while in 1954–55 it had not yet begun to affect inheritances in Fatata and had scarcely been heard about in Atea, it would inevitably bring about far-reaching changes in social relationships in both places.

always in terms of area or time. When a large parcel was used only or mainly for growing food crops there appeared to be little formalized allocation among its co-owners concerning who could plant where and for how long; in fact, in many such parcels even nonowners were permitted to garden for no more rent than the planting of a few coconut palms. However, when a cash crop was intended the co-owners were usually required to consult with one another regarding the intended site and duration of use, this having been particularly requisite in the case of vanilla. And with respect to the sharing of a productive grove of coconuts this was done, as previously noted, on a time-division basis, usually in six-, or less typically four- or three-month blocks.

Most instances of joint use of a coconut grove involved only two committees, each of which harvested the parcel's coconuts in six-month blocks—or rather, was entitled to do so, many (as described earlier) having leased their entitlements to a single harvest to a co-owner or some other person or having contracted with a co-owner for the latter to harvest the nuts in return for half the net profits therefrom. On the other hand, some instances of co-ownership and joint use were more complex, as the following two examples will illustrate.

Atitiao (Atea), a parcel of about twenty hectares, was jointly owned by seven committees, only one of whom, a late middle-aged widow, resided locally. About one-sixth of the parcel was planted in coconuts, the remainder having been used only for occasional food-gardening. Each of the seven committees owned harvest-rights of the coconuts for a six-month period every three and a half years, those of the Atean co-owner having been exercised by her adoptive son, who paid her one-half of his copra profits in return.

Omuna (Atea), a parcel of about forty-five hectares, was jointly owned by three committees (representing the surviving lines of the original owner of record, a *'piri-ari'i'* [near-aristocrat] who had resided in Fare).

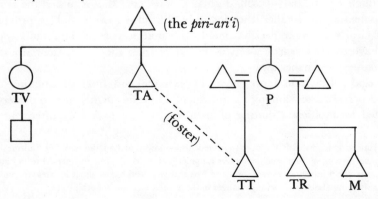

Tetua and her offspring resided in a neighboring district and owned one-third of the parcel's copra production. Tati had had no offspring of his own but had "fed" Poni and willed him his one-third interest in the land. As shown, Punu had had three offspring, each of whom inherited equal share-rights in her third. Manu subsequently moved away and relinquished his share-rights to Timi and Poni, leaving them each with one-half of his committee's one-third share of Omuna's coconut harvest, and thereby increasing Poni's total share to one-half (i.e., one-third plus one-sixth).

The co-sharing of land-use rights was verbalized in a way that was quite distinctive. *"Mātou,"* the exclusive form of the pronominal first-person plural, was sometimes used by a speaker to refer to his (or her) household, parish sodality, etc., in contexts where the reference was unambiguously clear, but it was my observation that its most common reference was to "we (exclusive) sharers of the same part of the use-rights of some land parcel." In other words, whenever I heard someone say *"mātou"* without specific reference to any other kind of social unit, I could be fairly certain that the term's land-tenure meaning was implied. Households, work groups, etc.—even families—were subject to unpredictable changes in membership, but the co-sharing subunit of a landowning "corporation" tended to remain stable for long periods of time.[30]

Having seen, quantitatively, how Fatata exceeded Atea with respect to the legally finalized fragmentation of land, it should now be asked how the two villages compared with respect to the unofficial kind of partitioning represented by division of use rights.

Of Atea's distinct, officially registered, privately owned land parcels thirty-three were generally acknowledged to be owned by one committee each and thirty-six of them by two or more committees each—the corresponding numbers for Fatata having been 184 and fifty-two. Thus from this statistic it would appear that Atea exceeded Fatata in this unofficial kind of fragmentation. But this is only part of the picture, in two important respects. The first has to do with the size of the parcels in question, the second with the partitioning process itself.

A large number of Fatata's 184 single-committee parcels consisted of small house lots or other lots so small that they had reached a stage of fragmentation where, possibly, their owners had concluded that further partitioning, even of use rights, would be impractical.

Secondly, in both Atea and Fatata, land partitioning short of legally registered land division must be viewed as having taken place in a continuous

---

[30]I write "tended" in order to reflect the fact that, in addition to the changes produced in each subunit membership through deaths, they were also altered occasionally by alienation, by legal partitioning, or by informal transfer of use rights (as in the case of Manu just cited).

and not always one-directional series of steps. A first step occurred, for example, when two brothers began to plant vanilla or coconuts on separate parts of their father's (or mother's) land, without any more formal agreement than the parent's consent. The division may have been sharpened somewhat when their own children began to help in the cultivation of each one's particular garden or grove, and it would have become more definite when the parent-owner died. On the other hand, that division may have eventually disappeared, either through infrequent use by one of the brothers or through the childlessness of one of them. Also, as indicated earlier, the partition may have been further sharpened nearly to—and in some instances, all the way to—legal division, through conflict of some sort between the brothers or their respective heirs. Thus, while *tōmite*-naming signified an advanced stage in this process of partitioning, it was only one of a number of fairly continuous steps.

Applying this yardstick to Fatata and Atea, I have the impression (which however I cannot quantify) that, with respect to the larger, *tōmite*-partitioned land parcels, the rate of divisiveness in land-use rights, in the sense just outlined, had progressed much further in Fatata than in Atea.

Finally, a *caveat* is required concerning a statement made earlier, namely, that "legal subdivision represented the extreme and final partitioning of a land parcel's assets among its co-owners" (p. 444). "Extreme," yes; but "final," not always so. That is to say, I came across several cases of parcels that bore identical ownership-name labels but that actually belonged, by legal registration, to different individuals. Inquiry revealed that those situations had come about as a consequence of the occasional practice of transmitting not only a person's surname (*i'oa paera'a*) but his or her "calling name" (*i'oa pi'i*) as well, to more than one descendant. Normally, such a situation would have occasioned no difficulty regarding property rights, so long as memories remained fresh and social relations congenial. With the passing of time, however, and the forgetting of pedigrees—a commonplace sequence in Te Piti, by the way—people sometimes "forgot," either unconsciously or deliberately, such things, and laid claim to rights in parcels on the basis of having a common registration name. In most such cases, a thorough investigation into *Etat Civil* and Lands Office archives would have settled the issue, but that would have involved legal fees and other expenses and initiatives that most Te Pitians were unwilling to undertake. Instead, a few of them (i.e., in Fatata) had possessed the foresight—moved probably by current property disputes—to secure their own and their heirs' rights in particular parcels through the expedient of changing their names (and their parcels' listings) by simply reversing their calling-names and surnames, thus, *Tautumataroa Henere* became *Henere Tautumatoroa*—an act that not only finalized a previous property division but that seems to have served to finalize other aspects of family segmentation as well, as exemplified in the statement of one heir to such a name-based division: "They (the other branch) are perhaps still kinfolk (*fēti'i*), but only distant ones (*mea ātea*)."

I turn now to the question of ownership—of who held the legal titles to Te Piti's land parcels, and of the distribution of those titles within each of the two villages.

The first statistics that need to be reported are the proportions between local and outside ownership of Te Piti's privately owned lands (that is, those not owned by the Administration, the parish, etc.).

Of the 673 hectares of such lands in Atea, one or more of Atea's Tahitian residents owned rights to about 140 of them, the corresponding figure for Fatata's 679 hectares of privately owned land having been 205 hectares[31]— plus the 71 hectares of a parcel of uncultivated mountainous wilderness in which one Fatatan resident shared title with numerous outsiders. (This individual knew only in a vague way who those co-owners were but not where they lived and had set foot on the land in question only to hunt for wild pigs.) Thus, leaving aside the unused parcel, it appears that Fatatans as a whole were more advantaged in this respect than Ateans. On a per capita basis, however, the Ateans were better off, having owned—per capita but of course not per owner—0.69 hectares, as compared with Fatatans' 0.58. But much more revelatory is the finding of how much of the private lands of both villages were owned by outsiders. I will return to this finding later, after describing how the locally owned land rights were actually distributed among the two villages' respective residents (i.e., those rights of proprietorship that were legally sanctioned—by purchase, testamentary disposition, inheritance, etc.—but not including an offspring's anticipated shares of its living parents' rights). A summary of these distributions is given in Table 11B.

Thus, actual ownership rights in local lands were more widely distributed among Ateans than among Fatatans, i.e., among 24.8 percent of the former as against about 21 percent of the latter. However, as will be shown, this seeming discrepancy is narrowed to the point of insignificance when account is taken of the relative numbers of Ateans and Fatatans owning land rights in places outside their respective communities of residence.

Another point of comparison is provided by figures for the numbers of residents of each place who not only did not legally own any land rights at

---

[31] These figures on local ownership were calculated by adding the land areas owned by Te Pitians in terms of percentages of ownership represented by their *tōmite* share in the title to all the parcels. For example, if a Te Pitian constituted one of the two coordinate *tōmite* of a parcel measuring two hectares he was credited with ownership of one hectare.

Table 11-B

Quantity Owned (hectares)	Number of Owners	
	Atea	Fatata
less than 1	13	32
1 to under 2	7	8
2 to under 3	5	11
3 to under 4	8	7
4 to under 5	1	5
5 to under 6	1	0
6 to under 7	1	6
7 to under 8	1	0
8 to under 9	1	0
9 to under 10	3	0
10 to under 15	7	3
15 to under 20	1	0
over 20	5	1
Total	54	73

the time of my 1954–55 visit but who also did not have any realistic expectations of obtaining any through inheritance or testament. In Atea, the number of such individuals was thirty-five, in Fatata seventy; or, expressed in terms of percentages of total populations, in Atea 16 percent, in Fatata 20 percent. Again, however, this kind of disparity turns out to be insignificant when account is taken of the relative number of these locally landless residents who held viable ownership rights in lands located elsewhere.

On balance, therefore, it appears that Fatata and Atea were much alike in terms of the proportion of their residents in possession of some ownership rights to land. Also the average local landholding residents of the two villages were about the same: 2.62 hectares for Ateans and 2.81 for Fatatans.

On the other hand, the *modal* distribution of these sizes of individual holdings differed markedly. That is to say, 24 percent of the Atean titleholders owned local land measuring less than one hectare, whereas the corresponding figure for Fatata was 49 percent. Moreover, the significance of this disparity is increased by the fact that most of the under-one-hectare holdings of the Fatatans were house lots and thus unproductive in terms of subsistence or cash incomes—a circumstance that tends to increase any economic significance that can be read into the figures on numbers of titleholders and average size of holdings given above.

In other words, when one views the land holdings themselves in terms of their economic productivity, the fortunate residents of Atea who owned land locally, and hence most accessibly, were considered better off in this respect than were their counterparts in Fatata.

Another aspect of landownership distribution that has considerable economic and social significance for this comparative study concerns the differences between households with respect to their members' *access* to productive land. (For example, even if, say, a man himself owned no productive land nearby, the fact that his wife did so served to place their household in a better position, economically, than one in which no member owned local productive land.)

The range of variation for this crucially important factor was very wide. At one extreme was the household of Tamu and his wife and one dependant, at the other hand that of Amaru and his wife and ten dependants. Between them, Tamu and his wife owned[32] about twenty-five hectares of land, most of it productive and readily accessible.[33] In contrast, neither Amaru nor his wife owned any land elsewhere and had no expectations of receiving any by inheritance or testament.

The distribution of land ownership by household is shown below:

Table 11C

Amount Owned (hectares)	Number of Households			
	Atea		Fatata	
	Number	Percentage	Number	Percentage
under 1	6	14	8	13
1 to under 4	10	24	18	29
4 to under 10	6	14	11	18
over 10	13	31	7	11
none**	7*	17	18*	29
Total	42		62	

*The number of households listed includes the two single-occupant ones that were excluded in the comparisons presented in Chapter X.

**Among those listed as having no land at present, three in Atea and four in Fatata had expectations of inheriting some.

---

[32]See footnote on page 36 for the basis of this calculation.

[33]Seventeen of these hectares belonged solely to Tamu's wife. Tamu's own land was his part of a very large tract, located outside the area included in this study, which was an inheritance from his part-European father. Since the holdings of Tamu's wife were more than sufficient for their needs, Tamu permitted his many siblings rent-free use of his own holdings.

The widest differences between the two villages revealed in the above figures pertain to households having very large land holdings and to those
having no land at the time of the survey and no known heritable interests in
any.

In communities as agriculturally oriented as these, possession by a household of very large holdings of arable land exerted a very weighty influence
upon the size of its monetary income, actual or potential. That is to say,
such households were in most cases assured of some money income from
their properties, by rent, even if they did not exert effort to exploit them
themselves. And by energetic exploitation, some of those richly endowed
households did in fact earn relatively large incomes from their properties. In
other words, in the absence of land property taxes, the possession of large
land holdings imposed no economic burden on a household—on the contrary. Thus, from this point of view the households of Atea were, on the average, considerably more advantaged economically than were those of
Fatata.

Similarly, Atean households were on the average much less disadvantaged than those of Fatata in terms of landlessness, i.e., only three of
the former possessed no land and no heritable interest in land, as against
fourteen in Fatata. (In this connection, it should be recalled that possession
of a heritable interest in land nearly always gave an individual the right to
use it at low rent or entirely rent free, depending upon competing claims.)
Moreover, this disparity was widened even further by the circumstance that,
with several of the Fatatan households listed on the "under-one-hectare"
line, their entire holdings consisted of houselots, i.e., of non-income-earning
land.

In the broader economic sense, my usage of "disadvantaged" in the preceding paragraphs is, however, more applicable to Atea than to Fatata. In
Fatata, the existence of a nearby market for fish provided landless men with
an alternative source of money income that was not available to Ateans. Indeed, some well-landed Fatatans preferred fishing to farming and made
little or no use of their land, either through personal exploitation or rental.
Moreover, I cannot attest that all or most of the landless Fatatans believed
themselves "disadvantaged" because of that fact. On the other hand, to be
landless in Atea, where agriculture provided nearly all of the community's
cash income, was clearly disadvantageous from any point of view (including
the expressed views of the Ateans themselves).

The same stricture applies to my usage of "advantaged" and to my
choice of "over ten hectares" as the criterion for this condition. Why ten?
Why not eight, or six, or four? In other words, how much land, as a minimum, did a household require to satisfy its money needs?

I could, of course, point out that, other things being equal, the money
needs of households would have differed according to the number and ages of

their members—but that would be only a partial answer in more senses than one. In addition to the circumstance that Ateans were more dependent than Fatatans upon land as a source of money, I would have found it difficult if not impossible to decide "how much is enough" for each village considered separately—or, for that matter, for any two households of the same size, etc., in each village.

Leaving such evaluations aside, it can nevertheless be reported that several Ateans *and* Fatatans had to (in the case of the former), or either had to or chose (in the case of the latter), to substitute their labor for land in order to satisfy their household and individual needs (whatever these may have been). I am unable to construct a general formula to quantify this connection between labor and land, but the cases of Amu and Pana in Atea were typical enough of that village to provide a fairly representative example of that connecton.

Amu (aged thirty-three) himself owned no land nearer than Taha'a Island (from which he received no money); his wife (aged thirty-one) shared use rights amounting to about 0.3 hectares in her father's Atean estate, but it contained few coconuts and was unsuitable for vanilla. For money, Amu cut firewood for the Chinese bakeries, grew vanilla on leased land, and made copra on a sharecrop basis from a nonresident owner's grove. His wife assisted him in vanilla pollinating and harvesting and spent much of her "spare" time making thatch-plates for sale. During 1954, Amu earned from his several occupations a net income of about 9,000 francs, from which was spent, or overspent, a total of 10,920 (bread–3,700, rice–400, sugar–2,500, tea–250, kerosenes–425, a new machete–320, fish hooks and lines–525, cinema–300, church contributions–500, and various sundries and "luxuries" such as razor blades, laundry soap, Christmas wine, ketchup, boat trips to Fare, etc.–about 2,000). His wife earned about 2,000 francs making thatch and she spent all of this on clothes and sewing materials for herself and their two young children. Amu and his family lived in a thatch-roofed single-roomed house (which was kept in good repair) and grew their own vegetables and coffee; Amu caught enough fish to provide them with relish four or five days a week. And husband and wife worked hard and continually for about five and a half days each week. Amu took part in one drunken bout during a trip to Fare and was mildly soused (on a friend's homemade brew) for two days during New Year—but that was about all the high life he indulged in while I was there.

In contrast, another Atean, Pana (aged forty-two) owned locally over three hectares of coconut- and vanilla-growing land, and his wife (aged forty-four) owned nearly fifteen. Pana made some copra and grew some vanilla himself but leased out much of their land on a sharecrop basis, thereby producing a total 1954 income of around 28,000 francs. (His wife helped some with vanilla pollinating and made thatch-plates for her sodality but engaged in no separate money-earning work on her own.)

Pana and his wife and two adopted teenage children lived in a large three-room metal-roofed house (in need of some repair). They raised most of their own vegetables but spent about 19,000 francs for other food and spent, or overspent, the rest of their income on cinema, travel, church, and Pana's large thirst for wine and beer.

Compared to Amu and his wife, they worked industriously but less frequently—I would estimate the equivalent of about four days a week. At the end of it all, Pana's house was larger and more solidly built than Amu's but in poorer repair, and the clothes of the two families were about the same in quality and quantity. Pana's family ate more store-bought foods than Amu's, but it is doubtful that its meals were any tastier or more nutritious. Also, at year's end both families were in debt for about the same amounts to the local Chinese storekeepers. In fact, the principal—the only really noteworthy—difference between the two households lay in the fact that Amu and his wife worked longer hours than Pana and his to maintain fairly similar material consumption standards (except, of course, for Pana's larger consumption of wine and beer). It would be an oversimplification to attribute this disparity in Amu's and Pana's working hours entirely to their differences in land ownership, but that disparity was certainly a factor, and probably the major one. Pana *could* of course have devoted his "free" time to earning more money and hence to widening the difference between his (nonalcoholic) material consumption standards and Amu's, but he did not do so—nor did many other Ateans who were similarly "advantaged" in terms of land ownership. The few Ateans who did convert their labor-freeing land ownership advantages into something more tangible than leisure or alcoholic euphoria (and hangovers) used the money earned through their "overtime" labor most typically for improving their housing—and only rarely for investment into more money-earning goods such as land or livestock or tools.

Turning now to Fatata, the advantages derived from larger-than-average land holdings were, as in Atea, more often than not converted into leisure and alcohol, and in a few cases into better housing, rather than invested in agricultural producer-goods.[34] But here the members of landless or "under-landed" households were presented with other sources of income, from commercial fishing and from wage-labor, at which they were able to maintain comparable material standards of consumption by working no more, or no more arduously, than their more land-advantaged farming neighbors. In

---

[34] Although the records show that in years just prior to 1954 some Fatatans had purchased local land (see below).

other words, although land was a very important resource in Fatata, it counted for less, economically, than it did in Atea.

Mention was made earlier of the large amount of Te Pitian land owned by outsiders and of ownership by Te Pitians of land elsewhere; I will now examine some of the more tangible[35] economic and sociological aspects of these two-way relationships.

To recapitulate figures given earlier: of Atea's privately owned parcels, 140 hectares were owned by local residents and 533 by individuals living more or less permanently elsewhere; the corresponding figures for Fatata were about 205 and 474.[36]

The outsider owners of Te Pitian lands who reaped monetary benefits from their estates did so either through flat-fee rents, through shares in crop profits, or through direct utilization.

During 1954, Ateans leased six parcels of land, totalling about forty-two hectares. Two of the parcels, totalling just over nineteen hectares, were leased from their Rai'atean owners by an Atean resident who owned no land in Atea. From this, he harvested copra, vanilla, and kapok, which he sold for 25,900 francs. Subtracting the rent he paid for his land (3,000 francs) and his other production costs (copra bags, etc.), he calculated his profits to have been about 18,000 francs—his labor having cost him "nothing." (Had opportunities been available, he could have earned 18,000 francs by working 180 days, instead of the 200 or more he devoted to his cash-crop farming.)

The third parcel of leased Atean land (nearly three hectares of mainly coconut land) belonged to the Administration, which rented it to the *tāvana* for 1,000 francs per annum. From it, the lessee obtained a net profit (excluding his own labor, of which he devoted about thirty days) of about 12,000 francs—obviously a favorable arrangement for him and transparently a perquisite of his office.

The fourth parcel of leased Atean land (just under four hectares) also belonged to the Administration, which continued to lease it to a former *tāvana* at a token rent of 1,000 francs per annum. In this case, the lessee (who was living in Pape'ete throughout 1954) subleased copra rights to another Atean on a sharecrop basis and received in return 7,000 francs, for which he expended no labor.

---

[35]The relationship may have had less tangible aspects, which, however, I was unable to uncover—e.g., feelings of confidence and security that may have been, and probably were, engendered in otherwise landless Te Pitians by the knowledge that, when all else failed, they could go to their distant lands for subsistence, etc. Or reciprocally, the similar feelings by non-residents towards their Te Pitian lands.

[36]The uncertainty for the Fatata figure is explained above, page 448.

The sixth instance of leasing, which was reported earlier, provides a telling exemplification of the restraints imposed upon the Ateans by their shortage of money capital. The thirteen-hectare parcel in question, containing some fine vanilla-growing land, was leased for a nine-year term by its absentee owners to an equally absentee Chinese, who in turn subleased it to an Atean man who produced vanilla on it on a half-share basis. In the event, the latter made a relatively attractive "profit" out of the transaction—which, however, he could have tripled had he leased it directly from the owners.

Finally, the parcel of land on which about half of Atea's dwellings were located belonged to a Ra'iatean Chinese, who charged his lessees only ten francs a year for each house lot—a fee which even his tenants considered inexpensive.

There appear to have been fewer instances of long-term rental by locals in Fatata than in Atea. Some instances may have escaped me, but I knew of only two that involved agricultural land and both of these had outside owners. Even houses and house sites belonging to outsiders were more typically "looked after" (*ha'apa'o hia*) rent-free than leased—usually by relatives or close friends of the owners.[37] Evidently, in contrast to Atea, most Fatatans who wanted more land for long-term farming preferred buying to leasing.

As described previously, sharecropping was practiced in Te Piti in several different ways. Considering copra first, the harvest in question was leased, more or less "commercially," on either a long- or short-term (i.e., four to six months) basis; or in the case of joint-owners, one of them undertook to look out for the others' interests by harvesting and drying the latters' shares of nuts and paying them one-half of his net profits.

As was the case with flat-fee land rental, Ateans engaged in copra sharecropping more actively than Fatatans, and with very few exceptions the owners of the groves in question were outsiders having no known kin ties with the croppers. According to my estimates (which are more accurate for Atea than for Fatata), about 80,000 francs were paid by Atean sharecroppers to their outside landlords during 1954, as against a corresponding figure of about 45,000 for Fatata.

The position was reversed with respect to groves owned jointly with outsiders but cropped by locals, the Fatatans having transferred about 17,000 francs of their revenues to outsider co-owners and the Ateans about 5,000. In this case, my estimates are more accurate for Fatata than for Atea. That is to say, the few Fatatans who regularly cropped the harvests of known

---

[37] Except, of course, for the ethnographer, whose Pape'ete landlady, however, charged only a nominal rent, i.e., *only* about four times the amount she would have obtained from a Tahitian, out of sympathy for the mysterious but doubtless important work I was engaged in!

nonresident co-owners tended to do so on a strictly commercial basis—keeping detailed accounts and remitting payments regularly no matter how small. To the best of my knowledge, only three of the many Atean share-croppers sent regular remittances to nonresident co-owners, most of whom were in fact fairly close kin. The others sent money only when it was demanded (which rarely occurred), or held it in reserve pending a visit by the other party, or, through negligence or design, paid little or none of it at all.

In Atea (mainly; in Fatata to a much less extent) visits by nonresident co-owners were regarded as the most convenient, the most appropriate (the "true Tahitian"), way of paying sharecrop rents. Moreover, in most instances I knew of, the visitors, upon receiving a payment, spent most or all of it in buying food delicacies to share with their sharecrop tenants, with whom they usually lodged when visiting Atea.

Deliberate nonpayment usually occurred when the due payment was considered by the sharecropper to be "too small" to bother about (say, less than about 200–300 francs), or when the cropper felt a grievance against a co-owner temporarily elsewhere (instances of this situation were described above and need not be repeated here).

The foregoing account of sharecropping applies mainly to copra. In instances where one of the owners produced vanilla on jointly owned land, he was not usually required to share his profits with the other owners. In most cases I knew about, the planter secured the consent of the other co-owners, specifically or by their lack of dissent, before proceeding to clear and plant, and that seemed to satisfy the latter.[38]

I wrote above that Fatatans who sharecropped copra regularly for known nonresident co-owners usually remitted the shares due the latter fairly meticulously—the emphasis in the statement having been "known" co-owners. In the case of many parcels of Fatatan land, the resident co-owners said they *believed* that other owners existed somewhere else (*i rāpae*: "outside"), or had existed in the past, but had lost all knowledge of their current existence or whereabouts. In fact, about twenty of the 250 parcels comprising Fatatan lands were in this category, including some with bearing coconuts or land suitable for vanilla. In all these cases, if the land in question were usable the resident co-owners used it as if it were wholly theirs. In addition, Fatata also included some parcels wholly owned by outsiders whose existence and whereabouts were completely unknown. In the only two instances of this

---

[38]The principal exception to this kind of arrangement had to do with the large (i.e., ninety hectare) estate inherited by the numerous progeny of a European who had died many years previously. During the decades that this estate had been in probate, the claimants—some of whom lived in Atea—were permitted use of the land in return for rent, which was paid to the trustee and was added to the estate's assets.

kind where the land had bearing coconuts, these were harvested by locals owning the adjoining parcels, but no one risked planting them in vanilla—for apprehension, it was said, that the owners would turn up and claim the crop. (Actually, the demand for vanilla-growing land in Fatata in 1954–55 was very weak anyway, compared to that of Atea.)

In sharp contrast with Fatata, *no* parcel of land in Atea remained in such a limbo of unknown ownership. Some parcels, it is true, were subject to competing claims (which court judgments had disposed of, although not to the satisfaction of the losing claimants), but the identities and whereabouts of all owners or claimants were well known.

I recorded several instances—proportionately about the same in both villages—in which the outside owners of parcels voluntarily and explicitly permitted their local joint-owners wholly rent-free use of their portions of the lands. In most cases, the latter were recognized as being poor and/or invalid and the concession phrased as based on *aroha,* but in two other instances the basis was said to have been based on the fact of kinship: *mea fēti'i.*

Finally, I recorded instances in which the nonresident co-owners of Te Piti land parcels periodically revisited them, for days or weeks at a time, to make copra or to plant, pollinate, and harvest vanilla. This occurred more often at Atea, where one joint-owner of a very large coconut- and vanilla-growing property retained an otherwise empty house there for his long and frequent visits. (In all other instances of this kind, in Atea and in Fatata, the visitors lived with relatives during the visits—some of them in houses which they also jointly owned.)

Now to reverse the direction, to consider how much land Te Pitians owned "outside"; how they derived benefits from it—and how much; and the social aspects of these procedures and benefits.

The question of "how much" land is impossible to answer. At one extreme was the individual who owned interests in three parcels in a neighboring district; he knew precisely the size of each of them, he personally harvested coconuts from them during his use-period, and he kept separate accounts of that income. At the other extreme were numerous individuals who "knew" or "thought" that they owned interests in land in distant islands but had never received income from them, had no intentions of going personally to collect their shares, if any, and did not even consider the possibility of writing to inquire. (Some of the latter, given the opportunity, would probably have sent verbal inquiries, but the act of writing and posting a letter, even for the more literate, was considered by many Te Pitians too formidable to undertake.)

Those Te Pitians who did receive money from their "outside" properties followed the kinds of procedures, just described, used by outsiders with respect to their Te Piti land interest—except for flat-fee rent. I recorded no instance of a Te Pitian leasing any of his "outside" land at a fixed rate of rent. Instead, those receiving any benefits from the land owned elsewhere did so either by exploiting it personally or by delegating someone else to do so on a sharecrop basis.

Some owners in both villages made almost daily trips to their "outside" properties to harvest their coconuts or to plant vanilla. This daily commuting was facilitated for Fatatans by the use of bicycles on the circumisland road; Ateans had to make such journeys by canoe. (One Atean used to spend four hours commuting each day during his "outside" periods; his overbearing and suspicious wife would not permit him to stay away from her overnight.)

Leaving aside the cases of bilocally residing producers, I estimated that during 1954 Ateans earned approximately 33,500 francs by personally working their "outside" land holdings as against the 18,700 or so earned by Fatatans. The greater ease whereby Fatatans were able to commute to distant parts of their island might lead one to expect that they would engage more often than Ateans in personally working their "outside" but same-island lands, but such was evidently not the case. Here again, the Ateans' paucity of alternative sources of money income appears to have motivated them to get their full shares of profit from the lands accessible to them—which means using their own labor in exploiting those lands, plus the extra labor of commuting, rather than sharing that profit with someone else. (By "accessible" is meant within their conventional means of access—travelling interisland, or writing letters, not having been considered practicable by most Te Pitians.)

In a few other cases, the owners of distant "outside" lands spent days or weeks at a time residing temporarily in the settlements nearest their land—usually, I was told, in the houses of kinsmen. In addition there were a few cases—two in Fatata and three in Atea—of whole families dividing their residence time about equally between the two communities in which their major landowning interests lay. These were usually young couples with no school-age children, and the separate properties were typically those of husband or wife. Sooner or later, however, most such bilocal couples settled down "permanently" in one or the other community—usually where their land-derived benefits were greater (as was noted in Chapter VIII).

Finally, it should be recalled that many Atean families had "country" homes in which they resided during the working days of some seasons of the year. These houses were located on their farming lands, and all of them that I knew of were situated within the territorial boundaries of Atea District. The most common time for this "country" living was the period of three to eight or so weeks that began in January, after the extended and evidently surfeiting holidaying attending New Year. In Fatata a few individuals or families had houses on their local but more distant plantations, and some of them overnighted there or lived in them for several days at a time, but on nowhere like the scale of Ateans' annual migration. Perhaps the Fatatans attached more value to the greater comforts of "town" living, or perhaps their more moderate New Year celebrations prompted less changing of gears, but another, more tangible explanation for this difference between the two villages is probably Fatata's superior roads, which brought all the cultivated portions of local lands within easy cycling or walking access.

The Te Pitians who received regular remittances from "outside"-owned lands numbered about sixteen—five Ateans and eleven Fatatans. During 1954, I was informed, these sixteen received a total of 27,000 francs from this source—8,000 to the Ateans and 19,000 to the Fatatans—and in shares ranging from 500 francs to one of 6,000.[39] As for the amounts received in less regular or less tangible forms, that is impossible to estimate. I recorded random anecdotal accounts about visits to distant settlements, where accumulated earnings (usually those too small to send) were paid to the guests by their hosts—either explicitly in the form of money (which the guests would usually repay in store-bought food) or tacitly in the form of hospitality.[40] A measure of the problem (though not the magnitude) of due money *not* received from lands owned elsewhere was evident in the statements I recorded from several individuals who attributed their cash shortages to that cause. In only one of these instances, however, was I able to pin down the complainer about the amount owed him, and even he expressed no intention to act beyond perhaps reporting the matter to the Administration.

Against all these efforts to receive one's share of profits from outside land holdings, and the grievances arising from nonreceipts, it must be recorded that many Te Pitians forbore obtaining such income, either through lack of interest, through cynicism, or through deliberate forfeiture.

Several individuals—more in Fatata than in Atea—asserted that they "supposed" they owned interests in land elsewhere but were clearly

---

[39]In fact, I believe that the actual figures were somewhat larger, both in numbers of individuals and in amounts received, inasmuch as some Te Pitians were obviously reluctant to reveal income magnitudes to their neighbors (or to me) except in situations where they knew the actual figures to be otherwise accessible, as, e.g., in publicly recorded vanilla sales, or in written store records.

[40]On one occasion prior to my visit, Atea's football team and many of its social supporters went to Taha'a for a match, to a place where some of them had small interests in local lands. They were so hospitably entertained, I was told long after the event, that their shares in Taha'a lands had been paid up for years to come. When I asked whether they had picked that destination for their match in order to collect their shares of land-profits the answer was: "Not really, or at least only perhaps (*mea paha*)."

uninterested in expending the energy required to pursue the matter any further. A few more—mainly in Fatata—said that they "knew" of the existence of distant land holdings but had no confidence in being able to prove their ownership or to obtain any benefits from it if they did.

And finally there were a few individuals in both villages who held demonstrable and capitalizable interests in distant land parcels and who purposely declined demanding their shares of the lands' profits. In two of these cases—one in each village—the holdings were large and evidently profitable, and the reasons given by each owner for his self-denial was that his spouse had enough land nearer at hand (which was true), and that he felt sympathy (*aroha*) towards his co-owning *fēti'i* (which may also have been true but would be difficult to demonstrate). In all the other cases the reasons for self-denial were also stated to be *aroha* towards the co-owning *fēti'i*, but the value of the portions in question were much smaller (hence the sincerity of the sentiments may have been genuine!).

Summary of Differences

One of the most noteworthy features of Te Piti's land tenure in 1954–55 was the large proportion of local land owned by nonresidents, i.e., about 74 percent in all.[41] For Te Pitians as a whole, this constituted an unfavorable circumstance in at least one important respect. To the extent that any of that outsider-owned land was used by Te Pitians for money-earning purposes—and much of it was—they had to pay rent, either in money itself or in the labor involved in sharecropping. Comparatively, the Fatatans were (per capita) more disadvantaged than the Ateans in this respect; but to counteract this "disadvantage" they were less dependent upon land than the latter for money-earning. Moreover, this disparity between the two villages in per capita land ownership was in the process of narrowing due to the faster rate at which the Fatatans had recently been buying back land locally, and which they would probably continue to do because of their greater money-earning opportunities.

Reversing the roles, some Te Pitians owned land elsewhere. I was unable to discover exactly, or even approximately, the extent of those "outside" land holdings, but my scattered evidence suggests that they were nowhere near as extensive as outsiders' holdings in Te Piti. Although my information regarding the income that Te Pitians received from their outside holdings is also incomplete, there is enough to indicate that it was considerably smaller than the external flow, and that more came into Fatata than into Atea in

---

[41]This includes the parcel of seventy-one hectares of Fatata land mentioned earlier (page 448), which, I deduce, was owned by outsiders.

terms of sharecropping "rent" (i.e., 19,000 to 8,000 francs, respectively, or at a per capita rate of fifty-six to thirty-six). But that position was reversed in terms of income obtained from their personal working of outside properties—33,500 francs to Ateans and 18,700 to Fatatans, or at a per capita rate of 151 francs to fifty-five, respectively.

The most obvious social-relational aspect of the situation just described was the influence it exerted upon kinship ties and vice versa. The communication engendered by co-ownership of a productive land parcel served to keep alive such ties between geographically separate kinfolk, whether those ties were "friendly" or otherwise. Moreover, when one or both of the co-owners visited each other's community (which co-ownership promoted but, of course, did not account for in all instances) the visitors were able to renew relations with other kinfolk there.[42]

There was also a negative side to Te Pitians' reciprocal land-tenure situation. History indicates that when, for some reason or other, Te Pitian kinfolk had become residentially separate most other dimensions of their social relations had become attenuated as well, including dissolution of co-ownership ties in several of the instances in which they existed. But along with this general trend, case studies show that the very fact of co-ownership had in some instances hastened overall attenuation and even complete rupture of social relationships; I refer to instances in which conflict over jointly held land had led the geographically separate parties not only to "divide the land" but to break off all other interactions as well.

In view of these islanders' aboriginal social structure, it may be relevant to inquire whether the principles of social hierarchy that were inherent in the land tenure of that era (i.e., in the hierarchy of residual claims) were preserved in the Te Piti arrangements of 1954–55. That is, were the outsiders who owned substantial landlord interests in Te Piti land considered, by themselves or by their Te Pitian tenants, to be socially "superior" to the latter in any discernible way? I would be hard put to provide explicit evidence of it, but I believe that answer to this question to be partly affirmative—at least from the side of the Te Pitian tenants.

The basis of my belief rests mainly on statements from tenants about the attitudes of their landlords concerning money due them either from flat-fee rental or sharecropping. Some of those landlords were characterized as hard and exacting—as taking unjust advantage of their "high status" (*teitei*)

---

[42]Thus, administrators and politicians intent on individualizing Tahitian land titles (i.e., for the stated purpose of "promoting economic development") should take into account the consequences this might have upon the archipelago's interdistrict and even interisland social networks.

vis-à-vis their low-status, "humble" (*ha'eha'a*) selves; while others were characterized as being "gentle" (*marū*) and *"généreuse"* (*hōro'a*)—as highly-placed persons *ought* to be towards their poorer and humbler selves. There were only two occasions when I was able to observe much interaction between Te Pitian tenants and their visiting landlords but not enough to draw generalizations from. However, in both of these instances I was struck by the solemn diffidence exhibited by the tenants, who were otherwise most unsolemn and undeferential men.

By 1954-55, the Western-inspired effort to transform Tahiti's aboriginal form of land tenure (which was a pattern of smaller provisionally held parcels integrated into larger unities by a hierarchic structure of overlapping residual rights) into a pattern consisting of even smaller, entirely separate, and individually owned parcels, had progressed a long way—and farther in Fatata than in Atea. This difference between the two communities was the result, probably, of several causes—*historical* (e.g., Fatatans' longer, more frequent and more direct contact with Europeans), *economic* (e.g., Fatatans' extra money for financing subdivision, and for buying parcels from one another), and *social*. With respect to the last, Fatata's more advanced progress towards parcel fragmentation and title individuation was both a consequence of and stimulant for "social fragmentation"—especially that of units comprising cognatic stocks and of cooperative work groups in general.

Fatata also differed from Atea with respect to local ownership rights in local land. While the percentages of local residents holding such rights were about the same in both villages—21 percent in Fatata and 24.8 percent in Atea—and while the average size of individual holding was also about the same—2.81 hectares in Fatata and 2.62 in Atea—the modal distribution of holding size differed markedly—i.e., 44 percent of Fatata's landowners had holdings of less than ten hectares, compared with 24 percent of Atea's. Moreover, a very much larger proportion of the locally owned Fatatan land holdings consisted of house lots, which could be valued in terms of money but which were otherwise unproductive of money income. Yet, however interesting this disparity may be from other points of view, it cannot serve as a measure of more general economic differences between the two villages, inasmuch as Fatatans had other and more copious sources of money than Ateans. In other words, land was more important as an economic asset in Atea than it was in Fatata.

As a corollary to this circumstance, to be landless was more disadvantageous, or to be land-rich more advantageous, in Atea than it was in Fatata—but mainly with regard to the number of hours people worked. For, in Atea as in Fatata, it was not the general practice to convert saved labor into anything except leisure, or wine or beer.

Aside from its more narrowly "economic" aspect, landownership was also important in some facets of social relations. As described earlier, it served occasionally as a weighty, even the weightiest, factor in choosing a mate and in choice of residence after marriage. Moreover, in marriages characterized by wide disparities in the spouses' land holdings, it tended to influence both the stability of the unions and the interaction of the mates, particularly when the woman was the richer mate in this respect.

Some behavior could also be viewed as connoting a positive correlation between landownership and social class—but in this connection it should be noted how ephemeral that correlation could have been. That is to say, because of the principles of inheritance that obtained (whereby each legitimate or officially acknowledged child inherited an equal portion of each parent's land) the offspring of prolific parents had to commence life with only a fraction of whatever wealth in land the latter might have possessed.

CHAPTER XII

RÉSUMÉ AND EXPLANATIONS
OF INTERVILLAGE DIFFERENCES

This chapter will summarize and account for the most noteworthy economic and economy-related differences between Atea and Fatata as recorded by this study in 1954–55. I will begin by listing those differentiating factors that seem to have been largely *extrinsic* to the two villages as they were in the mid-1950s.

Section One

1. Most obvious among those factors were the two villages' different locations with respect to other human settlements, or rather, their residents' accessibility to such settlements. In this, Fatata was much less isolated than Atea in several weighty respects: it had shorter and more frequent boat communications with Pape'ete, easier access by road to nearby villages and emporia, and—what Atea altogether lacked—direct proximity to labor-employing European plantations.

2. Another set of extrinsic factors in which the two villages differed had to do with their immediate physical environments. Topographically, the area comprising Fatata had a more ruggedly mountainous interior, but this was compensated in some measure by its wider coastal plain and by the location of its widest valley directly behind the settlement itself.

"Arability" is extrinsic only in terms of a society's perceptions thereof, but inasmuch as Ateans and Fatatans seem to have had more or less the same perceptions in this regard, the two areas did differ with respect to their distribution of "land types" as locally defined. In this sense, the Atean area contained a much larger amount of "arable" land than Fatatan, absolutely and proportionate to the whole; and in view of Atea's smaller population, this works out to a per capita advantage of nearly three to one (i.e., Atea having had 570 hectares of "arable" land and 217 residents, as against Fatata's 315 arable hectares and 348 residents).[1] Also, of the "arable" lands identified with each village, the Fatatan area lay under the additional disadvantage of containing much more "rocky" land, suitable mainly for melon growing, than Atea.

On the other hand, with regard to supplies of natural fresh water, Fatata was much better located than Atea, having had a large stream of clear water flowing through the settlement itself, in contrast to Atea's small and overworked springs and its far-distant stream.

Fatata's lagoon, being somewhat shallower, was better suited than Atea's for seine fishing, but a weightier difference between the two villages' marine environments was Fatata's closer proximity to a navigable break in their respective barrier reefs—a possible advantage in terms of the quantity and variety of marine life.

3. The age and sex profiles of a community's population may be said to be extrinsic to as well as conducive to the nature of its activities and institutions, but those profiles are also shaped by the institutions, etc., in some degree. Lacking sufficient historical data, I am unable to speculate credibly about the latter relationship but can say about the former that the age differences beween the Atean and Fatatan populations of 1954–55 were not wide enough to have had any discernible effect upon the activities, etc., that are this study's main concern. That is to say, in terms of the production, circulation, and consumption of the objects and services that existed in 1954–55, the two populations were nearly alike—51.5 percent of Atea's population consisted of individuals in the (culturally defined) productive stages of life, between fifteen and sixty years old, as against 54.5 percent of Fatata's. This is not to say that all such in those stages were, in fact, productive, or that all others were engaged only in consumption, but according to many of both villages' widely held norms, age was defined in those terms.

Within those more productive stages of life, there were relatively fewer females than males in Atea than in Fatata. There may be some correlation between this demographic difference and the observed circumstance that Atean women worked alongside their husbands in food and cash-crop

---

[1]This, of course, does not signify that actual landownership in the two villages was so distributed—only that, *ceteris paribus*, such lands were commonly identified with each village as a whole in the proportions given.

agriculture more so than did their Fatatan counterparts—however, I believe that this correlation, if it was in fact such, was not a direct adjustment to current statistical imbalance but one deriving from older mental attitudes about women's economic roles.

Again, as noted elsewhere, Fatatans were on the whole committed to longer schooling for their children, i.e., to postponing, hence currently reducing, their productive work, but a demographic basis cannot be used to account for this difference between the two villages, since the proportionate number of school-age children in both places was nearly identical.

In other words, the above differences between Atea and Fatata with respect to sex- and age-based roles cannot be attributed entirely or even in part to demographic patterns that existed in 1954–55. In this case, explanations of the differences must be sought in correlations with other differences and, ultimately, in "history" (where, it may be, but cannot be proven, that demographic factors did at one time exercise more influence in shaping the ideas and practices involved).

4. "History" must also be invoked to help account for the differences between Atea and Fatata with regard to the spatial arrangements of their residences, e.g., by the influence formerly exercised in Fatata by European missionaries and officials; and by the absence of such direct influences in Atea. But geography also was and continued to be a contributing cause. With the sites selected and with the numbers of people given—in the formative past and in 1954–55—Atea's crowded density can be seen as a necessary adjustment to its site's constricted size and Fatata's spaciousness as a preferred acceptance of its wider and longer coastal plain.

Having invoked "history" to help account for differences between the settlement patterns of Atea and Fatata, I must try to clarify my usage of the term.

Some of "history," i.e., what people did and thought in the past, undoubtedly determines what they do and think in the present. In this sense, much if not most of the behaviors described in this study were determined by history. (This is not a resurrection of the discredited theme of "custom is king." Some choice is probably involved in most of the things people do and believe, but just as probable is the circumstance that the various alternatives weighed by the chooser are also products of past doing and thinking.) But, instead of history in this very broad (and somewhat tautological sense), I invoke the term here for a more specific class of past events that were largely extrinsic to the Te Pitians themselves, things that *happened to them* and their settlements prior to 1954–55 and that were weighty enough to have brought about appreciable differences between the two villages of

1954–55.[2] In my view, those historical situations and events that have had most influence upon the matters examined in this study were the following:

(a) Fatata's greatness as a pre-European political and religious center, as contrasted with Atea's insignificance—or perhaps nonexistence as anything other than the site of a few socially inconsequential households.

(b) Fatata's prominence as a major center of European missionary activity, beginning as early as 1802, as contrasted with Atea's lack of even so much as a church of its own until 1921.

(c) Mo'orea's (including Fatata's) compliant subordination to direct French rule, from 1843 to the present, as contrasted with Huahine's (and hence Atea's, such as it was) experience, first with British "protection," beginning in the 1820s, and then with an unwelcome and militarily imposed French colonial rule only since 1898.

(d) In addition, Fatata's character as the headquarters of the French administration of Mo'orea for many years, and as a place subject to fairly close French attention ever since—which is to be contrasted with Atea's spatial remoteness from, and what seems to have been neglect by, French officials throughout its French-governed era.

(e) Along with the above, Fatatans' experience of a continuous stream of other Europeans—temporary visitors and "permanent" residents—as contrasted with Atea's paucity thereof. (Of course, some Ateans, like many more Fatatans, were able to observe Europeans elsewhere, but in contexts less relevant to life at home.)

(f) In connection with the last statement, both Fatatans and Ateans had for several decades been accustomed to spending weeks, months, or years away from home. And during those times they had acquired information and attitudes, not only from and about Europeans but about many other things as well, all of which were in a sense extrinsic to life at home and much of which had in due course some effects on the behavior of themselves and their neighbors at home. (Discreet anecdotes about such effects could be summoned by the score, but they do not fall into any patterns general enough to epitomize.) In any case, since some Fatatans had over the years spent more man-days away from home than their Atean counterparts, it is plausible to conclude that their home community acquired, or at least was exposed to, more of those nonindigenous ideas, etc., than Atea.

Now to summarize the more prominent[3] differences between the economy-related institutions and activities of the Ateans and Fatatans as

---

[2]Underlying this usage—and in fact underlying the whole of this study—is the assumption, stated in the Introduction, that the indigenous cultures ancestral to both Atea and Fatata were virtually identical.

[3]In the summaries presented in the descriptive chapters were listed some other differences that will not be repeated here—where only the most salient ones, and those with social-relational ramifications, will be recapitulated.

observed in 1954–55. And when listing them, I will also attempt to account for them—either as direct effects or consequences of the extrinsic factors just enumerated, or as effects of those or of other local situations. I begin with a recapitulation of behavior differences that had to do with the residents' consumption of material goods and with their actions in obtaining them.

Section Two

1. On the average, Fatatans spent about one-half times more money on store-bought food staples than the Ateans did—not because of a correspondingly higher preference for such foods (although their closer experience with Europeans did move them somewhat in that direction), but because of two other circumstances, namely their greater opportunities for money-earning, coupled with the choices, either relatively free or relatively constrained, made by more of them to avail themselves of those opportunities rather than grow their own vegetable foods. Had the Ateans enjoyed comparable opportunities, more of them might have made the same choices, but not, I suggest, to quite the same extent as was done by the Fatatans, because of the difference in food preference just mentioned and because of the smaller amount of suitable and readily available vegetable-growing land found in Fatata. In other words, even had a larger number of Fatata's food providers wished to spend more time growing their own vegetables, they would have been constrained, more so than their Atean counterparts, in doing so.

Fatatans also ate more locally caught fish than Ateans. Most of this difference came about as a spinoff from the Fatatans' overwhelmingly larger engagement in commercial fishing.

Chapter II also recorded some small differences between Atea and Fatata with regard to poultry raising and egg consumption, to wild pig hunting, and to the economic uses made of horses and dogs, but such differences were not consequential enough to engage more of our interest here.

2. Fatatans, mainly women and young men, spent about twice as much money as Ateans on clothing—a circumstance based partly on their possession of more money and partly on their proximity to Pape'ete, where island fashions were dictated and supplies of clothing more varied and plentiful.

Fatatans also spent nearly three times as much money as the Ateans did on physical health, again mainly because of their larger money resources, but also, I suggest, because of their better acquaintance with things European, including a somewhat firmer faith, or larger hope, in European medicine.

3. Fatata's houses, old and new, were more "European" than those of Atea in architecture and generally superior in size and quality of construction. The architectural differences were a reflection of Fatatans' closer relations with Europeans, recently and in the past, while those of size and construction were the result, mainly, of the latters' larger money incomes, also recently and in the past. (Implicit in this comparison is my assumption that Ateans and Fatatans were very much alike in their desire for, if not in their ability to acquire, what they, respectively, perceived to be European-style houses.

Although, as just stated, Fatatans' closer European contacts and larger money incomes were the main reasons for the differences between the two villages' houses, another factor must be granted some weight. I refer to the Ateans' frequent employment of organized labor-exchange crews for house building and repair—in contrast to Fatatans' utilization of paid and sometimes even imported expert house builders. Atea's dearth of ready cash may have been responsible for the persistence there of the practice of labor exchange, but only partly so; one cannot rule out the possibility that a highly valued and widely shared ethic of work-sharing was also involved— an ethic that was only feebly apparent in Fatata. As for the reason for that difference—I suggest that the ethic in quesion derived from the common, pre-European Tahitian past and that its stronger persistence in Atea represents one of a number of facets of Huahine's (and the Leeward Islands as a whole) generally less contiguous experience of and more conservative reaction to European influence. But whatever the explanation for the stronger persistence of that ethic in Atea, its implementation there by crews of enthusiastic but unskilled carpenters clearly contributed to the inferiority of Atea's houses *vis-à-vis* those of Fatata.

4. A survey of house furnishings found Atea and Fatata to be about the same with respect to the quantity and quality of basic furniture (e.g., beds, chairs, tables, lamps, stoves, and utensils) but established that Fatata's houses contained more radios, refrigerators, and phonographs (a situation that was reflected—but only faintly—in expenditures for house furnishings for 1954, when the Fatatans outspent the Ateans on the average of 385 francs to 339).

5. As already mentioned, both "historic" and "geographic" factors help to explain the difference between the spacing of Atea's and Fatata's houses; the same explanations may be offered to account for the presence, in Fatata, of well-kept lawns. Finally, "extrinsic" action by the colonial government was solely responsible for Fatata's having had a better distribution of running water than Atea.

Section Three-A

Next to be recapitulated are the more noteworthy differences between Atea and Fatata with respect to money earned by their residents from "outside" sources, i.e., from persons and organizations (including the local Chinese storekeepers) other than the Tahitian residents of Atea or Fatata. (How some of that money circulated among Ateans and among Fatatans will be treated below, in Section Three-B.)

During 1954, there was a wide difference in the total amounts of money Fatatans and Ateans earned from persons and organizations outside their own respective communities of Tahitians, and also wide differences in the ways in which that money was earned. In terms of the totals, Ateans earned about 7,573 francs per capita, and Fatatans almost 3,000 francs more. (The magnitude of this difference will be better appreciated by noting that 3,000 francs represents somewhat more than the average monthly wage of a Te Pitian at that time—had he been fortunate enough to obtain wage-work.) The differences between the two villages in terms of money-earning activities will now be summarized.

1. While Fatata contained less land suitable for growing coconut palms than Atea, it contained, overall, more palms—a heritage of its history of longer and closer European contact. On the other hand, Fatatans produced, per capita, less copra than did the Ateans—as result, partly, of the circumstance that they possessed more alternative (and what by many were described as more congenial[1]) ways of earning a living and, partly, of the fact that palm ownership among them was less widely distributed than in Atea (a situation that will be dealt with in Section Eleven).

While Fatatan palms may have been rendered more productive by banding (an antirat practice, which was rejected by Ateans), this advantage may have been neutralized in some measure by the Fatatans' more widespread harvesting practice of cutting the nut from the palm (a practice that probably resulted in some nuts having less meat).

Despite Fatata's smaller production of copra, it brought in over twice as much profit to its producers. This paradox resulted partly from Fatata's closer proximity to Pape'ete, the islands' only overseas transshipping port. And in addition, the Atea producers were persuaded, by their more chronic indebtedness to their local storekeepers, to turn over most of their copra to

---

[1] While there was a sentiment expressed by many residents in both communities, and not only by the older ones, that copra-making was a "good" activity, a "truly Tahitian" one, the fact remains that it was regarded by most of those whose opinions I sampled as onerous and relatively poorly paid work.

the latter in a green state, and hence at a much lower price, even correspondingly, than they would have received had they dried it themselves. (Although it may be argued that some labor time was thereby saved, many of Atea's producers lacked opportunities to apply that saving to other kinds of money-earning.)

Copra making was also revealed as having been less monetized in Atea than in Fatata, where more paid labor was employed in its processing and where the owners of dryers required even primary kinfolk to pay for use of their equipment. And the method of harvesting by nut-cutting, which was considered to be an act of selfishness when done by a time-alloted co-owner, was much more prevalent in Fatata than in Atea.

2. Vanilla growing was Atea's largest money-earning industry by far, whereas in Fatata it ranked below several others in this respect. In Atea, 35 percent of the population was deeply engaged in vanilla growing, as against a figure of 5 percent for Fatata; and of these, thirty Ateans produced green beans in amounts of sixty or more kilos, as against only one in Fatata.

Several explanations may be offered for this striking difference in the economic lives of Ateans and Fatatans.

In the first place, Atea contained more land naturally suitable to the growing of vanilla beans, including more land not already preempted to coconuts. But in addition to this geographic factor was another and probably weightier reason for the difference. Vanilla growing, as practiced in both villages, was regarded as a very onerous undertaking and one requiring a long time lag between initial clearing and first harvest. It was also thought to be risky (because of insect pests and disease) and uncertain (because of a history of sharp fluctuations in price). As a result, many Fatatans chose to concentrate their energies in other, less onerous, more congenial, and faster profit-earning activities, such as fishing and wage-work, alternatives that were not available to their Atean counterparts. In addition, it might be argued that Ateans on the average attached higher social value to farming, including vanilla growing (which in fact I believe to have been the case), but how much of that attitude was an accommodation to current necessity and how much of it a manifestation of a deep-rooted cultural heritage I cannot say. In any case, these contrasting attitudes, whatever their histories, did serve to reinforce, and possibly even widen, the gap between the amounts of time and energy devoted to vanilla growing in Atea and Fatata.

Another difference between Atea and Fatata with respect to vanilla growing was the lower price paid for Ateans' green beans—an average of 225 francs per kilo, as compared with the equivalent average of 250 paid to Fatatans. Some of this difference may have come about through competitive bidding by the Chinese buyers, which took place only in Fatata, but most of it was due, clearly, to Atea's greater distance from Pape'ete, and the higher transportation and handling costs that this entailed.

Finally, with respect to the differences that obtained between Atea and Fatata in the social ambiance of vanilla selling, i.e., Atea's festivallike atmosphere versus Fatata's businesslike mood, I believe that most of that can be accounted for by the difference in number of sellers, although the two villages' pervasive differences in ethos were undoubtedly also at play.

3. In contrast to Fatatans, who carded not even enough kapok fibers to fill their own local wishes (i.e., for mattress and pillow filling), Ateans processed enough to fill all local needs and in addition sold 68,685 francs' worth for "export." Since Fatata contained even more kapok trees than Atea (most of which went unharvested in *both* places), the reason why so many Ateans—thirty-seven in all—processed kapok for sale (a tedious and poorly paid work even by local standards) was avowedly their lack of opportunities for other money-earning jobs.

4. Two reasons can be offered to account for Fatata's lead over Atea in amounts of coffee bean exports—Fatata's per capita earnings in 1954 having been 285 francs from this source as against Atea's 122). First, was the circumstance that Fatata contained relatively more coffee trees than Atea, a heritage, perhaps, of its longer and closer European contacts. And second was the presence in Fatata of one individual—the producer of most of the exported coffee—who possessed a combination of attitudes and abilities that no Atean possessed in like measure. In neither village were all the productive coffee trees regularly harvested, and one would have thought that the Ateans, at least, would have exploited this valuable resource to its fullest extent. However, unlike kapok, the large-scale harvesting and processing of coffee beans for commercial export required an amount of entrepreneurial and management skills which no Atean appeared to possess.

5. Fatata's lead in sale of vegetables (the reported revenues amounted to five times those of Atea,[5] but the actual difference may have been even wider) can be explained by the circumstance that many more Fatatans grew none of their own vegetables, mainly because of their employment in other more profitable and less onerous work. Fatata's inferiority to Atea in terms of suitable vegetable-growing land may also have served to discourage some of the nongardeners, but is unlikely to have been the main cause.

---

[5]The reported figures on revenues from "export" sale of vegetables must be qualified by the likelihood that some of those vegetables were eventually resold to other Te Pitians.

As for Fatatans' lead over Ateans in revenues from "export" fruit sales—a conjectured ratio of eight to one—this may be explained by their proximity, and more frequent visits, to Pape'ete.

6. Since all of Te Piti's revenues from the export of cassava flour came from the production of two individuals, one in each village, Fatata's lead in this activity is to be "explained" in part by the greater zeal, energy, etc., of its producer (who was, incidentally, the major coffee producer noted above), and in part by Fatata's proximity and easier access to Pape'ete, where the cassava was marketed.

7. Fatatans cut and sold more firewood than did the Ateans—about twice as much per capita, but fewer Fatatans were engaged in this activity. The explanation for the first of these differences is quite simple: more bread was baked and eaten in Fatata, per capita as well as totally, and hence more firewood was required by the storekeeper-bakers. (The explanation for the larger per capita bread consumption is the same as that behind Fatatans' larger consumption of most other store-bought foods, namely, their fuller engagement in nonsubsistence enterprises and their larger money incomes.)

Concerning the greater specialization involved in firewood cutting in Fatata (i.e., only six men were thus engaged, and those part time but regularly, whereas in Atea nearly every youth and adult male was so engaged some of the time), a partial explanation may be found in the circumstance that the six regular Fatatan cutters owned little or no land suitable for cash-cropping and were reported to have been unsuccessful as fishermen and unable to secure regular wage employment.

8. The very wide differences between Atea and Fatata with respect to revenues from "export" sale of cattle, pigs, and chickens and eggs—1,140 francs per capita for Fatata, as against 187 for Atea—can be explained mainly by Fatata's proximity to Pape'ete, currently and in the past (i.e., in the past, because it had required a fairly long period for Fatatans to develop cattle-raising adjusted to Pape'ete's demands). Ateans were very familiar with pig and cattle "raising"—in fact more of their households kept cattle and pigs than did those of Fatata—but the difficulty and expense of selling more of them to outsiders evidently discouraged such commerce.

9. The existence in Fatata of a large and profitable commercial fishing industry, and the absence of such in Atea, can be accounted for, almost wholly, by the differences in the two villages' distance from and access to Pape'ete. The slightly better suitability of Fatata's adjacent lagoon for seine-net fishing may have made for larger catches there (as perhaps did its

possibly greater variety and quantity of fish), but the factor of location was the weightiest and most immediate cause of this most salient economic difference between the two villages.

In this connection, the difference between Atea and Fatata in amounts spent in 1954 for purchase of tools (700 francs per capita in Atea and 923 in Fatata) consisted largely of money spent on fish nets and other things connected with fishing.

10. As we saw, Fatatans earned in 1954 about three times as much as Ateans, per capita, by working for "outside" employers (including the local Chinese). Even eliminating the one-time windfall earnings obtained by working on the public works pipe-laying project (which brought in a total of 457,045 francs), their advantage over the Ateans in this sphere of money-earning would have been twofold. Nor is the principal explanation for this difference difficult to find: it was Fatata's geographic location in close proximity to several European plantations and Atea's isolation from all such places of potential employment.

11. As summarized in Table 3E, the more noteworthy differences between Atea and Fatata in amounts of rent received from outsiders had to do with dwelling houses, "theaters," land, and savings accounts.

The house-rent item, while small in amount, was yet another sign of Fatata's further progress in the monetization of its social relationships. That is to say, the outside schoolteacher who resided in the house in question was required to pay rent to its local owner. This contrast might, of course, be interpreted as a sign of Ateans' stronger support for education (which was, however, not otherwise evident) or for their closer identification with the Administration in general (which also was not otherwise apparent), but I believe that their less commercialized attitude towards social relationships in general is a better explanation for this difference.

As for the theaters, it turns out that while the film distributors had to pay higher rents in Fatata, they actually received—or so I infer from attendance figures—smaller revenues from their filmings there. If these figures are correct (and I am not sure that they are), it could mean either or both of two things—first, that the Fatatan landlords were harder bargainers than their Atean counterpart (another sign of a more pervasive monetization), or that the film distributors were obliged by their competition to pay higher rents for the privilege of operating in Fatata—another payoff to the Fatatans, deriving in part from their location and hence easier accessibility.

The Fatatans' larger incomes from land rental to outsiders—31,000 francs against the Ateans' 10,500—requires explanations of two kinds. First, for local lands, from which their Atean owners received 2,500 francs and their

Fatatan counterparts over 12,000, this difference is to be explained not by any higher rental rates (the rents received were about the same per hectare in both places) but by Atea's remoteness from prospective outside users, as contrasted with Fatata's proximity, expecially to the numerous Chinese vanilla growers living nearby, who at that time were eager to expand their plantings. As for the lands owned by Te Pitians and located elsewhere, lands for which the Ateans received about 8,000 francs in rent as against the Fatatans' 19,000, I suggest that this difference may have been due to two circumstances: the more extensive outside land holdings of the Fatatans (as inferred from the population's larger number of outside ancestral origins), and the Fatatans' somewhat superior literacy and better familiarity with the workings of modern communications, hence their larger propensity for keeping in touch with their outside properties by mail.

12. As for the Fatatans' interest earnings from savings accounts—which were said to have been "very small" but which were at least more than the Ateans' zero—this difference is also to be explained by their better familiarity with the modern world, including its commercial aspects plus, of course, the residence in Fatata of more individuals possessing unobligated amounts of money.

13. The only money earned in 1954 by Te Pitians selling "refreshments" to outsiders occurred at Fatata during interdistrict football matches and at New Year. My very rough estimate of the profits thus earned by sales to outsiders is about 5,000 francs. The reasons why Ateans earned no money in this way are very simple: their New Year celebrations did not include that kind of commerce, and in 1954 there were no interdistrict football matches played there!

14. The very wide difference between Atea and Fatata in amounts received in the form of remittances, about 2,000 francs in Atea and 85,000 in Fatata, is puzzling in one respect. That the Fatatans received more (about 25,000 per annum against the Ateans' zero) in the form of pensions, welfare payments, and family allocations from the government, is not very surprising; having greater familiarity with the workings of government they tended to utilize more of the latter's largesse. The puzzling aspect of this difference lies in the relatively larger amounts received by the Fatatans in the form of remittances from *kinfolk* living and working elsewhere. It might be thought that Atea, with its generally more conservative, less Europeanized social values, would have imbued its absent natives with stronger kinship loyalties, but such was evidently not the case—at least, not in terms of this form of manifestation of "kin solidarity."

Section Three-B

All of the money originally acquired by Te Pitians originated outside (*i rapae*), and nearly all of it eventually returned to that outside, but in the interim much of it circulated among the Ateans, or the Fatatans, themselves. In this section will be recapitulated the more important differences between the two villages in the ways in which money circulated locally, and an attempt will be made to account for such differences.

1. Despite the popular disclaimer that "no Tahitian would sell *ma'a* (vegetable staples) to another Tahitian," there was evidence, direct and indirect, that many of them did so.

While cassava flour was usually classified as *ma'a*, some of it was openly and avowedly bought and sold among Ateans and among Fatatans—an estimated 3,150 francs' worth among the former and 4,800 francs' worth among the latter—which, per capita, amounted to fourteen francs in both villages, and this requires no explanation in terms of a difference.

Most of the other vegetable staples—*taruā* (Xanthosoma), sweet potatoes, yams, and (in Atea only) taro—that were sold locally were sold through the local stores, but it is my estimate that Ateans sold at least 5,000 francs' worth of *ma'a* directly to other Ateans and Fatatans at least 20,000 francs' worth to other Fatatans—representing a per capita difference of twenty-three to fifty-nine, which is to be explained by the circumstance that many more Fatatans than Ateans grew no *ma'a* at all.

Some coffee beans were also bought and sold locally but I was unable to discover the volume of that commerce.

2. The Fatatans sold regularly more cattle, pigs, and chickens to outsiders than did the Ateans as a consequence of their proximity to Pape'ete. They also sold relatively more to their Tahitian neighbors, 295 francs' worth per capita against the Ateans' 239, as a result of the circumstance that fewer Fatatans raised livestock of their own and that more of them had such money to spend.

3. My estimate that Fatata's fishermen sold about 40,000 francs' worth of fish to other Fatatans is probably very conservative. In contrast, I doubt that Atea's expert fishermen (who included only one "regular") sold to their fellow villagers fish worth more than about 5,000 francs during 1954. (Most of the fish consumed by Ateans was self-caught, or obtained through reciprocal exchange with other households, or purchased from itinerant fish-sellers from nearby districts.) There is direct evidence for concluding that the principal reason for this large difference in volume of local fish

commerce was the Fatatans' fishing for the Pape'ete market. That is to say, most of the fish that I saw being sold in Fatata—by peddling, actually—was from catches originally intended for Pape'ete but not actually sent there, either because of there having been too few to justify sending or because of a breakdown in transport.

4. Some women in both villages engaged, in their spare time, in making palm-leaf thatch-plates for sale to their neighbors, those of Fatata about 6,000 francs' worth per annum and those of Atea about twice as much. The reasons for this difference were probably twofold. In the first place, the attitude that women ought to do some productive work on their own was more prevalent in Atea than in Fatata—a component of Atea's more conservative ideological heritage. And secondly, Atean women had fewer other kinds of opportunities for money-earning than did their Fatatan counterparts.

5. In all but three cases, all of the canoes in use in Te Piti during my visits there were of local manufacture, and during 1954 several men in both villages built or repaired canoes for themselves. There was, however, some specialization in this craft. In Atea there were eight men known as experts, in Fatata four; during 1954, three of the latter fabricated four canoes, worth a total of 11,250 francs, and two of the former made one canoe each, worth a total of 4,500 francs.

A possible reason for Fatata's having had fewer (and somewhat more expert) specialists than Atea is to be sought in the encompassing circumstance that division of labor in general, and specialization in particular, were more widely acknowledged and practiced in Fatata than in Atea, an explanation that would also help to account for the Fatatans' relatively larger expenditures in this category.

6. In only one kind of inter-Tahitian money-earning service—namely, unspecialized manual labor—were the differences in earned incomes between Atea and Fatata wide enough to invite attention and require explanation.[6] Here, as Table 3D shows, Fatatans earned nearly two and a half times as much, per capita, as Ateans did in working individually as laborers for other local Tahitians in a variety of unspecialized jobs; and Ateans earned about *two hundred seventy* times as much, per capita, in working for other

---

[6]Even though Fatata exceeded Atea by a very large rate in the amount of money earned by the services performed by copra-dryer owners, I exclude this item from consideration because of the inconsequential amount so earned—and by the uncertainty that attaches to the estimate thereof.

local Tahitians, also in a variety of such jobs, not as individuals but as members of organized work groups.

As described above, the organized work groups (*pupu rave i te ohipa*) of Atea—as distinct from the male (or female) memberships of the sodalities, who occasionally engaged in working together to earn money for their sodality treasuries—were of two kinds: work exchange and money-earning. The work-exchange ones engaged most typically in house building and repair; they worked on one another's houses without pay (but usually for food and drink) on the understanding that every member would eventually receive such help in return. The money-earning groups differed not only in working specifically for pay (which their members then shared) but in being smaller than the work-exchange groups. Also, the money-earning ones worked, more typically, on ground clearing and other agricultural tasks. And whereas they sometimes operated like the work-exchange groups, among themselves, their *raison d'être* was to earn money in a more congenial way, i.e., more congenial than working individually and alone. (In fact, so important was the congeniality factor to them that they were usually content to work collectively at rates less than those customary for individuals doing the same things.)

Fatatans also engaged occasionally in collective work as, e.g., members of sodalities (to prepare feasts), or as citizen-residents (to clean the cemetery). And, as was described, some fishermen regularly worked together for shares of the catch. But Fatata contained nothing like Atea's work-exchange groups and for the most part its residents were outspokenly opposed to participating in arrangements like Atea's money-earning groups.

To cite "cultural conservatism" as the explanation for Atea's commitment to organized work groups (as contrasted with Fatata's disdain for them) is to some extent tautological unless the assumption is made (which, in fact, is here the case) that such groups formerly prevailed throughout Tahitian society and that they have persisted in some places, such as Atea, while discontinuing in others, such as Fatata. The question then becomes: what has contributed to their discontinuance in Fatata? (Not, why they have continued in Atea, which is a more complex and difficult question to try to answer—unless one subscribes to the view, which is not the case here, that peoples' behavior will remain the same unless subjected to palpably different influences.)

The explanation for the discontinuance of organized work groups in Fatata is also complex but probably consists of several of the situations and events that have contributed to Fatata's other differences from Atea, i.e., location (with respect to Pape'ete, mainly), other contacts with Europeans, etc. But rather than evaluating all those situations and events here, in terms, say, of time sequence and weightiness, I will proceed with an itemization of other differences and postpone the evaluation to the end.

7. The more noteworthy differences between Atea and Fatata with respect to rent money received from fellow villagers has to do with copra dryers, agricultural land, harvest rights, and money itself.

That some Fatatan dryer-owners charged fellow villagers (especially close kinfolk) rent for the use of their dryers, whereas their Atean counterparts did not do so, is simply another example of the more pervasive economic individualism that obtained in Fatata, coupled with a stronger tendency to monetize social-relational transactions. The fact that Atean landowners received more rent money from fellow-villager tenants than did their Fatatan counterparts—58,400 francs to 25,400—might appear at first glance to contradict this interpretation, but in this case I believe that the explanation is to be sought in another direction, not directly connected with individualism or "monetization." That is to say, in this case the difference was due largely to Ateans' greater dependence upon agriculture as a source of money and hence their greater need for arable land. The landless or land-poor Fatatan had recourse to fishing or wage-labor for some money income, but his Atean counterpart lacked such opportunities.

As for the Fatatans' greater inclination to engage in crop purchasing (whereby coconut-grove owners earned 7,000 francs during 1954, in contrast to the Atean owners' zero), I believe that the explanation, again, lies mainly in Fatata's wider money-earning opportunities, i.e., fewer Atean grove-owners would have been willing to forego the maximum incomes that their groves could provide simply to spare themselves the labor of harvesting.

The Fatatans' acknowledged receipt of interest (i.e., 2,500 francs) from money lent to other Fatatans, as compared with the Ateans' none, might not be the whole truth about such local transactions but it does suggest that such moneylending (i.e., for interest) was less unethical in Fatata and hence more widely practiced than in Atea.

8. Most of the money earned by Te Pitians in the sale of alcoholic beverages and other "refreshments" came from other Te Pitians.

From the sale of the former, the Fatatan sellers (i.e., the official licensee and his retail agent) realized profits of about 25,000 francs, which was that much more than was earned by anyone in Atea in this way. The simple explanation of that difference is that there was no one in Atea licensed to sell alcoholic beverages. And the explanation for *that* was the opposition to such licensing, which was expressed by the village's civil and church leaders and reinforced by the island's gendarme. Some of Fatata's church leaders were likewise opposed to the licensing of beverages there but were either insufficiently influential to force the issue or insufficiently indifferent to tolerate it.

As for Fatata's lead over Atea in amounts of money earned—and hence spent—on cinema-time refreshments, I believe that this can be attributed directly, and mainly if not entirely, to Fatatans' larger supplies of ready cash.

In addition to the differences between Atea and Fatata in the amounts of money earned and in the ways it was earned, this study has revealed some noteworthy differences in the ways the two populations spent that money. Several such differences have been dealt with above, and the others will be discussed below, in appropriate contexts.

Section Three-C

During the year of survey—which was typical of several preceding years in this respect—Fatata's income from outside sources was, per capita, nearly 40 percent higher than Atea's. Two major questions posed by this superiority were: What uses were made of it? and, How did those uses serve to differentiate other aspects of the Fatatans' behavior from that of the Ateans?

First of all, while it would be difficult if not impossible to establish a direct causal relation between that income superiority and such specific uses, the fact remains that Fatatans did tend to invest more of their earnings than did the Ateans in interest-bearing savings accounts, in tools, in education, and (over a longer time period) in land. While the amounts kept in savings accounts were "small," they nevertheless exceeded the Ateans' none. And while some of the tools, e.g., the new copra dryers, may not have yielded the anticipated high money returns, they were at least technically capable of doing so. As for the Fatatans' larger investment in education, that was manifested in two ways: in the much larger amount of money (i.e., over five times as much per capita) spent in sending their children to Pape'ete for further formal schooling, and in the somewhat lighter work demands (in competition with their schooling) made on children at home.

No money was spent on land purchase in either village during the survey year 1954, but during the immediately preceding years Fatatans had spent considerably more on this form of investment than had the Ateans.

Again, while I cannot demonstrate a direct causal connection between earnings and expenditures during the survey year itself, the Te Pitians were limited over time—like most of the rest of mankind—to spend only what they earned, and it is reasonable to assume that they kept more or less within those limits during the survey year as well. Thus, another part of the answer to the first question posed above is likely to be contained in a comparison of money spending in Fatata and Atea.

After subtracting the sums invested (which also constituted "spending" but of a quite different kind), and after subtracting the sums paid in taxes and fines (over which the payers exercised little choice), the Fatatans are shown to have spent more in 1954, on both objects and services, than the Ateans, at the rate of about 9,292 francs per capita to 7,262. Moreover, their advantage in spending power was further increased—I cannot estimate how much overall—by the lower prices they had to pay for some of the things purchased. That is to say, not only were prices generally higher in Atea's stores than in Fatata's (a justifiable difference in view of the higher transport costs), but the Fatatans were also better able than the Ateans to avail themselves of Pape'ete's even lower retail prices, an opportunity that they frequently seized.[7]

Of course, the Ateans and Fatatans did not spend their earnings in entirely corresponding ways, and the nature and magnitudes of those differences require examination, as do their causes and consequences.

On Table 3H, the money expenditures of Ateans and Fatatans were listed in topical arrangement. Listed below are the same expenditures, minus those I label "investments" and "taxes," arranged by order of magnitude for the bigger-spending Fatatans and showing also how the Ateans' spending differed in both rank order and magnitude.

In terms of rank order, the widest differences between the two villages' expenditures occurred in the categories of "house furnishings and utensils" and "contributions to church affairs." These differences are further indications not only of Ateans' smaller amounts of ready cash but of their deeper commitment to their church.

Other wide rank-order differences occurred in the categories of cinemagoing and travel, explanations for which will be offered below, in Section Five. The remaining differences in rank order of expenditures revealed in Table 12A are discussed elsewhere or involved differences and magnitudes too small to require explanatory comment.

Finally, some discussion is called for concerning relations between the Te Pitians' expenditures and their earnings, specifically, concerning their "trade balances" with the outside world.

As shown in Tables 3F and 3H, in 1954 Ateans earned about 1,681,041 francs from outside sources and spent about 1,502,350 francs that returned during that year to the "outside,"[8] the corresponding amounts for Fatata having been 3,560,235 and 2,067,500. Thus, both villages had "favorable" trade balances—which in the case of Atea was about 805 francs per capita

---

[7]The store prices for foodstuffs, utensils, and clothes averaged about 2–3 percent higher in Atea than in Fatata and as much as 5–10 percent higher in Atea than in Pape'ete, but I am unable to estimate the price differences in many other goods the Te Pitians bought.

[8]This figure, and the corresponding one for Fatata, was arrived at by subtracting from total expenditures those amounts that went to fellow villagers, mainly for the latters' earnings as wage laborers and as vendors of food, alcoholic beverages, and "refreshments," or for activities involving *feti'i*.

**Table 12A. Per Capita Expenditures, 1954,
in Order of Fatatan Magnitudes**

	Fatata		Atea	
	Per Capita	Rank Order	Per Capita	Rank Order
Food	4,784	1	3,250	1
Clothing	994	2	596	3
House Building and Repair	800	3	550	4
Cinema	619	4	901	2
House Furnishings and Utensils	385	5	339	8
Fēti'i	365	6	406	7
Travel	318	7	463	5
Alcohol	310	8	182	9
Church	303	9	442	6
Medical	170	10	64	10
Cinema Refreshments	162	11	36	11
Musical Instruments	37	12	19	12
Vehicles	35	13	0	14
Political	10±	14	11±	13

and for Fatata about 1,748—but "favorable" to a precariously small degree. Moreover, it should be recalled that these "favorable" balances were in both villages due to the relatively large earnings of a very few individuals and that, were those fortunates and their earnings removed from the calculations, both villages would be revealed to have had "unfavorable" trade balances, the more so in Atea than in Fatata. Indeed, looking beyond the more comforting—or rather, less *dis*comforting—per capita averages, one would have seen in both villages (and more in Atea than in Fatata) many individual household units whose money expenditures were chronically larger than their money earnings—who were, quite literally, *always* in debt.

We turn next to Te Piti's storekeepers, the Chinese "outsiders" who constituted the villages' principal and perennial creditors, to recapitulate and try to explain some other sides of their social relations with their Tahitian customers and neighbors.

Section Four

In both Atea and Fatata, the Chinese storekeepers interacted with the local Tahitians in two ways—in commercial exchange of objects and services, and in informal and usually amicable discourse. Comparatively, the frequency and money value of the commercial exchange was considerably higher in Atea than in Fatata, a consequence, mainly, of Ateans' farther distance from other sources of merchandise, wage employment, and credit. Also, the noncommercial interaction between Chinese and Tahitians occurred more frequently and with more friendly familiarity in Atea than in Fatata, partly perhaps because of the Atean storekeepers' farther isolation from compatriots elsewhere. Also, the fact that all of Fatata's male storekeepers had Chinese spouses, as against only one of Atea's—the other two having been "married" to Tahitians—probably encouraged the former to lead more separate lives. In addition, Atea's Chinese participated, by explicit or tacit invitation, much more often than their Fatatan counterparts in their Tahitian neighbors' ceremonies and celebrations.

Against all the above (or more likely because of it), there were occasions in Atea (more frequent than in Fatata) when relations between Tahitians and Chinese became hostile. Such occurrences took place mainly in the context of commercial transactions, but the tensions engendered served to reinforce the Tahitians' more pervasive attitudes of distinctiveness *vis-à-vis* the Chinese.

Section Five

The only organized sport pursued during my 1954–55 visits to Te Piti was soccer, and that only in Fatata. However, its absence in Atea was only temporary; it had been played there up to two years previously and was to resume two years later. Just as in the case of Fatata, where playing halted a year after my visit, the Te Pitians' enthusiasm for and engagement in soccer appeared to have had a cyclical life of about three years on and three off—due, assertedly, to cumulative boredom (*fiu*) and to disagreements over use of club-treasury funds and augmented by cyclical buildups in attitudes against putting so much practice-work into an activity that produced no monetary rewards. (It was a similar attitude that finally prevailed against the continuance of the Te Pitians' only other recent organized sport, canoe racing.)

2. With respect to alcohol consumption, the Ateans differed from the Fatatans in three noteworthy ways. First, they spent less money on it and hence presumably drank less, a situation that is to be accounted for partly by their smaller resources in ready cash and partly by the greater effort required to purchase it (i.e., Fatata contained a licensed seller whereas Ateans had to travel an hour or so by boat to obtain their drink). Secondly, while a third of Atea's household units reported no alcoholic consumption at all by

its members, this was the case of only a fifth of Fatata's. Differences in availability of ready cash may have been responsible for some of this disparity, but another factor that may have contributed was the weighty personal influence exercised by Atea's nearly abstemious pastor over his flock.

A third conspicuous way in which Atea differed from Fatata in use of alcohol had to do with timing and degree—i.e., many of Fatata's drinkers tended to imbibe moderate amounts of wine or beer several times a week, sometimes with meals, while most of Atea's drinkers tended to imbibe only occasionally and then in large and inebriating quantities. Fatatans also indulged in occasional drinking parties, but those were on the whole less frequent and less saturnalian than those of Atea. To say that this difference was another manifestation of Fatatans' superior "urbanity"—i.e., more Europeanized habits—is tantamount to explanation by definition, but I know of no other way to express it. (I do not, for example, believe that the Ateans' feast-or-famine use of alcohol was part of a more general consumption pattern—based, say, on their smaller money resources.)

3. Relative to their other expenditures (and to comparable European standards) the amounts of money spent by Fatatans on cinemagoing were very high, i.e., 619 francs per capita, and were exceeded only by amounts spent for food, clothing, and house building and repair. And the Ateans' expenditures on cinemagoing were even higher, i.e., 901 francs per capita, and second only to amounts spent for food. The only explanation I can offer for the relatively large amounts spent in both villages for this form of diversion is—was—its power to divert; the weekly or semiweekly showings provided the most novel and entertaining means of escape from what many Te Pitians themselves characterized as a narrow, monotonous, and stale everyday life. And the Ateans' even larger expenditures than the Fatatans' on this diversion can perhaps be attributed to their even narrower, etc., way of life. This is not meant to imply that the Te Pitians' way of life was in fact "narrow," "stale," etc., by any hypothetical universal standards but rather that many Te Pitians did, in fact, consider it so—in comparison, that is, with Pape'ete, which many of them had seen at first hand and of which nearly all of the rest of them possessed colorful images.

4. Travel, no less than cinemagoing, was induced in large part by the Te Pitians' desire for diversion—for the pleasure of experiencing different events and scenes. Some trips were motivated by economic factors, others by illness of self or close kin, still others by obligations or attachments to kinfolk living elsewhere, but desire for amusement was paramount in many journeys and present in most others as well.

As revealed in Table 12, the Ateans spent more, per capita, on travel than the Fatatans (463 to 318 francs). And while some of this difference may possibly be attributed to the Ateans' greater isolation, narrower way of life, etc., and hence more wanderlust, I believe that most of it was due to the farther distances they had to travel to reach comparable places.[9]

5. Neither Ateans nor Fatatans made much of Bastille Day, which was marked at Pape'ete in a two-week carnival of huge cost and scale, but New Year was celebrated in both villages with well-attended religious ceremonies and protracted festivities. I will not digress to speculate about why both Atea and Fatata favored New Year over Bastille Day but shall propose explanations for why the Ateans exceeded Fatatans in their celebration of New Year, which they did in terms of duration, religious solemnity, social intercourse, festive revelry—and expenditures of energy and money.

History and location had much to do with the Ateans' deeper engagement in the celebration of New Year. The roots of the celebration probably go back to the pagan festival, "ripening of the year" (*parara'a matahiti*), which took place at the time of the year's most plentiful breadfruit harvest, a few weeks after the summer solstice (Oliver 1974:259). In due course, the English missionaries preserved and fortified this ceremonial climax with the addition of Christmas and New Year, and the Ateans' deeper engagement in New Year celebration is just one more manifestation of their generally greater preoccupation with the beliefs and activities that comprised that earlier Protestantism, which in itself resulted from their longer historical involvement in a British-missionary polity.

It might be argued that the Fatatans' emphasis on Christmas (the reverse of Ateans' emphasis on New Year) constituted an even more Christian, and hence more Protestant, stance, but I believe that we have here to do with chronologically different varieties of Tahitian Protestantism—an earlier one (the one represented more strongly at Atea), which, while very "fundamentalist" in most respects, also contained more elements of the pagan past; and a later one that contained less of the latter and that purveyed to, and hence was in part adapted to, a more secularly Europeanized congregation (one, for example, that was beginning to adopt the image of Christmas publicized by Pape'ete's retailers).

---

[9]I did not systematically collect information on numbers of trips taken or distances travelled so am unable to document this conclusion—except to repeat that the cost of travel from Atea to any non-Huahine destination was considerably higher than the price of passage from Fatata to Tahiti.

6. We will continue this discussion of the Te Pitians' practices of Protestantism after mention of three other forms of diversion in which the two villages differed.

That Fatata only had billiards and *pique-nicques* was unmistakable evidence of its residents' closer contacts, in recent decades, with Europeans. And that women's sewing bees persisted in Atea—they were formerly a part of Fatatan life as well—was still another manifestation of Atea's "earlier" variety of Protestantism, in which the worthy European missionary wives devoted countless hours to this most innocent, most practical, most Protestant kind of diversion.

Section Six

There were no large discernible differences between Atea and Fatata with respect to the *content* of Christian religious beliefs and only my undocumented impression that the Ateans were on the whole more accepting than the Fatatans regarding such beliefs, but there were some noteworthy differences between the two villages with respect to church attendance, to Sabbath observance, to the manner and amount of support rendered to the church, and to the relation between pastor and congregation.

1. The Ateans were much more faithful than the Fatatans in attending church services and in hallowing the Sabbath. As in the case of their deeper absorption in the celebration of New Year just discussed, I propose that these behaviors of the Ateans were additional manifestations of their commitment to the "earlier" form of Society Islands Protestantism, as conditioned by their different colonial history and as reinforced by their farther distance from Pape'ete.

2. In the year 1954, the Ateans made donations to their church amounting to 442 francs per capita, or about 5.8 percent of their earnings from outside sources during that year. (Or, put another way, the Ateans' church donations ranked sixth in their categories of expenditures, while those of the Fatatans ranked only ninth.) Moreover, in recent years the Ateans had contributed even larger amounts, to the building of a parish assembly house—something that Fatatans had not done and probably would have been disinclined to do. In addition, the Ateans contributed much larger amounts of their labor to the maintenance of parish buildings, whereas the Fatatans gave most of their contributions for this purpose in money alone, more in the form of individual donations (in contrast to the Ateans' giving as members of parish subgroups). The Ateans' way of making church contributions was not only a particular feature of that "earlier" Protestantism but

was more generally a residue of pre-European institutions, which the
Ateans, because of their location, their peculiar colonial history, and their
smaller amounts of ready cash, had succeeded in (or had been constrained
into?) perpetuating.

3. The main organizational differences between Atea's and Fatata's parishes had to do with the authority and influence exercised by their respective pastors—Atea's having possessed more titularly, and exercised more actually, than his Fatatan counterpart. The titular aspects of the office of the
former was, again, a continuation of the "earlier" Protestantism, which was
quite theocratic at one time, but the differences in the exercise of the office
can be explained in part by differences in the personalities of the
incumbents.

4. Turning now to Te Piti's parish sodalities, a comparison of them reveals differences in the amount and kind of support they received from their
members and in the activities they engaged in. As with the inclusive whole-
parish unit, the Ateans attended sodality meetings more faithfully and contributed more of their resources to them, not only in money but in labor as
well. In addition, Atea's sodalities played a larger role in its members' weddings than those of Fatata. The explanation offered for the differences in
analogous whole-parish phenomena just recapitulated apply equally to the
sodalities. In addition, the lively interest shown by Ateans to their sodalities
was probably due in part to their fewer diversions of other kinds—again, a
consequence of isolation.

Section Seven

Atea's governmental district unit differed from Fatata's in function, in
style of leadership, in cohesiveness, in relations with other local social units,
and in relations with the encompassing Administration of the territory as a
whole.

1. Atea's *tāvana, qua tāvana,* was more active and influential than Fatata's
in the management of local village-wide activities and in the resolution of
interpersonal conflicts. (The large public works project which the Fatatan
tāvana supervised and the cemetery cleanups and festive visitor receptions
which he perfunctorily oversaw had no parallels in Atea.) Ateans accepted,
even invited, their *tāvana*'s intervention in local affairs, whereas the Fatatan
tāvana tended to remain aloof from local affairs not included in his officially
prescribed duties and to refer to higher authority questions and decisions
that were.

Some of these differences may be attributed, directly, to factors of location and to the actions of higher Administration officials, i.e., whereas the Mo'orea gendarme made regular and frequent visits to Fatata (rendered easier by that island's encircling road), the Huahine gendarme tended to leave initiative in the hands of Atea's *tāvana,* who, as we saw, appeared reluctant to expose his district's affairs to outside supervision and his villagers' conflicts to outside judgment and penalty (an attitude, I believe, that was based, not on jealousy of his authority but on sympathy for his villagers).

In other words, much if not most of the interdistrict differences in district domain and management had to do with the leadership styles, hence the personalities, of the two *tāvana* involved. But, while helping to account for those interdistrict differences, the personality differences in question can also be viewed as reflecting the attitudes of the two populations as to what roles the Administration should play in their lives. In this sense, the Atean electorate can be characterized as wary if not actually hostile to the geographically and culturally distant regime, and as desirous of managing their own affairs in their more customary and hence congenial ways. In contrast, the attitudes of most Fatatans revealed a more cynical view of their fellow villagers' motives and actions and better acquaintance with—hence less generalized hostility toward—the colonial Administration.

This is, of course, all very tentative and impressionistic. To demonstrate any fundamental correlation between an electorate's attitudes and their leader's personality would require evidence over time and including several successive leaders, which information I do not possess. Also, to characterize an electorate's "attitudes," as I have just done, would require ideally much more systematic probings than I undertook—but, with all its shortcomings, I offer the above "explanation" as hypothetical and not entirely improbable.

2. My conclusions about the two district polities' internal cohesiveness and their relations with other local social units—namely, that Atea's polity meetings were better attended and that the polity itself was more conterminous with other local units—are interconnected. In a negative way, the Fatatans, through their lesser isolation, had recourse to more alternative, and evidently more attractive, ways of spending their time, whereas the Ateans gravitated towards any kind of assembly taking place: vanilla selling, cinema showing, sewing bees, etc., or even street-quarreling matches. As for the overlap in membership and leadership between Atea's district polity and other local social units, that involves more complex explanations. Geographic isolation may have been one indirect factor—but under some circumstances social isolation can lead to or be associated with social fissures of great width and depth (as the example of Atea's neighboring village, cited earlier demonstrates).

A more credible explanation requires comparison with those other social units with which the district polity shared memberships, namely, the parish and the RDPT political party. For historical explanations already proffered, the active membership of the local parish included virtually all of Atea's ambulatory residents, and the active membership of the local RDPT virtually all of its adult male residents. Hence, inasmuch as membership in the local district polity was also all-inclusive (but by legal definition rather than by historical happening), the memberships in those three Atean units were ipso facto conterminous. And, by the same token (i.e., because of its different history, etc.), Fatata's active body of parishioners and its fragmented party memberships did not share boundaries with membership in the district polity.

(If the reader is beginning to tire of the Euclid-like tread of this reasoning, he has my sympathy!—but I am unable to devise a more felicitous way to phrase what I want to say.)

As for the close overlap in leadership, de jure and/or de facto, between Atea's district polity and its parish and RDPT, I suggest that it derives from the overlap in membership just discussed. Indeed, what emerges from these reflections is that Atea was, as the time of my visit, a single all-embracing social unit, a community group, with a single set of de facto leaders who, so to speak, merely changed their official hats with changes in context. In contrast, Fatata was made up of several distinct categories of residents, e.g., parish faithful vs. parish defectives, RDPT vs. Poroists vs. de Gaullists, and hence had no leaders of comprehensive authority or influence.

Reasons why Fatata's parish was less cohesive than Atea's have already been offered, and reasons why its political parties were more numerous will be put forward in a moment, but first an explanation will be offered for the "closer" ties that existed between Fatata's district polity and the Territory Administration. The questions are: Why was it that exchanges between district polity and Administration (in the form of taxes, medical services, etc.) were larger and more frequent in the case of Fatata than of Atea? And why did the Fatatans look upon the relationship with less dissatisfaction than that expressed by their Atean counterparts?

Here again, I suggest that the factors of dissimilar geographic locations and of dissimilar histories *vis-à-vis* the Administration officialdom were decisive. Throughout the past few decades, the Fatatans had lived nearer and were more accessible, mutually, to agencies of the Administration; had in consequence interacted more frequently with the latter, including exchanges; and had thus learned by experience (what the Ateans had had less opportunity to learn) that the Administration, for all of its bureaucratic clumsiness, was (according to the Fatatans' own characterization) essentially *mārū*—soft, permissive, kindly.

Returning to the question of Fatata's division into three political parties, as against the Ateans' nearly unanimous commitment to one, I suggest that Atea's location and colonial history and consequent allegiance to rural Tahitian-ness and its culture hero, Pouvana'a (who was also a Huahine man), served to override all other disagreements they could have had (and that they did in fact have) regarding the economic and other kinds of issues that differentiated party allegiances elsewhere, including Fatata. For, in Fatata, not only were the residents on the whole better informed about differences in party ideologies, but they were more attentive to specifically economic issues than their Atean counterparts. In other words, although both Ateans and Fatatans were differentiated among themselves with respect to property and earnings—the former somewhat less so than the latter—only the Fatatans tended to express such differences in terms of political association and votes.

To some anthropologists reading the above, the questions will probably occur: What about kinship? What influence did ties of kinship exert on the Te Pitians' political associations? The domain of kin relations will be reexamined in Section Ten, but to anticipate a bit, it can now be said that kinship did in fact exert some influence on political party membership—but only in Fatata. Ateans were divided into separate kin constellations no less so than were the Fatatans, but for the Ateans the commitment to the Pouvana'a-led movement overrode differences in kin affiliation as well as differences in economic status.

Section Eight

1. The noteworthy differences between the two villages' marital union types concerned Type V ("firm" nonlegal unions prevented by technical considerations from becoming legally, and hence ecclesiastically, sanctioned), Type I (legal unions sponsored by the principals' kinfolk and ceremonialized in veiled-bride weddings), and Types II and III (legal unions sponsored by the principals' pastor or sponsored and ceremonialized by their sodality mates). Of these, Fatata contained a larger percentage of Types V and I, Atea a larger percentage of Types II and III.

On first impulse, I am puzzled by the finding that Fatata contained five "firm" unions of Type V as against Atea's one. Most of the technicalities that served to prevent a couple from becoming legally married had to do with information that was recorded, or should have been recorded, in civil registers and required written inquiries or assistance from officials to obtain or to have waived. And because of the Fatatans' greater propensity for letter writing, and their better knowledge of and less discomfort with officialdom, I would have expected them to have been more successful in removing the technical impediments to the legalization of their unions—if, of course, they had really wished to. So, perhaps the explanation is to be sought in the strength—or rather, weakness—of their motives. That is to say, in comparison with the Ateans, they were more indifferent to the church's moral norms in general and to its marriage codes in particular. Or, put another way, the Ateans were so much more strongly influenced by those norms that they persisted in removing the technical constraints in marriage despite their rustic disabilities.

The same explanation can be offered for Atea's superiority over Fatata in percentages of marital unions of Types II and III. (There is some tautology contained in this explanation, inasmuch as I draw on this bit of evidence, along with other bits, to build up my generalization about Ateans' "stronger commitment to Protestantism" but such reasoning is, I suppose, an inevitable feature of cultural studies of this kind.)

Type I (veiled-bride wedding) unions were, of course, also ceremonialized in church, but, as we saw, they were twice as numerous, relatively, in Fatata. There are, I suggest, two complementary explanations for this seeming paradox. The first explanation is economic, i.e., fewer Ateans were able to mobilize on short notice the larger outlays of cash required for a veiled-bride wedding. The second and more important explanation is to be sought in the high value, held by more Fatatans than Ateans, attached to family social superiority as expressed, in this context, by pride in a daughter's chastity and by display of family affluence. Historically, money affluence and social-class sentiment may have been dependently interrelated, but in 1954–55 they appeared to operate as separate, but associated, causes behind Fatata's preponderance over Atea in this type of marital union.

2. Atea's higher incidence of fidelity pledging between nonlegally-wed spouses was also caused by (as well as having served as tangible evidence for) its residents' stronger commitment to Protestantism.

3. With respect to the criteria used in selecting a marital partner, Fatata contained more widely age-discrepant couples than Atea (specifically, older women and younger men). Also, the factor of social class weighed more heavily in Fatata than in Atea when parents had voices in choosing spouses for their children.

Fatata's more numerous older woman–younger man unions were evidently due to the circumstance that that village contained a larger percentage of individually (land) wealthy women. There was a sentiment, voiced by the more faithful parish members in both villages, disapproving in principle of widely age-discrepant marriages of both kinds; the fact that more Fatatans than Ateans appeared to flout that disapproval could be seen as another manifestation of Fatatans' weaker commitment, on the average, to local Protestantism in general, but I think that the economic factor was the more decisive one in this case.

As for the importance of social class in spouse selection, the heavier weight that Fatatan parents—or at least, the *teitei* ones—placed on this criterion was (tautologically!) yet another manifestation of Fatata's deeper concern with class stratification.

4. Regarding postmarital residence, the stronger tendency of recently wed Atean couples to move into separate houses of their own—which 60 percent of them did, as against only 37 percent of their Fatatan counterparts—is best explained by the circumstance that fewer Atean houses were large enough to accommodate additional families. On first consideration, this might appear to have reversed an expected preferred choice, i.e., one might have expected that the Fatatans, who were generally more Europeanized, would have adopted a more Europeanized, neolocal, view about residence. It should be pointed out, however, that the early English missionaries, whose influence had remained less vitiated in Atea, also preached the virtues of the single-family household.

Our statistics on postmarital residence also revealed that in cases where the recently wed couples did not move into a house of their own, they tended in both villages to reside in the household where the husband previously lived, and this tendency was even stronger in Atea than in Fatata. In the absence of other, more palpable circumstances, economic or otherwise, that might be proposed to account for this tendency in both villages, I suggest that it occurred as another manifestation of the basic postulate of male superiority. As for the difference between Atea and Fatata in this regard, I suppose that this can be explained partly by attributing to Ateans a stronger male bias generally; but the fact that Fatata contained a larger percentage of relatively affluent females (in terms of land holdings) may also have served to render its residents' residence choices somewhat less virilocal.

5. In contrast to the larger land holdings that Fatata wives, on the average, contributed to their marital unions' resource pools, i.e., land used by their husbands for subsistence gardening and cash-cropping, Atean wives, on the average, contributed more of their own labor to the family's subsistence and money-earning enterprises. Two possible kinds of explanations may be offered here—the one ideological, the one technological. Concerning the former, it might be proposed that a woman was expected, by deep-rooted Tahitian tradition, to contribute a large share of objects and services (even larger than her husband's in terms of time) to their family pool and that

this tradition had persisted more tenaciously in Atea than in Fatata. Or, it might be suggested that, while the tradition had persisted equally in both villages, the larger average land wealth contributed by Fatatan wives had served to reduce their need to labor in family enterprises. While many Ateans and a few Fatatans acknowledged that Leeward Island, including Atean, women worked harder than those of Mo'orea, I heard no Fatatan explain the reason for the labor-division difference in such terms—although when discussing local cases of unions between younger men and older and usually wealthier women, my informants did justify the age discrepancy in similar terms.

The technological kind of explanation that can be offered (for Fatata women's smaller labor contributions, overall, to family subsistence and money-earning enterprises) is more palpable, namely: fewer Fatata families engaged in subsistence gardening than was the case in Atea, and far more Fatata husbands earned much or most of their money income from commercial fishing (which was not females' work) or wage-labor (at which males only were usually employed).

For my own part, I believe that both of these explanations, ideological and technological, have some merit.

6. In comparison with Fatata, although about as many, proportionately, of Atea's marital unions terminated in separations, fewer of them did so by means of legal divorce—this despite Ateans' higher percentage of legally wed couples. Two influences were at work in bringing about Fatata's larger percentage of legal divorces. First was the circumstance that Fatatans as a whole had more ready money with which to pay the high costs of a legal divorce. And second, with their readier access to Pape'ete officialdom, and their generally fuller information about how that officialdom worked, the Fatatans were less paralyzed than the Ateans in embarking on such a daunting enterprise.

Section Nine

The only noteworthy differences between Atea and Fatata respecting their residents' passage through life had to do with the place and management of births, with the conduct of funerals and the location of burials, and with attitudes and practices regarding the life stage of "childhood."

1. The fact that more Fatatan women than Atean gave birth in hospitals was due to two interdependent circumstances. First was the easier accessibility, over a long time, of such hospitals and the frequent prenatal visits by Administration *accoucheuse*. And second was the Fatatans' larger measure of

trust in European medicine. In other words, this difference is another specific outcome of the previously and frequently cited contrast between Fatata's and Atea's location and recent colonial histories.

2. In Atea, the dead were buried in places associated with—and usually owned by—their close kinfolk, whereas in Fatata all deceased residents were buried in a common village cemetery. Inasmuch as the Fatatans' practice was in conformity with the Administration's ordinance on the subject and the Ateans' in violation of it, it follows either that the Administration had managed to enforce the ordinance more effectively (because of its generally closer supervision over Fatata's affairs) or that the Fatatans were inherently more law-abiding than the Ateans (through that closer supervision and through other experiences of theirs during their colonial history). A third possibility is that the Fatatans, unlike the Ateans, would have preferred common-cemetery burial even in the absence of the ordinance.

In an effort to account for the intervillage difference in burial practice, I did ask Fatatans and Ateans their reasons for their actions and had to conclude that the Administration's *current* enforcement was probably the most decisive factor in causing the Fatatans to do as they did but that that sanction-backed rule was in fact reinforced by the conviction of many Fatatans that cemetery burial was in itself the right way to dispose of the dead. But as to why it was right, I got no further than eliciting vague and impromptu statements about "hygiene."

The Ateans were more positive in the reasons they gave for burying their dead in places associated with their living kinfolk, i.e., they (the living) wished to be near their dead loved ones, and the dead (they asserted) wished to be near their living kin.

At one point in my inquiries I tried to discover whether fear of ghosts played a part in persuading the Fatatans to bury their dead in a common, and distant, cemetery but did not succeed in eliciting any hint of such views and, in any case, had there prevailed such a view it would have operated with equal or even stronger force in Atea.

I also scouted such factors as differences in housing density, perceived economic value of land (i.e., an objection to "wasting" it in graves), etc., as possible explanations for the Fatatans' avowed preference for cemetery burial—but without finding any correlations credible enough to accept.

Turning now to the financing of Te Piti's funerals, it will be recalled that in Atea this was done mainly by kinfolk of the deceased, whereas in Fatata the cost was distributed throughout the community in the form of a self-imposed tax institutionalized as the Philadelphia Society. Inasmuch as the kin-financing of funerals had formerly been the practice in both villages, the question becomes: How did it come about that Fatatans had adopted the new arrangement and, after demise of the Philadelphia Society, were considering adopting another similar nonkin arrangement, namely the RDPT-based mutual-aid funeral fund?

I must confess that I can offer no satisfactory specific answers to that question. The larger amounts of unobligated cash possessed by the Fatatans may have been a factor, but not a persuasively decisive one. And the same pertains to "kinship sentiment" which, while in some contexts (e.g., in the lending of copra dryers) it may have been "stronger" in Atea, cannot be said to have been stronger enough, comprehensively, to serve as a more general explain-all. As for Te Pitians' predilections for community-wide (in contrast to individual or family or kin-group based) actions, the Ateans have been shown throughout this study to be more inclined in that direction than the Fatatans in several respects (e.g., in their festivities, and in matters of church and politics). In the end, I suppose that I must resort to the more general explanation, namely, that the Fatatans' adoption of the essentially new kind of funeral arrangement represented by the Philadelphia Society was yet another manifestation of their readier acceptance of innovations (which, again, is to be explained by their history of closer and more frequent experiences with alien ideas and institutions).

3. That same basic difference in their colonial histories also helps to explain why Fatata's parents tended to view their offspring's "childhood" as lasting longer (than was the case with Atea's parents) and as being a time when "consumption" and "learning" (including formal schooling) were more appropriate than productivity. Specifically, more Fatatans than Ateans had concluded, mainly from observation, that longer and more concentrated schooling tended in the end to result in larger money incomes. (In this respect, as was the case with bank savings accounts, the Fatatans may be said to have shown a greater propensity for "investment" than the Ateans.)

In some societies, the technologies of subsistence (or money-earning) serve either to encourage or discourage the use of child labor, but I cannot see how such factors can be pointed to here. Atea and Fatata did indeed differ in their *emphasis* on this or that technology, but the technologies themselves were much the same; and as far as I can see, there were no overall inter-village differences in technology emphasis that could have led to differences between the two villages in their attitudes towards "childhood."

Section Ten

The more noteworthy differences between Atea and Fatata with respect to their households had to do with size (i.e., the number of their adult members), kin-age composition, intrahousehold transactions, and monetization of supply. Individual households also differed, in some cases very widely, in terms of the distribution of authority and the degree of social harmony among their respective members, but I was unable to identify any criteria palpable enough to classify all households in these respects and hence cannot compare the two villages in this way.

1. With respect to size, Atea had a much larger number of single-adult households than Fatata and a slightly larger number of households containing three adult members. In comparison, Fatata had slightly larger percentages of households containing two or four adults.

The only explanations I can suggest for Atea's preponderance of single-adult households is that village's smaller population and its greater isolation from other settlements. That is to say, the adults in question, having been unmarried at the time (either widowed or "divorced"), had fewer opportunities than their Fatatan counterparts for finding new mates, either locally or "outside." (Indeed, some of Atea's older "singles" complained of their circumstance in those terms.) This kind of reasoning, turned around, may also serve to explain in part Fatata's preponderance, which was small but recognizable, of two-adult (i.e., mainly husband-wife) households. As for the intervillage differences in percentages of three and four adult members, I suggest that Atea's preponderance in the former was also due in part to the greater difficulty of its third household members (who were typically unmarried) in finding mates. But the only reason I can suggest for Fatata's preponderance in four-adult households was that village's larger number of more capacious houses (specifically, to their capacity to accommodate two families).

On the other hand, Atea's fewer number of capacious houses does not appear to have limited, relative to Fatata, the percentages of five-or-more-adult households there.

2. In the matter of kin-age composition, Atea contained proportionately a few more single-family households (both simple and complex), and many more of the residual extended-family type. Its preponderance of the former can be explained by that village's generally smaller houses. But the only explanation—and that not very persuasive—I can offer for its larger proportion of the latter is the village's smaller population and farther isolation, which may have combined to make it more difficult for the "residual" grandparent to find a new mate.

This latter circumstance may also have been partly responsible, in reverse, for Fatata's preponderance of full extended-family households—that, together with the village's larger number of more capacious houses.

3. With respect to transactions among members of a household, Atea exceeded Fatata in both *unity* and *equity*—unity having been the degree to which most objects and services used by members were pooled and redistributed among all of them regardless of subunit boundaries, and equity the degree to which all members conformed to local norms regarding the proper balance between what they put into the pool and what they took out.

Atea's lead in percentage of households with higher degree of unity was a direct reflex of its preponderance of the single-family type. The number of adults in a household may also have been a factor, i.e., 77.5 percent of Atea's households contained less than four adults each, compared with 72.5 percent of Fatata's, but the kin-age variable is the more predictive.

We also saw that Atea's households exceeded those of Fatata with respect to distributive equity by a margin of 82.5 percent to 74.5 percent. I believe this difference derived mainly from Atea's larger percentage of simple single-family households (i.e., 52.5 percent to Fatata's 48.3 percent), which in the combined two-village series tests were found to be almost invariably equitable.

4. The findings on monetization revealed that a much higher percentage of Fatata's households acquired relatively large amounts of their food and building materials by purchase than was the case in Atea. The questions are: Why was that so? and, What effects did it have on household unity and equity?

The answer to the first question is simple and direct, i.e., Fatatans on the average earned larger money incomes and were engaged less in food gardening; but answers to the second question are more circuitous.

It is perhaps plausible to assume some (negative) degree of association between household unity and monetization of supply, i.e., earning a separate money income may dispose people to spend some of it on their own; but this is not borne out consistently by the figures for the combined two-village series. And Atea's higher degree of household unity would thus seem to be, as just stated, a reflex of its preponderance of single-family type units and not of its lower degree of monetization.

The same finding applies, somewhat surprisingly, to the variable of household distributive equity. While Fatata's households were characterized by less equity and more monetization than Atea's, this association appears to have been quite fortuitous, inasmuch as the combined two-village series revealed little association, positive or negative, between the two variables with respect to individual households. In other words, money was not necessarily and directly the root of evil!

5. Turning to interhousehold relations (i.e., those which included household members *qua* members as a whole), these, it will be recalled, were characterized as having been either positive or negative. (The positive ones were those involving regular exchanges of objects and services; the negative ones those typified by mutual expressions of hostility ranging from "coolness" and "anger," to *enemi.*) Observation and inquiry revealed the existence in Atea of fifty-two well-established and mutually acknowledged positive linkages among the villages' forty multimember households, in contrast to the twenty-eight such linkages that prevailed in Fatata with its sixty-two multimember households—in other words, a ratio, proportionately, of three to one.

(Inquiry also revealed a number of negative interhousehold relationships in both villages, but, owing largely to the Fatatans' discountenance of public quarreling, I was unable to secure enough objective information to permit comparison of the two villages in this respect.)

Several factors contributed, directly or indirectly, to Atea's large preponderance of positive interhousehold linkages. One of these was its residents' frequently-voiced self-image as a friendly, cooperative community, a case of deliberate adherence to a proudly held ideal; another, perhaps, was the closer spacing of its houses. But I think that the larger part played by money in the internal economy of Fatata's households was perhaps the most directly-influential single factor that differentiated it from Atea in this respect. It boils down to the simple proposition that the residents of both villages were more generous with their services and with objects secured directly by their labor, than they were with money or objects purchased directly with money, e.g., they gave more freely of self-grown root crops than of store-bought bread, and of otherwise-idle labor than of labor-earned money income or of objects bought with such income. (As we saw above, Atea's more extensive use of money in the supply of individual household requirements does not appear to have reduced their internal unity—or equity, but the two villages appear not to have been structurally equivalent to their component households in this respect.)

But what about "kinship"? I noted earlier that many of the households engaged in regular exchanges were connected by close kin ties: Was "kinship" also influential in promoting Atea's preponderance in positive interhousehold links?

Section Eleven

1. In addition to their many extended families and sibling-connected families, both Atea and Fatata contained other kinds of clusters of consanguines, including large components of several cognatic stocks. However,

the sizes and shapes of these clusters varied so widely that it proved unfeasible to devise a classification of their genealogical structures whereby the two villages could be compared in this feature. Moreover, most of the consanguineal clusters were so intricately reticulated by affinal ties, present and past, legal and otherwise, that their boundaries were for most purposes quite indistinct.

In fact, in both Atea and Fatata, the ties of kinship were so numerous, manifold, and comprehensive that the most telling way to compare this aspect of the two villages is to indicate the percentage of household heads (male and/or female) who had *no* ascendant or collateral kin ties with members of other local households. In this respect, Fatata exceeded Atea by a wide margin, there having been thirty-three (or 27 percent) of Fatata's household heads, as compared with nine (or 12 percent) of Atea's, who had no such ties.

I can offer no general explanation for this difference. It cannot be accounted for by differences with respect to the heads' origin outside Atea or Fatata; as seen in the discussion of marital residence patterns (Chapter VII), the two villages did not differ much in the percentage of spouses that had married into the village from elsewhere. Nor can it be explained by differences in ages of household heads; proportionately Fatata's household heads included no more aged (hence ascendantless) individuals than Atea.

2. Returning to the question raised in the last paragraph of Section 10, nearly half of Atea's fifty-two interhousehold exchange links were based upon (or, at least, characterized by) primary or secondary kinship ties between heads of the linked households, as contrasted with only eight of Fatata's interhousehold exchange links.

Part of the explanation for this is statistical, i.e., as noted in the preceding paragraph, proportionately more of Atea's households were in fact interrelated by kin ties of their heads, hence there was a greater likelihood there of the exchange links having been between kin-related households. A second part of the explanation is ideological, which I offer in the form of another syllogism, namely, that it was a manifestation of the Ateans' sentiments about their stronger loyalties to kinfolk. In other words, I propose to view the Ateans' readier inclination to enter into exchange relationships with kinfolk (rather than with, say, neighbors or friends) as one expression of an ideological value to which they were more strongly committed than the Fatatans. Other expressions of that value or, rather, of Ateans' stronger commitment to that value, were their tendency to permit kinfolk rent-free use of copra dryers (referred to in Section 3A), their ways of sponsoring funerals, their choices of burial sites, and their expenditures (larger than the Fatatans') on *ohipa fetiʻi*.

3. Regarding funerals and burial sites, I make the assumption (based on general information on ancient Tahiti and on specific inquiry about early twentieth-century Mo'orea) that previous generations of Fatatans were like the present-day Ateans in their financing of funerals by kinfolk and in burying their dead on kin-identified land. Thus, the Fatatans' practice of village-financed funerals was a manifestation of their stronger commitment to different values that, cumulatively, ranked somewhat higher than their commitment to kinship and that included such attitudes as the desire to spread (hence minimize) money costs and their inclination, in some contexts, to favor common interest over common descent. As for the Fatatans' practice of cemetery burial, I suggest that that was a result of their more direct subjection to Administration control—reinforced somewhat by their new concepts of public "hygiene."

4. The Fatatans' smaller total expenditures on *ohipa fēti'i* (despite their larger money incomes) was another manifestation of their inclination towards association based on common interests and of their further "commercialization" of social relationships outside their own household. In addition, I suggest that some of the Ateans' larger expenditures on *ohipa fēti'i*, especially on its "hospitality" aspects, may be explained as a consequence of that village's smaller size and its farther geographical isolation. That is to say, social meetings with kinfolk provided one of the few forms of diversion accessible to them—fewer than those accessible to the Fatatans.

5. The heavier emphasis given by Fatatans to kinship in the sponsorship of weddings was explained above (Section 8) as having been the result of their larger supplies of cash and their somewhat greater preoccupation with social class.

A contradiction might appear to be involved between the first of these explanations and the finding, just discussed, that the Ateans spent more, per capita, on *ohipa fēti'i*, as a whole. The resolution to this is found in the ways money was obtained for such causes and ceremonies. Money for the kin-sponsored veiled-bride weddings (which were more common in Fatata) was usually obtained in both villages by direct and on-the-spot solicitation, whereas most of the materials (including money) needed by the Ateans for their *ohipa fēti'i* was obtained on credit from the local storekeepers. Inasmuch as few Fatatans "sold" their cash crops to or through their local stores, they maintained small, or no, credit accounts there. Not so with the Ateans, whose credit on future crop deliveries encouraged them to amass debts, which the similarly sanguine storekeepers were willing to permit.

6. Deriving "practices" from "values," as I have done in this section, is an exercise in analysis rather than of explanation; thus there remains the necessity to explain why the Ateans and Fatatans differed in their emphasis on kinship, as exemplified in the contrasting practices just discussed.

Following the reasoning employed about organized work groups (Section 3B), I propose that the Fatatans of earlier generations were much like the present-day Ateans in the importance they ascribed to kinship and that certain experiences they had undergone during recent decades had served to weaken that attitude—including their longer and more frequent contacts with Europeans of all kinds (and not just missionaries and officials), their deeper involvement in the money economy, and their contacts, locally, with more Tahitians who were not kinfolk (a situation that the Ateans, in their smaller and more isolated community, did not experience to the same degree).

Another domain in which kinship was involved was in the joint ownership of land, to which subject we now turn, as part of the protean topic of land tenure.

7. To begin with, large percentages of the areas identified both with Atea and with Fatata were owned by outsiders—79 percent of the former and 70 percent of the latter. The historical backgrounds of these situations were as follows:

As previously mentioned, Fatata had been an important political and religious center in pre-European times, and the present-day (i.e., 1954–55) land rights of some of its absentee owners—especially those who were living on Tahiti—probably derived from kinship relations dating back to the eighteenth century. (Also, as was mentioned earlier in Chapter XI, some of those absentees' rights derived from ceremonial "gifts" made by locals to visiting Tahitian aristocrats—"gifts" that the latter were ungracious enough to accept in a sense more literal than the donors had intended.) The absentee ownership of several other Fatatan parcels, large and small, stemmed from the long and close association of many Europeans—missionaries, colonial officials, planters, and rusticators—with this fruitful, strategically located, and beautiful natural setting. In addition, the lure and easy access of nearby Tahiti, especially Pape'ete, had for decades drawn Fatatans away from home, and some of their descendants had continued to reside on Tahiti.

The historical basis of this aspect of Atea's land tenure was markedly different. The village itself had been only recently established (by the clustering of several previously dispersed households), and few people from elsewhere (including very few Europeans) have resided there, and those mainly as marital mates of locals. Some of Atea's absentee landownership can be attributed to former indigenous residents, or their descendants, now living permanently or mainly elsewhere, but most of the outsider-owned land was held by the inheritors of some very large estates acquired by two French-Corsican immigrants several decades previously. A few of the latters' mixed-blood heirs resided locally in 1954–55, but most of them lived permanently elsewhere.

Thus, "historical" and "locational" explanations may be offered for the large magnitudes of outside ownership of both Atean and Fatatan lands—but what accounts for the differences between the two villages in this regard?

The differences in question present something of a paradox. On the one hand, Fatatans as a whole owned 9 percent more of their village-identified area than the Ateans did of theirs, but when expressed in of per capita terms the Ateans were the more advantaged of the two, at the rate of 0.69 hectares per capita to Fatata's 0.58. And the "explanation" for that difference is the obvious circumstance that the 348 Fatatans and the 217 Ateans were, respectively, identified with areas of almost identical size! As for why the Fatatans as a whole owned more of their geographic area than the Ateans, various particular events in their respective histories would have to be reviewed to account for the difference—those, along with the more general circumstance that the Fatatans had had, and continued to have, more ready cash with which to hold onto their properties against outside demands and, recently, to buy them back.

Within the decade prior to 1954–55, much more land had been converted, or reconverted, to local ownership in Fatata than had been the case in Atea. Some of this had been accomplished by swapping—local Fatatans having relinquished to Tahiti kinsmen their rights in Tahiti-located jointly owned land, in exchange for full rights in their jointly owned Fatata land—but most of it was acquired by purchase from the outside owners, either by new acquisitions or by Fatatans buying out the interests of co-owners residing elsewhere. The "economic" explanation I propose for Fatata's lead in such transactions is the larger supply of money that its residents, specifically its land-acquisitive farmers, were able to earn.[10]

The so-called "advantage" possessed by the Ateans *vis-à-vis* the Fatatans (i.e., the somewhat larger size of their holdings, per capita, in local land) was in fact more than offset by their greater dependance upon land for money-earning—a circumstance poignantly exemplified by the high "rents"

---

[10]Were this trend to continue, and if other factors were to remain constant, it is conceivable that Fatata's residents would eventually recover ownership of all local land—a situation that would undoubtedly have some ramifications in social relations, etc. But of course "other factors" seldom remain constant, and trends are subject to radical change of direction in monetary economies as vulnerable as Fatata's.

some of them had to pay, in labor, for their use of outsider-owned parcels of local land. Some individual Fatatans also paid such "rent" for the use of outsider-owned land, but the availability of alternative ways of money-earning reduced their necessity for doing so, and fewer of them actually did.

8. The Ateans' limitations also showed up in the price they paid in exploiting land owned by them in places "outside." I was unable to learn how much land either they or the Fatatans owned "outside," but judging from the circumstance that Fatata contained a larger percentage of persons one or both of whose parents had once resided elsewhere, it is plausible to suppose that their "outside" land holdings were larger as well. In any case, whatever the amounts of those "outside" holdings, the Ateans worked more and harder than the Fatatans to exploit their resources. The latter received more sharecrop rent money from their outside properties, at the per capita rate of 56 francs to 36, but the Ateans earned three times as much as the Fatatans (151 francs per capita to 55) by working their outside properties themselves—and despite the extra amount of commuting time and energy that their village's isolation required them to spend.

9. Turning now to the distribution of local landholdings among the Te Pitians themselves, it transpires that the percentages of residents owning some local land did not differ very widely in the two villages, and the same was true of the average sizes of individuals' holdings and of the number of individuals having no land in hand or in prospect. What did, however, turn out to be widely different between the two villages were the modal sizes of individuals' land holdings. In a word, of those Ateans fortunate enough to own land far fewer had very small holdings (i.e., under one hectare) and far, far more had very large holdings (i.e., over ten hectares) than their Fatatan counterparts. Moreover, a very large percentage of the Fatatan small holdings were house lots, i.e., land unsuitable for producing food or cash crops.

Thus, it would seem that comparatively, in terms of size of holdings, the Fatatan proprietors were doubly disadvantaged—first, with respect to the proportion of holdings of economically productive size, and second, with respect to the proportion of holdings of economically enriching size. But it should not be forgotten that such disadvantages would have signified more in Atea than in Fatata, where size of land holding was only one of several requisites for a better-than-minimum standard of material life.

Reasons for the caveat just stated were put forward in Section 3; explanation of the intervillage differences in modal sizes of land holdings is more elusive but is probably not unconnected with Atea's shallower history as a settlement and its smaller population throughout time—a matter that will be discussed below, in paragraph eleven.

10. In the context of everyday Te Piti living, the matter of how much or little land an individual owned was far less crucial than how much or little the combined members of a household owned or had free access to—for, as we have seen, access to land use was one of the basic kinds of goods contributed by the members of most households to their common resource pools.

Thus, using households as proprietary units, the differences between Atea and Fatata in land ownership modalities were also found to be very wide. Thirty-one percent of Atea's households "owned" (in the sense given) local holdings of ten or more hectares, as compared with only 11 percent of Fatata's. And 17 percent of Atea's households owned no land locally, as compared with 29 percent of Fatata's. And even more crucial, only 7 percent of Atea's households owned no local land, presently or prospectively, as compared with 23 percent of Fatata's.

On the basis of these figures, it would appear that Atea far surpassed Fatata in this important material resource—but again, it is necessary to apply the caveat previously expressed. Indeed, the three of Atea's households that owned no land, presently or prospectively, represented a measure of economic deprivation cumulatively larger than the fourteen Fatatan households which shared that plight.

11. If the objective of colonial policy had been to transform these islanders' land tenure pattern into one of small, distinct, and individually owned parcels, as some say it was, that policy had progressed much further in Fatata than in Atea. By 1954–55, Atea's 673 hectares of land had been subdivided, legally, into seventy-three distinctly owned parcels, and Fatata's 679 hectares into 248! Since explanations for this very wide difference required the addition of much descriptive material, they were put forward in Chapter XI, and will be recapitulated here.

First, it should be noted that, while topography undoubtedly influenced the locations of land boundaries, etc., in parts of Atea and Fatata, that influence was manifested in both villages to about the same degree. Also, while the technology (and, so to speak, the "sociology") of vanilla growing encouraged land subdivision more so than did copra production, one might have expected that it would have led to more subdivision in Atea, where vanilla growing was much more active—but it evidently did not have enough effect (if any) to offset other factors contributing to Fatatans' further "progress" in land subdivision. And third, while the Fatatans' larger cash resources and their better knowledge of and readier access to officialdom may have made it easier for them to bring about subdivision once the decision to subdivide had been reached, it is unlikely to have had very weighty influence on the decision itself.

In the end, I believe that the weightiest influences that contributed to Fatata's further fragmentation were some of the very general ones that have been identified repeatedly throughout this chapter, namely, Fatata's larger population and its longer and closer contacts with Europeans, including many who resided in Fatata itself. Some of the events, etc., comprising those influences produced direct and immediate fragmenting effects, as, e.g., in the case of Europeans purchasing lots only large enough to accommodate a house. But other such influences worked indirectly, slowly, and cumulatively—such as the numerous events, ideas, situations, etc., that changed Fatatans' values concerning the sharing of material resources and labor (values that had remained more intact in more isolated and insulated Atea).

12. Similar events and their consequent ideas and values were responsible for differences between Atea and Fatata with respect to the "unofficial" partitioning of land-use rights. Thus, while the proportion of single-committee to multiple-committee proprietorship was much higher in Fatata than in Atea, this comparison is rendered spurious by the irreducibly small sizes of most of Fatata's single-committee parcels—and was contradicted by my direct observations, which yielded the impression that with the larger legally undivided parcels, whether owned by one committee or more, the rate of unofficial divisiveness in use rights had progressed further in Fatata than in Atea.

Summary

Now to itemize the most salient differences between Atea and Fatata, and the factors—singly or cumulatively, directly or indirectly—that brought them about. First, those differences that had to do with the people's material standards of living.

The Fatatans ate more[11] store-bought, and correspondingly less home-grown, food than the Ateans (and paid relatively less for an item than the Ateans had to pay), but whether that food was more enjoyable to them, or more nutritious, I cannot judge. Fatatans also drank more alcoholic beverages than the Ateans, and that usually at a more regular and frequent but less inebriating rate.

Fatatan women and young men possessed more European-style clothes (and paid relatively less for them) than their Atean counterparts. Also,

---

[11]Throughout this section, the words "more," "less," "larger amounts," etc., mean "more than," etc., the other village being compared; and unless otherwise indicated, the stated comparison is on a per capita basis.

Fatatans on the average spent more money on European remedies for their physical ailments, but whether that had actually made them healthier, or had resulted in more birth survivals or greater longevity, I do not know.

Fatata's houses were on the average larger, more European-like, and better constructed; contained more luxury items such as stoves, refrigerators, radios, and phonographs; and, in contrast to Atea, were served by near-at-hand outlets of piped-in fresh water. They were also more widely spaced from one another and more usually surrounded by well-kept yards.

Generally speaking, the Fatatans had more leisure time at their disposal and a wider variety of "imported" ways of spending it, e.g., three to four film showings weekly (against Atea's two to three), easier and less costly travel, billiards, and the institution of the *pique-nicque*. (They also engaged in organized football during 1954–55, but so had the Ateans previously, and so they were to do soon again.) For their part, the Ateans used some of their (smaller amount of) leisure time in more old-fashioned European diversions, such as community-wide New Year festivals, parish and sodality meetings, and sewing bees. The Ateans actually spent more than the Fatatans on cinemagoing and travel but got less for their money in return.

Turning to the technology and economics of productive activities, while the Fatatans caught more of the fish that they ate, the Ateans produced much more of other kinds of subsistence goods, especially vegetable staples and building materials.

Conversely, the Fatatans earned much more money from "outside" sources—mainly through their incomes in commercial fishing, livestock raising, and work for wages. And even though the Fatatans actually produced less copra, per capita, they earned more from it. In fact, the only major productive activity in which the Ateans surpassed the Fatatans in income was vanilla growing—but even here their profits, kilo for kilo, were less than those of Fatata.

The Fatatans' productive activities not only earned them more money from "outside" sources (which helped to make possible their more European material standard of living), but that was accomplished at somewhat smaller costs of time and energy. Also, while Ateans wishing to earn "outside" money were restricted mainly to agriculture, Fatatans had some choice between agriculture, livestock raising, commercial fishing, and wage-labor.

Objects and services also circulated commercially among the residents of each village, and although the total amounts of money involved in such exchanges were not markedly different—1,240 francs per capita in Atea and 1,350 francs in Fatata—there were some noteworthy differences between the two villages in the kinds and amounts of goods bought and sold. The Ateans exchanged larger amounts of roof thatch (women's work), group-organized labor (mainly men's work), and rent money (for agricultural land). In contrast, the Fatatans exchanged larger amounts of locally grown vegetables, locally caught fish, locally manufactured canoes, locally vended alcoholic beverages and cinema refreshment, individually performed labor, and harvest rights in coconut groves.

Some conspicuous differences between Atea and Fatata were revealed in social relations.

To begin with, the differences in subsistence and money-earning activities just itemized carried with them certain differences in this domain as well. For example, women took no part in Fatatans' commercial fishing, which absorbed much of the time of many Fatatan males; on the other hand, women worked along with men in Atea's dominant vanilla growing. Again, the closer interdependence between the Ateans and their Chinese store-keepers in commercial exchanges (including credit) found parallels in other kinds of interaction as well. In addition, certain more general values, which were not directly associated with specific work techniques and in which the two villages differed, seem to have exercised direct influence on the social organization of some kinds of work. Thus, Atean women and children tended to work more than their Fatatan counterparts in both subsistence and money-earning activities. Also, Atean men frequently worked together in money-earning and work-exchange groups, whereas, with the exception of some types of fishing, Fatatan men preferred to work solo or on a wage-paid basis. And with respect to money-earning services in general, Fatatans tended more towards specialization than their Atean counterparts—a situation that resulted in the Fatata social system having contained more relationships of the specialist-client pattern.

The study also revealed some conspicuous social-relational differences between Atea and Fatata in marital unions, household groups, and other aspects of kinship.

Regarding the first, Atea contained more legally (and ecclesiastically) ceremonialized unions in general, and particularly more of the pastor- or sodality-sponsored type—but considerably fewer of the sumptuous kin-sponsored veiled-bride type. Of the rest, the two villages contained about the same percentages of the "temporary" and of the "firm but purposely nonlegalized" types, but of the couples who were firmly linked but unable to wed legally because of technical restraints Fatata contained four to Atea's one.

Atea's numerical superiority in officially ceremonialized unions was augmented by its lead in the percentages of nonlegalized couples subscribing to unofficial but pastor-sanctioned fidelity pledging.

In the matter of choice of spouse, Fatata contained more unions of couples of wider than average age-difference (i.e., older females, younger males) and more in which the parents had done the choosing (i.e., in connection with veiled-bride weddings).

The most noteworthy differences between the two villages in choice of postmarital residence had to do with neolocality—in which Atea had a larger percentage—and in "spouse pull." Regarding the latter, virilocality was more prevalent than uxorilocality in both villages, but the difference was even wider in Atea.

Regarding the spouses' respective contributions to their common economic "pool," Fatata's wives furnished more in the form of land, while Atean wives furnished more in the form of productive labor—both for subsistence and money-earning purposes.

And while the rate of marriage dissolution was about the same in both villages, the Fatatans finalized more of their breakups by legalized divorce.

Turning now to the Te Pitians' households, their most palpable social groups, more of Atea's were centered around one or three adults and more of Fatata's around two or four. In kinship ties, Atea contained more households composed of simple nuclear and residual extended families, and Fatata more of the full extended family type.

Despite the considerable amount of effort I devoted to studying this phase of Te Pitian social relations, only minor differences were discovered between Atea and Fatata regarding their households' transactional unity and equity (distributive justice)—and Atea's slight superiority in these respects seems to have been associated, functionally, with its higher percentage of single-family households and was evidently *not* an expression of inter-village differences in "values." And, while Fatata's households were revealed as having purchased (rather than self-produced) more of their food and building supplies (not a surprising finding, in view of the Fatatans' larger money incomes and smaller concern with subsistence gardening), this circumstance—to my surprise, I must confess—seems not to have been directly correlated with the unity or equity variables themselves.

Much wider were the differences between the two villages in regularized exchanges of objects and services between households. In this kind of social relationship, Atea exceeded Fatata by a very wide margin. Not all such relationships, in either village, were based on (or even associated with) ties of kinship between the connected households' heads, but kinship was a factor in Atea's superiority in this institution.

In fact, ties of consanguinity and/or affinity served to reticulate large percentages of the residents of both villages, but Atea contained fewer households not included in such networks and witnessed more occasions on which kinfolk interacted as such—particularly in connection with the inter-household exchanges, the sharing of tools and hospitality, and the sponsorship and financing of funerals. In only one kind of event did Fatata's constellations of kinfolk surpass their Atean counterparts, and that was in the sponsorship and financing of veiled-bride weddings, which were inherently kin-based events and which took place more often in Fatata than in Atea.

Kinship also was the basis of most of land tenure in Te Piti—in co-ownership, use rights, and title transfer. In some of these and other aspects of land tenure, the two villages were found to be widely different.

In the case of both villages, most of the areas conventionally identified with them were actually owned, legally, by persons living elsewhere, but the Fatatans owned a larger percentage of their village-identified land than the Ateans owned of theirs. Also, the Fatatans had been for several years gradually acquiring, or reacquiring, more of that land, mainly by purchase (which the Ateans had been unable to do). Notwithstanding, the Ateans made fuller use of their own local land holdings and, by lease and share-cropping, of the outsider-owned local land as well. (Although I could not discover how much land either the Ateans or Fatatans owned "outside," inquiry revealed that the former received more income from such land, mainly by dint of their own hard work and despite the greater disadvantages resulting from their isolation and modes of access.)

Another conspicuous difference between the two villages was in the number and size of legally distinct parcels contained within their village-identified areas. While those areas were of about the same total size, Atea's was divided into seventy-three distinct parcels and Fatata's 248—yielding per capita averages of 9.32 and 2.78 hectares, respectively. Even more indicative of the two village areas' rates of fragmentation were their numbers of parcels of under one hectare in size—the Atea area having contained four such and Fatata 160!

Returning to the Te Pitians' own land holdings in their village-identified areas, the most noteworthy difference between the two villages was not the percentages of resident-owners (which were also about the same) but the modal sizes of individual holdings. In this respect, the Atean owners appeared to have been better off than their Fatatan counterparts in having owned fewer very small holdings and more very large ones—a disadvantage for the Fatatans that was reinforced by the circumstance that most of their very small holdings were non-income-producing house lots. As was pointed out, however, this relative disadvantage of the Fatatans' *vis-à-vis* the Ateans was mitigated somewhat by the circumstance that land was not as essential to them economically as it was to the Ateans.

Even more salient was the statistical finding that Fatata contained far fewer households whose members, singly or collectively, had large local land holdings and many more households whose members had none—again, a disadvantage *vis-à-vis* the Ateans, but rendered less crucial by the Fatatans' other alternatives for gaining livelihoods.

Three other social institutions found in both villages, but participated and structured in conspicuously different ways, were the Protestant church parishes (and their component sodalities), the government district units, and the local branches of the Territory's political parties.

While all but a handful of the Te Pitians were more or less Protestant in the content of their religious beliefs and in their denominational commitment, the two parish memberships differed from each other in several other respects. In a word, the Ateans attended both church and sodality meetings more frequently and in larger numbers than the Fatatans, and they contributed more to those organizations both in money and labor. Correspondingly, the Atean pastor's influence over his parishioners was broader and more effective than that of his Fatatan counterpart, and he exercised more often his authority and prerogatives.

Similarly, the meetings of the Atean citizenry were better attended than those of Fatata, and Atea's *tāvana* played a more active and influential role in district (and nondistrict) village affairs. During 1954–55, Fatata's male citizenry engaged more often in district-wide projects; the two largest of these—pipe-laying and receptions for official visitors—had no parallels in Atea at that time but did have in previous or subsequent years. Fatata's district was also more closely integrated into the territory's Administration, in the form of more direct supervision by higher-ups—but looked at from below, this was both a cause and a consequence of the Atea District's superior autonomy and cohesiveness.

Atea's superior cohesiveness in district matters was matched in the political sphere, where its entire citizenry was united in the RDPT party—in contrast to Fatata, where two other parties were represented by small but influential memberships.

Finally, when viewing and comparing the two villages as whole communities, Atea was revealed as having been much more cohesive than Fatata, in the sense that its component social units were more conterminous and its leadership (official or de facto) more unified. In addition, the Ateans joined together much more numerously and frequently than the Fatatans in certain events—e.g., the New Year festival, wedding celebrations, and vanilla selling—that were not specifically connected with any of the villages' formal social units.

The differences between Atea and Fatata described in this study were the result of circumstance and events spread over two centuries and longer, and it would be patently impossible to document all the changes manifested in those differences in particular historical sequences of cause and effect. There are, of course, some exceptions to this limitation. I believe, for example, that

Fatata's proximity to Pape'ete, and Atea's remoteness, were crucial circumstances directly behind the Fatatans' adoption of large-scale commercial
fishing—once Pape'ete market demand had grown large enough, and once
some Fatatans had come to recognize that demand. Again, I think it highly
likely that some of the described differences between the current modus op-
erandi of the two villages' parishes and district governments were occasioned by dissimilarities in the personalities of their current pastors and *tāvana.*
On the other hand, I am unable to reconstruct the particular sequence of
events that induced former generations of Fatatans to abandon the practice
of group-organized work exchanges—and the Ateans to retain it. And it is
only guesswork on my part to attribute the Ateans' preponderance of neolocal residence to their smaller houses. Thus, the explanations I have offered
range from the clearly obvious through the plausibly likely to the wild-shot
guess.

Those explanations also vary between the sharply particular (e.g., the influence that Pouvana'a's Huahine origin had upon Ateans' political views)
to the broadly general (e.g., the cumulative effects that their closer European contacts had upon the Fatatans' architectural preferences, drinking
habits, and health practices).

In some instances I have resorted, *faute de mieux,* to syllogistic reasoning,
e.g., when ascribing the Ateans' greater propensity for kin-based interhousehold exchanges to a more general ideological set, a value; and when
ascribing some of the Fatatans' practices to their greater receptivity to
European-derived innovations. In extenuation, I will say that I am painfully conscious of the mushiness and circularity of this kind of reasoning but
do not in such cases have the data to build firmer foundations. (And I lack
the ingenuity—and the gall!—to pretend to be capable of devising a credible
hypothetical reconstruction of the sequence of events that produced or altered such values.)

In conclusion, I will only say that, while numerous particular circumstances, events, and individuals had served to create and widen differences
between the two villages under study, the single most potent factor in that
process—the one that had persisted for two centuries and more and had
shaped events in many kinds of ways—was the villages' spatial and travel-
time distance from northwest Tahiti, where Pape'ete is now situated and
which has been these islands' "urban" center since the earliest European visitors and settlers began congregating there. It is from this most decisive contrast that the two villages compared in this study were given their pseudo-
nyms—the one being *Fatata,* which in Tahitian means "nearby," the other
Atea, which means "far away."

POSTSCRIPT

Originally it was my intention to use my field observations for a study not only of culture variability but also of culture change. The differences between Atea and Fatata herein recorded clearly contain many implications concerning changes, i.e., it is my assumption, for example, that the type of group-organized work exchanges found in Atea in 1954–55 once existed in Fatata as well and that their absence in the latter in 1954–55 constituted a transformation that had taken place over time. And it was my original plan to deal not only with the kind of long-range changes inferable from contemporary differences between the two villages, but to describe and try to explain in comparable detail changes that had taken place in both villages between my first visits, in 1954–55, and my second ones, in 1959–60.

I have since decided to abandon that second objective—much to my own relief, I must confess, and doubtless also to the relief of any readers who have stayed the long course thus far and who, with dogged conscientiousness, might feel impelled to follow it to the distant end. There are several technical reasons for stopping here—in addition to the personal and, I suppose, unprofessional, one of wishing to terminate a job that has already consumed much time drawn out over many years.

The first of these is that, except as will be noted, none of the events and situations observed during my return visits were in my opinion markedly different enough from the earlier ones to warrant attention in this already lengthy report. Some changes in personnel had of course taken place—births, deaths, arrivals, departures, etc.—but none divergent enough from the earlier patterns to require attention. A few houses had been built or repaired, but in line with the previous trends. Two Ateans had purchased high-powered outboard motors, which propelled their small boats almost out of the water—but these were used mainly for breakneck pleasure excursions to Fare. One of Fatata's fishermen introduced from Tahiti a new technique for securing fish rounded up by the *hapua* method (p. 73), i.e., by driving the coralled fish into a net made of wire rather than of fiber fewer of them escaped. (The new technique was quickly adopted by all of the local seine-net fishermen.)

A few other topical items chosen at random:

—By 1959–60, Fatata's youths had abandoned competitive interdistrict football, and Ateans had resumed it—in line with the cyclical pattern remarked on in Chapter VI.

—One of Atea's vanilla growers had begun to dry his own beans—but his neighbors (who were still deeply in debt to the storekeepers) continued to maintain that vanilla drying was "too difficult for Tahitians."

—By 1959–60, Atea had obtained its own running water, by means of pipes leading from its stream-fed mountain reservoir. Water taps were located along the village street, each one serving one or more houses. This, of course, lightened the chore of water-carrying and resulted in an increase of water use, but women continued to gather around a certain few of the outlets to do their laundry.

—The Fatata billiard parlor was opened to (paid-for) play more frequently and regularly and partly replaced the football field as an evening rendezvous place for youths.

Several more such changes of this kind and magnitude were observable but will not be listed, inasmuch as they had not at the time brought about any conspicuous transformations in the economics or social-relational aspects of the Te Pitians' lives. Instead, I will focus, however briefly, on the local consequences of some political events that had occurred in Atea in 1958.

The events in question were touched off by a territory-wide referendum in which the voters were asked to choose between total political independence from France and membership in a new-style "French Community." As a result of interpersonal strife, the RDPT leadership had split and the Pouvana'a-led faction had declared for independence from France—a position that most (if not all) Ateans supported both on account of political sentiment and of personal commitment to Pouvana'a. In the end the Ateans and most other Leeward Island Tahitians voted for independence but in the territory as a whole a majority vote was cast for continued ties with France. The wider politics, etc., of this referendum (which are described in Thompson and Adloff 1971) do not concern us here, but what does is the way the campaign was conducted in Atea. (The referendum took place eighteen months before my return visit to Atea, but memory of it—doubtless highly selective—was still vivid during my stay.)

Predictably, the Atean voters, with one exception, voiced whole-hearted support for Pouvana'a's call for a vote for independence. The exception was the pastor, who repeated from the pulpit his mission superiors' call for continued ties with France. Most if not all Ateans past childhood appear to have resented the church's official stand, not only because of the "impropriety" (*e 'ere i te mea tano*) of the church leaders having taken *any* stand on a political issue, but also because of a statement allegedly broadcast by the church's highest officials, accusing proindependence persons of "stupidity" and of "following Satan's way." I was unable to learn with complete certainty whether Atea's pastor had spoken against independence and had made such accusations as reflecting his own views (which he subsequently disavowed) or whether he was only following the alleged commands of his superiors; at any rate, his actions aroused a storm of anger and protest locally, which led eventually to a split in Atea's congregation.

The pastor's statements about the referendum, whether personal or merely "official," was not the only event that produced the storm. Even during my first visit, there had been murmurings against him—partly for his uncompromising policy in prohibiting noncontributors the use of the assembly house (Chapter VI, pages 215–16), and partly for what was regarded by some of his parishioners as his practice of exploiting his official position for personal economic gain—a charge, by the way, that I often heard levelled against other Protestant pastors elsewhere. In 1954–55, however, the murmurings were no more than that; as I endeavored to show (Chapter VI, pages 215–16), the pastor and the *tāvana*, jointly and officially, most effective authority and influence over what appeared to be, by most definitions of the term, a unified, cohesive community.

The murmurings, I was told, increased after my first visit, when the pastor prevailed upon some members of the congregation to "donate" their labor in the construction of a European-style house, which he said was for his "retirement" but which he proceeded to turn over to his daughter and her European spouse. But even this discontent was contained until released by the referendum episode.

Leadership among the most vocal dissenters was assumed by one of the parish's deacons, a man of part-European descent (but totally Tahitian in way of life) and one of the village's best educated and most prosperous residents. This man, whom I shall call Marama, secured local support for a petition to the church authorities to remove the pastor from office—a move, he explained, that was commanded of him in a dream. Then, when the authorities refused to comply, Marama and a majority of the congregation "left" the church. Many of them joined with Marama to form a breakaway group, which held their own Sunday services in the residence of one of them. Others in the village formed the nucleus of a small Mormon congregation, whose American missionaries were quick to move into the breach. And still others used the break as a basis—an excuse, some of their neighbors charged—for attending no church services at all.

Subsequently, a few of Marama's original followers returned to the pastor's fold, having been persuaded to do so mainly by the *tāvana*, who had remained loyal despite (he informed me) his own disapproval of the pastor's political stand.

And so matters remained throughout my second visit. During the week, people went about their various economic activities much as usual, and I could detect no sign of "anger" or "coolness" between members of the factions and no lessening of the usual friendly chatter and banter that had accompanied casual interaction before the break. But on Sundays the lines were clearly drawn. The rival church services were held at the same time and two of them within deliberate hearing of each other, and the divisions thus exemplified tended to continue throughout the rest of the day. One of the fatalities of the schism was the midweek meeting of each sodality, but a much more obvious loss was the parish-wide Sunday night *tuāroʻi* session (p. 214), which, even more so than the midday church service, had served to exhibit and ritualize the village's character and cohesiveness.

As just noted, the breakup seemed not to have affected the Ateans' everyday modes of producing and consuming and of casual social interaction "in the street." Nor, according to my inquiries, had it diminished the numbers of interhousehold exchanges. And except for one marital separation, precipitated by the wife having joined with the Mormons, it had to my knowledge not yet resulted in any radical social-relational changes in families, households, or joint landowning units. The sodality-based labor-exchange groups were no longer functioning but other kinds of labor-exchange and money-earning work groups continued. Moreover, the young men of the village, regardless of church affiliation, had reactivated the football club and were playing interdistrict matches.

But, as every adult Atean I talked with in private readily said, the village was "not the same as before." Or to put it into the words used by most of them, "The village has become sick" (*ʻua maʻi hia teie nei vāhi*).

Many pages could be written about Atea's so-called sickness, but instead I will turn to Fatata and describe as briefly as possibly what changes the 1958 referendum had precipitated there.

In a word, such changes were few in number and very limited in scope.

During the campaign before the referendum, the Territory leaders of both pro- and antiindependence sides had visited the village and spoken to large turnouts, and (I was informed) many discussions, some of them heated, had taken place among the Fatatans themselves. The residents knew, from radio and word of mouth, of the Protestant leaders' antiindependence stand and of their pastor's agreement with it—but the latter did not urge others, from the pulpit or elsewhere, to follow suit.

In the end the majority of Fatata's voters declared for continued ties with France—evidently with the helping votes of some who had previously been supporters of Pouvanaʻa himself.

During the time of my second visit to Fatata, a year after the referendum, I could discern no noteworthy changes in the village's economy or social-relational patterns that could be traced, directly or indirectly, to the referendum—except in the RDPT, whose active members were fewer in number and, it seemed to me, very much on the defensive—even fearful of what they imagined the victorious French Administration officials would do to them in revenge.[1] I was told that the referendum had "broken up several families"—but on closer examination the quarrels and separations in question had been set in motion by other conflicts totally unrelated to politics.

The points of this postscript are two.

First is the methodological one, a reminder of the desirability—indeed, the necessity—of observing a society over a considerable period of time before drawing conclusions about its inherent character. I will not attempt to specify how long a time "considerable" should be nor spend any more words belaboring this widely acknowledged methodological counsel.

The second point concerns analysis and interpretation; and it consists of a question that I will not even attempt to answer in full. The question is: How did it come about that a community so apparently "cohesive" as Atea could split so widely apart? The fact that the more uncohesive social structure of Fatata did not become even more so, as a result of the referendum, did not surprise me—and, I trust, should not surprise any conscientious reader of this report. But Atea—how did it happen that such an apparently unified community had become so socially divided in this important respect?

The answer, I believe, is not to be found hidden behind the word "apparently"—that is to say, the problem is not largely a product of shallow observations nor an artifact of the analytical operations employed. Nor do I believe that it can be answered by use of a metaphor; however picturesque the Ateans' own characterization of their community it was not an organism, healthy or sick. Nor was it a machine, say, that split apart under intolerable inner pressures. Individuals, and thus psychology, would have to be dealt with in any systematic attempt to answer the question—as would individuals interacting and hence sociology as well. But rather than attempt to follow such courses of inquiry to the lengths that would be required—another tedious inquest in an already overlong research—I will add only my unelaborated conclusion that the factor of *distance*—which accounted for much of Atea's relatively tighter prereferendum cohesiveness, accounted also for much of its more divided postreferendum falling apart.

---

[1]A fear that was visibly increased during the subsequent trial of Pouvanaʻa, who was accused (and adjudged guilty and exiled) of attempting to put Papeʻete to flames after his referendum defeat.

APPENDIX

In a paper published in 1958,[1] I recorded some notions, still very tentative, about the concept of "social structure" and suggested a way in which they might be integrated into the subject matter of "economics" for cross-cultural comparisons. Like most of the programmatic statements put forward by social anthropologists in their early and optimistic days, this one was greeted by professional colleagues either with indifference or skepticism.

Subsequently I applied some of that paper's analytical suggestions in a library-based study on ancient Tahiti (Oliver 1974) but only for organizing the descriptive materials on social relations. That exercise was helpful to me but, evidently (from the reviews), did not exactly spark a revolution in methodology! (In fact, almost the only kind of published reaction to it was irritation with the scheme's turgid terminology.)

Notwithstanding that stillbirth of my brainchild, I am going to try to beget again—but this time in an appendix, where the approach will appear less obtrusively pedantic and the terminology less infelicitous. What I propose to do here is to compare what I will call the societal economy of Atea with that of Fatata, in terms of the following characteristics:

1. A list of each village's widely shared goals (arranged hierarchically when possible) and an estimate of the extent to which the achievable ones of those goals were actually achieved.

2. An examination of the factors, natural and cultural, which were responsible for the gaps between the achievable goals and their actual attainment by each village as a whole.

Throughout this exercise, the reference will be to each village as a whole, without attention to the actual distribution of the ideas or goods among

---

[1] "An Ethnographer's Method for Formulating Descriptions of 'Social Structure,'" *American Anthropologist*, Vol. 60, No. 5 (1958).

individuals or households. That latter is, of course, an important aspect of any specific "societal economy" (e.g., for the study of stratification) but will not be treated here lest it stretch too far both my data and the patience even of appendix readers. I will begin with the goals.

Part One

I have no illusions about the difficulty of drawing up a list of goals—especially a hierarchically ordered one—representing the consensus of a whole community of humans. In the first place, individuals in any community are known to change their goals and the rank-order among them (i.e., with advancing age, with realization of some of them, etc.). And, of course, females will inevitably differ from males not only in their rank-ordering of some goals but in the contents of their lists as well.

A second kind of difficulty has to do with procedures. Ideally, such an inquiry should be conducted by lengthy and carefully constructed questionnaires addressed to an appropriately representative sample, which would then be supplemented by observations on individuals making real-life choices. I hasten to concede that I did not follow such a course of inquiry. I used no systematic questionnaires for this purpose and recorded mainly what came my way. I did, however, draw up a tentative list of community goals about halfway through my first visit and corrected my rank-ordering of them from time to time, but more on the basis of passive observation than of experiment or leading question.

As in perhaps most other human communities, the matter of goals was further complicated in Atea and Fatata by the contextual presence of some more or less "official" ones representative of the larger, encompassing society. These were the goals, implicit or explicit, of the French government and of the territory branch of the Protestant church.

I cannot find an official statement listing the general goals enunciated by the French government of that period and applicable to French subjects residing in places like Atea and Fatata, and I will not attempt to put together an authoritative one from such of the political speeches, laws, welfare enactments, etc., that might apply. However, I suppose that such a list would be found to contain the following desiderata applicable to Atea and Fatata,[2] namely, a peaceful community relatively free of interpersonal conflict, and one made up mainly of French citizens, who were:

—healthy and long-lived;

---

[2]One such limitation (in 1954–55) having been the Ateans', Fatatans' (and other Tahitians') lack of voice in selecting their own governor, gendarmes, etc.

—educated at least to the point of literacy (in French) and with a "basic" knowledge of the sciences, the arts, and French history and institutions;

—provided with at least a (defined) minimum of food, shelter, and clothing, and a certain amount of innocent entertainment;

—accorded security for their rightful property; and

—provided with privacy and protection for their personal selves (particularly when they were handicapped, e.g., by "minority" age, or by senility or ill health).

Inferentially, such governmental goals would also have served to encourage durable and monogamous marriages and to discourage extramarital sex. As for the mechanics of citizenship, the government's official policy would appear to have been to permit, even encourage, the adult Atean and Fatatan a voice—although a very limited one[3]—in his own governance and to require him to contribute a share—although a smaller-than-national-average one[4]—to the cost of government.

Ateans and Fatatans were familiarized, week in and week out, with the Protestant church's goals—by their pastors and by their own reading of the (Tahitian language) Bible. From the countless hours I spent listening (yes; listening!) to the former I infer that the most important of those goals were the following:

—To attain Heaven after death and thereby avoid Hell;

—To abjure "pagan" beliefs and practices;

—To maintain and increase the strength of the Protestant Church at home and abroad (against, e.g., paganism, Catholicism);

—To maintain certain behavioral standards, such as honesty, extramarital chastity, sobriety, modesty, etc.

—To create and sustain certain social relationships, such as monogamous marriage and other family ties, good neighborship, wide fraternalhood, etc., and to devote special attention to the needs of the weak, the disabled, the bereaved, and the very poor;

—To become learned in the contents of the Bible; and

—To make an effort—which, however, could never be large enough—to repay God, in money and in worship, for His bounty.

Some of the above goals, both government and church, had become incorporated into the ideologies of the Ateans and Fatatans, but others had

---

[3]One such limitation (in 1954–55) having been the Ateans', Fatatans' (and other Tahitians') lack of voice in selecting their own governor, gendarmes, etc.

[4]As witnessed by the Ateans' and Fatatans' freedom from income taxes and by their low rate of military conscription.

been rejected or ignored, in whole or in part—as the text of this book has shown. In addition (or in transformation) it is possible to identify a number of "indigenous" goals shared by most Ateans *and* Fatatans past "youth" and by many of the youth as well. I will begin by listing these goals, first of the Ateans, and indicate later on if and how the Fatatans differed in this regard. (Despite the unsystematic nature of my inquiries, described earlier, I believe that the following inferences are accurate enough for present purposes.)

For the convenience of myself and of non-Tahitian readers, I will list the Ateans' ingredients of "The Good Life" under three headings: *Conditions, Activities,* and *Statuses* (although I feel quite certain that no Atean would classify them in this way—nor indeed even come up with a comprehensive list of such goals, without considerable prompting by the investigator). Also, I will arrange the items under each heading in a kind of rough-and-ready priority ordering, based on the number of individuals including them in their own personal goal inventories and on what I infer to have been their own priorities.[5] And finally, I will identify the items as concisely as possible on the ground that most of them have already been discussed in the text.

Conditions

1. **Comfort.** Tahitian words like *maita'i* ("good") and *ora* ("life," "health") express some of the implications of this term, but I know of no single close equivalent in Tahitian to it and I did occasionally hear villagers (specifically, Fatatans) use *bien-être* in this sense. And one of them who did so, prompted by my questioning, did in fact include most of the items which I place in my list (the one that now follows) in explaining what he meant by that French term.

A. Consuming enough of certain kinds of foods and beverages (for fuller discussion of this item, see Chapter II, pages 54–84).

B. Being free of physical pain. I should add here (to what was recorded in Chapter II, pages 54–84) that in my observation the Ateans appeared to tolerate considerably more physical pain than most Europeans I know—except for toothache, which seemed to induce a patterned response of utter, self-pitying misery.

C. Being bodily clean, except when work required otherwise.

D. Wearing clean clothing, except when work required otherwise; and (for most women and young men) wearing fashionable clothes.

E. Residing in furnished and rainproof houses. For most Ateans, to be "comfortable" in this sense such houses required only a few essential

---

[5] A Guttman Scale-Analysis test would have been useful here but was not applied.

furnishings such as bed, lamp, table, and some raised places—chairs or benches—for sitting. Other things, like elaborate bedsteads, *tīfaifai* (bedspreads), wardrobes, radios, and phonographs were for display and entertainment.

F. A proper balance between action (including work) and inaction. Ateans enjoyed being active some of the time, followed by periods—including *long* periods—of doing nothing. They sometimes admired individuals who worked *most* of the time, e.g., most Chinese and some Europeans, but criticized such habits in other Tahitians. Also, while they were equally critical of excessive inaction (*hupehupe*), especially when it brought hardships to others, they displayed no felt need to be "busy" merely to avoid inaction. (No precepts here about "the devil finding work for idle hands"!) In this connection, however, the periods of inaction, which they evidently enjoyed and felt no need to justify, were not so highly favored as a part of *future* well-being as to warrant extra *present* action. In other words, Ateans showed little inclination to work harder today in order to do less tomorrow.

G. Immunity from psychological "trouble" (*pe'ape'a*: anxiety, shame, consuming anger, boredom, etc.).

H. Nonentanglement in social conflict.

Now to estimate the extent to which individual Ateans actually achieved these goals constituting "comfort."

It is my conclusion that every Atean obtained enough *ma'a* (starchy staples) in his diet to satisfy his wishes for them but that most of them would have liked to be able to eat more *'ina'i*—fish and meat, and more imported packaged foods of all kinds. Most of them would also have liked to consume more imported confections and beverages—alcoholic and/or nonalcoholic.

Regarding physical pain: despite their apparent stoicism (except for toothache!) most if not all of them experienced more of it than they would have wished—headaches, gastric upsets, fevers, etc.

Being bodily clean and wearing clean clothes (except when working) were goals easily attainable by everyone and actually attained by most. Except for several women and a few young men, I will also judge that most Ateans were content with the amounts and kinds of clothes they owned.

Concerning "shelter," most Ateans appeared to be satisfied with their houses and house furnishings—except for a few who evidently wished to make them somewhat more rainproof and easier to maintain. There were, however, several individuals who, for reasons connected with status goals, had longings for larger and more European-style dwellings and for more European-type furnishings.

Individuals varied widely in the amounts of time they devoted to work, and I have the impression that many, from longest- to shortest-time workers, wished to devote less—and hence fell short of attaining their individual goal regarding a proper balance between action and inaction.

I cannot judge very accurately how many Ateans managed to achieve immunity from psychological "trouble." There were several individuals who obviously and almost continually harbored feelings of irritation or anger or discontent and several others who appeared to be perennially at ease with themselves and with the world at large. Again, there were some individuals who were notoriously quarrelsome and others who managed to stand continuously aloof. And in between those extremes were many others who, I imagine, wished for less social conflict than they were able to achieve.

2. **Body perfection** (an aesthetic, not a health-connected goal). The value in which this attribute was held was indicated, e.g., by the Ateans' disdain for "excessive" thinness or fatness, by their derision towards baldness and physical deformities, by young women's eagerness for tooth replacement, and (when one listened closely) by their contempt for the salient physical imperfections of many of the Chinese and most of the Europeans they encountered.

It is my belief that few Ateans were dissatisfied with their physiques or other physical features. The exceptions were those having baldness, or elephantitic or otherwise crippled limbs, or darker-than-average skins. (The latter were nicknamed *"Ere'ere,"* "Blackie," which was borne cheerfully by men but with evident embarrassment by young women.)

3. **Masculinity, or femininity** (as the case may be!). Notwithstanding the tolerance, even respect, shown towards the definitively transformed (and appropriately skilled) *māhū,* the Ateans esteemed highly those persons who behaved in ways conforming to their dichotomous sex stereotypes and were critical to the point of contemptuousness for those who did not.

Aside from the two who were outright *māhū,* the only persons in Atea who were judged by their neighbors to deviate from their appropriate sexual roles were a few notoriously henpecked husbands and a few loudly domineering wives.

4. **Having children.** As the text should have made abundantly clear, the desire to have children was evident in all Atean married couples—and in some unmarried young adults as well. Furthermore, this goal was largely achievable for virtually everyone—either through their own proliferation or through the widely prevalent custom of fosterage (*fa'a'amu*).

5. **Being with kinfolk.** Some Ateans expressed a desire to get away from their "too narrow," "too boring," "too prying" village, and from their "too importunate" or "too domineering" kin; but when they did leave, they nearly always sought out other kinfolk in the new place—or returned home again for lengthy visits or permanent stays.

6. **Being with other Tahitians.** Whether kin or not, Ateans were more at home with other Tahitians than with Chinese or Europeans—a circumstance that became clearly evident when they were away from their village.

7. **Being in the Society Islands.** Part of this goal, which was evident in all Ateans I talked with on the subject, was the wish, just listed, to be with other Tahitians, but another part had to do with geography and climate. Most Ateans appeared to enjoy travelling abroad, or the prospect of doing so, but seemed happier still to return to these islands, which to them were self-evidently the best places in the world to live.

8. **Control over one's own actions.** There was evidence of some ambivalence here. On the one hand, strong and charismatic Tahitian leaders were admired and often followed—provided, however, their authority was not too directly exercised or too close at hand. For, in the village itself, Ateans were quick to oppose anyone who took too much leadership initiative or who sought too strictly to impose even customary rules.

As for being controlled by non-Tahitians, there was also some ambivalence. Some older men harked back to the legendary "British" era as a time of more authoritarian but better-conducted government, in contrast to the more easygoing but allegedly ineffectual French regime. Some of those same men, along with others, voiced wholehearted support for Pouvana'a's "Tahiti for the Tahitians" program but also expressed a preference even for European (i.e., French) officials over Tahitian ones (other than Pouvana'a himself), their distrust of some of Pouvana'a's aides having been stronger than their irritation with the French.

In any case, in the political setting of 1954–55 there was little or nothing that the Ateans themselves could have done to achieve this goal—whatever it happened to be!

Some Ateans also expressed, in one way or another, a desire to end up after death in the Protestant Heaven, and a few of these evidently conducted their lives with that goal specifically in view. And some other Ateans expressed convictions that they would end up in Hell, no matter what they did or did not do. On the other hand, I believe that for the majority of Ateans the prospect of Heaven or of Hell was not a preoccupation that influenced their daily thoughts or actions in any large degree.

Finally, some Ateans may have striven to attain or to maintain other "conditions," such as chastity (a few young girls), or fidelity (a few wives), or sobriety, etc., but those I have listed above were I believe the most widely held goals in this category.

Activities

I reported above the Ateans' desire for activity (balanced, however, by periods of inactivity) and will list now the kinds of activities they wished mostly to engage in. Because of the wide variations in individuals' evaluations of some of those activities, I will not attempt to present them in an overall, community-wide rank-order—except for the very broad categories of social versus solitary activities.

I saw many instances of individuals doing something alone and evidently enjoying it: angling from a wharf or a solitary canoe; spearfishing for hours at a time; lovingly ironing and reironing a pretty dress; picking out a tune on a ukelele; patiently fitting new boards into a treasured old canoe hull; etc.—sometimes even reading (i.e., the Bible). But much more often the Ateans did those and other things in company, deliberately (it would seem) and with signs of heightened enjoyment from the company itself.

Keeping this distinction in mind, the kinds of activities Ateans past childhood appeared most to enjoy were the following:

1. **Attending social gatherings,** "profane" and/or religious, e.g., parties (i.e., *'arearea,* usually with drinking and singing), feasts, *tuāro'i* sessions, choir practices, and playing (but not practicing!) football.[6]

2. **Eating favored foods** (and for some, smoking tobacco).

3. **Fishing** (but not gardening, copra-working, or vanilla pollinating)—and, for some, hunting.

4. **Sewing** (by women)—especially bedspreads and modish dresses.

5. **Travelling** (except for health or on legal/government business).

6. **Attending cinema** (and discussing it ad infinitum!).

7. **Fondling infants** (and, for mothers, dressing them up and showing them off).

---

[6]In 1959–60. In 1954–55, football-playing was in abeyance in Atea.

8. And last, but not least, copulating.

(If I were to define "sleeping" as an activity, rather than inactivity, it would appear very prominently on the list.)

Again, it is necessary to inquire how far the Ateans succeeded in reaching these "activity" goals.

Regarding the attending of social gatherings, I concluded from several kinds of evidence—attendance (and voluntary nonattendance) lists, interviews, overhead conversations, vocal expressions of satiety, etc.—that nearly every Atean was able to satisfy to the full his wishes for this kind of activity. Such gatherings occurred very frequently and, within very broad limits, were nonexclusive. (The chief exceptions were adult drinking parties, from which younger persons were sometimes excluded.) People were even suffered to attend the meetings of sodalities other than their own (except when new songs were being practiced). Nor did the time demands of work appear to restrict any individual's participation in such gatherings, although fatigue from work occasionally induced some to stay at home. In fact, the only weighty restraint on social gathering was money, and that only for the kind of partying that required quantities of alcohol.

Shortage of money also restrained some Ateans from eating enough of some of the kinds of food they desired or smoking as much as they wished, from attending cinema regularly, and from travelling as far and as often as they would have liked. But as for *time,* the only preferred activity that some individuals had to forego on account of a shortage of it was fishing—which I do believe some Ateans would have spent many more hours at had gardening and cash-cropping been less urgent and time-consuming.

Statuses

I will make a distinction here between the statuses that betokened prestige and those that betokened social authority. The distinction is not entirely clear-cut, inasmuch as the social esteem—the "vote" or approval—that constituted prestige ipso facto endowed the incumbent with some measure of influence over the voters' actions; but, unlike what I call "authority," prestige alone was backed by few if any effective sanctions.

Prestige, the nearest Tahitian equivalent of which is *ro'o,* derived from the following types of attributes:

1. *Māramarama*—knowledgeable, enlightened, intellectually schooled, etc., in matters religious or secular. Only a few individuals, mostly male, were so characterized in Atea, and those who were were accorded universal respect.

2. **Respectability** included such behaviors as piety, marital fidelity, moderation in the use of alcohol, fair-mindedness, and nonbelligerence. Several persons, including a few women, were described as combining most or all of these attributes, and as such they were quite visibly deferred to.

3. **Skill** in certain activities. For men such activities included fishing, canoe-hull fashioning, carpentry, orating (on appropriate occasions!), growing large root crops and melons, singing (especially in a falsetto voice), doctoring, and money making; and those for women: sewing, roof-thatch making, vanilla pollinating, and singing (the louder the better). In 1959, skill in football playing was applauded during games but was not talked about later. Displays of physical strength or agility were also admired on the occasion, but I never heard a man described admiringly as being generally "strong." With Tahitian-style dancing it was the reverse; I heard several women (mainly younger ones) and men (of all ages) described admiringly as *numero ho'e* (number one!) in dancing, but except on a very few occasions the local experts did not practice their skills—the female having usually held back because of "shame" and males having performed only when drunk.

4. **Generosity**—i.e., doing more than the required minimum, for example, in the feeding and beveraging of guests, in contributions (particularly of money) to church and sodality, in money loans to acquaintances in need, and in services to community-wide undertakings. But there was evidence of some ambivalence regarding this status, in that some admiration, grudging but positive, was expressed towards the sparing and hard-bargaining man who also managed to acquire and preserve some wealth—but not nearly as much as for the openhanded one.

5. **Industriousness** (*itoitora'a*). This attribute was praised even if it failed to pay off—in which cases the persons in question were usually pitied. And it was especially praiseworthy when an industrious person succeeded, and then was generous with the fruits of his success. On the other hand, in the case of the person who became affluent through unceasing industriousness and then hoarded his wealth, the respect for that industriousness was outweighed by disapproval of his meanness—which brings us to the question of the Ateans' attitudes towards material affluence itself.

6. **Wealthiness.** There is no question in my mind but that nearly all Ateans would have liked to become or remain wealthy. The exceptions were a few realists who, recognizing the impossibility of their ever becoming so (and not because of any ideological opposition to material possessions) seem

to have expunged the thought of that goal from their calculations. On the other hand, Ateans' attitudes towards those of their neighbors who, by local standards, were indeed wealthy—in money incomes, in size of land holdings, in type and size of dwellings, in conspicuous consumption, etc.—were shaped by their feelings about the ways such wealth had been acquired or was used. I noted above their attitudes towards the wealthy but illiberal individual. Similar disapproval was voiced towards the individual who was thought to have acquired his wealth by cheating or exploiting his (Tahitian) neighbors. And while Ateans envied and were in some ways deferential towards those of their neighbors who gained relatively large means through possession of large inherited land holdings, they did not hold them, for that reason, to be praiseworthy.

In consequence of all these qualifications there was no one in Atea during the periods of my visits who was the object of universal admiration because of his wealthiness per se.

7. **European-ness.** Inasmuch as the principal criterion for occupying a superior (*teitei*) position in Atean (and Fatatan) society was descent from parents or grandparents who had been wealthy, this status may have invited some envy (and with some respect in connection with choice of an off-spring's spouse), but it was not one that could be aspired to. There was, however, another status in the Ateans' social universe which connoted "superiority" and which was accessible by individual effort—namely, European-ness.

Ateans were very ambivalent about European persons and traits. While they respected and/or envied many of the former they were contemptuous of persons of any degree of Tahitian descent who behaved as if they were largely European. And while many Ateans wished and worked to obtain European objects and skills, they disapproved of other Tahitians who possessed such things in large measure and correspondingly set themselves socially apart.

Another "status" occupied by some (male) Ateans and admired (and probably aspired to) by some of their fellow villagers, was sexual potency, as manifested in numerous sexual conquests. However, in my limited experience (I was assigned initially to a role of sedate respectability and kept there most of the time), public talk about this topic was limited to ribald jesting.

The levels of prestige status reached by any Atean were measured directly and exclusively by the number and the weight of the "votes" of approval of his fellow villagers. (In other words, during my visits no resident there was esteemed, or disesteemed, on account of his status *elsewhere*.) Furthermore, because of the very nature of these statuses their top levels were achieved by only a few individuals. And thirdly, in contrast to most of the goals listed under "conditions" and "activities," some of the prestige statuses just itemized were not wished for by some Ateans, however much these latter may have esteemed the current incumbents of those statuses. (If this strikes any reader as contradictory, I would explain that despite the high esteem in which I hold, say, the world's champion ping-pong player, I have no consuming desire to occupy that position.)

For those who desired them—who, as noted, did not include every Atean—the resources required for achieving the higher levels of prestige status were, singly or in various combinations: time, energy, intelligence, natural ability, and money. Of time not required by other activities, there appeared to be enough available to any Atean to achieve higher levels in such statuses as *māramarama* (which depended heavily on rote learning), respectability, skill, industriousness, and even wealthiness. As for the other resources required for prestige, in addition to differences in motivation (which I did not attempt to measure[7]), there were some fairly wide individual differences in energy, intelligence, and natural ability, as manifested by the stratified levels of actual achievement.[8]

Turning now to the statuses that betokened *authority*, i.e., those whose incumbents were characterized as having *mana*,[9] nearly every Atean questioned agreed upon a list of four: *tāvana*, pastor, schoolteacher, and *mūtoʻi*. Some informants added the office of parish orator (*ʻauahi paroʻita*) but conceded that, despite the authority that was potential to that office, the current incumbents were usually so senile as to be unable to exercise it. A few informants also included the offices of the district councillors and parish deacons in their lists but then acknowledged that the former were usually far "below" the *tāvana*, and the latter far "below" the pastor except, occasionally, in sodality affairs.

Although I list the four *mana*-laden offices among the Ateans' (and Fatatans') status goals, there were to the best of my knowledge very few Ateans

---

[7]Although I am persuaded that it can be done. See D. C. McClelland, *The Achieving Society* (Princeton: Von Nostrand, 1961).

[8]Since I also neglected to attempt to measure these variables separately (if indeed they were separable) this reasoning is of course syllogistic and *a posteriori*—a defect, alas, which I cannot now correct.

[9]The word *mana* connoted supernatural power, usually dangerous, when applied to places and objects associated with pagan times (such as temple ruins and ancient stone boundary-markers). When applied to a pastor, it also carried some meaning of supernatural power, as represented by that official's special link with God and hence a stronger-than-average ability to invoke supernatural sanctions. But in most contexts, when *mana* was applied to the pastor—and in all contexts when it was applied to *tāvana*, *mūtoʻi*, and schoolteacher—the word signified their power to invoke secular sanctions of either the government or the Protestant Church.

in residence during my visits who actually aspired to those goals. To most Ateans, the training required of a schoolteacher or a pastor was believed to be so long and difficult that it was not even contemplated. Some persons regarded the office of *mūtoʻi* as a sinecure worth having, but most Ateans believed that the kind of influence with Administration officials that was needed to secure that appointment was beyond their reach. It was only the office of *tāvana* that some individuals publicly aspired to, and that only in Fatata; in Atea, to state publicly a wish for the office would have been interpreted as disapproval of the current incumbent, and that would have been a most unpopular view to express.

Of the four principal authority statuses represented in Atea, and potentially achievable by Ateans, only that of *tāvana* was attained by approval votes cast (literally!) by the Ateans themselves, the others having been achieved by appointments by outsiders and based on attributes defined by outsiders and in part produced elsewhere. As for the nature of the resources needed for becoming *tāvana,* all I can suggest is that they were a combination of those needed for achieving certain of the prestige statuses—*what* prestige statuses having depended on the values held by the electorate when the choice was made. (In the case of the 1954–55 *tāvana* of Atea, the favored statuses were, clearly, generosity and respectability.)

Summarizing, it appears that shortage of money was the principal tangible resource that thwarted most Ateans from attaining all of their achievable goals. (By achievable I mean what lay in their capabilities to achieve—through increased effort, etc. By their nature some goals, such as to be the village's most *māramarama,* or most generous, etc., person were achieved by only a few.)

How much additional money was needed is difficult to answer. Leaving aside the possibility that, had additional money been available, their "felt" needs would also have expanded, I know of no cut-and-dried formula for measuring such "needs," as they were felt to be in 1954–55. Since no Atean appeared to be wasting away from starvation—or suffering unduly from exposure to weather, or rebelliously disgruntled by lack of desirable clothes, etc. (except perhaps for the wives of a few outstandingly lazy or improvident men), or bored to apathy by lack of money for cinema and travel—I suppose one could arrive at an "objective" estimate of "minimum" money needs by referring to the per capita income and expenditure figures for 1954 (which, as far as I could learn, were about the same as those of the immediately preceding years).

Of course, per capita figures do not represent actual individuals, nor can they be translated to represent actual households. And although differences in consumption levels, among individuals and households, were smaller in

Atea than in, say, Tahiti's 'A'ou'a community (Finney 1973), differences there were—in expenditures and hence (probably) in goal achievement as well. However, since I am unable to provide exact figures on specific individual (or household) incomes and goals (or goal shortfalls), I must fall back to the village as a unit and say that the money income of Ateans as a whole was insufficient to satisfy all of the money-requisite goals of all the residents. Such a statement would, of course, be applicable to most if not all money-using communities elsewhere; I will attempt to reduce its banality somewhat by comparing Atea with Fatata in this respect.

I turn now to Fatata, to list the ways in which its residents' ideas about "The Good Life" differed from the Ateans', and the degree, relative to Atea, to which they succeeded in achieving those goals.

To make matters simpler, I could discover only a few differences between Ateans and Fatatans in their goals—not surprising, in view of their common cultural heritage; and such differences that did occur can be traced largely to their different experience in the past and continuing colonial period of their histories (as described in the text of this book). The most salient of their differences regarding the goals having to do with "comfort" were the following:

- —The Fatatans expressed slightly stronger wishes for imported foods—and actually ate much more of them (though still not as much as they would have liked).
- —Their dislike of physical pain was no different from the Ateans', but they succeeded more than the latter in alleviating it—partly through larger expenditures and partly through their easier access to the Administration's medical facilities.
- —I cannot say whether their antipathy to interpersonal conflict differed from the Ateans' but they did manage better than the Ateans to keep their conflicts out of public view.

Among the other goals which I label "conditions," I found the Fatatans somewhat less rigid than the Ateans in their preferred masculine and feminine stereotypes and even less concerned than the latter about a "blessed future life." As for the desirability of exercising control over their own actions, the Fatatans appeared to me to be more predisposed than the Ateans to submission to outside authority and even less so than the latter to the exercise of authority by one of themselves.

With respect to preferable "activities," I gained the impression that the Fatatans were less fond than the Ateans of large social gatherings; this was clearly apparent in the characteristically small attendance at most organized meetings and was explicitly stated to be one of the reasons for their rejection of work groups of the labor-exchange and money-earning types (except for fishing crews).

Fatatans' criteria for their prestigious statuses differed from the Ateans' in several features. Not surprisingly, they awarded higher points to expertise in fishing and canoe making than in gardening and vanilla growing, and they spoke with less praise of the speed champion roof-thatch maker and the expert in bedspread sewing. Also, open-handed generosity was less practiced—and less highly esteemed. And Fatata contained a few individuals who were considerably wealthier than any of their neighbors and who were admired for their wealth (including one who was elected *tāvana* principally on that account). The *teitei* (upper)—*haeh'a* (lower) social contrast was talked about more frequently and openly in Fatata and exercised a weightier influence in mate choosing, but as upper-class status was ascribed by birth, lower-class persons could not aspire to it (except perhaps for their children). A high degree of European-ness could, however, be aspired to and was in fact sought after by several Fatatans and actually achieved by a few. As in Atea, the achievers were criticized if they set themselves socially apart from their neighbors, but the criticism here was less vocal and less severe.

In summary, I judge that the Fatatans came closer, overall, to attaining their achievable goals than did the Ateans theirs. Some of this came about through the differences in their definitions of those goals, but much more was due to the means at the Fatatans' disposal for achieving those goals, including especially their larger money incomes (which were augmented somewhat by the slightly lower prices they had to pay for some of the objects and services they desired). In saying this, I am not also saying that the Fatatans were on the whole "happier" than the Ateans. In fact, nothing I witnessed in Fatata equalled the intensity of the public expressions of pleasure that characterized Atea's large social gatherings—*tuāro'i* sessions, house-thatching parties, vanilla weigh-ins, etc., and the week-long carnival of New Year. But that kind of "happiness" is a different thing from the phenomenon of "goal achievement" I am attempting to measure and compare. In a word, if both Ateans and Fatatans would like to eat meat every day—or to go frequently on trips, or buy new clothes every year, or sell their produce to whomever they wished, etc.—and if the latter were able to satisfy those wishes more often than the Ateans, then they have come nearer than the former to achieving those goals, whether or not they experienced more "happiness" in the process.

I turn now to a more systematic examination of the factors that contributed to the Fatatans' advantage in goal achievement insofar as those had to do with money—which was one of the most instrumental, if not the most instrumental, of resources needed for achieving those goals.

Part Two

This section will consider the factors that had to do with money-earning in both Atea and Fatata, and attention will be devoted to those contributing to Fatata's larger income from outside sources—which in 1954–55 was 10,504 francs per capita as against Atea's 7,573. Even subtracting the windfall earnings by Fatatans from a one-time government-financed public works project (i.e., 157,045 francs in all), the difference between Fatata and Atea remained large, 9,154 francs to 7,573. The subject will be discussed under five headings: natural resources, labor, capital, technology and marketing, and social relations. No new facts or conclusions will be introduced, but the treatment of facts will differ from that contained in the text.

Natural Resources

The phyical features of the areas from which the Ateans and Fatatans earned most of their "outside" money were very much alike. The Atean area contained a larger proportion of arable land, but not crucially so. Conversely, the lagoon facing Fatata had closer sea outlets, a bottom better suited to seine-net fishing, and possibly more fish—but these did not add up to a decisive economic advantage over Atea.

The fact that Fatata's population was larger than Atea's in an area of near-identical size would have been a disadvantage had it not been that more Fatatans than Ateans made some or all of their livelihoods working outside the area.

Labor

Potentially, there were several circumstances that could have combined to differentiate the money-earning labor forces of Atea and Fatata, in quantity or quality:

1. Fatata contained a slightly larger proportion of females between the ages of fifteen and sixty, i.e., the period when females (and males) were usually most actively engaged in work.

2. However, it was my observation that Atean females of that age period actually worked more in money-earning agriculture (especially vanilla) than their Fatatan counterparts, and this disparity was increased by the circumstance that in commercial fishing (Fatata's principal money-earning industry), females worked not at all.

3. While there was no significant difference between Atea and Fatata in the proportions of residents aged five to fifteen, the attitudes of parents differed in that those of Fatata demanded less productive work of such children, including money-earning work.

4. Another cultural factor that influenced differences in work quantity was prescribed (or at least encouraged) work stoppages. That is to say, Ateans were much more strict than Fatatans in the observance of a no-work Sabbath, and the "vacation" that accompanied their New Year celebrations lasted much longer than that of Fatata.

5. And finally, there was more specialization (i.e., a potential for more expertise) in the Fatatan labor force than in that of Atea.

Regrettably, I am unable to weight the above factors and hence cannot compare the two labor forces in equation form. Moreover, I did not collect enough individual work schedules to provide a representative sample of actual working times. (Not only was there too much else to do but, except for a few individuals—all in Fatata—who were engaged in full-time wage work, I found it next to impossible to elicit dependable information about the relative amounts of time people devoted specifically to money-earning work.) So, in the absence of quantified data, I must again fall back onto that faithful crutch of ethnographers everywhere, and record my *impression*—which is that, per capita, the Ateans worked *harder* in money-earning jobs and the Fatatans worked with more expertise in those occupations that required such.

Capital

The principal types of capital available for money-earning in Atea and Fatata were land, plantings of bearing coconut palms and vanilla vines, roads, wharves, copra dryers, boats, horses, breeding pigs and cattle, various kinds of tools—and money itself. Listed below were the differences between the two villages in the availability of those goods.

1. The character of the land generally identified with either village was quite similar in terms of suitability for current uses, except that the Atean area contained a somewhat larger amount of arable parts.

2. Ateans held title to only 21 percent of the privately owned land in their village area, as against the Fatatans' 30 percent—but per capita the Ateans as a whole were better favored, each one having owned an average of 0.69 hectares to a Fatatan's 0.58.

3. Some of the land in both villages was devoted to subsistence gardening while some was taken up in housing and hence did not figure directly in money-earning. More of Fatata's land was given over to house sites, but much, much more of Atea's to subsistence gardening, so that in the end I am inclined to believe the amounts of land actually available for money-earning were about the same, per capita.

4. Some Ateans and Fatatans also held title to lands outside their village areas. I was unable to discover the whole amounts of such lands but some indication of their importance, as capital, may be inferred from earnings from them. Thus in 1954, the Ateans earned about 33,500 francs, and the Fatatans 18,700, by actually working those lands; and the Ateans received about 8,000 francs against the Fatatans' 19,000 in the form of rent. In other words, the per capita earning from such land by the Ateans exceeded the Fatatans' by 187 francs to 111—but much of that excess was due to the Ateans' own labor in working the outside lands.

5. More of Atea's money-earning lands were directly accessible by water (and hence canoes, of which Ateans owned a sufficient number) and more of Fatata's by roads (and hence by produce-carrying horses, of which the Fatatans owned a sufficiency). In addition, both villages were provided with adequate wharves for shipping their produce "outside."

6. The residents of both villages owned capital in the form of local bearing coconut palms and vanilla vines. Fatatans owned coconut groves two to three times as extensive as the Ateans. Conversely, the Ateans owned vanilla plantings twelve to thirteen times larger than the Fatatans; and these produced crops whose annual value more than made up for the Fatatans' superiority in the annual yields of their coconut palms. However, since the total bearing life of a coconut palm is about fifteen times as long as that of a vanilla vine—and the remaining bearing lives of Fatata's 1954 palms at least five times as much—the Ateans would over the years be required to invest a great deal more labor than the Fatatans to maintain their current advantage in this form of capital.

7. While Atea contained more copra dryers than Fatata, they were actually much smaller in size and more primitive in construction and had far less total drying capacity.

8. As for the other kinds of tools required in harvesting and processing their cash crops, these were all quite simple and inexpensive, even in Atean and Fatatan terms (e.g., axes, knives, coffee hullers, cassava grinders, etc.) and were owned in sufficient number in both villages.

9. Livestock was produced in both villages, the Ateans having had more pigs and the Fatatans more cattle—and as breeding stock parts of those herds constituted potential "capital." In actuality, however, a far larger number of Fatata's pigs and cattle were raised for sale to outsiders, and hence Fatata may be said to have enjoyed a considerable capital advantage over Atea in this respect.

10. Both villages possessed canoes and other tools required in subsistence fishing but only the Fatatans had the tools (e.g., larger canoes, nets, and holding baskets) needed for larger-scale commercial fishing (which, as frequently noted, only the Fatatans practiced).

11. I cannot estimate the amount of unobligated money owned by the Ateans and Fatatans during the survey year 1954 but am certain that the latter were ahead of the former in this respect. Thus, four Fatatans had bank savings accounts, compared to no Ateans. And while I could not discover how much money they lent to fellow villagers for interest, the fact that only Fatatans actually acknowledged having engaged in this allegedly "un-Tahitian" practice suggests that it was considered to be less unethical in Fatata and hence more widely practiced there—which suggests that there was more ready cash in Fatata for lending. Another sign of Fatata's larger supply of money—or, at least, of its residents' smaller degree of indebtedness—was the fact that fewer of them were willing (i.e., pressed by need) to engage in low-return sharecropping (and then only for shares much larger than the Ateans had to accept). But most revealing of all was the periodic spectacle of Ateans delivering their green vanilla beans *and* their green copra to the local Chinese storekeepers after harvest, and more often for reducing their debts than for cash or future credit. The Fatatans also sold most of their (small) harvests of green vanilla beans to their local storekeepers, for both debt reduction and cash, but they were evidently debt-free enough to be able to process and market their copra themselves (and thereby gain higher profits by doing so).

Summarizing these differences in the ownership of capital goods, the Ateans owned slightly more money-earning land than the Fatatans and somewhat larger numbers of currently bearing crops (in vanilla, at least), but the latter were better off in all other important capital respects, including the possession of unobligated money.

Technology and Marketing

The same kinds of tools and processes were used in both Atea and Fatata in the production of vanilla, cassava, and coffee, and the marketing of these products was carried out in similar ways. On the other hand, there were some important differences in the ways in which copra and livestock were produced and marketed, some equally important differences in the ways in which some labor was marketed, and a momentous technological difference between the two villages deriving from the circumstance that, unlike Fatata, Atea had no export fishing industry at all. Details of these differences are listed below:

1. The Fatatans' banding of their coconut palms against rats probably served to increase their yields over Atea's unbanded ones, but this advantage was as likely as not nullified by the practice of cutting down somewhat unripe nuts, which was done more in Fatata than in Atea. A difference that

was not nullified, however, was the Fatatans' more extensive practice of drying their own copra (and on their more efficient dryers) and then selling it themselves (or by agent) in Pape'ete's competitive and higher-paying market.

2. With the view to selling many of their pigs and cattle "outside," the Fatatans fed or grazed them more attentively and in ways that increased their weight and not, like the Ateans, with little more than household refuse or with what grew under coconut palms.

3. In Atea, the only local residents who received salaries or wages from "outside" sources were the pastor, the *tāvana,* the *mūto'i,* and a few part-time employees in the local stores. In Fatata, in addition to these, there were several residents who marketed their services to outsiders: two of the three schoolteachers, the reservoir inspector, and a number of individuals who worked full- or part-time at neighboring European plantations. (This was in addition to the large number of men who worked on a one-time government public works project.) The plantation workers owed their employment to Fatata's proximity to their places of work and not to any inherent skills of their own. The schoolteachers, however, owed theirs to skills—such as they were!—that no currently resident Atean could have matched—a difference that bears upon the characteristics of the two villages' labor resources discussed above.

4. The technology and marketing procedures associated with Fatata's commercial fishing had no counterparts in Atea. That technology made use of several very large outboard-motor-propelled canoes, several large (and very expensive) seine nets, several huge fishholding baskets, and quantities of imported spearguns. Some of the catch was made by individual anglers and speargunners but most of it by well-organized, and more or less permanent, job-assigned crews of three to five men who worked together one to three times a week throughout much of the year. Some of the marketing (in Pape'ete) was done by the fishermen themselves, some of it by one of them acting as agent. The profits from single catches ranged from zero (or less) to very large windfalls; averaged year-round, they provided some—or most, or all—of the annual incomes of most of Fatata's postchildhood males.

Summarizing the factors considered thus far: through a combination of advantages in:
—geography (mainly its location)
—labor resources (its somewhat more specialized and better trained personnel)
—capital (a larger number of long-term money-earning coconut palms, larger and more efficient copra-drying facilities, more marketable livestock, and more unobligated money)
—and in technology and marketing (the self-drying of copra, the whole technology and marketing procedures of commercial fishing, the selling

of labor outside the village, and the generally greater specialization of some money-earning jobs),

the Fatatans were able to earn larger money incomes from outside sources than the Ateans.

Let us now look at the social-relational arrangements associated with such money earning and enquire whether differences between the two villages in this domain had any influence on differences between their money incomes.

Social Relations

First of all we can eliminate from consideration certain kinds of money-earning in which endogenous factors, social or otherwise, played little or no part in promoting either village's advantage over the other; these were commercial fishing, wage labor, and the selling of fruits, vegetables, and livestock. In all these cases (in which Fatatans out-earned Ateans) the main reason for Fatata's advantage was its location—its proximity to Pape'ete and its contiguity to European plantations.

The preponderance of these occupations in Fatata unquestionably gave rise to some kinds of social relationships not found in Atea, e.g., to share-profit fishing crews and to some atypical division-of-labor in the households of full-time wage earners—but not the reverse. This is not to say that some of Fatata's traditional ways of interaction did not influence, say, the frequency of fishing and the organization of their fishing crews—and in the end, perhaps, the amounts of money earned. Indeed, I am quite certain that they did so. For example, many of Fatata's young women would have been quite capable of doing some of the lighter jobs involved in seining, thereby relieving more males for the more strenuous operations, but Fatatan conventions regarding sexual division of labor did not permit that "rational" measure to be tried out—or even considered. In this section, however, I am concerned with differences between Fatata's and Atea's *customary* forms of social interactions and the influences that these exerted upon inter-village differences in money income. Had the Ateans been close enough to Pape'ete to engage successfully in commercial fishing, I expect that they would have had all-male fishing crews just like those of Fatata—and despite the fuller use of females there in agricultural work.

We can also eliminate from discussion certain other categories of money-earning in which endogenous factors did play important parts in giving one village an advantage over the other, but in which the social-relational component was small or only very indirect: namely, in the production of vanilla, kapok, firewood, cassava, and coffee; in the vending of refreshments to outsiders; and in the salaries of schoolteachers. Local social-relational factors were implicated in the magnitudes of the differences revealed in some of these. For example, one of the factors contributing to Atea's superiority in vanilla production was the engagement of women and children in pollination and harvesting to a degree not practiced in Fatata; and this practice was but one manifestation of more general features of intrafamilial relationships in Atea. Again, the fact that two local women had become highly qualified enough to serve as schoolteachers in Fatata implies something about the wider "freedoms" permitted females there vis-à-vis males. However, these factors contributed only secondarily to the total intervillage income differences we are now concerned with.

Those categories of money-earning in which social-relational components contributed in large measure to intervillage income differences were: the renting of property, the receipt of remittances, and the production of copra.

Fatata's superiority in house-renting income—a small but noteworthy difference—was one more sign of that village's farther "progress" in the commercialization of social-relational transactions, i.e., in the replacement of non-reciprocable giving and gift-exchange by buying-and-selling. Its superiority in theater-renting income was another such sign (added to which was the bargaining advantage resting with the theater-building owners on account of the village's location). As for the Fatatans' lead in land-renting income, this came about through two separate circumstances. Regarding rents paid by outsiders for use of the Fatatans' local land, the area's location close to the residence of a number of landless Chinese vanilla growers resulted in more land being rented. But the village's lead in rent receipts from land owned by its residents elsewhere was due in large measure to their more frequent interaction with co-owning exploiters of those lands. Such interaction was conducted in large part through letter writing (in which Fatatans engaged more actively than the Ateans), but was no less "social" for that.

Fatatans' lead in remittance income may be attributed, in part at least, to the same circumstance. Their somewhat higher rate of literacy and their stronger penchant for letter writing helped to maintain "closer" communications between resident and absent kin, including the remittances in question.

However, the intervillage difference in copra income provides the nicest example of the influence of social relations upon profits.

Let me review the salient differences between the villages in this their oldest, most "traditional," most characteristic money-earning activity.

Fatata contained less land suitable for growing coconuts, but more nut-bearing palms. Of these the Fatatans themselves owned an average of eighty-three palms per capita, against the Ateans' fifty-eight. Even so, the Ateans produced more copra than the Fatatans (i.e., 192 kilos per capita to Fatata's 153) partly by harvesting more of their palms and partly by share-cropping more local palms owned by outsiders. But in spite of this, the Ateans' copra brought its residents only 706 francs per capita as against the 1,308 francs that went to Fatatans.

The main reason why the Ateans worked harder and harvested more of their local palms was their paucity of alternative ways of money-earning. And one of the reasons for their lower profits was the higher cost of trans-porting their copra to Pape'ete. In addition, Ateans on the whole had to pay a larger proportion of their total sales revenue in rent to the outside owners of local groves. But social-relational factors were also implicated.

The practice of banding coconut palms against rats (or in the case of Atea, of not banding them) had a social-relational basis, inasmuch as it de-rived from the palm owners' attitude toward the Administration—one of (some) trust on the part of the Fatatans, or *mistrust* on the part of the Ateans. However, since the effect was to reduce the copra yield of Atean palms it served to reduce the size of Atea's total copra harvest vis-à-vis Fa-tata's, but not the rate of profit per kilo of harvested copra.

Similarly, the wider prevalence in Fatata of the practice of nut harvest by cutting reflected a difference in social-relational ambience there, namely, a more selfish version of sharing among grove co-owners. And while this may have served to reduce Fatata's total copra harvest, it did so only slightly and did not influence the Fatatans' higher profits per kilo of harvested and dried copra.

Intervillage differences in social relations also served to affect, respective-ly, the profits of individual owners. In Fatata, the producer who needed ex-tra labor in harvesting had to pay wages for that labor at going rates, and the producer without a dryer of his own usually had to pay for the use of one. In Atea, it was otherwise. A producer requiring extra labor was usually able to employ a money-earning work crew at considerably less than the standard wage rate—plus a little food and wine. And for those few produc-ers who dried their copra before selling it, those among them who did not own dryers were usually able to borrow the use of one from a kinsman or neighbor without charge. But of course, these advantages enjoyed by Atea's producers reduced correspondingly the potential money income of the Atean dryer-owners and work-crew members, and did not affect Atea's rela-tively lower profit-per-kilo as a whole.

In the end, the circumstances that had most to do with Fatata's higher copra profits were that the Fatatans dried their own copra whereas the Ateans sold most of theirs green—and this contrast provides exemplification of a widely ramifying difference between the two villages' relationships with the encompassing world "outside."

The local parties to those two sets of relationships were the Tahitian copra-producers and the Chinese storekeepers. The formative dimension of those relationships was economic; it had to do with transactions between the parties—with the explicitly commercial exchanges of the storekeepers' goods for the Tahitians' money or copra. And unlike many kinds of exchanges between Tahitians, these did not even carry the pretense of being nonreciprocable, or of permitting nonequivalent or indefinitely-delayed returns. The dissimilarity between the two villages in this transaction lay in the circumstance that the Fatatans paid for their store goods in money, and usually after no very long delay. In contrast, the Atean producers paid for their store goods in copra, and usually after so long an interval that they were seldom if ever out of debt. Moreover, they paid in green copra, which fetched a much lower price than the dried, and hence increased their indebtedness even more.

The reason why the Atean producers paid their store debts in copra was that they seldom if ever had in hand enough ready cash for doing so. And the main reason why they paid in green, lower value, copra was the large amounts and the perpetuity of their store debts. In some cases in the past, the debts had become so large and old that the storekeepers had brought suit for settlement before the island gendarme—and had in the meantime denied further credit. And in several instances during my visits, they had cut off credit, or permitted the debtor to receive only bread. And it was these kinds of pressures that persuaded most producers not only to turn over their copra directly to their creditors, but to turn it over as soon as possible, i.e., green.

In contrast, the Fatatan producers, who were in most cases indebted to their local storekeepers either less so or not at all, dried or had others dry their copra locally and sold it at higher prices in Pape'ete itself. Several circumstances contributed to this procedure, e.g., the cash many of them earned from fishing or part-time work; the daily boat to Pape'ete (which served to speed up payment for copra shipped there on consignment—in contrast to the fortnight or so that would have attended the consignment-selling of Atean copra); the long-established ties many Fatatan producers had with Pape'ete buyers; their weaker dependance upon the local stores for imported goods; and possibly, the persuasiveness represented by the superior efficiency of Fatata's copra dryers, hence smaller chance of loss by spoilage during drying.

Thus, several circumstances, singly or in combination, were responsible for creating and maintaining the differences in transactions that obtained between copra producers and storekeepers in Atea and Fatata, but the dissimilarity in social relations characterized by those transactional differences was the culminating contrast and the weightiest cause of the Fatatans' larger money incomes from copra.

BIBLIOGRAPHY

Anderson, Eugene: "Tahitian Bonito Fishing" in *Kroeber Anthropological Society Papers*, Vol. 28, Berkeley. 1963.

Barrau, Jacques: *Subsistence Agriculture in Polynesia and Melanesia*. B.P. Bishop Museum Bulletin No. 223. 1961.

Chabouis, L. and F.: *Petite Histoire Naturelle des Établissements Français de L'Océanie*. 2 vols. Saint-Amand-Montrond: Imprimerie Bussiere. 1954.

Coppenrath, Gérald: *Les Chinois de Tahiti*. Publications de la Societe des Oceanistes No. 21. Paris: Musée de L'Homme. 1967.

Danielsson, Bengt: *Love in the South Seas*. London: George Allen and Unwin. 1956.

Danielsson, Bengt and Marie-Thérèse: *Moruroa, Mon Amour: The French Nuclear Tests in the Pacific*. New York: Penguin Books. 1977.

Davies, John: *A Tahitian and English Dictionary*. Tahiti: London Missionary Society Press. 1851.

Ellsworth, S. W.: *Zion in Paradise; Early Mormons in the South Seas*. Provo: Utah State University Press. 1959.

Finney, Ben R.: *Polynesian Peasants and Proletarians*. Cambridge (Mass): Schenkman Publishing Company. 1973.

Green, R. C. and Kay; Roy and Ann Rappaport; and Janet Davidson: *Archaeology on the Island of Mo'orea, French Polynesia*. Anthropological Papers of the American Museum of Natural History, Vol. 51, Part 2. New York. 1967.

Handy, W. C.: *Handicrafts of the Society Islands*. B. P. Bishop Museum Bulletin No. 42. Honolulu. 1927.

Henry, Teuira: *Ancient Tahiti*. B. P. Bishop Museum Bulletin No. 48. 1928.

Hooper, Antony B.:

    1966   — *Marriage and Household Structure in Two Tahitian Communities*. Unpublished Ph.D. Dissertation, Harvard University. 1966.

1970A — "Adoption in the Society Islands" in Vern Carroll (ed.) *Adoption in Eastern Oceania*. Association for Social Anthropology in Oceania Monograph No. 1. Honolulu: University of Hawaii Press. 1970.

1970B — " 'Blood and Belly': Tahitian Concepts of Kinship and Descent" in Jean Pouillon and Pierre Maranda (eds.) *Éxchanges et Communications: Mélanges Offerts à Claude Lévi-Strauss a L'Occasion de son 60ème Anniversaire*. The Hague: Mouton and Co. 1970.

1976 — " 'Eating Blood': Tahitian Concepts of Incest" *Journal of the Polynesian Society* Vol. 85 No. 2, 1976.

1978 — "Tahitian Concepts of Sickness and Methods of Treatment" *Publications de la Société des Océanistes* No. 39. Paris. 1978.

Kay, Paul:

1963A — *Aspects of Social Structure in Manuho'e*. Unpublished Ph.D. Dissertation. Harvard University. 1963.

1963B — "Urbanization in a Tahitian Household" in A. Spoehr (ed.) *Pacific Port Towns and Cities*. Honolulu: B. P. Bishop Museum. 1963.

1963C — "Aspects of Social Structure in a Tahitian Urban Neighborhood" *Journal of the Polynesian Society* Vol. 72 No. 4. 1963.

1963D — "Tahitian Fosterage and the Form of Ethnographic Models" *American Anthropologist* Vol. 65 No. 5. 1963.

1964 — "A Guttman Scale Model of Tahitian Consumer Behavior" *Southwestern Journal of Anthropology* Vol. 20 No. 2. 1964.

Lemaitre, Yves: *Lexique du Tahitien Contemporain*. Paris: O.R.S.T.O.M. 1973.

Levy, Robert:

1968 — "Tahitian Adoption as a Psychological Message" in Vern Carroll (ed.) *Adoption in Eastern Oceania*. Honolulu: University of Hawaii Press. 1968.

1973 — *Tahitians: Mind and Experience in the Society Islands*. Chicago: University of Chicago Press. 1973.

Marshall, Donald: *Ra'ivavae*. New York: Doubleday. 1961.

Moench, Richard:

1963A — *Economic Relations of Chinese in the Society Islands*. Unpublished Ph.D. Dissertation. Harvard University. 1963.

1963B — "A Preliminary Report on Chinese Social and Economic Organization in the Society Islands" in A. Spoehr (ed.) *Pacific Port Towns and Cities*. Honolulu: B. P. Bishop Museum. 1963.

Nag, Moni: "Economic Value of Children in Agricultural Societies" in J. T. Fawcett (ed.) *The Satisfaction and Costs of Children*. Honolulu: East-West Center. 1972.

Nag, Moni; R. C. Peet; and R. C. White: "An Anthropological Approach to the Study of Economic Value of Children in Java and Nepal" *Current Anthropology* Vol. 19 No. 2. 1978.

Newbury, Colin:
1956 — *The Administration of French Oceania, 1842–1906.* Unpublished Ph.D. Dissertation. Australian National University. 1956.
1961 — *The History of the Tahitian Mission, 1799–1830.* Cambridge (England): The University Press, for The Hakluyt Society. 1961.

Oliver, Douglas: *Ancient Tahitian Society.* 3 Vols. Honolulu: University Press of Hawaii. 1974.

O'Reilly, Patrick: *Le Tahiti Catholique.* Paris: Société des Océanistes. 1969.

Ottino, Paul: *La Pêche au Grand Filet à Tahiti.* Paris: Cahiers O.R.S.T.O.M.— Sciences Humaines Vol. 2 No. 2. 1965.

Pambrun, Henri: *Le Régime Foncier dans les Territoires d'Outre Mer et en Polynésie Française.* Papeete: 1958.

Panoff, Michel: *La Terre et Organization Sociale en Polynésie.* Paris: Payot. 1970.

Papy, H. Rene: *Tahiti et les Iles Voisines.* 2 Vols. Toulouse: Les Artisans de L'Imprimerie. 1954.

Republique Française: *Code Pénal.* Paris: Librairie Dalloz.

Republique Française: *Code Civil* (Edition no. 58) Paris: Librairie Dalloz.

Republique Française: *Recensement Général de la Population (Décembre 1956), Territoire de la Polynésie Française.* Paris: Service de Statistique Chargé des Relations et la Cooperation avec les Etats D'Outre-mer. 1960.

Republique Française: *Population de la Polynésie Française: Recensement du 9 Novembre 1962.* Papeete. 1963.

Teissier, Raoul: "Etude Demographique sur les Etablissements Française de L'Océanie de Cook au Recensement des 17/18 Septembre 1951" *Bulletin de la Société des Etudes Océaniennes* Vol. 9 No. 102. 1953.

Thompson, Virginia and Richard Adloff: *The French Pacific Islands: French Polynesia and New Caledonia.* Berkeley: University of California Press. 1971.

Vernier, Charles: *Tahitiens: D'Hier et D'Aujourd'hui.* Paris: Société des Missions Évangeliques. 1933.

White, B.: "The Economic Importance of Children in a Javanese Village" in Moni Nag (ed.) *Population and Social Organization.* The Hague: Mouton. 1975.

Wilder, G. P.: *The Breadfruit of Tahiti.* B. P. Bishop Museum Bulletin No. 50. 1928.

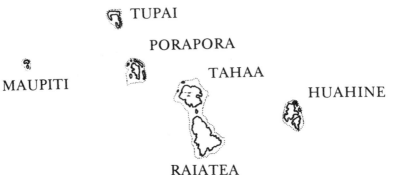

TUPAI

PORAPORA

TAHAA

MAUPITI

HUAHINE

RAIATEA

MAIAO

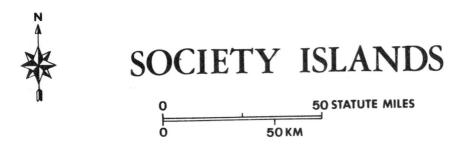

N

SOCIETY ISLANDS

0   50 STATUTE MILES

0   50 KM